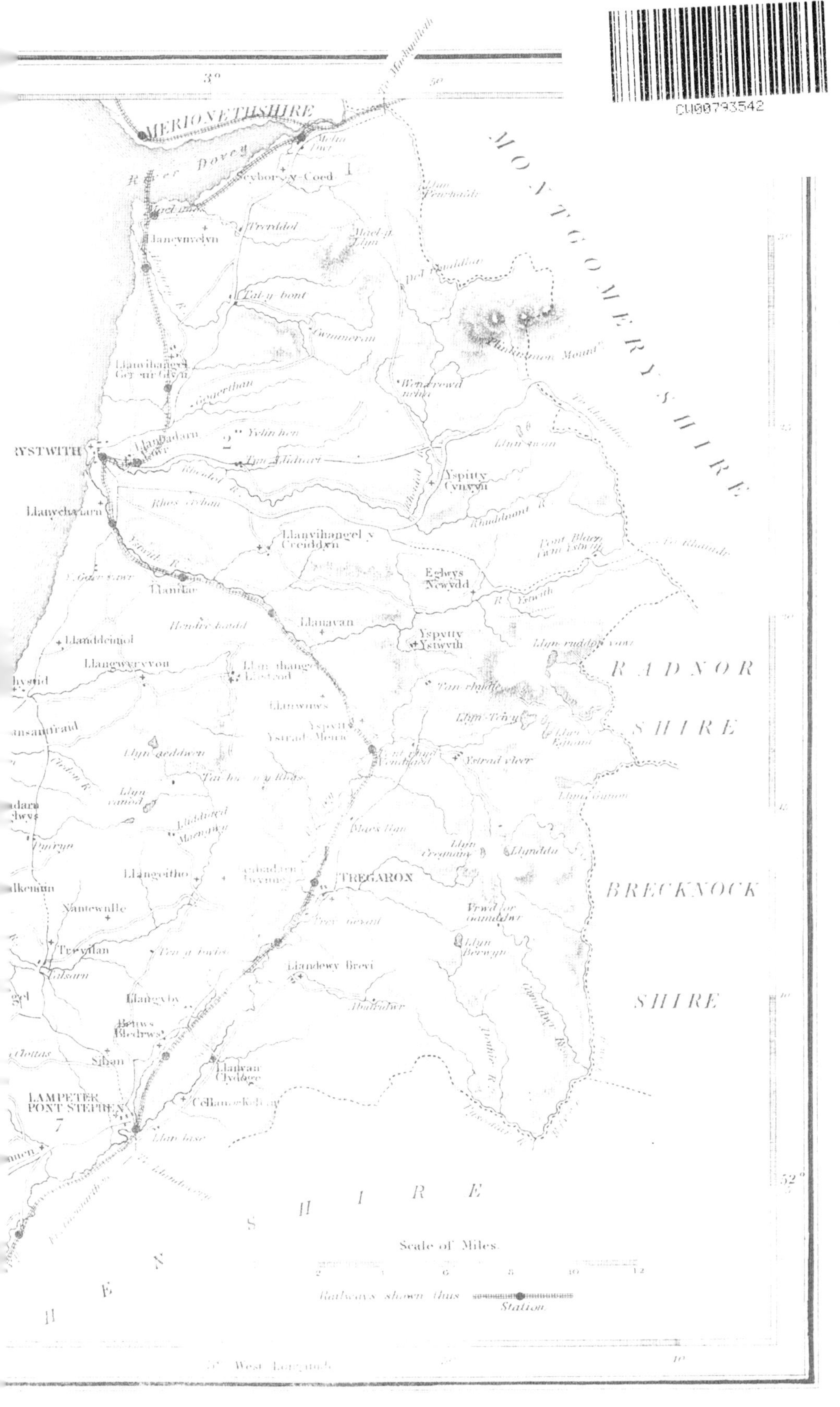

3°
50'
MERIONETHSHIRE
River Dovey
MONTGOMERYSHIRE
Tal-y-bont
Plinlimmon Mount
Llanbadarn Vawr
Llanychaiarn
Llanvihangel y Creiddyn
Yspytty Cynwyn
Eglwys Newydd
Llanilar
Llanavan
Yspytty Ystwith
Llanddeinol
Llangwyryvon
RADNOR
SHIRE
TREGARON
BRECKNOCK
SHIRE
Llangeitho
Nantewnlle
Llandewy Brevi
Llangyby
Silian
LAMPETER
PONT STEPHEN
S H I R E
Scale of Miles
Railways shown thus
Station
52°
West Longitude

CEREDIGION:

a Wealth of History

The Banc Ty'nddôl gold disc of *c*2000BC, discovered in Cwmystwyth in 2002: see p. 36.

CEREDIGION:

a Wealth of History

Yn rhagoriaeth ar bob tir,
Gorau yw Sir G'redigion,
Duw a'i cadwo yn ddi-warth,
Hon yw buarth yr haelion.

(Unknown, *c*1577)

GERALD MORGAN

Gomer

First Impression – 2005

ISBN 1 84323 501 3 (Hardback)
ISBN 1 84323 580 3 (Softback

This book is published with the financial support
of the Welsh Books Council

Printed in Wales at
Gomer Press, Llandysul, Ceredigion SA44 4JL

I
Phyllis a Merêd.

CONTENTS

Cwmystwyth, by Mary Lloyd Jones. [Courtesy of the artist]

PREFACE

Come with me up the muddy track, past the sign which says 'footpath closed for logging', on this afternoon of 8 December, 2004, with the low, watery sun in our eyes. We're walking up Trichrug, that prominent hill in mid-Ceredigion which for forty years has been blanketed by conifers, but is at last almost free of timber. As we pass the stacked logs and reach the heathery summit, a snipe bursts away from us, and in front of us are the most ancient visible monuments in our county, the three Bronze Age tumuli which gave the hill its name (a fourth exists, but is hardly visible). No matter that some vile person has abandoned a car nearby, no matter that one of these huge graves is crowned by a concrete Ordnance Survey pillar, Trichrug is the finest viewpoint in Ceredigion. It's true that on this hazy winter's day we cannot see Snowdonia, Cadair Idris, Pumlumon, the Llŷn peninsula, Bardsey, the Carmarthen Van or Preselau, but we know they're there, and on the right day next summer, now that the wretched trees have at last gone, we shall be able to acknowledge the mighty men of the past who chose this for their burial place, and enjoy an unparalleled view. In 1819 it was enjoyed by the traveller Jenkin Jones, who 'saw 13 Churches at once, the hills of Snowdon, Plynlimmon and Cader Idris, and the whole of Cardigan Bay.'

In spring I would invite you to come on a fine warm evening to stand on Craig-lais, Aberystwyth (Constitution Hill), with the rocky ribs of Wales corrugated under our feet, and enjoy this sea-washed country, where choughs make their clashing calls overhead, a kestrel hunts the slopes, and once in the past a peregrine flashed by. Thyme is purple in late summer; earlier, pinks and white campion are everywhere, and wheatears move northwards to Gwynedd. To the north, Sarn Cynfelyn projects darkly into the sea, and on a calm day its underwater line is clearly visible much further out. Borth and Ynys-las are hidden from us, but beyond are Aberdyfi and Tywyn, the peak of Cadair Idris, and even in the haze Snowdon and its attendant lords are easily visible. Further round is the Llŷn peninsula, with Bardsey clear on the horizon, nearly forty miles away.

To the south, beyond Aberystwyth are Pendinas and the wonderful cliffs of Ceredigion, all the way to Mwnt and Cardigan Island, largely unknown to the Cardis themselves, since they rarely walk the coastal path or take a boat to see the seals, the fulmars, the guillemots, and the strange pinnacles of clay at Mynachdy'r Graig, nor the gannets and, with luck, a leaping dolphin. Beyond Mwnt rise the Preselau hills; to their west the Pembrokeshire plateau creeps away into invisibility. Inland, the great wet sponge of Pumlumon is hidden by nearer hills, but to the right are the ramparts of Mynydd Bach, and everywhere are hedges and fields, the latest pattern imposed on the land by the millennia of farming. The poet Alun Lewis saw the superb embrace of Cardigan Bay from Penbryn:

> . . . like to swan or moon the whole of Wales
> Glided within the parish of my care:
> I saw the green tide leap on Cardigan . . .

And the great mountains, Dafydd and Llewelyn,
Plynlimmon, Cader Idris and Eryri
Threshing the darkness back from head and fin . . . ('In Hospital: Poona')

Others may see it all differently. A 'poor and remote territory' is the description of Cardiganshire offered by the distinguished English historian F.M.L. Thompson, reviewing volume 3 of the *Cardiganshire County History*. This verdict may seem natural to a reviewer based in the Home Counties of England, though he is as remote from me as I am from him, and his use of the word 'territory' seems to imply some far-flung area not yet brought fully under the rule of law. As for poverty, it is perfectly true that income per head in Ceredigion is roughly half that in the Home Counties, and that for almost all their history the majority of Ceredigion's population lived in grinding indigence on its poor soils, hence the savage description of the county as 'the devil's grandmother's jointure', and its mocking by the Morris brothers in their 18th century correspondence as *Sir Abernoeth*, roughly translatable as 'the naked county' (referring to the absence of trees, as well as to the poverty of the inhabitants). It is part of the intention of this book to counter the metropolitan viewpoint by suggesting that Ceredigion is not some Kerguelen or South Georgia, but is well-connected in the world, and that it enjoys a wealth not to be measured in gold or even Cwmsymlog silver, while its people, slanderously reputed to be 'Scotsmen without the generosity', often prove generous far beyond expectation. Furthermore, I hope to open the eyes of incomers to the rich history of their chosen home, and to remind the Cardis themselves of their inheritance.

The reader will see that after two scene-setting chapters there is an attempt to tell a general chronological story for some seven chapters before the book reverts to topics. Topics themselves present difficulties because some elements are common to several subjects. Thus, reluctantly, there is no separate chapter on riots, because Cardiganshire's not infrequent riots between 1730 and 1845 are relevant to a number of different topics. Within the chapters I have sought readability, hence no footnotes. I can only plead in mitigation that at least there is an index (it is amazing that people still publish history books without indexes), and sources and reading matter are named at the end. The intention is that this shall be a book for the public which, it is hoped, will also appeal to scholars.

Part of the original plan was simply to produce a one-volume popular digest of the three-volume *Cardiganshire County History*, of which Volumes 1 and 3 have by now appeared, and most welcome and authoritative they are. Volume 2 has unfortunately been delayed by factors beyond the control of the general editors, and though I long to see it, it seemed better to carry on. Chapters 1, 3-5 rely heavily on Volume 1 of the *County History*, Chapters 6-8 and 12 are fairly straightforwardly based on the work of a number of eminent historians. I discovered, however, that although the *County History* Volume 3 is outstanding in itself and I have used it, there might well have been a fourth volume in the series. Some episodes and chapters are based on personal research. If the book whets the reader's appetite for more, the *County History* and the volumes of *Ceredigion* should be consulted; the excellent Ceredigion museum at Aberystwyth, the Llywernog museum of the lead and silver-mining industry, the Red Kite Museum at Tregaron (which deals with far more than the well-known bird) and the Heritage Centre at Cardigan should be visited. Best of all, let the reader explore the county's fascinating landscape, the finest historical resource of all – preferably on foot, map in hand. Despite low-flying jets, tarmac and traffic, conifers and wind-farms, caravans and bungalows, Ceredigion is still a delightful county.

The reader might expect to find extended treatment of such well-known Cardiganshire figures as Thomas Johnes of Hafod, Sir Herbert Lloyd of Peterwell or Joseph Jenkins, the Welsh Swagman. But Thomas Johnes has been dealt with by several authors, while Bethan Phillips has made both Sir Herbert Lloyd and the Welsh Swagman her own. Nor is there – I hope – unnecessary repetition of what has been published in my books on Trawsgoed and Nanteos and their respective families, although these major figures of the gentry are not ignored. There is an effort to give due attention to the Pryses of Gogerddan, who, although the major political family in the county for over four centuries, still lack their historian.

Ceredigion may seem an easier choice to write about than some other Welsh counties; for example Carmarthenshire or Pembrokeshire have such obvious cultural and socio-economic divisions within them that it is in some ways difficult to conceive of them as single units. Ceredigion has been a regnal, governmental or administrative unit, with few boundary changes, for perhaps 1,400 years – possibly longer. Since it was known from 1536 until 1974 as Cardiganshire, and in Welsh as *Sir Aberteifi*, it might have been easier to use the term Cardiganshire throughout, as the *County History* does from the 13th century. But though one easily slips into using the old terms, 'Ceredigion' is both older and newer; David James uses it for his admirable *Ceredigion: a Natural History*, and I am glad to follow his example when dealing with it in general terms, or pre-1536 and post-1974. Related to this difficulty was the problem of a title for the volume. Sir John Edward Lloyd had already used *The Story of Ceredigion* and D.J. Saer had earlier appropriated *The Story of Cardiganshire* for a now rare volume, while *Ceredigion* is the title of the county's admirable historical journal.

I owe numerous debts: for points raised in discussion, for information, for reading chapters of the book, and for pictures. Many such obligations can no longer be acknowledged, drowned in Lethe, but I thank Owen Watkin, Ceredigion's chief executive, for contributing the Afterword, and I have been helped at one time or another by Dr Jill Barber; the editor of *The Cambrian News*; Arthur Chater, the Revd Canon James Cunnane, Alun Creunant Davies, David Davies (Pyllau Isaf), Dr Jeffrey Davies, Mrs J. Ann Davies, Dr Howard Davies, Dr Jeffrey Davies, Dr Susan Davies, Gwyneira Edwards, Professor Hywel Teifi Edwards, Robat Gruffudd, Richard Hartnup, Erwyd Howells, Dr John Hughes, David James, Dr Evan James and Mrs Auronwy James, Heather and Terrence James, David Jenkins, Professor Geraint H. Jenkins, Professors Emeritus Ieuan Gwynedd Jones and Dafydd Jenkins, Mary Lloyd Jones, Dr Anne Kelly Knowles, Ros Laidlaw, Thomas Lloyd, Dr Iestyn Morgan Watkin, Morfydd Owen, Dr Caroline Palmer, Mrs Mary Raw, Ivor Richards (who took me into the bowels of the Cwmystwyth mines), John Rowlands, Mike Snow, William Troughton, Dr Eryn White, the Revd David Williams, Dr Iwan Wmffre, to whom Chapter 2 is deeply indebted, and Martin Wright. As for institutions and their staffs, I warmly thank Dr Adam Gwilt of the National Museums and Galleries of Wales, Martin Fowler of the National Coracle Centre at Cenarth, Dr Michael Freeman of Ceredigion Museum, Charles Griffiths the archivist of Dyfed-Powys Police, Dr Helen Palmer and the staff of the Ceredigion Records Office, Dr Stephen Briggs, Toby Driver, Medwyn Parry, Richard Suggett as well as Penny Icke and the library staff all of the Royal Commission on Ancient and Historic Monuments (Wales); Nia Richards and William Howells of the Ceredigion Library, many members of the staff of the National Library of Wales; Neil Ludlow, Kenneth Murphy, Paul Sambrook and Richard Jones of the Cambria Archaeological Trust; Richard in particular provided me with four maps. I have attempted to acknowledge the origins of every picture, and offer sincere apologies if I have accidentally transgressed. I am particularly grateful to the National Library of Wales, the Royal Commission on Ancient Monuments, Wales, Ceredigion County Library and the Earl of Lisburne for permission to use many copyright pictures. Pictures without acknowledgements are my own.

My wife Enid has lovingly tolerated my long-term affair with the volume and read several chapters in draft; my daughter-in-law Patricia has also read a number of chapters in draft and helped eliminate repetitions and other errors. I owe particular debts to Dr John Davies, who read the whole text and made many valuable suggestions and corrections; to Richard Hartnup, Dr Chris Arnold, Professor J. Beverley Smith and Dr Llinos B. Smith for reading draft chapters, and in general to Professor Walford Davies, who opened a second career to me which made this and other books possible. I owe much to the extra-mural classes in Aberystwyth, Cardigan, Llanafan, Devil's Bridge, Ysbyty Ystwyth, Llanilar, Llanfihangel-y-Creuddyn, Bronnant, Llan-non, Llanrhystud, Caerwedros, Felin-fach and Cwrtnewydd with whom I discussed many of these subjects, and from whom I learnt a great deal. My apologies to anyone not named here. Any errors of fact and waywardness of judgement are my own. I acknowledge especially my debt to Ceri Wyn Jones and the staff of Gwasg Gomer. Thus far I have recognised academic titles (with apologies for any ignorant omissions), while in the text I have not. I hope my friends and others will forgive me this *lèse-majesté*.

Note 1: Orthography

In spelling Ceredigion's place-names, I have tried to stick to the guidance of Elwyn Davies's *Rhestr o Enwau Lleoedd / A Gazetteer of Welsh Place-Names* (Cardiff, 1967). This means that I have on occasion differed from the County Council's sign-posting and from the Ordnance Survey, notably in a more generous use of hyphens to indicate strengthening of the final syllable. Llan-non is hyphenated for its pronunciation and should keep the initial 'n' of the saint's name. Llannarth doesn't need a hyphen, since the accent falls on the usual Welsh penultimate syllable, but the double-n is correct. I have not however attempted to re-form spellings which have been so long accepted that it would be presumptuous to use an older form. For example, the early spelling of the well-known mansion and estate was *Gogerthan*, which demonstrates its root in the word *garth*, but it has rarely been used in print, and so I have used 'Gogerddan', and such other usual modern forms as Mydroilyn and Troed-yr-aur, rather than baffle the reader by reconstructing them.

Note 2: Metrication

Yards, feet and inches have not been taught in our schools for a generation. What should the historian do? I have tried to use metres where apposite, but when measurements are derived from a text of the past I have kept the imperial measure. However, I have clung to miles rather than taking up kilometres, an inconsistency for which I believe most readers will be grateful, for at least another generation. I have not attempted any decimalisation of money; the inflation of the past fifty years has in any case made it impossible to make comparisons with the past, and who knows, perhaps it will all be euros and cents in a few years' time.

Dyffryn Rheidol: the small lakes are in fact flooded gravel pits.

Pumlumon in evening sunlight. [Martin Wright]

1. The Nature of the Land

The best brief description of Ceredigion is a thousand years old:

> This land is like a four-sided table.
> A high mountain rears up as the source of the sun,
> Good to ensure grazing for the flocks.
> A large river waters the south of the land,
> And the broad ocean washes the western verge.
> To the north, a great river is the boundary.
> Thus do two rivers, the sea and a mountain
> Set off this fruitful country.

Ieuan ap Sulien, the scholar-priest of Llanbadarn, penned those lines in Latin a little before the year 1100. He knew his country well. Ceredigion can indeed be envisaged as four-sided; to the east the sun rises over Pumlumon and the Cambrian mountains, which provide extensive grazing. Together with the Teifi, the Dyfi and the sea, they define the boundaries of this ancient kingdom, still a separate area of administration after more than a thousand years. In fact the county boundary does not simply follow the Cambrian mountains' watershed; for a critical part of its course it runs roughly east from Lampeter towards Ystrad-ffin and Llyn Brianne, then north to touch the Claerwen reservoir, and thence north-west to Eisteddfa Gurig before taking in Pumlumon. This area south-east of the watershed, Fforest yr Esgob, is now the county's 'empty quarter', almost devoid of population, but it was not always so, as will be seen in Chapter 11.

The northern and southern boundaries, roughly Dyfi and Teifi, have occasionally fluctuated, and some details can be found at the end of this chapter. But what is obvious to everybody who lives near the Teifi is that the 'Vale of Tivy', to use the anglicised name by which it has often been known, may have been divided along the river by the ruling authorities, but it has long been its own social unit, which includes parts of three counties. Indeed, when the medieval Church authorities organised Wales into archdeaconries, that of Cardigan reached across the river to include a dozen parishes in what are now the counties of Pembrokeshire and Carmarthenshire. Nevertheless, the natural features described by Ieuan ap Sulien have set Ceredigion quite distinctly apart from the rest of Wales. That is not to admit too readily to the accusation of remoteness; the Teifi and Dyfi are fordable, bridgeable frontiers, and even the mountains had many routes across them, most of which are now green tracks.

As for the sea, Ieuan tells us that his father Sulien was educated in Scotland and Ireland. Ireland is visible from Wales and Scotland from Ireland. The western seaways, from the Mediterranean to the Hebrides, had been known for millennia, and were a principal route by which people reached the Hiberno-British archipelago after the ice retreated, bringing with them skills in tool-making, metalwork, the will to erect stone monuments, religious practices and world-views of which we know so little, and skills in navigation which we should not underestimate. It is of course true that the lack of shelter on the Ceredigion coast and its position in the lee, so to speak, of the Pembrokeshire peninsula, made it a less favourable landfall. But Ceredigion was not entirely bypassed either by early people or by the saints and scholars who certainly used the seaways between west Wales, Ireland, Scotland, and via Cornwall to Brittany – as did the Vikings, and later the zealous Methodists who came by boat from the Llŷn peninsula in the 18th century to receive communion from the hands of Daniel Rowland at Llangeitho.

However, it was by land that the Romans came, crossing the Teifi at several points; Saxon raiders and Welsh chieftains too came to Ceredigion by land. The Normans poured in both across the Teifi and down from the north-east; English lords and King Edward I himself marched through the county, crossing both Dyfi and Teifi, while the great rebel prince Owain Glyn Dŵr took the most difficult (and therefore unexpected) route of all, coming over the bleak Pumlumon massif to the river Hyddgen. Henry Tudor marched his little army up from Pembroke through the county on the way to his surprising victory at Bosworth.

THE county covers rather less than one-tenth of the surface area of Wales. Its 1934 area was 441,237 acres, that of Wales 5,098,878 acres. Within its boundaries of that date it was the fifth largest of the thirteen historic counties after Carmarthen, Glamorgan, Montgomeryshire and Brecon. Prior to the spread of afforestation, the county had fewer woodlands than any other county – 1.2%, compared with 5.0 % for Wales.

Ceredigion is not the most favoured of the thirteen counties of Wales. Thomas Phaer, writing in 1563, was damning: 'All this is a very bare country and mountainous . . . All along the coast is no trade of merchandise but all full of rocks and dangers.' The county has little really fertile soil; its only important mineral reserves were in lead, silver and zinc, not the coal and iron which created the recent wealth of the south-east and north-east of Wales. Much of the land is high and the rainwashed soil is acidic, unfavourable for the growth of crops. Its coastline has no good harbours, and still offers a menacing lee shore to sailing vessels. It has only one small island, less exciting than the islands of Pembroke, and its mountains offer good walking but no rock-climbing. It lacks the rugged magnificence of Caernarfonshire and Merionethshire. It is remote from present centres of government in Cardiff and London (which some would claim to be an advantage); it retains only one of its original standard-gauge railways, and at the time of writing it has, apart from the Cardigan bypass, no dual-carriageway roads.

Nevertheless, Ceredigion has much to offer both to its inhabitants and to its visitors. The splendours of Devil's Bridge, the delights of Llangrannog and Cenarth are well-known, but the fine coastal walks between Borth and Aberystwyth, Tan-y-bwlch and Llanrhystud, between New Quay and Cwmtydu, and around Mwnt, are less frequented than is the Pembrokeshire coastal path. The sandy beaches of Ynys-las and Borth, Cei Bach and Penbryn compete with the best in Britain. The wilderness country north of Nant-y-moch, the hills beyond Ysbyty Ystwyth and Strata Florida, the splendid valley of the Teifi and its lovely tributaries, the gorges of the Rheidol at Parson's Bridge and the Ystwyth below Pont-rhyd-y-groes, exquisite Cwm Einon and splendid Cwm Ceulan, are a continual delight to those who know them. There are many lesser pleasures: hill-forts great and small, the laburnum hedges of the south-west, stretches of beech-lined road in mid-county. In history and literature, too, Ceredigion has many treasures, and much work of interpretation remains to be done. This chapter offers a brief description of the physical make-up and natural life of the area, the stage on which Ceredigion's history has been played out. Geography is always a determinant of history, and geography has been a powerful moulder of the Welsh and their idea of themselves as a people, a nation. As time goes by, and the challenges of geography are met and overcome, it has less impact, while the sense of history and culture become more influential. So it is with our county, though it will be claimed later that Ceredigion, and its past as Cardiganshire, is too disparate and its people too scattered to be considered as homogeneous units.

* * *

Geologically Ceredigion does not have the same extraordinary variety of rocks, soils and scenery found in the other western counties of Wales. The county's foundations are thick layers of sedimentary rocks, with some metals but no traces of

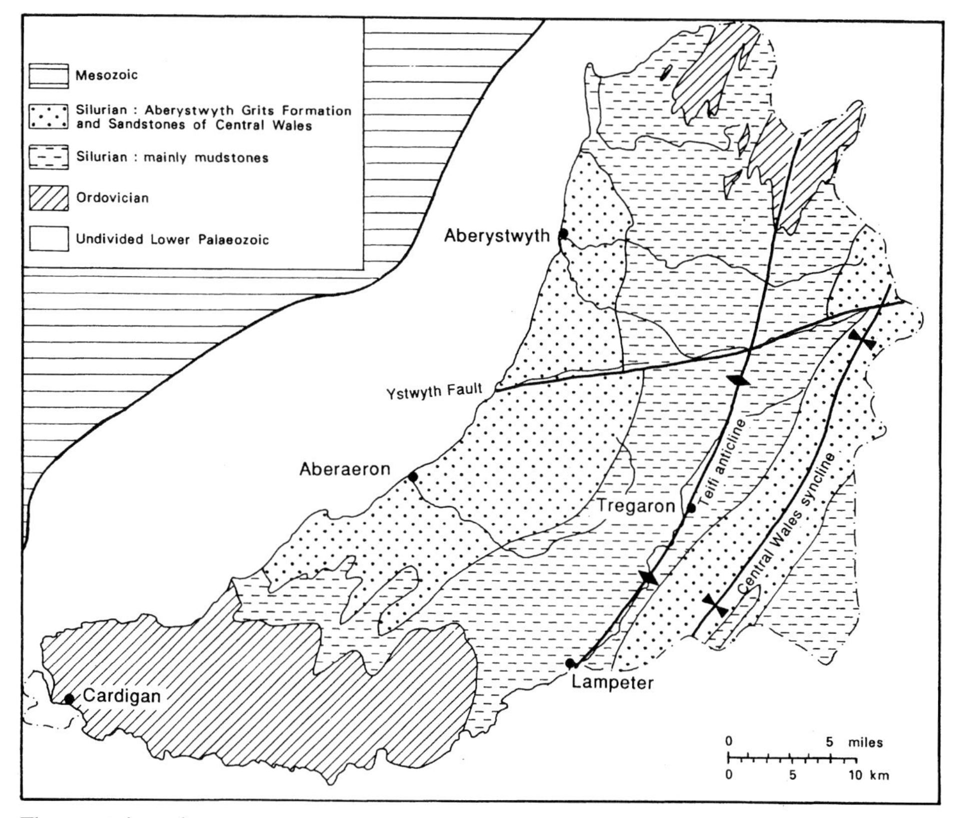

The county's geology. [From *Cardiganshire County History* Vol. 1, by kind permission]

volcanic activity, and with only a few fossils. However, the impact of nature's erosive forces has severely modified those simple foundations, and the county's complex landscape can be initially understood best in two ways.

The first way is to climb out of the valleys in which we pass most of our time. To those who spend their time living and travelling in the county's valleys, or driving out of the county along the A44 to Llangurig, Ceredigion appears to be mountainous enough, especially in the north and east. However, once out of the valleys it is clear to the viewer that the county is largely a plateau, or perhaps several plateaux or extended steps rising from the sea. Because the plateaux are largely covered with soil, supporting grass and trees, it is not easy to see how they are formed. A second way of understanding the structure of Ceredigion is to walk along the coast between Borth and Llanrhystud, between Llan-non and Aber-arth, or south from Aberaeron towards Aber-porth. This means walking either above or beneath a long series of sea-cliffs; sometimes these are formed of glacial rubble and clay, but mostly they are rock, laid down in a series of layers, some thicker than others. The strata do not lie horizontally for long; they swoop, rise, loop and plunge, and are broken by faults which have caused inconsistencies. They are the foundation of much of Ceredigion.

These strata of Silurian rocks, known as the Aberystwyth Grits, were formed some four hundred million years ago, when this area of the world's surface lay at the bottom of a now-vanished ocean. Somewhere south of this ocean was an ancient continent, whose rivers brought down mud and silt and deposited them in the shallow waters of its continental shelf. Earthquakes and storms caused these deposits to slide down the steep slope of the shelf like avalanches, so that they spread out in huge rolling cloud-like streams across the ocean bed, depositing grit and mud as they moved. Millennia passed, layer buried layer, and under pressure they eventually hardened. The ocean bed twisted and buckled as it rose from the depths to form a new continental plate, so that the layers of rocks developed faults, and the strata swelled and dived until they formed the extraordinary patterns so clearly to be seen along the coastline, especially at Craig-lais (Constitution Hill), Aberystwyth, and in the coves between Aber-porth and New Quay, particularly at Cwmtydu and Llangrannog. Inland, where great beds of mudstone were laid down at a rather later period, jets of hot mineral-laden waters rose from deep in the Earth's crust and forced themselves into the rock seams, leaving metallic deposits principally of lead and zinc, with silver, iron and occasionally copper present, often in association with layers of quartz.

The general grain of Ceredigion runs from the north-east to the south-west, as is clear from the line of the Cambrian mountains (which form an upward-bellying fold called a syncline), and the corresponding downward fold or anticline of the Teifi valley. Athwart these features runs the major geological gash known as the Ystwyth fault, which is visible from Cwmystwyth to Llanafan bridge, guiding the river Ystwyth on its way. The Ystwyth suddenly swings away north-westward, but the great fault continues straight on to Llanrhystud, forming a channel for the river Wyre. The area of Mynydd Bach between Bronnant and Trefenter appears to be an outlier which really belongs to the Cambrian range to the east. Partially ravaged by

Folded strata with cave at Cwmtydu.

the brutal planting of a wind-farm on its northern summit, Mynydd Bach – with its hilltop lake Llyn Eiddwen, its wintering geese, its stories of squatters and emigrants, and its Welsh poetic tradition – is still one of the most intriguing areas in the county.

One of the puzzles of Ceredigion's geology is the way in which these masses of sedimentary rock acquired their present shape, that is to say, the apparent steps or platforms referred to above. Another puzzle is how the area's drainage pattern developed. No later rocks overlie the great rock beds laid down 400 million years ago except rubble and clay, sand and soil, all of very recent origin. Why, when you climb out of the valleys, do so many Ceredigion horizons appear almost completely horizontal, as if drawn with a ruler? Were there later layers of rock, such as chalk, once covering the area, but which have now entirely vanished? If so, what wore them away? Geologists are still discussing these issues, and indeed the gently rolling triangle defined by the Aeron, the Teifi and the sea in the south of the county still awaits a thorough modern geological survey which might help us better to understand the area's development. Even the briefest comparison of the cliffs north and south of New Quay suggests significant differences in the processes to which the original layers of sediment were subjected.

However, it seems clear that the county's valleys began to be formed perhaps thirty million years ago, when the central mass of Wales started to rise higher and higher. Rivers drained off the high land towards the Irish Sea, finding their way along faults or areas of weaker rock and cutting into the overall surface. As the land rose, the rivers cut deeper. For example, it is easy to see from the Hafod Arms hotel at Devil's Bridge, or from the road just south of Ponterwyd, that the river Rheidol once ran in a fairly shallow valley. However, the lowering of sea level, when so much of the world's water was locked in ice, increased the river's power to erode, and it cut for itself the county's most spectacular gorge. The same events formed the gorge of the Mynach as it passes under the triple bridge and roars down its stepped waterfalls to join the Rheidol, and the fine gorge of the Ystwyth below Pont-rhyd-y-groes. The splendid gorge of the Teifi below Cilgerran was the result of somewhat different influences.

Unfortunately not all geologists agree even on whether Ceredigion really consists of platforms, though the views from a number of vantage points certainly give the impression that stepped platforms exist. The steep slopes of some of the county's valleys near the sea have been explained by the supposition that they are ancient sea-cliffs, but not everyone accepts this theory; they may have been caused by ice or snow. There is however general agreement that draining water has been the most powerful single influence on the shape of the Ceredigion landscape as a whole, with ice and snow playing an important secondary role.

The power of cold to change landscape is well known; it derives not only from the power of moving ice-sheets and glaciers, but from the impact of freeze-thaw-freeze on rocks, where water penetrates any faults and expands when frozen, thus further opening the rock. There have been successive Ice Ages during the past three million years; indeed, it can be argued that to be under ice has been the natural condition of much of Britain in recent ages, but that we are at present in a geologically-brief warm period. Ice certainly affected most of the Welsh landscape. Glaciers helped to sculpt the lower Rheidol and upper Ystwyth valleys, and they deepened the estuaries of the Dyfi and the Teifi. The rock-floor of the Dyfi estuary is so deeply hidden under mud and sand that when in the 19th century railway engineers hoped to built a bridge to connect Aberystwyth with Aberdyfi via Ynys-las they could find no rocky bottom on which to rest the foundations.

Moving ice-sheets and glaciers not only grind down rocks and deepen valleys; they carry huge quantities of material – boulders, pebbles, sand, silt and mud. When the thaw comes, these are deposited in layers and heaps on the surface which has been ground down by their movement. Where bedrock is exposed, fierce frosts broke up the surface

CWMYSTWYTH in particular bears quite spectacular evidence of the effects of snow and ice in the chill period following the disappearance of the last great ice-sheets ten thousand years ago, especially in the north-facing cirque of Cwm-du. Here the effect of freeze-thaw-freeze, the weight of snow and perhaps ice, sculpted out the best example in Ceredigion of a cirque not unlike (though greener than) the great cirques on Cadair Idris and Snowdon. A spectator standing on the Cwmystwyth-Rhaeadr road opposite the farm of Tŷ Mawr can see clearly that a great half-circle has been delved out of the steep valley side. The subsequent mass of rubble has slid, like a massive tongue, into the river valley, forcing the Ystwyth many metres out of its natural course. Into this huge green tongue of soil and stones a stream has cut deeply, up to ten metres in places, revealing the depth and nature of the rubble. At the back of the cirque, down the almost vertical rock, a small waterfall still contributes its mite to the process of erosion.

and reduced it to small stones and particles. A boat-voyage or a cliff-walk almost anywhere along the Ceredigion coast will reveal deposits of this rubble of clay, gravel, pebbles and boulders, usually called till. It forms weird cliffs in several places on the Ceredigion coastline, and the sea, wind and rain have sculpted these into strange forms. Between Aber-arth and Aberaeron the fields which run gently down to the sea are formed of this material, while the steep slope inland from the road represents an ancient rock sea-cliff (now made artificially steeper by road-widening). At Morfa Bychan too, and north of Aber-arth, the cliffs consist in part of clay or glacial till, often heavily undercut by the waves.

This overlay of clay, sand and earth was not the only result of the Ice Ages. The huge grinding sheets of ice, hundreds of metres thick, which sometimes stretched from Scotland southwards, brought material from far away; some of the most colourful pebbles to be found on Tan-y-bwlch beach, Aberystwyth, were carried all the way from Scotland. In the Teifi valley, when the ice retreated, great blocks broke off and were

THE natural lakes of Ceredigion are confined to the northern half of the county. Apart from the unusual cluster at Teifi Pools, there are other lonely, boggy lakes on the high Cambrian lands, like Llyn Fyrddon Fawr. Most accesible is the remarkable Llyn Eiddwen in the hollow on the top of Mynydd Bach. Llyn Eiddwen, like Cors Caron and the Dyfi estuary, attracts wintering geese from the Arctic, a shadowy reminder of colder times. Llyn Llygad Rheidol is a natural lake which has been increased in size by a dam. There are also several reservoirs, from the enormous and bleak Nant-y-moch to the attractive Cwm Rheidol, and numerous large and small ponds which provided water for the lead mines.

Cliffs of eroding glacial rubble, Gilfachyrhalen.

left behind. They were soon covered by glacial rubble and then slowly thawed, leaving behind small round lakes like that on the verge of the Tregaron-Pontrhydfendigaid road. These are known as kettle-holes. Perhaps the most spectacular single ice-made deposit in the county is Sarn Cynfelyn. This feature can be picked out on any map showing variations in the depth of the sea, or it can be seen by walking northwards along the clifftop from Clarach to Wallog at low tide. A huge bank of boulders and pebbles runs out some five hundred metres, and from the cliff-top its line can be traced much further out by the disturbance it causes in the flow of the tide. It is in fact nearly seven miles long, ending at the Patches shallows (in Welsh *Caerwyddno*), and was formed by glacial deposits carried from Mynydd Aran, Meirionnydd, and dumped by the retreating ice sheet. At the lowest spring tides, several miles out, the water on the Sarn is only a few feet deep. This and other *sarnau* (W. *sarn* = causeway) in Cardigan Bay gave rise to the legend of Cantre'r Gwaelod, Gwyddno's kingdom which was overwhelmed by the sea because the defences were neglected by the drunken Seithenyn.

Sarn Cynfelyn, between Clarach and Borth.

Although the effect of ice on the Cambrian mountains of Ceredigion is not nearly so spectacular as on Cadair Idris or in Snowdonia, its traces are clear enough. Llyn Llygad Rheidol, on the northern slopes of Pumlumon, is a typical ice-age remnant lake like those on the northern slopes of Cadair Idris, nestling in a cirque ground out by the ice. So great was the effect of ice on south Ceredigion that when the Teifi valley was blocked in several places the meltwater forced new channels which the river now follows near Cilgerran, Cenarth, Henllan, Alltcafan, Llandysul and Llanllwni. Further up the valley temporary lakes were formed, of which Cors Caron, at a thousand hectares the largest peat bog in southern Britain, is a remnant, built up behind a bank of ice-rubble or moraine. In many places the force of the meltwater running away towards the Irish Sea was so great that it created valleys which are now streamless. Meltwater under the ice-sheet also formed many of the smaller short valleys in the north of the county, like that at Coed Bryngwyn-mawr, east of the A487 between Tal-y-bont and Rhydypennau.

The Teifi flowing out of Cors Caron.

*　　*　　*

The formation of the county's rivers has already been mentioned. The Teifi, which for its entire length either flows through the county or forms its boundary, is by far the grandest river, and its course has been well described by Dr Richard Moore-Colyer. Its source lies in the remote pools called Llynnoedd Teifi, a group of natural lakes now partially exploited as a controlled water-source. The infant Teifi rushes steeply down into its first valley, on past Strata Florida abbey towards Pontrhydfendigaid; it dawdles lazily through the massive peat spread of Cors Caron, then rolls gently on between green fields and past Lampeter. Thence it runs through more green meadows to Rhuddlan Teifi, (where, according to the first branch of the Mabinogi, Pryderi, prince of Dyfed, held court), through a gorge at Maesycrugiau, thence to Llandysul, where the hills open out to allow the river a fine sweep before it eventually plunges into another gorge at Alltcafan. Then more meadows follow until the next gorge at Henllan, after which the river alternately meanders and rushes past Newcastle Emlyn, through the Cenarth gorge and over its low but spectacular falls, then beneath the beetling Pembrokeshire castle of Cilgerran and onwards through Cardigan town to its last, treacherous meanders into the sea. These gorges were forced through the rock by fierce flows of meltwater from or under great masses of ice, while silt and rubble blocked the original course of the river.

Ceredigion's other rivers (for despite its great influence the Dyfi can hardly be claimed for the county except in its last few miles) are much more abrupt than the Teifi. Some scurry steeply to the sea as fast as their slopes allow and some lesser streams even precipitate themselves over cliff-edges onto the beach below. The Rheidol, Ystwyth and Aeron have plenty of variety of scenery, their length allowing time for meanders and offering valleys broad enough, in places, to have allowed the spread of estate demesnes and the creation of country mansions – though the Rheidol has far fewer of these than the other two, since it is comparatively late in its course before it spreads out. Even some of the shorter rivers have their attractions; the Wyre and the Arth, for example, have both cut pleasant if inaccessible gorges into their bedrocks. The Teifi's Ceredigion tributaries, the Berwyn, Granell, Cledlyn, Clettwr and Cerdin, are particularly attractive but little visited.

With the disappearance of the ice ten thousand years ago came the growth of vegetation, but geological change had not ended – of course it never does end. Trees that grew near the land's edge from Borth to Ynys-las were slowly overwhelmed by the rising sea-level after the last great thaw. The north-running tides around Cardigan Bay built up great pebble beach-banks at Tan-y-bwlch and Borth, fronted by extensive sandbanks; behind the Borth pebble-bank, in the swampy debris, there grew the fine peat-bog of Cors Fochno, while inland the peat-bog of Cors Caron arose and continues to grow behind a bank of glacial rubble near Tregaron. Sand made by the grinding of the Irish Sea ice-sheet accumulated in the Dyfi estuary, especially at Traeth Maelgwn, where the great king of Gwynedd was said to have won the throne of Gwynedd by defying the tide more successfully than Canute,

Dunes at Ynys-las.

since he had his throne made of waxed birds' wings. Change continues today; Ceredigion is gaining land at Ynys-las with the slow extension of the sand-beaches into the sea, but is losing land at Aber-arth and at other places where the clay cliffs are eroding. The Ynys-las and Teifi estuary sand dunes grew rapidly during the medieval period.

It is the development of soil which has enabled men and women to populate Ceredigion since the last Ice Age. Ice, snow and frost, both by their sheer cold and by their movement, had created drifts, banks, sheets and cliffs of soil which was initially virtually sterile because of the low temperatures. During the centuries and millennia that followed the disappearance of ice permafrost, the soils were influenced by chemical change, by rainfall and wind, and by the slow spread of vegetation from the warmer south, along with the work of earthworms and other small creatures which helped humus to develop, thus assisting the growth of larger vegetation.

The actual nature of the soil, to what degree it is acid, aerated and base-rich, depends on the processes by which it has accumulated, and where. Erosion means that soil is thicker in hollows, thinner on hill-tops and steep slopes. Earthworms are more active in the better-aerated soils, mixing the original minerals of the soil with decaying organic matter and thus encouraging growth. Thinner, poorer soils lose their minerals, leached out by rain, giving less encouragement to strong vegetation. Where the soil is waterlogged, other processes take over, especially the growth of sphagnum moss, the base material of peat, and the resultant peat blankets grow strongly. Peat will also develop on high, well-drained land where low temperatures discourage earthworm activity. Road-works sometimes cut through and expose sections of the soil, showing an upper black layer of peat, with grey soil beneath, which in turn lies on an orange, iron-flavoured subsoil.

There is no natural limestone or chalk underlying any Ceredigion soil, and most of the surface is acid. For centuries farmers attempted to overcome this problem by buying quicklime from the lime-kilns whose ruins are still to be seen on many of Ceredigion's shores; the kilns were served by small sailing ships which brought limestone from Pembrokeshire. Even more discouraging than acidity is the poor drainage of much of Ceredigion's soil, especially on higher land, thus encouraging the development of peat. Peat was extensively exploited in Ceredigion for domestic fuel, lasting (on Borth bog on a very small scale) into the middle of the twentieth century. Virtually at the source of the Ystwyth is a pond created by peat-cutting, and many of the high peat blankets show miniature black cliffs where the cutters worked. Above Cwm-du, in Cwmystwyth, as well as in many other upland areas, are steep tracks down which the peat-cutters brought their fuel on sleds.

The soils of Ceredigion and the contours of the land greatly influenced the development of human movement and occupation. Drier soils made both communication and settlement possible, while the wetter soils discouraged both. Brown loamy soils, though often thin, have encouraged farming which until the 20th century was mixed arable and stock on all but marginal high land. Iron Age hill forts and the surviving cairnfields or burial sites in the Cambrian mountains might suggest that people clung to the high, less forested, ground, but this is misleading: hill-forts and cairns are not easily eradicated, and the high marginal land has been less worked over in subsequent ages, whereas lowland evidence of human settlement has most often been wiped out, to be revealed only by road-works or other human interference.

The soils of Ceredigion have been greatly influenced by human activity during the past seven thousand years. Burning of the primeval forests, grazing by domestic animals, ploughing and harvesting crops, building of houses, coppicing and barking of the remnant woodlands, the making of roads, the planting of forests, drainage, and the mining of lead and zinc, have all drastically altered the soil. For example, planting conifer forests involves large-scale drainage into streams and rivers, altering their nature and releasing minerals, including poisonous aluminium. Felling of conifer plantations, which are so often planted on the county's many slopes, brings swift erosion of soil into the drainage system. Lead and zinc mines have poisoned not only the rivers Ystwyth and Rheidol, but modified or wiped out vegetation in their vicinity and downstream. This can be seen in the remarkable area above Llanafan bridge, where the sweeping gravels are unable to produce any substantial vegetation, other than grasses and small shrubs, because of the underlying lead pollution which resulted from centuries of mining at Grogwynion.

Other human activities are also directly related to the county's geology. The county's largest quarry, at Hendrefelen, between Ystrad Meurig and Ysbyty Ystwyth, exploits the thickest available layers of the basic grits, capable of producing massive slabs or lesser stones and gravel as required. The thinner layers exposed at Aberystwyth were quarried for building the castle and the older houses in town; some small quarries can be seen behind the north end of Marine Terrace and in Pen-glais park. The cliff-slope at Allt-wen, at the south end of Tan-y-bwlch beach, was quarried for the new quay built in the 1830s to protect the harbour entrance. Although local stone has not been highly valued, the best of it is highly resistant to the weather, and has often lasted much better than softer sandstone and limestone imported from afar. The Rheidol and Teifi valleys have both provided sand and gravel; in the case of the Rheidol, small lakes have been created when the disused gravel pits were flooded.

The landscape of Ceredigion has also been modified by the need for water. The mountains in the lead-mining region bear the scars of leats which brought water, sometimes from miles away, to turn the waterwheels which were the only available source of energy for the crushing mills. Reservoirs were created; at Rhos-rhudd above the Newidion valley near Trisant, there are three large reservoirs, one dry and two full, created for the lead industry. By far the largest reservoir wholly within the county is at Nant-y-moch, between Ponterwyd and Tal-y-bont, made as a store for water to drive the hydro-electric plant at Cwm Rheidol, itself partly flooded as a reservoir for returning water to Llyn Dinas at night, with the added advantage of controlling river flow and thus reducing the risk of flooding once so frequent in the lower Rheidol valley. Part of the huge Llyn Brianne reservoir intrudes into the south-east of the county.

* * *

The peat deposits of Ceredigion offer valuable evidence for the history of vegetation in the county. During the millennia during which they grew, they have preserved twigs, leaves, seeds, pollen and spores of past times, so that peat cores drilled out of the bogs are time-capsules illustrating the appearance of the countryside in past ages, although they are not easy even for experts to interpret since, for example, some plants produce much more pollen than others. However, it is not difficult to imagine the development of vegetation in the county since the last retreat of the ice. Tundra conditions prevailed at first, slowly yielding to the spread of dwarf birch and willow, juniper and grasses, aided by the development of insect life. Naturally, trees would have grown taller on the lower land, where hazel shrubs would have formed an important element of woodland growth. It is possible to imagine quite thick birch-hazel scrub and forest covering much of the county during the period 7000-5000BC. Gradually the cover became more varied, with elm, oak, pine, and then lime, alder and beech increasing in numbers, while heather and bracken spread on a number of sites. The submerged trees at Borth, dating from about 4000BC, were alder, with some pine, birch, oak and hazel. Their stumps and logs appear after a winter storm, remaining visible for weeks or months until another storm covers them in sand. Trees and shrub cover must have reached all but the highest points in the county; the bleak, treeless horizons still typical of the Cambrian uplands are not in fact natural wilderness, but the work of humans and their farming activities.

Pollen samples show that, certainly from 2000BC and probably from much earlier, human activity was altering the county's vegetation. Trees were being destroyed for animals to graze and for crops to be planted; bracken, grass and sorrel

The sunken forest at Borth, showing peat beds.

increased in extent. Eventually, with the arrival of the Romans, the original woodlands were completely destroyed or totally altered by felling and regrowth. These changes would have caused considerable erosion of hillslopes and silting in streams and rivers, and would eventually have been accentuated by increased grazing, possibly associated with sheep-rearing under the Cistercian control of tens of thousands of acres from the 13th century onwards, and with woodland clearance by English military leaders anxious to afford their Welsh guerilla opponents as little shelter as possible. The pollen record also shows the peak of agricultural activity during the Napoleonic wars, when marginal land was put under cultivation and when the increasingly pauperized population squatted on common land.

Woodland on level ground is rare in Ceredigion, felled by neolithic farmers and their successors; most of the county's remaining broadleaved woods are on steep slopes, especially in the north of the county and in the Teifi valley and its tributaries, where farmers coppiced them, finding the crop of oak poles, posts, bark for tanning and firewood more valuable than the scanty grazing which clearance would have produced. Economic reasons now make it impossible for the trees to be managed as they once were, and their main value to farmers is as winter shelter for sheep. They are therefore often left unfenced, and the undergrowth, seedlings and shoots are grazed off, making new growth impossible. The rhododendron weed *ponticum*, the curse of the Snowdonia National Park, is making headway in a number of Ceredigion's woodlands. There are patches of richer woodland scattered through the county, most notably in the Teifi gorge at Coedmor and the fenced woods of the Rheidol slopes. A fine birchwood at Cwmnewidion Uchaf, like some of the area's other woodlands, has a rich variety of autumn fungi. The most freakish of Ceredigion's woods are the patches of stunted oaks which hang at several points on the cliffs between Morfa Bychan and Llanrhystud. Their leaves and shoots continuously burnt by the salt, they are only some three or four metres high, but gnarled and thick-trunked; they too were coppiced by the occupiers of the nearby farms.

Although much of Ceredigion's modern vegetation is grass for silage or acidic upland pasture, and although the variety of species is under constant economic pressure, there remains a diversity of interesting sites which show what must have been a comparatively rich botanical landscape. Insectivorous plants survive in favoured upland wet sites, and orchids thrive in dune-slacks at Ynys-las, and in a number of other favoured spots. The Teifi supports a variety of waterweeds, and interesting plant communities flourish along the county's cliffs; for example, low-growing sea-squills cast a blue mist over fields near Mwnt church. The rich plant communities once associated with traditional hayfields are now mostly remnants in church graveyards, but survive in the Aeron valley, on the slopes of Pendinas, Aberystwyth and in the Camddwr valley below Soar-y-Mynydd. Many surviving plant communities are now found in nature reserves, or are listed as sites of special scientific interest; the best-known are Ynys-las, Cors Fochno (Borth bog), Cors Caron (Tregaron bog) and the Cardigan wildlife centre.

The animal communities supported by this variety of landscape have been much

Penderi oakwood nature reserve.

reduced by human activity. The survival of the wolf into the medieval period seems well-attested by the place-name element *blaidd/bleiddiaid*, but the river-name *Arth* (i.e. bear) is actually a reference to the growling noise of the water. Gerald of Wales's late 12th century reference to the last British beavers on the river Teifi is well-known, but regarded by some scholars with scepticism. No species of deer is endemic to the county, and the deer-parks at Lodge Park (Tre'r Ddôl), Trawsgoed, Ciliau Aeron and Llanfair Clydogau have long vanished. Foxes, badgers and polecats are widespread, and elusive otters are known on most rivers; the pine marten is virtually unknown. Hares, unfortunately, have become much rarer in recent decades, and even more regrettably the red squirrel has entirely disappeared from the county. Eight species of bats occur.

The wild or feral mammal which has influenced the Ceredigion landscape more than any other is the rabbit. Rabbits were once preserved in warrens. The old name for the headland partly occupied by Aberystwyth castle was *Cwninger*, a warren; they were useful sources of meat and skins, and even in the 19th century shooting rabbits was reserved to the owners of game rights. By the 20th century they had become a serious plague, only moderated by the severe first outbreak of myxomatosis, which wiped out 99% of their population. However they are once more fairly common.

The largest breeding animal in Ceredigion is the grey seal, and specimens of seven species of whale and dolphin have been stranded on the county's beaches, including individuals from Cardigan Bay's breeding population of bottle-nosed dolphins, one of only two such groups round the British coast, and reckoned to be perhaps 130 in number. To see one of them leap eight or ten feet into the air is the finest wild-life spectacle in Ceredigion. As well as bottle-nose and Risso's dolphins, the waters of the Bay support a wide variety of fish, though heavy trawling and netting mean that the great shoals of the past are no longer known. The herring fishery once supplied part of the Cardi's staple diet, and either herring or mackerel formed the giant shoal which in 1206 filled the Ystwyth estuary, to the astonishment of the Welsh chronicler. Mackerel are still welcome summer visitors to the Bay, and sea anglers catch bass, skate, monkfish, gurnard and grey mullet, while fishermen concentrate on lobsters and crabs. Sturgeons were caught on two occasions in the Teifi, in 1878 and again in 1880; at that time they were still known in Irish rivers.

Dolphins (mother and young) off Cardigan Island. [Photo: Janet Baxter]

The varied landscape of the county, despite the impact of agriculture, still maintains a considerable variety of bird life. The large RSPB reserve at Ynys-hir stretches from the Dyfi salt-marshes through rich oak-woods to the high moorland above Furnace and Eglwys-fach, with a corresponding range of species. When the late R.S.Thomas, a keen ornithologist, was vicar of Eglwys-fach in the 1960s, he managed to observe ninety-nine different species in one day, and was mortified by his failure to see a short-eared owl normally resident on the Ynys-hir reserve; it would have given him his century. The maritime environment is naturally important, and summer visitors who take pleasure-boat trips will see gannets, auks and Manx shearwaters, while winter observers spot red-throated divers. Although the county's cliffs do not carry the rich numbers of seabirds to be found in Pembrokeshire, guillemots and razorbills nest south of New Quay, while cormorants, shags, fulmars, kittiwakes and herring gulls can be found at several spots. Above them hang scavengers and birds of prey: ravens, kestrels, buzzards and peregrines, and the clattering calls of choughs can be heard in many places.

Bird populations and species distributions vary considerably over the years, as a result of human interference and other more obscure reasons. Drainage of the great bogs drove away the bittern and spoonbill, while the loss of hayfields finished off the corncrake. On the other hand the slow spread of the fulmar southward and the recent dramatic occupation of all Europe by the collared dove are not easily explained. Other modern colonists now breeding in Ceredigion are the red-breasted merganser, the goosander and the goshawk.

Ceredigion will always be associated with the survival and revival of the red kite. In 1900 the entire Welsh population was a handful of birds surviving in Ceredigion and north Carmarthenshire, but the decline of gamekeeping and growing public interest and official support enabled that tiny population to grow and repopulate the whole of mid-Wales with several hundred birds, so that kites can sometimes be seen even over Aberystwyth, and large numbers may be seen at favoured feeding places. Another typical Ceredigion bird is the pied flycatcher, which like the two varieties of spotted woodpecker loves the hanging oak-woods. The county has heronries at Ynys-hir, Llidiardau (Llanilar), Llanllŷr (Tal-sarn), Cockshead (Olmarch), Llanerchaeron, Highmead, Llanfair (Llandysul), Henllan and Llechryd.

The herons live rather uneasily alongside the numerous freshwater anglers who enjoy Ceredigion's salmon, trout and sewin fishing on rivers and lakes. The only coarse fishing is to be found in privately-owned ponds, from one of which pike have escaped into the Teifi. Common frogs, toads, newts and slow-worms are widespread, while adders and grass snakes are scarcer. The study of insect life has been slow to develop in Ceredigion despite its rich variety; for example, it is difficult to know how much decline there has been in the county's butterfly population, while species of British moths are still being identified here for the first time, though it is not easy to tell whether they are new arrivals or have simply not previously been recognised.

Fluctuations in the numbers and species of living creatures are closely associated with changes in the landscape, which is so largely controlled by human activity. During the twentieth century there have been dramatic changes in the appearance of the rural landscape. Affluence and population growth since 1961 have caused some villages and towns to burgeon, with roadside ribbon development and the often heedless and poorly-planned scattering of bungalows built, until recently, with little consideration of their impact on the countryside or for the traditional appearance of Welsh country dwellings. On the other hand a number of the previously abandoned *tai unnos* (the one-night houses built by squatters) and smallholdings have been renovated as first or second homes, and some villages have been allowed only limited development, and so have retained something of their charm. But the fact is that, as elsewhere in Wales and England, most villages have become dormitories, losing most of their shops and post-offices, with chapels and even churches closing.

Afforestation has permanently changed much of the upland landscape, while the move from mixed farming (hay and arable) to the complete dominance of sheep and of silage for cattle, dictated by impersonal economic forces, has spread a dull green uniformity over a good deal of the enclosed land, but at least lowland areas have retained most of their hedgerows, although many have grown into lines of trees, because the expense of proper hedge maintenance is impossibly high. Subsidies intended to enable the survival of hill-farming have led to grassland reseeding which has impoverished the variety of flowering plants, and there is considerable overgrazing, giving some of the hill country an impoverished, shaven appearance. However, it seems clear that the countryside has long had problems of overgrazing; could we see the county as it was in 1750, when much of the land was still unenclosed and bare, we might not be particularly impressed. The main impact of tourism on the landscape has been the growth of caravan and chalet parks, most notably at Aberaeron, Llanrhystud, Clarach and Ynys-las. A more recent and more drastic menace to the natural landscape, however ecologically desirable it may seem to many, is the growth of wind-farms. The development newly completed at Cefn-coch, in the wilderness area above Cwmystwyth, is the fourth in the county, and the largest so far. Wales is being reindustrialised, but without workers.

Nevertheless, despite all these difficulties, Ceredigion continues to offer to the discriminating and patient observer a profoundly varied and interesting landscape with a wide range of natural inhabitants that survive mostly despite human interference, but sometimes only with our aid. Apart from the nature reserves already mentioned, the inquirer after Ceredigion's wild life may be referred to the Teifi wildlife centre on the south bank of the Teifi between Cardigan and Cilgerran; although the centre is within Ceredigion, it can only be reached by car through Pembrokeshire. Apart from having one of the finest modern buildings in the county, the reserve has splendid walks. The best way to see the magnificent Teifi gorge at this point is by canoe.

Note: Boundary Changes

Several factors have led to alterations in the boundaries of the county. In the north, the Dyfi boundary was not as firm as one might suppose, since Furnace and Glandyfi are nearer to Machynlleth than to Aberystwyth, so the former town acts as an alternative centre of gravity. Under the Poor Law legislation of 1834, the northernmost civil parish of Cardiganshire, Ysgubor-y-coed, was incorporated into the Machynlleth Union under the Poor Law of 1834, and became part of Montgomeryshire registration county and eventually of Machynlleth Rural District. However, in 1934 it was transferred to the Aberystwyth Rural District, and is again part of Ceredigion.

The southern or Teifi boundary has a more complex history, which it is not easy to elucidate. In 1832 the county parliamentary constituency was extended across the Teifi from Adpar to include the town of Newcastle Emlyn, while the Cardigan borough constituency was extended to include Bridge End and St Dogmael's. However, these enclaves south of the Teifi remained for some time in their respective counties for all purposes excepting parliamentary elections, and eventually Newcastle Emlyn returned to the Carmarthenshire constituency. The St Dogmael's story is more complicated. Bridge End was incorporated into Cardiganshire by the 1888 County Councils Act, and commonsense has decreed that it should remain in the county, along with Cardigan marshes. Part of St Dogmael's parish in 1894 became a new civil parish, Llandudoch-drefol, part of the urban district of Cardigan, and therefore within the county. In March 2003 it was transferred back to Pembrokeshire.

The end of wilderness? Cefn-croes, above Cwmystwyth, photographed in 2000 and in 2004 by Martin Wright.

2. Naming Ceredigion

There are some strange place-names in Ceredigion. Why are there farms with names like Denmark, Brysgaga, Wallog, Palmon? What is a non-Welsh-speaker to make of Pontrhydfendigaid or Bwlchyfadfa? Some names are delightful: Tafarnybugail, Castell Nadolig, Maesymeillion, while others are mysterious – Wstrws has baffled all the experts. A thoughtful tourist may notice a scattering of Hebrew names among the county's villages. Much, though not all, was explained in the year 2000 when Iwan Wmffre's enormously detailed thesis on Ceredigion place-names reached the National Library of Wales, and it will take a while yet for all its implications to be realised; such a brief treatment as this chapter can in no way do justice to Wmffre's remarkable work. Place-names have for thousands of years been a source of speculation by those keen to explain them in terms of history and personal relationships, but only in the late 19th century did people realise that there could be a science of place-name study, based on historical documents, local pronunciation and comparative linguistics. Here we can only touch on a few basic issues, not offer explanations of the thousands of place-names in Ceredigion.

Ceredigion's place-names are overwhelmingly Welsh in origin, but that does not always make them easy to explain, even for a Welsh-speaker. The oldest names in European countries are usually river-names, and Ceredigion rivers comply with that general rule. The earliest recorded place-names in the county are *Stuctia* and *Tuerobis*, river-names found in the classical geographer Ptolemy's list of place-names around the coast of Britain; he located the two rivers between St David's Head and the Llŷn peninsula. *Stuctia* is a form of a British word which developed into modern Welsh *ystwyth*, meaning sinuous or flexible, and obviously refers to the river Ystwyth. *Tuerobis* is a corrupted form of the British name which gives us the word Teifi, which is connected with other river-names such as Tâf and Thames, all derived from a British root meaning 'dark', as in modern Welsh *tywyll*. Another British name in Ceredigion known to us from classical sources is *Bremia*, which derives from the same root as modern Welsh *brefu*, the lowing or mooing of cattle, preserved in the name Llanddewi*brefi*.

The meanings of place-names can be exasperatingly elusive; the obvious explanation is not always correct, and difficult names lead to home-made explanations ('folk etymologies') which are almost always wrong. The river name Aeron is typical of the difficulties facing the amateur student. Welsh dictionaries give the meaning of *aeron* as berries, which could well explain the name of a river flowing among fruiting trees like rowan and hawthorn. Most scholars however have agreed that the name derives from the Celtic goddess of war, *Agrona*; in early Welsh *aer* meant 'battle, war', and those who have seen the Aeron in winter flood will understand how it acquired the name. Having said that, Iwan Wmffre is not willing to condemn the simpler explanation.

The names Ceredigion, Cardigan and Aberteifi are clearly linked together by history. Ceredigion is the oldest name we have for the early Welsh kingdom, while Aberteifi ('Teifi estuary') was the Welsh name for the area in which the Normans built their town. The Normans did not adopt that name, however; rather inappropriately, they borrowed the kingdom name Ceredigion for their town, corrupting it to Cardigan, while the Welsh kept the original name of Aberteifi. From the 1230s Cardigan was a local administrative and political centre, and remained so for several centuries before yielding place to Aberystwyth and, recently, to Aberaeron. Given Cardigan's borough status, the town's name was imposed very early on the district it controlled, hence *Cardiganshire*. The Welsh followed suit in their own way by calling the shire after the name of the town, Sir Aberteifi, although the version *Sir Ceredigion* was officially preferred in 1889 when the County Councils Act came into force.

The name Ceredigion itself transparently means 'the people of Ceredig', though who Ceredig was is obscure. He has traditionally been identified as one of the sons of Cunedda, a fifth-century North British warlord credited with driving the Irish out of north and west Wales. Some eminent scholars have doubted the very existence of Cunedda, while others have defended him. Certainly a parallel can be drawn with a number of Welsh district-names which derive from men's names: Meirion-nydd, Dunoding < Dunawd, Rhufoniog < Rhufawn. The personal name Ceredig can be

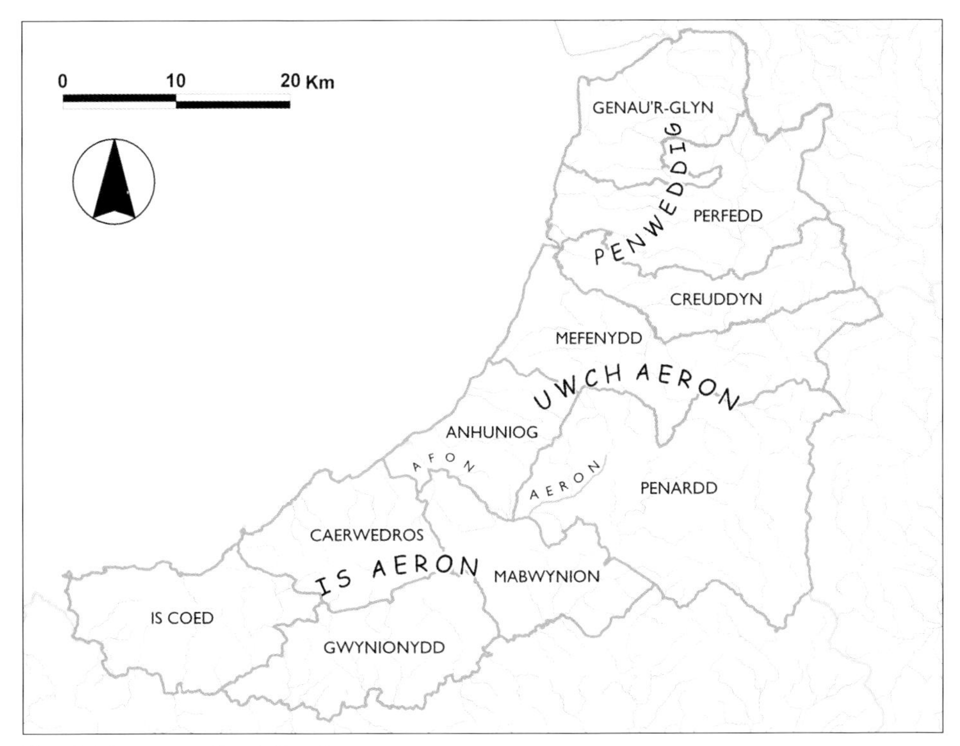

The divisions of medieval Ceredigion.

[Copyright Terrence James, drawn as part of his DIGIWATU project constructing a digital map of the ancient territorial and administrative boundaries of Wales].

associated with the Welsh *caru*, 'love'; *'câr'*, a relative. Other personal names used for places bear overtones of early Welsh legend. Thus Bedd Taliesin (Taliesin's grave) is a cromlech which has at some early period been given the name of the poet associated with the 6th century A.D., and his name was adopted in the 19th century by the village on the main road below the monument. Wallog mansion, between Clarach and Borth, carries the early male personal name Gwallawg; a 13th-century manuscript refers obscurely to Gwallawg ap Lleënawg (literally 'Hairy son of Literate'!), but who he was we shall never know. The saint's name Cynfelyn has been borrowed from the nearby church of Llancynfelyn for the great natural bank of stones (W. *sarn*) which runs from Wallog beach for nearly seven miles out to sea, terminating in the shoal called on Lewis Morris's map of 1748 Caerwyddno, but now prosaically known as the Patches. Gwyddno, of course, was the legendary king of Cantre'r Gwaelod, the drowned land off the coast of north Ceredigion and Meirionnydd.

Some of the oldest names in the county are those of its sub-districts. In the period of Welsh rule before the coming of the Normans, the whole of Wales was divided into *gwledydd* (singular *gwlad*), of which Ceredigion was one; *gwlad* might in this context be translated as 'chiefdom' or petty kingdom. At some unknown time these *gwledydd* were divided into *cantrefi* (literally translated, a cantref is a hundred settlements), which in turn were subdivided into *cymydau* (*cwmwd* = a neighbourhood). However, only one genuine *cantref* name survives in the county, that of Penweddig, between the Dyfi and the Ystwyth. This name is obscure, but possibly means 'the farthest land', and indeed Penweddig is the northern outpost not only of Ceredigion but of the larger early kingdom of Deheubarth. The commote names all survive; from north to south they are Genau'r Glyn, Perfedd, Creuddyn, Mefenydd, Anhuniog, Pennardd, Mabwynion, Caerwedros, Gwynionydd and Iscoed. Genau'r Glyn ('mouth of the valley') is a reasonable description based on the river Leri, while Perfedd ('middle, centre') is the middle commote of Cantref Penweddig. Creuddyn is more difficult; the late Melville Richards suggested that it meant 'fort', and could refer to Pen Dinas, the spectacular hill fort at the western tip of the commote. Mefenydd or Myfenydd, Mabwynion or Mebwynion and Gwynionydd all defy explanation, unless they are from putative personal names such as Myfan, Mebwyn and Gwynion. Anhuniog certainly derives from the man's name Anhun, from Latin *Antonius*. Pennardd simply means a hill-promontory. The only reasonable explanation of Caerwedros is that it was the fort of a man called Gwedros, though the name is not otherwise known. Iscoed simply means 'below or this side of the wood', that is, nearer to the centre of administration.

This original layer of Welsh administrative areas and their names was overlaid, in Ceredigion and Carmarthenshire, by units with the name *gwestfa*. This was in origin a food-tax for the support of the local ruler, and came to be applied to the areas from which it was collected. Ceredigion was divided into fifty-six of these units, whose names sometimes derived from kindred groups, sometimes from parish or local centre names, others are from personal names or are quite obscure in origin. The very smallest units of late medieval administration were the township and the parish. Township names were sometimes those of the largest farm in the area, while others are descriptive. Thus *Elgar* township in the parish of Llanfihangel Genau'r-glyn gave its name to a farm; Elgar is a rare early man's name, once borne by a medieval hermit on Bardsey. Other early terms which survive in place-names are *maenol* (estate) and *rhandir* (share-land); the latter apparently a subdivision of *gwestfa*.

Parish names often have a religious origin; *llan* (an enclosure), *capel* (chapel), and *bangor* (fenced enclosure), each referring to a place of worship, are all well-known elements. They are often followed by the name of the saint to whom the church was dedicated, either a native saint (e.g. Padarn, Dewi, Deiniol, Ffraid, Llwchaearn, Tysul) or a Biblical saint (Mihangel = Michael and All Angels, Mair, Pedr). Because the Biblical names are few, but frequently used, qualifying elements were added, hence Llanfihangel Ynys Edwin (now Eglwys-fach), and Llanbedr Pont Steffan; Edwin is of course an early English name, while the identity of Stephen of Lampeter is uncertain, as is that of the Walter of Llanfihangel Castell Gwallter and Bwlchgwallter (Ysbyty Ystwyth). Unfortunately, names in *Llan-* can be misleading. Llanfarian, south of Aberystwyth, has no church of that name, and there are examples elsewhere in Wales of other elements, notable *Glan-* and *Nant-* having been transmogrified into *Llan-* names. Llanfarian is recorded in a Gogerddan document as *Nantafarian*. On the other hand, a *Llan* lacking a church may nevertheless be genuine. Between New Cross and Abermagwr, on the Aberystwyth-Pontrhydfendigaid road, there is the farm of *Llanddwy*. The name is consistently found in this form from the 16th century. Despite the absence of any trace of a church, the element *–dwy* preserves an older spelling of the word *Duw*, meaning God. Near Devil's Bridge is the farm of *Llaneithr*. Here again, although there is no church, the element *Llan-* appears to be original; Eithr was the name of the man traditionally believed to have granted land to the church of Padarn.

The element *Tre-* or *–dre* could well confuse any learner of Welsh who knows that *tref* in modern Welsh means 'town'. In fact, the English original '-ton' meant a settlement, as small as a single farm, and the Welsh word developed in exactly the same way, from 'farm' to 'town'. Tregaron preserves the element, along with what is usually reckoned to be a personal name, an early saint. It may disappoint some to know that there is a more likely explanation – Caron is the name of the lordship and parish of the district, of which Tregaron developed as the centre. There is no particular reason why this should be a man's name; the only known linguistic parallel is the Scottish river-name Carron, a name which means 'hard', referring to the stony bed of a river.

Many of the country houses of Ceredigion bear ancient names. Some are easily understood, and seem to have survived unaltered since they were named centuries ago, e.g. Ynys-hir (at Eglwys-fach), Trawsgoed, Alltyrodyn, Ffynnon-bedr. The well-known name Nanteos is an example of a re-naming; the site and house were once known as Neuadd Lawdden (Llawdden's Hall). The name Nanteos in modern Welsh means 'nightingale stream', but despite the fact, referred to in Chapter 1, that bird populations have changed over the centuries, it nevertheless seems unlikely that the nightingale ever sang there. The more likely explanations are either that the squire who changed the name had an unusually poetic imagination, or that some other bird was meant, perhaps the linnet. Other mansion names are not so obvious at first glance. Gogerddan derives from Welsh *garth*, meaning a promontory, an element which occurs in numerous Welsh place-names such as Llannarth, Cenarth and Penarth. Brynog, in the Aeron valley, is nothing to do with the Welsh *bryn*; the first syllable rhymes with English 'brine', and almost certainly derives from *brân/brain* (crow, crows), and must originally have been Braenog, 'the crow-haunted hill'. The second element of Hafod Uchdryd is a personal name which died out after the 14th century; it is borrowed from an early English name which still survives as the surname Oughtred. Lloyd Jack, in the Aeron valley, is probably from Clwyd-jack (Jack's gate) or Clwt-jack (Jack's plot).

The farm names of Ceredigion offer a rich variety of descriptions. The simplest names consist of only one element, e.g. Cilie, Carrog, though some single-element names may have been whittled down from a compound original. Most names are made up of at least two elements, sometimes linked by the definite article *y/yr*. Most often these names consist of a noun followed by a qualification. These may be linked into one word (Glanystwyth, Hafodiwan, Felinbedw) or be separate words, either linked by a hyphen or hyphens (Tan-yr-allt) or not (Hafod Uchdryd). Neither the Ordnance Survey nor local custom are reliable in matters of hyphenation and compounding. At the risk of pedantry, the most accurate form of the name for a well-known coastal settlement is *Llan-non* – St Non's place of worship. The present common usage, 'Llanon', would mean 'enclosure of ash-trees', if it meant anything at all.

The first element of compound farm names may be a word denoting a settlement, including: *Tŷ* = house, *Tyddyn* = originally a farm, now meaning a smallholding, *Hafod* = summer farm, *Bod-* =

A few farm and house names.

dwelling, *Hendre* = home farm, *Lluest* = summer-grazing house. The common element *Ty'n-* should not bear an accent, since it is an abbreviation of *tyddyn*. A name may describe the position of the dwelling relative to a landscape feature: thus *Cefn* = rear, *Pen* = top, summit, *Tan/Dan* = under, *Blaen* = top. Then again the locational element may actually be the very feature of the landscape where the farm is located: *Bryn* = hill, *Aber* = confluence, *Rhyd* = ford, *Ffos* = ditch, *Rhos* = moor. Personal names occur quite frequently in farm names, suggesting the name either of the original pioneer or a subsequent owner, usually but not exclusively male, e.g. Hendre-Rhys, Llety Ifan Hen, Pantdaniel, Beddgeraint, Ffynnonmeredydd, Moelifor. Usually we have no idea who these people were, but Parcrhydderch, near Llangeitho, is an exception. Rhydderch was a 14th-century *uchelwr* whom we shall encounter in a later chapter. He was a landowner of free descent, a patron of poets and scholars, after whom the White Book of Rhydderch, the earliest surviving copy of the *Mabinogion*, was named. Many of these personal names connected with farms may go back even further than the 14th century.

Llwyn Merch Gwilym (the grove of Gwilym's daughter, in Lledrod parish) and Esgair Tanglwst near Rhydlewis certainly preserves the names of women (Tanglwst is from Tangwystl, 'hostage of peace'; *esgair* = ridge). Other colourful elements in the more easily understood farm-names include trees (*-ynn* = ash trees, *derw/en* = oak, *llwyn* = grove, *gwern* = alder, *celynnen* = holly), plants (*banadl* = broom, *craf* = wild garlic or ramsons), birds (*crychyddod* = herons, *brain* = crows, *barcud* = kite) and animals (*blaidd/bleiddiaid* – wolf, wolves, *cadno* = fox, *baedd* = boar).

This alarmingly brief treatment of farm names should not persuade the reader that this is an easy study. Some farms have changed their names. For instance, the 16th-century Strata Florida rentals for Cwmystwyth list the abbey's farms, including Dolybeudy. But where is Dolybeudy now? An 18th-century rental gives the clue: *Tŷ Mawr alias Dolybeudy*. Tŷ Mawr is to be seen below Cwm-du in Cwmystwyth; why the name was changed is a mystery. Other farm names have vanished because they were swallowed up long ago in a still-continuing process of amalgamation, though their names survive in documents as names of fields, recognisable as farm-names by the forms they contain, such as *Tŷ*, *Llety*. Some farm names have been altered over time to give an easier explanation: thus Cynhawdre (Swyddffynnon) became known as Gwenhafdre. The latter name means, literally, pale-summer-settlement, but it is actually a corruption of the original name, which derives from *cynhaeaf* + *tref*, meaning 'harvest-home'. The two farms on the same site, mapped as Gwenhafdre Uchaf and Isaf, have recently been renamed by the owners as Gwenhafdre and Cynhawdre, thus restoring the original spelling.

The vast estates of the monastery at Strata Florida left their mark on Ceredigion names. The name of the abbey itself is a latinisation of Welsh *Ystrad Fflur*, 'the strand of the river Fflur'. *Fflur*, like *(E)Leri*, seems to be a river-name derived from a female personal name. The blocks of land owned by the monks have names that include Tirymyneich (the monks' land), and individual farms include Cwrt (the court or administrative centre of a grange) and Mynachdy'r Graig. Some names are not religious; Hafodygofaint has nothing to do with 'convent'. *Gofaint* means 'blacksmiths'. Llety'r Synod is much more likely to be Llety'r Asynnod (the donkeys' lodging!) than a meeting of monks. Synod Inn is a puzzle; the tavern was originally called the Black Cock.

Every farm maintains a set of field names, for ease of reference. Field names in England have been studied fairly intensively, while in Wales the subject has barely been opened. Field names often change with a change of ownership, especially if a non-Welsh-speaker acquires the farm. They also change, naturally, when field patterns are altered, as they often have been over the centuries. Field-names may be found in the tithe map schedules of the 1840s, though not for all parishes, and can often be found in 18th-century estate surveys; unfortunately these, in Ceredigion, do not go back further than 1740. The majority of Ceredigion field names are extremely boring: translated, they simply mean Below the House, Above the House, Calves' Field, Colts' Field, Geese Field, Three-Cornered Field, Little Field, Big Field, Hay Field and so on.

However, poring over the tithe schedules and estate surveys or questioning farmers does produce a harvest of interesting and unusual names, often inexplicable. The following examples all come from the Ystwyth valley and its tributaries. Cae Pickpocket, for example, illustrates a farmer's sardonic humour; this was probably a field which no amount of expenditure of money or effort could make profitable. Cae Llaw Chwith (Left-handed field) is an odd name, which may refer to its position relative to the farmhouse. Why should 'Banc Ladies' have been so called? William Eardeley Richardes, squire of Bryneithin, Llanychaearn, called some of his fields Captain, Major, General and Governor, which seems odd, but he could never forget that he had been an officer on the field of Waterloo. The name Cae Dial seems exciting, since Welsh *dial* means 'revenge', but unfortunately for romance, this is the English word 'dial', meaning a place where the haymakers erected a temporary sundial with a pole and clods of earth to measure the passage of the hours. Some field names seem quite incomprehensible in their tithe-schedule spelling: what on earth are the meanings of Cae Llwst, Llanrabel, Cae Crank, and Ag Felly (which simply means 'and so on')?

SOME of the best Ceredigion place-names do not appear on any maps known to me – Banc Siôn Cwilt, by Talgarreg, for example; Siôn, whoever he was, had nothing to do with quilts, he was *gwyllt*, a wild man. The hill on the A487 which runs down from Waun-fawr towards Bow Street is *Rhiw Siôn Saer*, John the carpenter's hill, while the narrow unclassified hill climbing south-east out of Llanfihangel-y-Creuddyn is *Rhiw Harri*, supposedly named after an English king who passed that way, or after Henry Tudor on his way to Bosworth. Who knows?

If the overwhelmingly Welsh names of Ceredigion are to be thus brutally summed up in these few pages, the comparatively few names from other languages should surely be dismissed in a paragraph. Yet by their very scarcity and interest they demand notice. There appear to be no representatives in the county of the tiny group of pre-Celtic names in Wales such as Môn, Menai and (possibly) Ewenni. Nor are there any names of genuine Latin or French derivation, which are indeed scarce over the whole of Wales. The nearest we can get to a classical place-name is

The Hebrew element in local place-names.

the abandoned farm of Sarn Elen, south of Llanafan, named after the well-known Roman road whose name *may* derive from Helen the mother of Constantine the Great, but is more likely to be of Celtic origin. Irish settlement has been briefly mentioned in Chapter 1, and it left some mark on the onomastic landscape; for example *Clarach*, the river north of Aberystwyth, is usually explained as Irish, but Iwan Wmffre is sceptical. The commonest Irish element in Ceredigion is *Cnwc-*, meaning a small hill, obviously related to the native Welsh *cnwch*, found in the settlement name of Cnwch Coch, near Abermagwr in the Ystwyth valley. The element *cil-*, as in Cilcennin and Ciliau, may possibly be Irish, meaning a cell or even a church, but is perhaps more likely to be Welsh, and to mean a 'nook'. The word *Gwyddel* (an Irishman) is not necessarily connected with the early Irish migrations of the late Roman or early post-Roman period; names using this element may be later, or may even derive eventually from Welsh *gwŷdd*, meaning scrub or trees. Only one Norse or Viking name survived from the period when the longships were familiar with the Welsh coast; the earliest name for Cardigan Island is *Hastiholm*, uniquely found in a document of 1268, after which the name vanished. The main foreign elements remaining are Hebrew and English.

Wales is unique in Europe for the number of its Biblical place-names. Beulah, Joppa, Nebo and the rest all began their Welsh careers as names of chapels. When early 19th-century settlements began to form around them, the name was often adopted for the settlement. Thus north Ceredigion has Salem east of Penrhyn-coch, with Moriah, Capel Seion (= Zion) and Pisgah on the road from Aberystwyth to Devil's Bridge, Joppa and Nebo south-east of Llanrhystud, and Bethania, Horeb and Beulah further south still.

Early English place-names in Ceredigion are extremely rare: the only ones of which I am aware are Gwbert (from a personal name, Godbert), Y Ferwig (= Berwick), the farm and former monastic mill of Fulbrook, near Tregaron, which is named in Strata Florida documents of the 16th century, and Mwnt (= Mount) north of Cardigan. *Betws*, as in Betws Bledrws, is usually explained as being the English *bead-house*, a house of prayer, though the form isn't actually known in any English source. Later well-known and most obvious English intruders, cheerfully adopted by the Welsh, are the names of London derivation like Bow Street, Chancery (formerly Chancery Lane) and Temple Bar. Their origins are not entirely clear: Bow Street is believed to be the result of a local magistrate's jest as he set up his petty sessions in a tavern. Not only does Chancery match it to the south of Aberystwyth; the five-way junction at Southgate (named after the tollgate, cf. Northgate Street in

Aberystwyth) was once known as Piccadilly, and the name of Constitution Hill has been transferred from the heart of London and imposed on Aberystwyth's northern promontory, since climbing it is good for the constitution – a typical example of heavy place-name humour; the hill's proper name of Craig-lais has been almost forgotten, though the second element survives in Pen-glais. The hamlet of New Row, near Pont-rhyd-y-groes, was a 19th-century creation of the lead-mining industry. It is rather surprising that the industry did not have a greater impact on the nomenclature of its landscape. Even the Wesleyan chapel built near Pont-rhyd-y-groes for English immigrant leadminers to worship in, and which is now a ruin, is called Capel Saeson (Englishmen's chapel). However, one of the early mining sites in Cwmystwyth is on the slopes of Copper Hill, irritatingly rendered into Welsh as *Bryn Copa* (hill-summit), while the 18th-century iron forge at Furnace gave the settlement its present name. Perhaps the most comical of all the late English names in the county is at the settlement of Llundain-fach (little London) in the Aeron valley, where a tributary stream has been locally rechristened *Tems*, i.e. Thames, to match.

STREET names in medieval towns are intriguing, sometimes colourful. Aberystwyth's Queen Street was originally Lurkers' Lane, then Barker's Lane. Princess Street's pretentiousness is deservedly undermined by the pleasant Welsh *Lon Rosmari*. Vulcan Street suggests a smithy or foundry. Pound Place denotes the pound for stray animals. Windmill Place really was the location of a windmill, visible in the earliest pictures of the town. It is a shame that the boring South Road has replaced Shipwrights Row, and that Heol-y-moch (Pig Street) no longer exists as such.

Derwen-gam, a compromise after earlier battles.

The influence of the drovers who took cattle to England for the London market has been suggested as the origin of at least some English names. Oakford was the invention of a local landlord, and in the 1960s became the object of a long-running campaign to re-establish the Welsh name, Derwen-gam. Highmead and Falcondale are other examples of the work of anglicising landlords, while Derry Ormond is part Welsh (*deri* = oak trees), part personal name. In the late 18th century *Trawsgoed* was translated for its anglicised Welsh owners into the meaningless 'Crosswood', a name which still lingers, though the original Welsh form has largely displaced it. Taverns have also helped in the process of naming communities; thus Ceredigion has Synod Inn, New Cross and Cross Inn, where 'Cross' refers to a cross-roads. At Ysbyty Ystwyth the English 'beer-house' has become Welsh *berws* in the stream-name Nantyberws.

The imposition of Devil's Bridge on the properly-named Pontarfynach is an example of deliberately anglicising influence. The devil plays no part in earlier Welsh folklore, while stories such as that of the old woman and her cow or cat now attached to the medieval bridge are well-known in England. Devil's Bridge and

Thomas Johnes's nearby Hafod estate were a major goal of late 18th-century tourists , and the English name was adopted for the stiff tongues of English visitors, while the story of the bridge, like the story of Llywelyn and his hound at Beddgelert, was added as another tourist perk; both act as onomastic or name-explaining tales. Artists' Valley is another attempt to make life more comfortable for the tongues of visitors, intended to replace Cwmeinon.

There are of course English loanwords in Welsh which occur in place-names, but which usually occur in compound names and were not considered as English words by the time of the naming process. Thus English 'park', an enclosure, became the standard Ceredigion dialect word *parc* for a field at some quite early, though undateable, period. It is still the standard word south of Llangrannog, but its former extent is obvious from the Aberystwyth suburb of Penparcau, while field-name lists from the 19th century yield 'Cae Parc', suggesting the process by which the all-Wales element *cae* displaced *parc*. Another such element is *comins*, clearly an English loanword, which occurs in Comins Coch, Aberystwyth, and as the squatters' zone of Comins, now almost deserted, in the village of Llanfihangel-y-Creuddyn.

Some English place-names reflect a local sense of humour. It was sometimes the habit to give the most distant field on a farm a name like Newfoundland, or Australia. In the village of Llanfihangel-y-Creuddyn, the point furthest from the village centre which was still reckoned part of the village is known as Russian Steppes (wild, barren country!). A group of houses in Llan-non has been known for a century as Siberia. More grimly, two long-established houses in Ysbyty Ystwyth are called Tyburn and Newgate, after two of London's most notorious prisons.

There is a thin scattering of fairly recent English names for mansion houses and farms through Ceredigion. Falcondale and Highmead have already been quoted: further examples in the south are Scotland Hill, Bowls, Rocklands; in mid-county are Navy Hall and Green-grove (historically both were mansions of the minor gentry, and the latter is a translation of a Welsh original). In the north are Lovesgrove, Castle Hill (both minor-gentry houses), Brickyard Farm, and Staylittle (near Tal-y-bont). Peterwell is another English translation of the original Welsh Ffynnon-bedr.

Many names remain mysterious, especially farm names. What is one to make of Gelmast (Cwmystwyth)? Can it really be, as believed locally, named after a wrecked ship called 'Gallant Mast'? It seems highly unlikely. Why alter Gwar-caeau (1891, in Trefeurig) to Columbia (1982)? What of the ancient battlefield site of Antaron, at Rhydyfelin south of Aberystwyth? Some odd names yield up their meanings with the help of the dictionary: the unusual Grip (Llangwyryfon) is not English but Welsh *crip* (= a slope). The strangely Latinate Adsol-wen (Llansanffraid) is simply Welsh *adsol* (= dry grass), defying the local folk-etymology. Pantinker (near Llechryd) is an Ordnance Survey corruption of Parctincer. Mock (Ffostrasol) may be an anglicised form of the affectionate abbreviation of the name Morgan. What is the last element in Alltyblaca? Some of these questions, and others not here posed, may be answerable, but many will certainly remain obscure.

How many of these villages can you locate on a county map?

Because of the backward state of Welsh place-name studies, despite the heroic efforts of a handful of individuals, it is still too early to draw detailed conclusions about Ceredigion place-names, even though Iwan Wmffre's wonderful thesis is now available in print. Study of the distribution of place-name elements has far to go. Nevertheless, one conclusion stands out. The most fundamental lesson place-names have for the historian is to indicate the influences which have been brought to bear on the landscape throughout the centuries. Humans are creatures for whom naming is an essential process. If you had no name, how would you know who you are, and how would I speak about you in your absence? If this place has no name, how do I know where I am, and how do you know where you are going, or where you have come from? Through its names the landscape can speak to us, though dimly, of the past, preserving its memories in its nomenclature, and obviously it speaks much more richly to those who know Welsh.

3. Cairns and Hill Forts

Bronze-age ring-ditches at Llandysul.

[Copyright: Welsh Development Agency].

The historic landscape of Ceredigion is like an onion; we live on the skin, but in our imaginations we can peel away layer after layer to look for the people who came before us and the traces they left behind. A better comparison would be to describe the landscape as a palimpsest; this was a sheet of parchment which was so valuable that a medieval scribe would scrape off the original text and write out a new text – but a skilled reader can trace the original writing under the more recent one. Likewise, the archaeologist can 'read' the landscape, looking for banks, tracks, ditches, mounds and standing stones – all the scars left by the generations before us. Modern archaeology is barely a century old, and in the first half of that century skilled workers were few. Excavations were conducted at Strata Florida abbey in the 1880s, and later at the Roman fort at Llanio, but it was a long time before these pioneering efforts were followed up. In any case, much of our knowledge depends on random discovery. For example, when North Sea gas-pipes were laid south of Bow Street, the necessary digging laid bare a site used for thousands of years for habitation and burial. In 2002 the remarkable gold disc, illustrated on the cover and as frontispiece, was discovered in Cwmystwyth (see p. 36). In 2003 excavations in a field near Llandysul, in preparation for the building of new premises for the printing and publishing company which has produced this book, revealed an important prehistoric site. Although it has not yet been accurately dated nor the details published, references to it will be found below.

The layers of the onion are not as deep in Ceredigion's past as they are in many places in Britain. Prior to the last Ice Age (i.e. before 11,000BC) only a solitary flint tool from Dol-y-bont near Borth remains as possible evidence of human occupation, though humans must have been here in previous ages, before the deep cold drove them south. And when Ceredigion finally emerged from under that great sheet of ice, snow and frost, it would not have been recognisable to our eyes, especially since the sea-level was much lower than it is today, virtually linking Wales to Ireland. When it became warmer, the sea slowly rose and people moved back northwards, but they would have found better hunting and living conditions on land that is now submerged. The remains of pine-tree and alder trunks, with their beds of soil and twigs, that sometimes emerge from the sands of Borth beach, are testimony to woodlands that flourished six thousand years ago, and people certainly walked that land.

Scattered thinly over the Ceredigion countryside are monuments and other sites from the ancient past: standing stones, burial cairns, burnt mounds, hill-forts. Hidden in the earth, or occasionally scattered on the surface, are artefacts: flint and bronze tools and weapons, sherds of pottery – even the occasional unbroken clay vessel, and a single splendid bronze shield, found at Aberllolwyn two centuries ago – and fragments of bone. These are chance survivors; the weapons and tools of wood our ancestors used, the leather and cloth they made, have either vanished or remain undiscovered, yet they must have been common. European discoveries of frozen and bog-preserved bodies have given us a better understanding of the food people ate, the clothes and the tattoos that they wore, the hunting gear they carried. One such body was found in Tregaron bog in 1811; it is reported to have been headless, and may possibly have been an Iron Age sacrifice, but that is simply guesswork. It would be possible to write a wholly speculative chapter or book on pre-Roman (and indeed Roman) life in Ceredigion, drawing on the vast amount of material collected Europe-wide, but such a book would be full of conditional phrases, of words like 'possibly', and 'perhaps', 'we may guess that' and so on. It would be so vague as to be worthless.

Our difficulties in comprehending the ancient past are immense. It was indeed another country, where they did things differently, though we should not forget that they felt the same needs and some of the fears and hopes that we feel. They were far more subject than we are to the varying seasons and climate. A year with little sunshine made for hunger, even starvation, as did the exhaustion of the soil by cropping. The spread of peat over the hills during the second millennium BC drove people from the higher land. They left no written records, only artefacts, bones, food-waste and man-made features in the landscape. Their interpretation is a matter for specialists, and has become increasingly a matter of complex applied science. Our eyes are further fogged by preconceptions which are difficult to shed. For example, most of us were taught at school a prehistory which depended on a culture-population theory of invasion-conquest-occupation-replacement. Thus we may well have been taught that Neanderthal beings were exterminated by early Stone Age flint-working hunters who were replaced by later flint-working farmers, who were in their turn replaced by Bronze Age people, who were largely displaced by Iron Age people, whom we assume spoke a variety of dialects which we call Celtic. Yet we have only to look around Wales today to see that one technology can displace another, that one language can overwhelm another, without any absolute need for a massive replacement of population – although that process too is at work in Ceredigion and other rural areas of Wales today.

Who were the first post-glacial people who settled Ceredigion? Are they the direct ancestors of today's Cardis? The first serious scholar to attempt an answer to the question was H.J. Fleure (1877-1969), professor of Geography at Aberystwyth. He was among other things a measurer of heads, believing that the length-breadth ratio of the skull could denote particular racial types. He was fascinated by his encounter with the shepherd brothers John and James James of Nant-y-moch on the slopes of Pumlumon in the first half of the 20th century; he believed that they were representatives of the original population of Britain, their ancestors having survived in their bleak mountain hideouts for thousands of years. Fleure wrote eloquently of 'the Little Dark People' who in west Wales were still 'often a large majority in a religious or bardic gathering,' or on the streets of Aberystwyth, 'having a somewhat anxious look.' He actually persuaded James James to bequeath his skull for posterity in return for a down payment of £70 – a very large sum at the time in the context of a Pumlumon shepherd's life. The skull survives in the National Museum of Wales, but the gesture was futile; Fleure's theories have long been exploded.

However, it is now persuasively argued by the geneticist Dr Steve Jones, who happens to be a relative of James James, that many of today's Welsh are indeed the descendants of the 'original' inhabitants of the Western European archipelago. Testing the Y-chromosomes of thousands of men across the globe shows that many Welsh males are genetically related not to their English or near-European neighbours but to the Basques, to some inhabitants of Siberia and, through them, even to some Native Americans (nothing to do with the Madog legend!). Another interesting result of these tests is to show that, as can be demonstrated in other ways, women tend to be more migratory than men. Men, as landowners, farmers and labourers, have been more tied to the land; women may have married in their home church or chapel, but then they tended to join their husbands. In early times they may well have been captured and carried off as spoils of war, or simply traded. Exogamy ('marrying outside the group') may also have been seen as beneficial for social and hereditary reasons.

Certainly there were humans here six thousand years before Christ, people who made small flints into tools and weapons. The term used to describe them is Mesolithic ('Middle Stone Age'), and they were hunter-gatherers. Amongst the evidence for their presence is an antler shaft with a drilled hole in it, found at Ynys-las – probably used as part of an axe or adze. Further south is the site at Aberystwyth harbour, now improbably crowned by a World War II concrete pill-box, where tiny flint implements (a selection of which can be seen at the excellent Ceredigion Museum) were manufactured in large numbers; worked flints of a similar kind have also been found at Llangrannog. The tiny flints would have been set in wood to make points, barbs and teeth for weapons and tools; found with them are stones which have been used as hammers, possibly to knock limpets off rocks, to crush crab-shells or bones. The source of the flint from which they shaped their weapons is a subject for debate; was there sufficient flint available (as there are still occasional flint pebbles on Ceredigion beaches today, wherever they may have come from) or was it traded in from elsewhere?

This is little on which to construct any serious portrait of Mesolithic life in Ceredigion, but since these people were hunter-gatherers, they would have eaten everything edible that they could find, including much that we would wrinkle our noses at today. They may have spent winters on the coast (not today's coast, of course), eating shellfish and seaweed, moving inland in spring to hunt and to collect nuts, roots, fruit, birds' eggs and insects. They must have been very few in number at any one time, since a large area is required to support the hunter-gatherer life-style – even that of a single family. Nevertheless, they may have had a greater impact on the landscape than we imagine. They could use fire, and may well, like the American Indians of the Eastern Woodlands, have used it to clear undergrowth, and even to make glades in the forest to improve their hunting yield. They lived here for centuries, bred and died, leaving so little behind.

By 4000BC new lifeways, with new languages, were spreading across Europe from Mesopotamia and Asia Minor. To what extent they were brought by migrants, and to what extent by trade and other contacts, is a matter of current discussion. Animals (other than the dogs that people had already kept for millennia) had been recently domesticated, and therefore it was necessary to clear land for grazing, a process in which sheep and goats assisted by eating the shoots from the stumps of felled trees, preventing regeneration. Cereals were being cultivated, so land had to be cleared for planting, probably by the slash-burn-and-move-on method, which destroys the soil's fertility. Along with these developments came an invaluable new technology, the making of pottery, and a compelling need in these new circumstances to provide rather more permanent forms of accommodation than may have sufficed for hunter-gatherers. The tool and weapon technology was still based on stone (with wood, bone and horn), but the techniques of edging and polishing the stone had gradually improved. These developments had occurred in Wales by 3500BC, introducing the culture labelled 'Neolithic' (New Stone Age). To what extent they were brought in by outsiders, and whether and how they had been learnt by the already-present hunter-gatherers, it is impossible to tell. Inevitably the development of agriculture would have reduced somewhat the need for hunting and gathering, but they still continued. In addition, agriculture, fragile though it was, made possible a more complex society, in which food surpluses could be exchanged for services. As this developed, specialism became feasible: a ruler, a priest-shaman or a craftsman need not necessarily be a herdsman-farmer as well, and he could therefore devote his time to establishing himself as a specialist; the terms used assume that men took these roles, though it is perfectly possible that women took sacred roles, and women were certainly involved in crafts, though perhaps not working in stone; division of labour by gender is an ancient practice; basket-making, for example, is in many contexts an entirely female craft.

These developments were slow. The earliest farming practices were twofold: the use of domesticated animals, and the sowing of grain. The forests that blanketed

Wales up to 600 metres above sea-level began to give way. The discovery of Neolithic potsherds at Llanilar, dated to about 4000BC, may not prove absolutely that local manufacture was taking place, since the pottery may possibly have been brought in from more sophisticated settlements elsewhere. Meanwhile, studies of pollen from peat layers in sites all over Britain, including Ceredigion, show that about 3000BC there was a dramatic decline in the population of elm trees, perhaps reflecting human activity as well as disease, while the deforestation of the upland areas by human interference may have initiated or assisted the formation of the peat blankets which cover so much of upland Ceredigion today, and which may conceal information which we badly need about the lives of the earliest communities in the county.

The discovery over the years of twenty-two Neolithic stone axes and adzes, spread throughout Ceredigion, is perhaps the best indication we have of the widespread Neolithic human presence here. They were made from various kinds of stone, many of them produced not in Ceredigion but elsewhere. However, despite the seemingly numerous axes, the thinness of the local population during the fourth millennium is suggested by the comparative lack of Neolithic monuments, compared with the rich remains in Pembrokeshire to the south and Meirionnydd to the north. There is not a single surviving Neolithic chambered tomb or cromlech in Ceredigion, though several are known to have existed, for example at Wileirog Uchaf north of Llangorwen, (SN 616860) and in Llangoedmor parish: Llech yr Ast (SN 222483) and Llech y Gawres (SN 200449)). A large stone still remains in the village square of Llanbadarn Fawr which was once the capstone of a cromlech or burial chamber.

The largest of the Trichrug Bronze-Age tumuli.

Gradually the use of large burial chambers in Wales – massive cromlechs like that at Pentre Ifan in Pembrokeshire, covered with earth and smaller stones – lapsed; instead, people made circular monuments whose remains are less impressive, but which in Ceredigion have survived in much larger numbers than their Neolithic predecessors. These circular monuments are recognisable as earth barrows and as cairns, which are not to be confused with the stone heaps made throughout the centuries by farmers clearing stones from their land; these latter are known as clearance cairns, and may or may not be ancient. Burial cairns are found on Mynydd Bach and throughout the mountainous area east of the river Teifi. The finest complex is to be found on the summit of Trichrug (SN 541599), the landmark hill south of the Llanrhystud – Tal-sarn road, which was virtually hidden until recently by an ill-sited conifer plantation.

On its crest are the three mounds which give the hill its name, the largest still some ten feet high and over sixty feet across; a fourth much smaller mound was overlooked by whoever first named the place. When such a burial mound has been dug into by past treasure-seekers, or otherwise eroded, a small cist formed by slabs of stone is often revealed; two examples can be seen close by the track that leads from Bedd Taliesin (SN 671912), itself originally a Bronze Age kerb-cairn, to Cae'r Arglwyddes. Corpses would have been placed in these cists, doubtless with ceremonies long lost to us, or if they had been cremated, the ashes would have been put in an earthenware vessel. There are also burial pits without stone cists; examples were discovered at Llanilar by road-workers in the 1970s, some of which contained burial urns, while in others the remains were simply placed in the earth. At least sixty-seven burial urns are known to have been discovered in the county, of which only twenty-seven survive in museums or in private hands.

THE Banc Ty'nddôl 'sun-disc', a small decorated gold ornament illustrated on the cover and as frontispiece, was a surprise discovery made in Cwmystwyth in October 2002 by a team of archaeologists led by Simon Timberlake. They were investigating the site of Roman and medieval lead smelting hearths at Banc Ty'nddôl, below the Bronze Age copper mine on Copa Hill. Probably the earliest gold artefact yet discovered in Wales, it is over 4,000 years old and belongs to the earliest period of copper and bronze working in Britain. The disc (diameter 38.9mm, weight 2.51g) is made of thin gold foil, decorated with concentric line- and dot-circles and pierced by two central holes for attachment. It was probably made especially as an adornment on a funerary garment and possibly symbolised the life-giving power of the sun. Follow-up investigation of the find-spot showed it accompanied a skeleton in a grave, which was once covered over by a mound of stones, known as a cairn. Perhaps this person was in some way connected with early prospecting at the overlooking copper mine, which has also recently been investigated and published by Simon Timberlake on behalf of the Early Mines Research Group. This disc, the first from Wales, is very similar in style to other examples known from Ireland, the Isle of Man and Brittany. The disc was declared as treasure in December 2003 and has been acquired by the National Museums & Galleries of Wales. A full report on the excavation and the significance of the find will be published in the near future. (© Adam Gwilt, N.M.G.W.)

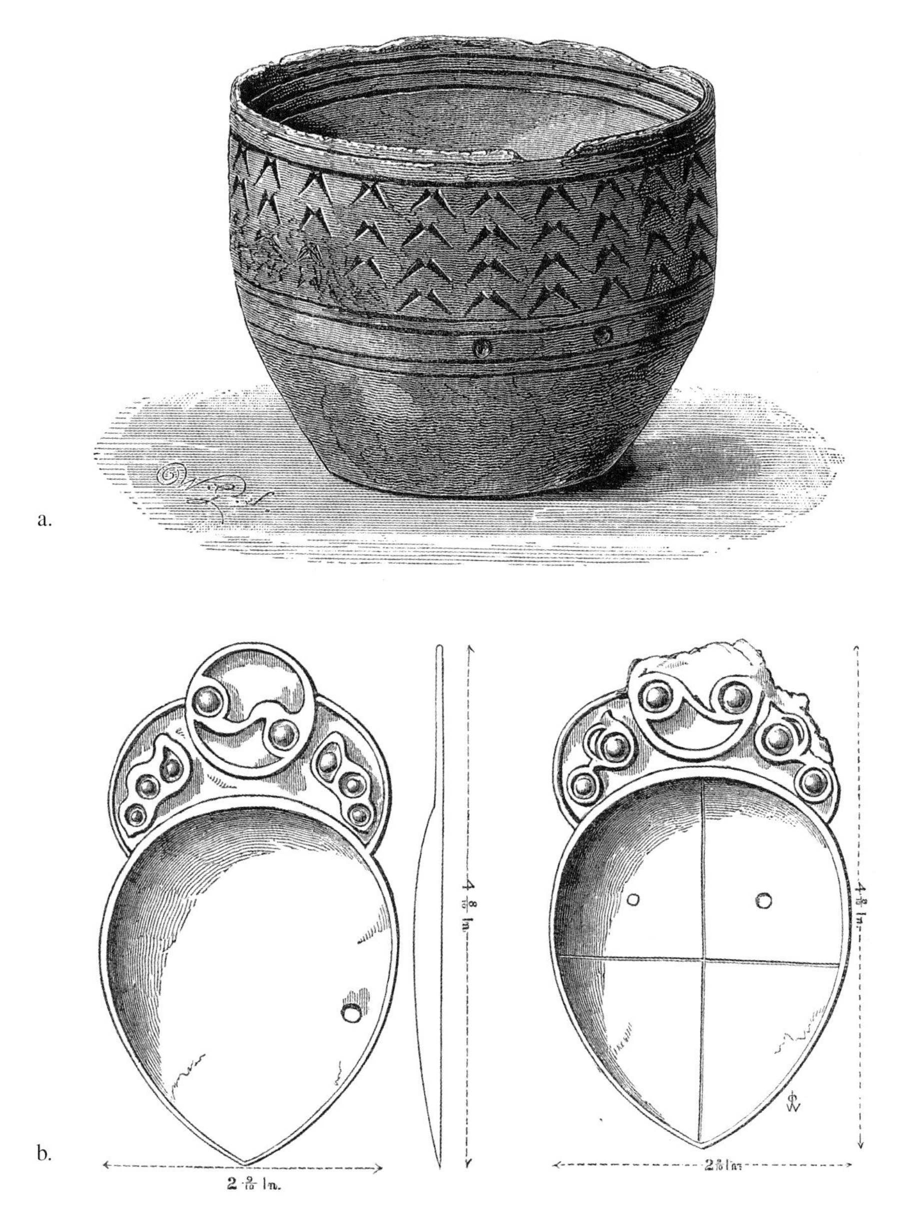

a. Bronze-age pygmy cup, Abermeurig. b. Bronze 'spoons' with La Tène (Celtic) ornament, Castell Nadolig.

[Illustrations from *Archaeologia Cambrensis*]

These urns were made of fired clay which to us seems coarse, but they were ornamented, and are the product of simple hand-throwing and firing. Other vessels must have been used as containers and for culinary purposes. Artefacts from early Bronze Age Ceredigion (up to 1500BC) include a few flint tools of high quality – a knife, and several arrow-heads – and items made from copper and from bronze, that alloy of tin and copper which was such a major technological advance in human development. Copper was mined on Copper Hill, Cwmystwyth, in this period; the only problem is the source of the necessary tin, which must have come from elsewhere. The rare bronze implements found in Ceredigion may be of local manufacture or may have come in through trade, while the copper implements – four axes and a halberd – may be local. Following years of work by the archaeologist Simon Timberlake, it now seems clear that not only copper but lead was mined in Cwmystwyth.

Typical stone-lined Bronze Age cist-grave, originally covered by a cairn.

Bronze Age monuments and clearances are the oldest traces of human activity which are easily visible in the Ceredigion landscape. Because such remains are so much more obvious on high ground than lower down, it used to be supposed that humans preferred settlement on land which was more easily cleared, while valleys were full of impenetrable woodland. This idea, which used to be taught regularly in schools, is now exploded; more survives today in upland Ceredigion than in the valleys, because the latter have been far more thoroughly reshaped by humans, destroying or burying earlier remains. Only by accident do sites like the urn-burials at Llanilar come to light.

The ceremonies which were held at these burial monuments, and at their earlier Neolithic counterparts, are unknown to us, but the investment of effort involved in raising a cromlech, or in creating a cairn, was considerable. These monuments, like the greater ones which preceded them, are more than signs of respect for the dead; they indicate possession of the land by its inhabitants and their ancestors; as the poet Elfed put it:

Yma mae beddrodau'n tadau / Yma mae ein plant yn byw . . .
Here are the tombs of our fathers / Here is where our children dwell . . .

These cairns are dated to the period 2500-1400BC, a period conventionally classified as the early Bronze Age, though stone continued to be used for most tools and weapons. There are no fewer than 346 cairns in Ceredigion known to us either through their physical survival or their recording by antiquarians in the past; there may be many as yet unrecognised, while scores of others will have been wiped out entirely. Only a few clearance-cairn sites have been recognised from the period; the most extensive is at Cae'r Arglwyddes on the northern river Clettwr, east of Taliesin village.

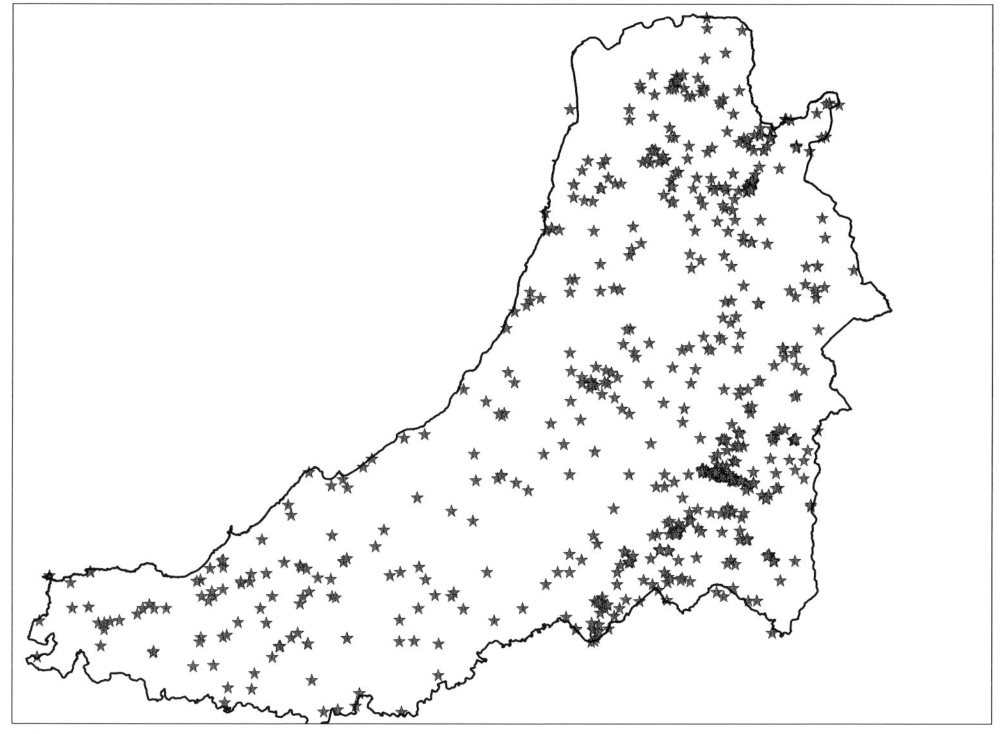

Map: Bronze Age Ceredigion [Richard Jones, Cambria Archaeology]. This simply acknowledges the cairns and other find-sites which show that virtually the whole county was occupied, however thinly. Compare this with the map on p. 42.

* * *

Menhirs or standing stones dot our landscape; the first volume of the *Cardiganshire County History* lists eighty-six, and who knows how many have been moved for reuse or simply destroyed. They are among the most baffling of landscape monuments. They are particularly difficult to date; they may have been moved or reused, and their purpose is often obscure: if ancient, were they markers for routes, gravestones, boundaries or meeting-places? Excavations at Stackpole in Pembrokeshire have demonstrated that a stone may be the only visible remnant of a long-buried and long-occupied site of some complexity.

Llech-gron, Cross Inn: is it a menhir, or a natural feature?

Some menhirs were named in the medieval period or later after earlier hero-figures: the original Arthur's stone at Maenarthur, Pont-rhyd-y-groes, has long vanished, leaving only its name on the farm, but three stones are named Carreg Samson, one south of Ysbyty Ystwyth (SN7414 7038), one in Gwnnws parish (SN 726712) and another above Llanddewibrefi (SN 6760 5380). Since Samson, though a Welsh saint by origin, is much better known in Brittany, it is more likely that the stones are named after the mighty man of Israel than after the saint; early Christians were not ignorant of the Old Testament. The finest stone in the county is surely Llech Gron (Nebo SN 542648), well worth a diversion from the Llanrhystud-Trefilan road, though some authorities suspect it of being a natural stone, not a menhir. Alas, the more spectacular stone circles of this period are only recognised at two much-spoiled sites in the county, one at Brynygorlan, Llanddewibrefi (SN749547) and the other at Moel-y-llyn, Ceulan-a-Maesmawr (SN 699910).

For the centuries following 1500BC we have far less evidence for burial practices, though habitation certainly continued, and Middle and Late Bronze Age metal implements survive to prove it. An axe, nine palstaves, a dirk, and a spearhead have been described by archaeologists, as well as four socketed axes, a pegged spearhead, a shield, and a stone mould for casting a chisel. These remains sound pathetically few, yet they are remarkable enough. They speak of professional metalworkers, whose products would have been greatly prized, though their frailer products (one imagines in particular brooches and mirrors) rarely survive the acid soils of Ceredigion. Bronze shields, such as the superb solitary Ceredigion example from Aberllolwyn now in the British Museum, would hardly have been used in serious warfare; weapon points would have pierced them more easily than they would layered leather-on-wood shields. As well as implements of bronze, stone continued to be used to produce axe-hammers and mace heads.

Even the scanty remains of landscape monuments, many of which have been destroyed, and artefacts, many of which have been lost after discovery, are enough to indicate permanent agricultural settlement in Ceredigion, though probably there were fewer people on the ground at any one time in comparison with either Pembrokeshire or Meirionnydd. On the other hand, the hard igneous rocks of these two neighbouring counties would survive better than most Ceredigion stone, which might account for the 'monument deficit'. Their beliefs and burial practices, their ways of thought, their political structures and relationships with other areas, are almost completely lost to us. But we can be sure they farmed, that they had some kind of political organisation which ensured the primacy of some individuals, leading to their endowment with wealth, influence and power, including the ability to procure valuable metal objects. Women, men and children would have laboured in small patches enclosed by walls, banks or hurdles; they would have grazed and guarded their cattle, sheep and goats, would have cut wood and hay, would have collected herbs and wild foods, and fished the rivers and inshore waters. They had hearths, and cooked at least in part by using potboilers, stones which were heated in the fire and then dropped into pits or containers to boil water. The so-called 'burnt mounds', heaps of red and black burned stone with charcoal or peat, bear witness to these practices. Some people, who in the surviving hunting-cultures have always been men, worked full or part-time as toolmakers in stone, and presumably in bone, horn and wood, and there were men of rare skills who could work metal. Others, possibly women, worked in clay to produce urns and food-vessels, and would surely have made baskets as well. What language these people spoke is a subject so controversial as to be best avoided; it may have been a form of Celtic, or some previously-established language now utterly lost.

Was there warfare in Bronze Age Ceredigion? Nothing survives to enable us to answer yea or nay; one can only suppose that human males were as belligerent then as they are now. The last millennium BC, which saw the introduction of ironworking into Britain, has left plenty of evidence to suggest that conflict was a regular threat to the safety of the communities which farmed Ceredigion. This was a period which, from about 1250BC, saw a slow but steady deterioration in the British climate, with a drop in average temperatures of two degrees centigrade, enough to curtail the growing season by more than a month. This must have particularly affected people living above two hundred feet in areas already affected by loss of tree cover, and by over-cultivation and consequent degradation of the soil. There may well have been a resultant drop in population numbers, but the fact that archaeology has as yet traced few remains other than hill-forts from the early centuries of the millennium before Christ does not prove the point.

Whatever the position during the first half of the last millennium BC, it is clear that there was plenty of human activity in Ceredigion in the five centuries before the Romans came. There was much burning of woodland, and there was almost certainly competition for usable farmland. By this time iron was being smelted widely in Britain, and must have been in Ceredigion too, though little evidence has yet been discovered. The language of the people of Ceredigion by this time was certainly Celtic, though there is no direct evidence before the Roman period. Until recently it was believed that the technology of iron, like that of bronze before it, had been brought either by waves of conquerors who had replaced or enslaved the previous inhabitants, or at least by war-leaders accompanied by their master-craftsmen, who had imposed the culture and language we call 'Celtic' on the resident population. But as has been already suggested, it does not require population replacement to explain technological advance and language replacement, despite the analogies one might draw with the Europeanization of North America. Both technology and language can be acquired by processes such as trade, neighbourly emulation and intermarriage, as well as by conquest.

* * *

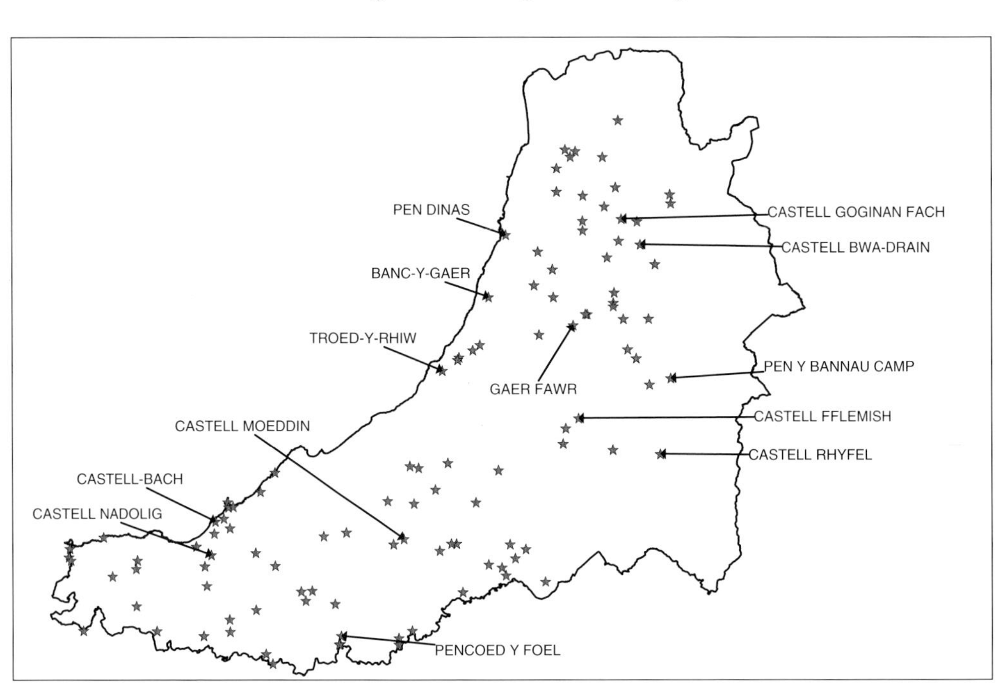

Map: Ceredigion hill-forts [Richard Jones, Cambria Archaeology]. Note the retreat from the higher ground occupied during the Bronze Age.

Quite the most splendid monuments to the past of Ceredigion are its great hill-forts. Although they must represent a troubled past, they give us a special insight into the ages for which we have no records, and some give magnificent views of the surrounding landscape. Y Gaer Fawr (SN 649719), for example, a prominent hill-fort on the left of the A485 road from Llanilar to Lledrod, gives us some glimpses of the way that nature and people have shaped the landscape of Ceredigion. East-north-east we look up the Ystwyth valley as the river winds its changeable way towards Llanafan bridge across the braided gravels. It flows down a great fault torn in the rocks of Wales, a tear which runs all the way from Blaen-cwm in Cwmystwyth to Llanafan bridge and beyond. The cleft is part-filled with rock debris and gravel from glaciation and other forms of erosion, over which the river runs. The gravels themselves might be expected to have sprouted dense willow-beds and alder carr, thus stabilising thc gravcl, but thc Grogwynion lead-mines poured centuries of poisonous waste into the river, so that nothing deep-rooted will grow in the polluted beds, even though frogs and toads flourish in the deep roadside ditches and rare plant-forms are found here. At Llanafan bridge itself, hidden from our view, the river swings away west-north-west, but the fault continues south-westwards; if we stand on the south-eastern flank of the fort, we can look into the valley, which eventually accommodates the river Wyre, flowing in a straight line all the way to Llanrhystud and the sea. How difficult it is to realise that both the Ystwyth valley itself and the hills around were once covered with trees, but the arrival more than four thousand years ago of domestic sheep and goats, along with men who ploughed and sowed the earth to grow cereals, eventually cleared away the forest, creating a totally different, wholly human-fashioned landscape, of which Y Gaer Fawr eventually became a part.

THE hill-fort names Caer and Castell can be confusing, since *caer* is often used of Roman forts, while *castell* suggests a medieval fortification. In fact the vast majority of place-names using these two elements are Iron Age hill-forts. The name Castell Fflemish (SN 654632) is particularly misleading; it has nothing to do with medieval Flemish colonisers, but is another Iron Age site. Other intriguing names are Castell Nadolig, Castell Rhyfel (SN 732599) and Caer Lifry (SN 516565).

Y Gaer Fawr (it means simply 'the big fort') is one of the finest hill-forts in Ceredigion, and has splendid views in most directions. The southern flank of the hill is so steep that fortification was barely needed at all, but the less demanding approach from the east follows an ancient curving track which must have been the main route for the fort's builders and visitors, and after passing a large white boulder which may possibly be a surviving landmark of a much earlier period, it reaches an obvious entrance between the ramparts to right and left. On the western flank of the hill the ramparts are double and triple, compensating for the gentleness of the slope; in places the ditches were cut into living rock, a hard task for men and women armed with tools made of wood, bone, horn and stone, though they may have eased the work by lighting fires and then pouring water onto the heated rock to fracture it.

Y Gaer Fawr was only one of several hill-forts in this vicinity, built in the centuries immediately before the Roman conquest of southern Britain in the first century AD; from the summit the less spectacular remains of smaller forts can be seen in the nearby plantations on Coed Allt-fedw and Cefn Blewog hill above Llanafan, while further west-north-west is the intriguing site of Penycastell (SN 630745) which gives Castle Hill, Llanilar, its modern name; it seems to be a prehistoric hill fort converted into a Norman ringwork-and-bailey castle. Its original Welsh name, no longer locally known, was Garth Grugyn, named after one of the boars slain there by Arthur in pursuit of the Twrch Trwyth, the giant boar of the Welsh saga, *Culhwch ac Olwen*. In the distance up the Ystwyth valley, perched high above the river, is a tiny prehistoric fortified Iron Age site which may have been the refuge for a farm close by, or even the habitation of the farm's family; it is now known as Castell Grogwynion (SN 721725). West-south-west, two miles away, is the hill fort of Argoed (SN 616710). All this activity suggests a flourishing and well-organised population, albeit anxious for their security, and judging by the varying sizes of these embanked sites, it may well have been a clearly stratified society of rulers and ruled, with complex degrees of subordination. Certainly the rulers who organised the building of these sites had considerable power, driving the labour-force to move thousands of tons of earth and rock with tools of wood and bone. It's obvious that the major sites were not merely for defensive purposes; they were perhaps rather like Edwardian castles, designed to stifle any thought of rebellion or attack, and to make clear the prestige of their creators. They are usually dated within the last three centuries BC, but it is possible that some at least were built on long-occupied sites.

The walker who climbs Y Gaer Fawr from the north-east will have a particularly privileged view. Halfway to the summit, anyone who pauses to look back will see the woods and gardens of Trawsgoed mansion. Close by, a period of prolonged drought such as the summer of 1976 reveals the grid plan of the Roman fort and its *vicus* or surrounding civilian settlement, a site which despite the droughts of the centuries was only rediscovered in 1959. The fort was approached from the south by Sarn Helen, the Roman road whose *agger* or elevation can be traced at the abandoned farm site of Sarn Elen, a mile south-east of Y Gaer Fawr.

The southern view from Y Gaer Fawr is dominated by the rugged mass of Mynydd Bach ('little mountain'), a kind of island cut off from the main body of the Cambrian range, its appearance now sadly altered by wind turbines. If we now fly in

Y Gaer Fawr, between Lledrod and Trawsgoed
[Crown copyright: Royal Commission on Ancient & Historical Monuments, Wales].

imagination from Y Gaer Fawr to Mynydd Bach, ignoring the turbines, another fine view faces us from Cofeb y Beirdd, a handsome memorial to the poets of the district. Behind us to the south is the natural lake of Llyn Eiddwen, while to the west and north-west we overlook the plateaux which seem to step down by stages to Cardigan Bay. Below us to the north is Trefenter, one of many areas where the land-hunger of the early 19th century drove desperate men and women to build their *tai unnos* (one-night houses) on common land, where was fought the conflict known as *Rhyfel y Sais Bach* ('The War of the Little Englishman'). Thousands of years earlier, their predecessors left their remains under the cairns still visible here and there, though many must have been swept away.

All over southern Britain, and almost throughout Ceredigion, the last centuries BC were the years of hill-fort building. Some one hundred and seventy hill forts and enclosures are listed in the *Cardiganshire County History*, but we should not imagine that they were all created or occupied simultaneously. Yet whether we consider them collectively or separately, they represent colossal feats of organisation and labour, since their creation meant shifting tens of thousands of cubic metres of earth and rock. This implies a comparatively high population level, a considerable degree of political control as already suggested above; it was presumably a response to political instability and a level of military threat. Whether the threat derived from outside, or whether it was a matter of inter-group strife within the area, we simply do not know.

It is possible, as R.A. Dodgson has suggested, that the communities of bondmen (and their families) which we know existed in the medieval period have their origin at this much earlier time. The evidence for such continuity is indirect but of great interest. Thus a common medieval Welsh term for a bond community was *maerdre* (*faerdre* in its mutated form). Crowning a steep hill north of the Teifi is the hill fort of Pencoed-y-foel (SN245428). On the southern edge of the hill, overlooking a bend in the river Teifi is Castell Gwynionydd, a medieval earthwork. Immediately to the west is a standing stone. Close to the eastern side of the hill fort is Faerdre-fawr. These features link together the Bronze Age (standing stone, though these are never dateable with certainty), the Iron Age (hill fort), the medieval earthwork (Castell Gwynionydd) and the *maerdre* or farmland owned by the local lord and worked by his tenants; finally of course the name of the earthwork suggests that this was the centre of the commote of Gwynionydd.

Naturally these embanked hill forts are not uniformly scattered through the county; we would not expect to find them in Ynys-las, Borth or Cors Caron; there are only two on the southern edge of Mynydd Bach, none survives on or near the coast between Llanrhystud and Cwmtydu (though one existed at the sea's edge at Aberaeron and others may have been swallowed by the waves), and there are virtually none in the inner heights of the Cambrian range. Nor are they of uniform nature or plan. Many are planted firmly on hill-summits, others on gentler rises or on cliff-tops, yet others on low ground, as in the Teifi valley. Some are small, others medium and some large; some have single ramparts, others more than one. The finest of all Ceredigion's hill-forts, Pen Dinas, Aberystwyth (once known as Dinas

Maelor), has both a single-rampart enclosure and a splendid multi-rampart enclosure linked to it. Such forts were probably multi-purpose; acting at times as permanent encampments, at other times as temporary refuges. At their most complex, they must have been impressive sights; the ditches deeper and the banks, much higher than they are now after two millennia of erosion, crowned with palisades of stake and wattle. The entrances would have been gated and guarded, watchtowers would have given sentries better vantage points, and inside were huts and smaller enclosures. It may be speculated that defence against siege would have been difficult, since by nature they tend to lack water, but any kind of enduring siege may have been unenforceable, until eventually a professional army appeared which could carry all before it. Whether any such siege of a Ceredigion hill fort ever took place is simply not known. If the people belonged to the apparently peaceable tribe of the Demetae, they may not have sought to imitate the fierce Silures or Ordovices, but rather yielded to the new and powerful Roman forces which confronted them so menacingly, yet with much to offer.

Pendinas from the air . [Crown copyright: Royal Commission on Ancient & Historical Monuments, Wales].

4. Romans in Ceredigion

News of the arrival of the Romans in Wales must have reached Ceredigion long before the imperial soldiers crossed the slopes of Pumlumon, or penetrated into the Teifi valley from Carmarthen or Llandovery. Although the emperor Claudius's armies had landed in Kent in AD43, and although they had engaged the Silures of south-east Wales and the Ordovices of north-central Wales before the year AD50, it was probably not until the governorship of Frontinus, AD74-77, that detachments of soldiers finally arrived in what is now Ceredigion. By that time there were already Roman forts at Llandovery, Pumpsaint and Carmarthen. The tribe of the Demetae, which may or may not have reached into southern Ceredigion, had yielded to Roman control, perhaps by agreement rather than after military conflict. Such compliance on the part of the Demetae is the best explanation for the apparent absence of Roman sites in modern Pembrokeshire. Nevertheless the Romans naturally needed to ensure against local opposition in Ceredigion, so in the course of building their road from south Wales to the north, they built forts at Llanio, Trawsgoed and Penllwyn, each guarding the road crossing-place of a major river. In the south, they were already linked to Carmarthen and to Llandovery; in the north the road crossed the Dyfi to Pennal. What did they expect to gain from their occupation?

This simple question is not easily answered, though it is obvious that since the Romans were bent on conquering Britain, mid-Wales had to be occupied. They would certainly have recruited slaves and soldiers from among the native population. It has long been uncertain whether they exploited the silver-lead ores of northern Ceredigion, the one other asset which might seriously have attracted them. The major lead-mining sites of later centuries – Cwmsymlog, Fron-goch, Grogwynion, Cwmystwyth – have been so heavily worked over since the medieval period that if there had been Roman mining, all traces of it may well have disappeared entirely. True, there are narrow tunnels in the Cwmystwyth complex of mines which have been traditionally known as 'Roman levels'; they show great skill and economy of effort in the way their creators tackled the hard rock, but no direct proof of their Roman origin has yet been found. Thus far, however, the only slight but definite evidence for Roman lead-mining in the county has been the discovery by Jeffrey Davies at Trawsgoed of a piece of lead chemically identifiable as being from the Tal-y-bont area.

All this demonstrates how difficult it is to view a period of history for which, in our area, we have no documents. Archaeology is all, and archaeology advances by fits and starts. Inevitably therefore, any effort to understand what what was going on, rather than simply describe what facts we know, is fraught with problems. Nevertheless, the effort in this case is worth making.

Even if entirely peaceful, the arrival of the Roman army in Iron Age Ceredigion must have been startling for the inhabitants, though the main body of soldiers took the form of units of auxiliary soldiers (some perhaps cavalry) rather than the still more impressive heavily-armed legionaries, a detachment of whom may nevertheless have surveyed the line of the road known centuries later as Sarn Helen, and supervised the building of the forts. The two cultures thus brought together were remarkably discordant. The mighty Roman empire reached from Britain to Syria and North Africa. Europe south of the Danube and west of the Rhine was Roman. Militarily, culturally, administratively, it was immensely sophisticated. The empire was organised in provinces, of which Britain was the newest, and within pre-Roman Britain, the area we know as Wales was certainly tribal; its inhabitants spoke the language we call British, ancestor of Welsh. By 'tribal' is meant here a culture divided into social groups owing allegiance to local leaders; we may call them chiefs, lords or kings, often hereditary. Their more privileged followers were their clients, including warriors and craftsmen, while the less privileged were slaves. We cannot know whether the whole of Ceredigion was controlled by one dynasty of chiefs; it is perhaps more likely that several dynasties divided the area between them. Theirs was a simple mixed-agrarian economy based on barter; unlike the Celtic kingdoms of south-east Britain, they did not produce coins. Surplus from their farming economy would have provided food-renders which sustained the chiefs of each group and their families, and their priests and other attendants. Britain was, by comparison with Rome, backward and unsophisticated, and within Britain, Ceredigion was a marginal area.

The invading Roman forces were masters of technologies unknown to the native British. Their administration was sophisticated, their weapons, forts and roads were startling in their power and durability, and they must have imposed immediate demands for labour and food-renders on the local populations, who would have been forbidden to occupy or reoccupy the more strategically-placed hill-forts. Recruitment of soldiers and the capturing of slaves probably ensued, disrupting the local society, while the presence of hundreds of husky, healthy auxiliary soldiers would have had its own impact on the local women, either with or without their consent, with further consequences for the local population. Readers old enough to remember the impact of American and Canadian troops stationed in Britain during World War II will not need reminding of what turmoil can be wrought among the women of a community by the arrival among them of vigorous and economically-advantaged young men.

Archaeologists tend to emphasise the brevity of the military occupation of west Wales, since the forts built in the seventies of the first century seem to have been abandoned by AD130. But that period of two generations was long enough for a good deal of social and cultural change and interchange. Some of the impact of the Romans on the local populations of southern Britain as a whole is clear from the surviving Latin loanwords in modern Welsh, not only the well-known terms for building (*mur, ffenestr, pont, pared, teml*), cookery (*coginio, cawl, cegin, ffwrn, torth*) and marketable goods (*bresych, pysgod, gwin, caws, pais, cyllell*), but words for captivity and punishment (*carchar, caeth, cadwyn, fflangell, ysbaddu*) and the body parts (*coes, braich*) on which fetters would have been placed. Latin-derived terms which might have borne particular relevance to Ceredigion include *plwm* (lead) and, because of its absence, *calch* (lime).

Like the British language, the landscape of Ceredigion certainly changed during the three and a half centuries of direct Roman rule. Apart from the abandonment of the hill-forts, and apart from the creation of forts, roads and bridges, the woodland cover which had already been drastically modified by millennia of human activity came under new pressure. Roman roads demanded widespread clearance to render travel safer, and the forts needed not only land clearance but large quantities of timber for ramparts and buildings, not to mention fuel. It is possible that Ceredigion was largely deforested by the fourth century AD, leaving a landscape which may have been mostly poor grassland and sphagnum bog. Although there is little evidence for the local cultivation of grain at this period, it is difficult to imagine that the garrisons of the forts, numbering many hundreds of men, could have brought in all the grain they needed either by road or by sea.

* * *

Modern exploration of Roman Ceredigion really began in 1959, although there had been some digging at the Llanio fort, between Tregaron and Lampeter, at the time the only known occupied site in the county (SN 644564), which was named *Bremia* by the Romans. The existence of a single Roman road was also known, that stretch of Sarn Helen stretching north from Llanio. It had long seemed to archaeologists that it must connect with the known stretches of Sarn Helen in north Wales, presumably with the known Roman fort at Pennal, Meirionydd. But the gap between Llanio and Pennal would have been at least two, possibly three days' march for heavily laden Roman soldiers. There simply had to be other forts, but where? In 1959 two scholars, the Roman archaeologist Sheppard Frere and the aerial archaeologist J. K. St Joseph, descended on north Cardiganshire and were able to locate the long-forgotten Roman fort at Trawsgoed (SN 671727). Bumps and ridges were and are still visible on part of the site, but it had never been previously noticed or examined. The fort is crossed diagonally by the modern B4340 on its way from Abermagwr to Llanafan Bridge. Part lies in Coedcae field on the river-side of the road, the rest behind the low wall that bounds Trawsgoed demesne. Its discovery was a fine piece of detective work involving the study of maps, the identification of possible sites, and visits by car, followed by aerial photography and trial excavation. Further research in the exceptionally dry summers of 1975 and 1976 revealed two further Roman military sites, a fort at Penllwyn near Capel Bangor (SN 650806), and a small fort at Erglodd, between Tal-y-bont and Taliesin (SN 653903).

Today the Roman site at Trawsgoed bears little evidence of its former size and status. The Roman surveyors chose an admirable position, on a broad flood-free shelf above the river Ystwyth. Water may either have been fetched from the river, drawn off from a leat, or taken from the small streams which drain the area. Ditches were dug to supply earth for ramparts surrounding five and a half acres, and the

Sarn Helen, looking north from above Bronnant. The line of the road is clear despite the modern deviation.
[Crown copyright: Royal Commission on Ancient & Historical Monuments, Wales].

ramparts were crowned by a solid fence of stakes. In each rampart was an entrance with heavy wooden gates, and the internal streets formed a grid within which the military offices, stores and barracks were situated, all built of wood and wattle-and-daub, save possibly the *principia* or headquarters building and perhaps the *horreum* or food-store, which may have been of stone. Drains were laid, latrines provided, and ovens strategically situated for the soldiers to bake their bread. A fort of this size could hold a thousand infantry or five hundred cavalry, but in the case of Trawsgoed we simply do not know what force was stationed there, since no inscription survives. In either case the men would not have been Roman citizens, as the legionaries were, but auxiliaries recruited in Europe or even further afield; the main reward for those who survived twenty-five years' service to retirement age was Roman citizenship. The fort may have only been partly garrisoned for much of its life; detachments could have been deployed as escorts on the network of roads, or further afield in putting down any sign of rebellion. While in residence, they would have spent time in weapon-drill and field exercises, and possibly in supervising the collection of food-renders. If lead (not to mention the accompanying silver) really was mined in Cwmystwyth, then the Trawsgoed forces would have been involved in supervision and escort work.

Some Roman forts in Wales were only occupied very briefly, but Trawsgoed and Llanio forts were of sufficient permanence, lasting perhaps fifty or sixty years, to attract camp followers of various kinds. In the case of Trawsgoed they lived and worked in the *vicus* or civilian settlement immediately outside the south-west and north-west ramparts, forming another grid system of streets. This area would certainly have been under the general control of the fort's commanding officer. Identification of the numerous buildings, many short-lived, is difficult, but they

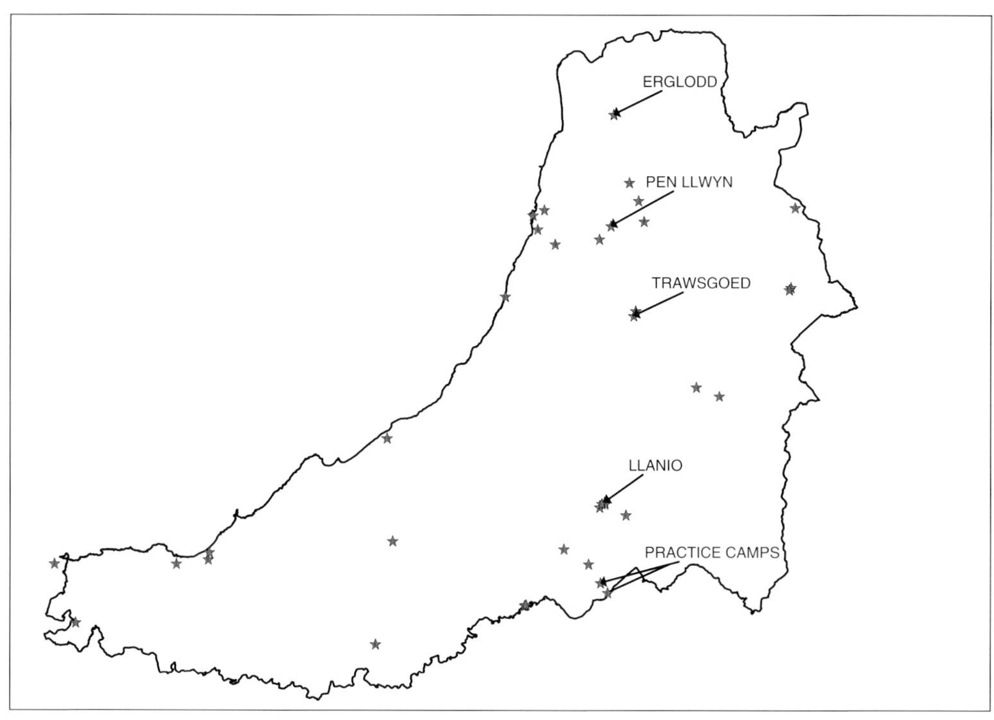

Map: Roman Ceredigion: forts and find-sites. [Richard Jones, Cambria Archaeology]

certainly housed metal-workers in bronze and iron who would have attended to the many needs of the garrison. There would also have been shops and taverns for serving the soldiery, and possibly the homes of women associated with the soldiers. At this period the Roman military were not allowed to contract formal marriages, but could hardly be prevented from fraternising with local girls, who may have found that there was marginally less drudgery in serving the needs of soldiers than of tribal agriculture. However, there was no long-term security for them; shortly before AD100 the fort was burnt down and abandoned briefly – why, we have no idea – before the reoccupation and rebuilding of both fort and *vicus*. When the fort was finally abandoned about AD130, the civilian settlement ceased to exist. In less marginal areas the abandonment of a fort did not necessarily mean the end of civilian life, but in Ceredigion there was no such continuity as is found, for example, at Wroxeter or Carmarthen, where forts were replaced by towns. What became of the Trawsgoed garrison and the inhabitants of the *vicus* is unknown.

One feature not yet located at Trawsgoed, though it must have existed, is the site of the bath-house, a usual accompaniment of any permanent Roman occupation. However, the bath-house at Llanio has been excavated. It lies a hundred metres south of the fort, with an excellent water-supply available from a nearby spring. The water would have been heated in a furnace to provide steam-heating for the *caldarium* and the *tepidarium*; after sweating profusely, the men using the baths (it is most unlikely that any women enjoyed this opportunity) cooled off in the *frigidarium*. We do not know what units formed the garrisons at Penllwyn or

Trawsgoed, but two inscriptions at Llanio tell us that the second cohort of Asturians served there. They would originally have been recruited in north-western Spain, and for obvious reasons the Romans followed a policy of not allowing men to serve in their native regions; it is easier to enforce military rule on strangers than on one's own people. Another inscription records the presence of 'the century of Artius; Marcus Ennius Primus built this'. Unlike the garrison, these men, eighty in number and not a hundred as often believed, were Roman citizen-legionaries, probably from Caerleon on detachment. Like Trawsgoed, Llanio had a *vicus,* and traces of its timber buildings and the debris of iron-working have been discovered.

Underfloor hypocaust at Llanio Roman baths.

[Crown copyright: Royal Commission on Ancient & Historical Monuments, Wales]

It may have been the garrison of Llanio or that at Pumpsaint that created the practice-camps close to Sarn Helen on the watershed between the Twrch and the Teifi valleys (SN 641493, SN 647485), which are close to what may have been a Roman watch-tower at Carregybwci (SN 645479). Creating such camps was part of the training of Roman soldiers. The soldiers in training had to create low ramparts with appropriate entrances to simulate marching-camps and the initiation of more settled camps, using the tools and stakes they carried with their other equipment.

Only one Roman road is clearly marked on the Ordnance Survey maps of Ceredigion. It is shown coming from Pumsaint through Farmers, climbing athwart the steep slope below Carregybwci, where it enters modern Ceredigion, with the practice camps on the right. It then drives directly towards Llanfair Clydogau, but its line is lost thenceforward, though it must have aimed at Bremia (Llanio). After Llanio it is shown as following the B4578 towards Bronnant, but diverges from it

(SN 645647) towards Trawsgoed. At Llwyn Merch Gwilym (SN 654685) the map gives up, but a little further north the ruined farm named on some maps and known locally as Sarn Elen (SN 655704) could hardly be more significant, and it is possible to trace a putative line on to the Trawsgoed fort.

The route northwards has been a matter of great debate, not simplified by the fact that any direct road northward has to climb and descend a number of steep slopes. It was thought to be – perhaps – the unclassified road that wriggles past Llanerch-yr-oen (SN 671749), plunges through Llanfihangel-y-Creuddyn and north-north-east past Sarnau Fawr (SN 660770). It reappears as an unclassified metalled road crossing the A44 at Penllwyn before arriving at the Penllwyn fort. However, recent aerial photography by Toby Driver has revealed a Roman road running northwards across the lands of Brenan farm (SN 644768), though no ground survey has yet been done. That remarkable group of Roman-road-hunters, the Viatores, were able to show that the English midlands had an extraordinarily dense network of Roman roads. Ceredigion would never have supported anything so complex, but the discovery of possible industrial working near the Erglodd fort, and the likelihood of Roman mining, makes some kind of network seem likely. Jeffrey Davies has suggested to me the use of the word 'route' rather than a formally-metalled 'road', and that such a route must have run from the little fort at Cae Gaer (SN 824818) through Eisteddfa Gurig towards Penllwyn, with the undated earthwork known as Llys Arthur (SN 787826) a possible resting-place en route.

As has already been suggested, the nature of Roman control in Ceredigion must have changed after A.D. 130. All the forts were abandoned and military rule must have been replaced by civilian rule, presumably from the little Roman town of Moridunum (Carmarthen). Ordinary life certainly continued in Ceredigion, though we know virtually nothing of it; among the few remains are those of a second-century cremation-burial at Penbryn which contained the only Roman gold coin found in Ceredigion, a few scraps of worked metal, a small wooden sculpture fragment (see p. 54) and some coins. The most important of these are coin-hoards found at Bwlch-bach, Nanteos (SN 608793), Rhiwarthen-isaf, Capel Bangor (SN 639795), Strata Florida (SN 746 658) and most recently at Salem near Penrhyn-coch. These may all have been buried in the last years of the third century AD, perhaps as a result of some military upheaval, though it is equally possible that the uncertainties of the money-market at the time may have driven the original owners to conceal their wealth, such as it was. But how were these deposits accumulated, and by whom? We have no idea, though the existence of travelling merchants or successful breeders of cattle or sheep cannot be ruled out. The long-used site at Gogerddan saw burials both early and late in the Roman period: a first-century cremation, and later corpse-burials in graves oriented east-west from the fourth or early fifth century – a possible but unproveable sign of Christian practice. Hen Gaer, the Iron Age fortification above Gogerddan, may have been the pre-Roman centre for the local population hereabouts.

Nothing emphasises the marginal status of Ceredigion when viewed from a British or European standpoint more than the sparseness of the evidence for Roman

Wooden carving of a woman's head, Llanio, perhaps a Romano-Celtic votive figure.

[Crown copyright: Royal Commission on Ancient & Historical Monuments, Wales]

occupation, and its virtually complete absence for the fourth century, even though we know that, for example, the Romans were active in the fourth century in north-west and south-east Wales. Although most of the evidence from Roman Wales is military, we have the remains of towns at Caer-went and Carmarthen (with its amphitheatre); we have villas from south Glamorgan; we have milestones from Roman roads, copper ingots from Roman Anglesey, the anchor of a Roman-period ship from the seabed off the Llŷn peninsula. Nothing of the kind survives from Ceredigion. There is, of course, a different but perfectly valid way of viewing this situation; if Ceredigion was marginal to Rome, so was Rome to Ceredigion. Despite the upheavals of the period AD 70-130, life went on, notwithstanding deforestation, slavery, military service and the birth of children to native women by foreign fathers.

To this point of view Welsh legend bears witness. The material, fragmentary as it is, shows that the memory of Roman occupation had completely disappeared by the early medieval period. There was in medieval Wales, it is true, memory of Julius Caesar, leader of the risky forays from Gaul into Kent in 55 and 54BC But that legendary memory claimed that Caesar's attempts at conquest had failed, that he had been driven back into the sea. No memory survived of the later, successful Claudian invasion and occupation. The other Welsh legend with Roman relevance is the 'Dream of Maxen Wledig', originally Magnus Maximus, the military adventurer who in AD383 apparently stripped Britain of such troops as it had to attempt the conquest of the Empire, but who failed and died. The legend, however, tells of him in splendid rule in Rome, yet falling in love with a beautiful woman whom he eventually finds in Segontium – Roman Caernarfon. She is Elen or Helen, at whose command the roads of Elen of the Hosts were built across Britain.

That virtual amnesia is perhaps surprising in view of the lasting impact of the Romans on the Welsh physical and cultural landscapes. On the physical landscape they left their forts and their roads. Culturally they left not only the elements of an aborted Romance language (those hundreds of Latin loanwords embedded in the Welsh language), but personal names (e.g. Edern, Meirion, Padarn) and, almost certainly, the foundations of Christianity, at least in south-east Wales. With Christianity they left some skill in Latin, and after their rule there remained a vague vision of Roman authority in which Celtic chieftains wrapped themselves. As Roman rule weakened, they may have brought in temporary allies to help keep their borders safe, including the Saxons in south-east Britain and even the Irish in south-west Wales. But once the 350-year yoke of Roman rule lightened and disappeared, a series of tribal kingdoms re-emerged across Wales, many of which must strongly have resembled those which the Romans had taken over or destroyed in the first century AD. So much had changed, and yet so little. One of those kingdoms was Ceredigion.

5. The Early Kingdom

So little was known in medieval Ceredigion about the area's early history that legend was able to flourish, especially in the north of the region. On the south bank of the Dyfi estuary is the great sweep of sand, sheltered by Ynys-las and laid bare at low tide, known as Traeth Maelgwn. Maelgwn is known to history as king of Gwynedd, who died in 549, but tradition commemorates him in Ceredigion too. It was asserted that in a peaceful competition at Traeth Maelgwn he had gained the kingship of Gwynedd by seating himself on a floating throne of waxed birds' wings, while his rivals were driven from their seats by the inflowing tide; the legend was obviously intended to demonstrate the political superiority of Gwynedd. Maelgwn's supposed contemporary Gwyddno, legendary king of Ceredigion, was believed also to have ruled Cantre'r Gwaelod, that realm defended against the sea by the great banks or *sarnau* which still stretch out under the waves, whose origin as we have seen was in fact natural, not artificial. Gwyddno was impoverished after the loss of this rich province to the waves, but tending his fishtraps on the banks of the Dyfi, he discovered the loquacious baby Taliesin among the salmon, and the infant poet soon defeated the bards of the tyrannical Maelgwn in the first *ymryson* or Welsh poetic contest.

These legends have no apparent historical grounding other than later propaganda on behalf of Gwynedd, though the repeated appearance of Maelgwn, a definite historical figure whom we shall brush past again shortly, is interesting. Ceredigion also figures in the Four Branches of the Mabinogi. Pryderi, ruler of Dyfed, had, according to the first branch, brought Ceredigion under his rule; in the fourth branch it was at his court at Rhuddlan Teifi that he welcomed the treacherous men of the North, who cheated him of his valuable pigs and eventually brought about his death at Maentwrog, far from home.

If we revert from legend to history, the mist of romance thickens to a fog of ignorance. Although the traditional date for the end of Roman rule in Britain is AD410, there can have been no dramatic Roman withdrawal from Ceredigion, for the simple reason that the garrisons had long since left the area, probably by the middle of the second century. Military control must have been almost non-existent, and any patrolling ships in the bay would probably have long been withdrawn from their task. By 400 whatever Roman control might have existed in south-east Wales had crumbled, though Romanised life there seems to have struggled on. The peninsula we call Cymru or Wales (neither name existed for many decades after the Roman departure) reverted to a pattern of tribal kingdoms not totally unlike that which had existed five centuries earlier. Even a few of the old names survived – Dyfed, for example, is derived from the pre-Roman tribe of the Demetae, and was retained to describe the area we call Pembrokeshire, though the Demetae themselves must have occupied a much larger area. For the historian, the period after AD400 remains almost totally obscure; we must grope in the murk for such clues as we may find. Nevertheless, despite this obscurity, the first surviving names of a handful of individuals who lived and died in Ceredigion are known to us through their tombstones, as will be seen.

Historically, Ceredigion became recognised as its own small kingdom or *gwlad*, protected to some degree by its natural boundaries of mountain and river from Dyfed in the south and Gwynedd in the north, and from Powys and the lesser kingdoms of mid-Wales. At some period whose date is lost to us, smaller lordships emerged all over Wales, called *cantrefi* and *cymydau* (commotes); we have already encountered them in Chapter 2. In the patterns beloved of early lawyers, the law-texts prescribe that there were to be so many commotes in a cantref, which in turn was to be a significant unit in a *gwlad*, or mini-kingdom. So obscure (or perhaps ineffectual) was this cantref system in Ceredigion that only the name of one cantref survives, that of Penweddig, also called Cantref Gwarthaf, both of which names indicate the 'furthest' place. Since Penweddig lies between the Dyfi and the Ystwyth, and is the northernmost cantref of the little kingdom, both names suggest, as would be expected, an administrative centre to the south, perhaps at Trefilan or even Dinefwr, the great centre of 12th-century Deheubarth. J.E. Lloyd's suggestion that such a centre was at Cardigan or Carmarthen would only apply if the names originated in the 13th or 14th centuries, which seems unlikely.

By the 12th century, and presumably earlier, the ten commotes of Ceredigion were small but significant petty lordships or units of sovereignty each under the rule of a Welsh lord, and they were partly retained after 1536 as *hundreds* under English rule. Some of their original administrative centres can be identified with varying degrees of certainty. The centre of Genau'r Glyn, for example, may have been at Henllys ('old court'), near Dôl-y-bont. In the case of Creuddyn, although its name probably refers to the Pendinas hill fort, the natural centre of the lordship was Llanfihangel-y-Creuddyn, as its name indicates. Five roads meet at the village, whose large thirteenth-century church indicates its former status. South of Creuddyn lies Mefenydd, between the Ystwyth and a complex southern boundary running up the river Wyre from Llanrhystud, then reaching across the Mynydd Bach to the Teifi. The centre for the next commote, Anhuniog, may originally have been at Llys-wen, which must have been replaced by Trefilan. The cantrefs of Gwynionydd and Iscoed were both subdivided, the former into Uwch Cerdin and Is Cerdin (respectively, above and below the river Cerdin), and the latter into Is Hirwern and Uwch Hirwern. This jigsaw puzzle of political and administrative units played a significant part in the later medieval history of Ceredigion.

Ceredigion, as we have seen, had its natural barriers which gave it some measure of defence; it was not however protected from the sea. The Irish of the fourth, fifth and sixth centuries AD were expansionist – or experiencing population growth. Their Ogam alphabet and their Irish names occur on memorial stones along the western seaboard of Britain; in Wales, they are most common in Pembrokeshire. Irish place-names occur sporadically through much of western Wales, and quite densely in Ceredigion. Churches were dedicated to indisputably Irish saints. Welsh legend, especially the tale of *Branwen*, tells of close Irish contacts. The Desi, a dynasty of Irish origin, the descendants of one Eochaid mac Artchorp (who may have lived about AD400-25), claimed to rule the seven cantrefs of Dyfed south of the Teifi. Even as late as the eleventh century, a king of Leinster claimed sovereignty over Wales. To what extent, then, did the Irish raid and/or colonise Ceredigion?

One of the county's surviving tombstones of the sixth century, now in the National Museum of Wales, is that of an Irishman buried at Llanwenog. His six-foot greenstone memorial bears his name in two scripts, Roman and Ogam, the notched Irish writing found only this once in Ceredigion proper (with another just south of the Teifi in St Dogmaels). In Ogam he is recorded as *Trenaccatlo*, in Roman letters as *Trenacat[us] filius Maglagni*. It is only to be expected that Ceredigion's sole Ogam inscription would belong in the extreme south of the county, bordering on Pembrokeshire where such inscriptions are comparatively common. The inscription, like the place-names, tells us of a community of people, perhaps second or third generation descendants of Irish immigrants, still speaking Irish but anxious to commemorate the dead man in a way comprehensible to such few Latin-literate people as might see the stone. Obviously some level of Latin had survived in Ceredigion, presumably among a small number of priests.

According to a tradition recorded in the ninth century AD, the fifth-century Irish settlers in Wales were driven out by the north Briton Cunedda, aided by his sons. The names of these sons appear for the first time in a tenth-century genealogy, and include that of Ceredig. There is no particular difficulty about believing that Ceredigion was named after a man named Ceredig; Glamorgan and Meirionnydd are reasonable parallels. As has been shown in Chapter 2, lesser regions within Ceredigion such as Gwynionydd, Mabwynion and Mefennydd seem to have been named after individuals. On the other hand, people were always willing to devise personal names to 'explain' a place-name, so Ceredig may be an eponymous figure without historical reality. But whether Ceredig, even if he was a real leader, was a son of Cunedda, is highly uncertain, not to say unlikely. The Cunedda tradition itself, whatever its foundation in fact or fiction, may have been strong enough to attract other names to it just as the Arthurian tradition did. Realistically it can be suggested that early Gwynedd propaganda incorporated Ceredig's name into the Cunedda family in order to justify the subordination of Ceredigion to Gwynedd. Ceredig, in turn, is recorded as the ancestor of the early kings of Ceredigion, the last of whom was Gwgon. The record of Gwgon's death by drowning in AD871/2 is probably reliable, as is that of his great-grandfather Arthen's death in 807. But the history of these men, and of their ancestors, is completely obscure. Another ancestor of Gwgon was Seisyll ap Clydog, who must have flourished in the eighth century, and who extended his kingdom into present-day Carmarthenshire, occupying the three cantrefs of Ystrad Tywi, and leaving behind him a realm known after him as Seisyllwg.

Whether Gwgon, last king of Ceredigion, ruled the whole of Seisyllwg is not known; it is possible that his kingdom had been reduced to the original Ceredigion. No son succeeded him, and it is therefore not surprising that the little kingdom should have been taken over by his sister Angharad's descendants through her marriage to the most powerful man in Wales, Rhodri Mawr, king of Gwynedd, who died in 878. This dynasty also took control of Powys, and therefore ruled much of Wales at a time when the land was under severe pressure both from Viking attacks by sea, and both English and Viking attacks across the eastern land border. Indeed, with the expulsion of Rhodri Mawr from Gwynedd in 877 by the Vikings and his death the following year at the hands of the English, the separate existence of the Welsh kingdoms seems, in retrospect at least, to have been seriously threatened. Admittedly, English influence helped sustain south Wales against the Vikings, but in 895 Ceredigion and Ystrad Tywi were devastated by Anarawd king of Gwynedd, who had English support. In 954 the north Welsh princelings Iago and Ieuaf, sons of Idwal the Bald, ravaged Ceredigion. There thus emerges from our fog of ignorance some anticipation of the wretched later period of Ceredigion's war-torn history between 1070 and 1295, the subject of the next chapter, although the long rule of Hywel Dda till his death in 950 may have been a period of comparative peace once he had united Gwynedd with his southern kingdom. It is certainly clear that Ceredigion, too small and weak to maintain any form of independence, was to be regularly contested between Deheubarth, Gwynedd, Powys, and eventually the Normans.

Passing references have been made in this chapter to the Vikings, but hardly anything is known of them in Ceredigion. There is the Norse name of Cardigan Island, Hastiholm, referred to in Chapter 2, and a single record of a raid on Llanbadarn Fawr, mentioned below. But whereas Pembrokeshire and Anglesey in particular have considerable evidence of the Viking presence in archaeology and place-names, the only archaeological evidence in Ceredigion is the hog-backed stone at Llanddewi Aberarth church, probably of Viking origin, which must have marked a burial. Obviously there must have been more to the story of the Vikings in Ceredigion; not every raid would have been recorded, and Llanddewi Aberarth as an early Christian centre may well have been the object of an attack.

Is there any way of understanding what life was like for the men, women and children of the little kingdom or chiefdom of Ceredigion? They certainly depended on agriculture, keeping cattle and sheep and growing crops on the land. A certain amount of woodland regeneration had happened after the early impact of the Romans, but although there was more woodland than there is today, there would have been large

A MAJOR archaeological discovery of 2004, that *annus mirabilis* of Ceredigion archaeology, was the finding on the edge of Cors Fochno of a medieval wooden trackway, apparently leading southwards from the church at Llangynfelyn. Similar trackways, some of them prehistoric, have been found in the Somerset Levels and elsewhere, but this trackway, made of adze-worked oak, has been dated to the 10th or 11th century AD. It is frustrating that we know so little about the men who built this track; it suggests a stable population cooperating in a long-term project – but where did they live? One has to wonder whether it has been the shortage of archaeologists rather than a supposed lack of sites which explains our ignorance of this difficult period.

stretches of open ground, sometimes boggy, sometimes yielding thin pasture. Houses would have been of the simplest – earth and timber, thatched, so that they have long sunk back into the soil, leaving no trace of settlement that we have so far been able to recognise, other than the mounds of burnt stone and charcoal at Morfa Mawr. The people's diet was supplemented by hunting, fishing and gathering; the ruling class would have depended on food renders from the bond population. Infuriatingly, they seem not to have made or used any pottery.

The Llancynfelyn wooden trackway. [Cambria Archaeology]

Equally uncertain is the organisation of landownership. It seems possible that the division between landowning free people and tenants of bond-land, known to exist in the 13th century, may well go back for centuries – even perhaps to the pre-Roman period. Free men owned land by right of descent, closed to women; they would have owed limited military service and some duties to their princes. Bond-people owned nothing, living in groups on land belonging to a local chief whose protection they earned in exchange for their labour. Bond-families probably outnumbered free. It would have been bond-land that the princes gave so lavishly to the Church. Some bond settlements survive as modern villages, for example Llan-non, while others have vanished; however one has been recently discovered at Llanerchaeron, and a hut excavated.

* * *

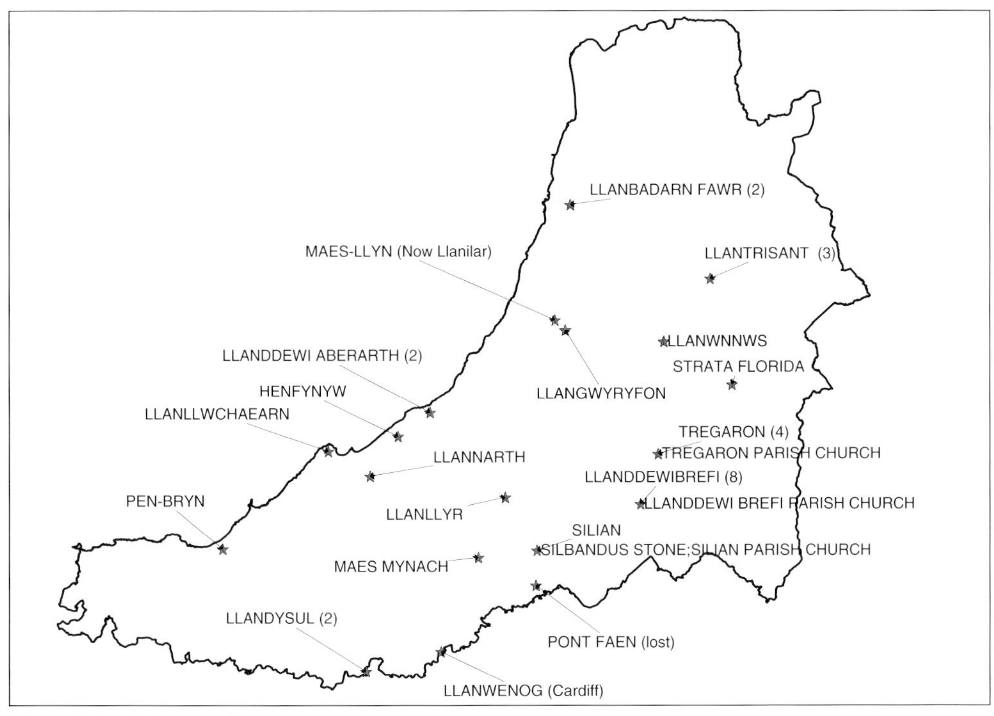

Map: Early Christian Monuments. [Richard Jones, Cambria Archaeology]

Nominally at least, the whole population of early Ceredigion may have been Christian, though it is difficult for us to imagine quite what Christianity meant to the vast majority who could not read. How they became Christian, who were their priests and how they gained an education, even the source of wine for the mass, are matters of great obscurity. The names of a number of the earliest Ceredigion Christians survive as 'saints', both men and women, though we know virtually nothing of them. Did early Ceredigion's Christianity derive from the Roman occupation, from Ireland, or from continental Europe? Did it come up the sea-coast from Pembrokeshire? Early Christianity in south-east Wales is certainly rooted in Roman times, but whether it spread into Ceredigion overland or by coasting missionaries from south-east Wales, or whether the Irish brought it, or whether other missionaries arrived here from elsewhere, is largely obscure – perhaps two, or all three sources were involved. Certainly there is evidence for Irish influence; indeed, Padraig O Riain has argued that Irish Christianity was the dominant influence, especially in southern Ceredigion. His case is founded mainly on the dedications of churches to saints of Irish origin: St Ffraid (= Bridget), commemorated at Llansanffraid on the coast between Llanrhystud and Aberarth is the most obvious, but O Riain argues for the Irish origin of the saints commemorated at Llanwnnws, Llanwenog, Llanwnnen and Capel Wnda (Troed-yr-aur), all connected by him with the Irish cult of St Finnian. A third source of Christian influence in Wales was Gaul, whence the idea of living in monastic communities seems to have reached Wales by the fifth or sixth centuries. Whatever the extent of Irish influence, native figures predominate in church dedications,

A POSSIBLE witness to the conversion of Ceredigion existed at St Tysilio's church (SN 363574). Before the church was renovated the pulpit rested on a huge stone. E.G. Bowen conjectured that it was an early megalith, incorporated into the church site in order to Christianise it, a possible example of a practice well-known elsewhere. (*Antiquity* 45 1971 213-5)

though interpreting these is controversial. Ceredig was believed, at least in the 12th century, to be a progenitor of saints, including Ina (Llanina), Tysul and Afan, not to mention Dewi.

It is certainly clear that the figures considered to be of the greatest importance were Padarn and Dewi, though of course the sources are biassed in favour of their own heroes. Padarn is a puzzling figure. The saint's 'Life', almost certainly written at Llanbadarn, claimed that he came from 'Llydaw' (the Welsh name for Brittany, but his place of origin may have been in south-east Wales). His cult is an interesting one. Llanbadarn Fawr, as is obvious from the name, was its centre, and the church was endowed early with lands between the rivers Clarach and Paith. Llanbadarn Odwyn (sometimes incorrectly written 'Odyn') and Llanbadarn Trefeglwys also survive as witnesses to Padarn's cult. Nothing visible survives of the early Christian settlement at Llanbadarn Fawr, other than two ninth- or tenth-century crosses and the fine manuscripts produced by the sons of Sulien at the turn of the eleventh century. It must nevertheless have been the major church in nothern Ceredigion, preserving a tradition that it had once been the seat of bishops in the pre-Norman days when Wales had bishops but no fixed dioceses or designated cathedrals. The visit of Gerald of Wales in 1188 records the survival or revival there of the Welsh *clas*; a similar ecclesiastical group existed at Llanddewibrefi, of which more below.

Other than Padarn, David is by far the most prominent of Ceredigion's saints and is strongly represented, both by the dedications to him at Llanddewibrefi and Llanddewi Aberarth, and by the traditions of his birth to Non (presumably of Llan-non) and her violater Sant 'king of the people of Ceredigion', and of his education at Henfynyw, immediately south of Aberaeron. An early carved stone was incorporated in the east wall of the present church when it was entirely rebuilt in the 19th century. Unfortunately there is nothing historical in his parents' names, since they simply mean 'saint' and 'nun'. It is interesting that there should be two quite separate places – Ceredigion and Dewisland – with such strong associations with the patron saint. They are of course connected by the place-name Menevia (Dewisland) and Henfynyw ('Old Menevia'). We can be sure however that the early Ceredigion dedications to

THERE has been hitherto no archaeological investigation of overtly Christian sites in Ceredigion. There are earthworks visible in a field north of the 1841 church at Llangorwen. Cellan church appears to have been built within a banked enclosure larger than the present churchyard. Llangoedmor too may occupy an ancient site. A significant number of churches lie on or close to the Roman road from Carmarthen which eventually forms Sarn Helen: Lampeter, Cellan, Llanfair Clydogau, Llanddewibrefi, Llanbadarn Odwyn and Llanfihangel-y-Creuddyn. This may be significant, as is the existence of many round churchyards, believed to be a sign of possible early foundation.

David are older than the eleventh century, and reflect the early influence of the saint's followers and successors.

Later tradition attributes a good deal of mobility to many of the early Christian teachers (or missionaries, or leaders), and there is no reason to doubt that. Many people were more mobile than we tend to think; local leaders would have been glad to encourage men of faith and learning from elsewhere, endowing them with land and assisting them with food and labour. Evidence of human mobility survives at Penbryn where a fine stone tells us that *Corbalengi iacit Ordous* – i.e. 'the body of Corbalengus lies here, an Ordovician', by which we should understand that he was from north Wales, the original tribal area of the Ordovices, and that he was a respected outsider in the community where he dwelt – and that he bore an Irish baptismal name; in him the Irish, Welsh and Roman Christian elements are

The Penbryn monument to Corbalengus.

Circular cemetery with 19th-century church, Pont-siân.

THREE Latin inscriptions are particularly intriguing. At Llanddewibrefi is the stone of Idnerth, son of Jacob, 'slain because of the spoiling of St David'; perhaps he was attempting to save the church from seventh-century robbers. At Gwnnws a cross-stone originally bearing the letters *IHS XPS* (the Greek abbreviation for 'Jesus Christ') appeals to the passer-by, ' whoever shall have explained this name, let him give a blessing for the soul of Hiroidil, son of Carotinn'. At Llanllŷr is an unusual and difficult inscription, apparently meaning 'the sacred place of Ditoc which Ollon, son of Asaitgen, gave to Domnuac'. Presumably it records the gift of land to a church of which no other early trace remains, save the name Llanllŷr, associated with a later nunnery. From such scant remains it can be seen that there was strife in Ceredigion, that people believed in the efficacy of prayer, that Old Testament names were used in baptism, that the church was being endowed with land, and indeed that there were enough literate people to make such inscriptions possible and worthwhile.

mingled. Moreover the stone was originally placed on top of a small cairn which contained a Roman burial urn with coins. Neither this stone nor that of Trenacatus mentioned above bears any visible Christian symbol, but the very literacy involved in inscribing the stones must be associated with an available Christian education – and why write it if nobody could read it? The survival of knowledge of the Ordovician tribal name is intriguing.

What kind of churches were there in early Ceredigion? Nothing was built in stone; rather, we may speculate that a site of Christian worship would have been a small wooden or wattle building, associated with a burial-place and before which stood a cross; within it the priest consecrated the sacred elements. Worshippers stood outside the building, but within the enclosure fence or *bangor* which surrounded it. At present archaeologists are sure that round churchyards can be a sign of antiquity, although they may have been altered by modern extensions, but how many round churchyards survive in Ceredigion is unclear. A well-known example is that at Ysbyty Cynfyn, near Devil's Bridge, though the long-held idea that the church was built within a prehistoric stone circle is now, at best, in suspension, and probably false. Several sites are known to be early, notably Llanbadarn Fawr and Llanddewibrefi. Both have Christian memorial stones from the pre-Norman period. Other inscriptions and crosses survive from Henfynyw, Llandysul, Llangwyryfon, Silian, Tregaron, Lampeter, Llandysul, Llanllŷr, Gwnnws, Strata Florida, Llannarth, Aber-arth and Cribyn, dating from the late fifth to the tenth century. Women as well as men were memorialised; the gravestone of *Potentina* is at Tregaron, that of *Velvor* at Llandysul; remarkably, Velvor has been revived as a female baptismal name in the area in recent times. Three stone crosses have survived in the churchyard of Llantrisant, north of Devil's Bridge, a site so completely abandoned between 1620 and its rebuilding about 1870 that the names of the three saints (*tri sant*) have been lost; the little crosses were only discovered in the early 1970s.

There is an apparent difference between such inscribed Latinate names as those of Tigernus (or Tigernacus) and Trenacatus on the one hand, and the non-Latinate Ditoc and Hiroidil on the other (for the latter, see the text box). Scholarship has shown that the Latinate appearance of the earlier names, with their inflected endings, is deceptive; the composers of the inscriptions were trying to record these Celtic names as they might once have been written in Latin form, but subtle indications show that, for example, *Tigernus* would already have been pronounced with only two syllables, not three, at the time when the name was inscribed; it was if the present writer were to be buried under the name *Giraldus*! However, the later inscriptions show that these archaisms were soon abandoned. Although such names in these inscriptions seem completely obscure to a modern Welsh-speaker, their meanings are not always beyond recovery; *Hiroidil* gives modern Welsh 'Hir-hoedl' – long life; *Tigernus* is modern Welsh 'teyrn', a ruler or chief.

Two Llanddewibrefi crosses.

The *clasau* to which reference was made above were communities of men, apparently monastic in origin, though not of the Benedictine or Augustinian traditions, some at least of whom were not celibate, living under the rule of an abbot whose position (at least by Gerald's time) was passed from father to son, and who was not an ordained priest. The community's economic survival was guaranteed by their communal, indeed clan-like, ownership of land in which sons had hereditary rights. In the case of Llanbadarn Fawr, these lands were, according to the legends incorporated in the *Life of Padarn*, the enforced gifts of Maelgwn Gwynedd (between the rivers Rheidol and Clarach) and of Eithyr (between the Clarach and the Paith). The name Eithyr survives in a significant farm name, Llaneithr, near Devil's Bridge. The function of such traditions, whether or not based on fact, was of course to justify the ownership of the lands by the community.

Even as the Norman menace developed on the eastern frontier of Wales, Ceredigion was preparing on its own account to enter documented history with something more to its Christian heritage than stone crosses, genealogies and brief entries in annals. By the mid-eleventh century a priest of Llanbadarn Fawr had gained a remarkably good education in Wales, Scotland and Ireland. His name was Sulien, and although a priest he was a married man with four sons, which was nothing unusual in the Welsh or indeed the European Church of the time. In 1072 Sulien was elected bishop of St David's, and his young sons must have benefited not only from their father's teaching but from the learning preserved in the cathedral's community. Sulien retired from his bishopric in 1078, but was persuaded to return in 1080 for another five years, during which time he encountered William I, king of England, on the latter's visit to the cathedral and pilgrim shrine.

We would know nothing of Sulien but his name in the annals and lists of bishops had it not been for two of his sons, Rhygyfarch and Ieuan. Ieuan lived till 1137, with the rank of archpresbyter of Llanbadarn. He copied out in his immaculate hand, with illuminated letters, a copy of St Augustine's work *De Trinitate*, and added to it a Latin poem about his father, which begins with the lines quoted at the opening of Chapter 1 above. He also added a verse in Welsh celebrating what may have been the major Llanbadarn sacred relic, Cyrwen, the staff of St Padarn. He is also claimed as author of the *Life of Saint Padarn*. Rhygyfarch's name is connected with a splendid psalter now in Dublin; it was not his own work, but was written by one Ithael, while the illumination was done by Rhygyfarch's brother Ieuan. Rhygyfarch's two major works were his Latin *Life of Saint David*, probably written at St David's, and his remarkable Latin poem on the ravaging of Ceredigion by the Normans, written in the margin of a commentary on one of Cicero's works. The poem, to which we shall return in the next chapter, is enough to show that the last and best flowering of independent Welsh Christian learning took place in menacing circumstances. The writings of Sulien's sons show a remarkably wide knowledge of Latin literature, and his grandsons served the Welsh Church with distinction.

* * *

The emergence early in the 10th century of Hywel Dda as king, first over the south-west, then over Powys and Gwynedd, must have brought change to Ceredigion. Suddenly the former kingdom may to some extent have lost its marginal status; it would have provided a natural routeway for Hywel and his servants to travel to and from Gwynedd. Hywel certainly saw that it was wiser to become a client kingdom of the powerful united English state rather than be defiant; faced with the variety of customs in various parts of his own expanded kingdom, he may perhaps have been responsible for the first codification of Welsh traditional legal practice. Despite his success during his long life, Hywel's death in 950 saw the immediate collapse of his kingdom, and war returned to Ceredigion, ravaged as it was by the princes of Gwynedd in 895 (with English assistance), and again in 952 and 954.

Thenceforward Ceredigion suffered the cut and thrust of internecine Welsh military politics, interspersed with seaborne Viking attacks, throughout the next hundred years. The area was mainly subject to rule by Deheubarth in the tenth century and by Gwynedd in the first half of the eleventh century. Some warlords, whether or not of royal descent, succeeded briefly in uniting disparate kingdoms as Hywel Dda had done; thus Ceredigion was ruled with Deheubarth and Gwynedd between 985 and 999 by Maredudd ab Owain. Such a union did not bring peace; in 992 Maredudd's lands were devastated by a rival who called in English aid. The incidental interference of the Vikings, who had attacked the monasteries at St Dogmaels and Llanbadarn Fawr in 988, was an added burden. In 1039 Gruffudd ap Llywelyn, king of Gwynedd, ravaged Llanbadarn Fawr and occupied Ceredigion, and in 1055 internal conflict again brought him on the rampage through the south-west. His rule over all Wales died with his defeat by Harold Godwineson (later briefly king of England) and his murder in 1063 or 1064. The less marginal status that Ceredigion had acquired under the rule of Hywel Dda did not prove beneficial in later years; the district provided a highway for the clashing forces of Gwynedd and Deheubarth. Moreover, Ceredigion was soon to provide a route southwards to Penfro for incursions by the Norman invaders who had overwhelmed the flower of the English military at Senlac, near Hastings, in 1066.

NOTE: CEREDIGION'S EARLY CHURCHES

It was only after the above was completed that I read the archaeologist Ken Murphy's report on Ceredigion's early medieval ecclesiastical sites, written on behalf of the Cambria Archaeology Trust for CADW, completed in 2004. The long-known difficulty of recognising pre-Norman ecclesiastical sites in Wales was the force behind CADW's desire to review the whole country, with a view to detailed investigation of promising sites. The Ceredigion report has not been published, but it is possible to read a copy at the Royal Commission for Ancient and Historical Monuments Wales's headquarters at Aberystwyth, and Dr Murphy kindly gave me a copy. He contrasts the poverty of the evidence for Ceredigion with the high potential of sites in Pembrokeshire, and the lesser but still considerable evidence for Carmarthenshire. The report follows CADW's guidelines for assessing and identifying early medieval ecclesiastical sites, considering the following:

- documentary sources
- dated archaeological evidence
- undated archaeological evidence
- early Christian monuments (ECMs)
- dedications and cults
- place-name evidence
- topographical evidence.

A total of sixty-one sites were considered, and divided into four categories:

A. High probability (9 sites)
B. Medium probability (13 sites)
C. Low probability (12 sites)
D. Possible sites with indirect evidence.

The names, sometimes reworded by me, follow in those groups, with the word 'church' usually understood unless indicated otherwise:

A. Aberporth (Llanannerch Chapel); Gogerddan burial site; Llanbadarn Fawr; Llanddewibrefi; Llangoedmor; Llangrannog; Llanwenog Church; Llanwenog Capel Whyl; Penbryn (Corbalengus stone).
B. Gwnnws; Henfynyw; Lampeter, Llanbadarn Odwyn; Llanddewi Aberarth; Llandysiliogogo; Llandysul (parish church – cf. group C); Llantrisant; Llanfihangel Ystrad (Capel St Silin); Mwnt; Silian; Tregaron.

C. Bangor Teifi; Cellan; Henllan; Llannarth; Llanbadarn Trefeglwys; Llandysul (St Winifred's chapel); Llangybi; Llangynfelyn; Llangynllo; Llanilar; Nancwnlle; Pen-bryn (church – cf. A. above).

D. Blaen-porth; Cardigan Island; Dihewyd (Llanwyddalus church); Lampeter (Hen-feddau); Llanafan-y-Trawsgoed; Llanbadarn Fawr (Maes Bangor); Llanddeiniol; Llandyfrïog church and Ffynnon Oer cist cemetery; Llandysul (Cwm Tri-beddau cist cemetery); Llanfair Clydogau; Llanfihangel-y-Creuddyn (Mynwent Fach, Llaneithyr); Llanfihangel Ystrad; Llanllŷr; Llangeitho; Llangoedmor (Five Beds cists); Llangorwen chapel; Llangwyryfon; Llangwyryfon (Maesllyn); Llanina; Llanllwchaearn; Llansanffraid; Llansanffraid Bryn-beddau; Rhostïe; Strata Florida; Ysbyty Cynfyn.

Murphy's discussion of evidence is followed by a description of groups A, B and C site by individual site, in summary form. It is impossible here to do justice to his dispassionate and careful handling of the difficult evidence. He points out that because a measure of independent Welsh control continued in Ceredigion through the 12th century and into the 13th, therefore churches founded during that time represent a continuum with the preceding period, and cannot be easily distinguished from it. Even the Cistercian foundations at Strata Florida and Llanllŷr are sites each with an Early Christian monument, suggesting that they were not entirely new.

The classification above does not mean that there were really only nine pre-1100 ecclesiastical sites in Ceredigion, at least two of which (Penbryn and Gogerddan) had never developed into churches, leaving only seven. There were certainly more, and for my own part it seems that Llandysul has a strong case for being considered as a centre of fairly early importance, though not as clear-cut as in Llanbadarn Fawr and Llanddewibrefi. So much is a matter of chance; the 1973 discovery of the three crosses at Llantrisant, a site hitherto regarded as insignificant, is a useful reminder that some evidence may yet reappear, while an enormous amount has simply vanished.

6. Resisting the Invaders

The entries in the *Chronicle of the Princes*, kept at that time in Llanbadarn Fawr, are bleak:

> 1073 The Normans ravaged Ceredigion
> 1074 A second time the Normans ravaged Ceredigion

The oldest inhabitants of that time could remember previous devastations. The fierce usurper king, Gruffudd ap Llywelyn, who for twenty years ruled almost all Wales by main force, had ravaged Llanbadarn Fawr in 1039; fifty years prior to that another warring chief had pillaged Ceredigion. This time, however, it would be different. True, there was a pause after 1074, but in 1093, says the chronicler: 'The Normans came to Dyfed and Ceredigion . . . and fortified them with castles.' This time the pillagers intended to stay, and the bare chronicle entry is vividly illuminated by an eyewitness. Rhygyfarch son of Sulien described the appalling behaviour of the new rulers of west Wales in his Latin *Lament*, which must have been written in the aftermath of 1093. Too long to be quoted in full, the poem demands nevertheless to be called in evidence:

> People and priest alike are crushed by Norman word, heart and deed.
> They extort new taxes and burn our belongings;
> One foul Norman enslaves a hundred by command and glance . . .
> We are mutilated, condemned, enchained;
> The honest hand is burnt with the thief's brand,
> A woman's nose sliced off, a man's testicles . . .

However, though they were brutal, the Normans' first occupations were brief, and Ceredigion passed under the rule of the last of the kings of south-west Wales, Rhys ap Tewdwr, who in 1081 had vanquished his Welsh enemies at the battle of Mynydd Carn somewhere between St Davids and the Teifi, and had achieved some form of recognition by King William I. But immediately after Rhys's death in 1093, Earl Roger of Montgomery came to the north bank of the Teifi and built his earth mound and stockade on an ancient site, Din Geraint. Inspired by the example of the men of Gwynedd, the Welsh rose in revolt the following year and destroyed Roger's castle; according to the chronicler, they left much of the countryside empty of men and cattle alike. Nevertheless, Norman earls still claimed the disposal of Ceredigion, and in 1099 Ceredigion was granted to the adventurous Cadwgan, son of Bleddyn ap Cynfyn, king of Powys, newly returned from exile in Ireland, who succeeded in establishing control, albeit fluctuating, over a considerable area of Wales.

Cadwgan had no rights in Ceredigion which local men would have recognised;

still, he seems to have been able to hold his place until 1109, when his wild son Owain, filled with lust, kidnapped from a north Pembrokeshire castle his own second cousin, the beautiful Nest, wife of the powerful Gerald of Windsor, and once mistress of Henry I of England. Anglo-Norman pride was outraged; Henry sent Cadwgan's Powys cousins to seek the miscreant, and with their allies they fell on Ceredigion. Once more the wretched province was overrun and its people terrorised, while Owain fled to Ireland and Cadwgan retreated to Powys. The plausible Cadwgan, who had a Norman wife and therefore allies, managed to persuade Henry that he was not to blame for Owain's ravishing of the not entirely unwilling Nest, and he was restored to rule in Ceredigion. However, Owain's return from Ireland caused havoc once again; there was no third chance for Cadwgan, so Henry gave Ceredigion to Gilbert fitz Richard, also known as Gilbert de Clare. Owain, evicted from Ceredigion, eventually met his death in 1116 at the hands of the supporters of Gerald de Windsor. The cuckold was avenged.

Aberystwyth's original Norman ringwork-and-bailey castle, above Rhydyfelin.
[Crown copyright: Royal Commission on Ancient & Historical Monuments, Wales].

Gilbert had seized his new lordship of Ceredigion with application and efficiency, and castle-building began on his own initiative and that of his followers. The Welsh chronicles names ten Ceredigion castles, and as Sir Goronwy Edwards pointed out, they matched fairly well to the lordship's nine commotes: Dingeraint and Blaenporth (both in Iscoed commote); Castell Humphrey (later called Castell Hywel, in Gwynionydd); Stephen's castle (i.e. Lampeter, in Mabwynion), Castell Fflemish in

Pennardd, Dineirth in Anhuniog, Ystrad Meurig in Mefenydd, Razo's castle at Peithyll (Perfedd) and Walter's castle in Genau'r-glyn. Mefenydd also had the first Aberystwyth castle, a ringwork and bailey, which stands on the hill above Tanycastell farm, south of Pendinas; its earthworks are still impressively large, and there must surely have been a civilian settlement on the hill's gentle westward slope. Thus the only commote without an early Norman castle was Creuddyn, easily supervised from Aberystwyth. There are references to 'Richard de la Mare's castle', whose whereabouts are not known, but there are a number of other earthwork castles in the county, and it seems possible that the tidy pattern suggested by Sir Goronwy did not actually exist on the ground. The Royal Commission on Ancient and Historical Monuments Wales lists eight ringworks and at least twenty-three mottes. Of the ringworks, Caer Penrhos above Llanrhystud (SN 552695), was a Welsh castle, built in 1148 by Cadwaladr ap Gruffudd by reusing an Iron Age hill fort. Of the surviving mottes, the most noteworthy in respect of its size is Trefilan, apparently built in 1233, and therefore another Welsh castle.

In addition to his castles, Gilbert reformed the *clas* at Llanbadarn, dismissing the ecclesiastical tenants and granting the church and its wealth to the monastery of St Peter's, Gloucester, who sent monks there. However, a Latin record of Welsh historical events continued to be kept at Llanbadarn, and later at Strata Florida, which was eventually worked up into a fuller chronicle and translated into Welsh as *Brut y Tywysogion*, the Chronicle of the Princes.

Gilbert's personal rule of Ceredigion ended with his death in 1117, and he seems only to have faced one serious interruption, albeit a dramatic one. When Rhys ap

The Trefilan castle motte, almost certainly of Welsh origin.

Ystrad Meurig castle. [Crown copyright: Royal Commission on Ancient & Historical Monuments, Wales].

Tewdwr of Deheubarth had been killed in 1093, his young son Gruffudd was taken to Ireland for his safety. In 1115 the young man returned to the south-west to claim back his patrimony from the Normans. According to the indignant chronicler at Llanbadarn, he gathered a band of hot-heads about him and in 1116 they irrupted northwards into Ceredigion. He first attacked the centre of Flemish settlement at Blaen-porth, slaughtering many of the settlers, and then moved north of the Ystwyth, to Cantref Penweddig.

Having crossed the Rheidol and seized and destroyed Gilbert's castle at Ystrad Peithyll, and having devoured many of the monks' cattle at Llanbadarn (thus provoking the indignation of the chronicler), Gruffudd and his men again crossed the Rheidol, climbed the short steep hill to Antaron (at today's Southgate) and looked across at Aberystwyth castle on the south side of the Ystwyth. They were unaware that the castle had been reinforced by night from the castle at Ystrad Meurig by Gilbert's resourceful steward Razo. Near the foot of the castle-hill was a bridge across the Ystwyth. As the Welsh moved down to seize the bridge, the Normans attacked and the Welsh, although they unhorsed a mailed knight, were routed and fled. The Llanbadarn chronicler's splendid account of this incident, the first blow-by-blow account of a battle in Wales, is somewhat undermined by the suspicion that much of the detail and excitement may perhaps have been contributed by the 13th century editor of the chronicle, a century or more after the event.

After the excitement of Gruffudd ap Rhys's unsuccessful incursion, the history of Ceredigion is a blank for almost twenty years; we can only speculate on the struggles of the ordinary people of the land to keep body, soul and family together. Gilbert's son Richard fitz Clare succeeded his father, but we know nothing of him in his western lordship until trouble boiled over at the death of the masterful Henry I in 1135. In April 1136 Richard hastened westwards towards Ceredigion to secure his interest there, but he was ambushed and killed near Crickhowell in the Usk valley. Suddenly the lordship of Ceredigion was a vacuum which the Welsh hastened to fill. Owain and Cadwaladr, the formidable sons of Gruffudd ap Cynan of Gwynedd, crossed the Dyfi into Ceredigion, where they were joined by other Welsh adventurers. A series of assaults on Ceredigion followed, and within three years every Norman castle had fallen except Cardigan itself, which held out even when a Danish fleet sailed up the Teifi to assist the Welsh. For a brief while Ceredigion was divided between the two northern princes, Cadwaladr son of Gruffudd ap Cynan north of the Aeron and his nephew, the poet Hywel ab Owain Gwynedd in the south; Humphrey's castle in the Clettwr valley was renamed Castell Hywel. However they eventually yielded control to their relatives, the sons of Gruffudd ap Rhys. It seems extraordinary that the Norman garrison at Cardigan was able to hold out for another eighteen years; admittedly the south bank of the Teifi was in also Norman occupation; the stand-off may have lasted through mutual consent.

Despite this failure to take Cardigan, the sons of Gruffudd ap Rhys consolidated their rule over the rest of Ceredigion, and in 1156 Rhys ap Gruffudd, the most formidable of the brood, built the castle at Tomen Las, overlooking the Dyfi, now crowned by a heronry in the Ynys-hir bird sanctuary; its purpose was to deter the men of Gwynedd from crossing the river into Rhys's domain. However the real menace to Welsh rule of Ceredigion came from England; the feeble king Stephen had been replaced in 1154 by the ferociously vigorous Henry II, who in 1158 turned his attention to south Wales, where Rhys and his brothers had so successfully turned back the Norman encroachments. Such was the strength of Henry's forces on this occasion that Rhys felt he had no option but to surrender without a fight. He thereby retained parts of his realm, but lost Ceredigion, where Earl Roger of Hertford, son of Richard de Clare, was reinstated as lord. Roger, like his grandfather Gilbert, lost no time in stamping his authority on Ceredigion, building or rebuilding castles at Castell Hywel, Ystrad Meurig, Dineirth and Llanrhystud. The common people of Ceredigion once again felt the burden of foreign occupation; whether it weighed more heavily than the yoke of the Welsh lords it is impossible to say, but it was certainly alien.

By 1164 the Welsh princes felt confident enough to defy King Henry. Rhys first overran most of Ceredigion, and in the following year finally took Cardigan castle. In 1171 Henry acknowledged Rhys's rule; indeed, following the death of Owain Gwynedd in 1170, Rhys was now the foremost of Welsh lords in both north and south Wales. He affirmed his status as 'the Lord Rhys' by rebuilding Cardigan castle in stone and mortar, and at Christmastide 1176 he held a great feast, with competitions in music and poetry. It is interesting that this famous occasion, retrospectively endowed with the title 'Eisteddfod', was held at Cardigan rather than

A GROUP of white-robed monks came, immediately before Rhys ap Gruffudd recaptured Ceredigion in 1164, from Whitland's Cistercian monastery to the banks of the Fflur, south of Pontrhydfendigaid, where the Old Abbey farm now stands. Although the monks had been invited by the Anglo-Norman Roger, who would have given the new abbey its original endowment of lands, Rhys took over its patronage and treated it generously. Strata Florida soon became a major political centre on its new site two miles from the original place of settlement. Abbots acted as ambassadors for the Welsh princes, and the abbey hosted the gathering of Welsh lords in 1238 referred to below. It was a major cultural centre, where the Chronicle of the Princes was kept, where major literary manuscripts were copied, and whose abbots patronised the great Welsh poets of the 14th and 15th centuries. Although stone churches, some of considerable size, were being built across Ceredigion, Strata Florida's refined Gothic and its extensive domestic buildings would have been enormously impressive, and considerable charity would have been dispensed at its gates, drawn from the abbey's estate of some 40,000 acres, divided into eight large granges in Ceredigion, with many smaller properties, and with rights of fishing along much of the northern coast.

at Dinefwr, which Rhys's propaganda claimed as the true power centre of Deheubarth. The feast itself may well have been imitative of Provençal culture, so well-known to Eleanor of Aquitaine, wife of Rhys's friend Henry II and therefore known to Rhys himself as a visitor to Henry's court. However there was already a long tradition of Celtic feasting, which would have involved poets and musicians. It may well, as J.E. Caerwyn Williams suggested, have been a festival both of propaganda proclaiming Rhys's power and prowess, and celebrating the rebuilding of Cardigan castle.

It should not be imagined that Rhys spent a great deal of his time in Ceredigion. His military campaigns took him to east and north Wales, not to mention visits to England, once as a prisoner, otherwise as an acknowledged Welsh lord and friend of Henry II. However, he made a lasting impression on Ceredigion. He had quickly taken over patronage of the abbeys of Whitland (which had a grange in the Teifi valley) and of Strata Florida, confirming and almost certainly extending its lands in a charter of 1184. He supported the priory at Cardigan, and himself founded the nunnery at Llanllŷr in the Aeron valley, as well as endowing the Knights of St John of Jerusalem with lands in Llanrhystud, Ystrad Meurig and Ysbyty Ystwyth. Indeed, to us it

Cardigan castle and bridge in the 18th century.
[Ceredigion Museum; National Library of Wales].

Cardigan castle today.

may seem remarkable how much land in Ceredigion was given away by Rhys and his family to the Church, including the whole valuable arable area between Llanrhystud and Morfa Mawr. So much is certain; it is less certain that it was Rhys who instituted the administrative unit of the *gwestfa* for the purpose of securing his income. It is interesting to note that non-Welshmen rubbed shoulders with the Welsh in Cardigan; when Rhys confirmed the priory charter, Lambert of Flanders, Ailbrutus of Bristol and others with surnames like Palmer, Parmenter and Cottrell were among the witnesses.

PRINCES OF DEHEUBARTH

Those who ruled Ceredigion or part thereof in **bold**

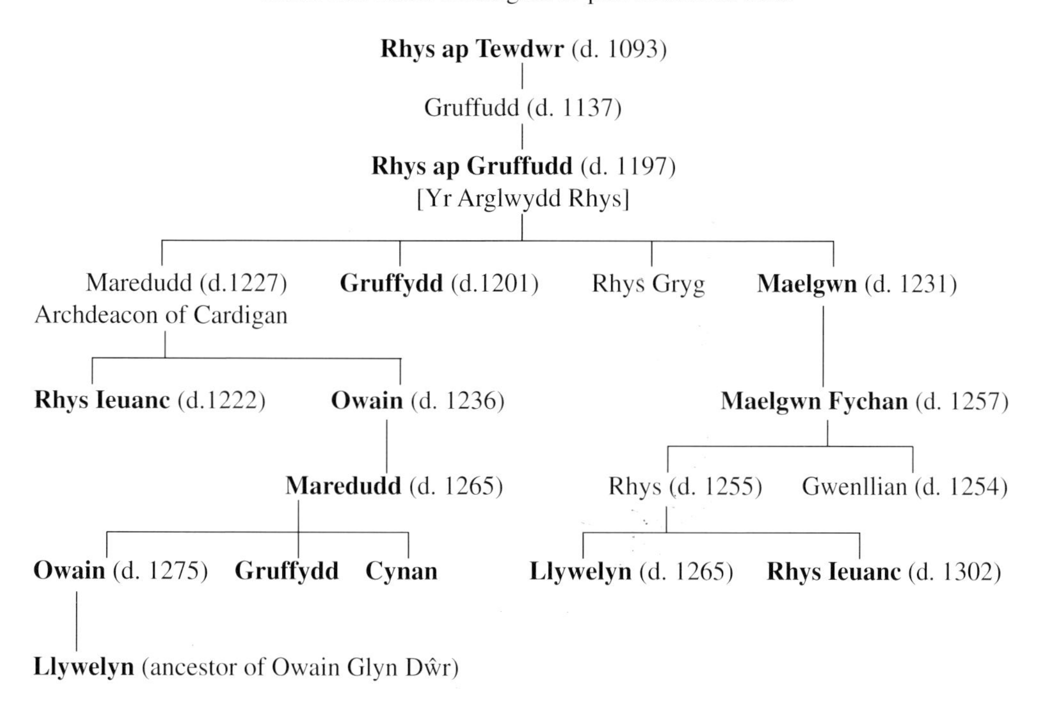

Rhys's reception and escorting of the Canterbury crusade mission in 1188 shows that he was familiar with the lordship, and must often have ridden its countryside in the company of his *teulu* or war-band. It was thus that he escorted Baldwin, archbishop of Canterbury, along with Gerald of Wales, through Ceredigion, having first entertained them at Cardigan. Gerald's famous description of the journey through Wales is muddled in its reporting of Ceredigion; he claimed that the party journeyed through Lampeter, Strata Florida and then via Llanddewibrefi to Llanbadarn, a most unlikely order of travel.

Although Rhys ap Gruffudd had done so much for the cause of Church reform by supporting the Cistercians, he seems to have allowed Llanbadarn to revert from the monks of Gloucester to its previous owners, the *claswyr* or monastic family body. This did not meet with the approval of Gerald, who was a leading exponent of church modernisation and reform, and had a horror of clerical marriage and paternity. His own words express his outrage: 'This church . . . has a layman as its abbot . . . We found the church of Llanbadarn Fawr reduced to this sorry state. An old man called Ednywain ap Gweithfoed, who had grown grey in iniquity, was usurping the office of abbot, while his sons officiated at the altar.' Although archbishop Baldwin was present, he seems to have done nothing immediately to change matters, but Ednywain and the *clas* are not heard of again.

Unfortunately for Rhys, after two decades of great success, his last years were bitter. This veteran warrior and statesman, who in youth had so loyally cooperated with his elder brothers, who had survived the wrath of a great European king and been his friend, eventually became the victim of his own fierce sons, who had begun to

Tomen Las, the Lord Rhys's northernmost castle near Glandyfi.

quarrel among themselves during their father's lifetime. Rhys had his son Maelgwn imprisoned, but the young man escaped in 1192, and the following year he brought siege engines to Ystrad Meurig and smashed his way into the castle, apparently to drive out his brother Gruffudd. The sordid details of the quarrel need not hinder us, but at one point Rhys himself was imprisoned, apparently by Maelgwn, though soon released by another of his quiverful of sons. Thereupon Rhys rampaged across Wales from Carmarthen to Radnor, crushing all opposition, but eventually dying in 1197, still in harness and splendidly eulogised in Latin by the chronicler, now based at Rhys's beloved Strata Florida where so many of his descendants were to be buried, though he himself was buried at St David's.

For twenty years Ceredigion had enjoyed a respite from warfare, thanks to Rhys ap Gruffudd, but the turmoil of his last years was a sure omen of a confused and confusing future. Rhys's numerous sons and grandsons fought ruthlessly in their attempts to control as much as they could of their father's domains. Gruffudd ap Rhys, acknowledged successor to his father, was at Aberystwyth (still on the hill south of Pendinas) when his rival brother Maelgwn, assisted by the fierce and ambitious Gwenwynwyn, prince of southern Powys, swept into the Ystwyth valley and stormed Aberystwyth. He captured his brother Gruffudd and handed him over to Gwenwynwyn before marching south to make himself lord of Ceredigion. The chronicler refers to 'the *town* and castle of Aberystwyth'; this settlement must have lain on the gently-sloping ground, now green sward, west of the castle mound, not on the present seaside site.

This victory of Maelgwn's did not bring further success. In 1198, his ally Gwenwynwyn was crushed by the English; his brother Gruffudd was released and swiftly regained almost all of Ceredigion. Maelgwn however, holed up in Cardigan castle, betrayed it to King John in exchange for recognition as lord of Ceredigion; an execrable act of treachery soon followed by Gruffudd's death. Maelgwn's hold on his lordship of Ceredigion was soon disputed by a new power in the land, Llywelyn ap Iorwerth ('the Great') who, secure in north-west Wales, was engaged in extending the hegemony of Gwynedd, and who first seized and rebuilt Aberystwyth castle in 1208. His domination was interrupted by the wrath of King John, who briefly humiliated Llywelyn, and whose French

THE Lord Rhys's descendants were not less active in Ceredigion than Rhys himself. Maelgwn ap Rhys, after a lifetime punctuated by fierce warfare and occasional treachery, died at Llanerchaeron in 1230, to be succeeded by his son Maelgwn Fychan, whose career, marginally less violent than that of his father, ended in 1257 only after the death of his only son Rhys in 1254 and two of his daughters; all four were buried at Strata Florida. Gwenllian had died at Llanfihangel-y-Creuddyn, suggesting – along with the name – that it was the centre of Maelgwn's commote of Creuddyn. Either Maelgwn or his grandsons Llywelyn or Rhys may have been responsible for building the large church there. The village itself, though its buildings are virtually all of the 19th and 20th centuries, may have had its origin in the settlement of the bondmen who worked the land for the lords of the commote. Into the 20th century some of the surrounding land was still worked by farms in the village, as opposed to the more usual scattered settlements.

military captain Falkes of Breauté started building another castle at Aberystwyth. Maelgwn, perhaps regretting his earlier treachery, drove out the alien and destroyed his castle; he and the other descendants of the Lord Rhys were now loyal adherents of the resurgent Llywelyn, who in 1216 divided the commotes of Ceredigion among them at a meeting held at Aberdyfi.

Llywelyn's control of Ceredigion, exercised through the southern princelings, lasted till his death in 1240. Two years earlier, before the high altar at Strata Florida, he had attempted to secure the recognition of his son Dafydd by all the Welsh lords who acknowledged his supremacy over more than half of Wales. The occasion must have been impressive; unfortunately, Dafydd was not the man his father had been, and Henry III did not allow him room to prove himself. Before the end of 1246 Dafydd was dead, and the Welsh lords had perforce to acknowledge Henry as their only overlord. In Ceredigion their lands were restricted and English officials ruled in Cardigan and Aberystwyth; the church, parish and tithes of Llanbadarn Fawr were taken by the king, and the building of the present great church was commenced. Crown lands in northern Ceredigion were administered by a Welshman, Gwilym ap Gwrwared, great-grandfather of Dafydd ap Gwilym.

While Ceredigion was fragmented between Welsh lords and Crown officials, a new power was rising once more in Gwynedd. Llywelyn ap Gruffudd, grandson of Llywelyn the Great, had overcome his brothers, swept the English out of north-east Wales and in December 1256 he appeared in north Ceredigion. English rule of Llanbadarn and control of the commote of Perfedd melted away before him; Llywelyn handed both over to Maredudd ab Owain. For twenty years there was peace in Ceredigion; Llywelyn left the English undisturbed in Cardigan castle and their tiny county of Cardigan, reckoning that the rest of Ceredigion was safe in the hands of the descendants of Rhys ap Gruffudd under his own overlordship. For twenty years he concentrated his energies further east, and Ceredigion may have enjoyed some semblance of peace.

* * *

The Ceredigion princelings acknowledged Llywelyn as their overlord, a state of affairs finally recognised by the distracted Henry III in 1267, when Llywelyn was formally confirmed as Prince of Wales. Llywelyn's iron control of his vassals cannot however have been entirely welcome, and when he came into conflict with the new king, Edward I, from 1273 onwards, his position became increasingly insecure but his attitude more intransigent. When war came late in 1276 it did not reach Ceredigion; Llywelyn's southern supporters abandoned him and hastened to submit to the Crown, led by Rhys Wyndod and Rhys ap Maredudd, the lords of Dinefwr and Dryslwyn, who were followed by their cousins of Ceredigion, Rhys Fychan ap Rhys ap Maelgwn, Gruffudd and Cynan, the surviving sons of Maredudd ab Owain, and their nephew Llywelyn ab Owain.

Little did their submission avail them; Pain fitz Patrick on the king's behalf seized Anhuniog, Mefenydd and Perfedd, and Edmund the king's brother arrived at

Llanbadarn; Rhys Fychan was now landless. At the king's command Edmund, already experienced in governing Cardigan, began building a castle on a fresh site, Pen Gwninger, a rocky knoll close to the sea and the Rheidol estuary, which Edward realised was vital for safety and provisioning in the event of siege; Welsh princes had never been able to afford a fleet. The authorities were careful to compensate the owners of the castle's site, almost certainly the monks of Strata Florida, with land elsewhere. This was no mere motte-and-bailey, but a massive stone castle intended to dominate the king's territory.

Cardigan was certainly the first substantial urban settlement in Ceredigion, founded by Gilbert de Clare between 1110 and 1117. Although no documentary evidence survives from the town's earliest period, it was clearly a mercantile centre for traders working both by land and sea. It was probably Gilbert who established the Benedictine priory east of the castle, the rebuilt church of which is still the town's parish church. St Peter's monastery at Gloucester claimed the priory as its offshoot, but the medieval documents maintaining this claim are forgeries; the priory was in fact dependent on the abbey of Chertsey in Surrey. The town claimed lordship over the half-commote of Is Hirwern immediately to the north and west, and by 1240 this was the acknowledged 'county' of Cardigan. The first description of the town, the date of whose borough status is obscure, dates from 1268, when Edmund, younger brother of Edward the later king, took over its control and commissioned a valuable survey, still unpublished. At this time the town had fairs, markets, mills and a salmon fishery. Most of the burgesses bore English names. Two of the gates of the town were known as East-gate and Bridge-gate; a document of *c*1301 names Wolf's gate, New-gate and Bartholemew's gate. Gerald of Wales describes his visit to the town thus: 'The next day we were in Cardigan or Aberteifi, which means the spot where the River Teifi meets the sea, and there we were entertained by Prince Rhys. A crowd assembled on the Cemais side of the river, not far from the bridge, with Prince Rhys and his two sons, Maelgwn and Gruffudd, in the middle, and the word of God was preached with great effect, first by the Archbishop and then by me . . . We persuaded a great number of people to take the Cross . . . In a green field just by the bridge-head where the sermons had been given those who had been present marked out a site for a chapel in commemoration of what had happened there.'

By the Aberconwy treaty of 1277, Edward confined Llywelyn to north-west Wales; only the lands which the prince had controlled before his breakout in 1256 remained to him, and only a handful of Welsh lords were allowed to do token homage to him, including Rhys Fychan of north Ceredigion, who had abandoned his allegiance to the king only a month after swearing it at Worcester, and was now a landless exile in Llywelyn's much-diminished train of followers. In Ceredigion, the Crown now ruled from the Dyfi at least as far as the Aeron, as well of course as the Cardigan area. The only areas still under some form of Welsh control were the commote of Pennardd and the district from the Aeron to Cardigan; some of this latter belonged to Llywelyn ab Owain, but he was a minor in the king's guardianship and his lands were therefore in royal custody. Gruffudd and Cynan

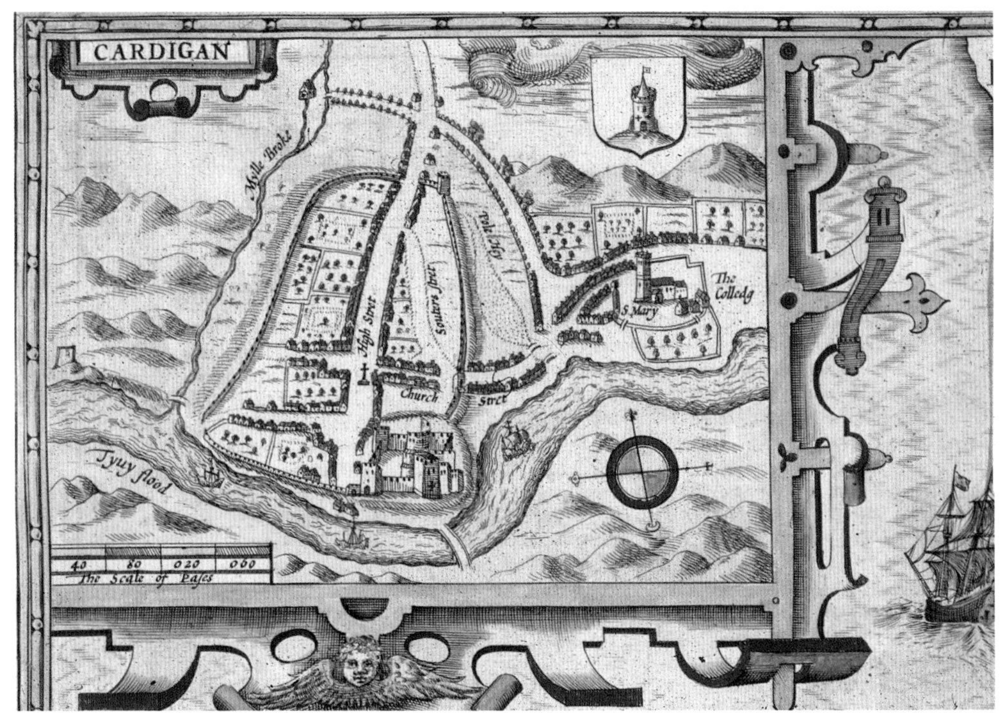

Cardigan borough, from John Speed's map of 1610.

were restored to mid-Ceredigion as royal vassals, their rights and privileges much reduced. This did not prevent them from claiming that the lands of Rhys Fychan were rightfully theirs, since Rhys was the bastard son of a prostitute! Such claims were hardly likely to trouble the masterful Edward, who had persuaded his brother Edmund to give up his position in Ceredigion in exchange for manors in England. The building of Aberystwyth castle and town continued; it needed lead, stone and timber, worked by 176 masons, 14 carpenters, 5 smiths, 2 plumbers and 1,120 other workmen. Once the castle was garrisoned, wine, coal and food had to be brought in by sea, not without difficulty.

The Welsh lords who had abandoned Llywelyn in 1277 soon regretted their bad faith; the oppressive exactions of royal officials in north-east Wales brought discontent, and at Easter 1282 there was a sudden and alarming uprising, initiated not by Llywelyn but by his mercurial brother Dafydd in north-east Wales. The first outbreak was on 21 March, but the news did not reach Aberystwyth for several days. On the 24th, Rhys Fychan and his cousin Gruffudd, who must have been apprised of Dafydd's plans, appeared at the new borough's gate and invited the castle's custodian to dine outside the castle walls. He fell into the trap and was seized, as was the castle; the Welshmen slaughtered the borough's inhabitants and began the destruction of the town and castle, sparing the garrison on the grounds that it was Easter. This return of Rhys, so recently the Welsh lord of Penweddig, did not last long; he was quickly driven out, and in May the king's great castle-architect Master James of St George was sent to examine the damage. In December 1282 Llywelyn was killed; his brother Dafydd was executed in October 1283. Edward's agents reported the discovery of 2000 cattle at Trefilan, presumably a Welsh attempt at a scorched-earth policy. Rhys Fychan was in royal custody along with his cousins Gruffudd, Cynan and Llywelyn. Rhys and Gruffudd had their lives spared by the king, but never returned to their lost lands; they were kept in confinement when they were not serving in the ranks of Edward's army.

Edward's 1284 Statute of Rhuddlan settled the governance of his conquests. Ceredigion was henceforth Cardiganshire, part of the southern division of the Principality (Carmarthenshire formed the rest; the remainder of south Wales consisted of marcher lordships). The king's only concession to the one-time Welsh lords was to allow Llywelyn ab Owain, presumably on account of his youth, to return to his lands. For the rest of his life (he died in 1309) Llywelyn was in effect a minor marcher lord within a royal county, his only claim to attention lying in his posterity; Owain Glyn Dŵr was by his mother the direct descendant of Llywelyn, and heir to his lands.

The 1287 revolt of Rhys ap Maredudd did not take fire in Cardiganshire; the men of Cardiganshire assisted vigorously both at the siege of the new castle in Emlyn, and in the hunt for the fugitive Rhys. However, in 1294 a much more serious revolt broke out in north Wales under the leadership of Madog ap Llywelyn, a direct descendant of Gruffudd ap Cynan of Gwynedd and fifth cousin to Llywelyn ap Gruffudd. His mother was that Gwenllian who had died at Llanfihangel-y-Creuddyn in 1254, and his father, also a Llywelyn, had ruled the cantref of Meirionnydd before his expulsion by Llywelyn ap Gruffudd. Madog was therefore kin to the Welsh ex-lords of Ceredigion, and was supported both by Cynan ap Maredudd and by Maelgwn, son of Rhys Fychan, both of whom had somehow wriggled free of Edward's custody. They rose once more in revolt, but failed in their attempt to capture Aberystwyth castle, and then fought their way southwards, failing again at Cardigan. Maelgwn was captured and sent to join his father at Bamborough castle in Northumberland, while Cynan, disguised as a leper, was captured at Brecon, condemned as a traitor, dragged through the streets of Hereford and hanged. Thus died the last free survivor of the Ceredigion descendants of Rhys ap Gruffudd whose fate is known. Two other sons of Rhys Fychan are known to have been in prison at Norwich in 1307, before they, like their father and their uncle Gruffudd, vanish from the record, without offspring.

Madog's failed revolt had galvanised much of Wales as a result of the oppressive nature of English rule. Edward had had to cancel his intended military expedition to France; once more he and his armies (many of whom were Welshmen) tramped through Wales, including Cardiganshire, to crush the Welsh, as they had done in 1277 and 1282/3. Despite these fierce upheavals, Edward's administrative machinery, already functioning in the town of Cardigan, spread very quickly through the Crown lands of Cardiganshire after the conquest of 1277. Despite the upheavals of 1282/3 and 1294/5, the year 1277 really marks the effective conquest of north Ceredigion, while 1282/3 completed control of Is Aeron. North of the Aeron formed a stewardship based on Aberystwyth, while the south formed another, based at Cardigan. The only lands not directly controlled by royal officials were the half-commotes of Gwynionydd Is Cerdin and Iscoed Uwch Hirwern, ruled by Llywelyn ab Owain and his descendants, which were not directly administered by royal officials; their lords collected their own rents, fines and dues, and administered Welsh land law in their own courts, but had to attend all major royal courts as tenants-in-chief. The descendants of Ednyfed Fychan, chief minister of Llywelyn the Great, held a number of townships in Cardiganshire; Ednyfed may have acquired them through his marriage to Gwenllian, daughter of Rhys ap Gruffudd; eventually these lands passed to Rhydderch ab Ieuan Llwyd, whom we shall meet again. Their owners enjoyed lesser privileges than those of Llywelyn ab Owain and his two sons, but they were not administered directly from Aberystwyth.

After acknowledging these Welsh lordships, Edward had a free hand to do as he would with the lands conquered from the Welsh princelings. He needed to reward loyal followers with land; part of Genau'r Glyn was given to Roger Mortimer, Aberaeron to John de Knovill and the whole commote of Pennardd to Geoffrey Clement, who later acquired Genau'r Glyn, as well as other interests in Cardiganshire. The commote of Mabwynion was given to Rhys ap Maredudd as a reward for his loyalty in 1282, and it was he who gave Lampeter its borough charter in 1284; the fledgling establishment survived the 1287 rebellion and consequent death of its founder. But the majority of the royal conquests stayed in royal hands, the domain of a prince of Wales when such existed, otherwise ruled by the king through his officials. Neither the Principality nor the Marcher lordships sent members to the king's parliaments save on one or two exceptional occasions. The Church, as we have already seen, owned extensive lands in Cardiganshire which were effectively independent of any royal administration, though certainly within the king's law.

For more than a century it seemed that, whatever unruly behaviour might take place on the streets of the boroughs, the king's county of Cardiganshire would never again know Welsh rebellion and royal retaliation. But it was not to be; eventually the county was to experience again the movement of armies and the fierce clash of war.

NOTE: LANDHOLDING AND SETTLEMENT

This subject is not easy to grasp; even the best individual witness we have, Gerald of Wales, was really an outsider whose understanding was far from complete. The terminology of the Welsh law-texts and the royal surveys of land post-1284 are far from simple; practice surely varied not only across time but from area to area. Thus in Cardiganshire the cantref divisions were less significant than the commotes, which lived on post-1284 as 'hundreds'. There were estates known as *maenorau*, a term which it seems is not derived from the word 'manor', but is older than the Conquest period. The *maenorau* were further divided into *trefi* or townships, small areas of settlement, consisting each of a number of *rhandiroedd* or sharelands. To complicate matters still further, the *maenorau* in Ceredigion were partly displaced by a system probably introduced during the twelfth century, namely *gwestfeydd*, which simply means 'taxable areas'. The elements *maenor* and *rhandir* both survive to the present day in Ceredigion place-names.

Some lands were held freehold by kin-groups claiming descent from a common ancestor; other lands were worked for the lord of the commote by bondmen. The kin-groups can be traced in Cardiganshire documents from 1268 onwards, but the system, known as *tir gwelyawg* ('resting-place land'), was certainly older. The men who held these lands counted themselves as free-born Welshmen, as opposed to the *taeogion* or bond-men who worked the lord's lands, the *maerdre*. These lands were characterised by areas of strips or furlongs, known as *lleiniau* or slangs, which can still be traced on 18th-century estate maps, and even on the tithe-maps of the 1840s. In the case of Morfa Esgob, the bishop's lands at Llansanffraid/Llan-non, they survive almost in their entirety, the largest remnant in Wales of a long-vanished system. Its survival here is probably due to the inefficiency of the bishops of St David's in exploiting their own land, which was given to the bishop by Rhys Ieuanc ap Gruffudd between 1215-1222. It was bond lands such as these which the rulers of Ceredigion gave to various agents of the Church, who became the greatest landowner in the county other than the princes and their successor, the Crown. As well as the tens of thousands of acres which belonged to the Cistercian monks and nuns and to the Knights of St John, the bishop of St David's held swathes of land not only at Morfa Esgob, but in Blaenpennal, Llanddewi Aberarth, Nancwnlle, Gartheli, Llanddewibrefi, Lampeter, Llandygwydd, Henllan Deifi, Bangor Teifi and Fforest yr Esgob.

Medieval strip fields at Llan-non/Llansanffraid.

[Crown copyright: Royal Commission on Ancient & Historical Monuments, Wales].

Periods of Norman rule certainly disrupted the pattern of land-holding. Gilbert de Clare settled immigrants in his lordship, both English and Flemish, summarily displacing some of the Welsh – a process which today we call 'ethnic cleansing'. He took over the existing system of taxation, which at this period was still largely in the form of food-renders. Agriculture was the essence of the economy, and so the burden of taxation was borne by Welsh farmers. Later in the century Gerald of Wales describes a pastoral way of life, with the people dependent upon their cattle and sheep, but his casual references to corn, bread and ploughing show that people were much more settled than his portrait suggests. Flocks and herds would have been shepherded over hilly ground, while plots and strips of crops would have been protected by moveable hurdles as well, perhaps, as hedges or fences.

7. Peace and Rebellion: Cardiganshire 1277-1543

The building of Edward's Aberystwyth castle and town walls from 1277 onwards was a spectacle of a kind never before seen on the west Wales coast. Edward had no interest in the former castle site above the Ystwyth; the new complex had to be accessible by sea, so that it might withstand any siege by the Welsh. He chose land originally belonging to the Cistercians of Strata Florida, who were compensated elsewhere. The influx of workmen was unprecedented (see the previous chapter for details). English masons, smiths, quarrymen and carpenters were brought from the West Country; many if not all came by sea with such necessary supplies as iron, lead, lime and nails. Some building stone for windows and doorways was also brought by sea; the best of the local building stone can be split for walls, but cannot be readily carved. The timber used would have been local. The plan suited the site; the result was a diamond-shaped fortification, while the long-vanished town walls girdled an area still roughly traceable on the ground today; from the castle to the main town bridge, along Mill Street and across to the promenade and back to the castle. The street plan was simple; what are now Market Street and Great Darkgate Street formed one axis, Bridge Street and Pier Street the other.

Celtic [?] motifs on the western arch at Strata Florida.

Building began on 1 August 1277; on 28 December in the same year Edward granted the new borough its charter. Building progress did not please the new justiciar and keeper of royal castles, Bogo de Knovill, when he visited Aberystwyth in 1280. There were no arms, garrison or provisions in the castle, and the borough gates, without locks, were open day and night; the gate tower had been sited too close to the sea, where it was continually shaken by the great crash of the waves. Repairs, modifications and additions to the castle were made, and work was still continuing in 1289. Once the castle was garrisoned, wine, coal and food had to be brought in by sea, not without difficulty. The total cost of the castle to the Crown was at least £4,300; at the same time Rhuddlan castle was being built, and large sums spent on the strengthening of the Tower of London. The sea remained a menace, and before the present promenade and road were built in 1903, much of the outer ward of the castle had disappeared under the waves. Bogo did not mention a problem which was to concern local people for centuries; no church was built within the new town, though there would have been a chapel within the castle. Citizens were presumed able, if not willing, to walk to Llanbadarn Fawr. The slaughter of the town's foreign inhabitants at Easter 1282 may help explain why the oldest list of burgesses, from 1300/1, indicates that half the inhabitants were Welsh, a situation which was not usually tolerated in other Anglo-Norman boroughs.

King Edward is known to have visited the castle works along with Master James, his architect; on such occasions he would have had his black-leather pavilion raised within the walls. At the end of September 1294 there was a widespread uprising across much of Wales, including Ceredigion. The king's steward Geoffrey Clement was killed, and his widow Matilda took refuge in the new Aberystwyth castle, which was besieged by the Welsh and only survived thanks to its strategic seaside position. In the spring of 1295 Edward was on his way south through Meirionnydd, and the Welsh rebels faded away. The king arrived in Aberystwyth on 11 May with 2,200 English infantry and 600 men from Anglesey. King and army moved to Llanfihangel-y-Creuddyn on the 12th, to Ffynnon-oer on the 13th and were at Llanddewibrefi on the 14th. From thence they went via Lampeter to Cardigan. It must have been one of the largest military hosts ever seen in the area. While the King slept in his pavilion and his lords in canvas tents, the soldiers would have wrapped themselves in their cloaks and slept under the stars in the rain. We know these details about the building of the castle and the movements of the king from the royal archives. The same sources tell us a good deal about life in Cardiganshire, especially the towns of Cardigan and Aberystwyth.

Within the walls of Aberystwyth the land was divided into 145 burgage plots, rented to those who could afford them; the present branch of Woolworths in Great Darkgate Street exactly occupies one such plot. Since Aberystwyth apparently could not attract enough colonists from afar, especially after the slaughter of 1282, Robert of Cherd and John and Robert Gotobed had to endure Ieuan Fychan ap Ieuan ap Rhys and Meurig Goch as neighbours (and vice versa). Ieuan Fychan ap Ieuan held four burgages in the town; Matilda Clement held two burgages. Many of the men and women listed as tenants also appear in the local court rolls which survive for the years 1301-02; they paid fines for selling fish on the beach, for falsely raising the hue and cry, for calling the town reeve a thief, and for numerous unnamed offences. Of the 112 listed tenants, some names are quite obscure; 45 are apparently English, 59 certainly Welsh.

A generation earlier in 1268 the king's tenants in Cardigan had been listed; it is more difficult to distinguish Welsh from English, but certainly the English were in a considerable majority, and along with them was Lambert of Flanders. By 1300 at least, many of the inhabitants of both towns were merchants who had exclusive rights to sell in the countryside, though an earlier generation of Cardigan men had been forbidden to sell to the Welsh. Markets were held on Saturday at Cardigan, on Monday at Aberystwyth; fairs were held regularly at both towns, while many other fairs in the county can be dated back to this period. The little port of Cardigan dealt in wine, herrings, wool, honey, corn, horses, cattle and beer. The sea was not always safe; a vessel sailing from Cardigan to Aberystwyth in 1230 was captured by Scottish pirates, which did not deter Cardigan men from crossing to Ireland and settling there.

Boroughs and burgages were new institutions in west Wales; as so often, the countryside was rather more traditional. A 1326 survey of the lands of the bishop of St David's indicates that at that time virtually all the lands in Cardiganshire over which the bishop had rights were still owned by kin-groups, who paid collective services and rents to the bishop. The individuals who made up these groups all had Welsh names, including some which were shortly to disappear from use, such as Gwasmihangel ('servant of Michael the archangel').

The financial records for west Wales, which at first seem to be dreary lists of taxpayers and sums owed to the Crown, actually throw interesting light into this apparently dark corner of Wales. A royal officer, Walter de Pederton, was responsible for buying honey, oat-malt, beef and bacon for the garrison at Aberystwyth, and for bringing wine from Haverfordwest. William Rogate, chamberlain of west Wales, was ultimately responsible for delivering to the Crown the king's income from 'the Welshry of Super Aeron', including payments for the tenure of mills, the right to graze pigs in woodland, to exploit river weirs and to the payments made by merchants for the rights to sell throughout the Crown lands. Teifi fishermen at Llechryd and Cardigan, many of them certainly coracle-men, had to pay either sixteen pence or four of the best fish. The fairs and markets of Cardigan paid tolls. In 1304 no money was paid for the hay on thirty acres of meadow in the Clarach valley because of flooding immediately after mowing, so that the crop had been ruined. 'The miners working in the lead mine near Llanbadarn' had to pay the Crown a foot of lead for every nine feet mined. The account adds that there were only four workmen available, though 'the mine is good if sufficient workmen could be found'. Apart from the *gwestfa* levied on each district, there were other important payments. These included, for example, the returns which had to be made for the fees paid by every office-holder; the Crown did not pay salaries to its minor officials, rather it sold offices to men who recouped their costs and hoped to make a profit from the taxpayers.

These payments represent an interesting combination of Welsh taxes originally paid to local lords, and new taxes and payments imposed by the crown. Doubtless the king's Welsh lands were seen as a lucrative milch cow for exploitation. Nevertheless, money had to be spent locally. The ministers' accounts include payments of expenses for falcons and sparrow-hawks, and for food, coal, wine, armour, weapons and chapel equipment for the castles. The greatest expenditure

SOME office-holders were less honest than others. Ieuan ap Madog Fychan (*fl.* 1312-50), reeve of Mefenydd, didn't keep accounts properly, stole a cow and protected a criminal. Despite being fined for these offences, he went on to assemble illegally a swathe of lands across the county, as well as the property of a criminal hanged at Llanbadarn, and was eventually sentenced to perpetual imprisonment, but escaped by paying a massive £400 fine. By 1346 his remaining lands were forfeit, and he may have died of the Black Death in 1349.

was of course on their building, intended as a massive deterrent to any idea of rebellion among the Welsh, but like later deterrents, costing huge sums of money.

All these accounts and innumerable other documents enabled Ralph Griffiths to build up an invaluable list of hundreds of men who held office in Cardiganshire between 1277 and 1536, justiciars and beadles, constables and reeves, and for many individuals and families he has constructed a *curriculum vitae*. For example, in 1268 Walter Blakeney occupied five and a half burgages of land in the borough of Cardigan; he was a juror in 1292, while in 1301 he leased Cardigan Island and the Netpool, and had increased his holdings in the borough to nine burgages. He was constable of Cardigan castle for the period 1298-1301. In 1301 a John Blakeney occupied a burgage in Vinny (= Fenny) Street, Cardigan, and a burgage and a half by Bartholemew Gate, and Elena Blakeney half a burgage close to St Mary's church. Other Blakeneys reappear later in the lists of Cardigan reeves and bailiffs; John Blakeney in 1388, William in 1403 (along with other posts including mayor in 1417 and 1423), another John in 1452 and 1475, Jankyn in 1467 and Thomas in 1492; clearly the Blakeneys were a leading family in the borough for two centuries. There is a general pattern visible in the allocation of offices; senior, especially financial, offices were largely in the hands of incomers, while more humble offices were usually held by Welshmen. It should be clear from this that local government, whatever its corruption and other deficiencies, was complex; there were structures of officials for the southern principality (justice, treasurer, deputies, attorneys, marshal), county officials (sheriff, steward, beadle, escheator) and commote officials (beadle, reeve, constable).

The most interesting family whose names appear in these lists is that of Dafydd ap Gwilym, whose poetry belongs to the second quarter of the 14th century. The poet's great-great-grandfather, Gwilym ap Gwrwared, was the crown's administrator of escheated lands in north Cardiganshire, and his death in 1252 was noted in the *Chronicle of the Princes*. Originally from south of the Teifi, Gwilym gained wealth through his office which made it possible for his grandson Gwilym Gam to be a holder of four burgages in the new town of Aberystwyth, as well apparently as land east of the town, for early tradition records Dafydd's birthplace as Brogynin, just south of a tranche of land, Tirymyneich or Doferchen, belonging to Strata Florida. Local tradition claims that his father Gwilym baked oats in 'Prior's Mill', almost certainly the mill at Cwrt, Penrhyn-coch, while the hill above Brogynin was once known as Dafydd ap Gwilym's Seat. Place-names in his poems demonstrate his familiarity with the area: Llanbadarn, Cellïau'r Meirch, Elerch, Bysaleg (the earlier name for the river Stewi), Nant-y-seiri are all within easy walking distance of

Brogynin. Apart from an occasional joke at the expense of the English, Dafydd's poetry seems far removed from that world where English armies had so recently tramped, where farmers struggled to pay their taxes, where life could be so nasty, brutish and short. Instead his work glows with love of birds and woodland, women and the good life, and above all with a delight in words, though he is well aware of the havoc time brings to female beauty and male endeavour. He commanded all the technical skills of contemporary professional poets without the need to earn a living as they did; he had a breadth of vision which they could hardly expect to attain, a vision which is recognisable in the work of his great near-contemporary Chaucer – they would have enjoyed each other's work and company.

Domestic ruin at Cae'r Arglwyddes, perhaps of medieval date.

Although Welshmen found it difficult to gain major administrative office, the more ambitious among them could not be kept down. Instead of opposition to the crown, it was cooperation which brought status and wealth. One of the descendants of Ednyfed Fychan, Llywelyn the Great's senior minister, was Rhys ap Gruffudd, who held lands in Cardiganshire and Carmarthenshire. Born in 1283, he was an exception to the ban on Welshmen in high office, and became steward of Cardiganshire in 1308. Loyal to Edward II during the baronial opposition, he attempted to rescue that wretched monarch from imprisonment in Berkeley castle, and had to flee to Scotland, but was pardoned, knighted, and made an English marriage, owning land around Lampeter and at Llanrhystud. Other descendants of Ednyfed held lands in the county; they ran out of heirs in 1367, and the lands passed to the Crown, but in 1391 were granted to Rhydderch ab Ieuan Llwyd, whom we shall meet in the next paragraph. Other men of less distinguished origin were determined to rise in society and bring their families with them, by holding office and exploiting it, and by acquiring land; unfortunately the shortage of documents from before 1536 makes it impossible to examine the earliest growth of Cardiganshire family estates.

The family of Parc Rhydderch, near Llangeitho in the vale of Aeron, was prominent during this period, surviving the Black Death of 1349-50 and its recurrence in 1361, of whose appalling havoc we have little direct Cardiganshire evidence. The family's ancestor, Ieuan ap Gruffydd, alive in 1344, was a patron of poets; his son Ieuan Llwyd was constable of Anhuniog in 1332, and his wife Angharad was elegised by Dafydd ap Gwilym. His son Rhydderch administered his native commote of Mabwynion during the years 1386-90 and held other important offices. More than that, he was an expert in Welsh law, consulted by others who sought his legal opinions, and it was almost certainly he who commissioned from the monks of Strata Florida the manuscript of the *Mabinogion* known by his name as the White Book of Rhydderch, which incidentally also contains a poem by Dafydd ap Gwilym, who must have resorted to this major nest of Welsh culture. Rhydderch's praises were sung in extravagant terms ('like Arthur . . . Bedwyr . . . Roland') by Dafydd y Coed, and surely by other poets whose works have perished.

The Buck brothers' print of Strata Florida in mid-18th century; note the parish church on the left and the Stedman mansion on the right. Today it has no gable windows. [National Library of Wales]

*　　*　　*

Into this network of minor Welsh gentry struggling to better themselves, enjoying the praise of poets and practising the art themselves, involved in local administration and interpretation of Welsh law, there erupted at the turn of the century the rebellion of Owain Glyn Dŵr. In Cardiganshire the events at Rhuthun on 16 September 1400 must have seemed a long way off, and for a while the revolt, despite the proclamation of Owain as Prince of Wales, was not an immediate threat to local security. However, even before the outbreak there was a link; Glyn Dŵr's mother was a granddaughter of Llywelyn ab Owain, lord of lands in southern Cardiganshire. The new prince might therefore hope for sympathy and support, both in those lands with which he was connected by family, and in every area where resentment against royal administration and taxation festered. In May 1401 Owain appeared in Cardiganshire for the first time, with a strong force of followers.

WELSH poetry flourished in the 15th century, and Ceredigion had its share. An important centre of patronage was Tywyn, overlooking the Teifi estuary. Now a farmhouse, Tywyn was then the home of an important family who patronised both the Ceredigion poet Deio ab Ieuan Du (see Chapter 22) and visiting poets from Gwynedd and Deheubarth such as Dafydd Nanmor and Lewis Glyn Cothi. Both poets sang the praises of Rhys ap Meredudd of Tywyn, whose father had been a Glyn Dŵr follower, and had married the daughter of the great rebel Rhys the Black, but the son survived the revolt and prospered, renting Cardigan Island and the town mills in addition to his lands. Dafydd Nanmor addressed at least nine poems to the Tywyn family, naming Rhys's wife, his two sons and three grandchildren.

The poet especially admired the feasts at Tywyn, which he describes with graphic hyperbole: Rhys's feast would feed the hosts of Asia, it resembles Arthur's feast at Caerleon and Caswallon's in London; Jesus fed the five thousand with a lesser meal. A thousand beasts were slaughtered to provide the dishes; his chief officers are his baker, carver, cook and the butler, who serves wine from a hundred barrels. Night will not come to Rhys's hall unto the ages of ages; he will live as long as the oak-tree, and the fall of rain and dew, so the poet's blessing falls on his patron. At Rhys's death Dafydd is distraught; he had been an Arthur to his people, poets had never called but they had been given wine so that none was thirsty. He consoles himself by praising Rhys's son Thomas, but soon he is in mourning again, and had to turn next to Rhys's grandson, Rhys ap Rhydderch, the flower of summer, growing like the ash-tree among princes, like wheat, like the vine.

Lewis Glyn Cothi, as well as visiting Tywyn, celebrated family members at Castell Hywel, Pantstreimon and Aber-mad, but did not apparently visit Strata Florida. Plenty of other poets did; abbot after abbot is praised, by Guto'r Glyn, Dafydd Nanmor, Llywelyn Goch ap Meurig Hen, Ieuan Deulwyn and Guto ap Siancyn. Guto'r Glyn laments the absence of Abbot Rhys from Strata Florida on a visit to Oxford; he has been away four Sundays, says the poet, but it seems like three months in prison, and each month like ten years. Dafydd Nanmor praises Abbot Morgan for his splendid building work; he has repaired the choir, fitted glass doors, and put enough lead on the roofs for a hundred mansions, and the weathercock on the tower is the highest in the land.

However, the most remarkable Ceredigion poem of the age is not the work of a professional, but of the Aeron valley squire, Ieuan ap Rhydderch ap Ieuan Llwyd. At some time between perhaps 1390 and 1420 he produced his *Boast*, telling of his education in the liberal arts, grammar and law, his familiarity with the Bible, his knowledge of French, of the astrolabe, of astronomy and the zodiac. He knows Ptolemy's geography and is familiar with Aristotle; he understands time and space. More frivolously (his word), he is familiar with the rules of Welsh poetry, he can shoot, run and swim; he is praised by men and admired by women, and at life's end he expects burial in Llanddewibrefi, and his soul to be received in heaven.

He chose the most difficult and therefore unexpected route, over the bleak shoulders of Pumlumon. After a night spent, according to tradition, in a cave, he moved his men down the Hyddgen valley, where he was met by a combined force of English and Welshmen. However, the Welshmen changed sides, and drove the English in flight. Two large white blocks of quartz, *Cerrig Cyfamod Owain Glyn Dŵr* ('the stones of covenant of Owain Glyn Dŵr'), still lie near the river, actually in today's Powys. It would be pleasant to imagine that the name derives from the events of that day, marking the point where the Welsh of Cardiganshire decided to follow a new leader. The triumphant force marched down to Aberystwyth and burnt the town, but failed to capture the castle.

On this occasion, Owain did not stay in Cardiganshire, so the young Henry of Monmouth, the prince of Wales, was able temporarily to occupy Strata Florida, filling the abbey church with troops and wreaking havoc in the country round about. However, Owain succeeded in establishing a headquarters in the county in 1404, when Aberystwyth castle and borough fell to his men. A considerable number of leading Cardiganshire people hurried to join him, including the family of Ieuan Llwyd of Parc Rhydderch, and Rhys Ddu (the Black) of Morfa Bychan, south of Aberystwyth. English administration in Cardiganshire had completely broken down; from 1401 in most areas no Crown officials were appointed and no taxes collected. Whether Owain's occupation of Cardiganshire was sufficiently well organised to take over the collection of taxes is not known, but the loyalty to him of many of the Welsh gentry with influence and administrative experience must have helped. It is difficult otherwise to imagine how he was able to continue campaigning.

It was at Aberystwyth in 1405 that Owain sealed his treaty with Charles VI of France, which brought French soldiers to Wales. But by 1407 Owain's star was on the wane. An English siege train arrived at Aberystwyth and besieged the Welsh in the castle, a scene which Edward I could hardly have anticipated. They had with them a cannon, the *Messenger*, but it was a case of return to sender; the gun exploded, killing its crew. That first attempt to take the castle failed, but in 1408 prince Henry was successful, the castle fell, and with it and the fall of Harlech, Owain's mission was doomed. So was Rhys Ddu, who led the castle's defence; he was executed. However, northern Cardiganshire remained one of the areas least willing (or least able on account of social disruption) to resume payment of Crown rents. The county as a whole had to pay a communal fine of £1,333, an astonishing sum if it were ever gathered, which is unlikely.

Thenceforward the comparative peace of Cardiganshire was uninterrupted for several generations – not that the leading men of the area did not create ructions

CHARLES VI of France not only sent soldiers to Owain's aid, he sent a Welshman to Scotland to seek help there. His messenger was a Cardiganshire man, Dafydd ab Ieuan Goch, who Adam of Usk tells us had been fighting the Moslems in the eastern Mediterranean for twenty years. He was presumably one of those Welsh warriors who sought employment in military service abroad, but was willing to aid his fellow-countrymen in their rebellion. Unfortunately he had no success in his Scottish mission.

from time to time. Since 1362 Llanbadarn Fawr parish and its income, with its dependent churches of Llanilar, Llanfihangel-y-Creuddyn and Llanfihangel Genau'r-glyn, had been in the possession of the Chester monastery of Vale Royal, given to the abbot by the Black Prince when importuned to help restore serious storm damage to the monastery. This claim to Llanbadarn's income was disputed by the monks of Gloucester, very willing, as was the fashion, to manufacture any 'missing' evidence, but they failed. In 1403 the long arm of the papacy had reached out towards Llanbadarn: the Roman pope Boniface IX appointed Gruffudd Young as its rector, only to be snubbed by his protégé; Young joined Owain Glyn Dŵr as his chancellor, and was thereby bound to support the Avignon papacy in the schism with Rome.

By the 1430s there were unseemly rows between the abbot of Vale Royal, anxious to collect all his tithes, and the abbot of Strata Florida, unused to having other princes of the Church trample his turf, some of which lay within the parish of Llanbadarn. Clerical violence flared in the streets of Aberystwyth. Three leading families in the town seem to have become involved in the troubles: the Rouburies, the Glais family, and the family of one John Fwyaf ap Jankyn. Two murders, in 1440 and 1456, and a series of enquiries and arbitrations bring these turbulent Welshmen vividly before us; for example, Jankyn Roubury was required to prove his innocence of the death of one Gruffudd Prouth, not before a jury under English law, but by bringing 300 oath-pledgers to Cardigan, while the Glais family paid blood-money to the victims' relatives – both practices reminiscent of Welsh law, not the English criminal law which was supposed to be administered in the county. Another of the accused, Dafydd Glais, was a scholar who translated two Latin texts into Welsh. The extent to which the Chester monastery became involved in Cardiganshire affairs is clear from the appointment in 1361 of abbot Thomas of Vale Royal as constable of Aberystwyth castle; he appointed himself rector of Llanbadarn Fawr.

Cast taken by George Eyre Evans from the abbot of Strata Florida's silver seal. [National Library of Wales]

Such ructions were generally more important in Cardiganshire than the distant civil strife known as the Wars of the Roses which from time to time convulsed many parts of England, and saw the throne of England usurped more than once. The major gentry of south-west Wales were Lancastrian in loyalty (i.e. they supported Henry VI as descendant of Edward III's third son John of Gaunt, Duke of Lancaster) as opposed to Richard Duke of York (descendant of Edward III's fourth son Edmund Duke of York); he enjoyed much support in east Wales. In 1456 the Duke of York's lieutenants seized Aberystwyth castle, only to be expelled by Jasper Tudor, but the Lancastrians suffered a huge reverse with the defeat of their forces at Mortimer's Cross, near Leominster, by a largely Welsh army led by Edward son of Richard Duke of York, who was crowned Edward IV.

There was no great increase in economic growth in Wales during the 14th and 15th centuries, as far as we can tell; indeed, given the setbacks of the Black Death, the Glyn Dŵr rebellion and the Wars of the Roses, this is hardly surprising. Instead, men would join royal armies during the times of war in France, or seek work in England. George Eyre Evans discovered in the Public Record Office an indenture of 1422 for the apprenticeship of a Cardigan boy, John Griffyn, in Wycombe, Bucks., suggesting that the later economic migrations of Cardiganshire men and women in search of work had at least one and probably many more early precedents. In the county itself Aberystwyth castle's garrison was small, Cardigan's was negligible, Ystrad Meurig's keep was probably already being pillaged for building stone, while Cardigan's town walls were falling into ruin. Aberystwyth town overtook Cardigan in size, but not sufficiently to fill the space within its walls, let alone overflow; Cardigan however remained the administrative and judicial centre for

Wern Newydd, near New Quay, where Henry Tudor is believed to have stayed on his way to Bosworth in 1485 [photo: Evan James].

Cardiganshire, especially after its long rivalry with Carmarthen was settled in 1395 to Cardigan's benefit. Both towns became more and more Welsh in character. The history of Lampeter at this period and of the other later claimants to borough status, Tregaron and Adpar, is obscure.

Also obscure, as far as Cardiganshire is concerned, are details of the last march of a medieval army through the district. News of Henry Tudor's landing in Pembrokeshire on 7 June 1485 must have spread quickly, but how many Cardiganshire men actually joined his mostly French and English followers as they doggedly made their way up the coast is not known. Indeed, it is not at all clear why Henry should have chosen the Cardiganshire route to the English midlands rather than passing through south Wales. Cardiganshire's major landowning figure was Rhys ap Thomas, lord of Dinefwr and grandson of Gruffudd ap Nicholas, who was a dominant figure in south-west Wales during the mid-15th century and a supporter of Henry's bid for the throne. Rhys owned lands in Cardiganshire, and may have drawn recruits from them, but he followed a separate route through Wales and only joined Henry near Welshpool. Various houses later claimed to have hosted Henry for a night, and certainly he must have spent two or three nights during his ride through the county. Apart from Wern Newydd, Llwyndafydd seems the most likely candidate; its owner Dafydd ab Ieuan is believed to have received from Henry the gift of a drinking horn mounted in silver, the *Corn Hirlas*, of which a 19th-century copy survives in the ownership of the Earl Cawdor. Henry and his men must also have stopped in or near Aberystwyth on their way to Machynlleth and Welshpool. He certainly gained supporters in Cardiganshire during his march, for several were rewarded after Bosworth, including Rhydderch ap Rhys of Tywyn.

Henry's victory at Bosworth seemed to bring little change to Cardiganshire. Henry's gift was for careful administration of the system as it was, rather than for reform. After his death in 1507 his son Henry VIII seemed at first even less concerned with Wales than his father. But in the 1530s, with the crisis of his divorce upon him and the possibility of war with Spain, Henry gave his great reforming minister Thomas Cromwell the opportunity to make changes. Change in Wales was long overdue; the country was divided between Principality and Marcher lordships, the administration of the law was a shambles, and economically the country was backward. A whole series of acts of Parliament relating to Wales were passed from 1534 onwards, bringing in parliamentary representation, Justices of the Peace and the Courts of Great Sessions,

DESPITE the apparent lack of dynamism in the little boroughs of Ceredigion, they were not without moving spirits. Wiliam John Fwyaf of Aberystwyth, who died in 1540, had established a new mill by the town bridge, known as Our Lady's mill, because the profit from the enterprise was dedicated to the support of a priest in the little church of St Mary which had been established at an unknown date on a site near the present pier. It was built too close to the sea, and by 1748 its ruins were being swallowed up. In his will Wiliam John left money to five local churches, to 'the working of Aberystwyth bridge' and for torches and tapers at his funeral. Wiliam had accumulated a good deal of land in and around Aberystwyth which eventually passed to the Pryses of Gogerddan.

administering the law of England. All Wales was divided into shires; henceforth Cardiganshire would have two Members of Parliament, one for the county and one for the boroughs. These reforms would bring plenty of opportunities for those families who already had some base on the land to reach upwards and outwards, as will be seen in the next chapter.

One no doubt unwelcome result of the new system was that Welshmen became liable for the 'lay subsidy', a tax on property which the crown levied from time to time. The long county roll for 1543 contained hundreds of Cardiganshire people who paid on a sliding scale per pound on their goods and cattle. Philyp Wiliam, son of Wiliam John Fwyaf (see p. 95) paid more than anyone in Aberystwyth – 13s 4d on his twenty-pound assessment. Unfortunately the roll has been badly damaged, but the lists for the parishes north of the Aeron survive, and they include the names of many men who were making their way in the new atmosphere of competition and gain which spread from England.

Viewed from London, the Welsh reforms of 1535-43 must have seemed small beer compared with the impact of the English Reformation, whose most immediate result was the dissolution between 1536 and 1539 of all monasteries and nunneries, and this of course affected Cardiganshire. It is true that the nunnery at Llanllŷr had never flourished, and Strata Florida had long been in serious decline. The tiny groups of monks and nuns could hardly have been able to sustain the sevenfold daily services, the *Opus Dei*. Their vast swathes of land had mostly been rented out on 99-year leases, particularly to the benefit of Strata Florida's abbots, under whose noses the illegal coining of money was taking place. With the closure of both establishments, the monastic lands were quickly leased or sold and resold, at first largely to the benefit of consortia of distant lay landlords, especially the Devereux family, the earls of Essex, who already had large interests in south-west Wales. Eventually, however, they were sold on to Cardiganshire families, as will be seen below.

How did life in the county change during the period covered by this chapter? There had been a long series of upheavals: armies had tramped through the land in 1277, 1282-3, 1295 and during the Glyn Dŵr rebellion. The Black Death reaped its dreadful harvest on more than one occasion. But by 1530 there had been a long period of comparative order. At the apex of society, the gentry class, though still ready to quarrel violently among themselves, were no longer the warlords of the past, but had given themselves to the building of estates, using inheritance, marriage and mortgage as their main weapons, aided when necessary by guile or force. They were still largely Welsh in speech and culture, but English culture and economic dominance were clearly at work among them. At the other end of the social ladder small farmers scraped a living from the acid soil; their womenfolk toiled unceasingly in their miserable homes and on the land, while their children herded the sheep and cattle, and picked stones and scared birds from the little fenced strips where crops were grown. For them little was to change in the near future.

Strata Florida before restoration [from a postcard].

Surviving gravestones at Strata Florida.

8. The Church: Llanbadarn Fawr to Llangeitho

Gerald of Wales's disgust at the state of the Welsh church in 1188, which he saw as corrupt, unchaste and disorganised, was entirely shared by the Norman invaders of Wales. They may have taken from 1067 until 1284 to achieve a military and political settlement of the country, but their stamp had been put on the Welsh Church long before the end of Welsh independence. The Normans are normally perceived as military conquerors, but in terms of the Church they saw themselves as reformers. They swiftly seized control of the English Church, and their prelates eagerly espoused the radical reform programme of Pope Innocent III. From the papal viewpoint the pre-Norman Welsh Church had been steeped in irregularities of all kinds: there was no proper archiepiscopal or provincial regulation, there were no fixed diocesan boundaries, no archdeaconries, no rural deaneries, there were not even parishes or tithes. Ancient institutions with a monastic tradition such as Llanbadarn Fawr were possessed by hereditary corporations, the *clasau*. Priests married, had families and ensured livings for their sons and grandsons. Perhaps most extraordinary of all to the eyes of the incomers, churches in Wales were not built of stone. All these perceived defects were true of Ceredigion, where the main Christian institutional presence, as in the rest of Wales, was one of mother-churches with subordinate chapels (a gross simplification, but surely pardonable in the circumstances).

All this the invaders sought to change, and there was no Welsh state nor a central power in the Welsh Church to offer resistance; the Welsh Church was not an organised province but simply, in papal eyes, an anomaly, almost a contradiction in terms. The Normans were able to achieve change in two major ways: by insisting on the appointment of Norman bishops who would acknowledge the supremacy of Canterbury and undertake reform, and by direct royal or lordly diktat. These controls were used in Ceredigion even before the final conquest, assisted by the willingness of native princes to conform. The Welsh Church had come under the formal administration of Canterbury by the time Archbishop Baldwin preached the crusade in Wales in 1188. The dates of the establishment of parishes, deaneries and archdeaconries is not certain, especially for Ceredigion, but guesses are possible. The archdeaconry of Cardigan, extending as it still does into what became the counties of Pembrokeshire and Carmarthenshire, may well have been created during the Clare lordship of 1110-36; the first archdeacon may have been Cydifor ap Daniel ap Sulien, who died in the post in 1163. Maredudd son of the Lord Rhys was archdeacon of Cardigan until his death in 1227, and he was succeeded by his son Gruffudd who died in 1242.

The first, incomplete, list of Ceredigion parishes dates from 1291, but the process of parochial division probably began under the Clare lordship (1110–1135). Alternatively it may just possibly have been carried out by the princes of Gwynedd during their occupation in the 1130s; Colin Gresham believed that it was under Owain Gwynedd (d.1170) that Gwynedd had been parochialised. A third possibility is that parochialisation happened under the rule of the Lord Rhys after 1165. Gresham argued that the parochialisation of Gwynedd was accompanied by the division of the land into townships; the Lord Rhys has been credited with the division of Ceredigion into *gwestfeydd*. All this is speculation; in 1291 eighteen parishes are listed south of the Aeron, and only nine to the north, partly because Llanbadarn Fawr's many subordinate chapels (e.g. Llanilar, Llanfihangel-y-Creuddyn, Llanychaearn, Llancynfelyn, Ysbyty Cynfyn) were not yet acknowledged as separate parishes. By 1563 the authorities counted eighteen parishes and seven chapelries north of the Aeron, with twenty-seven parishes and sixteen chapelries to the south; many of the chapelries eventually became independent parishes. At some early stage several parishes became divided into two or more fragments, by processes which are as yet poorly understood; other alterations may well have occurred before the parish boundaries were first accurately mapped in the 1840s. However, if the exact details of how church administration developed escape us, more is known about monastic reforms.

The Welsh religious community at Llanbadarn Fawr is better known to historians than the county's other important early centre at Llanddewibrefi. Its antiquity has already been indicated in Chapters 5 and 6. With the grant of the lordship of Ceredigion to Gilbert de Clare in 1110, there began a long struggle to reform Llanbadarn. Sulien and his son Rhygyfarch were already dead, but other members of the family were able to survive or adapt to the changes imposed on them. Gilbert's first move was to grant Llanbadarn and its lands to the Benedictine abbey of Gloucester, making it a subordinate priory, no doubt with foreign monks in charge. However, with the deaths of Henry I in 1135 and of Richard de Clare the following year, the invading warriors of Gwynedd expelled the Benedictines, and the restoration of Welsh tradition is indicated by the record of the death of Ieuan ap Sulien in 1137 under the unreformed title of 'arch-priest'.

Llanfihangel-y-Creuddyn church (note the John Evans sundial).

Meanwhile, following the expulsion of the Benedictines Llanbadarn Fawr was once again in unreformed hands, as we have seen from Gerald's account of his 1188 visit. However, Ednywain and the Welsh hereditary community are not heard of again; in 1211 the area was in English hands, and an English priest was imposed on Llanbadarn, at least temporarily. Eventually Llanbadarn emerged from all this chopping and changing as a parish church, owned by the Crown, at the heart of an area of more than 200 square miles, which over the following centuries was divided into seventeen separate parishes and ecclesiastical districts. Following the success of Henry III in the years 1241-45 in breaking up the commonwealth of Gwynedd, this great parish had become part of the spoils of war; successive royal monarchs and post-1300 English princes of Wales used the living as an income for important court officials. Thus a series of major figures of English government became rectors of a benefice they never visited, appointing vicars to officiate in their place, until 1359.

Henry III's control of Ceredigion, which lasted until Llywelyn's liberation of 1256, must have been the time when work began on building the present massive church at Llanbadarn Fawr. It is just possible that the splendid main doorway at Llanbadarn was brought, stone by stone, from Strata Florida abbey after the closure of the monastery in 1538. Cardiganshire is not rich in early churches, but the rugged building at Llanfihangel-y-Creuddyn was begun in mid-13th century, apparently in crude imitation of Llanbadarn. Medieval towers survive in a number of village churches, including Llannarth, Llanilar, Aber-arth, Llandysul, Tregaron and Llansanffraid. The medieval appearance of the tower of St Mary's, Cardigan, is however deceptive; it was rebuilt after collapsing in 1705.

Llanbadarn Fawr porch, the finest medieval stonework in the county.

Rhys ap Gruffudd may or may not have tolerated the unreformed 1188 state of affairs at Llanbadarn Fawr, but he proved himself an innovator elsewhere. He established a monastery at Talyllychau in his home territory of Cantref Mawr, and nurtured the newly-arrived community of Cistercian monks at Strata Florida. Its earliest surviving charter (1184) shows that the abbey controlled extensive lands north of the Aeron, some at least the gift of Rhys. As with a number of other Welsh Cistercian monasteries, Strata Florida's first site was temporary; well before the end of the century the monks had moved to the present site immediately south of the river Teifi, and in 1201 their new church was consecrated. The abbey's importance was spiritual, intellectual and economic as well as political. Poets sang the praises of the abbots, mainly for the standard of their hospitality and building work rather than their sanctity. Among the Welsh manuscripts copied in the scriptorium were the *Chronicle of the Princes*, the *Mabinogion* tales, and poetry addressed to the Welsh princes. Strata Florida was the burial place of several generations of the descendants of Rhys ap Gruffudd, though he himself was buried at St David's. Dafydd ap Gwilym may or may not have been buried at Strata Florida, but he was certainly known to the monks during his lifetime. The monastery's vast estates (including much poor mountain land) produced mainly wool, oats and horses. The initial impetus, which by 1200 had carried Cistercianism almost throughout Wales, and which had brought in useful numbers of lay brothers, began to wane after 1300. The abbey's lands were far more extensive than the dwindling community could administer directly, and by the 15th century they had been leased long-term to tenant farmers.

As well as profiting from the land, the monks had various other sources of income. Their famous fair at Ffair-rhos long outlived the abbey, but was profitable while the monks lasted. They had rights of shipwreck on parts of the coast, and the *goredi* or semicircular fishtraps still to be seen at low water between Llan-non and Aberaeron are traditionally attributed to them; whether the present *goredi* are actually those of the monks seems most unlikely in view of coastal erosion, but doubtless their servants fished in the same way, and in any case, the original *goredi* were probably created centuries before Strata Florida. The monastery had political and cultural functions too; various abbots acted as ambassadors for the princes of Gwynedd, and one of them hosted the gathering of Welsh lords in 1238 which acknowledged the right of Dafydd ap Llywelyn to succeed his father, Llywelyn the Great. Strata Florida played a leading role in Anglo-Welsh politics, always siding with the Welsh princes.

THE abbot of Vale Royal monastery at Chester, founded by Edward I, appealed in 1349 to the crown for financial help. The Black Prince, who as Edward III's eldest son was Prince of Wales, gave to the abbey the church and tithes of Llanbadarn Fawr, which was of course in his gift as titular ruler of the Principality. From then until the dissolution of the abbey in 1539, it was Vale Royal and not the crown which enjoyed the considerable parish revenue, appointing vicars to conduct local worship. With the dissolution, the tithes were leased and then sold to speculators. For centuries the Chichester family of Arlington in Devon drew thousands of pounds annually from the farmers of north Ceredigion.

There was a darker side to Strata Florida life, nevertheless. In 1212 King John ordered the destruction of the abbey; fortunately this was not completed. In 1217 the abbot was deposed, apparently for political reasons. The abbey was seriously damaged by royal troops in 1295, for which Crown reparations were paid. It was attacked by thieves in 1423 and assaulted by the abbot of Aberconwy and his followers, who imprisoned the monks and robbed the monastery. There was a disputed election to the abbot's chair in 1344, and another abbot was deposed in 1352. Reference has already been made to battles in the streets of Aberystwyth regarding the collecting of Llanbadarn's tithes between the supporters of Strata Florida and those of Vale Royal, who were not unnaturally regarded as intruders. In the abbey's last days two monks were arrested by the abbot for coining, a crime of the utmost gravity. Nevertheless, Strata Florida's contribution to Welsh politics, to Welsh culture, and to the economy of Cardiganshire were enormous, far outweighing the skirmishes and follies of a few of the personnel.

Strata Florida was not the only Ceredigion beneficiary of Rhys ap Gruffudd's generosity. He supported the priory at Cardigan, and founded the Cistercian nunnery at Llanllŷr in the Aeron valley, one of only three nunneries in Wales, where they were much less popular than elsewhere. It is therefore hardly surprising that Llanllŷr was a small establishment of which little is known. Rhys also endowed the Knights of St John of Jerusalem with lands in Llanrhystud, Ystrad Meurig and Ysbyty Ystwyth. Attention has already been drawn to the generosity of the princes towards the Church.

Episcopal reform in Cardiganshire is most evident during the time of bishop Bek of St David's. In 1287 he reconstituted Llanddewibrefi as a collegiate church, with twelve priests having the title of canon and, initially at least, serving the parishes round about. Their income derived from the tithes of a dozen local churches, including Llangybi, Llanbadarn Trefeglwys, Llanfihangel Ystrad, Llanerchaeron, Llanbadarn Odwyn, Llannarth and Tregaron. Bek's purpose was twofold: the canons were to pray for the soul of Edward I and his ancestors, and the twelve-fold appointment gave the bishop, and later the Crown, a measure of patronage. Sooner or later, probably sooner, canons were appointed who had no desire either to serve or live in Llanddewibrefi; by 1366 (admittedly after the disruption of the Black Death) virtually all the canons were absentees. This is hardly surprising given the low level of the collegiate income. Despite economic difficulties, the college was not terminated until 1549, when the rector was Rowland Meyrick, father of that slippery character Sir Gelly Meyrick. Meyrick senior, who became bishop of Bangor, managed to cling to the collegiate possessions until his death in 1566, when after a legal battle they passed to the Crown.

If Llanbadarn Fawr and Llanddewibrefi were pre-Norman in origin, the third major church in Ceredigion, Cardigan priory, was a Norman foundation,

ABSENTEEISM and pluralism were a problem in the ordinary parishes as well as at Llanddewibrefi. Figures survive for the southern half of Ceredigion in 1534. Of 24 parish livings, only twelve had priests in residence, and they were in the poorest parishes, each with a yearly income of £10 or less. Five livings were in the hands of Thomas Lloyd, precentor of St David's. Virtually nothing is known of the calibre of the resident parish priests in the 15th century, but it is easy to suppose that, given such poor rewards, they were unlikely to have been men of a high intellectual or spiritual calibre.

though there may have been a pre-existing church called Llandduw. The priory was established by Gilbert de Clare in 1111 and adopted as a Benedictine cell by Gloucester abbey. By 1166, when the conquering Rhys ap Gruffudd took over Ceredigion, it had been transferred to St Peter's, Chertsey, and Rhys confirmed the priory's holdings. When John Leland passed through in 1536 with the royal commissioners, only two monks were in residence, both Englishmen from Chertsey. The priory was dissolved in 1538, and passed into lay hands, becoming a gentry house. The church building, St Mary's, where two strange carvings survive in the chancel, has been the parish church at least since the 13th century.

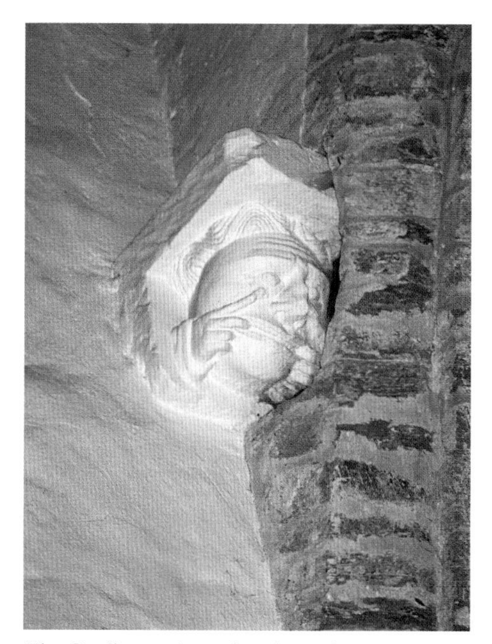

The Cardigan priory church carvings: a grotesque, and a woman in fashionable headgear.

Strata Florida was not the only Cardiganshire centre of church learning in the later middle ages. In 1346 an anonymous anchorite or hermit living at Llanddewibrefi compiled a remarkable manuscript for his patron, Gruffudd ap Llywelyn ap Phylip ap Trahaearn, of Cantref Mawr, known as *Llyfr Ancr Llanddewibrefi*, the Book of the Anchorite. It is a virtual library of Welsh religious literature in a single volume of 286 pages. With one exception, the works are translated from Latin, and cover a wide range of medieval devotional and apocryphal works, e.g.: 'How Many were Taken up into Heaven?', 'The Dream of St Paul', 'The Life of St David', and meditations on scripture, including the Annunciation and on the Lord's Prayer. The exception, 'Holy Living' has no known Latin original; it is probably an original work and is of considerable interest. It would be fascinating to know how the anchorite was able to bring together so many Welsh texts. Was he copying from the library in the collegiate church of Llanddewibrefi?

As might be expected in such a poor district, Cardiganshire is not well endowed with fine church architecture. Llanbadarn Fawr is quite the most impressive in terms of its massiveness. Built apparently by royal initiative, its 13th-century structure would still be recognised by its builders if they could return to see it today, although they would be surprised at the Victorian crenellations on the tower, and at the slated roofs, which were thatched at least until the early 18th century. As for the huge interior, little survives of its medieval nature other than the spiral tower-staircase and the rood-loft door in the chancel, the loft and screen having long succumbed to reform and restoration. Its monastic connections may have helped ensure the church's cruciform shape, although Cardigan church, also with monastic connections, was never cruciform. The only other cruciform churches in the county were at Strata Florida, now of course a ruin, Llanddewibrefi, which has lost its transepts, and the primitively impressive 13/14th-century church at Llanfihangel-y-Creuddyn, which has fine early timberwork in its roofs. Cardigan's chancel with its splendid arch, behind which peep down two extraordinary sculptures, and which contains its medieval piscina in its original position, is well worth seeing.

BETTER church accommodation was badly needed by 1600, and some small effort was made to improve matters. The Lloyds of Ynys-hir built Eglwys-fach church in 1620, the same year that Morgan Herbert built Eglwysnewydd in Cwm-ystwyth. Meyrick tells us that 'on Cwmsymlog hill are the remains of a chapel erected by Sir Hugh Middleton, in the reign of King James, for the use of his miners.' Thereafter there is little sign of church building activity until the rebuilding of Cardigan church nave in 1702, which was followed by the collapse of its tower.

Mwnt church.

Cardiganshire churches seem to have suffered more than most at the hands of restorers and rebuilders, not to mention Tudor and Civil War iconoclasm, though many of those rebuilt by the Victorians were in poor condition. Rhostïe church, now a slighted ruin, had the county's only surviving medieval bell, now preserved in nearby Llanilar church, itself possessor of an attractive little tower and some good medieval timber roofing. Several of the smallest churches charm by their simplicity, but whitewashed Mwnt alone can compare in situation and atmosphere with the numerous simple churches of Gwynedd. In common with the rest of south Wales, no early stained glass survives; alas, the medieval east window at Cardigan church, which had escaped the vandalism of the Puritans, was apparently removed by Thomas Johnes to decorate his library at Hafod, leaving only a few fragments behind; the fruit of his vandalism was destroyed by the Hafod fire of 1807. The only pre-Victorian brass memorial known to me, at Llwyndafydd, is not medieval, and there isn't a single effigy tomb in any of the county's churches, though the recesses in the wall of Llanbadarn Fawr's north transept may once have contained a couple. Llandysul's medieval stone altar (if it really was an altar) with its remarkable cross-marking has survived in the church's Lady chapel. There are attractive fonts at Llanbadarn Fawr, Llannarth, Cardigan, Llanwenog and Llandygwydd. A few fragments of roodlofts have survived at Mwnt, Llanina and Llansanffraid.

One Cardiganshire church stands out from the rest for its present attractiveness. Llanwenog is quite the most pleasing in the county, giving us some faint hint of the world of late medieval Welsh Christianity in Cardiganshire. Over the tower doorway a strange carved face looks down; inside, the holy water stoup, worn with much use, has been restored to its place. The church has kept its extraordinary primitive font with large Celtic faces, its timbered barrel-roof and screen, both of the 15th century, and some later wall-paintings. Even so, the rood-loft and its carved images of the Crucifixion, its stained glass windows, its early wall-paintings are all lost. Indeed, it requires a powerful effort of the imagination to recreate in one's mind some idea of what medieval churches were actually like, with their thatched roofs, with their underfloor burials, no seating but their benches against the wall,

St Ffraid's well, Cynhawdre, Swyddffynnon, with the owners' grandson, Ieuan.

their stained glass, their candle-lit murk, their rushes spread on the floor, and the congregation playing only a small active part in the worship.

The medieval screen at Llanwenog.

Some few of Cardiganshire's many holy wells (more than 200 according to Francis Jones) survive to remind us of their part in the county's Christian landscape, attractive as they were both to pilgrims and to devout and/or superstitious local people. Cybi's well at Llangybi is a still attractive example, and Ffynnon Ffraid at Cynhawdre (Gwenhafdre), Swyddffynnon, has been excellently restored through the initiative of its owners. Ffynnon Ddewi, by the main A487 south of Synod Inn, must have known generations of pilgrims and still has serviceable stone steps, but the well itself is much neglected. In addition to wells, the county's roadsides would have held little wayside shrines of the sort which can still be seen in the depths of Brittany, but which have vanished in Britain almost without trace.

There is abundant evidence for the dozens of small chapels which undoubtedly existed in the county; two at least are still intact church buildings, at Llanina and Ysbyty Cynfyn, not to mention those like Llanafan which were once chapels of Llanbadarn Fawr but became separate parishes. Others can be traced in field and farm names. In the lower Ystwyth valley lies the farm of Llanddwy (God's church), mentioned in Chapter 2. There is no sign of a church there now, but nearby is the little settlement of Ffynnon Drindod (Trinity Well), which had a reputation for healing eyesight. A Trawsgoed estate map of Tan-yr-allt farm, drawn in 1781 before the building of a single nonconformist establishment in the area, shows Cae Capel (Chapel Field); an aerial photograph in the collection of the Royal Commission on Ancient Monuments shows a grass crop-mark of a small building on what was once Cae Capel, so it may have been a little medieval chapel. A number of such chapels existed in the parish of Llandysul: Llanffraid, Capel Sulfed, Capel Gwenffrewi, Llanfair, Capel Dewi and Capel Martin – all vanished. They were dependent on a seventh district, long known as 'Y Fameglwys' – the mother church.

The cult of saints was certainly vigorous in Cardiganshire in the late medieval period, even though there is less surviving evidence than for some other counties. It was certainly believed by antiquarians from Meyrick to George Eyre Evans that a chapel to St Non existed in Llan-non; the latter gave a detailed description of it in 1903, but what he saw seems simply to have been a secular ruin, while the surviving battered carved figure (now in Ceredigion Museum) is more likely to have been an obscene Sheela-na-gig than the mother of St David. Much of the evidence for late medieval saints' cults comes from the poetry of the Welsh *cywyddwyr*; unfortunately Cardiganshire had only two such poets, Ieuan ap Rhydderch and Deio ab Ieuan Ddu, neither of whom devoted himself to pious verse. Dafydd ap Gwilym is silent on the subject of churches in his home county.

Pilgrimage would certainly have played a part in Cardiganshire's religious and social life in the 15th century: pilgrims from Cardiganshire would certainly have gone to St David's and further afield; Rhys ap Dafydd Llwyd of Gogerddan went to Rome and was praised by the poet Lewis Trefnant for so doing. His journey cannot be accurately dated; it may have been about 1500. Within the county the only direct surviving evidence we have is for pilgrimage to the miraculous statue of the Virgin at Cardigan, and even that knowledge only survives in the records of destruction by the Reformers. According to the legend propagated by the monks of Cardigan priory, the statue had been found on the shore of the river Teifi, with a lighted taper in the Virgin's hand. The priory church of St Mary itself had been founded, the legend continued, on a site of the statue's choosing, and the taper had continued to burn for nine years without renewal, 'until one forswore himself before it', upon which the flame vanished. The last prior admitted that the taper was actually a piece of wood, since pilgrims had long ago surreptitiously scraped away the wax of the original (and presumably any replacement tapers) to keep as holy relics of their visit to the shrine. The bitter reforming bishop Barlow (St David's 1536-47) who did so much to ruin his diocese, ensured the destruction of the statue. No credence whatever should be given to the tale of the Nanteos cup, which was not a sacred medieval relic, was not housed at Glastonbury nor preserved at Strata Florida abbey as a relic in the pre-dissolution days, and only gained a reputation as a healing cup in the late Victorian period.

Two remarkable relics of the old faith, unique not just in Cardiganshire but in all Wales, and which could not be touched even by Bishop Barlow, are the two songs to the Virgin preserved in the family of the poet J.Glyn Davies at Llanllwchaearn (New

Quay). The better-known is *Myn Mair* ('for Mary's sake'); the quiet melancholy of its tune is reminiscent of plainsong, and the words transport the hearer back to another time and mindset:

Fy hatling offrymaf dros enaid dan glo,	My mite I offer for a coffined soul,
Fy nghannwyll offrymaf yn eglwys y fro,	My candle I offer in the parish church;
'R offeren weddïa' saith seithwaith yn daer,	Seven times seven I pray the Mass
Er cadw ei enaid anfarwol, Myn Mair.	To save his immortal soul, by Mary.

A typical feature of pre-Reformation church life was the chantry. A visitor to some of the great English cathedral and abbey churches will see, perhaps between nave-pillars, tiny chapels, large enough to hold an altar and a few seats. These are chantry chapels, originally paid for by wealthy men and women who wanted daily masses to be said for their souls, to reduce their time in Purgatory. A gift of land in perpetuity would provide a stipend for the mass-priest. Cardigan priory had two such endowments supporting priests, though no separate chapels were created. Several Cardiganshire churches had chantry foundations of an intriguingly collective nature – farm animals. Ordinary people, probably on their deathbeds, could ensure a share in a parish chantry by contributing a goat, sheep or cow to their parish church's flock, managed by the church wardens; the sale of surplus beasts paid for the priest. Such chantries existed at Llanfihangel-y-Creuddyn and Llanbadarn Fawr; they were swept away by the Chantries Act of 1547.

Personal salvation, or avoidance of the pains of Hell, did not depend only on the prayers of a priest; it was a matter of good works on behalf of others. Many might be tempted to postpone charity until they were dead and buried, when their wills might reveal donations of money to churches and bread to the poor. Unfortunately hardly any Cardiganshire wills survive before 1540, when the country already hung on the cusp between Rome and Reformation. Wiliam John Fwyaf of Aberystwyth died in that year. He had already done a great deal for his town; because Llanbadarn church was a long and muddy walk from Aberystwyth's gates, he had founded a mill by the town bridge whose income endowed a priest to take services at the little chapel of St Mary, now long swallowed up by the sea. In his will Wiliam left generous gifts of money to five churches in north Cardiganshire. Twenty years after his death there was a serious legal conflict over the town mill; the Crown authorities insisted that it had been founded as a chantry, and was therefore Crown property, while the inhabitants were equally insistent that it had never been a chantry, and they won their case.

Although buried with the Latin Catholic rite, Wiliam John Fwyaf had already become involved with the first steps of the Reformation: he had been a local commissioner for the lands of Strata Florida after its dissolution in 1538, and may have benefited thereby. The country-wide closure of the monasteries was to change the nature of the land market in few places more than in Cardiganshire, with the lands of the monks, of the nuns of Llanllŷr, the priory of Cardigan and the Knights of St John all passing into lay ownership. Unfortunately there is much we do not know about the impact in the county of the dissolution, the re-Catholicisation by Mary between 1553 and 1558, and the shaping of the Church of England by Elizabeth and her ministers. The poor and sick could no longer seek help at Strata Florida or Llanllŷr; there was no further welcome for the poets at the once-great abbey. However, the gentry seized their new opportunities to flourish at the expense of the Church, as will be seen below.

Until recently it had been thought that Cardiganshire had been without a single squeak of resistance to the Reformation. The county justices never admitted the existence of recusant Catholics, whose names had to be reported to the authorities, though their absence of course may suggest some skill in dissimulation. However Father James Cunnane of Cardigan and Evan James have shown that there was indeed a Cardiganshire man who died for his Catholic beliefs. This was Hugh David, who in 1574 became vicar of Llannarth and Llanina. Nothing is known of his ministry until 1592, when he was brought before the Privy Council at Greenwich on a charge of treason, which was passed to the Court of Great Session in Cardigan. Witnesses averred that Hugh David had described Henry VII as a bastard, that Elizabeth should not be queen, that he had said 'woe to that realm that a woman is governor of'. He had been conducting 'superstitious ceremonies' and devotions to the saints, and accepting offerings for the dead. Judgement was extreme; Hugh David found guilty, and was hanged, drawn and quartered, quite probably at Cardigan, suffering for his political views as well as his religious practices. He has yet to be recognised by the Catholic church authorities as a martyr for his faith.

* * *

Evidence for church life in Tudor and early Stuart Cardiganshire is less scanty than for the medieval period. Gentry families certainly provided recruits for the reformed priesthood. The Lloyds of Castell Hywel produced Griffith Lloyd, principal of Jesus College, and Thomas Lloyd, chancellor of the diocese of St David's. Less exalted in church rank was Richard Lloyd, rector of Llangeitho, brother of principal Griffith Lloyd; the two were uncles of Sir Marmaduke Lloyd of Maesyfelin, one of the great men of Wales in his day. By the mid-16th century probate evidence is available; almost every priest who left a will and inventory was seriously involved in farming, a tradition which in an attenuated form survived into the early 20th century; the late Revd Noel Evans told me that his clergyman father could never have sent him to Oxford about 1920 if the family had not been able to depend on the produce of the glebe-land held by his father at his south Cardiganshire vicarage.

Most wretched of the county's clergy in the early 17th century was perhaps John Hughes of Trefilan, whose property at his death in 1614 was valued at less than five pounds; he had been too poor to marry, but left his doublet, shirt, shoes, hat and bands to his illegitimate son! Very different was the condition of Thomas Gwyn, vicar of Llanfihangel Genau'r-glyn, who had two oxen, fifteen milch cattle and 130 sheep and lambs, and who left sixty pounds to be divided among his poorer relatives

Parish life was probably rather more humdrum in the rest of the county than in Llanllwchaearn. Apart from maintaining Sunday worship, one of the parish priest's functions was to write out the wills of his parishioners, for which they might expect a sheep or a cash equivalent by way of payment. By and large their handwriting and spelling were no worse than those of other literate people of the age. Another function would have been to guide the church wardens in carrying out their duties, which gradually increased in number during the 17th and 18th centuries. Were the local clergy learned men? It is hard to tell; the great majority of those who made wills left no books at all in their inventories, but that does not necessarily mean a complete lack of culture.

Cilcennin church in 1683, sketched by Thomas Dineley. [National Museum of Wales].

when he died in 1598. Thomas Gwyn had aspirations, and married his daughter to Morris Vaughan, a J.P. and leading gentleman of the district; his morals were seemingly no better than the lay gentry, for at his death he left an illegitimate child.

More learned than most of his clerical brethren was David Griffith of Llanllwchaearn, son of a minor gentry family, details of whose life have been recovered by Evan James. David Griffith graduated from Jesus College, Oxford, in 1584, and after remaining for some years in Oxford as a lecturer teaching the Protestant faith to students, he illegally sold his Oriel College fellowship and returned to Cardiganshire to become rector of Llanllwchaearn in 1598. There he acted in an even more autocratic fashion than was usual among country clerics; he blackguarded his parishioners, arranged illegal marriages, and in 1604 (himself at least forty years of age) he abducted a fifteen-year-old girl, Gwenllian, who may have been his ward, and married her. Although this must have caused some scandal at the time, the dust certainly settled, for Gwenllian became the mother of his six children, and when he made his will in 1621, he appointed his mother-in-law as guardian of the children.

Although Puritanism was a growing force in English religious life from the mid-16th century, there is little evidence for it among Cardiganshire people for some decades. That it had gained local adherents by the early 17th century is clear from the 1612 will of Richard ap John ap Rhydderch of Llanfihangel Genau'r-glyn, who left forty shillings 'towards the mayntenance of fowre sermons to be quarterly prechede in the said parish church of Lanvihangel genglyn by my ghostly ffather Lewis Phillip'. Such a bequest was the Puritan equivalent of the late medieval chantry, and the priest Lewis Phillip too must have been a Puritan.

The outbreak of civil war and the victories of Parliament brought revolution to the Church; no bishops, no sports, no Christmas, and eventually no monarch. At the local level the new authorities in London were concerned above all with the standard of parish ministry. Wales was one of the dark corners of the land, considered to be full of ignorance and superstition, in desperate need of good preaching and teaching. In Cardiganshire approval was given in 1646 to fourteen ministers across the county, although several of these were later thrown out. For example, Morgan Evans was made rector of Ciliau Aeron in 1647 and ejected for drunkenness in 1651; he was back in the living in 1661. The 1650 Act for the Propagation of the Gospel in Wales expelled another eighteen Cardiganshire clergymen for the assorted offences of drunkenness, keeping an ale-house, simony, insufficiency, scandal, using the Book of Common Prayer, fornication, delinquency and incest. So great was the subsequent shortage of ministers that itinerant preachers were appointed, followed in 1657 by a drastic regrouping of parishes; Lampeter, for example, took in another four parishes, and Cardigan another six. Evan Roberts, the minister of Llanbadarn Fawr, was paid a salary of £100 a year to preach to his large parish.

Cardiganshire was visited by at least three of the major figures among the Welsh Puritan saints of the Commonwealth period. Walter Cradoc came to the county; in 1655 the Quaker John ap John walked the streets of Aberystwyth testifying to the inner light, and two years later George Fox sought to establish meetings in the county. The turbulent Fifth Monarchist Vavasor Powell was at least twice in Cardiganshire, once in 1654 to organise resistance to the newly proclaimed Protectorate, and again in 1656 at Llanbadarn at a gathering of several hundred men from eight Welsh counties. The meeting was held ostensibly to break bread together, but must have been part of a campaign against the Lord Protector Cromwell, whom Powell loathed. However, despite such visits, Cardiganshire was stony ground for the seed of Puritanism. It produced no great preacher or spiritual writer, no Morgan Llwyd or Walter Cradoc. John Lewis of Glasgrug in the Rheidol valley was the sole Puritan of real consequence in the north of the county. Appointed one of the commissioners under the 1650 Act for the Propagation of the Gospel in Wales, he favoured a Welsh college to educate ministers. An independent church was gathered together in mid-Cardiganshire during the 1650s and survived the return of the king and the bishops; it is particularly associated with Cilgwyn, Llangybi, and the beginnings of Congregationalism in the county.

The restoration of Charles II in 1660 and the reinstatement of the Church of England were welcomed by the populace at large, and by the gentry in particular, in Wales as in England. However, the *status quo ante* was not completely restored. In places as far apart as Llanfaches in Monmouthshire, Brynllywarch in the Llynfi valley, Ilston in Gower, Rhydwilym in Pembrokeshire, Dolgellau in the north-west and Wrexham in the north, the hearts of a minority of men and women had been changed. True, some of the old radical programmes had vanished; the restoration saw the end of Fifth Monarchy men in Wales and Diggers, Ranters and Levellers in England. But the inner light of the Friends, the espousal of adult baptism, the desirability of a gathered church governed by its congregation, all these, conveniently lumped together by their enemies as 'Dissent', had taken root, and could not be extinguished by the brutal Clarendon Code or the savagery of local magistrates.

Quakers visited the county after the Restoration. About 1668 Thomas Ellis of Montgomeryshire came to Aberystwyth and with others was imprisoned at Cardigan. Following his release and return home, he again came to Aberystwyth with Richard Davies of Dolobran; Thomas Pryse of Glan-ffraid imprisoned them, but at the next Quarter Sessions the justices decided to release both men. Charles Lloyd of Dolobran visited Cardigan in 1688, but the only place where Quakerism survived was at Wern-dryw, Llanddewibrefi. Although Wern-dryw is not mentioned by name until 1709, several men were imprisoned at Tregaron in 1659 and 1664 for Quaker practices, suggesting that it took better root in the upper Teifi valley than elsewhere. Several Cardiganshire men and their families emigrated to Pennsylvania and the West Indies; whether this was always for religious rather than economic reasons is not clear. The Quaker burial ground at Wern-dryw is still identifiable.

Despite the Church of England's continuing dominance after the Restoration, the people of Cardiganshire were touched by other forms of Dissent than the Quakers. In 1672 the Dissenters of mid-county took advantage of Charles II's Declaration of Indulgence; houses in Cardigan, Cellan, Dihewyd, Lampeter, Llanbadarn Odwyn, Llanddewibrefi, Llandysiliogogo and Llanfair Trelygen were licensed for dissenting use, and there may have been others that chose not to be licensed; five independent ministers were licensed to preach. One of them was Morgan Howell, born at Betws Bledrws. He had gone to an open-air meeting addressed by Walter Cradoc, and had attempted to disrupt the meeting by playing football, but sprained his ankle and was obliged to listen, and was converted. The licensed houses seem to have been attended by groups who recognised themselves as forming a single gathered congregation; its central meeting-place may have been Cilgwyn, Llangybi, though the vicar of Llangybi claimed in 1676 that there were no Dissenters in the parish – surely an untruth. Another of the five ministers was David Jones (d.1722), father of the extraordinary scribbler of the same name, who was the author of such works as *The Secret History of Whitehall* (1697), *A Compleat History of Europe* (1699) and *A Compleat History of the Turks* (1701). Apart from those whom we may call Independents, there were a few Baptists and a handful of Quakers in the county; the Baptists, who in their early days worshipped at Rhydwilym on the Pembroke-Carmarthenshire border, were eventually to increase, but the Quakers remained a tiny group at Wern-dryw. Taken all together, their numbers throughout the county were only a small proportion of the population. Cardiganshire Dissenters were fortunate in that the county's restored establishment of gentry plus clergy was somewhat more tolerant than that of Merionethshire.

The Church of England, although claiming the passive loyalty of the bulk of the county's population, was poorly endowed to maintain spiritual life. The church buildings were mostly in wretched condition. So small were the incomes of nearly all the livings that they would have been unattractive to well-educated men, supposing that many such had been anxious to work in the county. Equally unattractive was the virtual absence of vicarages; a parish priest had to find lodgings for himself, and on a typical Cardiganshire stipend could hardly contemplate marriage. There seem to have been even fewer graduates in the county's churches in the early 18th century than a century earlier; most were men who had been educated in grammar schools, or from the 1730s at Edward Richard's school at Ystrad Meurig. Despite all these drawbacks, the Church was nevertheless served by some able clergymen, and that despite the lack of support from many of the frequently-replaced bishops of St David's. Another sign of hope was the successful establishment of circulating schools by Griffith Jones, Llanddowror, from at least 1738 if not earlier, described in a later chapter.

The parish incomes for St David's diocese were set out in 1721 by Erasmus Saunders. Eighteen livings were over £50 per annum; 55 were less, and many of those less than £10. Indeed, £10 was the income of the vicar of Cardigan. It was essential either to have other employment, such as schoolteaching, which was equally badly paid, or several livings.

Llanwenog church.

The crowning individual achievement of any Cardiganshire clergyman at this time was the work of Moses Williams (1685-1742), son of Samuel Williams of Llandyfrïog, himself a clergyman and translator of religious works into Welsh. Moses Williams was also an Anglican clergyman and foremost of the Teifi valley scholars; he had at one time been an Oxford assistant to the great Edward Lhuyd. Apart from translating devotional works into Welsh and producing a thousand copies of a Welsh catechism for his Llanwenog parishioners, he was invited by the

SPCK to bring out a new edition of the Welsh Bible for domestic reading. Ten thousand copies are believed to have been printed of the 1718 edition, a thousand of which were given free to the poor. So great was the demand that another ten thousand were produced in 1727. Moses Williams was an exceptional man, the product of a Welsh Anglican milieu which was not as spiritually deaf and dumb as its fiercer critics were to claim. But the fire to be lit in Llangeitho in 1735 would mean that even the efforts of Moses Williams and his backers were insufficient to meet a new hunger for God's word.

* * *

With the passing of the Act of Toleration of 1689 it became safer for Dissenters, other than Quakers, to meet without fear of serious persecution. The Cardiganshire church first gathered in the Commonwealth period, referred to above, was well-organised, with its ministers, teachers, elders and deacons, and its circuit of meeting places at Cilgwyn, Caeronnen, Llwyn-rhys, Abermeurig and Crug-y-maen, all in mid-county. By 1715 its senior minister was Philip Pugh (1679-1760), a man of gentry family from Blaenpennal, educated at Samuel Jones's academy at Brynllywarch, and then Abergavenny. After his return to Cardiganshire he was first of a team of three men ministering to six congregations in mid-county. He was an outstanding figure, irenic and ecumenical of spirit, able to use such wealth as he had for the benefit of his churches, at least one of which he built himself. Pugh was vigorously active at the time of the conversion of Daniel Rowland of Llangeitho in 1735, and adopted a thoroughly supportive attitude to the early Methodists. It must have been a disappointment to him when they decided that they would no longer invite Dissenters to address their meetings.

The religious life of Cardiganshire had taken a radical turn only a few years before the outbreak of revival at Llangeitho in 1735. The Dissenter Jenkin Jones (*c*1700-1742) of Llanwenog, a combative theologian, had begun to preach against Calvinistic predestination in 1726, attacking the doctrine of original sin. In 1733 he built a chapel at Llwynrhydowen, where he could propagate his Arminian beliefs to a sympathetic congregation, and other ministers began to adopt his views, not without provoking a good deal of fierce controversy; Jones was accused by his enemies of teaching that Christ saved all mankind, including Jews, Muslims and pagans – an outrageous doctrine to the orthodox faithful. Religious radicalism in southern Cardiganshire would eventually develop into Unitarianism, with Llwynrhydowen an important centre; further north, especially beyond the Aeron, Dissent was always slower to develop. But 1735 was to mark the beginning of a huge change in the county's religious life.

9. Civil Society, Civil War

For fifteen years my home was Tan-yr-allt, a small farmhouse within view of Trawsgoed Park in the Ystwyth valley. A brief view of this one Cardiganshire landscape as it is today can demonstrate the power of the county's gentry, who from before 1536 until almost the end of the 19th century were its governing class. The farm had been a Trawsgoed tenancy from at least 1601 until 1947. The house had been rebuilt in the 18th century with bricks from a brickpit and kiln on the estate. Until the great gale of 1976 a splendid silver fir tree stood in the corner of the garden; in the late 19th century the Vaughans of Trawsgoed had planted trees hither and yon to improve the landscape, and some may still be seen about Llanafan bridge. Through the sessile oakwood above the house runs a path still known as 'the Lord's path', created for one of the earls of Lisburne to view his estate in the valley from on high. The B4340 road from Aberystwyth follows a line laid down by the Turnpike Trust about 1780 in consultation with the first earl, Wilmot Vaughan, who was then able to close the ancient road that ran close to the north front of his mansion.

Wilmot and his successors created a swathe of woodland along the new turnpike to cut off any view of the mansion, as well as planting hillside blocks of rhododendrons and other trees to provide cover for pheasants. Between the mansion and the woodland is what was until recently the largest and finest garden in the county, with a splendid arboretum – both in much need of care (and expenditure) at the time of writing. A turning off the B4340 leads to the village of Llanafan, with its Earl of Lisburne primary school and its Lisburne village hall, as well as the parish church rebuilt by the third earl and filled with family memorials. The villagers of Llanafan were nearly all employed either by the Trawsgoed estate or by the lead mines which paid royalties to Trawsgoed. Because the family disapproved of drink for the working classes there is still no village pub in Llanafan village or parish, even though the Vaughans moved from Trawsgoed more than fifty years ago. Llanafan was a 'closed' or estate village. A remark to a villager that the Vaughans had once owned every acre in the parish save one single farm elicited the blunt reply, 'Yes, and they owned the people too.'

Not every part of Cardiganshire's landscape and society was so overwhelmingly controlled by a single family as Llanafan and the mid-Ystwyth valley. Indeed, Cardiganshire had fewer truly large estates than some other Welsh counties of comparable size and population; the spread of minor gentry with small estates was extensive throughout the county, especially in the south. Nor was every man who claimed the rank of gentleman a power in the land; some were miserably poor, owning little more than their genealogies. Nevertheless, the power of the major landed gentry was formidable, thanks to their ownership of the vast majority of farms and their control of office. How had they achieved such dominance? It is clear that the revolution brought about in Wales from the 1530s by the joint impact of the Reformation and the Acts of Union gave a huge impetus to those Cardiganshire men who were ambitious to rise in the world, men like David Lloyd of Castell Hywel, Cardiganshire's first MP, and John Pryse of Gogerddan, his immediate successor in Parliament.

Prior to 1536 Cardiganshire had been in many ways a restricted little world of its own. A man who could boast of his free ancestry, evident from his genealogy, might well own some land. He might, if he had a little education and a patron, hope to purchase Crown office as a local administrator, particularly of taxation, enabling him to feather his nest. He would have to understand Welsh law, which in all its complexity still applied to land and property, the administration of which was conducted to a great extent by word of mouth, and in Welsh. His culture would be a Welsh-language culture, involving (certainly for the better-off) the patronage of poets. A man's estate was unlikely to grow greatly from generation to generation, because land held by Welsh law had to be divided between sons, while daughters could not inherit even in the absence of sons, so even a socially advantageous marriage could not bring an access of new land to a man's estate, unless it was land owned under English law; it has not yet been established how widely that was the case in Cardiganshire.

Thomas Cromwell's reforms of the 1530s changed all that. Cardiganshire was no longer cut off from England by the Marcher lordships, with all their uncertainties and anomalies of administration, and their multiple boundaries. The ten original commotes of the county were replaced by five 'hundreds': Troedyraur, Moyddyn, Penardd, Ilar and Genau'r-glyn. The thought-world of ambitious men was no longer hemmed in by the need for such specialised local knowledge as the law of Hywel Dda. New goals existed: the justiceship of the peace, influence in the county court of Great Sessions, membership of the Council of Wales and the Marches at Ludlow, the county and borough seats in London's Parliament. New land came on the market, thanks to the dissolution of the monasteries, including the broad acres of Strata Florida and the lesser lands of the convent at Llanllŷr. New skills were needed, especially a knowledge of the now-absolute law of England, which in its turn required a new fluency in the English language. Lands anywhere could in the absence of a son be inherited by daughters, thus creating in many parts of Wales a new and desirable class – that of the landed heiress.

THE threat of foreign invasion had its echoes in Cardiganshire. In the 1560s the government surveyed the whole coast to assess its resources and vulnerability to invasion. In 1597 a Spanish ship took shelter in the Dyfi estuary for some days, causing much excitement. It escaped, leaving the local leaders lamenting their lack of cannon to attack it. For the musters of men to serve as soldiers, see Chapter 14 below.

It is agreed by historians that the combination of Henry VII's victory at Bosworth and the Acts of Union of 1536 and 1543 increased the numbers of Welsh people who moved to England either for long periods or permanently. Temporary mobility is easy to prove in the case of the gentry; the universities and Inns of Court, the law-courts and Parliament all attracted Welsh gentlemen to England. But what of lesser folk? A will proved in London in 1568 is a stray pointer to their mobility. Margaret ferch David ap John wished to be buried in Tregaron church, and was presumably in the parish of Caron when she died. But she had goods in two Monmouthshire parishes, and appointed Lewis Aprice of Edington, Wiltshire, as overseer of her will. A long search of wills in English counties would reveal other native Cardis who had emigrated.

However, the Tudor revolution in Wales affected the gentry much more than it did those men and women who formed the infrastructure of society, whose labour, services, rents and taxes were the economic foundation on which all rested: farmers, labourers, shepherds, craftsmen, and their womenfolk. Ambitious men set about increasing their estates and seizing new advantages, and this inevitably brought about all kinds of changes. Suddenly education became vital, not in knowledge of Welsh law and poetry, but in the English language and English law. Schools appeared in many Welsh counties during the 16th century, but not as far as is known in Cardiganshire. The only alternatives were to use tutors or to send boys away to school (most girls would be taught by their mothers).

The vital step was higher education: Oxford or Cambridge, and/or the Inns of Court in London. This was valuable both for an eldest son and heir and for his younger brothers, who needed to make careers for themselves. Thus Griffith Lloyd, second son of Hugh Llewelyn Lloyd of Llanllŷr, graduated at Jesus College Oxford, became a professor of law and eventually principal of his college before his death in 1587, leaving his books of law and divinity to his younger brother Richard. John Pryse of Gogerddan was a member of the Inner Temple in 1553, but in September of that year he became Cardiganshire's MP. Although he continued his membership of the Inner Temple, other demands were made on his time, apart from managing his growing estate; he was High Sheriff of Cardiganshire in 1570 and of Merionethshire in 1580; he was Cardiganshire's leading representative at the Ludlow meetings of the Council of Wales and the Marches, and sat as MP in five parliaments before his death in 1584.

Never before had any Cardiganshire-born men enjoyed such careers as those of Griffith Lloyd and John Pryse. They adopted English-style surnames, they were fluent in English, they could hobnob with members of the elite of Wales and England. Yet it should not be imagined that everything was transformed at a stroke. John Pryse and several generations of his descendants continued to welcome Welsh poets to Gogerddan to sing the family's praises at least until the time of Sir Richard Pryse, baronet (d.1651). The process of anglicisation of the Welsh gentry was not quite as rapid as some have believed, nor was it complete by 1651, nor yet was it something planned; it is well described by J. Gwynfor Jones as a drift 'from one world to another without realizing that by entering the new they were in fact betraying the old.' Some men entered early into industry: James Philipps of Cardigan Priory was exporting Cilgerran slates to Ireland in 1620, while Nanteos and Gogerddan were involved in lead-mining early.

It should not be imagined that the leaders of Cardiganshire society in the Tudor and Stuart period were as polished and as genteel as their successors of, say, the late 18th century. The times could be violent; indeed, no county in Wales was more violent than Cardiganshire. In the south there was a fierce quarrel between the Leweses and the Birts; John Birt put John Lewes in irons in Cardigan gaol, accusing him of supporting the Earl of Essex's rebellion; Essex was a major landowner in south-west Wales with a Cardiganshire following. In the north John Pryse's son Richard, who held almost all the offices previously filled by his father and was knighted in 1603, made an enemy of a lesser man, David Lloyd of Aber-mad in the Ystwyth valley. In 1599 Lloyd brought Pryse before the court of Star Chamber in London, accusing him of misusing his office of Deputy Lieutenant for the county by converting the armour and ammunition of the county militia to his own use, of levying illegal taxes to replace the missing armour, of corruption in the Court of Great Sessions and of forgery. Unfortunately the verdicts of the court are all lost, so we cannot know whether Pryse really was proved to be a rogue, or whether David Lloyd was trying to ruin him by dragging him to London with a train of expensive witnesses rather than to the court of Great Sessions at Cardigan.

The feud was a serious one: in 1600 Richard Pryse's brother Thomas took the sons of David Lloyd of Aber-mad to Star Chamber on charges of assaults and riots at Aberystwyth and Llanbadarn Fawr, and of resisting arrest. The Pryses and the Lloyds, despite being landed gentry with JP status, were obviously at each others' throats, and their feud was only one of many which fizzed and boiled in the county. Gentlemen were accused by their fellows of perjury, corruption, falsification of documents, assault, attempted lynching, extortion, expulsion of men from their lands, abduction, false imprisonment and riot. In 1565 Richard Fychan of Trawsgoed, father of Morys ap Richard, brutally killed the local justice, Ieuan Llwyd of Llanychaearn, and fled the county. In 1590 Myles Gwyn, Deputy Sheriff of Cardiganshire, was murdered in Montgomeryshire. This was the period at which Welshmen became particularly known among the English for their hot blood. The gentry-sponsored street violence of Verona which Shakespeare portrays so vividly in *Romeo and Juliet* was well-known in Cardiganshire, nor would it entirely disappear before the late 18th century.

LOCAL gentry society was far from being a closed shop. Well before 1603 the major Carmarthenshire family of Jones, Abermarlais, gained lands in Cardiganshire in the person of James Jones of Dolaucothi, who had already been High Sheriff of his new county in 1586. Despite – or because of – their gentry status, the Joneses played a lively part in quarrels on the streets of Llanbadarn. The whereabouts of their Llanbadarn mansion is unknown; before the end of the century they seem to have moved from the district, concentrating their activies in Llanfair Clydogau and Aber-mad.

Electoral politics was a major concern of leading gentry families, and could be startlingly disputatious. The 1601 election for Cardigan boroughs brought to a head the contest between Aberystwyth and Cardigan for primacy in the county. County sheriff Richard Herbert of Park, Montgomeryshire, favoured Aberystwyth's choice of William Awbrey, but Cardigan returned one William Delabere, who reached

London first and was able to take his seat in Parliament because the clerk there did not insist on having the sheriff's notification. Awbery's protests did not bring about a resolution. At the next election, in 1604, the High Sheriff was Sir Richard Pryse, who sought the re-election of Delabere, but this time Cardigan by due process elected William Bradshaw, a man of the town; the Pryses had not yet secured the half-nelson hold which they would eventually impose on Cardiganshire politics.

It may surprise the reader to know that these ambitious, quarrelsome men were by no means eager to achieve royal titles or favour. When Charles I was crowned, the gentlemen of his kingdom were 'invited' to the coronation, a privilege which involved accepting knighthoods at considerable expense. Many refused the honour, and the King, who by 1630 was ruling without Parliament, sought to impose fines on the recalcitrants. Twenty of them offered their excuses: one was impotent and decrepit, another was four-score years old, several had 'a great charge of children', another owed a thousand pounds, while Morgan Lloyd of Abertrinant answered that at the time of the coronation he was possessed of no estate at all.

The 'great charge of children' sometimes resulted from the fact that gentry sexual morals were often far from genteel. David Lloyd of Llanfechan in the vale of Teifi, a JP in 1600 and a married man, begot eight illegitimate children by six different women. Rees ap David ap Jenkin of Aberpyllau in the Ystwyth valley, who was high Sheriff of the county in 1573, fathered four bastards by three women; his wife was childless. These men were not exceptional. The fate of many such offspring is usually obscure, but a few were fortunate. Thomas Jones, gentleman herald of Porthyffynnon,Tregaron, (d.1609; better known in folklore as Twm Siôn Cati, the outlaw scapegrace) was illegitimate, but held a small estate nevertheless, and bequeathed it to his own illegitimate heir. Another such man was Charles Lloyd of Maesyfelin. His father Sir Francis Lloyd had not produced offspring by his wife, but his mistress, Bridget Leigh of Carmarthen, bore him two sons, and one of them, Charles, inherited the estate in 1669, was knighted by William III and given a baronetcy in 1708 by Queen Anne.

Illegitimate daughters were even less likely to inherit an estate. Morgan ap Phylip ap Hywel of Llechwedd Dyrys (d.1622), did his best to ensure that one of his two illegitimate daughters had a £700 dowry, while the other girl was fobbed off with five pounds. To skip forward a little, Edward Lhuyd (1660-1709), the greatest Welsh scholar of his age and a figure of European significance in both science and linguistics, was born at Glan-ffraid, the illegitimate son of Bridget Pryse, gentlewoman, fathered by Edward Lloyd of Llanforda, Oswestry, who fully acknowledged his brilliant son and ensured a good education for him. The tradition of double moral standards for men and for women meant that such cases of gentry ladies bearing acknowledged illegitimate children were unusual (but see Chapter 10).

Some gentry attempted the improvement of manners, at least among their local inferiors. In remote and lawless Cwmystwyth the Herberts had established their Hafod Uchdryd estate on a freehold basis by 1640. Technically their parish church was distant Llanfihangel-y-Creuddyn; the local chapel of ease at Llantrisant had long been in ruins. In 1620 therefore Morgan Herbert built a new church,

Eglwysnewydd, at a convenient centre for the population and for his mansion. However, the Herberts were not exempt from the run of criminal violence, as will be seen below, and their frequent nomination in probate documents as guardians of minors may suggest intimidation rather than hope of protection. The gentry were in theory pillars of the established Church, but it was more usual for them to exploit the Church than to sustain it.

* * *

At this point it must be made clear that within a single chapter it would be impossible to detail the development of all the important Cardiganshire estates. So far Trawsgoed, Gogerddan, Llanllŷr, Ynys-hir, Aber-mad, and the Herbert family of Cwmystwyth have been mentioned, and of those, Gogerddan from the lifetime of John Pryse and his son gained a pre-eminence in the county which the family held until the decline of the landed estates in the late 19th century. Indeed, it may be useful to continue their story as a paradigm of the opportunities and dilemmas which befell gentry families. It can be argued that what gave Gogerddan that pre-eminence was simply that they were quickly away from the starting gate, and that others (like the Lloyds of Castell Hywel, Maesyfelin and Llanllŷr) who made a good start did not display enough stamina. The Vaughans of Trawsgoed eventually built up a bigger estate than Gogerddan; John Vaughan of Trawsgoed (1603-74) was incomparably more talented than any Pryse, and with the eventual acquisition of a peerage (admittedly an Irish one) the family gained aristocratic status. Moreover the Vaughans never lacked a male heir. Nevertheless, in county politics it was the Pryses of Gogerddan who dictated terms. Simply put, eleven Pryses and four of their in-laws sat for either the county or the borough seats, while only six Vaughans did so.

The Pryses had succeeded so well particularly because they married wisely. The Pryses devoted themselves for several generations to making good marriages. John Pryse's great-great-grandfather was originally of the Rhydderch family of Glyn Aeron, but an opportunity had arisen at some unknown date in the 15th century for him to marry the heiress of Gogerddan (land held by English law). Subsequently the Pryses married in all directions, in and out of Cardiganshire. John Pryse himself married, not an heiress, but Elizabeth Perrot, daughter of one of the most powerful and wealthy men in Wales, Sir Thomas Perrot of Pembrokeshire. Of their two sons, Richard

THE fortunate and audacious could climb a kind of marital ladder to fortune. A small landowner like Morys ap Richard Fychan of Trawsgoed would marry a local heiress, from the same valley. A son, or in the case of Morys, his grandson Edward and his great-grandsons John and Henry, would marry heiresses from further off (in this case, all were Stedmans, of Strata Florida and Cilcennin). The next generation might, as the Pryses liked to do, marry into a neighbouring county, but in the case of Trawsgoed, John Vaughan's son Edward jumped straight to an English marriage, with a rich London merchant's daughter. Finally *their* son reached to the stars by marrying Malet, daughter and co-heiress of the Earl of Rochester, and acquired his peerage as Lord Lisburne.

the elder (d.1622) married the heiress of Aberbychan, Montgomeryshire, and went one better than his father by gaining a knighthood. His younger brother Thomas also managed to win an heiress, a local one, Bridget of Glan-ffraid, Dôl-y-bont (Bridget, mother of Edward Lhuyd, was their daughter). Thus, although not a direct Gogerddan heir himself, Thomas became a squire in right of his wife, and provided in their descendants a useful source of cousins to inherit Gogerddan when the senior branch of Pryses ran out of male heirs. By 1640 the Pryses were allied by marriage, within Cardiganshire, to the houses of Strata Florida, Llanllŷr, Llanfair Clydogau, Noyadd Drefawr, Blaen-pant and Ynys-hir, and also to families in Montgomeryshire and Merionethshire.

To describe the Gogerddan marriages in too great detail would weary the reader, but the importance of wedlock as a means of securing land and influence is plain enough. Gogerddan took a step further up the prestige ladder when the second Richard Pryse (d.1651), grandson of the first Richard, married Hester Middleton, a daughter of the wealthy Sir Hugh Myddleton, the London Welshman who improved the city's water supply; Richard was created baronet in 1641. After Hester's death Sir Richard espoused Mary, widow of the great painter Van Dyck. Sir Richard's eldest son Richard Pryse III married Elizabeth Whitelocke, daughter of Sir Bulstrode Whitelocke, a significant figure in English politics during the Civil Wars. It was at this point that things began to go wrong. Richard Pryse III was obviously a disappointment to his influential father-in-law, on whom he called from time to time to bail him out of trouble, and he failed to produce children. Moreover his wife engineered a clandestine marriage between her sister, Hester Whitelocke, and Sir Richard's younger and penniless brother Carbery, thus incurring the wrath of Sir Bulstrode.

However, before moving with the Pryses and the rest of Cardiganshire's gentry into the alarming waters of the Civil Wars, some impression at least must be given of the whole county, and in particular of the general ebb and flow of family competition and collaboration. By 1640 the Pryses dominated much of Cardiganshire north of the Rheidol, if not through Gogerddan directly, then through Glan-ffraid and another subordinate estate, Bodfagedd (Lodge Park, Tre'r-ddôl); they also had lands in Merionethshire and Montgomeryshire. Between the Rheidol and the Ystwyth the Joneses of Nanteos and the Powells of Llechwedd Dyrys, opposite Nanteos, were already pre-eminent locally. The Vaughans of Trawsgoed had in 1632 enormously increased their Ystwyth valley estate by the purchase of eight granges of Strata Florida lands, thus making them the greatest landholders in the county. However, they sold the freehold of many Cwmystwyth tenements to the leaseholders, the Herberts of Hafod Uchdryd, while Ffosybleiddiaid (Swyddffynnon) was sold to Oliver Lloyd, thus creating two new estates. The Vaughans had not monopolised the Ystwyth valley; the substantial estate of Aberpyllau, already referred to above, had broken up before 1600 and its lands had been recycled, and there were other independent holdings which either were or eventually became estates at Cwmnewidion, Maesdwyffrwd, Llidiardau, Aber-mad and Aberllolwyn, three of which were eventually swallowed up by Trawsgoed. Castle Hill, Pen-y-wern and Tan-y-bwlch were later creations.

A Powell funerary hatchment at Nanteos. Heraldry was often used to conceal the humbler origins of rising families.

It is comparatively easy to describe the gentry world of northern Cardiganshire, since it was dominated by four estates (Gogerddan, Trawsgoed, Nanteos and Hafod Uchdryd). The rest of the county is more complex. Much of mid and south Cardiganshire was dominated by families called Lloyd, most of whom were related to the Castell Hywel family. Ffosybleiddiaid was the northernmost Lloyd house, and there were numerous estates which at some time or other were held by Lloyds around Llanrhystud (Mabws, Ystrad Teilo, Moelifor); in the Aeron valley (Llanllŷr, Green-grove, Lloyd Jack), and all down the Teifi valley from Llanfair Clydogau to Bronwydd, Cilgwyn and the Priory at Cardigan. The most important of these Lloyd estates in the 17th century was Maesyfelin, which in the 18th century was subsumed in Peterwell.

However the Lloyds were far from having it all their own way in the south. Two of the most important southern estates in 1640 were Abernant-bychan (Penbryn) and Noyadd Drevawr (Llandygwydd), the first of which is now scarcely a memory. John Lewis of Abernant-bychan had married Bridget, daughter of Sir Richard Pryse I, and thanks to his father-in-law's influence had been elected MP for the county in 1604 and gained a knighthood. He bought in the Coedmor estate east of Cardigan to swell his holdings. But neither the family nor the estate endured, and now the Abernant mansion site is occupied by a farmhouse with the grand name of Plas Glynarthen. Noyadd Drevawr was a major Teifi valley estate owned by the Parrys, who by judicious marriage gained land in Y Ferwig, and in St Dogmaels and other Pembrokeshire parishes. Mention too must be made of the Priory at Cardigan, where in 1640 the Philipps family was in firm possession (and which a hundred years earlier had been re-roofed with lead stripped from St David's cathedral by Bishop Barlow). It is clear that the Teifi valley was a social unit which largely ignored the county boundary running down the river to the sea.

What were these gentry houses like? Unfortunately, we hardly know. Only Wern Newydd near New Quay and the much-

WERN Newydd (originally 'Y Wern' now Plas-y-Wern) near New Quay is worthy of its unique status as the oldest house in Ceredigion. The main range is of *c.*1670, and much of the fine panelling and plasterwork, as well as the splendid staircase, belong to this period. The eastern part of the house is older, probably of the 16th century. The descendants of Einion ap Dafydd Llwyd, he who entertained Henry Tudor in 1485, moved away after the *c*1670 rebuilding, and little was altered thereafter.

altered Stedman house at Strata Florida, survive from this period. We may suppose that many of the gentry lived in hall-houses, using a great deal of timber, until the 17th century; Thomas Dineley's sketch of Trawsgoed in 1684 shows that a rebuilding must have taken place, presumably by Sir John Vaughan; the house is splendidly gabled, and set in a fine fashionable garden. Strata Florida is shown in a Buck print as apparently having three storeys, but the house was re-roofed and the roof-gables or attics disappeared, leaving a more modest farmhouse, though with a remarkable early fireplace. The prints do not make clear whether the roofing was new-fangled slate or the traditional thatch. Some idea of the size of what may be called a representative gentry house can be gained from the inventory of John Birt of Llwyndyrys, Llandygwydd, who died in 1623. The following rooms are named: dining room, chamber, parlour, kitchen, buttery and upper loft, with a separate dairy. Lodge Park, Tre'r-ddôl, in 1682 contained a kitchen, hall, parlour, wainscot room, green

Sir John Vaughan's Trawsgoed home in 1683.
[by courtesy of the Earl of Lisburne]

Interiors at Wern Newydd, New Quay (from postcard).

chamber, red chamber, matted chamber, 'the dark room at the head of the stairs', 'my lady's chamber', 'Mrs Lloyd's room', servants' chamber and cellars.

The Llwyndyrys rooms were filled with an assortment of tables, chairs, benches and bedsteads; the inventory names a close-stool and chamber-pots (there would have been no other sanitary facilities in the house, no running water or drainage), and Birt owned a small array of silverware and a battery of pewter dishes, brass pans and ironware for the kitchen. Small signs of luxury are the two velvet window-cushions, four embroidered cushions, tablecloths and a looking-glass. Other gentry inventories include muskets, fowling pieces, swords, pistols, a gold watch, tobacco boxes, books, and a coconut 'mounted and tipped with silver'. In the greatest houses family portraits were beginning to appear; Sir Marmaduke Lloyd of Maesyfelin stares threateningly out at us from the year 1642; Sir John Vaughan's puritanically pursed lips and splendid judge's robes formed part of a Trawsgoed collection which by 1700 included portraits of the children of Charles I, the Earl of Rochester, his daughter Malet, and a state portrait of William III. Books are rarely mentioned, but Sir Francis Lloyd owned 'a studdy of bookes', and Sir John Vaughan inherited part of the great library of the polymath John Selden, including one of the most important of early Welsh manuscripts, *Llyfr Llandaf*, which eventually passed with a daughter to a Flintshire family.

Sir John Vaughan, Trawsgoed.
[by courtesy of the Earl of Lisburne]

Most gentry inventories show that gentlemen were closely involved in farming, though they would have depended on their employees to do all the hard labour. Thus James Stedman of Strata Florida (d.1617) owned two hundred cattle and seven hundred sheep, twenty horses and a quantity of swine and poultry. Thomas Jones of Fountain Gate (Twm Siôn Cati) had sixteen oxen, 91 other cattle, 180 sheep and 83 lambs. Maud Birt of Llwyndyrys at her death in 1671 owned 31 horses.

* * *

By 1640 the pattern of Cardiganshire life had apparently settled down after the remarkable changes of the Tudor period. The gentry were in firm control of civil society, and though their frequent squabbles could become violent, serious disorder was not an apparent threat. The Anglican settlement was functioning, if not with unseemly enthusiasm, at least with some semblance of regularity, and with no apparent threat from that puritan dissent which was making itself known in England and the Welsh Marches. However, the changing political situation in England must for some years have been a topic of conversation among many Cardiganshire gentlemen and some of the clergy. John Vaughan of Trawsgoed in particular was, in his roles as borough MP, as a leading London lawyer, and as a friend of the intellectual lawyer and *eminence grise* John Selden, close to the heart of London political life.

King James I, despite his many personal weaknesses, had managed to balance the competing forces which threatened society until his death in 1625. But his son Charles, although personally a more attractive figure than his father, had such an exalted perception of his own divinely-ordained kingship that conflict with Parliament was inevitable. The House of Commons insisted on its right to approve taxation, and its puritan wing sought drastic reform of the Church of England, even to the point of abolishing episcopacy and replacing it with a Presbyterian system. The infuriated Charles dismissed Parliament in 1629 and ruled for eleven years as dictator, raising money by various quasi-legal devices. In 1635 Hector Philipps of Cardigan Priory wrote to complain that too much Ship Money was being levied in Cardiganshire; his family were to become local leaders for the parliamentary cause. In 1637 Thomas Bushell, a dynamic figure in the booming local lead-silver industry, opened a mint in Aberystwyth castle, obviously with royal approval; it was to supply the king with Cardiganshire silver coins until 1643. In 1639 fifty men were levied from the county to join the king's forces against the Scots. Even in Cardiganshire, so apparently distant from the great affairs of the kingdom, there must have been worried men.

The struggle lay between the king's supporters who, to put it crudely, maintained his divine right to absolute rule, and those, many of them puritans, who sought to insist on the sovereignty of Parliament and on church reform. A number of MPs, led by John Vaughan of Trawsgoed among others, sought a middle way, but as so often, the moderates were squeezed by the extremists. In 1642 Charles raised his standard at Nottingham, and was joined by his supporters. Parliament continued to sit in London, but the moderates left. The first Civil War had begun.

In 1642 the Cardiganshire gentry were virtually all royalists, as was most of Wales. A letter from John Vaughan to Morgan Herbert in 1643 laments the fall of Tenby to parliamentary forces. By 1644 John Jones of Nanteos was writing excitedly from the royalist headquarters at Oxford to his friends about events there, he having raised a hundred Cardiganshire foot-soldiers for the king. The Cardiganshire Lloyds were royalists to a man. Among the very few supporters of Parliament in the county were the Philippses of Cardigan Priory; Hector Lewis has already been mentioned, and his sons George and Hector were vigorous in the cause. James was a member of the Parliaments of 1653, 1654, 1656, 1659 and 1660; he and his brother were members of the Commission of Sequestration, which offered plenty of opportunity to inflict swingeing fines on royalist landowners. The only intellectual representative of the parliamentary cause in the county was John Lewis of the little Glasgrug estate in the Rheidol valley, already referred to in Chapter 8 above. Lewis was a zealous puritan, who joined enthusiastically in the pamphleteering warfare of the period; *The Parliament explained to Wales* is the most significant of his contributions. However, it brought him obloquy at home; at the Great Sessions he prosecuted Oliver Lloyd of Cwm-bwa for repeating a slander by Richard Herbert, saying that John Lewis was a traitor, and that:

> *y fynna weld i quartery fo, o blegid y llyfyr y nayth fo, oblegid y llyfyr y Cyhoyddodd fo yn erbyn y Brenin yn achose y parliament a Cookold yw John Lewis fach.* (I'd like to see him quartered on account of the book he made against the King in the cause of parliament, and little John Lewis is a cuckold).

The sound of tramping soldiers was heard in the county in 1644, when the parliamentary leader in Wales, Sir Thomas Myddleton, joined with soldiers from Pembrokeshire at Lampeter and drove northwards through the county, fighting a battle 'at a bridge near Machynlleth' against forces led by Rowland Pugh of Mathafarn, a relative by marriage of the Pryses. In 1645 the county was still reported to Charles to be 'wholly in order for the king'. Before the year was out, however, the scene changed drastically. The Pembrokeshire parliamentarians besieged and captured first Cardigan castle, then Aberystwyth, which they took with the aid of Colonel John Jones of Nanteos, recently so strong for the king. The castle was thereupon largely destroyed. King Charles surrendered to the Scots. The first Civil War had ended; the second Civil War, which in Wales reached its climax at the battle of St Fagans in 1648, was a briefer affair with little impact in the county.

Cardiganshire took longer to settle than the rest of the country. There was a battle at Llanrhystud in 1651 in which twenty men were killed. In 1652 there had been one last flurry of anti-Cromwellian discontent, confined to Cardiganshire, but it was soon put down by Rowland Dawkins. Oliver Lloyd of Ffosybleiddiaid was

Aberystwyth castle, from a Buck brothers' print of the mid-18th century, suffered severely in the siege of 1646.

summonsed for having tried to raise men and money against Parliament, saying, 'Where will you Roundheads appear, when Charles II, King of Scots and King of England, comes with an army to get his right? Then will you all be hanged.' Drums were beaten in Llanbadarn Fawr, to no avail. But the religious situation was far from happy; it was easier to expel parish priests for moral turpitude than to find worthy preachers to replace them. Parishes had to be grouped, as many as ten together, and could hardly have enjoyed an effective ministry. Whatever the failings of the episcopal Church, it was more easily overthrown than replaced, and the same was true of the monarchy; the frequent changes of government (the rule of Parliament, followed by the rule of the Major-Generals, followed by Oliver Cromwell's Protectorate) meant that the system was bound to collapse once Cromwell's iron will had faded into death.

The success of Parliament, thanks to Cromwell's army, was accompanied by ferocious bickering, and the sound of men changing sides. The triumphant parliamentarians set up committees to examine and punish their defeated opponents. Cardiganshire was punished with a £3,000 levy for 'delinquency', i.e. for supporting the king. Morgan Herbert of Hafod, Richard Lloyd of Ystrad Teilo and David Lloyd of Llanychaearn were accused of pressing men to fight for the king, and of imprisoning those who had refused. Thomas Evans of Peterwell and Morgan Herbert had been in arms for the king at St Fagans. John Vaughan of Trawsgoed, John Jones of Nanteos and Llewelyn Parry of Llanerchaeron were all reported as delinquents. John Jones vigorously denied all accusations; he was under threat of losing the Hampshire estate he had acquired by marrying an English heiress, and claimed that his regiment of soldiers had assisted at the siege of Aberystwyth, and that he had never been in the king's army – an outrageous lie! He so ingratiated himself with the new order that when John Vaughan of Trawsgoed sought leave to travel to London 'for the recovery of his health', he needed a certificate from John Jones. Nevertheless, Jones's memorial stone in Llanbadarn Fawr church, piously erected by his daughter long after his death in 1666, ignores these tergiversations, presenting him as a true loyalist. The punishments meted out to those royalists found to be disloyal varied considerably. Sir Francis Lloyd of Maesyfelin and Sir Walter Lloyd of Llanfair Clydogau were fined a thousand pounds each, truly enormous sums; Thomas Evans of Peterwell, however, seems to have escaped scot-free and soon gained a horrid reputation as an enforcer of parliamentary fines; he may well have been able to increase the extent of the Peterwell estate as a result.

While all this went on, Parliament attempted to bring order and reform to the governance of the country. As we have seen, John Lewis of Glasgrug became one of the commissioners for the propagation of the gospel in Wales by the Act of 1650. Some royalists and moderates sought to maintain their status by rejoining the administrative system. Lloyds and Herberts appear among the names of the high sheriffs for the Commonwealth period; indeed, Morgan Herbert achieved the remarkable distinction of serving the office, usually an annual appointment, for the four years 1657-60 under the four administrations of Oliver Cromwell, Richard Cromwell, Monck's administration prior to the Restoration, and Charles II. John and Henry Vaughan appear among the JPs of 1656. Sir Walter Lloyd of Llanfair Clydogau and Olmarch was one of the few who remained loyal to the Crown throughout, and appears never to have been compensated for his faithfulness; his loyalty to the crown was admired by Katherine Philipps, 'the Matchless Orinda', despite her parliamentary husband James Philipps:

> . . . he dar'd to be loyal, in a time
> When 'twas a danger made, and thought a crime.
> Duty, and not ambition, was his aim,
> Who study'd Conscience ever more than Fame.

* * *

The Restoration was not simply the return of the king, it was the restoration, as far as was humanly possible, of the pre-Commonwealth order, which meant the recall of Parliament, the re-imposition of traditional gentry rule under the Crown without the interference of London-based committees, and the return of the episcopate and Church order. Only the Commonwealth regicides were persecuted, which enabled the Philippses of Cardigan as well as the trimmers among the county's gentry to continue in ownership of their estates and control of office. The Gogerddan ascendancy was in temporary abeyance; Richard Pryse II had been MP for the county from 1646 to 1648 as a parliamentarian (although he had acquired a baronetcy from the crown in 1641), replacing the royalist Sir Walter Lloyd. After his father's death in 1651 Richard Pryse III remained a JP after the Restoration until his death in 1674, and engineered his return to Parliament for the county seat in 1660 in the brief Parliament of that year, but was quickly replaced in 1661 by John Vaughan of Trawsgoed. The county seat only returned to Gogerddan in 1690 with the election of Sir Carbery Pryse, Sir Richard's youngest brother. John Vaughan was able to continue his advocacy of the third way, neither on the side of the Cavalier revanchistes, nor an extreme critic of the Crown, but pleading for the rule of the king through Parliament, the classic Whig position, until he was made chief justice of the Court of Common Pleas in 1668, and earned his place in history by ensuring through his 1670 verdict in Bushell's case that the government authorities had no right to punish jurymen who brought in verdicts which the authorities did not like. This was a blow for civil liberty which still reverberates in the legal system, and Sir John Vaughan deserves to be more widely remembered as a great lawyer and a great Welshman.

The accession of the Catholic James II in 1685 and the subsequent birth of his male heir, who would obviously continue a Catholic monarchy, must have excited opinions in Cardiganshire, but we know virtually nothing of them. Even the 'Glorious Revolution' of 1688-89 which saw the king's flight to France seems to have had little immediate impact in Cardiganshire, though to be sure Sir Thomas Powell of Llechwedd Dyrys was one of the judges whose dismissal of the Crown case against the Seven Bishops in 1687 was instrumental in the downfall of the

Stuart regime. The Pryses of Gogerddan regained political leadership of the county from 1685 until the death of Sir Carbery Pryse in 1694. This was the end of the direct Gogerddan line; the estate passed to a Glan-ffraid uncle, Edward Pryse, and then to his son Lewis, who sat in Parliament from 1702 when he was only eighteen, and therefore technically disqualified. In 1715 Lewis Pryse forfeited his county seat in Parliament because, being sympathetic to the deposed Stuarts, and subsequent to the Old Pretender's rebellion of that year, he had refused to attend Parliament, complaining that he was suffering from gout; he was expelled from the House. Pryse's gout was genuine, but so was his disloyalty to the new Hanoverian dynasty of George I; he was a well-known Jacobite. He did further damage to the Gogerddan cause by remaining a bachelor and dying in 1720 at the age of only 37; his heir was a four-year-old third cousin, Thomas Pryse.

John Vaughan of Trawsgoed, first Lord Lisburne [by courtesy of the Earl of Lisburne].

Malet, Lady Lisburne, daughter of the Earl of Rochester [by courtesy of the Earl of Lisburne].

Although Gogerddan was acknowledged as Cardiganshire's foremost estate and the Pryses, however diluted their descent, as the county's most influential family, the hiccups of inheritance gave space for other families to share power, particularly the Powells of Nanteos, the Lloyds, and above the rest, the Vaughans of Trawsgoed. John Vaughan, who became the county's first peer (albeit with an Irish title, Viscount Lisburne) in 1695, saw the possibility of outflanking the Pryses by absolute loyalty to the Protestant succession of William and Mary, and he engineered the replacement of a number of the county's JPs by his own nominees. He embraced the Hanoverian succession in 1714 after the death of Queen Anne, but his death saw a temporary decline in the family's influence, since his son John was a dissolute gambling womaniser who almost ruined the estate before dying in 1741.

Chapters in books are entirely artificial; there is of course no absolute break in the development of a society, even during a revolution. But looking back from 1715 to the Elizabethan period it is evident that, though the gentry still ruled, much had changed. English marriages and English education reorientated the Pryses, Vaughans and Powells, connecting them firmly with English society. A Vaughan and a Powell had achieved high office in the great law-courts of England; a Vaughan wielded political and legal influence in London. The bards who had still visited the great houses until about 1650 no longer trod the roads of Wales. The houses themselves were becoming more comfortable, more fashionable, and English had largely replaced Welsh as their mode of intercommunication, though many minor gentry probably still used the language in everyday life. The period saw considerable strengthening of governmental interference in Cardiganshire; the consequences of the Acts of Union were slowly being worked out. At the same time, little can have changed for the majority of the population, engaged as they were in the grim struggle for survival in a difficult environment.

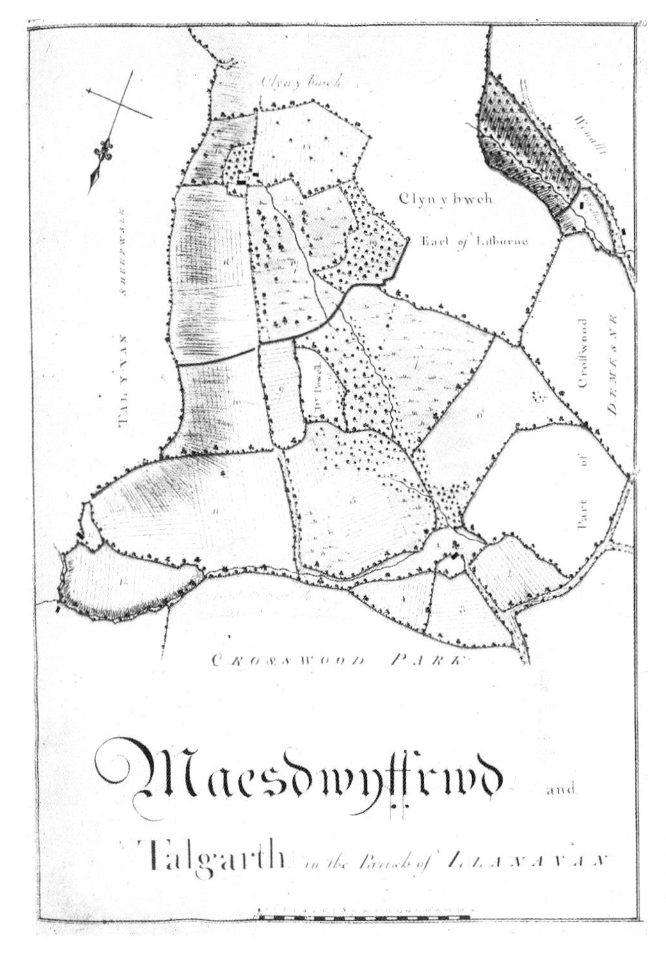

Maesdwyffrwd, mapped in 1781, was a tiny estate swallowed up by Trawsgoed before 1700.

[National Library of Wales]

10. Women's Lives in Cardiganshire

On 12 February 1667 John Vaughan of Trawsgoed, although a leading figure in the House of Commons and shortly to become Chief Justice of the Court of Common Pleas in London and a knight to boot, was at home in his Trawsgoed mansion listening, in his capacity as a justice of the peace, to depositions of evidence in a local case:

> concerning a felonious Rape praetended [= alleged] to bee committed upon the body of one Katherine Phillip of Blaenpennall . . . by Rees Thomas of Blaenpennal.

Cases of rape were rarely brought before the courts in 17th century Cardiganshire, probably because it was even more difficult to gain a conviction then than it is today. On the face of it, the case was simple. Katherine claimed that as she was walking home from a wedding on the morning of the 27th of the previous May, she had been dragged into an empty house by one Rees Thomas, and had made such efforts to resist his forceful advances that she fainted. She had gone straight home to her father, Phillip Pugh, and told him of the incident, showing the bruises she had suffered. However, she claimed that she had not realised that intercourse had happened until she found she was pregnant, a claim which a modern midwife would find unlikely. Rees Thomas, of course, claimed consent.

In the ordinary way it seems probable that any other young woman in such a case – assuming her to be innocent – would have had to resign herself to her wretched lot. However, Katherine was something of an exception. Her father Philip Pugh was a gentleman, a puritan, and a minor landowner, grandfather of Philip Pugh the minister referred to in Chapter 8. The loss of her honour would have been considered a blemish, rendering her less acceptable in the marriage market. It must be assumed that it was Pugh's social status which made him insist that the law should take its course, whatever the risk. Unfortunately the verdict in the case is not known, but it brings the plight of a Cardiganshire woman vividly to life. At least one case is known, from 1565, where a Caron man, Morgan ap Llewelyn, was sentenced to be hanged for breaking into a house and raping a woman, along with five men of Montgomeryshire. The housebreaking undoubtedly compounded the felony.

* * *

Before the mid-16th century there is only scanty surviving evidence about the lives of women in Cardiganshire. Women could not hold office under the Crown, there are few court records, no wills, no parish registers – only bald genealogies, which often disagree even on individual women's names, or simply omit them altogether.

Widows' names do appear in tax lists, but one cannot link them to their families. However, from about 1550 onward it is possible to know a good deal about women from several sources. As in the case of Katherine ferch Phillip, the records of the Courts of Great Sessions throw dramatic light on their lives.

Women appeared before the court at Cardigan as accused criminals, as defendants in civil suits, and as plaintiffs, though in that case they had to be represented by a suitable man, as was Katherine by her father. A woman without a male protector in case of need could be in great difficulties. Women also bore witness, though this involved appearing before a local Justice rather than at court. Women were accused of all kinds of offences, from infanticide to slander, from witchcraft to selling ale without a licence. Infanticide seems rarely to have been prosecuted; one of the few surviving Cardiganshire cases was that of Jane Evan, of no fixed parish, accused of murdering her bastard child in 1661. Again, the verdict does not survive. As for slander, in 1615 Elizabeth ferch Griffith Mason, a widow, was ducked at Cardigan as a common scold. Scolding, slandering, gossiping and fomenting of lawsuits are mentioned quite often in the court files, though women were as often victims of slander as perpetrators thereof; the mere accusation of a woman as being a witch or a whore could do her serious harm. Thus Thomas David and Katherine his wife brought a suit at Cardigan for slander against Thomas Bevan, since he had said *Witch, Witch, me vinna gweld dy grogy dy* (Witch, witch, I'm determined to see you hanged.') Jonet Owens, a widow, sued William Williams for £500 for saying *fe yddarfy y fy mam yn y gyfreth Ledratta tri oene a hi gynygodd share ohonynt ymmi* ('my [Jonet's] mother-in-law stole three sheep and offered a share to me [William].' He had to pay an undisclosed sum of money.

As for theft, while men most often stole farm animals, women stole clothes. In 1580 Margaret ferch John David Jenkin of Llanfihangel Genau'r-glyn stole seven kerchiefs, three shirts, a cloak and other garments from Jenkin David ap Ieuan, worth rather more than a pound, and was sentenced to be whipped. She could be considered fortunate; two centuries later she might well have been transported. Normally women seem to have stolen from other women, but one woman who dared steal a man's property was Eva ferch Ieuan of Llandysul, a spinster, who in 1566 stole goods from one David ap Ieuan Deio. Eva was found guilty, and asked how she pleaded. A man might plead benefit of clergy (in effect, the ability to read) and escape serious punishment, though his hand would be branded to ensure that he could not escape punishment for a second offence. Eva took the only resort open to a woman; she pleaded her belly, because the law was not willing to kill an innocent child when executing the mother. So the judge ordered the sheriff

> To bring her before . . . a panel of virtuous matrons of Cardigan who can establish the truth. She is to be palpated and inspected as the custom is to see if she is pregnant.

The list of matrons survives, and they were not impressed by Eva's plea; the words *non est pregnans* were inscribed on the writ. Whether punishment followed is not known.

Women could also give evidence as witnesses when depositions were made about any crime, and seem to have been as willing as men to accuse other women of offences, including witchcraft, though only one case is well documented for Cardiganshire, and that as late as 1691, when Katherine Rees of Nancwnlle was accused on obviously trumped-up charges. From the ludicrous evidence of the man who accused her, and the farrago of nonsense presented by the male and female witnesses who supported him, it is possible to extract a few facts which explain the hostility towards Katherine: she was a woman with a wall eye, a sharp tongue and an uncompromising manner – one of whom her neighbours were afraid.

The picture of women that emerges from the court records is obviously distorted, since most women never went to court, and in any case are far outnumbered by men in offences of all categories except slander. However, incidental references portray women as economically active, engaged in the cloth industry, working in agriculture, running ale-houses and involved in casual prostitution, as well as attending social functions, especially weddings.

Female innkeeper at a Llannarth inn, *c*1813; note the *crogloft* with ladder. [National Library of Wales].

Two other kinds of court records extend our knowledge. The court records include coroners' verdicts in scores of cases of sudden or unexplained death. Thus in 1551 Ieuan ap Rees of Lledrod murdered Elen ferch Griffith with a reaping hook; the poor woman lingered for three weeks before dying of her injuries. In 1565 Dyddgu ferch Jenkin was drowned in the Ystwyth, while in 1580 Alice ferch David of Llanddewibrefi hanged herself 'with a rope fixed to a beam'. Most inquests were on the deaths of men; of the women whose deaths were investigated most had either hanged themselves or accidentally drowned.

A different legal source bearing testimony to women's lives is the records of the Quarter Sessions, which only survive from 1739 onwards. The majority of cases recorded are to do either with pauper women and parish maintenance, or with unmarried mothers and the unwillingness of parishes to pay for their confinement and for the support of them and their children. In 1739 the overseers of the poor in Caron parish persuaded two JPs to allow them to move Anne Jenkins, 'a poor woman', to the parish of Llanddewibrefi, but the Quarter Sessions reversed the verdict, and charged Caron with costs. Diana Martin, 'a poor prisoner in the County Gaol' was to be allowed a pound towards her relief. At a second meeting, the justices decided that she should be discharged from prison, with two pounds from the county funds to assist her.

A major source of evidence is the wills made by Cardiganshire women, though since it was usually only widows and the occasional spinster who made wills, the source is imperfect. Widows who were the mothers of children only inherited a third of their husbands' goods, and since those might have to be used to pay debts, the widow's lot was not particularly happy, though she had a right to bed and board from her children. Though women had less to bequeath, they often made their wills in loving detail, naming individual items of property. Margaret ferch David of Tregaron died in 1568, and because she named Lewis ap Rees of Wiltshire as overseer (perhaps she was in England when she died), the will was proved in London. As well as five cattle and twenty sheep, she named her flock bed, coverlet, blanket, five pairs of sheets and one odd, two pans of seven and four gallons respectively, a three-gallon crock, a coffer containing the sheets, eleven pieces of pewter and a candlestick.

Wills were usually made on one's deathbed, and occasionally the scene can be recreated in some detail. Thus Margaret William of Caron was dying in April 1631. She was the widow of Rosser Jenkin, and Rosser's executors contested the will in the church court, claiming that Margaret had not been in her right mind. The lawyers drew up a questionnaire, to which the witnesses to the making of the will had to respond. Three local yeomen testified that Griffith Morgan, who had copied down Margaret's wishes, had at first doubted whether she was in her right mind, to which she had replied:

> It is somewhat dark. Light a candle. Although I am sick and feeble, yet I thank God I am of as perfect memory as ever I was . . . and she lifted herself in her bed and sat and then declared her will.

Many widows' wills and inventories of their goods demonstrate how they had to scrape a living as best they could: a cow, a few sheep, a salting trough and a flitch of bacon, a kneading trough for baking, all help to portray women getting by with occasional periods of casual labour on the land, assisting in childbirth, sitting with the sick, cleaning and watching by corpses, brewing ale, and when there was no more urgent task, forever spinning and knitting. Jane Daniell of Llanddewibrefi, who died in 1712, had survived thanks to her single cow, which she would have been able to graze on common land. Lesley Davison has cited the evidence of English travellers to show that in Wales women did not only care for cattle and poultry, but would drive the plough as well, supposedly a male-only task.

Clearly widows, who if they had children would have only inherited a third of their husbands' property, tended to be poor, but not always. Jane Vaughan of Cardigan was richer (at least in goods) than almost any woman in the county outside the gentry class, but her circumstances were difficult at the time of her apparently sudden death. Her husband had died intestate in May or June 1649, and Jane had found herself in charge of four young sons, a farm and the early modern equivalent of a supermarket. But the grieving Jane had little time to reorganise her life; she died only a few weeks later, having made a will in favour of her children, and a splendid inventory was made of her property. Her shop sold twenty-nine varieties of cloth, a dozen different kinds of buttons, whalebone stiffeners, ribbons, spices (ginger, cloves, pepper, cinnamon), whale-oil, gunpowder, saddlery ware, salt, hops, soap and leather girdles. It may be presumed that before her death her husband had spent more time dealing with the farm and Jane with 'my shoppe' as it is called in her will.

Wealthiest of all were the great widowed ladies of the county, such as Dame Gwen Pryse of Gogerddan, who died in 1637, leaving sums of money to local churches and to the maintenance of Aberystwyth bridge. Much of the money she left to her grandchildren was in the form of debts owed to the family, some of them not recent, and one may wonder whether every legacy could have been paid except as credit. More vivid is the will of Margaret Stedman of Strata Florida. She was a Breconshire heiress, whose great wealth (by Cardiganshire standards) is reflected not only in her 180 cattle, but in the splendid dresses she divided among her daughters, and the gold chain and bracelet, and gold collar with pearls, which she left 'as a relic of memory of my love' to her grandson John. However, even Margaret Stedman did not possess a diamond ring as did the widowed Maud Birt of Llwyndyrys, who died in 1671.

Dyddgu ferch David of Llangrannog, who died in 1630, was not of the same social status as the Pryses and the Stedmans, but she certainly died a wealthy widow. Much of her wealth lay not in her land, stock and farm and household materials, but in the amount of money she had lent out to some forty men and one woman from a dozen different parishes across the county. Such lists occur more frequently in women's probate documents than men's, suggesting that a number of women, including some who had little property, supplemented their incomes by lending money at interest, a useful service in a cash-scarce economy. Of these female money-lenders, the most remarkable was Mary Lloyd of the small estate of Ynys-hir, on the county's northern border. She died a spinster, and to judge by her inventory, she must have engaged herself in embroidery and cloth-working, since she left twenty yards of white serge, twenty yards of coloured flannel and eighteen turkeywork seats and backs for chairs. But these were of little value compared with the £564 cash she had out on loan, a remarkable sum.

* * *

Wills made by men also throw much light on women's lives, since they appear as wives, mothers, sisters, daughters and granddaughters. Rees Morgan of Lledrod in his will of 1662 names not only his father, brother and three nephews; he was generous to his mother, his four sisters and three nieces, all named. In particular, wives were often entrusted with carrying out the executorship, and usually did so rather than nominate a substitute as they were entitled to do. A woman as executrix, widow and mother had a great deal of work on her hands, and she would always take a male relative or neighbour with her on the journey to Carmarthen to have the will proved. When David Lloyd of Crynfryn, Nancwnlle, died in 1613, he left all his property to his wife in care for his eldest son, a minor, on condition that she kept and maintained the children, and did 'her best to maintain and keep my sons at school as she shall think fit'. His wife was one of four executors, but the others were not to act without his wife's agreement, nor she without theirs.

Men often stipulated that their wives should have their property only whilst they remained widows, losing most of their legacies should they remarry. This was not a matter of retaining male control from beyond the grave, but was the result of a practical concern for the dying man's children, who might find themselves deprived of property which should have come to them from their mother, if she were to marry again and have more children. Thus Griffith Lloyd of Llanllŷr, dying in 1583, left his only child Jane to the care of his wife, but should his wife remarry, then guardians were to have care of Jane and ensure a good marriage for her, rather than that she should be controlled by a stepfather.

Wives are sometimes described as 'dear' or 'beloved' in men's wills, though this may often have been common form. However, there is no doubt of the affection felt by Evan ap Henry of Llanfihangel Genau'r-glyn before his death in 1608, leaving his pathetic belongings to his daughter Margaret:

> As well for the natural love and fatherly affection I bear . . . [as] for her filial obedient and tender care of me her father, old and bedridden, being languishing after the death of her mother.

When Rees Vaughan, a minor gentleman of Pyllau in the Ystwyth valley, died a widower in 1637, he left among his property his late wife's cloak and 'safeguard', the hooked stick with which a woman lifted her skirts when walking on wet or muddy ground; these were obviously treasures by which he remembered her.

Men on their deathbeds who had wives who were known to be pregnant, or of child-bearing age so that they might be pregnant, would show concern about unborn children. John ap Edward ap John, who had married the heiress of Nanteos, believed himself to be on his deathbed in 1600, and so laid down that if his wife were with child, it should inherit £30 if male, £20 if female; in the event he did not die until 1607. Rees ap Jenkin David ap Ieuan of Llanfihangel-y-Creuddyn, dying in 1601, knew his wife to be pregnant, and decreed: 'to the child unborn whether it be manchild or a womanchild two heifers or two bullocks five sheep'.

Premarital sex is evidenced by an occasional probate reference: in 1584 Rees

Lewis of Troedyraur refers to 'my bastard son George Lewis, begotten on Anne daughter of Oates Ashurst, now my wife'; the boy was marked with illegitimacy for life, since his parents had not married until after his birth – why, we do not know. Marriage could not bestow legitimacy on a child born before the union was legalised. More unusual is the case of Catherine ferch Griffith, who lived as the concubine (the word is used in his will) of Lewis David ap Evan of Llanfihangel Genau'r-glyn, who died in 1612. She had borne him six children, half-siblings to his legitimate children. What had happened to his wife? If she was dead, why had he not married Catherine, whom he appointed his executrix? What did the legitimate children think of the equality of treatment given to the illegitimate? What did his legitimate son Morgan feel about the fact that the illegitimate son Philip was appointed to execute the will jointly with Catherine?

Women had to cope with the unfaithfulness of their men as best they might. Many men left bequests both to their legitimate and illegitimate children, though there was rarely parity of treatment. David Lloyd of Aber-mad in the Ystwyth valley, dying in 1631, left a wife and three illegitimate sons, one of whom, unusually named Brochfel, managed to make his way in the world and himself left a will. However, the estate went to Lloyd's grandson, James Lewis, his deceased daughter's legitimate child. Another long-suffering wife was Mary Vaughan, daughter of the earl of Carbery and wife of Sir Francis Lloyd of Maesyfelin. She bore her husband no children, and during her lifetime he conducted a sexual relationship with Bridget Leigh of Carmarthen. Bridget bore him two illegitimate sons before the death of Mary, after which he married Bridget, who then produced a legitimate daughter. Before his death in 1669 Sir Francis had ensured that his son Charles, though illegitimate, should inherit his estate despite his status. Women also had to deal with the illegitimate offspring of their own children. So Dyddgu ferch Nicholas of Cardigan, in 1608, left property and furniture to her granddaughters Mary and Esther, 'supposed daughters of Philip Griffith'. It is clear from the will that Dyddgu's daughter, mother of the two girls, was already dead, but that she felt no particular animus towards her daughter's lover is evident from the fact that she left him some furniture. However, she made her brother guardian of the younger girl, and his wife was to advise her.

There is a great deal of evidence in men's wills about the provision they made for their daughters' dowries, which could be a considerable burden. Thomas Pryse of Glan-ffraid in 1623 left his six daughters sums of £500, £400, £300 and three of £200 respectively, Whether these sums were ever paid over in cash is open to question; in some cases at least such dowries seem to have been simply notes of credit, to be drawn on at need. Even the poorest did what they could for their daughters. In 1635 Howell David ap Rees of Llanilar could only leave two or three cows to each of his six sons, but his only daughter Mary was to have four pounds in money as well as a cow, a heifer and a large chest. In the case of numerous daughters, the sums of money or numbers of farm stock bequeathed are largest in the case of the eldest daughter. This was not favouritism; the younger daughters would normally have longer to wait before marriage, and their money or stock could multiply in the meantime. If a daughter is named in a will, but only receives a token gift, it is because she was already married and had had her share.

Mothers-in-law appear in men's wills from time to time. In 1624 David Jenkin of Ystrad Aeron made a complex will dividing his property between his wife, his mother-in-law and his children. His wife was given the third part of his moveable property as was customary, along with the lease of a small property. The rest of his goods and chattels were divided with his mother-in-law taking half and the four children the rest. In 1655 David Lloyd Meredith, gentleman, of Cwm-bwa (Llanbadarn Fawr) appointed his mother-in-law Katherine Lloyd of Wern Newydd (near New Quay) one of three guardians over his children.

If a father had died without providing for his daughter, then a grandfather might help out, as did Griffith ap Ieuan Trahern of Llanddewibrefi in 1629, leaving his granddaughter Joan ferch Rowland 'forty pounds and a pair of bedclothes and wearing apparel fitting for her at her marriage, my Executor to find her meat drink lodging and apparel until she attain to the age of sixteen years or be married, whichsoever thereof shall first happen.' Grandmothers too might play a role, as we have seen in the case of Dyddgu ferch Nicholas cited above. Rees ap Rhydderch of Lledrod, who died in 1611, had eight grandsons by his three married daughters; he left his one unmarried daughter in the care of her three sisters, who were to keep her 'in meate, drinke, Lodging and apparell sufficientlye during her naturall lyf.'

The marriage market among the gentry class has already been discussed in a previous chapter, but it also deserves to be considered from the women's point of view. Some surprising characters appear as wives of Cardiganshire gentlemen. For example, the 54-year-old James Philipps of Cardigan Priory married in 1647 as his second wife the 16-year-old Katherine Fowler, daughter of a London merchant, who became famous as 'the matchless Orinda', poet and woman of letters, the centre of a circle of writers and admirers, and author of a remarkable poem in praise of the Welsh language. It seems likely that she spent much of her short life alternating between London and Cardigan, writing poetry and letters to her circle of friends. Her translation of a play by Corneille was the first drama by a woman ever to be produced on the London stage. She died in London of smallpox in 1664.

Katherine Philipps, the Matchless Orinda [National Library of Wales].

Untalented, but still interesting in view of their family connections, are the two daughters of Sir Bulstrode Whitelocke, a major figure in the politics of Commonwealth England. Following her mother's death when she was only 11, Elizabeth the elder sister had been sent to Mostyn relatives in Flintshire, and her marriage with Richard Pryse of Gogerddan followed through a family connection. When she was pregnant and depressed at Gogerddan she sent for her younger sister Hester, who fell in love with Richard's penniless younger brother Carbery, and as we have seen in a previous chapter, she married him against her angry father's wishes. Whitelocke's journal gives occasional glimpses of Elizabeth's loneliness in Gogerddan and of his grim tolerance of his unsatisfactory son-in-law.

A Pryse lady of Gogerddan, exact identity uncertain. [National Library of Wales]

Aristocratic women who gave birth without benefit of clergy were rare; two examples from Cardiganshire had very different fates. Bridget Pryse of Glan-ffraid was the lover of Edward Lloyd of Llanforda and mother of his child, the great scholar Edward Lhuyd (1660-1709). Lloyd, a married man, paid for his son's education and though Bridget never married, there is no surviving evidence that she had to endure any major humiliation. Much worse was the fate of a daughter of the first Viscount Lisburne of Trawsgoed. One Edward Jones wrote in 1739 from Worcester to Thomas Pryse at Gogerddan, asking him to intercede with his friend Lord Lisburne for the sake of his sister,

> who is now in great Want and distress about a month ago she came to this town with a young Child about eight Months Old from a place Calld Rhoss in

> Herefordshire the Child was only Lap'd up in a pice of flanen and she all in rags Like a begar Woman that comes from one doore to another . . .

This woman, unnamed in the letter, must have been the Letitia Vaughan who supported her brother, the dissolute second Viscount Lisburne, in the break-up of his marriage in the late 1720s. A lawyer in the case, scribbled on a document that she, not being married, was the mother of twins. Since her brother by 1739 was in the last stages of debauchery it seems unlikely that he took any action. Letitia Vaughan's fate makes a sad contrast with the wealth and security of Margaret Stedman.

Marriages were usually negotiated by fathers, whether at a gentry or a more humble level, though it would be foolish to assume that mothers did not have their say; indeed, in cases cited by Lawrence Stone in his studies of problem marriages, the mother kept the father in utter ignorance of the behaviour of his children, though evidence of that kind does not emerge from wills. Yeoman farmer Lewis David ap Evan, already encountered above, was on his deathbed concerned about his daughter Catherine. He had given thirty cattle and sixty sheep to John ap Rees David Goch as a dowry in anticipation of Catherine's pending marriage to John's son. Fearing that with his death the marriage-pledge might not be honoured but the dowry retained, Lewis David provisionally left the stock to be divided between his other children should the wedding not take place. As for negotiations at a higher social level, in 1720 William Powell of Nanteos was concerned about his son Thomas's apparent lack of interest in the opposite sex. However, Thomas mentioned to his father his interest in a Miss Mary Frederick, sister of Sir John Frederick and daughter of the wealthy London businessman Thomas Frederick of Westminster. William Powell lost no time; although personally unknown to the widowed Mrs Frederick, he wrote to her in the most polished and diplomatic manner, begging permission to bring his son to visit her and her daughter with a view to marriage, which duly took place; Thomas used his wife's large dowry to rebuild Nanteos in the fashionable Palladian style.

Fathers frequently laid down in their wills that their daughters should marry only with the consent of surviving relatives and friends. Guardians were often appointed, whose agreement also had to be sought. The sanctions against disobedience were fear of disapproval and loss of dowry. However, not every daughter was willing to obey either a dead or living parent. Take for example the wretched case of Jane Lloyd of Green-grove. This was a small estate in the Aeron valley, owned in the late 17th century by one Morgan Lloyd. He died in 1688, leaving his estate to his daughter Jane, wife of Charles Lloyd of Maesyfelin, who had a daughter, also Jane. After his wife's death, Charles Lloyd married again, and fathered two sons. Now the elder of the two boys was heir to Maesyfelin, but their half-sister Jane was still heiress of Green-grove, her mother's estate; Charles had control of it by his marriage, but not ownership. Jane's was a lonely life, dependent on the goodwill of her stepmother, while her father looked after her inheritance. No doubt he intended either that Jane shouldn't marry at all, so that Green-grove would pass to his son and heir, or that Jane should at least marry well.

But poor Jane fell in love quite unsuitably. The Lloyds were accustomed to exchange visits with the Cornwallis family, and the Cornwallises brought their servants with them, as one did when travelling and visiting. One of the servants was a James Tanner. Years later his brother Henry, a glovemaker, described going to Maesyfelin to see his brother, and finding him in the cellar with his arm round Jane Lloyd's waist. She said to Henry: 'Isn't your brother ungrateful, refusing me when I am ready to give myself and my fortune to him.' Then, when James agreed to marry her, she threatened that if he didn't keep his word, she would drown or burn herself, and haunt him to destruction afterwards. So Jane and James eloped to Llanpumsaint, Carmarthenshire, where a drunken priest agreed to marry them. He had to be bribed to get out of bed to perform this clandestine, midnight ceremony, and then the couple, with their witnesses, returned to Maesyfelin and got into bed together. The marriage, though clandestine, was legitimate.

Jane's father was outraged when he heard the news. James was summarily seized by Charles Lloyd's men and carried off to be pressed into the army as a common soldier, and then sent straight off to Flanders. Jane's case was taken to the bishop of St David's, thence to Lambeth palace, and finally the marriage was annulled. Jane was compelled to sell her inheritance to her father for £700, and she was married off to a Carmarthen lawyer, with the money as her dowry. Nothing better illustrates the power of the gentry in society and of the paterfamilias on his hearth.

Even though thus treated, Jane Lloyd's life can never have been quite as wretched as that of the indigent poor women of the past of whose misery so little evidence survives. Women have always been, and still remain, a much larger percentage of the poor than their numbers warrant. Evidence for their lives in the early modern period only comes into focus in Cardiganshire in the late 18th century, with the keeping (and survival) of parish vestry books, which recorded the taxes raised for the maintenance of the poor and the decisions made on their behalf. (See also Chapter 20 below).

A girl might begin her life in poverty with her birth to a single mother. In 1783 Evan David, farmer of Llety Twpa, Lampeter, agreed to take Lucretia John, a bastard child, for a period of ten years. The parish would pay him a guinea a year for the first five years; after that it may be assumed that the little girl, if she survived, would be expected to work for her living. When in 1792 the case of a pair of illegitimate twins came before Lampeter vestry meeting, the boy child was adopted by the paternal grandfather, while the girl was left to be supported by the parish. The next stage might be an apprenticeship; in 1779 William Davies of the Nag's Head Inn, Lampeter, took Mary Lloyd from the care of the parish, which paid him three guineas for giving her a five years' apprenticeship, with 7s 6d legal costs. Cast loose early, with no parental support and no dowry, the next stage might well be for a girl seeking love and comfort to become pregnant by an absconding male, and the sad cycle would begin again.

Jenkin Jones gives a grim eyewitness account of life at the bottom of the heap in 1819 after sheltering from the rain in a cottage near Aberystwyth. The wife was scraping a few potatoes for her husband and six children, and 'there was every proof of the poor woman's exertion to keep this hovel and her children clean', but there was only one chair, and the bed on which the whole family slept was 'some straw laid on a few boards and covered with a blanket.' This contrasts fiercely with his description of Mrs Evans, wife of the vicar of Cilcennin, who was 'a stout middle sized woman, looking as if she had worked hard, dressed in the homely woollen cloth of her own making and the round hat.' Her kitchen, heated by a peat fire, was 'well stored with sides of bacon, hams, hung beef and smoaked herings, ornamented in the fashion of all the Welch cottages, with the large well-polished pewter dishes and plates, and the brass dairy utensils, the which are always supplied by the bride's friends on the day previous to the marriage.' Mrs Evans's overwhelming hospitality included an offer to find her visitor a wife from among the local girls.

Less unfortunate than women who fell on the parish were the young unmarried women who in mid and later 18th century filled the majority of seats at Methodist society meetings, the *seiadau*, especially in mid and south Cardiganshire. William Richard reported in 1743 from Dyffryn Saith that 'Jane Rees had a plain Discovery of her Justification has walked much in Liberty, but now under some trials', while Margaret Thomas was 'under some Conviction, much in the dark.' From Lledrod came a report that 'two parties in the Society are intending marriage, and in the Lord as far as we can tell'. The collective excitement of praise in worship, the importance given to individuals and their problems in the *seiat*, must have been intoxicating for younger women, who normally lived a life even more restricted than that of their male contemporaries. No doubt too they hoped to find husbands who would be faithful in both senses of the word, would not get drunk, and who would pray with them rather than beat them. Wholly exceptional was Elizabeth Thomas of Blaen-porth, who was allowed by Howel Harris to act as leader or 'exhorter' in the privacy of the *seiat*. Women were otherwise debarred from any leadership role.

Evidence of abuse of women is rare before the 19th century, which of course does not mean to say that it did not happen. Jill Barber has researched the case of women farm servants in the 19th century, for which a good deal of evidence survives. Young women were regularly sent out to work in farms, and many were abused and raped. All the complaints of rape which survive in the archive of the Ystwyth valley Llidiardau estate (the Parrys were solicitors and local magistrates) concern female farm servants under the age of 20; complaints were often withdrawn, and of the men brought to trial, only 13% were found guilty. This is not surprising; for a start, rape was a hanging offence until 1842, and all-male juries could hardly be relied on to take an objective view; their own attitudes included the usual excuses: 'the woman tempted me', 'women secretly enjoy force', and 'it was only meant as a bit of fun'. On the other hand innocent girls were supposed to be ignorant about sex, and yet a modest refusal to describe what had happened could lead to dismissal of the case, because a demonstration of sexual knowledge meant automatically that the girl was unchaste. How farm girls, however innocent their lives, were supposed to be ignorant of sex when surrounded by horses and cattle, sheep and poultry is a mystery!

Some cases were truly appalling. In 1805 one Mary Morgan, aged 16, was executed for infanticide, though juries would often bring in verdicts of accidental death to avoid such a consequence. Jane Evans of Bow Street, aged 13 and pre-pubertal, was severely maimed in a sexual assault by a Gogerddan gamekeeper, Simon Frazer, but the case against him was thrown out; one cannot help suspecting Pryse influence as the true reason for this. In 1866 Sarah James, aged 11, had been raped by one Evan Davies; the defence cross-examined the girl about supposed sexual misdemeanours two and three years earlier, and the case was dismissed.

Young women were particularly at a disadvantage in dealing with unscrupulous employers and their sons. It was after all a crime to run away from one's master or disobey him. Farm employment often left girls in lonely situations; sleeping arrangements were often far from satisfactory, and the time of worship on Sunday mornings left the house quiet and gave predators a particularly good opportunity. Jill Barber has described one case where the farmer's wife actually urged her sons on to take advantage of the female servants. This must have been exceptional, especially in view of the increasing cult of respectability during the 19th century. There is a last extraordinary case of the *ceffyl pren* (see Chapter 14) being used in Lledrod in 1875 by the family of a wife whose husband had misbehaved with a female servant.

Women at the Trawsgoed harvest, 1888. [by courtesy of the Earl of Lisburne].

Pregnancy was of course a frequent consequence of this abuse, as well as of consenting sex as a result of 'bundling'. As ever, it affected the women rather than the men, who might seek to escape by moving or brazen out the consequences. Before 1834 a mother could go to the magistrates to swear an oath that X was the father of her child; it was then up to the constables to seek out the man and extract payments for maintenance, which was often difficult. In default of such support, the young mother (if, as might happen, she had been dismissed from her post and had no available family willing to maintain her) would go 'on the parish', and minimum regular payments would keep the child alive; if an orphan, it would be farmed out. A parish vestry would only pay if it was the woman's parish of last full employment; otherwise the officers would appeal to the magistrates to move the mother and child to her 'true' parish.

Women's work in 19th-century Cardiganshire was overwhelmingly domestic. Daughters would either be sent out into domestic service, though the lead mines employed a number of women, mostly in sorting and washing ore, or they might be kept at home to assist in the chores of home and farm, while learning the skills they would need after marriage. The never-ending chores for farm-women are described in Chapter 11; they caused several early 19th-century travellers to comment, as did one Mr Martyn on his tour of Cardiganshire: 'I cannot speak too highly of the industry of the Welch women nor of the Idleness of the Men.'

Census studies of women's employment are interesting, though rendered frustrating by lack of consistency; for example, the term 'housekeeper' includes daughters looking after their widowed fathers' households as well as widows looking after their children – and some of the latter group describe themselves as servants. The 1881 census for the parish of lower Llanfihangel-y-Creuddyn, demonstrates the general pattern for females aged 16 and over:-

Wife: 104
Servant: 44
Daughters-at-home: 33
Housekeepers: 29
Dressmaker: 15
Farmer: 5
Pauper: 3
Lead mine work: 2
Publican: 2
Others: 5 (subpostmistress, governess, visitor, widow, scholar).

Gogerddan serving girl.
[National Library of Wales].

To attempt a description of women's lot in 19th-century Cardiganshire would require a whole research project in itself. There is a great deal of evidence to be derived from newspapers alone, as well as from the growing documentation of local government and the census. While women's status in every aspect of public life remained wholly subordinate, increased access to education and therefore literacy, and the reforms brought about by the Divorce and Married Women's Property Acts, as well as slow improvements in sanitation and health-care, formed the foundations of the slow

20th-century revolution in the status of women throughout the kingdom. Such diverse changes as the slow reduction in the average size of families, improved domestic appliances, the bicycle and 'rational dress' all helped the process of liberation.

Among the first manifestations of women's activism was their involvement in the temperance movement. This, which had its origins in the United States, was originally a male-organised movement which welcomed female involvement, especially since women were the most frequent victims of domestic abuse as a result of drunkenness. One of the earliest Welsh branches was the Aberystwyth Auxiliary Temperance Society (1835) which had a number of women in its membership, and many women from the town, domestic servants included, signed the pledge in subsequent years. The British Women's Temperance Association, formed in 1876, had its origin in the Order of Good Templars, but for some time made little progress in Wales. The founding of *Undeb Dirwestol Merched Gogledd Cymru* (the North Wales Women's Temperance Union) in 1892 saw the movement gathering vigour, with a branch in New Quay. The veteran educationist, public lecturer and woman of letters Cranogwen (Sarah Jane Rees, 1839-1916) in her sixty-third year, 1901, led the movement in the south with the founding of *Undeb Dirwest Merched y De*, the South Wales Women's Temperance Association, which expanded successfully through the south, including Cardiganshire.

Ceridwen Lloyd Morgan has drawn attention to the natural link between the temperance and suffrage movements; the temperance movement, climaxing in the

A group of unidentified Aberystwyth suffragettes, *c*1905? [National Library of Wales]

Welsh Sunday Closing Act of 1881, was obviously political. Like the women's temperance movement, the suffrage movement in Cardiganshire has yet to be researched. There were occasional public meetings in favour of suffrage at Aberystwyth in 1874 and in 1895. Emmeline Pankhurst spoke twice in Aberystwyth in 1911, supported on the second occasion by a Mrs Davies of the Cymric Suffrage Union (ironically based in London); both meetings were chaired by Rachel Barrett of Carmarthen, an Aberystwyth science graduate. In 1913 a Miss Brown spoke at a public meeting of the Aberystwyth National Women's Suffrage Society; this was the non-violent women's movement, as opposed to Mrs Pankhurst's Women's Social and Political Union, which also had a branch in Aberystwyth at some stage. John Gibson, long-time editor of the *Cambrian News*, was a vigorous campaigner for women's rights.

* * *

Although the past conditions of Cardiganshire people's lives often reflect that dreadful verdict that most men were slaves, and women the slaves of slaves, and although the evidence is not as rich and as varied as a historian would like, it is clear that from the late 19th century many women's lives did improve thanks to the reforms already mentioned, to the slow diminution of poverty, and to the practice of birth control. Moreover, although many women suffered the wartime losses of sweethearts, husbands, fathers, brothers and sons (I think particularly of an acquaintance of mine, the late Mrs Mary Davies of Llanfihangel-y-Creuddyn, whose three brothers were all killed in World War I), they did not have to endure the appalling conditions and dangers of combat endured by so many men, nor the horrors of the Blitz. But the difficulties of wartime life in domestic circumstances, even in an area far removed from actual danger, are not to be lightly dismissed.

Women at Aberystwyth market, early 19th century. [National Library of Wales]

11. Growing, Getting and Spending

Tourists who cast a casual glance over the agricultural landscape of any part of Cardiganshire, whether green-hedged valley or bare and acid upland, may suppose that the appearance of this landscape has changed little for centuries, save for the upland planting of conifers and wind pylons. They would of course be entirely wrong. Even within living memory farms had their pigs and poultry, and many grew cereals and potatoes. The last generation of men who, as lads, drove horses has not yet entirely vanished, nor have all the women who once milked by hand and made butter and cheese. About 1990, on the uplands of Gwnnws parish between the Ystwyth and the Teifi, I saw sheaves of oats neatly arranged in a field, and spoke with the 90-year-old farmer who supervised the building and helming of stacks of rough hay in traditional manner. He remembered how as a boy he had driven a sow all the way to Llanfihangel-y-Creuddyn to be serviced by a boar, at a cost of seven shillings and sixpence. As recently as the early 1940s stallions were still being taken from farm to farm by the *gwŷr meirch* (stallion-men) to serve the mares.

Today the pigsties have no pigs, the old cowsheds no cows, the stables no horses, the farmyard no poultry, and the barn, if it is full of anything, contains silage. The passing of this agricultural heritage, its horses and machinery, was wonderfully elegised in the sonnets of Alun Jones ('Alun Cilie'). The old breeds are gone or altered, and a whole range of varieties of cattle and sheep, and crosses between those varieties, form the bulk of the stock. The farmer's wife probably works in the nearest town or welcomes summer tourists, and she buys her butter, milk and eggs in a supermarket. The corn mills are silent or have vanished altogether; the few surviving blacksmiths deal mainly with agricultural machinery and ornamental ironwork, and shoe only horses kept for leisure. All seems changed – not least, at the upland level, by the invading armies of conifer plantations and wind pylons.

However, an earlier half-remembered landscape of, say, 1920, with its neat hedges and mixed farming, had itself changed from earlier times, though it is certainly true that during the 20th century change accelerated. Travellers in Cardiganshire, from John

PERHAPS the greatest change of all has been in land ownership and the pattern of labour. In Cardiganshire in 1887, approximately 80% of farmland was tenanted and 20% in individual ownership; the demise of the greater and lesser estates had hardly begun. Even so, Cardiganshire had more owner-occupied farmland than any other county in Wales. Despite the dramatic increase in the sale of estate land, by 1906 the percentage of owner-occupied land actually dropped to 16%, and there was a similar fall in eight other Welsh counties. However, by 1970 the position was completely reversed, with almost 70% of land being owner-occupied, the highest percentage in Britain. All these figures suggest that Cardiganshire farmers have always been especially keen to occupy their own land. Over the same period the number of full-time farm labourers dropped to virtual extinction.

Leland in the 1530s to Benjamin Malkin in the early 1800s, spoke of a landscape more bare and open than we or our grandparents would recognise, while 17/18th-century road maps indicate much arable cultivation in the south of the county. In 1795 unenclosed land totalled over 200,000 acres; by 1853, despite popular resistance like that expressed at Trefenter against Augustus Brackenbury in *Rhyfel y Sais Bach* ('the war of the little Englishman'), five-sixths of those acres had been enclosed and parcelled into fields either by local agreement or by Acts of Parliament, with consequent hedging or walling. As late as 1780 some ancient enclosure was in the form of strips of land, *lleiniau* or slangs; a map of 1781 shows that the farms of Ysbyty Ystwyth were not compact units, but intermingled strips and small fields. This medieval landscape is still remarkably preserved at Llan-non, the best example in Wales. Much other land in the early modern period was cultivated in temporary strips, fenced off from open grazing ground by the hurdles which figure in numerous early 17th-century probate records. Some upland farms cultivated the little fields directly around the house, on which they would keep some stock during the winter to dung the ground for summer crops.

As for the bleak and barren uplands, Ceredigion's generous share of the Cambrian mountains, they too have changed drastically. In the far south-east of the county, bordering on the historic counties of Breconshire and Carmarthenshire, lies Fforest yr Esgob, the Bishop's Forest (the name doesn't necessarily indicate a great swathe of trees; 'forest' meant a hunting-ground). Part of the area is the mountain of Cnwcheithinog, which thrusts down between the rivers Pysgotwr and Doethïe towards Rhandir-mwyn. Terry and Heather James have walked this once-inhabited area and photographed it from the air as well as the ground. Their presently unpublished work shows extensive evidence for cultivation ridges over large swathes of the mountain, which cannot be detected except from the air, while several deserted settlements of uncertain date are visible on the ground. What was hunting ground and is now sheep-walk was once heavily cultivated – but at what period is as yet uncertain.

* * *

Our earliest documentary sources of knowledge about Cardiganshire farming are the records of Strata Florida abbey. The lands given to the monastery by the Welsh princes would have been bond-land which together with the bondmen (serfs) and their families, became the tax-free property of the monks. They organised the land into 'granges', areas which originally would have been supervised by monks or lay brothers and worked by the bond-men who were virtually tied to the soil and lived in grouped hovels; each grange had an administrative centre. The Cistercian order is usually credited with the improvement of sheep-farming in Britain, though it is hard to know how much difference they made in Cardiganshire, since we know so little of what went on before their arrival in the mid-12th century; certainly wool was an important product on the Strata Florida farms. With the 14th-century passing of the great Cistercian enthusiasm, the lay brothers disappeared and the monks were fewer in number, so that it was more convenient to rent out farms to tenants, usually on 99-year leases. The tenants paid the monastery various dues, mostly in oats, poultry, sheep and wool, but with a certain amount of cash as well. It is clear from the records that even in high Cwmystwyth the farmers were growing corn-crops which would sustain them and their families as well as their landlords.

Much used to be made by commentators of the phenomenon of transhumance, the spring transfer of stock from the lowland *hendre* or home farm to the upland *hafod* or *hafoty* for summer grazing, followed by a return in the autumn. That this was at some time a regular feature over much of Cardiganshire seems certain, but when did it cease? In a sense it has never entirely disappeared; some highland farms winter their stock on lower ground to this day. But the old system meant the involvement of much labour, and the use of a summer habitation. By 1530 the Strata Florida farms with *Hafod* names (most famously Hafod Uchdryd) were already permanently-occupied tenancies. Instead, on even higher ground the name *lluest* occurs, meaning a temporary establishment originally for summer-grazing. Some of the *lluestau* eventually became permanent farms under the pressure of land-hunger. In the valley of the Dilyw, a tributary of the Ystwyth, Lluest Dolgwiail had become a permanent farm by 1800 – probably earlier. It only fell into ruin after the brutal winter of 1947 broke the hearts of the occupants and drove them out. The high western slopes of Pumlumon and its outliers carried dozens of *lluestau* on land claimed by Gogerddan; tenants paid rent to the Pryses and installed their own shepherds to care for the flocks. Here and there the ruins of their rough homes protrude through the wiry grass where no one now would dream of living.

Estate archives, particularly those of Trawsgoed, tell us a good deal about tenancies, though of course not nearly as much as we should like to know. On the estates from at least 1550 if not earlier, tenancies were granted, not for 99 years as in the case of Strata Florida lands, but for periods of up to 21 years or for 'three lives', named at the time of making the lease. Several difficulties drove landlords to abandon the three-lives and fixed-period tenancies. Under such agreements the annual rent would be fixed for the whole period, meaning that inflation might well erode the value of the rent, although some evidence cited below suggests that from 1600 onwards prices of farm stock hardly

TITHE was a burden on Cardiganshire farmers; this levy of one tenth of a farm's annual produce (i.e. one calf out of every ten, one measure of hay out of every ten, and so on) had originally been a levy for the maintenance of the Church. However, in this county nearly all the tithes had been alienated and were in the hands of landowners. The dissolution of Vale Royal Abbey, Chester, meant that the tithes of the parish of Llanbadarn Fawr passed back to the Crown; by 1660 they were in the hands of the Palmer family, and in 1699 passed to the Chichesters of Arlington, Devon, who by the 19th century were drawing thousands of pounds a year from their tithe-tenants without even meeting their obligations as tithe-owners, which was to maintain the church's chancel in good repair and to pay the vicars properly. The Chichesters often had difficulty in collecting their tithes; there was a long dispute in the early 19th century, and the whole scandal became even more irksome as the Nonconformist percentage of the population increased.

rose at all during the 17th century. It was the landlord's practice to levy an entrance fee over and above the rent on the new tenant, or an inheritance fee (heriot) on a tenant succeeding his father, but this was not adequate to compensate for any anticipated inflation. Additionally it was feared that the tenant, especially if he had no heir in the offing, would squeeze everything out of his holding by the end of his tenancy, leaving the soil exhausted. So it was that by the early 19th century annual tenancies had almost entirely replaced the customs of old.

Leases give some insight into farming practice. Several Cardiganshire estates had farms which right up to the early 19th century paid rents partly in kind. In 1756 Robert Roberts of Grogwynion took a lease on his farm from Lord Lisburne which obliged him to pay £5.12.0d a year in rent, a hen and twenty eggs at Shrovetide and a goose at Christmas, as well as promising to grind his corn at Pontrhydfendigaid mill. Such rents were still being collected in the Ystwyth and Aeron valleys and at Gogerddan as late as 1820. Apart from rents, conditions might be laid down: the tenant might have to lay so many yards of new hedge every year, or maintain a dunghill, and not cut wood or in any way infringe the landlord's mineral rights. A particularly galling general restriction was that on the control of vermin; by law only heads of gentry families, their heirs and their gamekeepers could own and use guns. By the 19th century, if not before, rabbits were a plague in the land, but farmers and labourers could not even net or snare them, let alone shoot them. Poaching was rife; it was not only a source of protein for the pot, but a gesture against the perceived tyranny of the landowners, as will be seen in later chapters in the case of the poacher-murderer Wil Cefn Coch.

DROVES of cattle, sheep and pigs plodded every August for centuries from Cardiganshire farms to English fairs and south Wales markets. From Cardigan via Newcastle Emlyn to Lampeter, from the Aeron valley to Lampeter and Tregaron, from the northern farms to Tregaron, Pontrhydfendigaid, Pont-rhyd-y-groes or Machynlleth, the drovers and their hangers-on plied their trade to Shrewsbury, Worcester and Hereford, then on to London. The drovers, some of them Englishmen, were key figures in the economic life of the county, and were only displaced in the 19th century by the railways and in the 20th by the lorry. The Aeron valley drover David Jonathan kept a diary of his trade for the years 1842-81. Several of the drovers' routes are followed today by tarmac roads; others, like the route from Strata Florida past Teifi Pools, are now green and silent trackways.

For greater detail of early farming practice we must turn to the probate records – the wills and inventories which survive in increasing numbers from 1520 onward. They have their drawbacks, of course. Wills naturally name the individuals involved, and the parish in which they lived, but only in the case of wealthy gentry are their homes named. This is particularly frustrating in the case of the county's largest parishes, only divided centuries later; Llanfihangel-y-Creuddyn stretched virtually from the sea-shore to the mountain boundary with Radnorshire. Llanbadarn Fawr was vast, and Caron too was huge. An inventory listing ten cows and fifty sheep might derive from a small lowland farm or a larger upland farm. True, some properties are named, but except in particular cases they are usually lands involved in mortgage rather than the testators' homes.

There are other difficulties with

inventories and wills, because the documents can sometimes be inconsistent with each other. In 1616 David ap Jenkin ap John of Caron parish left seven sheep in his inventory and virtually nothing else. In his will, however, he bequeathed a cow; the inventory was presumably incomplete – or had the cow been sold at his death? At the other end of the scale of wealth was Phylip ap Howell of Ysbyty Cynfyn, ancestor of the Powells of Nanteos, who at his death in 1589 left 132 cattle and 600 sheep. In his inventory there is no reference either to corn or to implements of husbandry; nevertheless, he was owed substantial quantities of corn which he had lent to 13 different individuals. Nor is it possible to imagine that a man farming on such a scale was *not* growing corn; again, the inventory is incomplete. Another, more speculative problem, is that of a man's age at death. True, it is possible to suppose that on average a man who names young children in his will may well be comparatively young himself. But a man who leaves little property may have in fact been originally more comfortably off, but having provided for his sons and daughters, and being himself past his prime, he may have retained no more than what was necessary for subsistence in old age.

Despite these problems, leases and wills, and especially inventories, still offer more information than any other single source about agriculture prior to the first descriptions of Cardiganshire farming, which date from the second half of the 18th century. Rearing stock was obviously the first priority then as now, and care was often taken in detailing cattle in particular, by age and price. Although prices tend to to be consistent, there are exceptions. Inventories of substantial gentlemen tend to value stock at higher prices. Thus Rheinallt Jenkins of Carrog, a gentleman of Llanddeiniol (d.1618), owned animals which were virtually all valued at higher prices than those cited in the rest of this paragraph: his best cows were priced at £1.13.4d each, his oxen at an average of £2 each and his sheep at four shillings each (double the usual two shillings). In general, cattle are classified as oxen, 'great kine' (meaning mature milch cows), steers, yearlings and calves, while bullocks and heifers are often detailed by age. Bulls are rarely mentioned. The values given are surprisingly uniform, although they correspond to what little is known of west Wales market prices. Oxen are the most valuable stock, usually at £1.3.4d, with milch cows at £1 and the rest between 15s and 5s according to age. There are puzzling references to 'wild beasts', even to 'wild beasts on the mountain', which suggest a measure of transhumance. References to

GOATS, those symbols of Welshness, are mentioned frequently in the years up to 1640, valued at a shilling each, half the value of sheep; after that date they become rarer and had nearly vanished by 1700. Pigs are mentioned fairly often, but poultry, which must surely have existed on most farms, are not mentioned so frequently, perhaps because they were so cheap; when they do occur, it is usually as 'poultry' or 'cocks and hens', with geese mentioned occasionally and ducks very rarely. Remarkably, turkeys occur in the inventory of David Lloyd of Crynfryn in 1613, having arrived in Britain from America only a generation or so earlier (the inventory of Sir Edward Littleton, a Worcestershire gentleman who died in 1586, mentions turkeys), and they occur again in later gentry inventories. Hives of bees were valued at a shilling or 1s 4d each.

individual cows left as legacies may detail them as red, pied or brown, but it is clear that the majority of cattle were black. Sheep are less categorised than cattle, and rams hardly ever mentioned. However, some inventories detail lambs, wethers, yearlings and 'old and poor sheep'. Lambs and old sheep were valued at a shilling each, good sheep at 2s each, wethers at 3s 4d. The 74 'milking ewes' owned by David Lloyd of Ffosybleiddiaid in 1714 constitute a rare reference to what may have been a common practice.

Many but not all inventories mention horses, sometimes in detail as geldings, 'labouring nags', mares, fillies and colts. 'Horse' seems often to mean a stallion. Prices varied between five shillings and one pound. One would hardly suppose from this evidence that Cardiganshire would eventually become an important centre for horse-breeding, with fairs at Lampeter and Llanybydder attracting buyers from afar, reaching a peak in 1910 with the shipment by rail of 1,100 horses from Ffair Ddalis, Lampeter. In the earlier period ploughing was done not by horses but by oxen, which were only gradually replaced by horses. It must be assumed that the known practice of later centuries, whereby small farmers would have their ploughing done by their larger neighbours' animals, in return for labour, was already the custom. Alternatively, some ploughing was probably done by the terrible drudgery of the breast-plough, an instrument forced through the soil by the ploughman himself.

It is not as easy as it might seem to use the price of animals in inventories to check on inflation. While the stock prices of 1600-20 are fairly consistent throughout the county, prices in the 1660s are less so. Thus Morris John Prichard of Llanbadarn Fawr in 1662 had his bullocks valued at a pound each, a higher price than earlier in the century, while his cows were unchanged at a pound each, and his calves were priced at only a shilling each. Phillip Griffith of Llanbadarn Fawr

Ffair Ddalis, Lampeter. [National Library of Wales]

(1662) had his sheep valued at only eighteen pence each, less than the previous two shillings a head, though of course his fifteen animals may have included lambs. By the end of the 17th century prices are still low, but erratic. Hugh David of Llanilar (1693) left oxen of a greater value than in 1600; they were priced at £1.15.0d each, but his milch cows were only a shilling a head more valuable than the usual 1600 price. Edward Lloyd of Cwmnewidion (1714) had oxen valued at three pounds a head and his sheep at three shillings a head, but his lambs were still a shilling each. David Lloyd's milking ewes, referred to above, were valued at three shillings each. By 1765, however, it is clear that prices, at least on a gentleman's farm, had risen further. John Griffiths of Pantyswllt, Llandysiliogogo, left a pair of oxen valued at £7.10.0d and a lesser pair at £5.10.0d, while his cows were priced at £2.10.0 each and his sheep at four shillings a head. Occasional references to stock bought at fairs, and surviving details from Pembrokeshire fairs which are lacking for Cardiganshire fairs suggest that probate values were usually fairly close to market prices.

Although details of trade in early Cardiganshire fairs are mostly lacking, there were plenty of fairs in existence from the 13th century onwards, and they were the fixed points in the agricultural year by which the passage of time was measured, even though fairs were not necessarily fixed occasions over the centuries. Five fairs on feast days of the Virgin Mary were gradually established in medieval Cardigan, lasting until the 19th century, save that the August fair (of the Assumption) moved to June. Llanbadarn Fawr's fairs were eventually merged with those of Aberystwyth. Cribyn's fair of St Silin and Dihewyd's 'Ffair Ddalis' were moved from their respective villages to Lampeter. The most famous fair in the county was Ffair Rhos, where the Strata Florida fairs outlasted the monks by centuries before moving to Pontrhydfendigaid and eventually fading away. Other major fairs long vanished were those once held at Capel Cynon (between Synod Inn and Llandysul), at Llanrhystud, Lampeter, Llandysul, Ponterwyd, Tal-y-bont and at Adpar. In 1671 the Birt family of Llwyndyrys sold cattle at Abergwili, Llandysul, Capel Cynon, Cardigan and Newcastle Emlyn fairs.

Some fairs were occasions for selling sheep, or cattle, or horses; others were more general, for the sale of home-knitted stockings, beer, farm tools, domestic and

Cardigan Fair notice. [National Library of Wales]

kitchen implements, cheese, clothes and cloth; some were hiring fairs, where men and women hired themselves out to farmers for a year's service. Fairs offered a rare opportunity for a break from the daily grind of work for both men and women, and could on occasion be the scenes of savage fighting; in 1627 at Ffair Rhos, Evan Rees had his skull split open by William David ap Rees of Radnorshire, who was wielding a billhook and claiming: 'he stole forty of my sheep, and if he's dead there's no harm done!'

A particular puzzle occurring in wills and inventories of the period up to 1700 is that of animals in separate keeping. In 1589 Phylip ap Howell left to his son Thomas seven cattle 'now in the keeping of Ieuan Lewis', and to his daughter Elen cattle, sheep and a horse in the keeping of four different men. There are scores of examples of this practice. Why did Cardiganshire farmers, greater and lesser, so often have much of their stock in the care of others? Was it a matter of sickness or old age, naturally to be associated with the time of will-making? Was it a matter of transhumance, of animals being on pastures rented from others? Was it, as is provable in the case of Maenarthur farm in the 1650s, that a landowner might rent out not only land, but the stock as well, to be repaid in ten years' time with animals of equivalent worth? Is it possible that these references are related to the previously-mentioned 'wild beasts', to animals 'on the mountain', 'in the forest' or to the 1636 entry in the inventory of David Rees of Llanychaearn for his '14 heads of sheep which be a herding in the Commons'? The only answer specified in any will I have yet read is to be found in that of Edward ab Evan of Llanfihangel-y-Creuddyn (1607). Under debts due to the deceased is a list of eight cattle owed him by Hugh ap Rees, 'which I deemed to be kept for part of this summer unto the said Hugh, and he was to redeem them upon demand and to have one quarter of pilcorn for the keeping of them.' So it seems likely that in some cases men were leasing out animals, with the lessee paying for them out of profits from calves and lambs, while in others they were simply paying others to care for them.

Corn is mentioned often in inventories, hay less often. Corn is often detailed as barley, oats, or the less common rye, but very rarely as wheat. Distinction is made between 'corn in the barn and haggard' and 'corn in the ground', or in one case 'winter corn in the ground', and pilcorn, a mixture of barley and oats, is often mentioned. Occasionally more detail is available. Richard ap Lewis of Llanfihangel-y-Creuddyn (1616) left corn in ricks and barn, and three acres of rye in the ground. Watkin Morgan of Abertrinant (1628), a richer man by far, had four acres of rye, 26 acres of oats and half an acre of wheat all in the ground. Other inventories refer to 'corn in the ground £6', '3 bushels of oats and rye in the house'. Quantities could be substantial; Rheinallt Jenkins of Carrog, already mentioned above, left twenty-five pounds' worth of corn in the haggard and barn, and an additional stack of corn is valued at £4.6s.0d, indicating how productive Carrog was.

The agricultural implements necessary for the growing of corn are rarely mentioned in these early modern Cardiganshire wills, but there are references to 'a plough and one harrow', 'one plough, two harrows with irons', 'winnowing sheets' and to 'implements of husbandry'. Watkin Morgan's inventory is a rare example of great detail in the matter of implements: he had two ploughs, six harrows, shovels, spades, pickaxes, hatchets, axes, hurdles, and a turf-iron for cutting peat. Unique among the hundreds of wills I have read is the reference to two pounds owed to Griffith Thomas of Llangeitho (1630) 'for his pains in ploughing other lands'. Another rarity is the 'dunghill or mixen' of John Meredith of Llanfair Clydogau (1631) valued at ten shillings, though every farm certainly had one. More common are references to 'cars', namely *ceir llusg* or wheel-less drag-sleds. No early Cardiganshire will has yet yielded vehicles like those of John Griffith, priest of Trefgarn in Pembrokeshire, who in 1603 owned 'one ironbound cart with two bodies, viz. a dung body and a long body'.

Other than corn, farm produce is rarely mentioned in the inventories, though obviously it was common enough. In 1632 Edward Lloyd of Llanfihangel-y-Creuddyn died possessed of quantities of wool, cheese and butter. There are occasional reference to beef and bacon. Quantities of malt were kept in store for home brewing. In 1605 Rees David ap Llewelin of Cardigan left, as well as his nine cattle and two pigs, and a good deal of corn, 'the fruit of a garden' valued at ten shillings, not to mention two stones of cheese.

THOMAS Johnes was not alone in his enthusiasm for improvement; the demesne farm of Werfilbrook, Llangrannog, owned by the Revd Lewis Turnor, was highly praised by Samuel Rush Meyrick in 1810. The English enthusiasm for turnips did not fire Cardiganshire's farmers, who believed their soil too poor and the expense too great to be worth the effort. The Turnor family played an important role in the county's farming. Lewis Turnor's father, the Reverend David Turnor (1751?-99) bought Wervilbrook and was one of the founders of the Cardiganshire Society for the Encouragement of Agriculture and Industry. He collaborated with Thomas Lloyd of Bronwydd to write *A General View of Agriculture of the County of Cardigan* (1794).

* * *

By the middle decades of the 18th century some attempts were being made to improve Cardiganshire's agriculture, reflecting new English practices. Abernantbychan tenants in 1739 were obliged to plant oak, ash, elm or sycamore trees yearly, and the agent recommended enclosing fields and liming the soil. The county's Agriculture Society was founded in 1784 by a group of landlords, but Samuel Rush Meyrick in 1810 commented that improvements had been 'rather limited', for which he blamed absentee landlords. The most enthusiastic improver was Thomas Johnes of Hafod, one of the Society's founders, who from 1780 attempted what was little short of a revolution on his estate. He planted vast areas of trees, he brought in cattle from Holland ('my Dutch ladies') and housed them in better conditions than most labourers and small farmers enjoyed. He published, in English and in Welsh, *A Cardiganshire Landlord's Advice to his Tenants*, advocating the rotation of crops, drainage, the planting of turnips and the proper use of lime. He claimed to be able to improve the exhausted upland soil from a rental value of two shillings per acre to forty shillings per acre. Johnes vainly petitioned the government to have families from Switzerland brought in to replace some of his tenants, whose conservatism exasperated him. Nevertheless, the government acreage report of 1801 referred to below observed of Cardiganshire that its agriculture was fifty years behind the rest of south Wales, particularly because of the shortage of lime and culm.

Similar comments had been made in a government report of 1794, which contrasted what the authors felt was the valuable potential of the county with the 'bad husbandry' and 'wretched management' of its farmers and the quality of their implements, e.g. 'the ploughs are too bad for description'; 'the farm houses are, almost without any exception, placed in the very worst situations for conveniency and profit'. The report was particularly sympathetic towards the farm labourers, abominably badly paid, overworked, underfed and living in hovels. The report provides particularly valuable data on the destinations of produce: 'the black cattle are all taken to Kent and Essex; the pigs and salt butter to Bristol; and the barley and oats to Bristol and London'; livestock went overland, produce by ship. At this time, as the report observes, much of the upland was still open country, unenclosed, which was beneficial to the poorest people scratching a living as best they could, but it was soon to change.

Many details of these changes are lost to us for lack of documentation. For example, although landlords had been far from ruthless in combining small uneconomic tenancies to form larger units, preferring their status as lords of many tenants, and although Cardiganshire is short of documentation before 1780, the process of change can be traced on maps. For example, the 1781 map of Wenallt farm in the Ystwyth valley shows clearly that this one farm had swallowed up holdings whose names survive as field-names: Trawsgoed Uchaf, Tyddynyfedw and Tŷ-cam. What the landowners were especially keen to do in the late 18th and early 19th centuries was to exchange lands in order to consolidate their holdings and remove anomalies such as the hay-strip belonging to Hafod Uchdryd in the middle of Trawsgoed's home demesne. But changes greater than these were being brought about by outside forces.

These changes were surveyed for the recently-established Board of Agriculture by Walter Davies, assisted by Edward Williams; the two are much better known by their bardic names, Gwallter Mechain and Iolo Morganwg. Gwallter had been commissioned in two stages to survey the whole of Wales, a task which took him from 1802 till 1815, when the report on south Wales, including of course Cardiganshire, was published. He took particular interest in those estates where improvements were being attempted by the owners, especially Thomas Griffiths, vicar of Llandyfrïog, secretary of the county Agricultural Society, and his brother David, both farming in the lower Teifi valley, as well of course as Thomas Johnes at Hafod.

In 1801, during the tremendous struggle with France which lasted from 1793 to1815, the government attempted to survey the crop acreage of England and Wales, parish by parish. The chosen crops were wheat, rye, barley, oats, potatoes, peas, beans, and turnips or rape. In Cardiganshire only the upland parish of Ysbyty

Ystwyth grew no wheat whatsoever, while Llanbadarn Fawr had 482 acres of wheat, 182 of rye and more than a thousand acres each of barley and oats. Rye had become a rare crop by this date; a third of the county's parishes grew none at all. Only one parish had more than a hundred acres of potatoes, but a good deal must have been grown in cottagers' gardens; at a pinch they could be imported from Ireland. Llanrhystud, in addition to its extensive acreages of barley (649) and oats (630), grew 240 acres of peas. Beans were hardly grown anywhere, and the only significant acreage of turnips (49), was in Llandygwydd, encouraged by Thomas Lloyd of Bronwydd. The county's tithe maps of the 1840s confirm the considerable extent of arable land in the county at the time, and although acreages certainly declined with the arrival of cheap wheat from the New World, mixed farming, with stock rearing very much in the ascendant, was still practised as late as the 1940s at low and medium altitudes. Perhaps the best evidence for the growth of corn in the early 20th century is the existence of eighty working corn-mills in the county in the 1920s. At the time of writing, however, virtually the only corn grown is maize for fodder.

Tato! Tato! Tato!

Y mae llwyth llong o Dato iachus at had, newydd ddyfod i

LANGRANOG,

o'r Ywerddon; ac ar werth bob dydd tra y parhaont,

GAN OWEN JONES,

RHIPINLLWYD,

am bedwar swllt a naw ceiniog y cant.

Ebrill, 1862.

M. THOMAS, ARGRAFFYDD, HEOL-FAIR, ABERTEIFI.

Importing potatoes from Ireland, 1862. [National Library of Wales]

19th century parliamentary enclosure, N.E. of Cellan.
[Crown copyright: Royal Commission on Ancient & Historical Monuments, Wales]

PARLIAMENTARY enclosure in the 19th century affected Cardigan Common and the parishes of Gwnnws, Llanrhystud, Lledrod, Llanfihangel-y-Creuddyn, Llanddeiniol, Llanychaearn, Llanfihangel Genau'r-glyn, Llangynfelyn, Nancwnlle, Cellan, Llanfair Clydogau, Lampeter, Llangeitho, Llanddewibrefi and the district of Rhos-y-garth, south of Llanilar. These enclosures can sometimes be recognised by the chessboard pattern in which the fields have been arranged. Some enclosures were small, others extensive, like the 1812 enclosure of Rhos Haminiog (5,000 acres) south of Llanrhystud and the 1815 enclosure of 10,000 acres in eight parishes east of Llanrhystud. The piecemeal sale of Cardigan borough council's commons was only completed in 1870.

Agricultural enclosure, the division of open lands and strips into hedged fields, is an ancient process which could be carried out by the landowners' agreement, and records rarely survived. However, in the modern period it became a matter for Parliament. Many of these enclosures brought hundreds of men, women and children out in protest to threaten the surveyors with hideous fates and to steal their equipment. Soldiers had to be stationed at Aberystwyth and Lampeter from 1816; the county's magistrates were pathetically inadequate to their task. Common and waste-land were of particular value to a growing population of landless people desperate for a few acres of land, however poor, on which to survive.

To remedy his wretched situation a man might seek to create a *tŷ unnos* on marginal

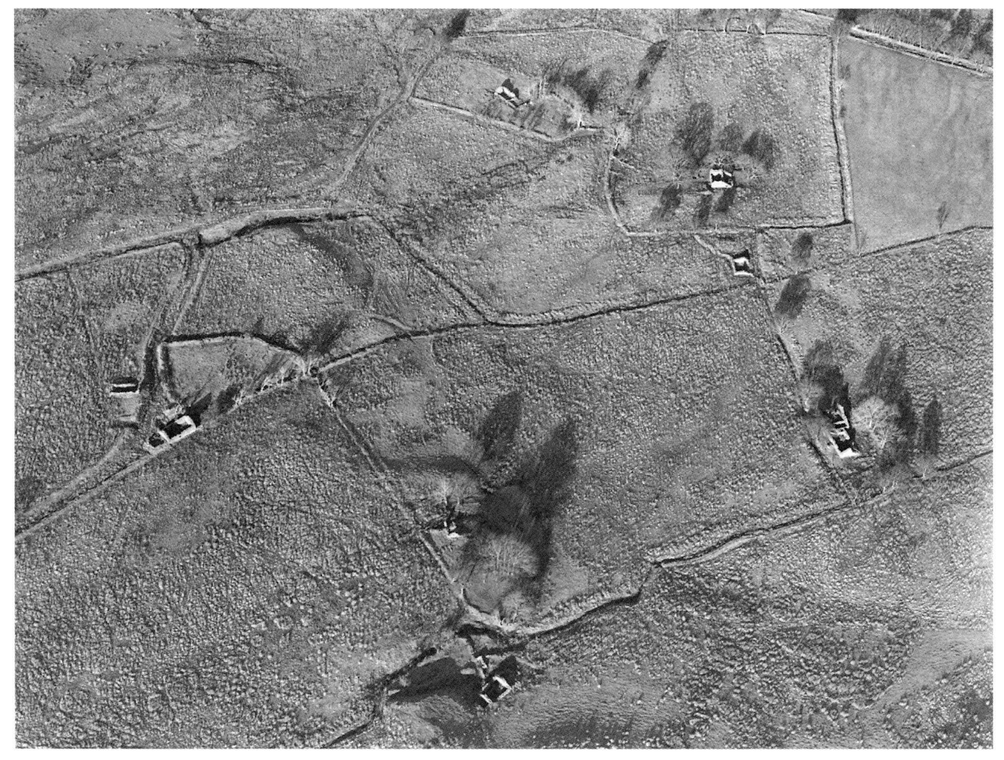

'Tai Unnos' (squatters' settlements) Bryngwyn Bach, Tregaron.

land, by a roadside or on common land. The common belief that the practice of building a clod-house overnight gave a man right to an axe-throw of land roundabout was popularly attributed to the law of Hywel Dda, but without the slightest foundation. A map of squatters' enclosures in the parish of Ysbyty Ystwyth in 1836 shows dozens of these places, and they are indeed round, suggesting that the 'axe-throw' was taken seriously. A year's occupancy was believed to give freehold to the squatter, who then rebuilt his turf-walled hovel in more substantial form. The hamlet of Cnwch-coch in the parish of Llanfihangel-y-Creuddyn was entirely created by squatters after 1781 on a small area of common land jointly owned by the estates of Cwmnewidion, Nanteos and Trawsgoed, and within clear view of Trawsgoed's front door. Even the wrath of the first earl of Lisburne did not succeed in evicting them; by the time of the tithe map the little tenements were freehold. Indeed, the parish might even give assistance to a squatter: in 1815 the Llanilar parish vestry loaned eight pounds to John Morgans of Llangwyryfon to pay the costs of his house Rhosgron 'on Wasteland'. Thus, with his promise to repay, Morgans ceased to be a burden on his parish rates; whether he ever actually repaid is not known.

The best-known case of popular unrest caused by enclosure is that of Augustus Brackenbury's attempts between 1820 and 1828 to enclose lands on the western slopes of Mynydd Bach and to build himself a mansion, which provoked *Rhyfel y Sais Bach* (the war of the little Englishman). This arose from an enclosure Act of 1815 covering six parishes south of the river Ystwyth. The enclosure commissioners were able to sell land to cover their costs, and it was thus that Brackenbury bought 850 acres, presumably with a view to their sporting rights. His first house was soon burnt at night by a mob, and it was in vain that the magistrates offered £100 reward for information. Brackenbury returned in 1826 and built another house, this time with a moat and tower. A mob soon captured the house in its owner's absence in Aberystwyth, looting it so thoroughly that there was little left. Soldiers were now drafted into the area, and a number of men were arrested, but their fate is uncertain, though it may be that the jury acquitted them. Brackenbury tried yet again in 1828, building a third house on a new site, but after two years of peaceful occupation he sold up and left.

It was not only the enclosure of waste or common land which caused difficulties. There had long been a tendency for smaller freeholdings to be swallowed up by larger neighbours, with the subsequent abandonment of the domestic accommodation. Some landowners became increasingly ready to join together small vacant tenancies to form a larger unit. Such practices seem to have been unusual before 1800, but as the century progressed, landowners were being forced to retrench, an economic trend which was reinforced, as Richard Moore-Colyer has argued, by the social and political changes of the time which increasingly separated owners from tenants – changes which included ever more rigid enforcement of the Game Laws. Even so, ancient practices died hard; the leases for three lives so prevalent before 1800 were not entirely replaced by yearly agreements, at least for cottages, and we have already seen that the medieval food-renders on several estates continued to be paid well into the 19th century.

Rents in Cardiganshire tended to be high in comparison with many other areas; this was mainly the result of land-hunger caused by population growth. It meant that there would usually be competition for vacant tenancies even when the rent might be so unreasonably high that the new tenant would in his turn be forced to beg for relief or vacate. This was not in the landowners' better interests, and they or their agents would frequently offer rebates or postponements, rather than either send in the bailiffs or permanently reduce rents. Most tenants had to engage in long struggles with landlords and agents about who should bear the expense of improvements; this was one of the issues which eventually led to the setting up of the Royal Commission on Land in Wales in the 1890s.

* * *

A report on sheep-farming in Cardiganshire published in the *Aberystwyth Observer* in 1864 gives a lively idea of problems and practices. The annual rent of sheep-walk land was between sixpence and a shilling per acre. Mountain tenants wintered many of their sheep on lowland holdings, bringing them up in the spring; after lambing and shearing, the sheep were left to themselves until Michaelmas, when wethers were sold to English butchers and graziers. Too much land was overstocked and undrained; shelters were not provided and no burning done. Any Englishman taking a tenancy would be driven off by his neighbours' combining to drive cattle and horses onto the unwanted neighbour's land to graze, thus ruining him. The report's recommendations for improving the situation would meet with any modern farmer's approval.

As for grain, although prices in Britain were affected by the growing imports of cheap cereals, most Welsh farms were little affected, since so much of their grain was grown for their own consumption. But the arrival of refrigerated shipping in the 1880s brought in cheap meat, and thus directly hurt the stock rearers of Cardiganshire. Rent rebates, either permanent or temporary, were necessary, thus reducing the incomes of landowners who were also facing increased taxation and contemplating their weakening political power-base as Liberalism drove out Toryism. The sale of estates was nothing new, but there was a sudden growth in the numbers of farms sold off and a shrinkage of the great estates, described in another chapter. In 1887, 19% of the county's agricultural land was owner-occupied; by 1970 it was 69%, the highest percentage in Britain. In the opinion of some this was not necessarily to the good. An English expert visiting the county in 1913 was told: 'the worst farmers were the small men who owned their own land, because, as owner, a man gets careless and neglectful about matters for which he would be taken to task if a tenant.' But this may also have been because the mortgage involved in buying land was a greater drain on resources than paying the rent, and so the farmers were unable to invest in their holdings. John Davies suggests that the change was partly responsible for some of the peculiarities of the county's demography, by which tenants forced their children to remain at home, unmarried, thus creating childless sibling households, a phenomenon which survived well into the second half of the

20th century. Meanwhile the shortage of tenancies meant that the ladder from labourer through smallholder to farmer was rendered ineffective.

Mr Unwin of Tŷ Mawr taking feed to sheep sheltering in Cwm-du. Note the lazybeds centre-left.

It was not only the change of land ownership which revolutionised Cardiganshire farming: it was permanently changed by mechanisation. Even before 1800 change was affecting farm work; John Davies of Ystrad Aeron noted in his diary in 1798 that he had seen 'the Buckwheat plowed with a new plow English fashion with foure Horses.' A steam-powered threshing machine was operating in the south of the county by 1875, though it was actually pulled from place to place by horses; a traction engine for the purpose only arrived in 1905. Hay-mowers arrived about 1890, tedding machines, potato diggers, corn-reapers and self-binders had followed by 1914. Some machines encouraged social co-operation in work-groups, but others, especially the self-binder, had a negative effect. David Jenkins has described the consequences; how 'the knot that bound farmers and cottagers together was severed', since the work-groups which helped on each farm at harvest were no longer necessary, and the cottagers no longer set potatoes on farmers' land. The horse, however, remained essential until the spread of tractors in the 1940s, a development which was accompanied by the almost total disappearance of mixed farming. Dairying and stock-rearing became the staple of Cardiganshire agriculture. Welsh Black cattle had served both purposes for centuries, but Shorthorns and even Jerseys had begun to appear before the end of the 19th century, improving the milk yield. More drastic change came in the 1920s and '30s with the replacement of butter-sales by bulk milk-sales. Associated with this development was the disappearance of dairy-maids; social change made it easier for young women to leave the land for alternative work.

Shorthorn cattle at Glanystwyth, 1988. [by courtesy of the Earl of Lisburne]

Between 1851 and 1901 the number of farm labourers in the county fell from 10,077 to 2,774; most migrated to the industrial south-east and beyond. Grim as was the life of a farm labourer (see Chapter 19), even worse was the fate of English orphan boys sent to work for local farmers; a government report of 1919 described them as being treated worse than dogs, and victims of worse treatment than Welsh boys received, though some farmers behaved honourably enough.

David Bateman has described the problems of agriculture as being the actual driving force for rural decline in Cardiganshire. General economic development has meant a decline in the status of agriculture within the British economy as a whole. Mechanisation not only drives out labour, it reduces food prices, so that agricultural incomes decline: there is, after all, only so much food that a population can eat – and cheap imports worsened the farmers' lot. With the decline in Cardiganshire of both shipping and lead-mining by the end of the 19th century, even the brief boost of World War I demand was not enough to secure farmers against the threats of eventual bankruptcy. In the past a broken farmer could become a landless labourer, but by the end of the 19th century such employment was disappearing. Men and their families were driven out of the business altogether – with nowhere else in Cardiganshire to go.

A perceived remedy after World War I was forestry. In the centuries before World War I, hedgerow trees and coppiced sessile oak-woods were the main sources of timber, whether for building houses, outbuildings, gates and fences, or ships.

Tenants could be obliged to plant trees; thus in 1732 the thirty-two Cardiganshire tenants of Abernantbychan had to plant certain numbers of oak, elm, ash and sycamore annually. Many landlords planted trees for ornament, and plantations for game, but only Thomas Johnes could be called a serious developer of forestry before the 20th century; half his huge acreage in and around Cwmystwyth was devoted to softwoods. But the timber crisis of World War I, and the agricultural collapse of the 1920s, meant that the government's decision to create the Forestry Commission was comparatively easy to carry out on the high marginal lands of mid-Wales, and the Commission's Welsh headquarters was located in Aberystwyth. Enormous swathes of land were bought cheap and planted up before, and especially after, World War II. For a while these developments brought employment and new housing to a number of communities in northern Cardiganshire. Public hostility to the Sitka spruce monoculture was mollified by the eventual adoption of more varied planting patterns, attractively pioneered on the steep slopes of the Ystwyth gorge around Pont-rhyd-y-groes. Gradually however, the opportunities for employment were reduced by the widespread adoption of mechanised techniques of drainage and planting, and the housing has been sold off. Forest Enterprise was hived off from the Commission with a new role, to deal with issues of conservation and public access; in Ceredigion it has a visitors' centre at Nantyrarian.

* * *

Who were the men and women who won their livings directly from the difficult Cardiganshire terrain for so many centuries? They bore varying titles: the esquires and gentry are dealt with in other chapters, but there were no rigid boundaries between them and the group of three other classes headed by the yeomen, with husbandmen and cottagers propping up the system. Husbandman is a title perhaps more used by others than by individuals of themselves. Yeomen usually owned their own land, and might on occasion lever themselves into the gentry class; they were often wealthier than some poor men who still described themselves as gentlemen. Evan James has traced the lineage of William Jones III of Llanllwchaearn, who died in Aberaeron workhouse in 1887. He had come down in the world with a bump: his father William Jones II had been a tenant farmer, and his grandfather William Jones I styled himself a gentleman, though he owned only 20 acres of land. William Jones I's great-grandfather, probably born about 1590, owned two farms of 100 acres in all, and had been content to be called 'yeoman'. Such freeholders were all bred to the soil, working as boys on their home farms, then perhaps sent out as servants (not labourers) to other farms where they would live in the stable loft and eat in the house, though not the main kitchen, in a virtual continuation of medieval household patterns; although not members of the farm's blood family, they were part of the *tylwyth* or household.

With the many skills he had acquired, with his small savings, and with the aid of his father, a young man might in his mid or late twenties approach a young woman to propose marriage. She would have spent time, first on her home farm and then in service, and she too would have acquired valuable skills to complement those of her would-be husband, would have saved a little money, and might also expect help from her father. With good characters and good fortune they might acquire a small tenancy prior to marriage, and with a growing family might then move to a larger tenancy, perhaps on the same estate; until, if they survived towards old age and their children had left, they would seek a small tenancy to sustain their last years. Other couples might remain on the same tenancy for life, handing it on to a son, and so a family connection might build up with the same farm over generations. Another pattern which certainly survived well into the 20th century was sibling ownership, with a brother and sister, or a set of brothers, owning one or more farms, and a deliberate choice made, either by their parents or by the siblings themselves, that they should not marry. It has been suggested that this was an unexpected consequence of the move to owner-occupation.

Landless men might have to sustain lifelong bachelordom for want of means to marry, or else they might diversify their skills, surviving by seasonal labouring, practising crafts of varying levels of skill for the rest of their time, gardening, poaching and perhaps keeping a pig. Then they would marry as best they might, and give labour in exchange for the right to set potatoes on part of a field, using manure supplied by their employers. Living conditions and diet, whether for labourers or for most tenant farmers, were grim, and were the object of comment by contemporaries. 'Hovels' is the commonest word to describe labourers' cottages, and many farmhouses were no better; it is hardly surprising that so many present-day Cardiganshire farmhouses, although on ancient sites, were rebuilt during the 19th century. Even the recreated cottage interiors at the Ceredigion Museum, the Llannon museum-cottage (open each August), or the cottages at the Museum of Welsh Life are highly sanitised versions of homes that endured the permanent siege of vermin of all kinds, that were dark, smelly and totally lacking sanitation or running water; no doubt the majority of women waged a daily and exhausting struggle against their difficult circumstances. English travellers in 18th-century Wales, and the Education Commissioners in the 19th century all give stomach-churning descriptions of Welsh peasant poverty. Doubtless there is an element of imperial rhetoric in their work, but travellers from Europe confirm the perception of Welsh poverty, inevitably shared by Cardiganshire.

Labour for both men and women was never-ending; when the stock did not need tending, when the butter and cheese had been made, when animals had been sold and bought at the fair, when ploughing and sowing and harrowing and hay-making were done, then there was bark to be cut and taken from the oak-woods to be sold for tanning, bracken to be burnt for the sale of the ashes to soap-makers, wool to be washed, carded, spun and woven, stockings to be knitted, straw ropes to be twisted, peat to be cut, dried and carried, rush candles to be made, corn to be taken to the mill, manure to be shovelled, stones to be picked, tools to be repaired, horses to be taken to the smithy, fences to be mended and hedges to be pleached, the house and outbuildings to be kept in repair, the garden to be dug, water to be drawn and carried, beer to be brewed. Then there was an endless round of house cleaning, washing and of food preparation by the women, even though the diet was simple in the extreme; coarse bread, oatmeal porridge, potatoes and buttermilk were its staples, with little meat other than bacon, and little by way of fruit or green vegetables. This dismal dietary regime was slow to improve; in the 1920s the County Medical Officer complained about the unhealthy diet of white-bread-and-butter and tea which was a rural staple.

David Jenkins has described the complex layers of status in 19th-century agricultural society in fascinating detail, too minute to repeat here in full. All depended on the size of the farm and the family in occupation. Thus the more sons, the less need for live-in servants or hired labour, and the more daughters, the less need for maids. Working with horses was the most prestigious occupation, monopolised by the men, while dairying and the care of poultry was carried out by the women, who would also assist at the hay harvest. Then there was an even more complex set of relationships between farmers and labourers, who might work a part of the farm for themselves in return for their labour, and between farmers and cottagers, who would be allowed to set a row of potatoes on the farm, and receive buttermilk and oatmeal at the house, in return for their labour when necessary. This was a society tightly knit in its family and social relationships, where shearing and harvesting demanded neighbourly assistance, to be repaid in turn.

Farming the Trawsgoed demesne, 1888.

Emigration, discussed briefly in Chapter 20 below, took Cardiganshire people in many directions; the best-known escape for the county's surplus population was to London, where from the 19th century till as late as 1950 the supply of milk from small dairies was undertaken by hundreds of Cardi families. If any of them went to London lured by pavements made of gold, they were soon disabused. The roads and pavements along which they pushed or (if lucky) drove their vehicles were hard-hearted indeed; only a few made enough money to buy land at home or retire in comfort (see Chapter 25).

David Bateman has laid out some of the consequences of the roller-coaster of depression and change for Cardiganshire's farmers during the early 20th century. In the 1911 census 10,663 people were recorded as making their living from agriculture; this represented almost 40% of the work force, compared with 12% for Wales as a whole. World War I led, as wars do, to an increase in prices, but after the war prices dropped and went on dropping. Wheat in 1930 was cheaper than it had been in 1771. Fat cattle in 1935 were back to their 1911 prices. Overall farm prices dropped between 1920 and 1933 by 62%. Farm labourers, already a disappearing breed, were also earning less. Profit in cash hardly existed; subsistence was all. These are facts often forgotten by historians involved in studying the dreadful industrial depression of the time. However, Cardiganshire's farmers were rescued in 1933, at least in part, by the establishment of the Milk Marketing Board, part of a belated but significant effort by the government to assist farmers. Previously only 500 of the county's 5,000 holdings were selling milk off the farm, but regular payments meant the monthly milk cheque was always a most welcome sight, and in consequence dairy cattle numbers rose. Working horses disappeared with the ubiquity of the tractor, but horse-rearing, especially of Welsh cobs, remains important, and Lampeter and Llanybydder horse-fairs are major occasions in the agricultural year.

Despite a sense of gathering gloom over the recent history of agriculture in Cardiganshire, there have been passages of great good cheer. 1902 saw the establishment of four agricultural co-operative societies in or partly in the county, inspired by Augustus Brigstock; in the same year he persuaded a delegation from the three south-western county councils to visit Ireland. Before long there were thirteen co-operatives in the county, 'accounting for a quarter of the total turnover in the whole of Great Britain' (D.I.V. Bateman), but their later history is not easy to trace. In 1904, driven by T.L. Loveden Pryse of Gogerddan, the first Welsh National Agricultural Show was held at Aberystwyth, where it remained until 1909. T.L.L. Pryse's brother, Sir Edward Webley-Parry-Pryse, led the establishment of branches of the National Farmers' Union from 1911 onwards. Brigstock and the Pryses were the last of the local gentry to make major contributions to the county's agriculture. The co-operative agricultural movement eventually failed in England but flourished in Wales from 1922 under the umbrella of the Welsh Agricultural Organisation Society, with headquarters in Aberystwyth, inspired by A.W. Ashby, professor of Agricultural Economics in the University College, a man who believed there was more to farming than stock, crops and income. Another enormous contribution to

Welsh and world agriculture was made by Sir George Stapledon (1882-1960), director of the Welsh Plant Breeding Station (now the Institute of Grassland and Environmental Research), Wales's only government scientific research centre.

*　　*　　*

Of the many craftsmen whose work sustained the agricultural communities of Cardiganshire, some can be recognised in the probate records. Blacksmiths flourished; Evan Clayton of Llanfihangel Genau'r-glyn (1661) left to his son Thomas 'My shop Coals and all Tools whatsoever and all horseshoes and Irons steel Anvil or any thing else that belongs or appertained to My Said Trade'. Blacksmiths were the crafting mainstay of the rural economy, manufacturing every kind of agricultural hand-tool and ploughing equipment, as well as shoeing all the horses, and the cattle to be driven to England. J. Geraint Jenkins has counted 104 smithies in the county which were still working in the 1930s. William Evans of Llanfihangel-y-Creuddyn designed and manufactured a horse-plough which attracted purchasers from near and far.

Other trades flourished, though some craftsmen were not at all prosperous, like the cobbler John Llewelyn of Llanfihangel-y-Creuddyn, who died in 1665 worth only 19s 9d. Spinning was a homebody activity for women, although spinning wheels appear in men's inventories (the husband of course owned all a married couple's property); weaving was a job for men. The only yarn woven locally apart from wool was hemp; small quantities of both seeds and yarn are named. In 1608 David Morris, vicar of Llanilar, left six yards of white cloth 'now with Ieuan ap William of Llanychaearn, weaver', to his daughter. Looms, 18 wool combs, wool cards and quantities of yarn and raw wool are named in various inventories. Glovemakers would have depended on working for the gentry; Morgan David, glover (1693) of Cardigan, left 'white leather' and 'half a dozen of small gloves', but also a spinning wheel and a pair of woollen cards', suggesting that he and his family worked at more than one trade. Tailors are named in wills; hat-making was a separate craft, for which Llancynfelyn had acquired a reputation by the early 19th century. I have not yet discovered a hatter's will, but several communities of hatters worked well into the 19th century, before the arrival

Abermagwr's blacksmith, Clive Davies, at work.

of the railway bringing cheap manufactured goods killed off not only the making of hats, but many other rural crafts.

The woollen industry was at first a home-based affair, though served by the *pandy* or fulling-mill for cleaning the wool, a task beyond home resources. From the beginning of the 19th century, if not earlier, woollen mills were built to spin, card and weave wool. The earliest mills served the lead-mines in the north of the county, and others appeared throughout the county, with a particular concentration in the Teifi valley and a lesser concentration in Tal-y-bont. Many of the mills were in fact on the Carmarthenshire-Pembrokeshire side of the valley, emphasising again the need to understand the valley as a single social and economic unit despite the function of the river as a county boundary. By the mid-19th century Cardiganshire with the whole Teifi valley was, J. Geraint Jenkins tells us, one of the most important textile manufacturing regions in Wales, with dozens of mills in operation employing hundreds of men and women. Their products were much in demand in the south Wales coalfield, which continued to flourish into the early 1920s, while World War I brought government orders for flannel, blankets and uniform-cloth. Irish immigrants joined the work-force, community billiard-halls, football and cricket teams appeared, industrial disputes occurred.

All was not well, however. In the north of the county the five mills on the river Eleri serving the lead-miners lost their market with the decline of the industry, though tourism helped keep two of them alive for several decades longer. Units were too small to be able to invest in new machinery or develop new markets. Business methods were dire and accounting inadequate. At the end of the war the government sold off cloth surpluses at low prices. The decline of the Welsh coalfield from the early 1920s was slow poison to the industry. Other factors contributed; village tailors could not compete with ready-made clothes and more fashionable wear from England, and there ceased to be a market for tweed. Across the Teifi, 21 mills closed at Drefach Felindre and their machinery went for scrap. Some mills kept going as late as the 1960s, but they were unable for lack of capital to accommodate themselves to an ever-changing market, so that only one Cardiganshire mill, the Rock mill at Capel Dewi, still functions at the time of writing, worked as a one-man unit by the great-grandson of the man who created the mill in 1895. It is noteworthy that like men, buildings could adapt to new economic uses; thus the Glan-ffraid forge established at Dôl-y-bont in 1723 was converted after 1808 to a woollen mill.

Brewing was a major activity throughout the land in the early modern period, and many farmers owned the usual apparatus of barrels: kinderkins, kives and casks, as well as quantities of barley malt, all used by their wives. The existence of numerous alehouses is well-known; Justices of the Peace were expected to regulate them, and a number of male and female keepers of unregulated alehouses were brought before the Court of Great Sessions from time to time. Alehouse-keepers can be distinguished in the probate records by the lists of tables and pewter drinking vessels which they kept. Edward Vince of Cardigan, whose father's 1618 will shows him to have been an innkeeper, was brought before the Court of Great Sessions in

1627 for keeping a brothel, and another Cardigan man was arraigned for keeping a bowling alley and assaulting a constable. More reputable, surely, was the innkeeper Samuel Davies of Aberystwyth (1752), whose dining room contained nineteen old oak chairs, two oak round tables and twelve pictures, and whose garrets had seven beds; unfortunately the inn is not named. There were many more inns and beer-houses than survive today, both in towns and in the countryside; some are recognisable from their surviving names or from their architecture and roadside positions. James Raw, the mining engineer and farmer of Tŷ Llwyd, Cwmystwyth, ran his farmhouse as a tavern, and the next generation continued the practice; some of the pewter mugs and the bar accounts still survive in family ownership. It would be interesting to know whether Llanafan was unique among Cardiganshire villages in never having had a pub, a mark of the Lisburne disapproval of drink for the *werin* at a time when one head of the family rejoiced in the nickname 'Fruity Port'. The largest and longest-lasting Cardiganshire brewery was Roberts of Aberystwyth, whose oast-house by the harbour can still be seen; brewing ceased in 1952.

The people of early modern Cardiganshire society practised self-sufficiency to a considerable extent. Men, and especially women, were not necessarily tied to a single trade. As has been seen, lead miners kept farm stock, while neighbouring farmers kept pack-horses to carry lead ore to Aberystwyth or Derwen-las. Evan Clayton the blacksmith kept 24 sheep; vicars were also farmers. Women, whether spinsters, married or widowed, spun yarn, baked bread, cured bacon and did whatever else was necessary to keep the wolf from the door. But some, as will be seen in another chapter, fell into dire poverty.

Despite self-sufficiency, shopkeepers played a vital role in the economy, particularly for the supply of goods other than food. Several long inventories testify to this; the longest, that of Jane Vaughan (d.1649) is described in Chapter 10. To judge by his inventory, David Richard of Tregaron (d.1601) only operated in a small way, selling linen, canvas, fustian, soap and flax. Ieuan Lloyd of Cwmsymlog (d.1629) was a more prosperous mercer, supplying silk, lace, gloves, combs, hatbands, buttons, stockings, gunpowder and a wide range of cloth, including fustian, calico, baize, buckram, canvas, kersey, broadcloth and cotton. His three scales and weights are listed. His will shows him to have belonged to a regional network of tradesmen: he appointed Esay Thomas of Bishop's Castle in Shropshire as his executor, and refers to Thomas Alderhey, a mercer of Chester. Cwmsymlog in 1629 was not the empty site it is now; it was full of the hurly-burly of the lead and silver mining industry. Englishmen were part of the county's commercial network. Richard Newell, merchant, born in Westbury, bought the now-vanished mansion of Glanleri and hobnobbed with John Vaughan of Trawsgoed; at his death in 1643 he left lands in Cheshire, Shropshire and Staffordshire, and a share in one of the Cwmystwyth lead-mines, which may have been what brought him to the county in the first place; his will was proved in London. In 1638 he had witnessed the will of his nephew Thurstan Radford of Llanbadarn Fawr; his livelihood is not apparent from his will, but he was obviously part of the immigrant commercial community.

Manufacturing industry on any scale larger than that of the individual woollen mill, the blacksmith's forge or the workshop has not played a large part in most of Cardiganshire's commercial history: shipbuilding was perhaps the most long-lived exception, and is dealt with in Chapter 13, and printing in Chapter 20. Careful examination of a few manhole covers in Aberystwyth will reveal that the town was home to iron-founding in the second half of the 19th century; there were several independent foundries, of which the largest was Green's, on what is now Alexandra Road. Green's exported its products internationally, difficult though it may be today to imagine it. One fine surviving example of Aberystwyth ironwork is the arched bridge at the foot of Jacob's Ladder, Devil's Bridge, dating from 1867. Cardigan too was a busy centre of commercial activity for centuries; the local economy was fuelled not only by agriculture, but by iron foundries, slate-quarrying at Cilgerran, a tinplate works at Llechryd, a brickworks, and by the long-flourishing Cardigan Mercantile Company. For a generation after the arrival of the railways the county's economic ventures continued to flourish (though not on a scale to prevent steady emigration), but with the general growth of larger enterprises in south Wales and especially the English midlands, small foundries and woollen mills alike were doomed.

It was only after 1945 that governmental and county efforts began, slowly at first, to support occupations other than agriculture and forestry, the chosen method being the industrial estate, with pre-built workshops and stores ready for occupation by tenants who might expect various forms of official encouragement, since by choosing Cardiganshire they were putting themselves at a distance from the populous markets of south-east Wales and the English midlands. Clothing factories at Lampeter and Cardigan, now closed, were important local employers of women workers, offering an alternative to migration. Despite setbacks, these estates have expanded, though there is little actual manufacturing; the companies involved are mostly engaged in services and distribution, whether of cars, groceries, building materials, dairy products, skateboards or books.

Note: Banking

When Sir Walter Lloyd of Llanfair Clydogau had to pay a fine to the Commonwealth government in 1651, he sent the money to London by a drover, 'but the drover neglected to pay it, to his great prejudice.' This demonstrates succinctly both the use people had to make of drovers for financial business, and the dubious reputation they acquired. Although there are several short books on banking in Wales, they contradict each other seriously on dates and relationships. However, it is clear that the need for banks was perceived in Wales by the late 18th century. The North Wales Bank, established in 1785 or 1792 according to whom one believes, became Williams & Co., and by the time of Pigot's 1822 Directory a bank called Davies, Williams & Co. operated in Bridge Street, at the house known as the Old Bank, but no other banks are mentioned in the county. Other banks came into existence in Aberystwyth: the Aberystwyth & Tregaron, which issued the famous 'black sheep' notes, with the number of sheep indicating the number of pounds for the benefit of the illiterate, and the Aberystwyth Savings Bank was in existence by 1830, opening for two hours on Mondays.

By the time of Slater's 1858 directory, Aberystwyth had branches of the National & Provincial and of the North and South Wales Bank, which had taken over the Aberystwyth & Tregaron. In Cardigan the South Wales Bank had a branch in High St. There were still no banks in Lampeter or Tregaron, but by 1868 Lampeter had two, its own Lampeter Bank, and a branch of the National Provincial Bank of England. By 1880 Tregaron had a sub-branch, opening Tuesdays, of the London and Provincial Bank, and there was another branch in Aberaeron, opening on Thursdays. The Lampeter Bank, like the North and South Wales, had disappeared by the end of the 19th century. The London banks were in charge.

12. Lead, Silver, Zinc

In the tree-filled canyon of the Ystwyth below Pont-rhyd-y-groes, accessible only by a narrow path, there suddenly rise up, like Mayan ruins in the Yucatan jungle, the huge concrete supports of a wrecked timber dam which in the early 1920s briefly held back the Ystwyth to provide a head of water for a lead-waste washery downstream at Grogwynion. Over a large area of northern Ceredigion there are barrack ruins, chimneys, massive walls, great piles of rock waste, tunnel entrances, tramway paths, huts for explosives, bridge foundations, unprotected shafts and occasional brilliant orange pools of water, which are only some of many traces of the county's defunct mining industry which may startle the visitor. To many they are hideous reminders of a rampant capitalism which enriched a few and ruined many in both health and pocket; the few were usually outsiders, the many more often local men whose lungs were destroyed by their work – they 'coughed black'. To others they are one of the many complex remains of Wales's rich and ancient industrial history, witnesses to centuries of toil and conflict. Both opinions are valid.

Y Graig Fawr, Cwmystwyth's mighty crag created by centuries of mining.

In some areas the walker should tread with care, since there are still open and unprotected shafts to menace the unwary, some of them half-filled with rusting vehicles, rolls of barbed wire, refrigerators, television sets, sheets of corrugated iron and other throwaway rubbish, even dead sheep. Grass refuses to grow wherever lead waste lies; the tiny percentage of lead that not even reprocessing could extract is enough to poison the soil and the water that seeps through it. The county council has landscaped several sites, filling in shafts, sometimes with a drastic loss of historical knowledge, though an improvement in terms of safety. The Rheidol and the Ystwyth, although now in better condition than they were sixty years ago, are still among the most polluted rivers in Britain. The little river Newidion has no life at all in its waters after flowing round a huge heap of lead waste at the Wemyss mine on its way to join the Magwr and eventually the Ystwyth.

The scenery underground can be even more remarkable than the surviving remains above ground. On both counts Cwmystwyth is an extraordinary site. A splendid view can be had from the south side of the great natural fault down which the Ystwyth flows. The steep north side has been sculpted into terraces, with a huge artificial cliff, created by hacking away at a colossal crag; photographs survive showing the wooden scaffolding which supported the miners at their task. Ruined buildings are still there: offices, barracks, the foundations of a large ore-dressing shed, a gunpowder magazine. Huge masses of rock rubble from the belly of the mountain spread on either side of the road. Simon Hughes has listed 84 levels, adits and cuts made over at least five centuries to give access to the lead ore (galena) and zinc ore (blackjack); lead usually fetched a better price, and zinc was only exploited when the lead market slumped.

Inside the mountain the scene can be alternately oppressive and dramatic. It has been estimated that there are thirty miles of passages in the Cwmystwyth complex, a third of which are now flooded, a third collapsed, and a third are still negotiable by the careful, fit and skilful who have a knowledgeable guide. Entry to one main section of the mine is by a straight and narrow tunnel which, after a few hundred metres with

Ivor Richards leads the way underground in Cwmystwyth.

Intersection of miners' passage with chamber emptied of its ore.

water half a metre deep, branches in several directions. There are mud and puddles underfoot as well as iron rails which carried the last generations of ore-wagons, and pipes which took pumped fresh air into the depths of the mountain. Here and there a wagon or a wheelbarrow still survives. Where the miners found ore they followed the vein whatever the angle at which it lay to the horizontal. The passage may suddenly open up to reveal a steeply angled and massive slot carved out of the rock, and here the explorer must climb, partly with the aid of the beams athwart the slot, partly by ladders over a century old. The rock is usually its native murky grey, but the depth of colour varies, and it may be streaked red or white with leaching chemicals. Care must be taken to avoid the shafts whose unshielded openings gape in mid-passage. Now and then the passages open into large chambers where masses of rich ore had formed, only to be ripped out. At convenient spots the miners collected together the useless rock (known as 'deads') from their labours in piles which are held in place by wooden grilles; this saved them the labour of carrying the material out of the mine.

Even a visit to the mine as it is today, alarming though it may be to the uninitiated, cannot convey the grimness of the miners' toil a century and more ago. The air was often foul, and made fouler by the lack of any toilet accommodation underground. Conditions were usually sodden with water and slimy mud. Shot-holes were drilled by hand, the heavy trams were pushed by men, women and children, not pulled by ponies as in the coalmines. Underground windlasses could not be worked by the surface waterwheels; instead they were wound by hand.

Back in the open air, moving eastwards towards Blaen-cwm, the hillside bears the long scars of a leat, a carefully engineered trench which carried water for miles to the ever-thirsty waterwheels. The Cardiganshire mines were absolutely dependent on water as their only source of power; coal was too expensive, wood too scarce, and peat would have been ineffective, since it cannot generate enough heat. The perennial problem was that although the mines flooded easily from the superabundance of subterranean water, there was rarely enough on the surface to secure regular working; the hint of a drought could stop the wheels turning and throw the men out of work. The chief task of the wheels was to pump out water, and to wind the ore to the surface; the luxury of a cage to carry the miners to and from the depths was unachievable, and they had to climb scores of metres on wooden ladders at the end of their long shifts. Water could of course be stored in reservoirs, and some of north Cardiganshire's most attractive lakes, like that at Trisant (Fron-goch) and the two (a third is now empty) at Rhos-rhudd above Cwmnewidion, were in fact created as reservoirs.

Water made possible the ancient technique of hushing, traces of which can be seen on Copper Hill high above Cwmystwyth. An earth dam would be made in a convenient spot, and when full of rain or stream-water, the dam would be breached and the water then rushed downhill scouring the hillside to the rock, where the veins of ore might then be exposed. The grassed scars of the process survive on the hillside to this day. The name Copper Hill is of course significant; there was copper mining here during the second millennium BC; the Ordnance Survey rendering of the name as Bryn Copa is unconvincing.

Hushing dam on slopes of Copper Hill, Cwmystwyth (note the break in the earth dam).

As well as shafts, waste-tips, leats and reservoirs, the ruins of mine buildings can be seen in many places in the Ceredigion hills, though they are not easily interpreted by the uninitiated, especially as some buildings served different functions at different times. At the largest mines – for example at Pont-rhyd-y-groes, Cwmsymlog, Fron-goch – there are entrances to passages, powder-magazines, the floors of crushing mills, the beds in which the water-wheels turned, the sloping beds of cableways, the ruins of offices, barrack-rooms, all now entirely abandoned but once furious with activity. Some of the houses owned by mining 'captains', as they liked to be called, are still occupied; they were of course of a much higher standard than the miners' cottages. Several attempts were made to establish smelters in the county, but none succeeded because of the shortage of fuel; the mining companies preferred to send their ore by packhorse to Aberystwyth and Derwen-las harbours, to be shipped for the most part to Neath and other south Wales smelters.

* * *

Lead is found in most if not all of the thirteen historic Welsh counties, but it was in Flintshire, Montgomeryshire and Cardiganshire that the erratic veins were most vigorously worked. The southernmost mining activity in the county was at Llanfair Clydogau, with a brief attempt at New Quay, but the main area where metal could be found stretched northwards from the river Ystwyth and from Strata Florida almost to the Dyfi. Whether the Romans mined lead here as they did in Flintshire seems recently to have been proved beyond doubt after years of work by Simon Timberlake, following suggestions by recent historians of the mining industry.

David Bick has suggested that certain earth workings above Llanfair Clydogau may be traces of a Roman aqueduct; mining certainly took place there in the modern era. Then there is the indirect evidence of the tiny Roman fort in the Tarenig valley over the county boundary in Montgomeryshire, visible from the A44. It is hard to imagine what purpose it could have served other than as a mini-garrison post to protect investment in the nearby lead-fields. Some narrow, beautifully chiselled galleries in the depths of Cwmystwyth, although known to tradition as 'Roman work', do not contain any convenient proof of Roman origin. The technique of 'hushing' referred to above was a common Roman mining practice, though that does not mean that the scars visible today are Roman in origin. Certainly the Cwmystwyth veins were worked on behalf of Strata Florida monastery well before 1530. It was in the 1530s that the Englishman John Leland visited the area, and in his journal he described how the great rock-face had already been cut away, and how pits had been sunk; he tells us of the first known death in a Cardiganshire mine, when the pit collapsed on a worker just as his fellow-miner had leapt out of the pit to rescue his lunch from a thieving crow.

The usual mode of managing an enterprise varied according to the period, but at bottom it was a matter for negotiation between the landowner and the entrepreneur. For much of the period the Crown was also involved, since it claimed ownership of precious metals and therefore expected royalties on the ore raised. Some landowners played a part themselves in the management of mining enterprises; others were content simply to draw the royalties per ton which the company paid. Since any serious mining enterprise meant the expenditure of much capital, money had to be raised by floating shares. All kinds of problems would arise: the weather and season could be difficult; the workforce might desert the mines for the potato harvest; the veins of ore were temperamental in the extreme, thanks to the multiple faulting of the rock in which they lay, and would suddenly disappear. Flooding was a particular curse. Tunnels could be driven through the hard rock to no avail whatsoever. Promoters of mining

'Roman workings' in Cwmystwyth mine.

companies could be dishonest in the extreme; a favourite trick was 'salting' samples, i.e. persuading investors that a load of ore was rich in metal – metal which had actually come from another enterprise altogether. Some fortunes were made in Cardiganshire mining, but many were lost.

Improvements in mining technology in the 16th century, mostly developed in Germany, made it increasingly possible to win large amounts of lead from the Cardiganshire mines, some of which also yielded much silver. In 1568 the courts had determined that any mine containing gold or silver, however mixed with other metals, was a 'mine royal', and therefore a Crown monopoly: thus was born in that year the Society of Mines Royal. The entrepreneurs who took Crown mining leases only reached Cardiganshire in 1586, when they found the existing mines in ruinous condition. Their agent, Charles Evans, hired German miners to work at Cwmsymlog, and soon lead and silver were being produced in significant quantities.

Hugh Myddelton, a London-Welsh goldsmith, took a lease of the Cardiganshire mines in 1617, working at Cwmsymlog, Cwmerfin, Goginan and Tal-y-bont. Conflict with local landowners made Myddelton's life difficult, but he bought off his most significant obstructor, Sir Richard Pryse of Gogerddan, by giving his own daughter Hester to Pryse in marriage, presumably with a large dowry. Coins made from Cardiganshire silver were minted with the Prince of Wales's crest of plumes to denote its origin. Meanwhile the non-silver-bearing lead mines south of the Rheidol were also being worked, especially Cwmystwyth and Grogwynion. Myddelton's success was carefully observed in London; James I appreciated the access of silver from a native source, and Myddelton was praised for giving employment to many poor men and serving the general benefit of the kingdom. In 1624 the rent of the mines royal in Cardiganshire was set at the enormous sum of £1,200 minimum.

After Myddelton's death in 1631, his leases were developed by Thomas Bushell from 1636 onwards, and as has already been seen in Chapter 9, Bushell set up a mint at Aberystwyth castle in 1637, supported at first by local gentry, who later turned against him; Sir Richard Pryse had his men throw rubbish into the mines and wreck the pumps. Sir Richard was briefly imprisoned for his trouble-making, but was not deterred from his opposition. Coins actually minted at Aberystwyth bear the tiny device of an open book, and the larger denominations have the Prince's feathers on both sides. With the arrival of parliamentary armies in Cardiganshire, Bushell fled the county, but the mint was briefly continued at Furnace by Edmund Goodere. Bushell had greatly improved mining techniques, digging long

A Description of the Mines in Cardiganshire by William Waller (1704), recently reproduced with a valuable commentary by David Bick, is an extraordinary description of the lead-silver mines at Esgair-hir, Cyneiniog, Cwmsymlog, Goginan, Bryn-pica, Cwmerfyn, Pencraig-ddu, Ystumtuen, Cwmystwyth and the 'silver mills' at Garreg, with maps and illustrations in a primitive but still useful style; they were the first British attempts to depict mine-workings. It is the most important of Waller's numerous publications. Walking the remains of these sites described by Waller, preferably on a fine day, is one of the most direct ways for one's imagination to enter the county's past.

adits on an upward slope from the entrance so that they acted as drains, improving the recovery of silver from the ore, and using bellows to try to improve the quality of the air. He was also popular with the ordinary people of the county, who were willing to side with him against his gentry enemies.

After the Restoration, mining in west Wales began to regain some shadow of its former importance, a period associated with the arrival of the Cologne engineer Cornelius le Brun, who later became squire of Nanteos by marrying the Jones heiress, and Anthony Shepherd, manager in the county for the Society of Mines Royal. But it was the discovery in 1690 of an apparently rich vein of lead at Esgair-hir which changed the mining landscape, and another English mining engineer, William Waller, was brought in as manager. Sir Carbery Pryse of Gogerddan owned Esgair-hir, and in 1692 he challenged the monopoly of the Society of Mines Royal in the House of Lords. Although Pryse may have falsified the evidence, he won the case, and was so excited that he is said to have ridden from London to Gogerddan in forty-eight hours, stopping only to change horses. Early in 1693 the Lords enacted that landowners had the right to mine on their own land so long as they sold the metal to the Crown at a fixed price. Coincidentally with this change in the law the use of gunpowder reached the Welsh mines.

Sir Carbery Pryse's dreams of boundless treasure were not fulfilled; the Esgair-hir mine ran into difficulties, and by May 1694 Pryse was dead. The leading role in Cardiganshire mining passed to the Neath coal-owner Sir Humphrey Mackworth, who in 1698 took over the Pryse family's mine-shares and formed the Company of Mine Adventurers; shares were launched by lottery. The whole episode was remarkable for its hyperbole, much of it the work of William Waller. Daniel Defoe, visiting the county in 1724, described the mines as 'the greatest, and perhaps the richest, in England' (*sic*). As he also commented on the coal found in the district, we may wonder at the general accuracy of his work. But Waller and Defoe were not the only ones to talk up the value of Pryse's claim. It was said that Esgair-hir had riches like those of the great Potosi silver mine in Bolivia; rash promises of charitable giving were made, and dubious samples were exhibited to persuade people to invest in the lottery. A specially minted set of Welsh silver coins was presented to Queen Anne.

A refinery was built at Ynys-hir, thus causing the community which grew up there to be named Furnace; it is not clear to what extent the work was fuelled by local charcoal or by coal brought in by sea. The silver mills are described and pictured by William Waller; the site was later re-exploited to create the Furnace iron-smelter, fuelled by charcoal, which still stands beside the A487. Lead smelting never flourished in Cardiganshire, despite other efforts at Aberystwyth and Devil's Bridge; it was easier to carry the ore via the ports of Derwen-las or Aberystwyth to Flintshire or, more usually, to south Wales. Mackworth's company quickly became mired in scandal, Esgair-hir in particular never lived up to its promise, and Mackworth himself, though elected as Cardiganshire's MP in 1701, 1702 and 1710, eventually abandoned the county's lead-mines. For twenty years they worked only fitfully, but in 1731 there was an outburst of activity and an influx of entrepreneurs, followed by agents of the Treasury; it had been realised that mining was taking place on common lands belonging to the Crown. In that year Thomas Powell of Nanteos, grandson of Cornelius le Brun, led a mob to expel intruding miners from Cwmystwyth – a rehearsal of what was to follow some twenty-three years later.

Lewis Morris (1701-65), the Anglesey polymath and poet who had surveyed much of the coast of Wales for the Admiralty, had also worked on a survey of the manor of Creuddyn and knew the north of the county well. In 1746 he was appointed deputy steward of the Crown Manors of Cardiganshire. Local landowners fiercely opposed the crown's intrusion; claiming ownership of all open and waste land for themselves. The Crown, on the other hand, though it had lost its monopoly on precious metals, was determined to exert its rights as landlord. Lewis Morris, a spiky character at the best of times, soon fell foul of the brothers Thomas and William Powell of Nanteos, especially after he began work at Esgair-mwyn, south of Ysbyty Ystwyth, on land claimed both by the Crown and the Powells of Nanteos. His efforts on behalf of the Crown were rewarded by his appointment as superintendent of the king's mines – but the king was far away, and the Cardiganshire gentry still effectively ruled the land. On 23 February 1753 a mob of several hundred miners and Nanteos tenants, led by Thomas Powell and Herbert Lloyd of Peterwell, arrested Lewis Morris and carried him off to Cardigan gaol. He was soon released, and soldiers were sent to guard Esgair-mwyn; a compromise was eventually reached, but Lewis Morris's financial affairs came under suspicion. He was investigated at length, and in 1756 was dismissed from all Crown employment, including his sinecure as controller of Customs at Aberdyfi, but he continued to be involved in mining in a personal capacity.

Work continued in various mines, some with the involvement of Lord Powis of Powis Castle, Montgomeryshire, his manager John Paynter (who leased Hafod Uchdryd), John Probert, and the energetic Chauncey Townsend, M.P. for Westbury, alderman of the City of London and owner of extensive interests in Glamorgan. Exploitation of zinc began alongside the production of lead-ore. Some mines were worked to little avail, while others boomed; between 1751 and 1771 Cwmsymlog yielded £11,500 profit to the Gogerddan estate. Thomas Bonsall (d.1808) of Derbyshire arrived in the county, took over the management of the Townsend mines, became mayor of Aberystwyth and built himself a mansion, Fronfraith, just outside the town. In 1796 he gained a knighthood for his diligence in presenting a loyal address to the king, who had not heard of his sharp practices in the mining industry. Bonsall was particularly notorious for his exploitation of the 'truck' system, the supply of goods (foodstuffs and mining equipment) to the workmen at extortionate prices.

Disturbed political conditions at the end of the 18th century, and increasing difficulties in working the mines after the easiest veins had been worked out, brought troubled times to the Cardiganshire lead-mines. First Spain and eventually the U.S.A. developed powerfully competitive mining industries which drove down the price of metal. Nevertheless a new generation of entrepreneurs emerged; Job Sheldon (d.1844), a man unusually concerned for the welfare of his miners, followed Bonsall as mayor of Aberystwyth. Sir George and Thomas Alderson, London Yorkshiremen, took over the lease of the Nanteos-owned Cwmystwyth mine in 1822 and began production there on a large scale, at a rate of nearly 2,000 tons of ore a month. However, in 1834 their financial affairs collapsed, and the lease was taken over by an Aberystwyth man, Lewis Pugh.

Meanwhile the mines owned by Trawsgoed and Gogerddan were all leased to the Williams family of Cornwall, marking a shift of influence. Prior to this lease the dominant English figures in these Welsh enterprises were from Derbyshire and the north of England, but henceforth Cornwall was to contribute more. However, despite their skill and efficiency, falling market prices drove the Williamses out in 1833, though one of their partners stayed on. He was John Taylor, a man with much experience elsewhere in Wales; by 1835 he and his sons were paying dividends to their shareholders, helped by improving market prices, but particularly as a result of their success at Fron-goch, between Trisant and Pont-rhyd-y-groes. The Taylors were efficient, energetic and sagacious, as well as being less dishonest than most in the cut-throat world of mining malpractice; gradually they took over the leases of nearly all the worthwhile mines in the county. In the mid-19th century the Lisburne mines alone were paying over £60,000 a year in wages, and spending over £30,000 among the tradesmen of the county.

As a result the upland mining sites buzzed and heaved with life. Men came from Derbyshire, Flintshire, Yorkshire and Cornwall to work as engineers and labourers, many bringing their Wesleyan Methodism with them. Some settled down, married, and integrated; James Raw of Yorkshire (d.1864) not only opened Raw's Level in Cwmystwyth in the 1820s, he leased land from the Trawsgoed estate, including his home at Tŷ Llwyd, which flourished as both farm and tavern; his great-great-great-grandson, also James Raw, farms Tŷ Llwyd today. As well as underground workers, the mines needed the craftwork of blacksmiths, coopers, masons, sawyers and carpenters. Miners who lived too far from their work to walk there every day had to sleep in squalid barracks whose ruins can be seen on many sites; they shared beds whose blankets were rarely cleaned. They worked by candlelight, often in oxygen-starved conditions even where air-pumping was used; hygiene facilities were non-existent, the stench

James Raw I, the Yorkshire mining captain, innkeeper and farmer.

vile, the threat of flooding frequent. On Saturday evenings, exhausted by the endless climbing of ladders to reach the surface at the end of the shift, they trudged home, only to trudge back to work by Monday morning carrying a week's supply of basic foodstuffs. They worked sometimes for weekly or monthly wages, sometimes on piece-rates for 'bargains'; in either case the rewards were not generous, and often slow in being paid. When Harry James, miner, of Llanafan died in 1641, he was owed no less than £20; like many other miners he kept cattle and sheep, especially valuable when the mines closed, as they did frequently. William Hedley of Llanbadarn Fawr (1706) refers to 'implements of minery' in his will; his inventory only mentions '3 tubbs, 1 buckett, 6 pickens', which seem to be the tools referred to; he like Harry James kept cattle and sheep.

Cardiganshire lead-miners. [Ceredigion Library]

Miners' cottages and gardens occupied any spare corner of roadside land, and their remains can frequently be traced today, for example in Cwmystwyth, while others in the mining villages are still occupied, though of course much altered. Some men spent their money in beer-houses; others were more serious, and ready to respond to the religious revival of 1859, which was particularly successful in Ysbyty Ystwyth. Their health was not good; they coughed black and died young. A particular complaint was *y belen* ('the ball'), the feeling that there was a heavy lump in a man's chest, as indeed there would have been from breathing so much dust. Tuberculosis was also a serious problem. Women and children worked mainly on the surface for a pittance, breaking, sorting and washing the ore. When a miner married, his wife's first task was to prepare a shroud, in case of a fatal accident. These were not as frequent or catastrophic as in the coal mines of the south, but they happened; at least five men were killed in a fire at Fron-goch mine on 29 October, 1859, an event commemorated in a Welsh ballad; the year 1876 saw four deaths in four different mines. Despite the often wretched conditions in which they lived and worked, the miners were not without pride. Lewis Morris's papers contain a miners' drinking song, probably of his own work:

In Sump or in Drift we work for a Shift
Thro' Fire and Water we'll venture,
To make it all level we'll drink and we'll revel
Twill help us go down to the Center.

A VIVID account of the lead-miner's life is given by W. Jones-Edwards in his *Ar Lethrau Ffair Rhos*. He worked at Glôg-fawr in the slime-pit and then underground with his father. A miner wore greased boots, with long thick socks knitted by his wife, a shirt, a woollen vest and flannel pants, with white moleskin trousers strapped below the knees, a leather belt, a sleeved moleskin waistcoat, an old coat, a cravat and cloth cap; the latter was changed at work for a leather hat with a soft cap underneath. To go underground the miner stuck a candle in a lump of clay on his hat.

The 19th-century ballad-singer Ywain Meirion also celebrated them in a song, *Mawl-gerdd Mwyngloddwyr Ceredigion* ('In Praise of the Cardiganshire Miners'). Theirs was a particular culture with its own folk-beliefs; they knew the signs which might reveal the existence of lead under the earth's surface, and of the spirits or 'knockers' which, it was supposed, could lead a prospector through the rock to a rich vein.

Decline set in after 1871, slowly at first, then accelerated by a fall in prices in 1878; the Taylors began to withdraw, and ceased activities in the county in 1890. Many workmen moved south to the coal mines, where the danger was greater but the pay better. Some took their families with them, while others sent remittances home to Cardiganshire. Local mining continued, but zinc was now more profitable than lead,

A relic of mid-20th century optimism at Esgair-mwyn.

thanks to the booming market in galvanised iron. Local men attempted small developments in some mines, while the larger mines passed from entrepreneur to entrepreneur; Fron-goch, for example, was worked from 1898 to 1903 by a Belgian company who brought in Catholic workers from the Continent; for a brief period they worshipped at the now ruined Capel Saeson (Chapel of the English) near Pont-rhyd-y-groes, built originally by the mine-owners for Wesleyan immigrants. Occasional profitable bodies of lead-ore still came to light from time to time between 1880 and 1920, but the great days were gone. Esgair-mwyn continued production until 1928, and efforts were made, including new buildings, to recommence there in 1948, but they had no success.

The most remarkable surviving and functioning institution created for the mining industry is the Vale of Rheidol Light Railway, built in 1901-02, whose history is dealt with in another chapter, but which was originally conceived as benefiting not only the Rheidol mines, but those at Fron-goch, Cwmystwyth, Ystumtuen and Dyffryn Castell. Even the World War I demand for lead could not revive the Cardiganshire industry, though much money was spent at Cwmystwyth in 1916 on new machinery, and in 1919 the Welsh Mines Corporation Limited was formed with all the usual optimistic rhetoric to exploit the Lisburne holdings north of the Ystwyth. With wartime government help a spectacular aerial ropeway had been built from Fron-goch over Grogwynion mountain and down to the Ystwyth, where a dam of concrete and logs was made in the river's gorge to provide a head of water. During the 1920s and 1930s the waste-heaps of Fron-goch were carried by the ropeway over Grogwynion and down to the Ystwyth, where the channelled water was used to wash the waste. At least one small boy who sneaked rides in the ropeway's empty tubs is still alive at the time of writing this chapter. Meanwhile work was carried on at Esgair-mwyn until 1928. The very last underground mining effort, near Tre'r-ddôl, was closed by fire in 1939. In 1940-42 the Ministry of Supply was involved in efforts to find a good supply of zinc either from the old mines or the waste dumps, but the difficulties proved too great. A post World War II effort to process the dumps at Esgair-mwyn eventually failed,

The wrecked dam at Grogwynion.

leaving an interesting complex of buildings which still stand at the time of writing. A Canadian company which drilled in the 1970s in the metalliferous areas of Wales did not return, and it is difficult to believe that there will ever be mining again in north Ceredigion. A visit to the Llywernog mining museum on the A44 near Ponterwyd is the best practical introduction to this remarkable and long-lived episode in Ceredigion's history; there are numerous modern publications and reprints available on the history and technology of this major feature of the county's history.

Into the depths of Cwmystwyth mine.

13. The County Gentry: Zenith and Nadir

An event which took place in the Ystwyth valley in the 1880s was described to the members of the Royal Commission on Welsh Land as they collected evidence in Cardiganshire in 1895. David Morgan, a Trawsgoed family tenant, had been offered a better tenancy as a result of his hard work, and he had spent much money preparing to move. Then his 13-year-old son was caught with a rabbit in a plantation belonging to Lord Lisburne's uncle, Captain Vaughan. As a result, Morgan was told that his promotion had been withdrawn. He sought an interview with Lord Lisburne, who swore at him repeatedly, until Morgan rebuked him, 'Do not you think, my lord, that I am a dog. I am a man, and you are only a man.' The radical ideals of Rousseau and Tom Paine had at last begun to take root in Cardiganshire. Centuries of complete gentry dominance was coming, apparently quite suddenly, to an end.

JOHN Nash made other contributions than Llanerchaeron mansion and church to the county's architecture, all sadly lost. He designed Cardigan's new gaol, completed in 1797, but demolished less than a century later. His bridge at Trecefel, Tregaron, was later replaced, and his five-arch Trefechan bridge at Aberystwyth was destroyed by floods in 1886. His Priory mansion at Cardigan has been almost entirely altered; Llanfechan villa (very like Llanerchaeron) was a ruin by 1861, and his extraordinary triangular Castle House at Aberystwyth was eventually swallowed entirely by Savin's hotel, now the Old College building. He provided designs for out-buildings at Nanteos, but if ever built, they have not survived.

John Nash's villa at Llanerchaeron, before the National Trust restoration.

With the passing of the generations who remembered the Civil Wars and the Glorious Revolution, and with the alarms of the Jacobite rebellions of 1715 and 1745 having little effect in distant Cardiganshire other than the dismissal of Lewis Pryse from Parliament, those gentry families who had estates and produced heirs were able to enjoy a long period of successful rule of the county. Between 1700 and 1850 they almost all rebuilt their houses in a variety of styles according to taste and period: the fine Palladian of Nanteos, the duller classicism of Trawsgoed and Gogerddan, the more elegant late classicism of Mynachty, the delightful Nash villa at Llanerchaeron, the comparatively restrained Strawberry Hill Gothic of the Baldwin Hafod and the exuberant Victorian Gothic of Bronwydd, the ugly blockishness of Castle Hill. They remodelled their gardens, emparked their demesne lands, largely though not entirely abandoned the Welsh language (see below), and held to the Church of England. Many had their estates surveyed and mapped, reorganising their holdings, and those lucky enough to own veins of lead ore continued to exploit them. The greatest families controlled the two parliamentary seats, held the lord lieutenancy and commanded the county militia, while lesser men used their positions as justices of the peace to run local government. True, it became gradually more and more common for the gentry to neglect the office of JP, leaving it to clergymen and doctors to do the work. From 1780 the gentry invested in the turnpike trusts, not simply as a financial speculation but to ensure the roads ran where they wanted them. Thus Thomas Powell of Nanteos (d.1797) was able to close the ancient road that ran past the front of his house, and instead directed the road to the other side of the valley, from which his mansion could be admired without intrusion on his privacy, while Thomas Johnes drove forward the road from Cwmystwyth to Rhaeadr.

Llanerchaeron: John Nash's staircase, before restoration.

It would therefore be a mistake to imagine this as an age without change or conflict. While there were Pryses (not in direct line of descent) at Gogerddan, Vaughans at Trawsgoed and Powells at Nanteos almost throughout the period, other families rose and fell. Gentry families became separated from their estates in a number of ways. They might run out of both sons and daughters, so that the estate would have to be sold, or otherwise disposed of, perhaps gifted to a distant relative, friend or neighbour; thus Henry Lloyd bequeathed the little Maesdwyffrwd estate to his Vaughan neighbours of Trawsgoed in 1687. The unusually high failure rate of male heirs is a feature of the whole gentry class during this period in Wales and England alike. An estate might have to be divided among heiresses, and thus lose its integrity, as when the Cilcennin estate was divided among the married daughters of Rowland Stedman, the core of the estate passing for a while into the sphere of Trawsgoed. The owner might become so poverty-stricken and debt-ridden that sale was the only choice available, as when about 1785 the wretched Cornelius Griffiths sold to Trawsgoed the Cwmnewidion estate in the Ystwyth valley, which he had acquired by marriage and then proceeded to ruin. A fourth kind of failure, the loss of an entire estate by gambling, is not unknown elsewhere but did not happen in Cardiganshire, though farms were apparently lost and won.

THE Pryses of Gogerddan were not proof against dynastic upheavals, though the name remained a talisman in the county. We have already seen that they ran out of direct heirs in 1694, and again in 1720, when a second cousin once removed, Thomas Pryse, was brought in to succeed. His son and heir Lewis died unmarried in 1774, and Lewis's cousin and heir, another Lewis, died in 1779, so the estate devolved on his daughter Margaret Pryse, who had married Edward Loveden Townsend of Buscot, Berkshire. Their son, Pryse Loveden (without the appendage Townsend), succeeded in his mother's right, adopted the surname and arms of Pryse, and moved from England to Wales. He entered vigorously into county life, becoming a JP and High Sheriff, but the Pryses were not quite the power in the land that they had once been; he had to be content with the borough seat in Parliament rather than the county seat, but he remained in place from 1818 until his death in 1849, and was succeeded in the seat by his son Pryse Loveden.

Margaret Pryse of Gogerddan, d. 1784. [National Library of Wales]

GENTRY estates naturally ignored county boundaries, especially the Teifi and Dyfi. Trawsgoed acquired estates in Middlesex and Northumberland, the Pryses in three of Cardiganshire's neighbouring counties, the Powells in Breconshire; similarly, families from 'outside' acquired land in Cardiganshire. One such was the Saunders-Davies family of Pentre, Maenordeifi (Pembs), who by the mid-19th century owned swathes across the south of the county. One unfortunate son of this family was Lt. Owen Saunders-Davies, killed in the Crimea at the age of 21. Many Cardiganshire gentry sons were killed on military service in the 19th century.

So after a century and a half the Herberts vanished from Hafod Uchdryd in 1704; the estate passed by marriage to a Carmarthenshire family, the Johneses of Dolaucothi, and it was only in 1780 that a Johnes, the famous Thomas, took up residence there, his precedent relatives having rented the house to lesser men. Maesyfelin, once so great but eventually heir-less, had vanished long before 1850; its companion estate, Peterwell, fell into ruin. Llanllŷr passed from Lloyds to Leweses. Lesser estates also changed hands; Ynys-hir passed by marriage from Lloyd to Knowles. The Stedmans of Strata Florida ran out of direct heirs in 1744 with the death of Richard Stedman, who had married Anne Powell of Nanteos. There were collateral heirs, but the estate was seized by Anne's brother Thomas, to whom money was owing, and the Nanteos estate was immediately increased by this highly questionable act. The widowed Anne foolishly married the insufferable Sir Herbert Lloyd of Peterwell, but eventually separated from him.

The sons of Pryse Pryse of Gogerddan, by Hugh Hughes, 1826. [National Library of Wales]

While some estates were swallowed up or disintegrated, other entirely new estates appeared. The Richardes family of Pen-glais emerged at the turn of the 18th century, and then produced a cadet branch which created the Tan-y-bwlch estate in the early 19th century. Other new mansions appeared round Aberystwyth, especially in the 19th century: Cwmcynfelyn to the north, Bryneithin (another Richardes house) and Ffosrhydgaled (now the Conrah hotel) to the south. Some estate lands appear to have been recycled from an old estate to its replacement on a nearby site; thus the Rhoscellan estate, between Aberystwyth and Borth, re-emerged in the 19th century as Wallog, with a mansion almost on the beach. William Williams of Pantysiryf, Tregaron, known as 'the king of the mountains' and 'the Job of the West' on account of his enormous sheepflocks, left his wealth to his nephew Nathaniel Williams in 1773. Nathaniel abandoned the family's mountain home and built a new house, Castle Hill, in the more temperate landscape of the lower Ystwyth valley above Llanilar, and his estate passed by the marriage of his daughter to owners from Shropshire, the Loxdales, who are still there. It was no new thing for Englishmen to establish dynasties in the county, as the story of Llwyndyrys (Llandygwydd) demonstrates. Robert Birt, whose family came originally from Essex, commuted between Llwyndyrys and Carmarthen, where he was mayor in 1564. The Birts flourished for over a century, but terminated in an heiress, who sold the estate to Sir William Wogan (d.1710) and it passed via another Pembrokeshire family called Simmons into the hands of the Revd Thomas Griffiths.

Owen Saunders-Davies. [Courtesy of Thomas Lloyd]

Another Englishman, Thomas Bonsall, the 18th-century lead-mining entrepreneur from Derbyshire, bought Fronfraith mansion, just east of Aberystwyth. Herbert Lloyd's Peterwell passed eventually into the hands of 'an outsider and foreigner', the Bristol banker Richard Hart Davis. The Lloyds of Cilgwyn yielded their home and estate to an English family, named Fitzwilliam, who became Hall for several generations before reverting to Fitzwilliam. Ironically it was one of this family, E. Crompton Ll. Fitzwilliam, who in 1853, disillusioned by the poor quality of Welsh gentry MPs, wrote, 'It is a pity that we cannot get someone to represent us who has both the strength and nerve, as well as the capacity to fight the battle of Cambria in Parliament.' He was a man of sufficient independence of mind to befriend the well-known radical and Unitarian Gwilym Marles, and to preach in his chapel at Llwynrhydowen, not at all the behaviour expected of a Cardiganshire gentleman.

Younger brothers of heirs to estates occasionally found themselves, when the heir died, heads of families. Normally they were expected to find their own way in the world, and a study of Welsh gentry younger brothers as a class would be an interesting project. They usually entered the Church or the armed services, or the law; eventually medicine, too, became a tolerated profession. The Revd Dr William Powell inherited Nanteos on the death of his elder brother Thomas in 1752. As a clergyman he could not follow his brother to Parliament, but he was a prominent figure in county life until his death in 1780. Dr Powell's younger brother John had moved in search of his fortune to Africa, where he died. Other younger sons went to Barbados (Carbery Pryse of Gogerddan, whose son eventually inherited the estate), or Jamaica (Thomas Lloyd of Llanfechan). For a later generation, there is a memorial in the Anglican cathedral at Calcutta to two Pugh brothers, administrators of the British Empire, whose bodies had been sent for burial 'to the land of their fathers at Llanbadarnfawr in Wales.'

Illegitimacy remained an obstacle to worldly success as a gentleman, but it was not insurmountable, at least for a man. In 1730 the dissolute second viscount Lisburne was abandoned by his wife Dorothy, who had entrapped him into marriage when drunk; she herself was involved in an adulterous affair, and bore a son, Edward, three years after leaving her husband. She made huge but mendacious efforts to secure the Trawsgoed estate for Edward, which technically should have been his anyway, since a man's wife's child is legally his unless proved otherwise. But the dead earl's brother Wilmot was in possession of the estate, and Dorothy's efforts came to an end in 1754 when the young man accepted a settlement from Wilmot. Edward thus acknowledged his own illegitimacy in return for an allowance of £200 a year. However, he was well looked after. David Lloyd of Brynog (Felin-fach), who was almost certainly his real father, gave him the little estate of Green-grove nearby, once the property of the Lloyds, thus incidentally denying the claim of his own legitimate blood relatives. In his turn Edward Vaughan begot a dynasty of soldiers and sailors whose memorial tablets fill the walls of Llanfihangel Ystrad church; eventually a direct descendant married the heiress of Llangoedmor and moved there. She was Sarah Millingchamp, whose father Benjamin had risen to the ranks of the gentry by

Herbert Millingchamp Vaughan, gentleman-author. [Courtesy of Thomas Lloyd]

ability rather than inheritance. Millingchamp was the son of the chief Customs Officer at the port of Cardigan, and after Oxford graduation and ordination he became a naval chaplain before gaining a chaplaincy with the East India Company at Madras, which made his fortune, and he had been able to buy Llangoedmor in 1801 for £3,500. New blood came into the gentry class from many quarters.

It is difficult to know whether the rate of production of illegitimate children by the county's gentry declined after 1700 or not; my own suspicion is that, particularly in the 19th century, gentlemen were less willing to acknowledge their extramarital offspring than they had been, so counting heads is difficult. Thus William Edward Powell (d.1854) of Nanteos made a youthful marriage and kept his increasingly unhappy wife at home while creating in London a new and extra-marital family. When his wife died Powell remarried, while still maintaining the second family in London, before they finally emigrated, presumably at his expense; his secret was only revealed in the 1990s by the research of Janet Joel. Leslie Baker-Jones has chronicled some of the more obvious cases of immorality among Teifiside gentry. Some involved men who simply did not marry the women they lived with, like William Brigstocke of Blaen-pant; he was only exceptional in that when in 1739 he found a 'suitable' wife, he dismissed his housekeeper, the mother of his six children, and she successfully sued for maintenance, admittedly not very generous.

Some other members of the gentry were more generally immoral. Thomas Bowen (d.1842), rector of Troedyraur and a man of good education and family, was described during his lifetime as being guilty of 'adultery, fornication and incontinency, neglect of his ministerial duties and other enormous Crimes.' The most startling of all Cardiganshire's wayward gentry was the homosexual masochist George Powell (d.1882) of Nanteos, a character of extreme contradictions and a patron of Icelandic culture and politics, and of the arts (see Chapter 23). When in 1878 he finally inherited Nanteos he undertook what must surely have been a frivolous marriage with a chambermaid from Fishguard, and in a letter to a friend wrote a hilarious account of his shambolic performance as High Sheriff for the county. His rival in eccentricity was Squire Treadwell of Aberllolwyn, who harnessed twenty horses to draw a miniature steamship from Aberystwyth to Llyn Eiddwen on Mynydd Bach!

Despite the colourful appeal to a modern reader of the sexual antics of the gentry, we should not be deceived; the vast majority of gentry offspring were lawfully begotten. Marriage was a serious business rather than a matter for romance, though real affection might well follow; the inclinations of the individual had to be weighed against the greater needs of the estate. An eldest son was expected to marry well; preferably an heiress, but failing that, a substantial dowry had to be sought. Other than the drunken second viscount Lisburne, the heirs of Trawsgoed in the 18th century all married sensibly and acquired estates in Devon, Middlesex and Northumberland in consequence, the eventual sale of which enabled the estate to survive massive debts. Indeed, from 1770 until 1820 the Devon estate at Mamhead was the Vaughan's main home, but it had to be sold to relieve the Trawsgoed estate of its many mortgages. It is to be noted that Sir John Vaughan (d.1674) had been the

SUBSCRIPTION lists for Welsh books may be taken as a sign of at least token interest in the vernacular culture. The 1718 edition of *Holl Ddyledswydd Dyn* was bought by William Powell of Nanteos and Lewis Pryse of Gogerddan; the second edition of *Drych y Prif Oesoedd* (1740) by Theophilus Evans, himself a Teifiside squire-parson, was bought by, among others, John Bowen of Troed-yr-aur, John Viscount Lisburne (d.1741), Walter Lloyd MP of Foelallt, Richard Lloyd MP of Mabws, David Lloyd of Lloyd Jack, John Lloyd of Peterwell, Sir Lucius Lloyd of Maesyfelin and Richard Stedman of Strata Florida.

last of the Vaughans of Trawsgoed to marry a Welsh wife; from then on they have always married women from England or beyond; an English wife was considered a desirable asset by Welsh landowners, while English squires were always willing to take on a Welsh heiress.

One major result of these marriages was that they accelerated the decline of the Welsh language on the hearths of the great houses, though surviving to a degree as a means of communicating with tenants. This decline was inevitable in a world where education meant school in England, further education at Oxford or the Inns of Court, and a career administering the law in English. Some gentry went so far as to translate the Welsh names of their houses into English; thus in the 18th century Trawsgoed became Crosswood, Rhydycolomennod became Pigeonsford and Gwernant became Alderbrook. However, as in Ireland, this attitude to the language did not prevent members of the squirearchy from considering themselves to be Welsh (or Irish), even in a world where 'England' usually signified Great Britain. This may be contrasted with the attitude of Welsh-speakers, to whom *Cymro* meant 'a Welsh-speaking Welshman' and *Sais* a person who spoke English, an attitude which has not entirely disappeared even today. Thus Welsh harpists continued to be welcome at Gogerddan and Nanteos well into the 19th century as signifiers of identity, whereas the bardic circuit was long dead – though Welsh doggerel might be recited at the coming-of-age of an heir.

It has already been noted above that William Powell I of Nanteos (d.1738) wrote eloquently to Mrs Frederick, a rich London widow, on behalf of his son Thomas (d.1752), who had been reluctant to show any interest in young women until he met the widow's daughter Mary. The result was a dowry that enabled Thomas to build a mansion worthy of his wealthy wife, but since the couple were childless, it was Thomas's brother, the Revd Dr William Powell, who benefited. In that instance the amount of the dowry is not known, but in 1750 John Lloyd of Peterwell married Elizabeth le Heup and a huge dowry of £50,000. His notorious younger brother Herbert, who succeeded him, had had to be content in 1742 with a (still considerable) dowry of £15,000. Lesser men naturally expected less; Thomas Lloyd of Abertrinant married Elizabeth Vaughan, a daughter of Trawsgoed, and must have been glad of her £3,000, which was five times his own annual rental. It is most unlikely that these sums of money were always paid over in cash at the time of the wedding; they were more probably used as accounts on which to draw as needed. In any case dowries were a contradictory blessing; a wife might bring in money, but daughters took money away. When a husband died leaving a widow she had to be provided with a dowager's income; Dorothy Countess of Lisburne lived on for fifty years as widow of the second viscount after his death in 1741, a severe drain on the debt-burdened estate of a brother-in-law who loathed her.

Among many of the gentry there was an obvious tendency to live well beyond their means, and although this may seem irresponsible it is understandable, since they had to bear the heavy expectations of their contemporaries. A true gentleman was in theory expected to 'live of his own', although as we have seen certain occupations were acceptable. A true gentleman should never be stingy; he should dress himself, his wife and family well, keep open house and a good cellar, take his family to London or Bath, give to charitable causes, subscribe to the publication of books, make a generous allowance to his eldest son and provide dowries for his daughters, buy places in the Church or the Army for younger sons, provide education for all his children and annuities for many dependants. Add to all these the obsession of the age with gambling and the temptations of alcohol and it is easy to see how income was more than swallowed up by expenditure, especially when further added to by hunting and shooting. The Vaughans of Trawsgoed, solvent in 1684, were involved in mortgaging the estate and selling unentailed lands from 1720 onward because of the second viscount's reckless gambling; the family was never again free of debt. Thomas Johnes of Hafod claimed never to have refused a man employment, but could not pay his wife's haberdashery bills or the curate of Eglwysnewydd's salary; eventually, and unusually for so influential a figure, he was declared bankrupt. William Edward Powell (d.1854) of Nanteos airily dismissed the pleas of his agent and trustees that he should live within his means. While keeping his first wife seriously short of cash and simultaneously running his second and illegitimate family in London, Powell ignored the pillaging of his birthright by his bailiff, by mining agents and by his famously red-nosed butler, and simply carried on spending. A new carriage, a new columned portico for the house, splendid new

The Nanteos stables, by an unknown architect *c*1840.

stables, all were necessary in Powell's eyes to maintain the port of a gentleman, especially one who was county MP and Lord Lieutenant. As for debts to mere tradesmen, whether butchers, vintners or haberdashers, any importunity on their part could be dismissed by the unspoken but known threat of the withdrawal of all gentry custom. Even the Duke of Newcastle, eventual owner of the Hafod Uchdryd estate, ran up debts of £900 in Aberystwyth. Jill Barber has described in detail the common gentry practice of ignoring their basic legal obligations by ruthlessly exploiting their social power, even to the extent, in the case of Roderick Richardes of Penglais, of blackguarding his servant to lend his savings for his wife's use. Richardes, a wife-beater, who at one stage fled to France to escape his creditors, has left no evidence of any virtue to offset his vices.

There were exceptions to these lists of debts and debtors. Lewis Gwynne of Mynachty, we are told, 'had in his house when he died, such a quantity of gold, that a horse could not carry the weight . . . and when put on a sledge it was with difficulty he could draw it . . . The amount in gold is about £100,000, besides £50,000 in the stocks . . . He was generous to the poor, always a friend to the necessitous, and an upright gentleman.' It is not clear how Lewis Gwynne acquired such enormous wealth, other than by being a careful bachelor, but at least much of it was eventually put to good use by his heir. This was Gwynne's cousin, the Revd Alban Thomas, a Hampshire clergyman, who had persuaded Susannah Jones the heiress of the Tyglyn estate to marry him after a lengthy courtship, and he added her surname to his own. He was further enriched when in 1805 he and his wife co-inherited the wealth of Lewis Gwynne, and he then added Gwynne to his already-lengthened surname. A man of vision, he spent much of the money in the creation of the harbour and town of Aberaeron. The rest of this fortune was squandered after his death when various claimants to the estate went to law against each other.

Outright conflict among the gentry seems to have declined as manners slowly improved during the 18th century, and after the disappearance of the Court of Star Chamber in 1689 they were somewhat more wary of taking each other to court. But clashes there certainly were. There was a standing feud between the Parrys of Llidiardau and Thomas Johnes of Aber-mad who, provoked by Thomas Parry's legal actions against him in 1741, set some thugs on Parry who was severely wounded, and brought a mob to attack Parry's Aberystwyth house. The convicted smuggler and murderer William Owen confessed in 1747 before his execution that on one occasion he had led some 'gentlemen and others' to attack Aber-mad, rolling a flaming barrel of gunpowder down the slope in the hope of blowing the house up. In 1753 Herbert Lloyd of Peterwell and a mob of Nanteos supporters arrested the Crown's agent for the county's mines, Lewis Morris, at gunpoint and carted him off to jail in Cardigan. In 1798 James Parry of the Llidiardau Parrys murdered a young man at Llwynhywel, Parry's home, and was eventually convicted of manslaughter, but probably never served his laughable three-months' sentence. Doubtless some gentlemen thought they were maintaining, if not the law, at least their idea of social order, by persecuting Methodists. Many districts have traditions of mobs, urged on by local gentry and clergy, attacking Daniel Rowland and other Methodist preachers. Perhaps the best-known example is of Richard James, an Aber-mad servant, sent to disrupt Daniel Rowland's preaching, and being converted by it.

Such behaviour was no longer practicable during the 19th century, with its extraordinary growth of Nonconformity which embraced the great majority of the Cardiganshire population, but most gentry families remained resolute for the Church, though the practice of actual piety was neglected. A distinction must be made between the majority of gentry, who were sufficiently tolerant to give or lease land for the building of chapels but who expected their tenants to be loyal politically, and the extreme exemplified in Miss Morrice of Carrog (Llanddeiniol), who only allowed tenancies to Church members; this was ironic, since Carrog had once welcomed and defended Methodists. There was another gentry minority, only to be found in southern Cardiganshire, who actively supported one or other manifestation of Nonconformity. One of the first had been Phillip Pugh of Blaenpennal (1679-1760) whom we have already encountered; he ministered to Cardiganshire's Independent congregation, and built Llwynpiod chapel, Llangybi, at his own expense.

SOUTH Cardiganshire's best-known estate was Bronwydd, always associated with the Lloyd family. Over some 250 years the Lloyds had successfully pursued at least four heiresses, acquiring six estates in the process, so that by 1880 the Bronwydd income was some £6,000 a year, much of it from Pembrokeshire. Thomas Lloyd (1740-1807) was a leading agricultural improver and tree-planter, himself farming his 250-acre demesne. Thomas Davies Lloyd (1820-77) was keen to see the development of harbour facilities at Newport (Pembs.) and New Quay, and sold land for railway development. He sought to gain a peerage, but had to be satisfied with a baronetcy (1863). He was the family's only MP, in the Liberal interest. His son Sir Marteine Lloyd encouraged his tenants to appear before the Land Commission, and followed the family tradition of never evicting a tenant. By the end of the 19th century the estate had debts of £94,000, which were not allowed to hinder the early acquisition of electric light and the telephone.

The great majority of the Cardiganshire gentry, however, like their class throughout Wales and England, supported the established Church. They might find themselves as JPs sanctioning the registration of dissenting chapels, but their own interest, whether spiritual or socio-political, kept them loyal to the parish church, not least because many of them had a vested financial interest in it – their ownership of tithes and of the patronage of livings. It must of course be allowed that many were sincere in their beliefs and practice; John Lewis of Gernos, Llangunllo, Walter Lloyd of Coedmor and Stephen Parry of Noyadd Trefawr, Llandygwydd, were all involved in the publication of religious literature before the Llangeitho revivals. The challenge of Methodism inspired some of them to repair and restore the county's churches, many of which had remained in dire condition through most of the 18th century. True, a goodly number contributed to the major repair of St Mary's, Cardigan, after the tower collapsed; Herbert Lloyd provided a new clock for the restored tower in 1762. But it was after 1800 that the serious renewal of the county's churches began, often led by the local gentry, whether in setting an example or bearing all the costs. New churches were also seen to be necessary; Sir Pryse Pryse of Gogerddan built Penrhyn-coch church, and his family were thenceforward buried there rather than at Llanbadarn Fawr. Matthew Davies Williams of Cwmcynfelyn, inspired by his younger brother Isaac's Tractarianism, provided a new church at Llangorwen (1841) north of Aberystwyth, the first 'Oxford Movement' church anywhere in Wales.

Bronwydd mansion. [Courtesy of Thomas Lloyd]

The attitudes of the Cardiganshire gentry to secular culture were, like their attitude towards religion, highly mixed. Some doubtless were not wholly unlike Squire Western in perceived hostility to literature and the arts, preferring the art of the fishing rod, the craft of the gun and the furore of the hunting field to all indoor sports other than gambling and wenching. On the other hand, education did a good deal to produce a man like Wilmot Vaughan (d.1800) of Trawsgoed, first earl of Lisburne, whose 'understanding was superior to most, equal to the best. His classical attainments were extensive, possessing all the elegance without the pedantry of the professed scholar.' While this is taken from his obituary in *The Gentleman's Magazine*, in which the writer was not upon oath, the earl's excellent written English is certainly adequate proof of his good schooling; he seems to have added considerably to the Trawsgoed library, seeking out French and Italian classics in particular. Thomas Johnes (d.1816) of Hafod, admittedly not a native of the county, set an even higher example of the gentleman dillettante, with his splendid library and collection of works of art, his bringing of Gothic architecture to the county's remotest valley, as well as a printing press, the first ever in mid-Wales, on which were produced his splendid translations of the French chroniclers, Froissart and Monstrelet, a task in which he was encouraged by his remarkable wife Jane. In the south of the county there were worthwhile libraries at Blaen-pant and Alltrodyn. Gentry patronage of painting and sculpture is dealt with in Chapter 23 below.

Some of the greater gentry combined a certain level of culture with a love of the blood-sports to which others were totally dedicated. The right to shoot game of any kind, indeed the right to own a gun, was ferociously guarded by law; only the landowner, his immediate heir, and friends he might nominate, were entitled to shoot. While pheasant, partridge, snipe and winter wildfowl did little direct damage to the crops of tenants, the latter's inability to defend their fields, gardens and poultry against the ravages of rabbits and foxes meant that in effect they paid a high tax in kind for their landlords' sport. The Cardiganshire gentry were mostly enthusiastic supporters of the whole framework of law which prescribed savage punishments for offenders; it is pleasantly ironic that a degenerate son of the Richardes family of Penglais was prosecuted in an Aberystwyth court for poaching.

The war between poachers and landlords which went on all over Britain culminated, as far as Cardiganshire was concerned, in the 1868 murder of a Trawsgoed gamekeeper by the poacher Wil Cefn Coch, who for months was hidden from the law by the populace before being spirited away to America with the aid of the respectable Aberystwyth grocer, man of letters and Sunday School superintendent John 'Ivon' Jones. During the 19th century the cult of pheasant-slaughter seems to have gained in intensity even as the gentry lost their political supremacy. As for fox- and otter-hunting in Cardiganshire, the history remains to be written; the subject is dealt with briefly in Chapter 23 below. It is claimed that the Teifiside hunt dates from *c*1700, while the premier hunt in the north was that of Gogerddan, but virtually all the gentry kept horses and dogs for hunting and shooting, and would attend hunt balls and dinners. The arrival of the railway helped the movement both of hunters and hounds from one venue to another.

* * *

By 1880 virtually all the old Cardiganshire families had been replaced by newcomers of various origin; only the Vaughans of Trawsgoed had occupied their ancient dwelling-place without interruption or inheritance through the female line. Nevertheless, it might have seemed to a bystander that little had changed, that the gentry still held pride of place in all the county's affairs. However, much had already changed, and more would change again. Not only were rich men moving into the county to take over estates; some of the men of Cardiganshire were upwardly mobile too. John Evans, a merchant of Commerce House, Aberystwyth, bought Lovesgrove in 1843 and married Elizabeth Pugh of Aber-mad, two steps which made a gentleman of him. Morris Davies combined gentry origins in Montgomeryshire with a flourishing business in Aberystwyth selling corn and lime, and his family acquired Ffosrhydgaled, Llanfarian.

The Government Return of Landowners 1873: Cardiganshire.

The following owned estates of 2000+ acres within the county:

Landowner	Home	Acreage	Rental Income
James Bowen	Haverfordwest*	3649 acres	£1918 *Pembs
A.H.S. Davies	Pentre*	2930	£1760 *Pembs
J.M.Davies	Antaron*	3984	£565 *Ab'wyth
Lewis C. Davies	Ysgubornycoed	3153	£898
Matthew V. Davies	Tan-y-bwlch	3674	£974
Col. H.D. Evans	Highmead	2808	£1863
F.T.G. Gibbs	Greenford*	2320	£620 *Middlesex
A.Gwynne	Aberaeron	3794	£3678
J.B.Harford	Falcondale	5782	£4256
T.R.H.J.Hughes	Castell-du*	2240	£1331 *Llanwnnen
John Inglis Jones	Derry Ormond	4782	£2570
William Jones	Glandennis*	2744	£1424 *Lampeter
Mrs M. Ashby Lewis	Llanaeron	4397	£2591
Earl of Lisburne	Trawsgoed	42,666	£10,579
John D. Lloyd	Alltrodyn	5417	£2429
Robert L. Lloyd	Nantgwyllt*	3521	£1393 *Rads
C.K. Longcroft	Llanina	2709	£1158
James Loxdale	Aberystwyth	4915	£2458
R.H.W.Miles	Bingham*	2135	£1739 *England
Mrs Morris	Capel Dewi*	3993	£246 *Carms.
George W. Parry	Llidiardau	3561	£1947
Major Lloyd Phillips	Mabws	2682	£1561
W.T.R. Powell	Nanteos	21,933	£9024
Sir Pryse Pryse	Gogerddan	28,684	£10634
Lewis Pugh Pugh	Aber-mad	6894	£2369
J.E.Rogers	Abermeurig	3263	£896
Mrs Saunders	Cwrt Henry*	2133	£875 *Carms
David Thomas	Llanfair	2560	£1204
Gwinnett Tyler	Mount Gernos	2051	£778
Capt H. Vaughan	Brynog	3561	£1927
John Waddingham	Hafod	10,963	£1638
D.K.W.Webley-Parry	Noyadd Trefawr	2105	£1021

Commentary. Even allowing for the variety of land in the county, there are several remarkably low rentals listed above, *vide* J.M. Davies, Antaron and Mrs Morris of Capel Dewi. Not one Cardiganshire landlord achieved an average value of £1 per acre per annum. Lord Dynevor's 7208 acres in Carmarthenshire just reached that level, earning him £7253. Even Earl Cawdor's 51,517 acres in Pembrokeshire and Carmarthenshire 'only' brought in £34,987. In practice rentals always fell below these figures on account of late or non-payments and rebates. Two well-known Cardiganshire estates fall below the 2000-acre figure: Sir Thomas D. Lloyd of Bronwydd owned 1974 acres (rental £1,287) and Thomas E. Lloyd of Coedmor held 1519 acres (rental £1,046), but both men owned considerable lands south of the Teifi, as did Gogerddan.

The weakening of the older families brought a certain amount of political change, which is dealt with in more detail in Chapter 19 below. It can be briefly summarised here as, firstly, the displacement of the Gogerddan-Trawsgoed-Nanteos nexus from the parliamentary seats by lesser landowners, and secondly, the latter's eventual disappearance from the hustings in the early 1920s. The change was more gradual than it may have seemed in 1868 when E.M. Richards, an avowed Liberal, defeated the Trawsgoed candidate for the county seat. After the defeat of Richards in 1874 the county returned landed gentry until 1921, a period during which constituencies in north Wales had replaced their controlling gentry families with men like David Lloyd George, T.E. Ellis, J. Herbert Lewis and George Osborne Morgan.

Although until 1889 the Quarter Sessions still controlled elements of local government, many gentry had long withdrawn from the responsibilities (though not the title) of being JPs. New functions of government, such as the provision of workhouses, water and sanitation, and compulsory education, had by 1880 brought about the introduction of elected local boards which wielded considerable influence and acted as an apprenticeship in local democracy. More fundamentally, the power of land in the British economy had been largely replaced by that of industry. Indeed, the main prop for the continuance of country houses was the desire of so many industrialists and wealthy tradesmen to become gentlemen themselves, but most baulked at the responsibility of land management. Land was not profitable; agriculture suffered a series of depressions, and was increasingly marginalised both by cheap imports, first of corn, then of frozen meat, while labourers migrated steadily to the ironworks and coalfields, where, however dire the living conditions, they were not so likely to starve.

The coup de grâce was delivered to the gentry of Cardiganshire and nearly all the rest of Wales by the results of the first county council elections in 1889. Of the thirteen Welsh counties, twelve had chosen what were in effect Liberal majorities; only Breconshire held out for the Tories. Many squires had stood for election, either expecting or hoping against hope that the deference on which they had insisted for so long would stand them in good stead. The sixth earl of Lisburne was unopposed for Strata Florida, and was appointed an alderman, but must have been disappointed that a Liberal coal-merchant was chosen over his head as first chairman of the county council; a number of other Cardiganshire gentlemen were less fortunate, losing their contests.

In retrospect, land sales by the larger estates seem to have begun in earnest in the 1880s, though estates had come on the market from time to time over many generations. In the late 18th and mid-19th centuries some sales had been in aid of consolidation. Now, however, death duties, chronic debt, declining incomes, agricultural gloom, shortage of servants and political castration drove the landowners of Cardiganshire, like many across Britain and Ireland, to sell in all seriousness. Tens of thousands of acres of Nanteos, Gogerddan, Trawsgoed and other lands were disposed of. Thus by the end of 1886 parts of the Gogerddan estate had been sold for a total of £118,783, much of which had to be used to pay off mortgages; at the same time, Sir Pryse Pryse could not resist the temptation to buy from Trawsgoed the 2000+ acres of Penrhyn-coch lands (known as Tirymyneich or Doferchen) which had once been the property of Strata Florida.

True, some landowners continued with their high lifestyle, in which shooting and the south of France figured prominently. In the 1890s Trawsgoed mansion was doubled in size with the addition of a hideous wing in sub-chateau style, thanks to borrowed money. Trawsgoed's gardens were splendidly remodelled, with a magnificent arboretum and a huge glasshouse. Then came the World War. Most affected was Nanteos, whose squire, Edward Athelstan Powell, lost his health in Mesopotamia and his only son and heir, indeed his only legitimate blood relative, William ('Billy'), in the last week of the war. It is said that the young man was shot by his own men, who may have been reluctant to join in a suicidal infantry charge when the war was so clearly ending; such a story can never be proved or disproved. Other losses are recorded in Chapter 24 below. The young Earl of Lisburne, serving in the newly-formed Welsh Guards, survived the slaughter, but the lifestyle at Trawsgoed was much curtailed during the interwar years despite the Earl's marriage to a Chilean beauty from a wealthy family. Eventually the mansion was sold along with its most of its remaining farms in 1947, though the family still retains a substantial acreage, mostly for shooting. The most successful survivor of World War I was Lewis Pugh Evans of Lovesgrove, grandson of John Evans of Aber-mad. He followed a military career, and as a lieutenant-colonel won the Victoria Cross for gallantry, eventually retiring as Brigadier-General to follow a successful farming career.

Sir Marteine Lloyd of Bronwydd.
[Courtesy of Thomas Lloyd]

While so much was changing between 1880 and 1930, one Cardiganshire country house seemed totally unaffected. At Hafod Uchdryd the lifestyle of the 1880s was maintained, with morning prayers every day for the servants, with the postman bringing fresh fish daily from Aberystwyth as well as the *Times*, which had to be ironed before being read to the elderly Thomas Waddingham. In 1930 the nonagenarian gentleman had to move to Aberystwyth for the sake of his health and he died there in 1937, aged 97. Within fifteen years his mansion was empty and roofless, and like much of the estate was in the hands of the Forestry Commission; in less than thirty years its ruins had to be destroyed. Waddingham's death in 1937 coincided with that of the popular Sir Marteine Lloyd of Bronwydd. Born in 1851, Sir Marteine's father Thomas had continued to build up the family estate while other landowners were starting to sell. Like Edward Powell of Nanteos, Lloyd lost his only son in World War I. Bronwydd was abandoned after the sale of 1937 following Sir Marteine's death, and it too is now a ruin, in process of clearance.

The fate of Gogerddan mansion was far more dignified that that of Hafod and Bronwydd; it became the home of the Welsh Plant Breeding Station, now the Institute for Grassland and Environmental Research. But the Pryse family had to endure numerous humiliations before vanishing entirely from the county they had dominated for so long. Sir Pryse Pryse (1838-1906), a well-travelled Welsh-speaker, had a brood of sons. One worked in the Daimler factory in Coventry and another finished his life as a vagrant, dependent on charity. Sir Pryse's heir was Sir Edward Lewis Pryse, who had been a major supporter of his younger brother Lewes in the development of the Royal Welsh Agricultural Show from its early Cardiganshire days, and was a prominent figure in many county activities. He died in 1918, shattered by his wartime experiences in France; his brother and heir Sir Lewes died in 1946 and another brother, Sir George, in 1948, who fifty years earlier had been the estate's steward. Sir George's son Pryse Loveden Pryse-Saunders sold Gogerddan, which had never been his home, to the University College at Aberystwyth; the last of the Pryses, he died in 1962. But Sir Lewes Pryse's much younger widow Marjorie, Lady Pryse, continued as the family's last representative, following a colourfully eccentric lifestyle in charge of the Gogerddan hounds, and gradually declining into a wretched yet cheerfully endured poverty before her death in 1993.

A Gogerddan monument in Llanbadarn Fawr church.

A few Cardiganshire houses and estates still remain in private hands, some with family connections to the county's past. A Loxdale still owns and runs the small Castle Hill estate in the Ystwyth valley, though not living in the mansion itself. Llanllŷr is still owned by Mrs Loveday Gee, daughter of the late Captain J. Hext Lewes, last of the county's Lords Lieutenant. Aberllolwyn is a small but attractive house in private ownership at Llanfarian; Alltyrodyn, Llidiardau, Mabws, Wern Newydd, Wallog, Noyadd Trefawr and Mynachty are all in new hands. Bryneithin has reverted most attractively to private ownership after a period as Welsh headquarters of the British Geological Survey.

Other mansions have endured various fates. Highmead, south-west of Llanybydder, was originally Rhuddlan Teifi, a court of Pryderi, Lord of Dyfed, wronged hero of the fourth branch of the Mabinogi. Historically it was the centre of a grange belonging to the Cistercian abbey at Whitland, then home to a branch of the Lloyds of Castell Hywel; it passed by marriage to the Evanses, and after several recent decades as a local authority residential school for disadvantaged pupils is now occupied by the European Institute of Human Sciences, and signposted in English and two Asian languages, but not Welsh. Castell Hywel became a school, then a farm, and was recently a holiday centre which closed in November 2002; the food company of that name operates from Carmarthen. Pen-glais is the property of the University at Aberystwyth, used until 2004 as the Principal's official residence. The Victorian Aber-mad, a fine building by J.P. Seddon, became first a school and then an old people's home; Cwmcynfelyn is also an old people's home, conveniently but depressingly next door to the new Aberystwyth crematorium. Derry Ormond was demolished in 1953 and Penywenallt in 1985. Ynys-hir, Abermeurig, Tyglyn Aeron and Falcondale are hotels; Pen-y-wern is a caravanning centre. Nanteos, well-preserved, has been available for bed and breakfast, but was recently sold, and will become a Japanese language school. Trawsgoed is in process of restoration after its years as the Welsh headquarters of the Agricultural Advisory Service, its future not decided at the time of writing. Llanerchaeron is unique – the only National Trust mansion in Ceredigion, along with its core estate; Cardigan Priory is also unique in the county, being now a hospital. Waunifor is now home to the Template Foundation, which runs educational courses on a wide range of subjects. Cilgwyn (Adpar) is empty, Lovesgrove divided up.

Llanerchaeron, after restoration.

Note 1: Garden History

Garden history is a latecomer to historiography; a certain ignorant snobbery, now defunct, once decreed that – apart from Powis Castle and Bodnant – there were no *real* gardens in Wales. Not only are there many – there were a good few in Cardiganshire and several have survived into the new Ceredigion era. A landowner had to have a good garden to match the status of his house; the oldest of which we have any knowledge is the formal garden at 17th-century Trawsgoed. The line between garden and park was a fine one, sometimes drawn by a ha-ha; the garden was domestic, the park was the world beyond (at least in the imagination), and each had to be carefully planned. At the turn of the 20th century Trawsgoed had one of the finest gardens in mid-Wales, and though various difficulties have wrought some havoc, it is still possible to appreciate the magnificent late Victorian arboretum, with many specimen trees, the fine oak-grove, and the remnants of the water garden and flower beds around the defunct fountain. The walled garden at Nanteos must have been splendid in its time; the walls now surround a wilderness. Restoration of the historic landscape at Hafod Uchdryd has been in progress, not without controversy but with some obvious benefits; the gardens as such are lost beyond recall. The most rewarding site at present is the restored Llanerchaeron walled garden, intricately patterned and wonderfully fruitful; other gardens at Ynys-hir, Llanllŷr, Penglais, Cwmcynfelyn, Ynys-hir and Pigeonsford all have their attractions. Their histories, and those of other great houses, have been well catalogued by Dr Caroline Palmer.

Llanerchaeron from the air.
[Crown copyright: Royal Commission on Ancient & Historical Monuments, Wales]

Note 2: The Earls of Cardigan

Thomas Lord Brudenell (d.1663) was elevated to an earldom in 1661 for a £1,000 payment in addition to the £5,000 he had already paid Charles I for his barony. I cannot discover why Cardigan was the chosen title; he was an Englishman without any apparent connection with the town or county.

14. Order and Disorder

In Cardiganshire, as elsewhere in early modern times, the majesty of the law was frequently mocked by public attitudes, by the feebleness of its personnel and by the tyrannical inclinations of local gentry and officials. There was often widespread popular sympathy for criminals. Mayors of Cardigan sometimes acted as petty kings; when in 1729 two of the county's JPs arrested a rioter in the town streets, the deputy mayor attacked them and forced the release of the rioter, telling one of the magistrates: 'No Justice shall Intermeddle in my Corporation, I'll wipe his Commission in my Backside.' Gentry feuded with each other when not ensuring that the poor knew their place; violence was commonplace, both social and domestic. Those who still dream of the good old days would be horrified to see the levels of past crime and the brutality of the courts, where accused men and women had absolutely no right to defend themselves, where trials lasted a few minutes, where verdicts were delivered in batches, and where judges were always in haste to move on.

It is of course true that the acts for reforming the administration of Wales, passed in 1535, 1536 and 1543, had done a good deal to improve the organisation of justice throughout the country, though its actual administration left much to be desired. There was a uniform system of courts in every county, though it is not always simple to understand their relationships with each other. Elementary matters of trespass by people or animals, and such matters as road maintenance and the allocation of welfare according to the Poor Laws, were dealt with either by a local court leet or by the parish vestry meeting. Immoral behaviour was supposed to go before a church consistory court, but this does not always seem to have functioned in Cardiganshire, and every so often a higher court had to deal with a string of cases of morally offensive behaviour, such as adultery and rowdy behaviour on Sunday.

Petty crime could be dealt with either by two Justices of the Peace sitting informally, or by the county's justices in Quarter Sessions – a court which also functioned as the controlling body in local government. Crime and civil suits (e.g. for slander, for debt) were intended to be taken before the court of Great Sessions, meeting every spring and autumn in Cardigan; in 1605 the judges were instructed to hold 'an assize or great sessions' at Aberystwyth, but this does not appear to have happened. It had been the Crown's intention that these courts should cover all offences and appeals except cases of treason. Unfortunately the London authorities had reckoned without the ingenuity of the Welsh. Some took their prosecutions to the Council of Wales and the Marches at Ludlow, which was a court as well as a council. Many Welsh gentry preferred to drag opponents before various courts in London, and many cases must have occurred which it is no longer easy to trace in surviving records, except those of the court of Star Chamber, which have been indexed.

Magistrates had little official guidance, and could be suspected of operating in their own interests, particularly in cases of trespass and poaching. Constables in the countryside and watchmen in the towns were reluctant to undertake such unpopular duties for little reward and much obloquy. Smuggling was commonplace throughout the 18th and early 19th century, and was widely connived at, to the despair of the authorities. Prisons were usually disgusting places and often insecure. The inadequacies of trial procedure are described below. It is hardly surprising that small, close-knit societies preferred their own methods of policing, which by the 19th century, if not before, included 'rough music' and the *ceffyl pren*.

It is fortunate that the records of the courts of Great Sessions in Wales are, despite lacunae, a major source of information about crime, justice and punishment in Wales; the surviving gaol files and the many plea rolls are a mine of information of a kind not available for the same period in England, where disposable records were deliberately weeded out when assizes finished. Huge mounds of these Welsh court documents, often filthy, rotten and rat-eaten were found in Carmarthen when, after the abolition of the courts of Great Sessions in 1830 and their replacement by assizes on the English model, the surviving archives were carted off (literally) to the new Public Record Office in London, and thence, a century later, to the National Library of Wales, where most have been cleaned and repaired – an enormous task.

The *ceffyl pren* or 'cock-horse' of the nursery rhyme was a means of social humiliation of people whose behaviour was unacceptable. A man who allowed his wife to rule his home, a man who beat his wife too harshly, a man or woman behaving scandalously, would be bound and mounted on a pole and carried about the village to the banging of pans. The custom lasted in Cardiganshire until the mid-1860s.

Thus witness statements made to a justice of the peace in cases of murder and theft survive in some numbers. Prisoner lists are sometimes available, listing all the men and women in prison, with the punishments to be inflicted noted beside each name. Jury lists are numerous. Coroner's jury verdicts survive. Latin writs set out the accusation made against a prisoner, and on the back may be written the verdict of the grand (preliminary) jury, saying that the case was either good (i.e. it should go before the court) or not good, in which case the prisoner would go free. Civil cases are preserved in plea rolls; reading them is like fighting with a vellum hydra, since the parchment scrolls, all bound together and tightly rolled up for centuries, have a life of their own.

As an example of a witness statement, consider the following. On July 21, 1657 Nicholas Morgan of Llangoedmor, a young man of 24, gave evidence before justices of the peace in the case of the murder of Morgan Robert, a two-year-old child. 'I came to Robert Morgan's house near Llechryd,' he said, 'and there was the body of Morgan Robert, only son of Robert Morgan, murdered. I asked, "Who killed the child?" and Robert Morgan replied, "I did, with my knife."' According to another witness, the father was actually holding his child's corpse. That information is adapted from the witness statements taken soon after the incident but some time before the actual trial. Robert Morgan was held in Cardigan gaol for two years before being found guilty and then reprieved, as we are told by the calendar of prisoners. Alas, no explanation is offered in the surviving documents for either the behaviour of the killer or for his reprieve. A century later William Morris of Anglesey commented to his brother Lewis that homicide was now held as cheap in the island as it always had been in Cardiganshire.

A JP had far more to do than simply take witness statements. He could command the local annually-appointed constables to assist him in apprehending a suspect. He could not release, except on bail, a person whom he suspected of a crime following his examination of witnesses. He had to bind by oath both the complainant (who was in effect the prosecutor) and the witnesses to appear at the next Sessions; if they were absent, the case had to be held over or else fail. He also of course had to ensure the production of the accused at the Sessions, and was expected to attend in person.

The arrival of the lawyers in Cardigan for the spring and autumn Great Sessions was a grand occasion, largely paid for by the High Sheriff for the year; expenses included travel, dinner and wine for the judges, trumpeters and their clothing, cockades, javelin- and pike-bearers and bell-ringers. Many JPs would be in attendance, together with wives and daughters, for whom this was a serious social occasion. On Monday the court would be formally opened, but no business would be conducted. On Tuesday the two judges would parade in full legal dress to attend church, waited upon by the county's lord lieutenant or his deputies, the county high sheriff and an array of lesser officials. In the afternoon the grand jury of JPs would be given their charge for the occasion, and have to decide which of the accused men and women should go forward for trial (*billa vera*) and which not (*ignoramus*). On Wednesday business postponed from the previous session would be dealt with. On Thursday the defendants in criminal cases would be tried in rapid succession before the petty jury of citizens from Cardigan and thereabouts; the jury would wait until all cases had passed before them and then deliver a string of verdicts; it is hard to believe that such a peremptory system was just. New business would be dealt with on Friday, and on Saturday the court would move on to its next location, Haverfordwest.

The clerks of the court had a great deal to do before and during the court's week of meetings, preparing the calendar of prisoners and bills of indictment, while the sheriff had to call juries together. Prisoners had a few rights; they could plead guilty or not guilty, object to jurors and make statements after the verdict prior to sentencing, though how many were capable of doing so may be doubted, though this was the occasion on which a man could plead benefit of clergy and a woman plead her belly. Before 1695 there was no such person as a defence lawyer. Hearsay evidence was admitted. It should be noted that for the first century of the Great Sessions in Cardiganshire, every judge was an Englishman; the first Welsh judge was only appointed in 1642, and subsequent Welsh appointments were not common.

The majesty of the law, however impressive it may have appeared on the streets of Cardigan when the Great Sessions opened, was far from commanding universal respect. George Owen gives a lively description of Cwmystwyth as it was about 1594. He tells us that many thieves lived there as outlaws, and 'the place itself is very wild and desolate, full of great and wild mountains and few inhabitants'. The thieves had an interesting mode of operation. 'Any true man that has lost any cattle may come and talk with them at a place appointed in those mountains . . . and if any of the company of thieves have the man's cattle unsold or unspent they will deal honestly with him, and take a reasonable sum of money of him to redeem his cattle'! Owen explains that Cwmystwyth was unique in Wales in being on the boundaries of three separate legal circuits, those of south-west Wales (Cardiganshire), south-east Wales (Radnorshire) and north-east Wales (Montgomeryshire). He also accuses the sheriffs and local justices of accepting bribes from the thieves.

Although the county's Great Sessions records are too patchy to allow of statistical reckoning, it is possible to draw tentative conclusions. Murder was apparently far more commonplace in early modern Cardiganshire than it is today, even though the population has at least trebled. In 1616, at a wedding ale at Cogoyan, Llanddewibrefi, one John ap Jenkin was beaten senseless by a gang of guests with clubs and hedge-stakes, and eventually died. One of the gang was eventually arrested, tried and hanged. In August 1627 at Ffair-rhos, William David ap Rees, a Radnorshire shepherd, attacked Evan Rees with a billhook, opening his skull, so that he died three days later. There was apparently a long history of violence between the two men, and William David's billhook brought him to the gallows at Cardigan.

A third savage murder took place in Cwmystwyth in 1648. By that time the Herberts of Hafod Uchdryd had made an effort to tame the violence of the area; Morgan Herbert founded the church of Eglwys-newydd in 1620 as part of that concern. But violence still lurked close to the surface. On 15 August 1648 John Rossey, an English soldier, was apparently making his way homeward, possibly as part of a troop of men from whom he must have become separated. Four local Welshmen, two of them surnamed Herbert, attacked Rossey with swords and pikes, wounding him twice, once an ugly wound on the knee, the other piercing his throat and killing him instantly. It took three years to bring one of the four before the court at Cardigan, where he was found not guilty. One can only speculate that it may have been a Welsh versus English assault under guise of royalist supporters attacking a parliamentarian. But what then of the verdict? Was this a Welsh jury refusing to convict a fellow-countryman of a crime against an Englishman?

The year 1648 was certainly a violent one. Apart from the death of John Rossey, several other homicides were committed. One Owen James murdered his wife Grace James with a stone. John Vaughan of Tal-y-bont attacked Morgan Thomas with a sword:

> in his right hand then and there held on the left side neere the hart in two severall places of the body of the said Morgan Thomas then and there did stabbe and thrust . . . two mortall wounds of the breadth of one ynche and the depth of sixe Inches . . .[so that he] languished from 15th to 18th November.

Richard Thomas of Llanrhystud, using a stone, killed Morgan ap Evan Lewis, who died nine days later. Both John Vaughan and Richard Thomas were able to plead benefit of clergy and got off scot-free! Benefit of clergy by this time simple meant the ability to read a few verses from the Bible. From the criminal's point of view, its only drawback was that it could only be pleaded once, since the reprieved person would be branded before release, and his previous conviction would be obvious were he to be caught again. Apart from benefit of clergy, prisoners, including those condemned to death, might be reprieved by royal proclamation, or by the need to recruit men for the armed forces. It may seem a travesty of justice that so many condemned criminals should avoid their due punishment, but the laws were so savage that had they been administered with full rigour, then the legal slaughter might well have been appalling. As it was, prosecutors would sometimes claim a lesser value for stolen goods in the hope of persuading the jury to bring in a guilty verdict which would not involve the death sentence; juries would pass riders to the same effect.

The other common crime among men (women's crimes have already been dealt with in Chapter 10) was stealing animals. Thus in 1648 Griffith Jenkin stole a sheep; Rhydderch David ap Evan Jenkin of Llanddewibrefi stole nine lambs and six yearling sheep, but escaped the hangman by benefit of clergy – reading from the Bible. Jenkin David ap Evan Goch of Gwnnws stole five oxen and a cow from Thomas David ap Evan Lloyd – it's hard to imagine how he thought he could get away with it. Jenkin David of Gwnnws stole a heifer across the county boundary at Gwngu. One investigation at Gynnull Mawr led to the discovery of a sheep's carcass under the dunghill, a favourite place apparently for stolen meat, since dogs could not easily detect it.

Not all offences were so serious. In 1627 a whole list of offences was presented which seem more suitable for a church consistory court. Edward Price and Mary Lloyd were presented for living in adultery. Morgan John of Llangoedmor was presented as a common drunkard and a disturber of divine service. Thomas James of Cardigan was presented for keeping a bowling alley and for beating the constable, while Edward Vince was accused of keeping a brothel. (Remarkably enough, a number of Cardigan women were imprisoned in 1942 for keeping 'disorderly houses' frequented by locally-billeted soldiers). Also in 1627 George Lewis of Ferwig was accused of bringing two car-loads of sheep into the market place on a Sunday at the time of evensong. Other such early 17th-century presentations include attempts to control vagabonds, such as Griffith ap Evan of Caron:

> for livinge in no Lawfull Calling, or Course of life, but wandring upp, and downe, with a taber and pipe, roguinge and bragginge.

On one occasion all the arraignments were of citizens of Cardigan: two had not cleared a gutter in Heol y Sarn, Cardigan; Thomas William, miller, had been drunk and had allowed fiddlers to play in his house and abused the constables when they came to arrest him; three men of Bron-gwyn were accused of being 'common proffainers of the Lords day by bowling, and hunting with Doggs'. In addition another jury was told that the chancel of Llannarth church needed repairing, and that Aberystwyth sorely lacked a shire hall. All human life came before the court at Cardigan.

Most colourful of the civil actions appearing in the Great Sessions records are those for slander, and since virtually all the prosecutors and defendants were Welsh-speakers, and since the law required the actual words used to be set down, records of slander contain the only Welsh written down in the court records. The language used was vigorous. Morgan Owens, gentleman, and Anne his wife sued William Williams for £3000 (*sic*!) for saying of Anne *Puttein Morgan William yw hi* ('She is Morgan William's whore'). William Jones, also claiming gentry status, and Jane his wife claimed that one Will Jenkin had said to Jane *Nydr wyt ty onyd whore Bytten Llydrones, llydrones yneved i* ('You're a viper, nothing but a strumpet whore and thief, thief of my sheep'). It is unlikely that anything remotely approaching £3000 would be awarded in such cases, which largely disappear from the records after 1660. A rare surviving document from the court of the Council of Wales and the Marches details an Elizabethan case from Llanfihangel-y-Creuddyn where a girl sang a rude song in Welsh about one of her neighbours, and was dragged to Ludlow; unfortunately the words were not recorded.

Aberystwyth had its own *dyn hysbys*, a cunning man or 'conjuror'. John Miles of Trefechan, who claimed to be 'a disciple of Agrippa Cornelius', was brought before Cardigan assizes in 1840 on four charges of obtaining sums of money under pretence of charming away diseases. He persuaded one victim that he would introduce him to the woman who had bewitched him, and prescribed a hideous mixture of the victim's hair, nail-clippings and salt to be spread around his house for protection, and a potion of weeds boiled in vinegar, which had made the poor fool ill. Miles was sentenced to three months' imprisonment. (From *The Demetian Mirror or Aberystwyth Reporter,* 15.8.1840.)

One accusation particularly resented by women, as already mentioned in Chapter 9, was that of witchcraft. Wales is unusual for its lack of court cases of witchcraft when compared with such areas of England as Lancashire and Essex. This was not because witchcraft was not believed to exist, on the contrary, 'everyone' knew of witches, *dynion hysbys* and witchcraft; the belief persisted well into the 20th century. Only two cases survive in the Cardiganshire records, both from Nancwnlle, both from the 1690s. In one case the evidence is lost, in the other the witness evidence is utterly ludicrous, and was obviously perceived to be so by the court. Both cases were dismissed.

The court immediately below the court of Great Sessions in the legal pecking order was the Quarter Sessions, the three-monthly meetings of JPs held in various places across the county, which dealt not only with minor crime but with a whole range of local government issues, including alehouse licensing, bridges and county buildings such as the gaol and shire hall, poor law disputes and gun licensing. It was only with the appointment from the 1830s onwards of elected boards with responsibilities for such matters as Poor Law administration, sanitation and education that the Quarter Sessions began to lose overall control of local government. Unfortunately the minutes for Cardiganshire Quarter Sessions only survive from 1737, and are largely taken up with allowing expenditure on bridges and on the settlement of bastardy cases, with notes such as 'Peter Bizard to pay Jane Jenkin Single woman the weekly sum of sixpense towards the maintenance of a female Bastard Child by him on her body begotten.'

Cardiganshire's justices of the peace continue to hold their courts to the present day, though stripped of all their local government powers (the last of these, the granting of licenses for alcohol, is about to be abolished at the time of writing). The Courts of Great Sessions, on the other hand, were abolished in 1830, not without opposition, and replaced by the assizes system long practised in England. The new court continued to meet at Cardigan until 1889, when it began meeting at Lampeter.

The Judge arrives at Lampeter Assizes. [National Library of Wales]

The violence of 17th-century Cardiganshire society did not die out during succeeding decades. Neighbouring farmers fought each other over boundaries and disputed grazing. The coracle men of Cilgerran fought with those of Llechryd over fishing rights. Mill dams might be destroyed in disputes over water rights; 'troi'r dŵr i'ch felin eich hunan' (diverting the water to one's own mill) is still a Welsh saying. Drunken brawls were frequent and constables helpless to intervene.

Thus far the criminals described have been individual men and women. But the county has had its share of social turbulence and unrest in response to harsh conditions. There were food riots in Aberystwyth in 1783 and again in 1795 when prices had risen and supplies were short: lead miners broke into storehouses and took away the corn. The Earl of Lisburne wrote to the Home Office that the working classes 'were much discontented and restless at the present exorbitant Price of all grain in the County.' By the late 1810s Cardiganshire was the most disturbed county in Wales. Inflation of prices and rents, population increase, the enclosure of land and amalgamation of tenanted farms, were all blamed, and at the end of the French war in 1815 there was sudden and severe depression. For some time illegal squatting (the building of *tai unnos*, one-night houses) had been spreading in the north. Official attempts to enforce the latest enclosure acts led to violent resistance in late 1815 and early 1816, and soldiers and militia were sent to Lampeter and Aberystwyth.

Rhyfel y Sais Bach, the War of the Little Englishman, is the best-known episode of the Cardiganshire land riots. The commissioners enforcing the 1815 enclosure act had to defray expenses by selling common land on which local people had traditionally enjoyed grazing and turbary (peat-cutting) rights. In late 1819 one Augustus Brackenbury bought 900 acres on the slopes of Mynydd Bach from the commissioners, following the purchase by building a house. Threats were made, and the house was attacked, looted or burnt on three occasions. He eventually sold his land in parcels and decamped. Not surprisingly he had a low opinion of the people of Mynydd Bach, calling them 'deceitful, treacherous and false swearers', and was highly critical of the magistrates for their lax attitude. However he understood something of the situation, referring in a letter to the Home Office to the lack of employment and overpopulation in the area, suggesting that land enclosure should be followed by improvement and the renting out of land with cottages, thus reducing the burden on the Poor Rate. The memory of *Rhyfel y Sais Bach* has not entirely faded from popular memory even today.

The moated site of Augustus Brackenbury's 'castle', Trefenter.

[Crown copyright: Royal Commission on Ancient & Historical Monuments, Wales]

A decade after Brackenbury's departure another kind of riot affected Cardiganshire. Whereas the upheavals on Mynydd Bach were the protest of cottagers and craftsmen, the Rebecca Riots were largely the work of farmers. Financial worries, including the commutation of tithes from payment in kind to payment in cash, were certainly at the root of these riots, which convulsed parts of rural south-west Wales between 1839 and 1844, though Rebecca had only a limited impact in Cardiganshire. Toll gates were broken in the Teifi valley in May and June 1843, and dragoons were stationed at Newcastle Emlyn and marines at Cardigan. More gates were broken, and in September there was a riot at Llan-non. In March 1844 a gate was broken at Pen-parc. The tithe problem flared up in Penbryn, where almost all tithe-payers were not Anglicans; the vicar called in the bailiffs, who sold one protestor's Bible as a contribution. Rebecca threatened the vicar so fiercely that he was given military protection. The worst was past, however, though Penbryn had not finished with the tithe problem, as will be seen in the next chapter. The Home Office showed some sympathy with the plight of the rioters, and the turnpike trusts were phased out by legislation.

The principal legacy of the riots in Cardiganshire was that the reluctant magistrates were forced to agree in January 1844 to create a police force of eighteen men, the first Cardiganshire constabulary. They were belatedly following the example of the Aberystwyth borough council, which had already acted. Taking advantage of the Municipal Corporations Act of 1835, two full-time constables for the town were appointed in 1837, aided by 33 occasional constables, paid by the day. After the Act of 1839 permitting the establishment of county constabularies (they only became obligatory in 1856) the reluctant magistrates were eventually obliged in 1844 to establish the Cardiganshire force, with a chief constable, a superintendent and sixteen constables; they absorbed the miniscule Aberystwyth force in 1857. This force was far from adequate, and occasional constables continued to be appointed; in 1849 the mayor of Cardigan published a list of 46 men sworn in, including labourers, a smith, a sail-maker, a hatter and 'William Allen, Kilgerran, Police Officer.'

There was at first considerable hostility to the police, who were certainly not above suspicion; the first constables were rather rough-and-ready appointments, and the first Chief Constable was sacked for using his policemen as river bailiffs. As for their unpopularity, in 1866 for example a policeman attempted in a Cardigan public house to arrest a wanted man, but the landlord seized the policeman and pinioned his arms so that the suspect could escape; the landlord was sentenced to three weeks' imprisonment with hard labour, which at that time meant eight hours a day in the prison treadmill. To complete the story, the Cardiganshire constabulary joined forces with that of Carmarthenshire in 1958 to become the Carmarthenshire and Cardiganshire Police. In 1968 this force amalgamated with the forces of Mid Wales and Pembrokeshire to become the Dyfed-Powys Constabulary (Dyfed-Powys Police since 1974).

Punishment in Cardiganshire's judicial system gradually altered over the years, following practice across Wales and England. Before 1700, offenders could be whipped, branded, pilloried, put in the stocks or ducked (a punishment usually reserved for women), and of course hanged for a range of offences which went on increasing until after 1800. That the countryside was not depopulated was due, as suggested above, partly to sympathetic juries and even judges and prosecutors, to successful pleas of benefit of clergy, and to frequent crown amnesties. With the

A

LIST

OF

CONSTABLES

SWORN IN BY

William Phillips, Esquire, Mayor,

FOR THE YEAR

1849.

Thomas John, Weaver, Muldan
James Sais, Shoemaker, Saint Mary's Lane
William Davies, Shopkeeper, Finch's Square
Edward Williams, Blockmaker, Muldan
David Williams, Smith, Market Square
Thomas Davies, Smith, near the Churchyard
Evan John, Weaver, Pendre
Dan Griffiths, Tailor, Carrier's Lane
Thomas Davies, Hatter, Pendre
Jonathan Thomas, Clothier, Greenfield Row
John Sais, Shoemaker, Carrier's Lane
William John, Butcher, Saint Mary's Lane
John Thomas, Shoemaker, Saint Mary's Lane
John Phillips, Shoemaker, Bridgend
William Phillips, Shoemaker, Muldan
Thomas Jenkins, Shoemaker, Saint Mary's Lane
David Davies, Shipwright, Muldan
Thomas Harries, Shipwright, Saint Mary's Lane
James Jenkins, Weaver, Muldan
David Phillips, Carpenter, Catherine Row
William Davies, Cooper, Saint Mary's Lane
James Thomas, Shoemaker, Finch's Square
John Thomas, Ostler, Saint Mary's Lane

David Augustus, Shoemaker, William Street
David Thomas, Carpenter, West Street
John Evans, Labourer, Muldan
William Davies, Gardener, Mr. C. Lewis's Yard
David Davies, Shoemaker, near the Bridge
John Morgan, Brickyard, Labourer
John Morgan, Catherine Row, Labourer
John Owen, Catherine Row, Labourer
David Davies, Catherine Row
Dan Richards, Finch's Square, Ostler
Thomas Evans, Kilgerran
William Allen, Kilgerran, Police Officer
David Jenkins, Kilgerran
William Davies, Pontycleifon, Carpenter
John Joseph, Carpenter, Pwllhay
Griffith Griffiths, Bath-house
David Thomas, Saint Mary's Lane, Lighterman
Thomas Williams, Bridge End, Carpenter
Thomas Davies, Carpenter, Pencraig
John Davies, Carpenter, Strand, Cardigan
William Edwards, Sailmaker, Cardigan
Benjamin Evans, Tailor, Pontycleifon
George Davies, Hatter, Muldan-ucha

February 8th, 1849.

ISAAC THOMAS, PRINTER, ST. MARY-STREET, CARDIGAN.

Cardigan borough constables. [National Library of Wales]

growth of British colonies in the 18th century transportation became an option. In 1822 Eleanor James became the only Cardiganshire woman actually to be sentenced to transportation; she had stolen clothing from a home in Tre-main near Cardigan, and was sent to Tasmania for seven years. The last public whipping in the county happened at Cardigan in 1830; the last use of the stocks was at Adpar in 1872. Ducking and pillorying seem to have ceased before 1800, when branding was long obsolete. I cannot discover when the last hanging took place in the county. The prisons at Aberystwyth and Cardigan were grim places, and seem originally to have been used as holding places for remand prisoners and debtors; judges preferred more physical modes of punishment. However, gaol sentences, often with hard labour in the treadmill, became increasingly common after 1700, with transportation for more serious offenders.

It is clear from 19th-century records that by 1840 murder had become a most unusual crime in Cardiganshire when compared with the homicide rate of the 16th and 17th centuries. True, a triple murder at Llanwenog in 1849 erupted from a husband and wife each accusing the other of infidelity. One case is reported for 1860, for which no one was arrested, and in 1868, as we have already seen, Wil Cefn Coch killed Lord Lisburne's gamekeeper, but escaped to Ohio, aided by a respectable citizen of Aberystwyth and the silence of his local community. In 1885 John Price of Aberystwyth shot his wife dead, but his death-sentence was commuted to life imprisonment. In 1894 Thomas Richards of Borth murdered his sister-in-law, and was tried and hanged at Carmarthen.

Almost all crime in 19th-century Cardiganshire must be considered petty; of 760 Cardiganshire prisoners held in custody between 1858 and 1867, 358 were tramps and vagrants, reflecting an age-old fear of outsiders. Chief constables had considerable trouble with arson from time to time, usually on farms, but arsonists also struck at the woollen mills when economic hardship brought layoffs. The tithe protests of the 1880s caused the police a good deal of trouble. Cases of domestic violence, paedophilia and incest appear in the *Cardigan and Tivy-side Advertiser*; several young men were rescued by the Cardigan solicitor William Mitchell from entrapment by young women anxious to find a father for their babies; in one terrible case the baby had obviously been begotten by the girl's own father. W.J. Lewis has described a Lampeter street fight of 1884 between two women armed with cudgels. The town crier had announced the battle beforehand, but the police interfered to prevent murder. There is no denying that violence, especially domestic violence, was still endemic in society, though to a lesser degree than in earlier centuries.

John 'Ivon' Jones, Aberystwyth litterateur and radical who helped Wil Cefn Coch escape to America. [National Library of Wales]

* * *

Reviewing in 1897 the achievement of the county's police, J.W. Willis-Bund, chairman of the county's magistrates, could claim that highwaymen had ceased to exist, the *ceffyl pren* had vanished, the selling of unlicensed ale had virtually ended, fairs were less rowdy, sheep-stealing much reduced, and the number of criminals on trial each year had lessened from 48 in 1851 to seven in 1896. He could have added that smuggling had been stamped out. Judges at Cardigan assizes would congratulate the authorities whenever there was no criminal case to try, and the police were keen to take the credit. But the whole movement of society was involved; as living conditions slowly improved, as people saw how desirable the goal of respectability appeared, as the chapels strengthened their social control, the temperance movement took effect, public behaviour improved and cooperation with the police increased. Emrys Jones has described the grasp the Tregaron Methodist chapel had on public behaviour:

> During the last [i.e. 19th] century its control over the behaviour of members, and in this way over much of the community, was near absolute, for it controlled the right of a Presbyterian to be a member of that church, and deprivation of membership meant an enormous loss of prestige and a lowering of status.

But by 1960 when that was written little remained of such power.

Today Ceredigion is one of the safest areas in Britain as far as crime is concerned, although statistics must be used with caution. As a senior police officer observed to me in the late 1970s: 'We didn't know there was a drugs problem in west Wales until we formed a drugs squad. No doubt if we formed a vice squad we'd find vice here too.'

The Cardiganshire Musters, Militia and Volunteers

The threat of invasion of England and Wales during the late 16th and 17th centuries was felt to be very real, and in the absence of a standing army, the government depended on mustering men in the way parodied by Shakespeare in *Henry IV* part 2. Records survive of the mustering of Cardiganshire men in 1572 and 1578; on the latter occasion fifty men of the county were to be trained for service in Ireland, fifty to be trained with calivers and seventy-five 'to be trained and kept in readiness upon an hour's warning.' At the same time deputies were appointed to keep an eye on all the county's 'creeks and landing-places'. In 1585 men were to be raised in the counties of south Wales to serve in the Low Countries. Abuses like those caricatured by Shakespeare seem to have happened in the county; in 1583 one Francis Jones had pressed six soldiers into service and then released five of them.

Mustering men virtually disappears from the Calendars of State Papers after 1597; the alarms and excursions of Elizabeth's reign seem to have calmed down greatly. However, in 1625, fifty men had to be levied from the county for service in Ireland; the men were sent to Plymouth, presumably for embarkation, and the deputy lieutenants billed the Crown for £90.10s.0d. for expenses and clothes. They were part of a body of some 1,700 men, whose officers at Plymouth complained to London of the expense of maintaining such a large number, and that many were running away.

The Militia Act of 1757 sought to bring order to the long-standing system of securing order by the recruitment of musters. Thus in 1539 it had been reckoned that Cardiganshire had 2,858 men between 16 and 60 open to serve in the musters when called upon, and the leading gentry were responsible for the care of their armaments, a responsibility which they did not always honour. The 1757 act decreed that Cardiganshire had to recruit 120 men, the responsibility lying with the Lord Lieutenant, and this seems to have been effected fairly quickly; in 1764 the men were involved in salvaging and protecting the cargo of a wreck at Llanrhystud. Ballots were held to choose the recruits, who could seek replacements for a payment. Their families had to be supported by their parishes. They trained in separate companies scattered across the county. The French declaration of war on the side of the American rebels in 1778 brought the first embodiment of the little regiment, which was marched off to Swansea. They spent time at Ross-on-Wye, Carmarthen and Pembroke, where they guarded prisoners-of-war. By 1781 the regiment had almost doubled, to 228 men. After Pembroke they served at numerous bases in England before returning to Carmarthen and briefly, in 1783, to Aberystwyth. With the end of the war in 1783 the regiment was disbanded.

Ten years later war with France was renewed, and 120 Cardiganshire militiamen marched to Sussex, then north to Chester, and by 1795 they were in Whitehaven, Cumberland, and the following year in Pembrokeshire, by which time the regiment consisted of 474 private soldiers. In 1797 a detachment was guarding prisoners-of-war at Pembroke when they were suddenly marched to Fishguard to help capture the French invaders and witness their surrender. At Swansea in 1801 they helped put down a food riot, and the following year peace broke out for a few months.

An act of 1802 tightened up the militia system; men chosen by ballot had to serve for five years. Any married man thus recruited would have to leave his family on the parish, and it became the responsibility of the parish vestry to seek for a single man who would accept payment as a substitute. In 1820 the parish of Llanfihangel-y-Creuddyn formed a society to enable subscribing members to pay for substitutes. With the renewal of war in 1803, the Cardiganshires were marched off to Woolwich, and in 1804 they became the Royal Cardiganshire Militia. After periods at various spots in the south of England they were redesignated as The Royal Cardigan Light Infantry Militia, and volunteered for service in Ireland, sailing in 1811, and the next year were again redesignated as the Royal Cardigan (Rifles) Regiment. They returned in 1813 to Portsmouth, and in 1814 to Aberystwyth. They were then discharged after eleven years' service, except for a small body of men based in the town, including a regimental band which was in some demand.

Militia recruitment and training recommenced, sporadically, in 1821, and the ballot was drawn for the last time in 1831. However the regiment's activities were limited until 1856, when they were called together and billeted in Aberystwyth for annual training, a burden on the townspeople which was eventually relieved by the building of barracks in 1867, designed by Sir James Szlumper, architect of, among other public works, the present Aberystwyth-Trefechan bridge. In 1877 the regiment was yet again rechristened, this time as the Royal Cardigan Artillery, with a battery of guns set up in the grounds of Aberystwyth castle; in 1882 the regiment was reorganised again, this time into the 5th Brigade of the 9th (Welsh) Division, Royal Artillery, and yet again in 1887, as the Cardigan Royal Garrison Artillery Militia of five hundred men. The regiment's final period of activity was during the Boer War, from May to October 1900. A final change of name, the Cardigan Royal Field Reserve Artillery, was imposed in 1908. The barracks buildings were demolished in 1979, a minor but depressing piece of vandalism. Among the few surviving dumb witnesses to the history of the Cardiganshire militia are Gogerddan house, Bridge Street, Aberystwyth, which was the regiment's headquarters from 1855 till 1867, and the name of Aberystwyth's North Parade.

For more than a century-and-a-half the militiamen of Cardiganshire, although never involved in battle except for those men who volunteered to leave the militia to join the regular Army, were drilled, marched and exercised in ways which must have left their mark on them in various forms, including the lash for infractions of discipline. It also left a burden of resentment among the civilian population who saw their men marching away behind the regimental drum, leaving their wives and children on the parish. I can testify that although it is (at the time of writing) forty-six years since I finished two years' National Service, the experience has had its lasting effects. How much more must that have been true of men who must have become fairly fluent English speakers during the French wars, and who otherwise would never have spent time in Ireland.

The militia's officers were invariably of the gentry class, including members of the families of Vaughan of Trawsgoed, Powell of Nanteos, Pryse of Gogerddan, Campbell of Stackpole, Brooks of Neuadd Lanarth and several branches of Lloyds. Interestingly, the only English recruit among the commanding officers was John P. Chichester of Arlington, Devon, who owned a swathe of tithes in the north of the county, but little or no land. Cardiganshire also contributed some of its landowners to hold commissions in the militias of other counties, not just Carmarthenshire and Pembrokeshire as was natural, but the Gloucester Militia and the Royal Clarence Militia. Many of these officers might well have struck full-time professional soldiers as laughable figures, though presumably not all; and of course the county's gentry did produce some professional officers who reached levels of distinction, among them General Lewis Davies of Tan-y-bwlch (d.1828), Lt-Col. Edward Crawford Lloyd Fitzwilliams and Brigadier Lewis Pugh Evans, VC, who is referred to elsewhere.

However, the disbanding of the Militia did not mean the ending of military activity in the county. W.E. Richardes of Bryneithin, who was something of a military fanatic, was the first commanding officer of the Cardiganshire Volunteer Rifle Corps, formed in the north of the county in 1860. Like the militia, they were redesignated a number of times. The Aberystwyth Drill Hall was built for their use in 1904; in 1908 they became part of the Territorial Army.

NOTE

Cardiganshire men who visited England could well finish up in court. On 26 April 1786, David Josiah Jones was found guilty at the Old Bailey of stealing a large quantity of cloth, and despite the character testimony of his fellow-Cardi Edward John Lloyd, he was sentenced to transportation for seven years. Unfortunately his local community is not mentioned in the trial papers, which can be read on the remarkable web-site www.OldBaileyOnline. It is just possible that he was not sent overseas; the American War of Independence had halted the process of transportation to America, and Australia was only substituted for it in 1787; in the meantime the condemned were held in the Thames hulks. However, these were probably emptied with the first transportation to Australia.

15. 'Boanerges was his name': Christianity in Cardiganshire

On the evening of Sunday March 30th, 1851, Tabernacl chapel, the largest in Aberystwyth with 1240 seats, had 1,022 worshippers; today the chapel is empty, its remnant congregation elsewhere, its fate uncertain. The changes wrought in our lives in the past forty years – the chapels and churches converted to housing, garages and warehouses, or simply pulled down, the busy Sunday supermarkets, and our changed leisure habits – make it almost impossible for us to grasp either the nature or the importance of religion in recent Welsh history. Students of the past find it much easier to concentrate on subjects which are of interest to us today: thus we have 'history from the bottom up', women's history, the history of medicine, sport, immigrants, while religion languishes.

Rhyd-y-gwin Unitarian chapel, one of the most attractive in the county.

Yet whatever the supposed hypocrisy of the Welsh manifestation of Christianity, whatever its hostility to secular pleasure and broader uses of the intellect and imagination, whatever the dire pettiness of its sectarian conflicts, it provided for a majority of people an extraordinary social cohesion. It provided a narrow but badly-needed form of education; it provided a ladder out of the lower depths both for the

Daniel Rowland, Llangeitho.
[National Library of Wales]

ambitious and the socially needy; and it swayed politics and gave a huge boost to the growth of Welsh national consciousness. In Cardiganshire a good deal of the original impulse which drove that great movement came from the man whom William Williams of Pantycelyn called Boanerges, the son of Thunder; he was Daniel Rowland of Llangeitho (1713-90).

Whatever the supremacy of Dafydd ap Gwilym as a poet, or the long-term importance of Sir John Vaughan as a lawyer, there can be little doubt that the influence of Daniel Rowland on the Welsh people and on Welsh history was greater than any other son or daughter of Ceredigion. It is therefore all the more frustrating that we know so little about him personally, compared with our knowledge of the two men with whom his name is always associated, Howel Harris and Williams Pantycelyn. Rowland was indeed a son of thunder – his voice in the pulpit was both loud and terrifying, and for half a century it echoed through the land; he was generally recognised as the greatest Welsh preacher of his time. Yet it is possible that he took holy orders as deacon in 1734 and priest in 1735 not from real conviction but simply because he was the son of a clergyman, also named Daniel Rowland, the vicar of Llangeitho and Nancwnlle. The son was certainly ignorant of the fact that at Whitsun 1735 Howel Harris, forty miles away at Talgarth in Breconshire, had an experience of religious conversion which set him, although a layman, preaching and counselling in the area round about his home. Nor would Rowland have known of the concurrent revival convulsing parts of New England, and perhaps not of the stirrings of English Methodism at the same time.

It was in 1737, three years after his ordination as deacon, that Daniel Rowland seems to have undergone his own conversion experience as a result of listening to Griffith Jones, Llanddowror, preaching at Llanddewibrefi. A short while later in the same year, 1737, Howel Harris heard Rowland preach at Defynnog, and was so impressed that he visited Llangeitho twice before the year was out. Rowland's preaching became more and more passionate, so that men and women crowded to hear him, and as his reputation gradually grew, they came from near and far to receive communion at his hands; people would come by boat from the Llŷn peninsula, landing at Llanrhystud or Aber-arth, and then walking to Llangeitho. Nor did he confine his dramatic ministry to his own neighbourhood; he travelled to the counties of north Wales several times, drawing both praise and abuse on his head. There is plenty of evidence for the ill-treatment he endured, such as this from a letter from Howel Harris to George Whitefield in 1743:

> I saw Bro. Williams [i.e. Pantycelyn] on his return from Bro. Rowland. He informed me that while he and Rowland discoursed at the seaside in Cardiganshire, ruffians with guns and staves beat them unmercifully, set on them by a gentleman of the neighbourhood. Rowland had a wound on his head.

Nor was it only the ignorant gentry and their hooligan followers who persecuted the early Methodists. Shortly after the beating of Rowland and Williams, the priest Peter Williams lost the curacy of Llangrannog on account of his Methodism. The gentry seem to have preferred violence to the use of the law; the story of the only early Cardiganshire Methodist to be dragged before the courts has been traced by Eryn White. He was Morgan Hughes, who was imprisoned and brought before the court of Great Sessions on charges of vagrancy and holding an unlawful assembly; the prosecutor was Richard Stedman, last squire of Strata Florida. However, Stedman did not attend the trial, so the case was thrown out.

One reason for such hostility was the memory, still preserved, of the behaviour of the religious sects who had convulsed the religious life of England and Wales a hundred years earlier, behaviour which was associated in public memory with rebellion, civil war and regicide. Fortunately the persecution did not last, though Evan Evans 'Ieuan Fardd' (1731-88) and the Morris brothers certainly detested the Methodists, and Theophilus Evans published *A History of Modern Enthusiasm* in 1752 which was fiercely critical of the movement. This was ironic, in that Evans's brother was accustomed to welcome the early Methodists to the family home at Penywenallt in the Teifi valley. It was also ironic that Ieuan Fardd, ordained priest as he was, should have been so hard on the Methodists, since he well knew the weaknesses of the established Church and was savagely critical of its ineffectiveness. Unfortunately he himself had his own weaknesses, particularly for the bottle, and on the rare occasions when he obtained a patron, he was inclined to test his patience to breaking point and beyond.

HOWEL HARRIS was a frequent visitor to Cardiganshire in the early Methodist years: at Morfa Mawr (Llansanffraid), Ystrad Aeron and Lampeter in 1739; Penywenallt (Llandygwydd) in 1740; Penywenallt and Blaen-porth, Llechryd, Cardigan, Tŵr-gwyn, Llangrannog, Henfynyw in 1741 (many of these places several times on each trip), and these visits, totalling 47, were largely made before the 1752 rift with Daniel Rowland. Some of these visits led to the foundation of *seiadau* and the recruiting of stewards and overseers, such as William Richard of Abercarfan, Llanddewi-brefi. Harris was present in the first monthly Cardiganshire Association (*Sasiwn Fisol*) at Tŵr-gwyn in 1743; he and Rowland both preached there. His diary records his rebuking of ship-wreckers and smugglers. In 1745 he commented in his diary: 'I go now to Cardiganshire where I see they are Stronger than me in faith and know more of Christ.' However, his savage comment on Aberystwyth was 'tis like that is the last place God will take'!

Believers did not come to Llangeitho simply to listen to Rowland in respectful silence. Many are the accounts of the extraordinary behaviour he inspired:

> Such Crying out and Heart Breaking Groans, Silent Weeping and Holy Joy, and shouts of Rejoicing I never Saw. Their Amens and Cryings Glory in the Highest &c would enflame your Soul was you there.

That is the generous report of Howel Harris himself, unmarred by any professional jealousy; on another occasion he commented on Rowland's sermon, 'I never heard such wisdom and Divine Light'. There were hostile reports too, such as this by an Anglican visitor to Llangeitho:

> His preaching again flung almost the whole society into the greatest agitation and confusion possible, some cry'd, others laughed, the women pulled one another by the caps, embraced each other, caper'd . . .

However, Harris did not always approve of 'such Extravagancies – crying out, falling on the ground, beating each other etc before carnal People,' as he commented at Llangeitho in 1743.

Despite his growing reputation and the personal loyalty he inspired in many, Rowland's followers were at first a small minority of the Cardiganshire population. Even smaller was the number of those sufficiently convinced to join the little confessional *seiadau* ('societies') which Harris and others began founding from 1737, and not all of those felt their faith to be certain. It would be a great mistake to suppose that the Revival of 1735 swept all before it; on the contrary, its growth was slow and uncertain in Cardiganshire as elsewhere. By 1745 there were thirteen *seiadau*, none of them in the north of the county. In spite of the rift between Rowland and Harris in 1750, each with his loyal followers, the cause continued its slow growth in Cardiganshire with the building of a number of meeting-houses for the *seiadau* at Llanbadarn Odwyn, Llandysul, Cardigan, Lledrod, Llanbadarn Trefeglwys, Llanddewibrefi, Henfynyw and Llansanffraid.

The early *seiadau* in the county were supervised by William Richard and William Williams, Pantycelyn. Naturally Pantycelyn became involved with the people of the county on a personal level. The first elegies he wrote were to folk of the county, and later he was to eulogise William Richard, his former colleague, who had proved himself particularly effective in his spiritual supervision of individuals. 1744 was the year in which Pantycelyn began his supervisory work in Cardiganshire, and also the year of his first published collection of hymns, *Aleluja*. Pantycelyn preached on a number of occasions at Tŵr-gwyn, the first Methodist meeting-house to be built in the county, and was a welcome guest at the Morris household which was the mainstay of the Tŵr-gwyn ministry. It was fitting that, just as his first elegy had been written to a group of Cardiganshire Methodists, so the last, composed a year before his own death, should have been on the death of Daniel Rowland in 1790.

TŴR-GWYN meeting-house was built in 1750 for the *seiadau* of Troed-yr-aur, north of Newcastle Emlyn. The appointment of Dafydd Morris in 1774 to take charge there was the first Methodist appointment of its kind in Wales. A great preacher, Morris was succeeded by his son Ebenezer, perhaps an even greater preacher, who would preach three times every Sunday as well as travelling throughout Wales; he frequently preached on board ships on the south Cardiganshire coast. He was among the first Methodists to be ordained in 1811, and took a leading role in drafting the Methodist Confession of Faith at Aberystwyth in 1823.

In 1762 a renewed revival broke out at Llangeitho; sceptics who came to scoff at the 'Welsh Jumpers' were far outnumbered by huge crowds who came to sing, to shout, to pray and to return home, many of them, as transformed beings. Nor was Daniel Rowland alone in the task of renewal. Not only did Howel Harris restore the bond of association between the two, but Cardiganshire began to produce a new generation of men, in or out of Anglican holy orders, to support and supplement Rowland's work: Dafydd Morris, Tŵr-gwyn (1744-91) and John Williams (1747-1831), curate of Lledrod, were among the foremost. Gradually the movement spread through the county, with Daniel Rowland continuing his passionate preaching for most of the rest of the century, until his death in 1790. It was strengthened by revivals in 1781 and 1790 at Llangeitho, in 1784 at Tŵr-gwyn, and the 1805 revival at Aberystwyth ('the Children's Revival').

The tomb of Ebenezer and Dafydd Morris at Troed-yr-aur

The slowness of the growth of Methodism in north Cardiganshire is intriguing. Dr Geraint Jenkins attributes it to the negative influence of the great landowners of the area, the Powells, Pryses and Vaughans, and it is true that they were not supportive as were for example the Lloyds of Bronwydd or the Bowens of Llwyn-gwair (in Pembrokeshire, but who had considerable influence in Cardiganshire). These Bowens were not related to Thomas Bowen of Waunifor, Llandysul, who built a meeting house for the Methodists and purchased fifty copies of Daniel Rowland's *Tair Pregeth* (1772); other gentry subscribers were John Edwards of Abermeurig, for thirty copies and Thomas Rogers of Brynele, for twenty. Thomas Lloyd (d.1793) of Bronwydd and his wife Mary read widely in theology and kept family devotions with great sincerity. Eliza Price of Pigeonsford, Llangrannog, was a regular attender at the Penmorfa Methodist meeting house. Indeed, even the notorious Sir Herbert Lloyd of Peterwell was involved with Methodism for a while. All these gentry lived south of the Aeron. However, such was the developing strength of Methodism that growth in the north of the county was inevitable. Gosen chapel, founded in 1770 in the parish of Llanychaearn south of Aberystwyth, was effectively the mother-church for north Cardiganshire; Tabernacl was founded in Aberystwyth in 1785 with only ten members, but soon began to grow, and further congregations hived off. It must of course be remembered that there was as yet no formal rift between Methodism and the Church of England; the buildings were not registered as meeting-houses, they were simply places for the *seiat* and worship.

While only a handful of the gentry involved themselves in Methodism, many were willing to offer their names and some financial help to the British and Foreign Bible Society, a branch of which was formed in Cardigan in 1813. John Vaughan of Trawsgoed, the boroughs' MP was nominated as branch president, and nine gentlemen and four squarsons (squire-parsons) were chosen as vice-presidents. The branch's annual reports survive for the period 1813-20; £210 pounds was sent to the London headquarters for the year 1813; the sums for following years were somewhat smaller. In exchange the society received Bibles and Testaments for distribution in the county. The branch's hope that more branches would be formed within the county was only partly successful; branches appeared at Newcastle Emlyn and Llwyndafydd. Despite the Anglican background of the branch's senior officers, donations and subscriptions were received from Baptist and Methodist congregations.

Meanwhile that majority of curates and vicars who held aloof from Methodism must have plodded on much as they had done before 1735, while complaining about the increase in the number of 'jumpers' and enthusiasts. Very few new churches were built in the county, but the desperate need of a church in the town of Aberystwyth, which had been churchless since Capel Mair had fallen into the sea at some time before 1730, was finally met in 1787 by the erection of a small new building where the present parish hall now stands. Thus the conscientious no longer needed to struggle to the parish church at Llanbadarn Fawr, while the less conscientious may have had their consciences pricked. Many parish churches continued to serve purposes other than worship; vestries would meet in them before adjourning to the (usually nearby) tavern, with the curate or vicar often keeping the minutes. The graveyards, largely unencumbered by gravestones until after 1750, were playgrounds, especially for the *gwyliau mabsant*, the annual patronal festivals.

Some nonconformists could be really generous to their causes. When Evan David of Cardigan died in 1794 he left £40 to the Revd William Jones, minister at St Dogmaels and £10 to be divided between the poor of that church and the 'New Chapell', with £5 more towards building the latter. He left his best suit to Richard Morgan, 'now keeping a Welch school at St Dogmels.' As a bachelor he had no family commitments.

The state of religion in the county in 1800 was complex. The Welsh Methodist movement, Calvinist in its theology, was still engaged with the Church of England, and still involved only a minority of those whose allegiance was Anglican. But under the new generation of leaders, especially Thomas Charles, Thomas Jones and John Elias, Calvinistic Methodism grew rapidly, as we shall see. The doctrinally-different Wesleyan Methodism, despite visits by John Wesley himself, only made ground with the arrival of missionaries in 1804, and though it gained many adherents in Aberystwyth and in the lead-mining district, especially when reinforced by the arrival of Cornish miners, it never achieved the success of the other movements.

Quakerism had maintained a shadowy presence in Cardigan, Llanddewibrefi and Aberystwyth, but had disappeared by the end of the 18th century, though there is now once more a small Quaker presence in the county. The old Dissenters, particularly the Independents (Congregationalists) and Baptists, could not avoid being affected by Welsh Methodist revivalism. Philip Pugh's successor as the leading Congregationalist in the county was Thomas Gray, whose ministry was far more charismatic than Pugh's. Many of Cardiganshire's leading dissenters were from outside the county: Pembrokeshire-born Benjamin Evans (1740-1821) was instrumental in founding several new congregations north of the Teifi, and in mid-county the Carmarthenshire man Thomas Phillips (1772-1842) set up his academy at Neuadd-lwyd, south-east of Aberaeron, in 1810, after establishing Congregationalism at Llanbadarn Fawr in 1802 and Tal-y-bont in 1804. His work in the north was taken up by another Pembrokeshire man, Azariah Shadrach (1774-1844), who established a congregation in Aberystwyth; his first chapel in Penmaes-glas (1823) is the oldest chapel building in the town, now used by the Merched y Wawr movement. Shadrach published numerous books on religious subjects, whose flamboyant titles are betrayed by their now-unreadable texts.

Hawen Independent Chapel, Rhydlewis.

Baptists made slower progress in Cardiganshire than either the Congregationalists or the Methodists. D.C. Rees, in his *History of Tregaron* claims, on rather fragmentary evidence, that an early congregation was established at Argoed, south of Tregaron, in 1718; there was a Baptist congregation at Llangoedmor by 1750 and a chapel was built in Cardigan in 1775, the work of Pembrokeshire-born William Williams (1732-99). But whereas Williams was a stern character opposed to religious emotionalism, Cardiganshire's most famous Baptist, Christmas Evans of Llandysul (1776-1838), was a preacher of passion who spread his beliefs successfully in Anglesey, returning on occasion to preach in Aberystwyth and Cardigan. Early Baptist congregations in the north of the county were formed at Penrhyn-coch

(1786), Aberystwyth and Llanrhystud (both 1787), and more were to follow. The first two of these causes were sponsored by the stewards of Gogerddan, who lived in the mansion during the time when the Pryse-Loveden owners were based in England. Despite this promising beginning, the Baptists registered a number of early failures; several of their chapels had fallen into ruin even before 1900.

The most remarkable manifestation of extreme Dissent in the county was the growth of Unitarianism in the Teifi valley. The ministry of Jenkin Jones at Llwynrhydowen, who preached universal redemption and free grace, has already been referred to in Chapter 8 above. The six congregations he established before his early death in 1742 slowly grew in numbers and influence, reinforced by the education offered at the Carmarthen Academy. Jones's successor, David Lloyd (d.1779), was a charismatic figure whose preaching encouraged thoughts of political liberty, sympathy with the rebellious American colonists and the Arian doctrine, teaching that Christ is not consubstantial with God – all of which doctrines were loathed by both gentry and Methodists. Lloyd's successors were his son Charles Lloyd of Coedlannau (1766-1829) and David or Dafydd Davis (1745-1827), whose name is always linked with his school at Castell Hywel, discussed below. Davis was a friend of most leading Welsh libertarians, including Richard Price, Iolo Morganwg, Thomas Roberts of Llwyn'rhudol, Jac Glan-y-gors and Tomos Glyn Cothi. Davis and Charles Lloyd fell out, and Lloyd, who had declared himself a Unitarian (believing that Jesus was simply a human being, and no more the son of God than other men), was involved in the division which saw the establishment of Unitarian churches at Pantydefaid and Capel-y-groes in 1802, followed by others. Thus came into being *Y Smotyn Du* (the Black Spot), the only rural Unitarian community in Britain. Their chapel with chapel house at Rhyd-y-gwin (SN534539) is perhaps the most attractive Nonconformist building in the county.

Pisgah Chapel is now a private house.

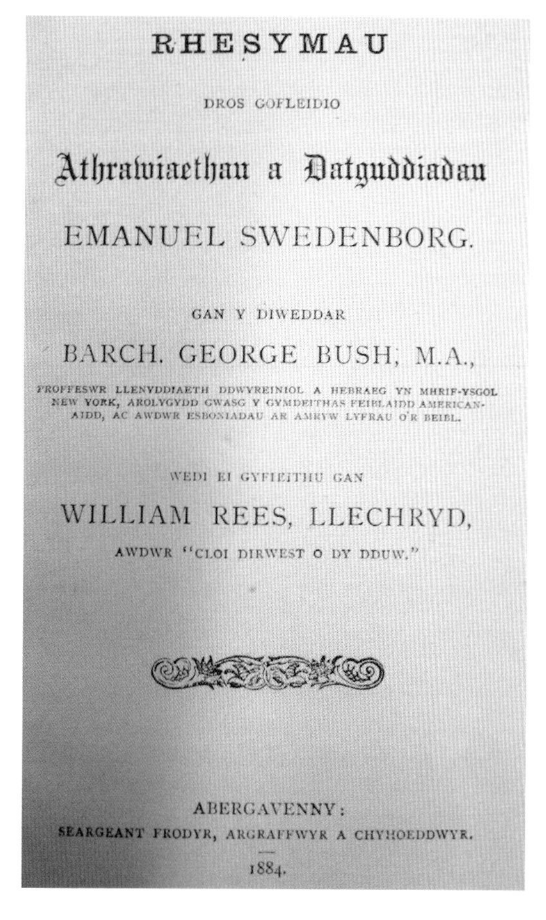

RHESYMAU

DROS GOFLEIDIO

Athrawiaethau a Datguddiadau

EMANUEL SWEDENBORG.

GAN Y DIWEDDAR

BARCH. GEORGE BUSH, M.A.,

PROFFESWR LLENYDDIAETH DDWYREINIOL A HEBRAEG YN MHRIF-YSGOL NEW YORK, AROLYGYDD GWASG Y GYMDEITHAS FEIBLAIDD AMERICANAIDD, AC AWDWR ESBONIADAU AR AMRYW LYFRAU O'R BEIBL.

WEDI EI GYFIEITHU GAN

WILLIAM REES, LLECHRYD,

AWDWR "CLOI DIRWEST O DY DDUW."

ABERGAVENNY:

SEARGEANT FRODYR, ARGRAFFWYR A CHYHOEDDWYR.

1884.

The further reaches of Victorian religion were not unknown in Cardiganshire. The Church of Latterday Saints (Mormons) was active in south Wales, but although they are known to have visited Cenarth and Machynlleth, I have not yet traced any activity in the county. The last and quite the most unexpected manifestation of sectarianism in Cardiganshire was the appearance of Swedenborgianism at Llechryd. It seems that in 1881 the Congregationalist minister, William Rees, and many of his congregation had come under the influence of Swedenborg, and were shut out of their chapel, and so built a new one, Y Tabernacl. From 1909 until 1921 a bilingual publication, *Y DYN / THE MAN*, printed at Port Talbot, appeared as the magazine of the New Church. The sect's Temple was at Ynysymeudwy, near Swansea, but the near-majority of subscribers to the magazine in 1914 (50 out of 109), their President David Jones, and their pastor the Revd William Rees were all from Llechryd. By 1919 there were only fifteen subscribers, the majority living in Ynysymeudwy, and William Rees was dead.

*   *   *

The increasing success of Methodism, and the inability of the Anglican Church to adapt to changing circumstances, was bound to lead to separation, and it finally came about in 1811 with the ordination of ministers at Bala and Llandeilo. In 1823 leading Methodist divines met in Aberystwyth to draw up the Confession of Faith of the Calvinistic Methodist Church of Wales, which was in effect the only body of any kind in existence covering Wales and only Wales. In Cardiganshire the leading advocates of change were Ebenezer Morris (1790-1867) of Tŵr-gwyn, son of Dafydd Morris, and Ebenezer Richard (1781-1837) of Tregaron (though originally from Pembrokeshire); both were ordained at Llandeilo in 1811. This new independence was not quite as radical as it seems; relations between local church and Methodist congregations were often friendly, and at an individual level there was a good deal of movement between one and the other. Many churchmen sent

THE Williams dynasty of Ystrad Teilo and Cwmcynfelyn were leading men in the county's church life. Isaac Williams I was vicar of Llanrhystud, Llansanffraid, Llanfihangel-y-Creuddyn and Penbryn and dean of Ultra Aeron; his son, Isaac Williams II, married the heiress of Cwmcynfelyn. Their eldest son Matthew led the building of Llangorwen church, inspired by his younger brother Isaac Williams III (1802-65), who was a leading member of the Oxford Tractarian (high church) movement, and an interesting poet. Llangorwen had the first stone altar in any Welsh church since the Reformation, when they had all been thrown out. The first vicar of Llangorwen, from 1841 till 1852, was Lewis Gilbertson of Elerch, north-east of Penrhyn-coch. After a period as vice-principal of Jesus College, Oxford, he returned to found a second Tractarian church at Elerch, and was briefly the first vicar there; his remains lie in a founder's grave outside the east end of the church. Plain-chant was used in both churches for several generations.

sons to be educated at Castell Hywel; like the old Dissenters, they had more respect for education than had the Calvinistic Methodists. Divisions could occur internally; chapel splits are notorious, and the Church was not immune; the building and dedication of the first Oxford Movement church in Wales at Llangorwen in 1841 caused ructions.

It should not be imagined that because there were about 140 churches and chapels in the county in 1812 the whole population were therefore pious and practising Christians. Geraint H. Jenkins has drawn attention to the prevalence of superstition and religious indifference among a large, if indefinable, section of the population. Despite the heroic efforts of so many ministers and priests, despite the growth of rational thought, the superstitions so deplored by the 17th-century Puritans were slow to die. The Hafod Uchdryd ghost convulsed the house's occupants more than once in the mid-18th century. It was still possible to collect stories of the *toili* or phantom funeral even in the late 20th century. Following burglaries at Llangeitho during the Methodist *sasiwn* of 1817, a *dyn hysbys* or cunning man was asked to identify the criminal. Indeed, the last *dyn hysbys* at Llangurig still exercised influence in the north of the county until his death in the 1950s. Nevertheless the influence of organised religion was powerful in Cardiganshire, particularly with the growth of the temperance movement in the mid-19th century. The *gŵylfabsant* or church patronal festival vanished comparatively early from the county, but the ferocious annual games of football continued at Llandysul on *Hen Galan*, Old New Year's Day in January, because the calendar revision of 1753, which altered the calendar by eleven days, was largely ignored in the Teifi valley and north Pembrokeshire. The event was replaced by Sunday School activities, originally organised by the vicar of Llandysul, Enoch James, including performances of the *pwnc*, or chanted catechism.

* * *

The 1851 religious census figures suggest that, over Wales as a whole, only some 50% of the population seem to have been worshippers, whereas in contemporary England the figure was nearer 25%. However, the claimed percentage for

Cardiganshire is certainly higher, though difficult to ascertain exactly, because some returns were either never made or have been lost, and of course the figures were self-assessed. Worse still, since many places of worship had two or three services on Sunday, it is impossible to know how many attended twice. The figures for the county are so complex as to defy a summary suitable for this book.

Buildings are easier to count than people, and it was of course the aim of all denominations to extend their membership, which meant the increased provision of buildings. At first the nonconformist denominations had the advantage of administrative and democratic flexibility as well as the zeal of converts, and there was a burst of building activity up to 1830. By 1851 there were 240 places of worship in the county, including purpose-built schoolrooms, with Calvinistic Methodists owning the largest percentage of available seating (32%) and claiming the largest number of worshippers. It was they who began the custom of creating 'English causes'; concern about the souls of non-Welsh-speakers led to groups of mainly Welsh-speaking members hiving off from their Welsh chapels to begin new chapels, staffed by Welsh-speaking ministers but providing spiritual homes for incomers and visitors. In Welsh-speaking areas of Wales these efforts on behalf of the *Inglis côs* were confined to towns. The table which follows is an attempt to count all the chapels, functioning or defunct, known to have existed in the county, drawn from the lists of chapels in Volume 3 of the *Cardiganshire County History*. Such totals of buildings according to denomination are crude in the extreme, since some chapels were large and splendid, others tiny and obscure; they are also disputable because a few chapels changed denomination; these have been counted according to their original founding congregation:

	Chapels	**Schoolrooms on other sites**
Calvinistic Methodist	113	45
Congregational	67	5
Baptist	29	3
Wesleyan Methodist	26	-
Unitarian	17	-

The investment of money, time, organisation and labour represented by those totals, without a penny of the government support that went to the churches, is remarkable indeed; anyone seeking to understand the *mentalité* of the recent past in Cardiganshire must keep it firmly in view.

Meanwhile, perhaps tardily, stout efforts were made to improve church buildings; of the 75 churches now standing in the county, 53 were entirely rebuilt or newly provided during the 19th century and the remainder

LLANGYNLLO church, built at the expense of Thomas Lloyd of Bronwydd, is a fine example of a High Victorian estate church, and matches the fantastic Gothic of the ruin of Lloyd's Bronwydd mansion. The interior is a riot of colour, with polychrome bricks, marble columns, angel-musicians and other elaborate ornaments and fittings. It was built in 1868-70 by John Middleton & Son of Cheltenham. The Lloyd vault is immediately to the west of the church.

Llansanffraid church: medieval tower, 19th century nave.

heavily restored, while many vicarages were built. Perhaps the Church's most remarkable product in Cardiganshire was the phenomenal number of young men who became ordained priests, creating such a surplus that many moved to other areas of Wales and to many areas of England; perhaps the best-known was Thomas Jones of Creaton (1752-1845), born at Cefnyresgair in Cwmystwyth, one of the founders of the Bible Society. Another, now forgotten, was John Davies (1795-1861), a graduate of Lampeter and Queens' College Cambridge, who served his entire career in England, was a respected philosopher and father of Emily Davies, founder of Girton College, the first women's college at Cambridge. A single parish, Llanwenog, produced twenty-seven priests as well as twenty-seven ordained non-conformist ministers, and it was not exceptional.

William Butterworth's church (Y Santes Fair) for Aberystwyth's Welsh congregation.

Cardiganshire's religious life was suddenly convulsed in 1859 by the outbreak of revival on the largest scale seen in Wales for decades. Humphrey Jones of Llangynfelyn (1832-95) was a Wesleyan Methodist who, after failing to gain acceptance as a candidate for the ministry, joined his parents who had emigrated to America. There he developed a powerful preaching ministry among Welsh emigrants. He returned to Cardiganshire in 1858 and began preaching at the Wesleyan chapel in Tre'r-ddôl. He soon encountered Dafydd Morgan (1814-83), a newly ordained Calvinistic Methodist minister at Ysbyty Ystwyth, who was deeply concerned at the deadness of religion in Wales. After a little scepticism Morgan seized the day, and while Humphrey Jones was laid low by a long illness, Dafydd Morgan spread the fire throughout Wales. Scenes like those of Llangeitho a century earlier were repeated in chapel after chapel. Lead-miners far underground laid down their picks and shovels to pray and sing. The revival of 1859 had a dramatic effect on attendance at both chapels and churches. Of Aberystwyth it was said:

> In the town of Aberystwith about four hundred members have been added to the Calvinistic Methodist Church alone. Several of the most ungodly people of the town have been converted. Eight publicans have taken down their signs, and become teetotallers.

Archdeacon John Hughes, the evangelical vicar of Aberystwyth, wrote:

> The religious revival, on the whole, I firmly believe, has been a great and extensive blessing to the principality. Multitudes of the most thoughtless characters have become, in outward conduct at least, correct and respectable.

Not every Cardiganshire landowner would have approved of such sentiments from a Churchman implicitly acknowledging the virtues of Nonconformity. The most extreme High Church landowner in the county was Miss Mary Morrice, owner of the Carrog estate, Llanddeiniol. In 1860 she offered her tenants an iniquitous Hobson's choice:

> I feel myself morally bound to set before you two alternatives, and you are at liberty to choose for yourself, namely to attend our Church service with your family and thus to support its principles, or otherwise (if your conscience will not allow you to comply with my request) you must quit the farm which you now hold of me.

Humphrey Jones, the 1859 Revivalist.
[Ceredigion County Library]

Her tenants revolted en masse; in 1861 fourteen farmers and thirteen cottagers with their families left their tenancies. Only two were prepared to attend church. There can hardly be stronger testimony to the power of belief.

Naturally enough, the religious passions of the 1859 revival eventually cooled, and all denominations settled down to what may have seemed to them a period of consolidation, though the shrinkage of the county's population from 1871 onwards did not bode well; 'complacency' would perhaps be a better term than consolidation. The building and rebuilding of churches and the founding and rebuilding of chapels and schoolrooms continued, and famous preachers thundered, chanted and virtually crooned from pulpits in church and chapel alike. Preaching festivals flourished, known in the trade as 'double-barrelled' when by custom two preachers were involved; indeed, no fewer than four of the *hoelion wyth* (pillars of the cause) of Congregationalism preached at the opening of Seion, Aberystwyth, in 1878.

From mid-century onwards Welsh Nonconformists were increasingly aligned with the Liberal party, although they were more conservative (but not Tory) than radical. The subject of tithes and church rates caused much irritation to nonconformist landowners and tenants (described below), alongside the cause of land reform to which they were inevitably linked, and from 1869 onward the issue of Church disestablishment was increasingly popular. Feelings did not run as high in most of Cardiganshire as they did in parts of north Wales, although there was a protest against church rates in Aberystwyth in 1847; as Ieuan Gwynedd Jones suggests, 'socially and economically, the county had fallen into a kind of torpor in which politics of a confrontational kind could hardly survive.' Ironically enough, the established Church did much to mitigate the criticisms deservedly levelled against it by providing more and better church accommodation, as well as more clergy and of a higher standard. Pluralism was ended; the scandal of half-starved curates

Parade through Aberystwyth to protest against Disestablishment. [National Library of Wales]

scurrying from church to church on a Sunday faded away. But after 1850 the Nonconformist denominations felt themselves to be in the saddle, and a triumphalism manifested itself in the architecture of such urban chapels as Seion and Bethel, both in Baker Street, Aberystwyth. Indeed the chapels competed not only against the Church but against each other. Historians are agreed that by the turn of the 20th century the case for disestablishment was not as strong as it had been, but the Liberal party was committed, and after endless shenanigans between 1870 and 1920, and despite vigorous protest by many Church leaders and people, the Church in Wales was created as a disestablished body.

If most of the county's religious life was respectably well-behaved, one area had its rebels. The 'Tithe War' of the 1880s and 1890s affected the parishes of Llangrannog, Betws Ifan, Bron-gwyn and especially Penbryn, where there was vigorous resistance to the payment of tithe, perhaps inspired by the events of the time of Rebecca, referred to in Chapter 11. It should be remembered that much tithe was paid not to the local church but to lay owners of tithe; at Penbryn however the tithe was owed to the church, and from the spring of 1889 until 1895 many nonconformists refused to pay, leaving the unfortunate vicar without an income. He reported some forty defaulters, so the association of tithe owners brought in bailiffs from Newcastle Emlyn, and for the next six years Robert Lewis, auctioneer and tithe collector, escorted by as many as eighty policemen, did his best to exact payment in the parish of Penbryn by auctioning the goods of those who refused payment. The scenes could be quite menacing and very noisy; blowing horns in the ears of the policemen and the horses drawing the bailiff's brake was a favourite ploy, coupled with threats of violence and death, and frequent throwing of stones and dung. Penbryn church windows were smashed twice. Some of those involved were elders or deacons in their local chapels, and it is clear from the newspaper reports that the Chief Constable, who was expected to be present, was not always in sympathy with the bailiff, who protected himself from injury by wearing a fireman's brass helmet. Some county councillors and their relatives, as well as Nonconformist ministers, were strong in support of the anti-tithe activists.

A number of prosecutions were brought against these anti-tithe protesters by the police, and one by Treasury officials after questions had been asked in the House, but with a few exceptions offenders were bound over with small fines; the Treasury case was dismissed by the magistrates. Among the exception was John Davies of Pant-yr-holiad, who was imprisoned at Carmarthen for three months in 1893 for assaulting the wretched bailiff. When he arrived back in Cardigan by train after serving his sentence he was given a hero's welcome, and a large public meeting in his honour heard the Carmarthen Boroughs Liberal MP, Major Evan Jones, a Tregaron man who had fought bravely at Gettysburg in the American Civil War, defending Thomas's stand. Thomas himself was presented with an address and a purse containing forty sovereigns. Another tithe 'martyr' welcomed home on return from prison was Evan Evans of Llandysul. The unrest was not entirely limited to the south of the county; John Morris of Glancarrog, Llanddeiniol, was distrained on for his tithes in 1889. However, by 1895 protest in the county had ceased.

One of the apparent triumphs of Welsh Nonconformity had been the passing of the Welsh Sunday Closing Act in 1881. In retrospect its political significance was to establish a precedent for separate legislation for Wales, a precedent which would be used again in dealing with education and disestablishment of the Church. Wales certainly had (and has) a problem with alcohol; during the years 1874-93 crimes of drunkenness were commoner in Wales than in England, though the overall crime rate was lower. Russell Davies has demonstrated the extent of the problem in Carmarthenshire, and there is little to suggest that the legislation was not as widely defied in rural Cardiganshire as were 'closing hours' in more recent times. Cardiganshire kept its 'dry' Sundays through the votes of 1961, 1968 and 1982, but another vote in 1989 finally opened the county to Sunday drinking. The importance of the tourist trade and the hypocrisy of the closed-pubs-open-clubs situation, together with the near-collapse of communal Nonconformity, overwhelmed teetotalism; many of those who voted for continuance of Sunday closing were simply registering a protest against the steady anglicisation of Welsh life.

The weaknesses of Welsh Nonconformity seem obvious to us today, and they were lashed by their contemporary critics such as the Churchman David Owen ('Brutus', 1795-1866), who attacked quack preaching, and Caradoc Evans of Rhydlewis (1878-1945), whose savage stories lampooned the hypocrisy of religion as practised in rural Cardiganshire. The ultimate chapel sanction against unacceptable behaviour was expulsion; figures published by Nerys Ann Jones for Capel y Garn, Bow Street, show that during the years 1875-1880 fifteen chapel members were expelled. In a sense expulsion was no more than a continuation of the practice in Anglican churches of penance for adultery (appearing in church wearing a white sheet and carrying a candle) or excommunication. It also seems that in the late 19th century the denominations became less tolerant of each other, while internal divisions made matters worse. This became painfully obvious in Aberystwyth in 1890 when a quarrel in Seilo over the appointment of elders led to the founding of the 'split' congregation of Salem; ironically, a century later, Seilo is no more and the two congregations are joined together contentedly in Salem, rechristened Capel y Morfa, where they have been recently joined by the former members of Tabernacl.

* * *

One advance for Christian witness which was decidedly unwelcome among Nonconformists, and regarded askance by Anglicans, was the slow increase in the Roman Catholic presence in the county. Regular worship in Aberystwyth began in 1867, and the attractive St Winifred's church and presbytery were opened in 1875. In 1923 Castell Brychan (now headquarters of the Welsh Books Council) became St Mary's seminary for training priests, and churches were opened at Lampeter (1940), Aberaeron (1958 – in a former Wesleyan chapel), Borth (1969) and Penparcau (1970). Several efforts were made to establish a presence in Cardigan; a little monastery was established in 1904 at Caermaria by French monks expelled by the anticlerical French government of the time, and a new shrine and church of Our

Lady of the Taper was created in 1956 as a centre of Marian pilgrimage in Wales. The Catholic presence in the Teifi valley was given a considerable boost by the post-World War II settlement of long-suffering Polish ex-servicemen and their families, a community which flourished for more than two decades but by now has been almost entirely absorbed or scattered.

More difficult for Christians to deal with than human weaknesses, and far more menacing than the supposed dangers of Catholicism, were the advances of science, philosophy and general secularism, associated with the spread of popular pastimes and entertainments. The higher criticism of new generations of learned theologians slowly undermined the authority of lectern and pulpit, while many within the chapels felt that worship had become desiccated and formal, and that they had been deserted by the Holy Spirit. Quarrels between and within the denominations, the ongoing difficulties between Nonconformity and the Established Church, hatred of Catholicism and Anglo-Catholicism were unattractive features of a Christianity which taught higher ideals, but often failed to live them. Revival was perceived as the answer, and many prayed and thirsted for it. True, there had been numerous regional revivals in Wales after 1859 as there had been before, but none had spread throughout the country; Cardiganshire experienced one brief revival in the late 1880s. In 1904 Welsh Nonconformity staged – so it seems in retrospect – one last Canute-like stand against the encroaching tide of secular indifference and stagnation. It began in Cardiganshire.

Joseph Jenkins (1861-1929), originally of Cwmystwyth, was the Calvinistic Methodist minister at New Quay. Towards the end of 1903 he had begun to experience a new warmth in his ministry, and in February 1904 he witnessed a passionate response from at least a few of his worshippers, including one Florrie Evans, a local young woman who was to play an important role in the revival. Other chapels across south Wales were experiencing similar outbreaks, followed by scattered manifestations across the north, but there was not yet any sense of a 'national' phenomenon. The experienced missioner Seth Joshua (1858-1925) came to New Quay, Newcastle Emlyn and Blaenannerch in September, 1904, and was amazed by the manifestations of revival – spontaneous prayer and singing, rejoicing and repentance. Among his hearers at Blaenannerch was Evan Roberts (1879-1951), a young ex-miner from Loughor who had intended starting a course of preparation for the ministry that month. Roberts was already a man of rich and complex spiritual experience who nevertheless felt unfulfilled, and who had prayed eagerly for revival. His response to Seth Joshua was to break out into prayer, and to many present he seemed as if he was on fire, so that his hearers were convulsed with feeling. He visited at least one other Cardiganshire chapel, Capel Drindod, before setting out to spread the message around Wales, leaving Sidney Evans of Gorseinon to keep the flame burning in south Cardiganshire. Although Roberts was widely regarded as the torch-bearer of the Revival, meetings did not necessarily require his presence. During November and December 1904 there were fiery meetings at Aberaeron, Bwlch-llan, Llanddewibrefi, Blaenpennal, Tregaron, Swyddffynnon, Pontrhydfendigaid, Tal-y-bont and Aberystwyth.

But the emotionalism of the Revival was to prove its own undoing. Although it swiftly became famous through the newspapers, awakening echoes in England and worldwide, it could not last at such intensity. Evan Roberts, after several campaigns during which his behaviour became more and more eccentric, eventually withdrew exhausted. It was unfortunate that, though many were engaged in the work which could never have been achieved by one man, the revival became identified in popular memory with Roberts's personality. Although new chapels were founded here and there in the aftermath, they were few; there were already sufficient buildings, especially in Cardiganshire with its declining population. Certainly many lives were changed, many improved, but it seems likely that those most affected were not the unchurched, but members and hearers whose convictions had lapsed or grown cold.

Chapel life was as active after the 1904 Revival as it had been before. For example, Bethania Baptist chapel, Cardigan, had at various times between 1870 and 1930 a Band of Hope, a Choral Society, a Dramatic Society, a Literary Society, a Temperance Society and a Young People's Guild. But there were to be no more revivals in Wales, and although religious life in Cardiganshire was to remain for some decades apparently unaffected by change, change there most certainly was. There were factors we can describe as negative: the impact of two Great Wars, of economic depression and the continued bleeding away of the population. Other factors may be described in a sense as positive; improved education led to a greater level of sophistication and willingness to question received ideas. A higher standard of living offered alternatives to the chapel as the sole fount of cultural and social life.

Over Wales as a whole, and despite the losses of the First World War, the number of members claimed by the Nonconformist denominations continued to increase until 1926, though its growth had been slower than that of the Welsh population, which itself had begun to decline after 1921. The population of Cardiganshire had already been falling since 1871, so the slow growth in chapel membership at the turn of the 20th century certainly justified some slight Nonconformist optimism. Thus in north Cardiganshire, Calvinistic Methodist communicants rose from 5,617 in 1873 to 6,750 in 1906, perhaps reflecting the '04 Revival. Then however a long decline began, briefly chronicled in the final chapter below.

16. The Cardi goes to School

Cities such as Oxford, Cambridge, London, Paris, Dublin and Edinburgh have a long and remarkable history of contributions to education; schooling on a large scale is always more easy to organise in urban centres enjoying at least some degree of prosperity. It is worth while keeping that in mind when considering the remarkable standards which have been achieved from time to time in Ceredigion, a poor rural area with only a few small urban centres and a thinly scattered population. The cultural achievements of Llanbadarn Fawr and Strata Florida, and the work of the anonymous anchorite of Llanddewibrefi, have already been noted above, without drawing particular attention to the fact that these could only be achieved by good schooling. Obviously the status, requirements and resources of the Church made that schooling possible. But how did the laymen of the family of Rhydderch of Dyffryn Aeron, especially Rhydderch's son Ieuan and their family and the lawgivers of that area, gain their education? Did the family's young men study at Strata Florida? Gain education they did, and not simply in the bardic or legal schools of which we know so little. Ieuan boasts of his knowledge of languages and liberal culture in a way which suggests attendance at Oxford – but how did he achieve that? Of course it is known that Welsh students went to Oxford to study; they flocked home to support Owain Glyn Dŵr's rebellion, but Cardiganshire connections escape us.

Other areas of Wales had their *clasau*, their Cistercian abbeys and their cultural achievements, though Llanbadarn Fawr and Strata Florida were outstanding at a national level. Following the Acts of Union and the dissolution of the monasteries, a number of grammar schools were endowed across Wales – at Bangor, Botwnnog, Rhuthun, Abergavenny, Carmarthen and Cowbridge, to name only some – but Cardiganshire was left without a single recorded institution. The monastic assets which elsewhere partly funded schools were in Cardiganshire entirely swallowed up by land-grabbers. Suddenly there is a virtual blank in the county's educational history; although it is known that there was a school at Lampeter in 1642, run by one Thomas Evans, no details survive.

Education was of course available at a distance, at least to sons of the major families, for whom there were two alternatives, either to import tutors or to send their boys away to school. Where did the Lloyds of Castell Hywel, the Pryses of Gogerddan, the Vaughans of Trawsgoed, send their sons? Only two places can be named with some confidence; John Vaughan of Trawsgoed (b.1603) was apparently sent to school in Worcester. As eldest son he was fortunate; a younger brother of his was sent to Shrewsbury, not to the school there but as an apprentice. John Jones of Nanteos was sent to school at Gloucester (later going on to Oxford and Lincoln's Inn). Other schools were certainly available; if the grammar schools at Presteigne or Carmarthen were not considered suitable, then Shrewsbury, Hereford, Worcester and London provided opportunities. But who took them? When Edward Jones of Nanteos made his will in 1636 he was determined that his eldest son John should remain at the Inns of Court, while his second son was to complete his MA at university, which we know from the Latin law-texts he wrote at Cambridge. The other four sons were to be 'maintaiened at schoole with meate Drinke cloathes and lodgeing' until sixteen, and then be placed in apprenticeships. The school or schools are not named. The Inns of Court in London were virtually a third university, after Oxford and Cambridge. Some young men went from university to the Inns of Court, others went straight there. A legal training was valuable to the heir of a landed estate. Morgan Lloyd of Rhiwarthen, gentleman, insisted in his will of 1640 that his son Thomas should go to school, and David Lloyd of Crynfryn, who died in 1621, charged his wife with ensuring the same for his son. Philip Pugh of Llanddewibrefi, who died in 1674, asked his son and namesake, who became convenor and minister of the county's Independent congregation, to see that his younger brother should have two years' schooling, it is not known where.

What about people of lesser wealth? Again, examples survive in probate records; Richard Powell, a mercer of Cardigan, on his deathbed in 1621, sought a year's schooling for his son. When Rees Thomas of Caron made his will in 1614 the curate of Gwnnws took notes, but since he was unavailable at the time of Thomas's actual death a local yeoman with the unusual name of Palaemon Lewis wrote out the will in full. It is clear from enquiries made by the church authorities in the case of disputed wills that gentry were able to read, but Cardiganshire yeomen almost invariably had to have the documents read aloud to them, either because they were illiterate, or could read only Welsh. But Palaemon Lewis could write good English – indeed, in 1629 he wrote out his own will, ending it by committing his wife and children to the care of 'the Allmightie whoe hath promised in his hollie Worde ever to be a father to the fatherless and defender of the widowes I ende with this Caveat, burum celum est necessitas.' He had obviously had a good education, but seems to have been a tenant farmer of limited means. His baptismal name, derived from classical legend, suggests an unusual family background, now apparently untraceable (could there be any connection with the farm name Palmon, in Llanddeiniol parish?). The most likely suppliers of education at a local level were parish priests, whose qualifications seem to have varied greatly. Girls would have been educated, insofar as formal tuition was considered of any value for them, at home.

The first endowed school in Cardiganshire was at Cardigan, the result of a petition organised by the parliamentarian squire James Philipps of Cardigan Priory in 1647. Confiscated church income from Llansanffraid was used to endow a 'free grammar school' at Cardigan for boys under the 1650 Act for the Propagation of the Gospel in Wales, with provision for lodging and maintenance for the poorest pupils. It was one of a large number of schools established under Cromwell, and at the Restoration in 1660 it was apparently the only one to survive, thanks to the support of the town's corporation and a measure of re-endowment under the will of Lady Laetitia Cornwallis. The boys were taught the Classics, French, English and Welsh.

Numbers never seem to have been as large as at the later Ystrad Meurig and Lampeter schools. The Cardigan school received a tolerably good report in 1847. In 1860 it was housed in the new and remarkable Guildhall designed in the Gothic style by R.J.Withers, and survived until the Welsh Intermediate Act of 1889 brought other arrangements into existence, described below.

Whatever schools they may have attended, Cardiganshire men were able by reason of their education to make their mark in the world of the Tudors and Stuarts. Reference has already been made to some of their achievements: Griffith Lloyd (d.1587), a younger son of Llanllŷr, rose to become principal of Jesus College, Oxford; his younger brother Thomas (d.1613) became chancellor of the diocese of St David's, and sent his son Marmaduke (d.1651) to Oriel College, Oxford, and then to the Middle Temple. David Lloyd of Llwyndafydd, no relation to the greater clan of Lloyd as far as I know, became a fellow of Oriel and a university lecturer before returning to Llannarth; his story is told in the previous chapter. Thomas Powell (d.1703) of Llechwedd Dyrys became a judge in the court of King's Bench. The Pryses of Gogerddan were attenders at the Inner Temple; members of the Philippses of Cardigan Priory went to Oxford or to the Middle Temple. By the 18th century we know that the major families were patronising Westminster and Harrow schools, with Oxford to follow. But what of lesser folk?

The Puritan initiative of 1650 did not die with the Restoration; instead it was taken up, first by the Welsh Trust founded by the Dissenter Thomas Gouge (d.1681), but although a school may have been established at Lampeter, the Trust seems to have had little success in the county. Schools however continued to be established in Wales by the Society for the Promotion of Christian Knowledge, which was active in the country from its foundation in 1699, not only in opening schools but in publishing Welsh language material for pupils and general readers. The Society had considerable success in Pembrokeshire, but little in Cardiganshire. A school was established in the county at the Esgair-hir mines, sponsored by the Company of Mine Adventurers of England, along with a chaplain; the only other SPCK school in the county was founded at Llandysul in 1727, for ten boys. The simplest explanations for the failure of both the Trust and the SPCK in Cardiganshire may be simply poverty and the use of English as a medium of instruction; another possibility is the lack of interest among the gentry. There was certainly no one in the county remotely like Sir John Vaughan of Derllys or Sir John Philipps of Picton Castle.

Instead it required an entirely new initiative which would emphasise teachers not buildings, and Welsh rather than English. The circulating schools of Griffith Jones are comparatively well-known and understood, partly because for many years Jones published an annual report listing all the schools and numbers of pupils, and partly from their overwhelming success. Griffith Jones taught the teachers himself, and gave them a clear and simple aim – the teaching of Biblical literacy for the salvation of souls, tested by a public oral examination in the parish church. Jones did not push his schools on anyone, instead he tried to meet demand from churches and parish gentry as it arose, providing a trained teacher if the local people would provide accommodation. Details do not survive before the winter of 1738-39, when there were ten schools scattered through the centre of the county. The number of schools in Cardiganshire varied from year to year; as low as six in 1743-44, as many as forty in 1765-66. Emphasis has been laid in the past on the total number of students registered, but this is bound to give a false impression, since it is quite clear that some students attended for more than one winter. However, a winter like that of 1764-65 saw 2,454 children and adults registered, perhaps ten per cent of the whole population, and since children were comfortably in the majority, the total percentage of the county's children in these schools must have been considerable.

The obstacles faced by the pupils must have been great, and are occasionally referred to in school reports. Thomas James, curate of Bron-gwyn, wrote in 1771, 'About Nine Days ago, I had the Pleasure of examining the Scholars privately, (they being so poor as not to appear in Church for want of Clothes).' The schools met with the general blessing of clergy and gentry; Lewis Gwynne of Monachty, Pennant, wrote to say that the teacher there had had 137 pupils, so that a second teacher was called in. It would be good to know more than we do about the teachers themselves, of whom at least one was a woman. The only identifiable and well-known figure is Morgan Rhys (1716-1779) the hymn-writer of Cil-y-cwm, Carmarthenshire, who taught in Llantysiliogogo in 1757-58, and later in Llandysul and Llwyndafydd. The suspension of the circulating schools in 1779 after the death of Madam Bridget Bevan was a severe loss to the whole country. In 1807 her endowment was released from Chancery, and there were six 'Bevan' schools in Cardiganshire in 1818; in 1854 the surviving schools were taken over by the National Society.

While the circulating schools were being established in the county, Cardiganshire's first schools of real note since the Cardigan Grammar School were also being created. The first was at Motygido, Llannarth, the work of John Pugh (1690-1763), curate of nearby Llanllwchaearn. He knew Greek and Latin, Hebrew and Arabic, and he had quite a good library. The school, which ended with his death if not before, was only one source of income for Pugh; as well as his inadequate stipend and fees, he had to farm to keep his household going. It was a hard-working life, and never a rich one. It is not certain when Pugh began teaching, but it must have been before 1733, if it is true that Edward Richard spent time with him before taking over and eventually expanding the second school of note.

This school was originally begun in his native village of Ystrad Meurig in 1732 by Edward's elder brother Abraham Richard; their parents, apparently of humble origin, had nevertheless been willing to secure good educations for their sons, it is not known where. Abraham died the following year in an unexplained accident, so Edward Richard, then not yet twenty-one, attempted in 1734 to carry on the school. However, about 1740, he decided he needed to improve his own education, and the school closed for several years while he honed his Greek and Latin, reopening in 1745. In the following year Dorothea, widow of Thomas Oliver, an Anglican priest in Dudley, endowed a school in Oliver's native village of Lledrod, and the trustees appointed Edward Richard its first headmaster, to manage both establishments. The relationship between the two neighbouring schools is both complex and obscure; the 1818 government Report on the Education of the Lower Orders (the Brougham Report) asserts that they were then under one roof. After Edward Richard's death in 1777, the headmaster was invariably an ordained clergyman, and was given charge of Ystrad Meurig parish. His successor John Williams (*yr Hen Syr*) was almost as well-known and respected as Richard himself.

What differentiated Ystrad Meurig from the Welsh Tudor grammar schools and from the unique institution at Cardigan was that Ystrad Meurig began simply as a one-man school of the kind which tended to live and die with its founder, but its status was transformed by Edward Richard's generosity; he endowed it with lands worth £128 a year, spending £200 on buildings, and he ensured its recognition as a 'grammar' school with trustees. He also founded a small library for his school, surely the first in Cardiganshire outside the mansions of the gentry; he also cultivated valuable acquaintanceships with the local gentry, particularly John Lloyd of Ffosybleiddiaid. Ystrad Meurig became a well-known producer of ordinands for the Church at a time when graduate candidates for holy orders were rare in rural Wales, and when a degree was not considered essential; most ordinands had grammar school educations.

The curriculum at Ystrad Meurig was, like that of the contemporary grammar schools, fundamentally classical, but under several, at least, of the headmasters Welsh was also taught there, and was certainly used in exposition for the benefit of pupils, many of whom arrived with little or no English. The backbone of the school's reputation was the number of its students who went on to have distinguished careers, mostly in the service of the Church, but also in the Nonconformist denominations. The most famous of Edward Richard's own pupils was Evan Evans, 'Ieuan Fardd' (see Chapter 22). Other former students included John Williams, son of William Williams of Pantycelyn, John Williams of Lledrod, another leading Methodist, Evan Richardson of Caernarfon, David Richard ('Dafydd Ionawr') and John Phillips, founder of the Normal College at Bangor, as well as several bishops, a general and a royal physician to George IV.

Ystrad Meurig resisted takeover attempts in the late 19th century by St David's College, Lampeter, and then by the local education authority. Like many another school, it flourished under good headmasters, and was fortunate in most of its leaders. However the creation of St David's College in 1827 and Bala Theological College in 1837 took away many of its best pupils; the Taunton Commission of 1868 reported damningly that 'it was absolutely destitute of any school building worthy of the name'. Nevertheless, its classical tradition was maintained into the 20th century by several outstanding headmasters, though the small size of the establishment and the growth of secondary and tertiary education throughout the land meant that Ystrad Meurig could no longer attract students of the same calibre as those who once had been glad to attend. The school enjoyed an Indian summer after World War II, when a number of ex-servicemen took advantage of government grants to gain a pre-university grounding there. Once they had moved on, the school shrank again, until closure became inevitable in 1974. The buildings still stand forlornly in the churchyard; the library was moved to St David's College, Lampeter. Cherished locally is the legend that Oxford scholars who came to investigate the school's remarkable and deserved reputation for classical learning were astonished to find that even the local peasants (students dressed for the occasion) answered their queries in Latin and Greek.

In the meantime many of the county's children were without education or the opportunity thereof. The first statistics available come from a governmental report of 1818 on the education of the poor. The report names fourteen Cardiganshire educational endowments totalling £1,191, of which £915 was the Bevan endowment for the county, much of it not apparently used; £215 belonged to Ystrad Meurig, leaving only £61 for other projects. Altogether these endowments accounted for the education of 415 children. In addition, fifty-five day schools provided places for 1,160 children, and twenty-six Sunday schools accommodated 512 pupils. If that was the sum total of Sunday schools, then the level of literacy must have dropped since the best days of the circulating schools. There were thirty-three parishes in Cardiganshire with no day-schools at all, and many of those without even a Sunday school. The same comment is repeated, with variations, of parish after parish: 'The poorer classes, though very desirous, are without sufficient means of instruction.'

Today the distinction between primary, secondary and tertiary education is well understood, but the categories are impossible to apply retrospectively. By 1847, and surely earlier, Ystrad Meurig was educating two categories who may be crudely called elementary and advanced pupils; its long record of providing 21-year-old men for ordination is sufficient indication of that. But more clergy were needed than one school could produce, and the grammar school at Lampeter was created for that purpose by Eliezer Williams (1754-1829), clergyman son of the Methodist pioneer Peter Williams. Williams had returned in 1805 from working in England to be vicar of Lampeter parish, and although at 51 he might have been pardoned for resting on his oars, he was an energetic man, and immediately began his grammar school to prepare young men for the Church, with considerable success. As well as studying Greek and Latin, the boys performed Latin plays in public. Eliezer's successor as headmaster was John Williams, son of *yr Hen Syr*, who was so well-known and respected that Sir Walter Scott sent his son to be taught at the school; he knew of Williams through his son-in-law J.G. Lockhart, who had been at Balliol with Williams.

The Nonconformist equivalent of schools like Ystrad Meurig and Lampeter were the dissenting academies. Two establishments described without apparent differentiation as academies or schools were Castell Hywel and Neuadd-lwyd. The former was the creation of David Davis (1745-1827; he is often referred to as Dafydd Dafis Castell Hywel, after his home). David was a teacher, libertarian, poet and preacher, who as well as teaching his students exercised a vigorous ministry to the Arian congregations of the Teifi valley. He had been educated in the Carmarthen academy, a hotbed of Nonconformist theological debate, and from 1782 until his retirement in 1820 his Castell Hywel establishment produced a regular stream both of Nonconformist ministers and Anglican priests, until bishop Horsley refused to ordain Davis's students on theological grounds.

As well-known in his day as David Davis was Thomas Phillips (1772-1842) of Neuadd-lwyd, inland from Aberaeron. A native of Carmarthenshire, he had been a pupil at Castell Hywel. His was to some extent a peripatetic ministry; although installed as minister to the Neuadd-lwyd congregation in 1796, he also shepherded the Independents of Tal-y-bont and Llanbadarn Fawr until 1810, which must have meant long hours on horseback. Whereas David Davis can fairly be described as a figure of the 18th-century enlightenment, Phillips's was a narrower concept of education than those of Ystrad Meurig or Castell Hywel; his whole emphasis was on scriptural knowledge, and on preparation for God's ministry. Any student who spoke Welsh was fined; the contributions supported the headmaster's tobacco habit. His most famous students were both local young men, Thomas Bevan and David Jones, the first Christian missionaries to Madagascar.

Unitarians, who were enthusiastic for education, established several small but highly effective schools in the 'Smotyn Du'. John Thomas kept a school at Llandysul between 1813 and 1861, and Thomas Thomas another at Pont-sian. John Thomas was effectively succeeded at Llandysul by William Thomas (Gwilym Marles), minister of Llwynrhydowen and a graduate of Glasgow University. The last school of these schools was at Cribyn, run between 1886 and 1906 by David Evans, whose pupils went on to university at Oxford, Aberystwyth and various other colleges and professional organisations.

It was only in the early years of the 19th century that Aberystwyth developed as a centre of education. The first school of note in the town was 'The Mathematical and Commercial School' founded about 1819 by John Evans (1796-1861), a native of Blaen-plwyf, at the south-east corner of Chalybeate Street. Evans was of a scientific and technical bent; he built a clock which crowned his school building and was apparently the first public clock in the town. He also made sundials, one of which survives over the porch of Llanfihangel-y-Creuddyn church. He was particularly famed for his teaching of navigation. Among his former pupils were Lewis Edwards, one of the greatest of Welsh educationists, founder of Bala Theological College, and Henry Richard, the first radical MP in Wales. J.C. Symons praised Evans's work highly in the 1847 Blue Books.

John Evans's Aberystwyth school; note his sundial.
[National Library of Wales]

John Evans's school, as its

title suggests, was not intended for young men seeking entry to the ministry of church or chapel, but that was the main function of the Ystrad Meurig and Lampeter schools. Bishops of St David's would never have been able to staff the underpaid livings in the diocese with Oxbridge graduates. Instead they had for generations been able to ordain men who had come from a grammar school or academy. However, a remarkable new initiative was taken by Thomas Burgess, bishop of St David's 1803-25. In 1804 he established the 'Society for Promoting Christian Knowledge and Church Union in the Diocese of St David's', and conceived a plan to build a college which would provide young Welsh ordinands with an education to degree standard. He canvassed vigorously for money, setting an example with a tenth part of his annual income. George IV gave a thousand pounds, J.S. Harford of Falcondale another thousand; archdeacon Thomas Beynon contributed £750 and Bishop Barrington of Llandaff £500. The universities of Oxford and Cambridge each gave £300; a Crown charter of incorporation was secured, and an income of £400 a year from the Privy Purse. By 1820 there was £13,000 available for building, to which the government added £6,000. Burgess's original intention was to build the college at Llanddewibrefi, but he settled for Lampeter, where J.S. Harford gave land, and the foundation stone was laid on 12 August 1822. Burgess was so overcome with emotion at the initial ceremony that he was unable to continue his address. C.R.Cockerell, the architect, based his plans on Oxbridge colleges, the obvious model of the day. Twenty-nine students attended when the college opened on St David's Day, 1827.

The college curriculum was straightforward: Theology and Christian Morals, Hebrew, Greek and Latin, Elocution and the Welsh language, Church history and the duties of the clerical profession. There were four members of staff. The principal was a young Oxford graduate from Coity, Glamorgan, Llewelyn Lewellin, a name whose orthography is not consistent. Born in 1798, he held his principalship for fifty-one years, until his death in 1878, by which time he had become vicar of Lampeter (1834) and dean of St David's (1843), but he stayed at Lampeter to the

St David's University College, Lampeter, in mid-19th century, by Emily Nares, daughter of Principal Llewelyn Lewellin.

end. His daughter Emily (Mrs Nares) painted the watercolour of the college which illustrates this chapter. Of the same age as principal Lewellin was his deputy Alfred Olivant, who moved from Lampeter in 1843 and eventually became a great reforming bishop of Llandaff; he and Burgess are both examples of the kind of talented Englishmen who gave the best of their careers to Wales and the Welsh Church, serving them outstandingly well. Lewellin appointed his former Oxford pupil, Rice Rees (1804-39) of Tonn, Llandovery, another young graduate, as librarian and lecturer in Welsh – the first such academic post for Welsh ever created anywhere. Eventually the college broadened its curriculum to include a professor of Natural Philosophy and Chemistry. From 1852 the college was empowered to grant degrees to its students.

What might have been the destiny of St David's University College had it been founded at Carmarthen? Less isolation and securer transport might have enabled it to grow more steadily. As it was, the college cherished its Church and Oxbridge links; relations with the nondenominational University of Wales were very slow to develop. For much of its life there were fewer than 200 students, and the two World Wars brought virtual, if temporary, closure. Only in 1963 were there more than 100 new admissions. Women students were not accepted until 1965. Eventually, in 1971, the college joined the University of Wales. The closure of Burgess Hall in 1976 meant that no student could be ordained directly into the Church in Wales, the original purpose of the college. While retaining theology and a chaplaincy, and developing a centre of Islamic studies, the institution has been largely secularised; since 1996 it is no longer 'St David's', but 'The University of Wales, Lampeter'. Partnerships with other colleges have been mooted but not fulfilled at the time of writing. The present total of nearly 2,000 students is still not enough to guarantee its long-term stability, but the closure of the college would be a local catastrophe.

THE mark of the voluntary societies is still to be seen in many Cardiganshire villages. Some pre-Victorian and Victorian schools are still in use, for example the little building of 1835 at Llanfihangel-y-Creuddyn, and the nearby Earl of Lisburne school of 1865 at Llanafan, complete with its school house. Others are falling into decay, such as the interesting school building at Llannarth and the remarkable little school at Elerch, all of a piece with the little Gothic church. The foundation of board schools after 1870 saw the creation of some good buildings, such as the Aberystwyth school next to the railway station, designed by Szlumper and Aldwinckle, now used for a variety of purposes.

* * *

As well as famous schools such as Ystrad Meurig, Neuadd-lwyd and Castell Hywel, there were in the county many town and village schools whose history is often difficult or impossible to trace, but were the result of private initiative, sometimes in connection with the National (C. of E.) or British (i.e. Nonconformist) Societies. Others drew on Madam Bevan's bequest. Those in existence in 1818 are summarised in the Brougham report of that year, referred to above. They all

The Earl of Lisburne School, Llanafan, in 1888. [Courtesy of the Earl of Lisburne]

suddenly swim into more detailed view with the publication in 1847 of the 'Blue Books', the report of the commissioners appointed by Parliament to examine the state of education in Wales, inspired by alarm at the state of unrest in both industrial and rural Wales. The report has been attacked ever since its publication for its criticism of Welsh morals and the Welsh language, written by three young English churchmen, of whom J.C. Symons was responsible for Cardiganshire. Although their reports were by no means totally negative, one can imagine the patriotic Welsh reaction to the comment on Tregaron, though it only echoes the opinions of all English travellers who passed through the town:

> The extreme filthiness of the habits of the poor [is] observable everywhere. There seemed seldom to be more than one room for living and sleeping in; generally in a state of indescribably [Is there a word missing here?] order and dirty to an excess. The pigs and poultry form a usual part of the family . . .

However, the report admits that crime rates in Cardiganshire were one-fifth those of Herefordshire. It would be otiose here to discuss all the general issues raised by the report; they have been splendidly addressed by Prys Morgan and Gwyneth Tyson Roberts. The report is still valuable for the detailed evidence it provides of the number of schools, their accommodation and their curricula, much of it written by the Welsh-speaking assistants to the three commissioners. Social and personal comments are also provided, which betray a complex set of values and attitudes alien to the people who were the subjects of their report.

There were schools of some kind in forty-two of the county's sixty-four parishes, but their quality varied enormously. Praise was bestowed on a number of buildings: 'a very convenient schoolroom, a very substantial building, and well fitted with school apparatus' (Betws Bledrws); 'very excellent schoolrooms . . . chiefly due to Mr Brigstock of Blaen-pant' (Llandygwydd); 'a sightly and substantial building, in excellent repair' (Borth). Other buildings are damned: 'a very comfortless room' (Mr Forrester James's school at Cardigan); 'a cow-shed . . . the walls were of mud; the roof of decayed thatch . . . neither fire nor fire-place . . . the ground being wet and muddy' (Llanwenog); 'a miserable, small, cold room' (Cwrtnewydd); 'a wretched place without any floor . . . a heap of mortar and rubbish encumbered the area' (Troedyraur).

While critical of many of the buildings, Symons and his assistants were even more critical of the teaching, the low standard of which was to be expected in view of the utterly miserable salaries and total lack of training of the great majority of the teachers, and the virtual absence of resources, problems acknowledged by Symons. The teacher at Llanwenog was described as 'a poor half-starved looking man [who] knew very little more than the scholars, nor is it at all expected that he should. His total income was £12 per annum, out of which he paid 10s for the rent of the school shed.' Sometimes the inspector emphasised contrasts within individual schools; for example, the Trawsnant school at Llanrhystud had an excellent building but 'the master was an uneducated person', previously a farmhand and dockyard labourer, whose little English was his sole qualification. By contrast the dismal cottage-school at Pen-y-garn, Bow Street, flourished despite its circumstances 'owing entirely to the natural ability and unusually good education of the teacher, a young married woman, named Jane Thomas'. Nobody commented, as would county councillors of a later generation, that married women however talented as teachers should stay at home.

Commissioner Symons reserved his highest praise for the Aberystwyth Wesleyan Day School, despite its lack of facilities: '[it is] the only really good day school I have yet seen in Wales. It is conducted by a trained master . . . The obedience of the children, and order and discipline of the school, were admirable . . . No child is ever struck . . .' Symons included a copy of the school's timetable in his report; every day began with 'Praise and Prayer', and lessons included not only English and Arithmetic, but Bible study, Geography, History and singing lessons, including brief sessions of 'Singing and Marching'. Aberystwyth's Sunday Schools also drew the commissioner's approbation.

The Blue Books offer more than a straightforward commentary on the actual state of the schools. There are frequent references to the poverty of the pupils and their parents, who often could not afford the pence necessary for attendance at many schools, nor could they afford to lose children's earnings, however miniscule. Bad weather affected the attendance of children who were inadequately dressed. Symons commented particularly on the small number of girls attending schools; their child-minding and domestic help was valued by their mothers, and small worth set on their need for education. His report did not bring about an immediate revolution in Welsh or Cardiganshire education, but there were improvements; the National and British Societies both made efforts to found more schools, though in some places there was Nonconformist resistance to government aid, which it was feared would promote the cause of the Church of England. In the second half of the 19th century such hostility seems to have intensified, as shown for example in the deliberate exclusion of Ystrad Meurig and Lampeter grammar schools from the developments that took place after the Education Act of 1870.

Cardiganshire was ill-prepared for compulsory education after the 1870 act. While Flintshire already had places for 78% of potential pupils, only Merthyr Tudful (22%) was lower than Cardiganshire's 38%. The act led to the formation of thirty-five school boards in the county by 1880 – the first in all Wales was that established for Aberystwyth, but some areas were reluctant, and eighteen areas of Cardiganshire had boards thrust upon them by the Education Department. Board members were elected every three years, and elections sometimes led to denominational and political conflict. Robert Smith has noted that some board meetings could not raise a quorum of members, because many (usually Nonconformists) had sought election simply to keep out the (Anglican) opposition rather than from a serious interest in education. Many of the problems which Symons had noted in 1847 – poverty, poor attendance, unpaid fees – continued to be a problem forty years and more later. The Welsh language was of course also seen as a problem both by Symons and by the school inspectors of the next generation; by the end of the 19th century official attitudes were more relaxed, but the Cardiganshire schools remained a powerful force for Anglicisation. Many head teachers were English born and bred, and few were as sympathetic to Wales as Mr Herring of Llanafan, who learned Welsh and took a serious interest in local history.

The next upheaval in Welsh education was the 1889 Welsh Intermediate and Technical Education Act, driven by the shortage of schools able to provide more than elementary education. The results were slow but welcome; Llandysul gained its intermediate school in 1895, as did Cardigan (swallowing the old Grammar School and moving site); Aberaeron and Aberystwyth were next (1896), followed by Tregaron (1897); Eliezer Williams's Lampeter Grammar School, later known as the St David's College School, continued in existence until *c*1950. By 1900 there were more pupils aged 16+ in the county's intermediate schools than in any other Welsh county except Glamorgan, an astonishing achievement considering the state of the county in 1847 and 1870. Unfortunately the syllabus and language of instruction (which was entirely English) were largely alien to rural Cardiganshire's children. Comment in the local newspapers criticising the anglicising effect of the schools was offset by the desire of many parents to see their children rise above agriculture; intelligent pupils were seen as potential bankers, lawyers and teachers, not as farmers, and since rural west Wales could not support many such aspirants to the *bourgeoisie* in the local economy, emigration was seen as necessary and natural, especially for the most intelligent.

A severe dispute followed the 1902 Education Act, which set up Local Education Authorities in place of the school boards. There was widespread resistance, known as the 'Welsh revolt', since ratepayers were now to become responsible for the maintenance of denominational schools – especially Church schools. However, protest eventually subsided, and the authority began to bring its disparate inheritance of some 106 elementary schools into some kind of order. Many school buildings had no running water and sanitary arrangements were crude in the extreme. But by 1914 ninety-one schools had been rebuilt or refurbished, and a programme to improve pupils' health was in train, as well as a programme of evening classes, which was eventually to develop into the Cardiganshire College of Further Education (now Coleg Ceredigion), with campuses at Llanbadarn, Felin-fach and Cardigan. Not all was well with what we now call secondary education; the percentage of pupils passing the 'scholarship' examination to attend the intermediate or grammar schools was small, and the numbers going on to university smaller still, despite the urging of Principal T.F. Roberts of the University College of Wales and the registrar, J.H. Davies, both of whom were members of the County Education Committee.

The state of the county's elementary schools in the 1920s was laid out in the County Medical Officer's annual reports, and from the viewpoint of 2004 they make grim reading. Few schools had flush toilets; most were provided with buckets, some with dry earth closets, which were considered an improvement on buckets 'if the teachers exercised vigilance'. Thirty schools had no running water; at Aber-porth water had to be carried from a neighbouring house; there was of course still no running water in much of the county's housing stock. At Penrhyn-coch in winter time the children 'had to wade ankle-deep in mud' to reach the toilets. Efforts were made to improve the lighting in school buildings; it is hard to believe, but a fact, that the original architects of many schools had been told that smaller windows with frosted glass would *benefit* the pupils' eyesight. Dr Ernest Jones, the M.O.H., campaigned vigorously for more sunshine. His nurses visited all schools regularly to examine children for lice, ringworm and other infections. In 1927, a bad year, there were 96 school closures because of infection, most often influenza.

Cardiganshire's elementary schools were fortunate during the interwar years in benefiting from the enlightened help of the county's inspector of schools, David Thomas. He encouraged head teachers to establish local studies in the curriculum, and his papers in the National Library of Wales contain some interesting folklore material. But the interwar years were not altogether

THE children's point of view is not often considered by historians. Two 20th century Ceredigion authors have written savagely about their experience of school. Caradoc Evans was fairly respectful of his first head teacher at Rhydlewis, but the second drew from him all the venom he could muster. Idris Mathias, at elementary school in Cardigan in the late 1920s and early 1930s, saw his teachers as brutes, ruling by violence and crushing the Welsh language. Other witnesses are more positive; W.T. Hughes as a child in Cwmystwyth about 1900 was taught by a Patagonian Welshman whom he obviously adored.

Children playing at the Lluest Welsh-medium primary school. [National Library of Wales]

Old College, Aberystwyth, prior to the fire of 1885; note the second St Michael's church right, whose roofless porch survives, and the original Aberystwyth pier. [National Library of Wales]

Women students, 1890. [from *The College by the Sea* 1928]

happy ones for the county's schools. The intermediate schools at Cardigan and Llandysul were blacklisted by the National Union of Teachers in the 1920s following a pay strike; the echoes of this were still to be felt when I taught at Cardigan in the 1960s. Money was short and necessary reorganisation did not happen. The school-leaving age was raised to 14 in 1918 and to 15 in 1944, putting pressure on buildings despite static or falling school populations. The arrival of evacuees at Aberystwyth drove Ifan ab Owen Edwards to establish in his own home a private Welsh-medium primary school in 1939 for seven pupils, thus initiating a movement which spread throughout Wales and flourishes today. After 1945 the county produced a development plan which foresaw the end of all-age elementary schools and the concentration of all pupils of 11+ in secondary schools.

* * *

It was purely by accident that in 1872 Cardiganshire acquired a second establishment of higher education, the University College of Wales, and it is impossible to do any justice whatsoever to this major Welsh institution in a chapter such as this. The committee responsible for attempting to establish a national university for Wales, lacking any serious resources, had been unable to determine whether to go ahead in north or south Wales when the extraordinary seafront railway hotel created by Thomas Savin and J.P. Seddon came on the market at a bargain price, and was snapped up. The college began modestly enough with few students and very few staff, and survived a serious fire which destroyed a section of the building; in the 1880s it was under pressure to close after the founding of university colleges at Bangor and Cardiff. It survived, and in 1893 became the senior college of the federal University of Wales; by 1900 it had 474 students, easily outstripping St David's, Lampeter. 1914 saw the frightful scandal of an ignorant Aberystwyth mob intending to lynch Hermann Ethé, one of the greatest scholars of Oriental language of the era, because he was German; the college authorities behaved with credit, insisting on paying his pension despite the chauvinistic attitude of local authority members of the college Court. But however accidental the creation of the University College at Aberystwyth, the situation created was surely unique; from 1872 this small rural county had and still has two degree-awarding university institutions. From the outset, despite its miniscule number of students in the first years, the University College of Wales was to make a huge contribution to culture in Aberystwyth and its environs, and an increasing contribution to the county's economy. As late as 1945, however, the future growth of those contributions could hardly have been foreseen.

ABERYSTWYTH'S Old College building, Savin and Seddon's wonderful Gothic fantasy hotel, swallowed up John Nash's strange, three-sided and triple-turreted Castle House, itself a Gothic fantasy built as a summer home (the first in the county?) for Sir Uvedale Price, friend of Thomas Johnes of Hafod. The long narrow triangular plot available was an architectural challenge which J.P. Seddon triumphantly overcame. Sadly the fire of 1885 destroyed many colourful features such as the half-timbered southern section visible in the earliest photographs.

17. Living by Water

In 1866 a 15-year-old Aberystwyth boy, Isaac Hughes, joined the brig *Lois* for a voyage to South Africa. The *Lois* displaced 215 tons, not a large vessel by the standards of the day, but robust, Sunderland-built and Aberystwyth-registered and owned. Although so young, Isaac Hughes was no longer an apprentice, bound to stay with the captain and ship for several years, but an ordinary seaman, bonded into the rough fellowship of the sea on which he had already spent several years. He could have expected to be away from Britain for anything up to a year or even more. But on 22nd September, way out in the Atlantic, at four in the morning, Isaac Hughes was sent aloft by the bo'sun. A few minutes later the bo'sun heard, as he told Captain Lewis, 'his noise in the water'. The bo'sun threw out a rope, put the vessel about, and cast a wooden bench overboard. The captain and crew rushed to the desk on hearing the cry 'man overboard'. The captain reported: 'the Boat was put out as quick as possible. While the men was getting the Boat out I heard him screaming astern and I have no doubt but he was drowned . . . The Men was so much excited the Boat leaked a little they did not go far and did not know w[h]ere to go as it was dark . . . saw the bench but seen nothing of him as he could not swim.' Sailors didn't learn to swim, so the belief holds, because there was so little chance of rescue that swimming simply prolonged the agony.

The captain of the *Lois* conscientiously listed Isaac's belongings after the lad's death. They included a lot of clothes, three copies of the New Testament, a Bible, books of arithmetic and spelling, and a volume entitled *Moral Courage*. Isaac Hughes was obviously a serious lad, concerned with self-improvement. Normally his property would have been auctioned among his shipmates, but the captain gained the permission of the Shipping Master to whom he reported the boy's death at the next port of call to send all his clothes and books home, 'since the deceased family are personal friends of his [i.e. the captain's] and he thinks the clothing would be of more value to them than the sum they are likely here to bring by sale.'

Many Welsh sailing ships were romantically painted in full sail, furrowing the ocean or the Bay of Naples, to hang in genteel parlours at home, but Isaac Hughes's death is a reminder that this was the most dangerous of livelihoods. Most young Cardis only had a few choices of career. If their fathers had a trade, a farm tenancy or a business, then they might follow them. But in a growing population there were more sons than fathers. Labouring on the land was miserable, going into the lead-mines even in their times of prosperity was miserable. But for those born in the coastal parishes of west Wales, the sea was a temptation: travel, adventure, tradition. It was also harsh. The pay was poor – a pound or thirty shillings a month in mid-19th century – the food often grim, the discipline harsh, the conditions dire, and mortal dangers ever-present. A century before the death of Isaac Hughes, when shipping logs were unknown, the Llannarth poet Evan Thomas Rhys (see Chapter

22) wrote elegies for three Cardiganshire crews lost on separate occasions, one for eight fishermen from New Quay, another for ten New Quay fishermen and a third for a Cardigan crew of three sailing with a cargo of corn to Barmouth.

* * *

Although the *Lois* was built in England, and although Isaac Hughes died far from home, both ship and boy were typical in many ways of the remarkable maritime culture of west Wales in the 19th century. At first glance, Ceredigion is ill-suited for the development of such a culture. The coast is a difficult one, a lee-shore controlled by the prevailing westerly winds, and lacking any natural harbours other than the treacherous estuary of the Teifi and the even more dangerous Dyfi. Coves like those at Aber-porth and Llangrannog provided landing-beaches for small vessels; New Quay's natural headland gives little shelter, while the Aeron estuary was narrow and shallow, and like the Ystwyth-Rheidol estuary, tidal and easily blocked by banks of pebbles and sand. The open beaches at Borth and Cei Bach, like the coves, could only cope with small vessels; the wreckage of the wooden jetties built to help them are only now disappearing into the sea. The original estuary of the Leri between Borth and Ynys-las, before it was canalised to flow into the Dyfi, can have offered little protection.

Llangrannog beach. [Ceredigion County Library]

Borth, however, like Llan-non/Llansanffraid, developed a remarkable maritime community despite the lack of anything like a harbour. Stout fishing-boats, some of them with three small masts, set out regularly for herring while they were still in the bay, and when the herring disappeared, mixed fishing, crustaceans and cockling in the Dyfi estuary were the mainstay of Borth fishing. Generations of young men turned to the sea for a career, signing on with Aberdyfi and Aberystwyth ships, and those with ability rose to be master mariners, while some of the stay-at-home population owned shares in the same vessels. Terry Davies, in his attractive history, reckons that the village produced at least 160 master mariners in the 19th and early 20th century, many of whom retired home to gossip in the sun. Dr Reginald Davies has traced over 8,000 Welsh master mariners and certificated mates, more than 2,000 of them from Cardiganshire. New Quay produced the largest number, followed by Cardigan, Aberystwyth and Aberaeron.

Despite the problems described earlier, all these places and others saw the building of hundreds of wooden sailing ships, while the coastal parishes provided men who were surplus to the agricultural population and willing to crew them. The reason for maritime development was simple: given the state of the roads, commerce was more swiftly conducted by sea. During the medieval period shipping may have been comparatively sparse, though the provision of wine, coal and building materials for Aberystwyth and Cardigan castles and their garrisons certainly brought ships bearing these and other goods, but most people lived simply on the land. However, there was a creeping increase both in the population and the standard of living, particularly in the little towns, and in the many mansion houses scattered through the county. Before the end of the 18th century a wide range of goods was being imported by small ships, and large quantities of salt and especially limestone were brought to the beaches for use by fishermen and farmers. Indeed, the port of Cardigan's trade was already beginning to prosper before 1700. Welsh and Irish ships visited Cardigan as coasting traders, exporting corn, slate and salted herrings.

The government of Queen Elizabeth I, anxious for the security of the country against foreign invasion, had surveyed the whole coast of Wales and England in 1563. The surveyor Thomas Phaer spoke sternly of the poor nature of the county's sea-shelters and the scarcity of shipping, but little or no action seems to have been undertaken, unless it was the diverting of the Ystwyth into the Rheidol at Aberystwyth in an attempt to clear the constant blocking of the latter's estuary by sand and shingle, though this event cannot be even approximately dated, save that it happened before 1750. Before that date a pier of stakes and stones had been built in the shelter of the only large promontory on the county's coast, probably in the 1690s, and the tiny village there had been christened New Key or Quay by 1704. It was a notorious centre for smuggling, particularly of salt since that essential commodity was taxed, as well as the usual brandy, wine and tobacco. There was a fierce encounter in 1704 at New Quay between eight customs men and a crowd of men with horses unloading several boats full of salt that had not paid their dues. More dramatic still was the encounter between the authorities and the notorious smuggler William Owen, whose well-armed ship came to Cardigan Bay in 1744. He had the effrontery, after driving off the Customs vessel, to land his goods by Cardigan's Custom House. The Collector boarded Owen's vessel with a gang of men including four Spanish prisoners-of-war from Cardigan gaol, but Owen and his

Aberystwyth jetty in the 19th century. [National Library of Wales]

crew drove them off, killing four before sailing to the Isle of Man. Owen was eventually executed at Carmarthen. Smuggling only became unprofitable with the abolition of excise duties in the pursuit of Free Trade in the 1870s.

In 1700 the days of New Quay's prosperity were yet to come. Cardigan was certainly the busiest centre in the county during the 18th century; the first stone quays on the river may date back to 1700, and the fine warehouse which still stands on the south bank of the Teifi by the town bridge was built in 1745. In 1785 the Cardigan Mercantile Company was founded, whose former offices bearing the company's title stand by the road south of the town bridge. Cardigan had long enjoyed the status of a port, with Customs officers and registration of vessels; Aberystwyth gained similar status in mid-18th century at the expense of Aberdyfi, and a third harbour was created at Aberaeron by act of Parliament in 1807, driven forward by the squarson landowner Alban Thomas Jones Gwynne, already referred to in Chapter 15. Both Aberystwyth and New Quay followed suit a generation later with harbour improvement acts which led to the creation of the present quay at New Quay and the jetties at Aberystwyth.

CARDIGAN produced a major dynasty of mariner-merchants in the Davies family, who were also involved in Newport (Pemb.). Thomas and John Davies imported iron ore for the Llechryd works, lime, culm and general goods, chartering vessels to join the Atlantic trade, acting as the town's first bankers, and owning warehouses on both sides of the river. They profited by the French wars of 1793-1815 even though one of their ships had to be ransomed after capture by the French. Another was captured off the Irish coast by an American vessel during the war of 1812-14. After the wars, they restarted emigration from west Wales to the U.S.A. in their own ships. Members of the family were usually the masters of Davies vessels, and the family suffered severe losses at sea. Second and third generation members of the family remained dominant in Cardigan's maritime, business and municipal affairs into the 1880s.

Even before these improvements, small ships were being built along the coast, and by the early 19th century if not earlier, shipwrights and carpenters were busy in every port and creek, and even on some beaches. All the vessels involved in the coastal trade were of wood, while iron and steel only came into the deepwater aspect in the latter half of the 19th century, when steam was also seriously affecting the industry. In west Wales, a ship might even be built half a mile inland and shifted on rollers to the nearest beach. Shipbuilding and chandlery were major employers in every small coastal community, but especially Aberystwyth, New Quay and Cardigan. The majority of Welsh sailing ships were locally built, using a mixture of local oak for the frame, with pine imported from Canada for the planking. However, many were built entirely of pine in Canada on commission from Welsh owners. These were cheaper but less well thought of, tending quickly to become 'sea-soft'. Other vessels owned in Welsh ports might have been built in English or Scottish ports and bought second-hand by their Welsh owners. Once registered a vessel would be insured. During the 18th and early 19th centuries this might be in London or Bristol, but by mid-century the larger ports had their own insurance companies; New Quay had three, and even tiny Aber-porth briefly boasted its own Mutual Ship Insurance Society.

The record of the county's shipbuilders is remarkable. Counts of the total ships built at the various harbours and beaches vary and are probably not complete, especially because the Aberystwyth registers from 1780 to 1824 are lost. Margaret Hughes claimed that a total of 278 ships were built at Aberystwyth up to 1882; about 240 are believed to have been built at New Quay and 160 (surely too modest a figure) at Cardigan. These figures do not include the minor creeks and beaches; for example, twenty-five vessels were built at Aber-arth and twenty-four at Llansanffraid, four of the latter each displacing two hundred tons.

It is likely that early shipbuilding in west Wales involved the buying-in of specialist items from elsewhere, but during the 19th century everything from anchors to blocks to sails was made locally. Foundries at Aberystwyth and Cardigan provided chains and anchors, and the county had its own sail-making lofts – six in New Quay alone. Ropes were also produced locally; Aberystwyth had two ropewalks, one at Trefechan, the other running parallel to Queen's Road, Aberystwyth.

Shipping registers of the Welsh ports make fascinating reading, to some at any rate. They are enormous volumes, with a double-page spread for each registration. A ship had to be registered before it could sail, and re-registered every time the ownership changed substantially, or when the vessel was modified. A registration gives the name of the vessel and her master, its tonnage and style – brig, schooner, brigantine, sloop – whether it has a figurehead, details of its decking and measurements. Their building was financed by groups of small investors.

FOULK EVANS and his son John were the best-known Aberystwyth ship-builders. They worked in Shipbuilders' Row (now Prospect St.). In 1839 Foulk Evans divided between his sons, his daughter, grandsons and other relatives his shares in no fewer than twenty-one vessels, all of which would have been built by him. He sent his son John to study shipbuilding in Aberdeen, and John's vessels were reckoned to be of the highest quality.

Every vessel's building costs were met in terms of sixty-four shares, of which the builder and the prospective master usually held a few, while the others would be sold in twos, fours or eights. It was quite rare for a single person to own all sixty-four shares; commercial wisdom dictated a spread of investment to those who could afford it. The master would invariably have a share in his ship, obviously helping to ensure his loyalty and application. The shipbuilder, too, often had a share, thus reducing the cost in cash to the purchasers. The majority of shareholders were shopkeepers, farmers and widows, who if they could afford it would spread out their savings between two or more vessels. The actual management would be carried out by a 'managing owner', often a man involved in running a number of vessels.

Before the introduction of registration, details of shipping in west Wales survive largely by chance. Probate records give tantalising references. In 1721 the Aberystwyth mariner Evan William of Heol-y-Wig left to his son Nathanial his share of the *Swan* and ten herring nets. In 1752 Lewis Evans of Aberystwyth left to his son Lewis Evans 'the Sloop or Vessel lately built by me'. In his inventory the 'small ship' is valued at £85; he also owned nineteen herring-nets and a fishing boat with mast, sails, cable and anchor. In 1808 John Rees of Aberystwyth died possessed of 'the Good Sloop Called *Fancy*' and a fishing boat called *Favorite*.

Unfortunately little personal documentation has survived for the county's ports like that which has been published for Gwynedd, especially Porthmadog. A brief diary, that of Simon Jones of Llangrannog, has been published; it sheds interesting light on his religious turn of mind. Only from 1860, for deep-water voyages, do log-books exist, now kept in the National Library. Alas, the great majority contain no more than the barest details of the crew. However, a few, like the log of the *Lois* quoted above, give much more detail, especially of indiscipline. A major cause of trouble was cooking; ships' cooks were often incompetent, and liable to demotion in favour of some wretched ordinary seaman. In 1866 the cook of the *George Reynolds*, one Ferdinand Roberts, was reported thus:

> He burnt the pease soup then came aft to ask the Master would he oblige him as to put another in his room, that he never cook a pease soup before in his life. Obliged to put Enoch Owens in his place . . .

Drink was another difficulty; in 1863 John Parry of the *Lettice Catherine* of New Quay broke open a case of champagne and drank thirteen bottles. William Lewis, a Cardiff sailor on the New Quay vessel *Ann Warren*, died at Alicante. The master recorded that he 'was found drowned under the ship's bow at 5 a.m. supposed to have gone in the ship's head to ease himself whilst in a state of intoxication.'

The shipping communities of west Wales which bred young men like Isaac Hughes were tight-knit societies in which, because their menfolk were so often absent, women played prominent if unofficial social roles. For example, the 1851 census for Borth lists some thirty-one household headed by mariners' wives in the absence of their husbands, and another seven headed by mariners' widows. Quite the most famous woman connected with the sea was Cranogwen (Sarah Jane Rees, 1839-1916: see Chapter 10 above), who taught navigation to generations of Llangrannog sailors.

From 1841 the sailors, shipwrights, sailmakers and their families may be traced through the census, and before that in parish registers and graveyards all along the Welsh coast. A remarkable gravestone in Llansanffraid cemetery records the drownings of four members of a single family on three separate occasions during the 1840s; an elderly widow lived through the deaths of a daughter, her two sons and her grandson. The most obviously distinct of the Cardiganshire maritime communities were Aberystwyth's Trefechan and Cardigan's Mwldan. Both were largely devoted to shipbuilding, equipping and preparing, with casual labour always ready to work the ships in and out of harbour, to load and unload their cargoes; a certain amount of lawlessness was associated with both places. But the coastal villages were all sea-oriented, from the communities of retired ships' officers scattered all along the coast, to the chapels which had, as does the Llan-non Welsh Presbyterian chapel to this day, signs to remind worshippers: *Cofiwch y Morwyr* – Remember the Seamen.

Despite all the difficulties of access and safety, maritime trade was all-important to the whole Welsh coast and beyond. Before the railway network began and spread, shipping was the cheapest and easiest mode of transport around the whole British coast for goods between many British destinations. The majority of small Welsh vessels, unlike the deepwater *Lois*, worked in the coasting trade. At the humblest level, thousands of small boats, from five to twenty tons displacement, carried lime and culm from Pembrokeshire to almost every beach in Ceredigion. At high tide the limestone and culm would be thrown overboard, and at low tide they would be carried to the omnipresent lime-kilns. The culm provided fuel, and the limestone, once burnt, would be carted away by farmers to spread on their hungry soil. The little ship would already be on its return journey southwards.

Craig-las lime-kilns, N.E. of Llan-non.

[Crown copyright: Royal Commission on Ancient & Historical Monuments, Wales]

The coasting trade might involve fairly regular trips such as those plied by the carriers of lead ore to the smelters at Deeside, Bristol and south Wales, or the carriage hither and yon of a whole variety of cargoes. A detailed Aberdyfi account of inward cargoes in 1785, carried by the *Peggy*, tells that she brought into port a cargo of sundry goods including 15 tons of fullers earth, 2 tons of sugar, 316 pounds of tea, a bottle of oil of vitriol, a complete printing press, a 'Water Engine', two boxes of perfumery, 5 hundredweight of alum, 2 hundredweight of hard soap, three half-firkins of soft soap and 18 puncheons of molasses. The 'water engine' may have been a pump for the lead mines. The reference to a printing press is intriguing; the first press known in Cardiganshire (other than the brief existence of Isaac Carter's press at Adpar) was established by Thomas Johnes at Hafod, but only began printing about 1805. Large quantities of slates were arriving at least from 1785 onward, and the decorative building stones and pillars used at such mansions as Hafod, Nanteos and Trawsgoed were all brought in by sea.

In comparison with the range of imports and the sheer bulk of lime and coal, the county's exports were limited. Cardigan exported much corn during the 18th century, and Pembrokeshire slate was also a Cardigan staple. Aberystwyth sent out the weighty products of the lead and zinc mines, taken to smelters in south Wales, Bristol and on Deeside. For many decades during the 19th century the county's oak woodlands produced oak-bark for export to the tanneries of Ireland, which had lost all its woodlands. However, ships must often have left port in ballast, lacking regular cargoes.

* * *

A rare documentary treasure is the accounts book of the 82-ton Aberystwyth brig *Renown*. This scruffy little book covers the years 1817 to 1830. Captain David Julian, a leading member of a well-known Aberystwyth family, was the ship's master throughout the period. The little book tells us to the nearest ha'penny how David Julian kept the ship's running account, and incidentally tells us what cargoes he carried, the wages he paid, and the harbours visited. Thus during 1817-18 the *Renown*, usually a coasting vessel, sailed from Aberystwyth to Newport, thence to Waterford with coal, to Liverpool with coal (he must have returned to Wales in ballast to fetch it), to Galway with salt, to Sligo with oats, to Cardiff (presumably for coal), to Cork with oak-bark, Cardiff again, Liverpool with iron, Ostend with salt, Wexford, Galway again, Bristol, Lydney, Kinsale, Cardiff, Dublin, and back to Aberystwyth. The total income for the two year period was £1,169.0s.4d., of which £530 went on food and expenses, £190 on wages, including the captain's own at £4 per month, and £451 was profit for the shareholders. At each port the entire crew other than the apprentice boy would leave, and a new crew would have to be recruited. At each port too the master would have to look about him for a new cargo, or else sail in ballast, without income, to a more promising port. The *Renown*'s cargoes included coal, iron, salt, tallow, oats, slates, tin, and sundry goods.

The *Renown* made one exciting voyage – to Kronstadt and to St Petersburg in Russia. Unfortunately a page is missing, so the cargo is unknown. But at Elsinore in

Denmark David Julian paid £3.5s.0d. for what he called 'sea-store', in other words alcohol for himself and his crew. Many Welsh skippers ran 'dry' ships, with no alcohol allowed, but the *Renown* was decidedly 'wet'. The little account book lists a phenomenal number of petty expenditures. Pilots, customs officers, carpenters, blacksmiths and hobblers to bring a vessel into place, all had to be paid. Horses for towing, mops, buckets, paint, oil, nails, oakum, all had to be paid for, and a comic entry in Liverpool records: paid 10s for 'damage dun by us'. David Julian was often away from his Aberystwyth home and family for two years at a time, though on one occasion he did hire a horse at Bristol and ride home for a visit. On his returns, the profits for all the voyages since his last return would be divided among the shareholders.

Like so many of his kind, Captain Julian came to a wretched end. On October 23 1841, on a voyage from Poole to Liverpool, the *Renown* was lost with all hands, including both David Julian and his son John. David's brother had already died at sea, and although another brother survived the sea and retired to land as a Lloyd's inspector, the family did not survive these catastrophes, in the Aberystwyth area at any rate.

The fate of the *Renown* is recorded in the Aberystwyth shipping registers, like that of most other vessels. Of course many ships in Aberystwyth ownership were sold on elsewhere, but even for some of those, and certainly for all those remaining on the Aberystwyth register, their destinies were noted. The lucky ships finished up as firewood or scrap – 'lucky' because their crews had survived and moved on. Other crews survived wrecks unscathed while the vessel was a total loss. For example, the 157-ton *Albion* of Llansanffraid sailed home from Demerara in 1868. En voyage the crew spotted a dismasted Newfoundland ship, the *Zero*. The boat was launched and the nine men of the *Zero* were brought aboard to squeeze in with the eight men of the *Albion*. Conditions on board must have been appalling. As if that were not bad enough, a few days later the *Albion* herself succumbed to dreadful winter weather and had to be abandoned; all members of the two crews were rescued by an American vessel.

THE lifeboats of Cardiganshire share the great lifesaving traditions associated with the Royal National Lifeboat Institution. Lifeboats powered by oar and sail were established at Aberystwyth in 1843, Cardigan in 1848 and New Quay in 1864. The Cardigan lifeboat, based at Poppit, is mostly manned from St Dogmaels. The *William Cantrell* at New Quay was the last oar/sail lifeboat in service in the United Kingdom; it was retired in 1949. All three ports are now served by inshore inflatables, as is Borth.

Cardiganshire ships were wrecked all over the world. In 1855 the *Claudia* went down off Gallipoli, the *Rhydiol* off Newfoundland in 1845; in 1875 the *Strata Florida* sank at Rangoon, Burma, the *Lady Pryse* at the Cape of Good Hope in 1880, the *M.A.Evans* at Buenos Aires in 1884. The second-biggest ship ever owned at Aberystwyth, the 663-ton *Caroline Spooner*, too big ever to have actually entered Aberystwyth harbour, was declared a wreck in Chile in 1893, and the leviathan of all Aberystwyth ships, the 1000-ton *Ralph Waller*, built in Canada in 1855, sank the following year on her way home from Callao. Sometimes we actually have the

Aberystwyth harbour, *c*1850, by R.G. Roberts. [National Library of Wales]

master's account of the disaster. In 1837 Richard Penhelog, master of the little smack *Albion*, declared on 13 April 1837 that she had been 'driven on shore near Aberdovey . . . and that I secured myself in the rigging of the Vessel for the preservation of my life'. But often there are simply the melancholy words: 'Lost with all hands' or 'sailed from port N on such and such a date, and not heard of since'.

The wealthiest man involved in Ceredigion shipping in the 19th century was almost certainly Thomas Jones of Aberystwyth (1804-80), known as 'the Younger' to distinguish him from his father, an Aberaeron man who moved to Aberystwyth in 1797 and took a partnership in a ropeworks. Jones the Elder brought up his children at Ropewalk (now Sandmarsh) cottage in Queen's Road before building, with his son, numbers 1 and 2, Marine Terrace, the attractive Georgian houses between the Gothic buildings of Old College and the former Theological College, and his son went on to become the richest and most influential man in Aberystwyth. At his death in 1880 Thomas Jones owned at least twenty-one freehold and leasehold houses, the tithes of the parish of Nevern, the Prince of Wales public house in Borth, a large timber yard, a considerable portfolio of shares, and had recently distributed five thousand pounds each to his four surviving children. He had loaned twenty thousand pounds in mortgages. He was also the owner of shares in twenty Aberystwyth-registered ships, of which he was the managing owner; during his career he had held shares in at least a hundred Aberystwyth vessels.

For years Thomas Jones had been at the head of Aberystwyth's mercantile and municipal life, a driving force on the town council, and the mainstay of the port of Aberystwyth. Until 1864 the port was vital to many aspects of the town's life, but the arrival of the railway from Shrewsbury via Machynlleth was to prove a death-blow, despite Thomas Jones's best efforts. He was concerned that if the shipping trade died, then the railways would have a monopoly of carriage, able to charge what they pleased, whereas ships had always competed against each other, thus keeping freights low. Even in his seventies he was engaged in new ventures, and several of the last ships to be built at Aberystwyth were on his initiative.

Ellen Beatrice drying her sails, the last sailing vessel built at Aberystwyth. [Courtesy of David Jenkins]

Two years after Thomas Jones died, the year 1882 saw the launching of the last sailing ship built at Aberystwyth, the *Edith Eleanor*, and in 1883 the *Cadwgan* of Aberaeron was the very last in the county. The county's maritime tradition and culture took a long time to decay. A few of the county's schooners and ketches survived to trade in the 20th century; the *Edith Eleanor* was sold to Wexford owners in 1916 and the *Ellen Beatrice* of Aberystwyth was broken up at Weymouth in 1924. But even before the arrival of the railway in west Wales, ambitious men like John Mathias, owner of the 1000-ton steamship *Glanrheidol*, had launched steamship companies in Aberystwyth (1856), Aberaeron (1863), and Cardigan (1869), where the railway did not appear until 1885, but they tended to concentrate management in Cardiff. Steamships continued to carry coasting cargoes round the shoreline from Liverpool to Bristol and back, called at Aberystwyth, Aberaeron and Cardigan. Heavy goods continued to arrive direct from European ports: Antwerp, Fredrikstad, Gothenburg, Roscoff, Landernau and Calais. Timber came straight from Nova Scotia and Finland. Such visits were fairly regular until 1914, but after the First World War they were seen less and less often. A few attempts were made to revive shipping even after 1945, but none succeeded.

A steamer visits Aberaeron harbour. [National Library of Wales]

SOME entrepreneurs, like Anne Jenkins of Aber-porth, were determined to stay nearer home. John Mathias of Penparcau set up the Glanrheidol Steamship Company in Aberystwyth in 1883, but the company's vessels traded out of Cardiff as coal carriers, and eventually an office was opened there. The Aberporth Steamship Company, founded by another member of the Jenkins family of Aber-porth, and the Glanhowny Steamship Company, were both based at Aber-porth in 1903, but their vessels never visited the county's shores, and both companies were bankrupt by 1910. The Aberaeron Steam Packet Company was wound up in 1918 with the repayment of stock.

Although ships along the Ceredigion coast became rarer towards the end of the 19th century, the maritime tradition did not die, but migrated elsewhere. Already in the 1880s a Cardigan man, Lewis Davies, an ex-skipper with the notorious Black Ball line of Liverpool, had set up a shipping company in his adopted city; his first vessel was of iron, named by him *Cardigan Castle*. But most ambitious Cardis went to Cardiff, and their ventures have been traced by the marine historian David Jenkins. For example, Evan Thomas of Aber-porth went into partnership with Henry Radcliffe of Merthyr Tudful, and by 1890 their company, Thomas and Radcliffe, was managing sixteen ships. Another such Cardiff company of Cardiganshire origin was Jenkins Brothers. David and James Jenkins were actually two cousins from Aber-porth, but they were also brothers-in-law, hence the company name. They operated a number of small shipping companies out of Cardiff as well as Jenkins Brothers between 1904 and 1927, when James retired. He died in 1940, leaving an estate of almost £250,000. Until 1929 his cousin Anne Jenkins was still managing a little sailing ketch, the *James*, out of Aber-porth.

The gatherings of retired master-mariners in their home villages, which lasted at least into the 1960s, have already been mentioned above. One of the last of his generation was Captain John Jones of Aber-arth, who died in 1965. In 1937 he had gained the nickname 'Ham-and-Eggs' Jones by a journalist anxious to distinguish him from Captain 'Potato' Jones and Captain 'Corn-cob' Jones, other Welsh

The *Ellen* unloading Scandinavian timber at Aberystwyth *c*1926. [Courtesy of David Jenkins]

captains who were involved at one remove in the Spanish Civil War. Jones's vessel the *Sarastone* was involved in trade with the Republican forces, who by early 1937 were on the retreat in northern Spain; hunger and illness were rife in the population. After a vain attempt to get food to Santander, Jones made two voyages to rescue refugees, the first with British naval protection, the second unprotected and with hostile shells dropping around the ship. In his courage and humanity, John Jones represents the best of the long Cardiganshire tradition of seamanship.

* * *

So far this chapter has dealt with Ceredigion's shipping. But more ancient than any traceable details of shipbuilding is the practice of fishing. Among the oldest visible signs of Ceredigion's relationship with the sea are the *goredi* or fishing-weirs already referred to in Chapter 6, which can be located by anyone who drives north along the A487 from Aberaeron. Just past the highest point on the cliff road towards Llan-non there is a convenient lay-by. From it, when the tide is halfway between high and low, it is possible to see arcs of stones lying in the water. Access to the beach from Aber-arth at the right tide-time gives access to more of these *goredi*; only a close approach gives a true idea of the strength of their storm-resistant foundations. With the falling tide, in days when fish were far more plentiful than they are now, many would be trapped and easily taken. This ancient form of fishing must go back centuries, probably millennia, though the present ruins must be more recent. The last weir-keeper was still alive in the 1920s.

Fishtraps, Aber-arth.
[Crown copyright: Royal Commission on Ancient & Historical Monuments, Wales]

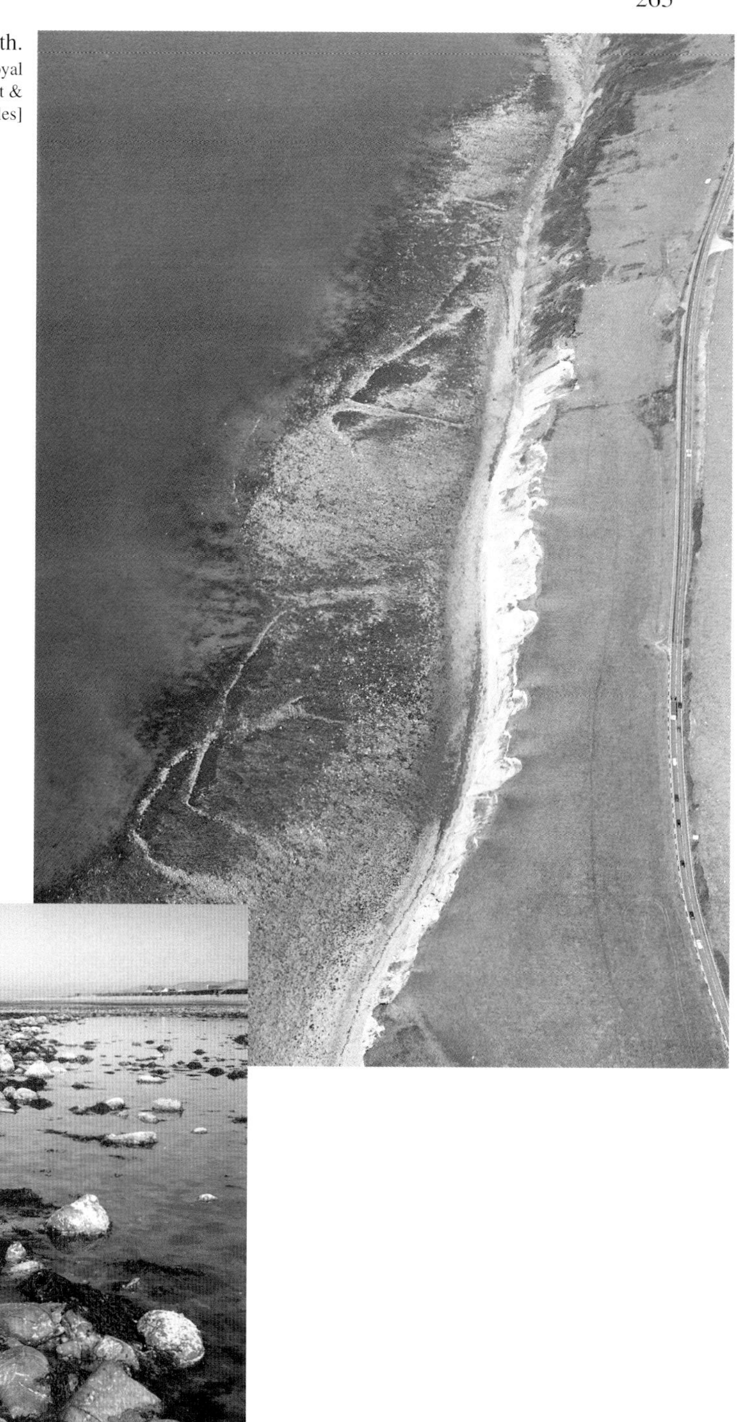

Fishtrap foundations, Llan-non.

Salmon-fishing in the estuary of the Teifi and the river's coracles are equally ancient modes by which the men of Ceredigion exploited fish. On the Teifi itself coracles worked from Llechryd, Cenarth, Aber-cuch and Cilgerran, each group having its own stretch of the river. The complex culture of the coracle fishermen, with their intimate knowledge of the river and their extensive vocabulary describing every part of the coracle and all the rules and practices of their work, has been well described by J. Geraint Jenkins. There were in 1861 some three hundred coracles on the river, but the declaration of a close season and the imposition of licenses, the hostility of anglers and of the estuary fishermen, all brought about a drastic decline in their numbers. An attempt in 1915 to buy out the river-coraclemen brought a defending lawyer's comment: 'German militarism is nothing compared to landlordism.' By August 1939 the riparian landlords had succeeded in eliminating coracle-fishing from the non-tidal waters above Llechryd. The present-day generation of twelve license-holding coraclemen, who fear they may be the last, practise a craft described by Julius Caesar, and highly attractive to tourists. The end of coracle fishing would be a drastic impoverishment of Welsh culture in the county. At the time of writing the fishing barely pays the annual cost of the licence.

Coracle fishermen at Cenarth bridge.

In 1603 George Owen described seine netting in the river estuary. Other early references to Ceredigion fishing include that in *The Chronicle of the Princes*, describing the huge abundance of fish, either herring or mackerel, which filled the Ystwyth estuary in 1206. From the 14th century onwards there are scattered references to the Cardiganshire fisheries, particularly to Aberystwyth, Aber-porth and Cardigan. Herrings were exported from Cardigan not only to other British ports, but to Madeira and the Canaries. For generations the Teifi yielded a rich harvest of salmon both to the seine fishermen and the coracles. Seine fishermen used a much larger net than the coraclemen, two hundred metres or more in length and some three metres deep. The net was paid out over the rear of the boat, which followed a semicircular course out from the beach and back again. The few remaining fishermen are based in St Dogmaels.

SS *Drumlough* approaching Cardigan [National Library of Wales]

For centuries the Cardigan Bay herring-fishery was hugely successful, with scores of boats gathering in September off Aberdyfi to take advantage of the annual migration of herring northwards through the Irish Sea. Lewis Morris, who knew Cardigan Bay as well as any witness, counted fifty-nine boats out of Aberystwyth alone, virtually all of which, according to custom, would have borne English names. In 1745 forty-seven boats caught over a million herring, most of which were salted or smoked and sent to England, and Morris refers to a glut of cod, whiting, pollock and ray (or skate), on which the fishermen set no value. *Slettan* was the Welsh name for these small fishing-boats; the word occurs in a number of probate inventories. By the late 19th century Aberystwyth boats were known as 'nobbies'. Herring continued to be a valued but dwindling catch until the early 20th century, after which they seem to have disappeared from the Bay for some years, but have now returned in small numbers. With the serious decline of fish stocks in the Irish Sea, fishermen turned to fishing for lobsters, crabs and scallops, to providing angling trips for rod enthusiasts, and to fair-weather trips for visitors. A few fishermen still earn money from the lobster-crab fishery, and a processing factory is still at work at New Quay. The shoals of mackerel are today much reduced by deepwater trawling, but fried swiftly after the catch, fish fresh from the Bay are one of Ceredigion's finest dishes, worthy to set beside the county's splendid sea-trout.

The Daniel brothers of Aberaeron repair their lobster pots.
[Ceredigion County Library]

18. Getting About, Getting Out

'Why don't we have a dual-carriageway from Carmarthen to Aberystwyth?' demanded an acquaintance. To which the best reply was, 'Is that why you moved here, so that you could turn the place into Surrey?' The protestor paused for thought. That was twenty years ago; now that Surrey-style planning has arrived in the Parc-llyn development at Aberystwyth, perhaps the dual carriageway will follow. It is true that travellers have never found Ceredigion easy going; the roads used to be unsigned, muddy, potholed and ill-maintained. English visitors would get lost in the dark, struggling belatedly to the next hostelry. Yet people have always travelled through the county, by horse, by coach, by water, but mainly on foot. There are plenty of recorded examples of people moving into, through and out of Ceredigion apart from invading Roman, Saxon, Welsh, Parliamentarian and Norman warriors: Gerald of Wales attending Archbishop Baldwin through the land in 1188, Henry Tudor travelling from Cardigan to Machynlleth on his way to Bosworth in 1485, the trudging drovers, peripatetic labourers and *merched y gerddi*, the travelling garden-women who walked to Glamorgan and the Home Counties of England and back every year.

One of Ceredigion's old green trackways.

The most obvious routes in Ceredigion, geographically speaking, can easily be picked out on a map: travel from north-east to south-west near the coast would not have been too difficult, either staying close to the sea or turning inland up the Ystwyth valley and over the watershed to the Teifi. The main obstacles would have been the rivers, particularly when in flood. The western slopes of the Cambrian mountains may seem seriously forbidding to us; the A44 and the A482 are the only comfortable tarmac routes. But the range offers a series of valleys and ridges which could be used to penetrate and cross that difficult obstacle by drovers, soldiers and labouring people. Alas, it is impossible to reconstruct the pattern of ancient trackways which, long before the Romans, were trodden by the men, women and children of Ceredigion.

Many of their routes may now be under tarmac; others would have been used later by the drovers, or may survive as the hollow ways and green tracks still visible in the countryside. Yet others have been wiped out in the process of creating forestry roads, and by the plantations themselves.

Here and there one can identify what may have once been an ancient trackway. An apparently simple example is visible on the north slope of Y Gaer Fawr, near Trawsgoed, where a green way can be seen gently climbing the easiest slope to the hill fort; it still serves the farmer but was worn into the hillside over two thousand years ago. Less accessible, but fascinating, is the line of standing stones and cairns which apparently marks an ancient route running SW-NE along the Craig Twrch ridge east of Llanfair Clydogau, now just outside the county boundary. Such stone-marked routes are more common on the Meirionnydd slopes of Cadair Idris and Ardudwy than in Ceredigion. North of Lampeter is the small Iron Age hill fort of Castell Olwen, and to the north-east is the Allt-goch ridge which has two more such hill forts, Castell Allt-goch and Castell Goetre; the present-day path along the ridge may perhaps follow the line of an ancient roadway. Another such track links Trefilan and Cilcennin, along the south-western slope of Trichrug. Neither village can be proven to be pre-Roman sites, but the route passes by a hill fort from which another track climbs to the Bronze Age graves on the summit of Trichrug, many centuries older than the hill fort below.

A network of such routes would have been ancient when the Romans arrived and drove a roadway from Pumsaint up the Twrch valley and over the watershed past what is now Llanfair Clydogau, building a fort at Llanio, then onwards north to Trawsgoed, Penllwyn and eventually to a ford across the Dyfi. Long after memory of the Romans vanished and the forts sank into the ground, the route was recognised as *Sarn Elen* or *Sarn Helen*, even though much of it has long vanished from view. Today the straight unclassified road running north from the Roman fort at Llanio to its junction with the A485 at Tyncelyn is recognisably Roman. From Tyncelyn it can be seen to run north with the present A485 for a while before veering away, and is traceable only in short stretches, such as the *agger* or raised mound of the road which is visible crossing soft ground to the south of the significantly-named farm-ruin of Sarn Elen. Northwards the land has been thoroughly altered by forestry, but a lane running athwart the northern slope of Y Gaer Fawr to Trawsgoed probably follows the line of Sarn Helen. The route from Trawsgoed to the Dyfi has already been described in Chapter 4.

Sarn Helen certainly continued in use after the Roman occupation ended, as did the ancient trackways, but our knowledge of early medieval roadways is as obscure as that of early medieval settlement. There must have been routes to and between early Christian sites, but they have been subsumed by later roads or have vanished. Trackways of some sort there must have been; a coastal route from Llanbadarn via Llanychaearn, Llanddeiniol, Llanrhystud, Llansanffraid/Llan-non, Llanddewi Aberarth, to Henfynyw surely existed. But what then? Did travellers cross steep-sided valleys to link with Llanina, Llanllwchaearn, Llandysiliogogo and Llangrannog, or were these each linked to a route via Llannarth, roughly following the present A487?

There must surely have been a route down the north bank of the Teifi from Llanwnnen via Llanfechan, Capel Dewi, Llandysul, Capel Bangor, Henllan and Llandyfrïog. But all is speculation, despite the intriguing references to roads and paths in the Laws of Hywel Dda, save only for the remarkable 10/11th-century wooden trackway at Cors Fochno, already mentioned in Chapter 5.

The old footbridge at Parson's Bridge, Ysbyty Cynfyn (note the lead-mine waterwheel in the background). [National Library of Wales]

Nor does speculation cease with the clearer view we have of the period following the Norman invasions. Obviously the Normans saw Cardigan and Lampeter as bridging points over the Teifi; the Teifi was bridged by the early 12th century, and the Welsh name of Lampeter indicates at least a 13th-century bridge. The same must have been the case when the new Aberystwyth castle was built from 1277. An apparent chain of earthwork castles can be followed from Lampeter via Llanio to Ystrad Meurig and down to Llanilar and Aberystwyth. There is another chain of such castles down the Teifi valley, and a thinner chain north-eastward from Cardigan to Aberystwyth. The Normans, the men of Gwynedd and the Welsh of Deheubarth marched and counter-marched through the district. The Clettwr Fawr valley, tributary to the Teifi, seems to have had some routeway importance; it was controlled by the Norman earthwork of Castell Wmffre, seized in turn by Hywel ab Owain Gwynedd and renamed after him as Castell Hywel. As well as soldiers, medieval Welsh roads carried tradesmen, tax-collectors, law enforcement officers and priests, pilgrims and visitors to fairs. In theory at least such roads were to be maintained by the lord of the manor, meaning of course his tenants; eventually responsibility was shifted to parish overseers under the supervision of JPs in Quarter Sessions.

Oral tradition has speculated on the medieval roads which would have been created by or used by the monks of Strata Florida. Tradition links the monastery with the little creek at Llanddewi Aberarth along a routeway known as Lôn Lacs. The monks certainly would have had connections to the coast; they had lands at Morfa Bychan and Morfa Mawr, and owned right of wreck and fishing weirs at several points. More readily traceable on maps and on the ground is the route known to tradition as the 'Monks' Trod', running eastwards from Ffair Rhos to their sister-establishment at Abbey Cwm-hir, over twenty miles away. A mountain road linking Machynlleth and Ponterwyd was followed in the 19th century by Michael Faraday and George Borrow, and must earlier have borne travellers southwards en route to St David's. They would have lodged at the vanished hospices for which Ysbyty Cynfyn, Ysbyty Ystwyth and (Ysbyty) Ystrad Meurig are named, with a connection to the Knights of St John of the Hospital, and then moved onward to

CEREDIGION is well-endowed with bridges. The oldest must surely be the lowest of the three bridges at Devil's Bridge, from the medieval period, followed later by Cardigan, Llechryd and Henllan. John Nash's five-arched bridge at Aberystwyth was swept away in a storm and replaced by the present hefty design of Sir James Weeks Szlumper; the other distinguished architect of a county bridge was Thomas Baldwin of Bath, who built Pont Blaen-cwm over the Ystwyth in 1783. Other attractive bridges are Llanafan bridge, Pont Einon near Tregaron, and the two arched bridges at Pontrhydfendigaid, the latter the work of John Edwards, son of William Edwards who built the famous bridge at Pontypridd. Squires often presided over the campaigns to secure bridges; John Lloyd Davies of Alltrodyn claimed the credit for the well-known bridge at Pont Alltcafan, and Jordan of Pigeonsford and Parry of Ffynonlefrith for Blaenbedw-fawr Bridge east of Pentre-gât.

The old Penparcau-Llanbadarn bridge. [National Library of Wales]

cross the little medieval bridge at Devil's Bridge; there is no reason to doubt the tradition which attributes the bridge to the monks of Strata Florida. The road led onwards to Pont-rhyd-y-groes and Pontrhydfendigaid, with their references respectively to the Ford of the Cross and the Blessed Ford.

Ponterwyd's old bridge.

There must too have been a route from Strata Florida to Llanbadarn Fawr, a route followed by Edward I in 1295 on his way via Llanfihangel-y-Creuddyn with an army to Strata Florida, Lampeter and Cardigan. Richard Moore-Colyer traces it, not along the present B4340 via Trawsgoed, which is essentially a creation of the turnpike period, but from Pont-rhyd-y-groes past New Row and Llety Synod via Llantrisant and Rhydypererinion (ford of the pilgrims) to Llanfihangel-y-Creuddyn and on to Llanbadarn. Dr Moore-Colyer has explored other possible routes joining Strata Florida to the coast: from Llangwyryfon via Lledrod and from Llanrhystud via Lledrod. Then of course there were routes south-eastwards in the general direction of the Tywi valley, one directly south past the remarkable earthwork of Cwys yr Ychen Bannog (the furrow of the horned oxen), and a roadway towards Lampeter. The monks' fair at Ffair Rhos would have brought plenty of traffic along these roads.

Other mountain roads certainly existed in the medieval period; travellers bound for England from Tregaron, Llanddewibrefi, Llanfair Clydogau and Lampeter would all have had routes east, as would northern settlements in the county. Many of these are still known as drovers' roads, which were certainly in use as early as the 13th century and surely earlier still. From Pembrokeshire to Anglesey the drovers were figures of major importance in the economy, collecting and driving tens of thousands of cattle eastwards to the great English fairs, even as far as Essex, and bringing home the money gained from sales, less commission. Photographs of the last of the 19th-century drovers show them wearing the kind of bowler hat still worn today by transhumant shepherds in the mountains of Romania, and like those shepherds, they were reputedly men of considerable wealth and toughness.

From northern Cardiganshire cattle could either be driven to Machynlleth and then eastwards, or to Devil's Bridge, whence a droving track ran eastwards past Bodcoll and through Cwmystwyth, giving access either to Llangurig by crossing the river Dilyw, or more directly to Rhaeadr, or again by moving south to Ffair-rhos and then along the ancient roadway east. For mid-Ceredigion, Tregaron was the major centre for bringing together large droves of cattle from dozens of farms before they began the journey eastward up the Berwyn valley past Diffwys and onward to Nantystalwyn and Abergwesyn; the road is now metalled and can be followed all the way by car. Another modern road, the A482 from Lampeter to Pumsaint via Tafarn Jem, was a major droving route, with an alternative way past the Lock and Key inn over the hill to the Drovers' Arms at Ffarmers. Yet another route, eastward from Llandysul, crossed Llanybydder mountain via another Drovers' Arms and Heol Lloegr ('the England road') to Rhydcymerau.

Apart from the drovers' roads eastwards, there was certainly a network of ways linking settlements to each other, and in 1555 an Act of Parliament laid down that, along with the necessary bridges, they should be maintained by parishes. Able-bodied adults were expected to labour for six days a year without reward to keep the parish roads and bridges in repair, under the supervision of surveyors appointed by each parish. The system's weakness is evident from the number of complaints, in the files of the Court of Great Sessions and Quarter Sessions, that parishes were 'presented' for not doing the job.

THE droving roads in their heyday would hardly be recognisable to us as roads. Although there were places where stone walls and thick hedges limited the animals to a narrow way, they would spread out wherever possible, churning up the turf and creating large tracts of mud. Today's tarmac roads, following certain of the old routes, still carry large numbers of livestock eastward to the markets of England, but the lorry-driving farmer has entirely displaced the pony-riding drover.

The late 17th-century 'Ogilvy' route maps indicate that there was, in theory at least, an adequate road-plan for Cardiganshire, with mileages given; they resemble the individual routes which the AA and RAC used to supply to drivers for particular journeys. A map by Thomas Gardner, undated, gives routes from Carmarthen to Cardigan, Cardigan to Lampeter and Lampeter to Aberystwyth. The mileages, not surprisingly, are eccentric and the spelling more so, but they must have lessened the hazards of travel. Streams and rivers, hills, marshes and swamps are all shown, with orientation to magnetic north.

It must be remembered that all this time the sea provided an alternative means of travel and trading; indeed, by the 18th century, as described in another chapter, the Cardiganshire coast was buzzing with activity from spring to autumn. Even the arrival of the improvements that came from 1780 with the turnpike trusts did not seriously affect maritime trade; heavy loads in particular were much more easily carried by sea, and passengers could reach Bristol or Liverpool much more cheaply than by the coaches which lumbered from Aberystwyth via Machynlleth to Shrewsbury. After about 1750 travellers had begun to penetrate west Wales in search of the picturesque and sublime. As we have seen, they complained vigorously about the roads, whose wretched condition led to parties getting lost or travelling miles out of their way; they were advised to carry compasses and a telescope. It was only with the development of the turnpike system that coach travel began to improve.

Turnpike trusts were essentially commercial companies sanctioned by Act of Parliament, in which shareholders dictated what should be done and how. Since only the wealthier gentry had the means to invest, they had the chief say in what should be done, although after the initial enthusiasm declined it was often difficult to get a quorum to take decisions. The idea was simply to provide more roads with better surfaces. However, the activities of the Aberystwyth trust from 1780 show clearly that it was the shareholders who would benefit most; it must be admitted of course that they bore the expense of securing the necessary Act of Parliament and of raising capital. Some of the gentry undertook contracts themselves: James Lloyd of Mabws and William Jones of Llanbadarn undertook for forty pounds to make up the road from Devil's Bridge to Eisteddfa Gurig, a wildly optimistic offer, whereas Edward Hughes of Aberllolwyn undertook the road from Rhydyfelin to the Aber-mad turning for forty pounds a mile. Thomas Johnes of Croft Castle, owner of Hafod Uchdryd, undertook the whole road to Rhaeadr for a hundred pounds, but a year later the contract was revoked, presumably because it could not possibly be carried out so cheaply. Thomas Powell of Nanteos and the Earl of Lisburne used their influence to ensure that the old roadways passing close to the front of their respective mansions should be closed. In the case of Nanteos the road was relocated to the southern side of the Paith valley, giving a splendid but distant view of the house, while at Trawsgoed the road passed well behind the mansion, and trees were planted to screen it off.

It was ordinary users of the roads who paid the costs, since it became impossible to travel without paying at the toll gates. Some

THE publication *Patterson's Roads* set out for its readers the coach connections available for Aberystwyth: to Cardiff via Builth and Merthyr Tudful; to Chester via Machynlleth, Bala and Llangollen; to Cowbridge via Merthyr Tudful and Llantrisant, to Holyhead via Dolgellau; to Hay-on-Wye via Builth, and to Milford via Cardigan. Carmarthen was accessible via Talsarn and Lampeter. All eventually ceased with the arrival of the railways. John Rea, guard on the last Aberystwyth – Shrewsbury coach, was commemorated by the splendid art deco window in the White Horse Inn, Aberystwyth, which he owned. He would hardly approve of its recent pretentious change of name, nor of the drunken imbeciles who smashed the original glass in 2003, fortunately now replaced by an excellent copy.

of the toll houses still survive; the cottages on the roads northwards and eastwards from Aberaeron are perhaps the best known, though the most visited is of course the Aberystwyth Southgate cottage, now re-erected in the Museum of Welsh Life. The turnpike trustees as a body did not manage the toll-collecting themselves but let out the work to the highest bidder. However, gentry were able to take the contracts themselves if they chose; Thomas Lloyd of Abertrinant was given the tolls of the north and south gates at Aberystwyth for three years at the price of £250 a year. Gentlemen were also able to negotiate terms; in 1772 William Powell of Nanteos paid two guineas for a year's passage through the Aberystwyth south gate for his family and servants.

Aberaeron north toll cottage, with modern extension.

The county's turnpike trusts floundered for some time, and profitability was only restored when the Earl of Lisburne steered the second Cardiganshire roads bill through Parliament in 1791. Despite a slow start, the state of the roads was greatly improved by the turnpike system. Although the first post office had opened in Aberystwyth in 1769, the service was erratic in the extreme; only in 1807 did a regular mail-coach begin to run to Shrewsbury via Machynlleth. Jenkin Jones appreciated the road from Lampeter to Tal-sarn, 'an excellent road with fine hedges a great part of the way.'

By 1829 Aberystwyth was linked through Ponterwyd and Eisteddfa Gurig to Llanidloes and Rhaeadr (now the A44); the coach journey from London to Aberystwyth was reduced from 48 to 24 hours. Coaches linked Aberystwyth to Machynlleth, to Aberaeron, Lampeter and Cardigan. Cardigan in turn was linked to Carmarthen at least from 1831 if not earlier, as well as to Narberth Road. Lampeter appears to have had no regular links eastward until the coming of the railway. But there were drawbacks to the turnpike system. Towns were surrounded by gates; free escape was impossible! Lanes were closed in order to force traffic to pay toll. It may seem strange that, at a time when food riots could convulse towns (as Aberystwyth suffered in 1795), several generations passed before there was a popular revolt against the turnpikes; perhaps protest was stifled by the passage of the fourth Cardiganshire roads improvement act in 1833. The Rebecca riots (1839, and again in 1843-44: see Chapter 14) mainly affected Pembrokeshire and Carmarthenshire, but they certainly overflowed into Cardiganshire, as described earlier. It is accepted by historians that the riots were not simply a revolt against paying toll, but rather that an accumulation of financial burdens in the 1830s and early 1840s drove men to protest against the most visible and therefore vulnerable of their burdens, the toll gates.

The Rebecca rioters gained considerable success; in 1844 county road boards replaced the south Wales turnpike trusts, whose debts were paid by the government, and for a generation south Wales arguably had the best road system in the kingdom. In turn the county road boards were taken over by the county councils in 1889, and though improvements have been made, such as better surfacing, improved bridges, altered bends and junctions, by-passes at Tre'r-ddôl, Llanbadarn Fawr and Cardigan, and one-way systems introduced in Cardigan, Llandysul and Aberystwyth. Otherwise the plan of the county's roads changed little during the 20th century compared with more populous areas of the country. The First World War in particular had a dire effect on road surfaces, since steam road-engines hauled huge loads of timber from the county's depleted woodlands, to the constant lament of councillors and the local press ('Cardiganshire roads are the worst in the kingdom'), but better surfacing slowly spread as the heaviest wartime traffic disappeared. Other recent improvements made it much easier for visitors to enjoy the mountain roads from Penrhyn-coch and Tal-y-bont to the Nant-y-moch reservoir, and to traverse the Cambrian mountains from Tregaron to Llanwrtyd Wells or to Llyn Brianne.

* * *

If the roads of Cardiganshire have been rather neglected by historians, the same cannot be said of the railways; only the lead-mines have been studied in as great detail. Two explanations may be offered; prosaically, far more paperwork has been generated by railway companies than by the ancient process of road-making, while there is no doubt that railways excite the (male) imagination more readily than do roads. There have been three periods of serious railway activity in Cardiganshire: the creation of a standard-gauge network, then the building of light railways at the turn of the 19th century, and thirdly the period of closures during the 1950s and '60s. Welsh railway fever developed during the 1850s, and all kinds of schemes were mooted for mid-Wales. Simply understanding the complexities of the period is a mind-stretching exercise, so many schemes were touted, but to put it at its least complicated, Oswestry was linked to Newtown, Newtown to Llanidloes, with a junction before Caersws so that a line was driven through David Davies's huge cutting at Talerddig and down through Llanbryn-mair to Machynlleth, arriving there in 1863.

David Davies's business partner, Thomas Savin, was keen to push on to Aberystwyth, a plan which Davies opposed because of the extravagance involved, and the partnership ended. Savin was determined to build large hotels at Borth and Aberystwyth, and he formed the Aberystwyth and Welsh Coast Railway so that trains could reach Aberystwyth and then go directly northward to Aberdyfi, Porthmadog and Pwllheli. He was at the same time juggling contracts for building and operating other lines; it is hardly surprising that his wonderfully extravagant Gothic folly hotel at Aberystwyth (now of course the Old College building) broke him financially. The line from Machynlleth to Borth was opened to traffic on 23 June 1863, with much rejoicing and nude sea-bathing by overheated passengers of both sexes; the fun was shortly followed by two fatal accidents, one a poor deaf lady who never knew what had happened to her. Savin's original intention to carry a line northwards to Aberdyfi by means of a viaduct across the Dyfi was frustrated by the difficulties of finding bedrock at Ynys-las, so the northward line separated at Glandovey (later Dovey) Junction and clung delightfully to the north bank of the Dyfi.

THE Carmarthen & Cardigan Railway Company laid a broad-gauge track from Carmarthen to Pencader and Llandysul before going bankrupt in 1864 and running in receivership before being taken over by the Great Western, which eventually extended the line through Henllan to Newcastle Emlyn in 1895. Cardigan was never reached by this line. Instead, the Whitland and Taf Vale Railway, which had reached Crymych in 1875, was finally brought by the Great Western to Cardigan in 1885, and the service was affectionately known as the 'Cardi Bach'.

On 1 June 1864 a train full of navvies reached the new station at Aberystwyth, though the line was not yet officially opened. They were splendidly entertained at the town's Assembly Rooms, and the line eventually opened to the public on 22 July with a 35-coach train carrying 1,800 passengers. Again there were junketings on a grand scale. While these events were taking place on the coast, changes were being made elsewhere. Four of the mid-Wales railway companies were joined together by Act of Parliament in 1864 to form the Cambrian Railways, and they were joined in 1865 by the Aberystwyth and Welsh Coast. The Cambrian Railways had an impressive mileage of track in mid-Wales, but the area was already losing population and sliding into economic decline; the company nevertheless survived on the verge of bankruptcy until the amalgamation of 1923. Travel was not swift; leaving Aberystwyth at 8 a.m., the traveller could not expect to reach London until 5.15; the Sunday 5.00 a.m. train took twelve hours. But for the first time a journey to London could be measured in hours not days.

While the first trains were arriving at Aberystwyth, a railway with a strange title was being driven through the rest of Cardiganshire. The Manchester and Milford Railway was intended to join the great manufacturing city of the north to the reputedly greatest harbour in the Old World at Milford Haven. The idea was conceived as early as 1845, and given the title Manchester and Milford Haven

Trawsgoed station ready to welcome the newly-wed Earl and Countess of Lisburne, 1888.
[Courtesy of the Earl of Lisburne]

BOTH the lines to Aberystwyth were frequently affected by floods washing away the ballast, both on the Dyfi estuary and in the Ystwyth valley. The experience of travelling on the M&M line especially provoked the imagination, most intriguingly in Saunders Lewis's radio drama *Yn y Trên*. Real dramas also occurred. The steep Trawsgoed bank sometimes meant that trains roared down through the station unable to halt, and one locomotive, *Lady Elizabeth*, jumped the rails near Aberystwyth and finished in the ditch. In the hard winter of 1947 a passenger train was buried in a snowdrift near Lampeter for three days.

Railway. Another such scheme was the Great North and South Wales and Worcester Railway, only memorable for its title. In 1852 the North and South Wales Railway was planned to link Milford Haven to Carmarthen and then northward to Llanybydder and Pontrhydfendigaid, then up the Ystwyth to the Dilyw valley and through the mountain to Llangurig, Newtown and Oswestry.

Other versions of this plan appeared, constant changes being necessary because new lines were actually coming into existence; one scheme envisaged a 17-arch viaduct across the Ystwyth gorge at Pont-rhyd-y-groes. By 1860 plans hardened into activity; the Manchester and Milford Railway Company Bill went through Parliament, thanks at least in part to William Chambers, owner of Hafod Uchdryd. The standard gauge M&M line was intended to connect Llanidloes with the proposed Carmarthen and Cardigan Railway at Pencader; the whole plan was crazily optimistic, especially in view of the looming Cambrian mountains which would have to be crossed. The company, soon desperately short of money, ran into all kinds of other difficulties, and the directors gave up the Llanidloes plan and decided to bring the line from Tregaron down the Ystwyth valley to Aberystwyth; it was easier to cross Caron Bog than Pumlumon. This meant conflict with the Aberystwyth and Welsh Coast's plans for the town. In addition the company was at loggerheads with three other projects, the Mid Wales Railway and the Swansea and Aberystwyth Railway, both aiming to reach Aberystwyth, and the Llandeilo and Teiffi (*sic*) Railway; these last two never materialised, and the Mid Wales never reached Aberystwyth.

The Aberystwyth-Carmarthen train at Tregaron. [Ceredigion Museum]

In 1863 the M&M directors had invited David Davies to build the line from Pencader to Pontrhydfendigaid, and eventually the line from Pencader to Lampeter was opened on New Year's Day 1866; it was not much use, as the Carmarthen to Pencader line was broad gauge! However, the work went on; Ystrad Meurig was reached in August, and its station named 'Strata Florida', which was actually three miles away. Simultaneously a third rail was laid from Pencader to Carmarthen, thus linking the M&M to the South Wales Railway. In August 1867 the link to Aberystwyth was completed, together with a branch to the harbour. The company was so short of cash that David Davies had to spend much of his own money building the line, which was financially handicapped from the start. Travellers rash enough to travel from Manchester to Milford via Aberystwyth, as was now technically possible, faced a long and difficult journey with an overnight stay en route. Even the 40-mile journey from Aberystwyth to Pencader took between three and four hours. The kind of blind optimism which spurred railway ventures forward is evident from the fact that the directors of the M&M, short of cash and with an unsatisfactory railway service under their control, obtained an Act in 1873 for a branch line to Devil's Bridge, which was never built. Part of their trouble was caused by conflict with the Cambrian company, and by unpaid debts which led to a crisis in 1875, when a receiver was appointed, and the line, though still operating, remained in Chancery. After 1900 the company began negotiations for leasing the

M&M to the Great Western or the Cambrian, trying to play one off against the other; in 1906 the Great Western took over, and in 1911 absorbed the company. In turn the Great Western Railway created by amalgamation in 1923 swallowed the Cambrian company, and was itself nationalised in 1947 as part of British Railways, later British Rail.

Already the overwhelming use of cars and the closure of so many Welsh railways has blotted from public memory the original impact of the train. It was an invasion like none before it, not only because of the unprecedented movement of goods and people, but for its power to unite the country culturally. Cheap goods could be carried easily and in bulk, edging out handcrafted local products. Cheap building materials were available – bricks and tiles – ending local distinctiveness. Cheap newspapers could be brought from London, tying Welsh readers more closely to English media culture. Cheap travel brought tourists, who had to be spoken to in their language, and their tastes catered for. Cheap coal replaced peat. The flourishing shipping industry died. True, Nonconformist preachers could travel more easily to Sunday appointments, and railways made the National Eisteddfod a viable possibility. But the routes ran more easily from east to west than from north to south. In a word, the cultural distinctiveness of Wales, of which Cardiganshire was one of the most isolated areas, a distinctiveness which had long been in a process of dilution, was even further drawn into the thought-world and material culture of London, Birmingham and Manchester. 'London House' became a favourite shop title – countered in Cardiganshire, it is true, by the local patriotism of 'Lampeter House' and 'Cardigan House'.

Aberystwyth railway poster [National Library of Wales]

The second period of the railway industry in Cardiganshire was the age of the 'light railway'; the phrase is used to cover both standard and narrow-gauge lines. Two narrow-gauge projects were launched in the county at the end of the 19th century; one a success, one a disaster. The disaster was the Pumlumon and Hafan Tramway, which linked the station at Llandre to the Hafan quarry via Tal-y-bont. It was opened in May 1897, and it was ambitiously intended for the use of passengers as well as carrying rock from the quarry to the Cambrian standard-gauge line at Llandre for onward despatch. Despite their initial problems with the first locomotive, and despite the accidental deaths of an adult and a child in separate accidents, the owners went ahead with the purchase of a single passenger coach, but so few were the passengers that it was only used for a few weeks, and the line closed altogether in 1899.

The success was of course the Vale of Rheidol narrow-gauge railway. Several plans had been laid for trains to reach this popular tourist resort, but it was the combined efforts of the Aberystwyth foundry-owner George Green and Sir James Szlumper, who had at one time been the Manchester and Milford's chief engineer, which finally succeeded in linking Aberystwyth to Devil's Bridge in 1902. As well as passengers, it was intended that the line should carry ore from the lead-zinc mines to Aberystwyth harbour, and there was an extension to the quayside, but by this time the mines were not a long-term economic proposition, though their product certainly gave the line an initial boost. It was also a great success with tourists. However, the arrival of petrol-driven buses and the drastic decline in mining meant that by 1913 the line was taken over by the Cambrian and so on through G.W.R. ownership to its status as the last regular steam on British Rail before its sale to the present owners.

THE Aberystwyth Cliff Railway, begun in 1896, was run until 1922 on hydraulic principles; the upper carriage had its water-tank filled, and the weight of the descent drew the lower carriage up on a cable. The water was emptied on arrival at the lower station, and the same routine performed again. Erratic water supply on the hilltop meant that electricity was eventually substituted.

The last standard-gauge line built in the county was the Lampeter, Aberaeron and New Quay Light Railway. Aberaeron was the last urban settlement in Cardiganshire without a railway, despite various schemes laid in the 19th century but not hatched, including the dotty proposal for a narrow-gauge line from Devil's Bridge to Aberaeron. Eventually the L.A. & N.Q. Light Railway Company began work in 1908, and by agreement the Great Western began running trains over the new line from Lampeter to Aberaeron in 1911. Despite its initial popularity the company was deep in debt by the time the line began working, and J.C. Harford of Falcondale gave £12,000 to keep the enterprise afloat, a huge sum for a Cardiganshire squire; at one point he had to act as guarantor to the creditors. In 1922 the G.W.R. took over the company and line, and kept it going despite competition from renewed competition from buses, which at one point had given up. The last phase of railway history in the county, the closures, is described in Chapter 25.

* * *

Although there are separate books about each of Cardiganshire's railways, no one has yet thought to write the story of the county's buses, even though during the 20th century they carried far more passengers. The lack of such a history is not surprising; even in a small area like Cardiganshire the story of bus operations is highly complex, and only a crude outline is possible here. Although the railways displaced long-distance horse transport as soon as they opened, horse-drawn coaches continued to operate on many short routes until the arrival of petrol-driven buses. These suddenly proliferated from 1904 (Cardigan-Newcastle Emlyn), 1905 (Aberystwyth and district, run by 'Jones and Co.'), and in 1906 the Great Western Railway began bus connections between Aberystwyth-Aberaeron (New Quay was added on in 1907) and Aberaeron-Lampeter. The latter was withdrawn when the Lampeter-Aberaeron railway line opened in 1911, a rare reversal of fortune. Cambrian Railways used a hired bus for tours from Devil's Bridge to the summit of Pumlumon, an idea imitated in the 1920s by the G.W.R. By 1923 the G.W.R. was running between Machynlleth and Aberystwyth, followed a year later by Corris Railway Motor Services in competition.

A passenger train leaves Aberaeron for Lampeter [postcard].

It was in 1924 that Crosville Motors of Chester established a depot in Aberystwyth, and after a dispute with the G.W.R. and other operators, north Cardiganshire was divided between them: the G.W.R. and Corris Railways would run Aberystwyth-Machynlleth; Crosville and Corris would run Aberystwyth-Devil's Bridge-Ysbyty Ystwyth, and the G.W.R. would run Aberystwyth-Cardigan. Jones & Co, the local Aberystwyth company, retained some services. Crosville was soon planning serious expansion, and took over several routes from small companies. Crosville recruited local drivers and conductors, who paid their own wages out of the week's takings and banked surplus money.

In 1929 Crosville was bought by the London, Midland and Scottish Railway, and a series of amalgamations brought the G.W.R. bus services into a company originally called Great Western Welsh, later abbreviated to Western Welsh, a company which many older readers will remember. Many piratical practices (actually more common in densely-populated areas rather than in deepest Cardiganshire) such as racing and more devious tricks, were outlawed in 1930 by a Road Traffic Act. Jones & Co., the largest independent operator in north Cardiganshire, was taken over by Crosville, and in 1934 the company acquired an independently-developed route from Aberystwyth via Tregaron to Lampeter. Even at the time, when cars were still few, some of Crosville's rural routes were uneconomic.

As well as these in-county developments, efforts were made to connect Cardiganshire to the rest of Wales not only by the Aberystwyth-Machynlleth link already mentioned, but by extending the New Quay-Llandysul and Cardigan-Newcastle Emlyn services on to Carmarthen; a route was also developed from Aberystwyth via Lampeter to Ammanford, and in 1929 there began a service from Aberystwyth to Wolverhampton and then a service to Birmingham, followed by a service from Aberystwyth to London, all the initiative of national operators working together as 'Associated Motorways', with its headquarters at Cheltenham. All these express services ceased between 1942 and 1945. Crosville was transferred from the LMS to the Tilling consortium, and adopted the green livery which remained familiar for the next half-century, though in 1948 Tilling became government property. The ownership of large bus companies has a history of Byzantine complexity.

Buses had generally flourished in the 1930s, and despite severe regulations were in great demand during wartime. Post-war, Crosville began town services in Aberystwyth in 1948, but from 1949 the company's Welsh traffic began a slow decline. There were of course small independent companies still running minor services side-by-side with the large groups, which had realised that they could not take over every B-road service in the countryside. It seemed that rail closures might give buses a boost, but the services provided to replace rail links did not flourish, and the steady increase in car ownership began to impress itself on bus company balance sheets. Companies large and small therefore sought subsidies from local authorities, which tended to favour small independent operators, who could run more cheaply from villages than from town bases. The Western Welsh title disappeared from Cardiganshire in 1972, its routes transferring to Crosville; Crosville became Crosville Cymru, with a succession of owners, until in 1997 the Arriva name began to appear on the buses, a process completed in 1998.

If it is complex enough to attempt even an outline of major bus operations in Cardiganshire, to chronicle the myriad single-coach entrepreneurs on every mini-service between villages is quite impossible. At one time or another there were independent bus operators at Penrhyn-coch, Cwmerfin, Pont-rhyd-y-groes, Pontrhydfendigaid, Llangeitho, Llangwyryfon, Tal-sarn, Tregaron, Aberaeron and Llanrhystud, while services around Cardigan were provided by operators in St Dogmaels and Moylgrove. Many services only ran once or twice a week. The two operators with the most extensive services in the county are Richards of Moylgrove, now operating out of Cardigan's industrial estate, and James of Llangeitho, running an extraordinarily complex network of village and town services in the area bounded

Early bus at Llanrhystud [National Library of Wales]

by Aberystwyth-Aberaeron-Lampeter-Tregaron. The Post Office also offers a daily mail-bus service between Aberystwyth and the Llangwyryfon-Trefenter district.

Political pressures on bus companies ranged from the financial to the linguistic. By the 1970s bilingual signing had become increasingly common in the Welsh environment, and many bus companies responded with Welsh and English titles and logos. Less easy was the problem of balancing subsidies, losses and fares, an impossible conundrum; one result was the closure or reduction in status of small Crosville depots such as Aberaeron and New Quay. There was also pressure to improve North-South communication in Wales, and as a result Crosville's Aberystwyth-Cardiff express service became in 1980 part of a Traws-Cambria route from Cardiff via Aberystwyth to Rhyl, later transferred to Bangor.

The future of the county's bus services must be fragile as long as car ownership is rampant; both trains and buses throughout rural Wales are heavily subsidised, and only this help and school services prevent the virtual shutdown of Ceredigion's buses. It is worth remembering, incidentally, that buses and to a lesser extent trains transformed the lives of country children attending secondary school. The usual practice was for those who gained places at the grammar schools to live in lodgings from Monday to Friday during term-time. This may have helped them mature, but it may also at a crucial age have widened the gap between their rural Welsh-language culture and the Anglicising effect of town life added to that of the schools.

19. Politics and Local Government

Occasional convulsions have punctuated the long uneasy sleep of Cardiganshire's electoral history. The extended parliamentary reign of a Pryse, a Vaughan or a Powell might end in sudden controversy, with drawn swords or pistols, with subsequent legal disputes at Westminster; even in more peaceful times there were ructions and excitement, with tenants expelled from their farms, with the sudden emergence of tradesmen and farmers as county councillors in 1889, with the election of the first Labour MP in 1966 and his defeat in 1974. But it is true that, compared with the politics of Carmarthenshire, and especially Carmarthen borough, this county seems, at least in retrospect, to have been a matter of small groups of men – always men, never women – meeting in smoke-filled rooms to arrange affairs to their own best advantage. Indeed, such meetings are still held, though not necessarily reported in the local press. If this sounds like Tammany Hall, so be it; electoral business everywhere has always been open to manipulation, and still is, though the extension of the vote from the comparatively few to the many has made such arrangements less certain than they used to be. It will simplify matters to treat local government later in the chapter, though county officials and town councils played their parts in parliamentary matters throughout the early modern period.

Even before the 20th century, when MPs had no salary or expenses (while government ministers were well rewarded), the status of MPs was enviable. They enjoyed status in their constituencies and could hope for honours and office; in particular they could use influence on behalf of their relatives, friends and neighbours, soliciting posts in the Civil Service or the armed forces, and other favours. They also enjoyed a certain degree of legal immunity; an MP could not be arrested for debt. For example, John Vaughan of Trawsgoed sat for the boroughs from 1796 onwards while the estate sank deep into debt thanks largely to his spendthrift behaviour. He was able nevertheless to survive, despite his utter inefficiency as a Member, until by 1818 his affairs were so befouled that he retreated from the Commons and from Britain, taking up residence in France until he was able, as head of the family after 1820, to sell his Devon estate and retrieve his situation.

How then, briefly, did parliamentary matters run as far as Cardiganshire was concerned? The Acts of Union granted the county one Member of Parliament and a member for the county's boroughs. These

COUNTY-TOWN status was once a matter of competitive pride in many counties, but in Cardiganshire the issue was never as clear-cut as in Pembrokeshire and Carmarthenshire. Cardigan had a head start, being the oldest borough and the original administrative, parliamentary and law-court centre, but in size it was overtaken by Aberystwyth. The latter however never consolidated its hold; the county assizes were established at Lampeter and the main county offices and meeting-place have for several decades been at the small but conveniently central Aberaeron.

originally numbered five: Cardigan, Aberystwyth, Lampeter, Tregaron and Adpar (claims for Trefilan as a borough never seem to have been successful). After 1732 Tregaron lost its borough status, while Adpar simply fell out of the reckoning. Burgesses of the boroughs were entitled to vote; the borough councils were entitled to create burgesses and the mayor of Cardigan was the returning officer, and so control of the boroughs was essential to the great men of the county. In the county itself, where the sheriff was the returning officer, freeholders were entitled to vote, and among them were reckoned the more substantial tenant farmers, thus giving major landowners, heads of the county's great families, a vast amount of influence, because their tenants were expected to vote as directed. Since MPs were not salaried, only the rich could offer themselves as candidates, and since a contested election meant a great deal of expenditure, it was much easier for the men of influence to carve up matters between them. Canvassing might well be necessary; voting was to be avoided as far as possible. For example, there was no contested election for the county seat from 1747 to 1859, and the borough seat was frequently uncontested.

Such lack of contests did not mean that politics were moribund. When there was an election, intimidated officials might return both candidates rather than admit defeat. In 1601 the borough election was stoutly fought; the sheriff declared at Aberystwyth that one Dr Awbrey of Brecon was elected, but the mayor of Cardigan declared for one Richard Delabere, who hastened to London and was admitted to the House despite Awbrey's appeal. Even without a contest there would be a great deal of canvassing. In 1784 the first Earl of Lisburne, Wilmot Vaughan, was deeply concerned that young Thomas Powell of Nanteos was determined to displace him at the election of that year. Wilmot wrote from London seeking the advice of his friends, hastened down to Wales and scampered round his estates and the houses of his friends to make sure that Powell realised he had no choice but to back away.

Family mattered far more than policy – indeed, to speak of political policy is largely anachronistic, though of course controversial issues would be fiercely debated. Following the flight of James II and the accession of William III and Mary II, the Pryses were Jacobite, to the intense rage of the Vaughans of Trawsgoed. The Secretary of State in London was told that at a meeting in Aberystwyth Lewis Pryse, William Powell and others had drunk a toast to the Old Pretender on their knees. In 1715 Lewis Pryse, though sick with gout, put himself forward successfully for the county seat but was expelled, having avoided enforced attendance at the House. He remained in correspondence with the Old Pretender's general the Earl of Mar, but like other Welsh Jacobites was keener to drink to the king over the water than to rise in his favour.

In so far as there were political parties at all, they did not in the least resemble today's organisations with their subscribing membership, conferences, manifestos and parliamentary whips. Rather they were shifting coalitions of greater and lesser families with their varying interests; the underlying issue of the period 1560-1780 was between those who gave more or less unconditional support to the monarchy and those who sought the de facto supremacy of Parliament – the 'court' and 'country' parties, names eventually replaced by Tory and Whig respectively.

For centuries the Pryses of Gogerddan were the county's dominant political family. The Trawsgoed estate might be larger, other individuals could muster considerable wealth, and the Pryses themselves often lacked an adult male as head of the family, but, from the time of Elizabeth I till the mid-Victorian period, the Pryses could to a great extent control the field. They had to be tactful; it was not always possible to control both county and borough. The boroughs of Cardigan and Aberystwyth were usually in the family's pocket, but this in itself cost money; in 1767 the election of the mayor of Cardigan cost John Pughe Pryse £102 in meat, drink and grazing for horses; by 1839 the cost of a contest for the boroughs was estimated to be between three and four thousand pounds. Elections for the county seat were not so easily controlled; the voters were too numerous to be easily corralled or to bribe, hence the meetings of county families in smoke-filled rooms.

No fewer than twelve Pryses sat for one or other seat between 1567 and 1868, not to mention their in-laws, especially the Leweses of Abernantbychan. When a Pryse was unavailable or unwilling to offer for one or other seat, then the family and their trustees (who included figures of great status such as Sir John Philipps of Picton and Sir Watkin Williams Wynn) would be consulted by would-be candidates hoping for support through the family's influence. It is true that a wealthy outsider might disrupt the pattern of any county's politics. In 1701 the hugely rich industrialist Sir Humphrey Mackworth of Neath bought his way into Cardiganshire's politics. The Pryses were facing financial difficulties which Mackworth solved by buying into the Gogerddan mining interests for £15,000; this effectively gave him the county seat in 1701, again after a break in 1705, and for a third time in 1710. In 1714 he left the county with the Pryses back in charge and much richer.

Nothing better illustrates the Gogerddan influence than the county election of 1761 and the borough election of 1774. In 1761 the sitting member for the county was Wilmot Vaughan, Viscount Lisburne (peers with Irish titles could not automatically sit in the House of Lords). Wilmot had been unopposed at the 1755 by-election, but now John Pugh Pryse was of age, and Wilmot was obliged to stand down in his favour rather than lose an expensive election contest. He regained his place in 1768 when Pryse inexplicably gave up the seat. In 1774 Pryse was in Paris at the time of the nomination; he wrote to Cardigan borough council instructing them that they were to elect a very distant relative of his, Sir Robert Smyth, an Essex man with no interest in the county. The council obeyed, but Thomas Johnes (later of Hafod), contested the election, and when Smyth was returned by the obedient council, Johnes petitioned Parliament and carried the day; Pryse had suddenly died, and though Gogerddan's influence might sway Cardigan borough it could not move Parliament; Smyth was replaced by Johnes.

The Pryses' first rivals were the Lloyd clan; between 1545 and 1880 the various Lloyd families provided eleven MPs, while the Vaughans of Trawsgoed produced seven between 1628 and 1859, not to mention General Sir John Vaughan, who sat for Berwick-on-Tweed. The Vaughans produced the only county members of any serious talent before the 20th century; Sir John Vaughan was a major leader of the moderate party which endured a squeeze between parliamentary cavaliers and roundheads and an important figure during his times in the Commons between 1628 and 1667. Wilmot Vaughan the first Earl of Lisburne held minor government office from 1768 until 1782. Uniquely among the county's families the Vaughans remained 'parliamentarian' into the present era; the seventh earl was an unsuccessful candidate in 1923, and his grandson, Nigel Fisher, represents at the time of writing an English constituency in the Labour interest and has held government office.

The Powells of Nanteos only produced three MPs, but were closely involved in the county's politics from 1710 onwards. Eventually Thomas Powell took the borough seat in the by-election of 1725, but in 1729 the Gogerddan interest put forward Richard Lloyd of Mabws, a relative of the family. Swords and pistols were brandished on election day at Cardigan amid riotous scenes, and the mayor cautiously declared both candidates elected, leaving it to the House of Commons to decide. The relevant committee disqualified Tregaron as a borough and declared Lloyd elected. The Powells had thenceforward to compete without the support of their Tregaron voters.

Quite the most controversial Cardiganshire politician in the 18th century was Herbert Lloyd of Peterwell. His elder brother John had sat for the county without fuss between 1747 and 1755, and Herbert hoped to replace him. However, this one-time friend of Howel Harris had become a widely-hated figure in the county and beyond, and had even been ejected from the magistrates' bench; Wilmot Vaughan of Trawsgoed was able with governmental support to claim the seat unopposed. Lloyd continued his rambunctious behaviour, forcibly arresting the equally unpopular squire Thomas Johnes of Aber-mad for debt and securing Johnes's incarceration in London's Fleet prison, where he spent nearly three years. However in 1761 John Pugh Pryse had come of age; Wilmot Vaughan as we have seen could not compete, while Herbert Lloyd had ingratiated himself so far with Gogerddan, and indeed with the great Duke of Newcastle, while reneging on promises made to Sir John Philipps, that he was able to secure the unopposed nomination for the borough seat, which Wilmot Vaughan might otherwise have gained.

Herbert Lloyd was triumphant: 'it must have mortified and hurt Vaughan beyond expression', he pronounced. Nor was this the end of his triumphs; thanks to his manipulation of royal favour and a down-payment of a thousand pounds, he secured a baronetcy in 1763. His kissing of the King's hand provoked the squarson John Lloyd of Alltrodyn to verse. Referring to the defunct habit of kingly 'touching for the King's Evil' (i.e. scrofula), Lloyd wrote:

O! had our gracious sovereign's touch
But cured him of his evil,
I'd own St George ne'er boasted such
A triumph o'er the devil.

Lloyd's behaviour, and his nomination of his friends as magistrates, brought chaos to the administration of law and order in the county, hardly secure at the best of times. He had also got himself into massive debt, and therefore badly needed to retain the seat at the election of 1768, but by then he had lost virtually all his allies, particularly John Pugh Pryse, who claimed nomination for Merionethshire instead of Cardiganshire, but had no intention of ever supporting Lloyd again; instead he successfully supported Wilmot Vaughan for the county and his own cousin Pryse Campbell of Stackpole for the borough seat.

With the eventual deaths of both Pryse and Campbell, Gogerddan's involvement was reduced to the use of influence by the estate's trustees and by Edward Loveden of Buscot, husband of the Gogerddan heiress, and by the end of the 18th century the county's parliamentary politics were dominated by Trawsgoed and Thomas Johnes of Hafod. There was only one contested election between 1790 and 1832, that for the boroughs in 1812, nevertheless there was plenty of manoeuvring at election time. But although the great families would continue to dominate politics through much of the 19th century, there was change in the air. Ordinary men might not be able to stand for Parliament, they might be unable to vote if they lacked qualification or if there was no outright contest, but there was a long-standing alternative – the petition to Parliament. In 1792 the whole county, as well as Adpar and Cardigan separately, petitioned for the abolition of the slave trade; in 1813 the clergy of the archdeaconry of Cardigan and the inhabitants of both Aberystwyth and Cardigan petitioned against Catholic emancipation. From 1816 it became more common for petitions to be sent to London on behalf of local causes; for aid against distress after the end of the Napoleonic wars in 1815, and against coal and culm duties. Southern Cardiganshire was canvassed for signatures to the great Chartist petition of 1839, and the Unitarians did not fail; among the 27,147 signatures from south Wales organised by Hugh Williams of Carmarthen, 1,026 Cardiganshire names were listed, including many from Llandysul and Cribyn, heartland of the *Smotyn Du.* Not that every Cardiganshire radical was a Unitarian; John Davies, the Ystrad Aeron bookbinder and diarist (*c*1722-99), who records his reading of Tom Paine's *The Age of Reason* over three days in 1798, was a churchgoer, while his wife attended chapel; as parish clerk, he could hardly have joined her. He was a reader of newspapers (unnamed) and copied a Welsh translation of the *Marseillaise* into his diary.

Thomas Johnes's death in 1816 brought Gogerddan and Nanteos back into the field in competition for the county seat. Pryse Loveden Pryse and William Edward Powell both coveted the place. At a meeting of interested parties both men were nominated; according to Job Sheldon, mayor of Aberystwyth, the two were persuaded to toss a coin in order 'not to disturb the peace of the county'. Powell won, was returned unopposed, and survived every election without a contest until his retirement in 1854. As he had also secured the lord lieutenancy of the county, W.E. Powell was for a generation the county's leading figure. Pryse Loveden Pryse contented himself with the borough seat in 1818; the two men usually voted on opposite sides, with the Tory Powell against Catholic emancipation. The only Cardiganshire people to petition on behalf of Catholic emancipation were the Unitarians of Capel-y-Groes; the Whig Pryse Pryse favoured it privately but would not vote in favour. The replacement of the courts of Great Sessions by assizes in 1830 was the object of vigorous protests across Wales, including Cardiganshire, but they did not prevail. The Reform Act of 1832, supported by both Powell (rather reluctantly) and Pryse made little difference to county politics.

It was at this time that the first rustlings of radicalism are detectable in Aberystwyth. Prior to the municipal reforms of 1835 the town had been held in the grip of an oligarchy of townsmen favoured by the Pryses, and only the still quietist Calvinistic Methodists formed any sizeable alternative to the Church of England. In 1832, when the second St Michael's church was being built, funds ran out, and the defensive sea-wall could only be completed by levying a Church rate. Suddenly the church vestry meeting throbbed with conflict; counsel's opinion was sought, and almost overnight the Methodists were radicalised. Nevertheless the wall was built, but change had been wrought. In 1836 the first of three numbers of a bilingual periodical was published, the *Cambrian Gazette: Y Freinlen Gymroaidd,* with the slogan 'Political Intelligence for the Welsh'. News of the Irish campaign against tithe payments and of Welsh church vestries refusing to allow Church rates appeared. An anonymous author or authors appealed vigorously for political education for the Welsh since 'the only stronghold of Toryism is popular ignorance', for which the stamp duty on newspapers was a major culprit:

> We have laws which the Welsh cannot read, a government whose language they cannot understand, and a constitution which . . . has never once been exhibited in the language of the people.

Who can have been behind this publication? Ieuan Gwynedd Jones has identified some of the individuals who were summonsed for not paying Church rate for the wall, but none is an obvious candidate for authorship of the little paper. Nevertheless the publication, short-lived though it was, must surely be linked to the Church-rate upheaval which was a catalyst for radicalism in the county's largest town.

John 'Ivon' Jones was a central figure in Aberystwyth's commercial, political and cultural life in mid-century. At one level he was a pillar of Nonconformist respectability and commercial values, who acted as secretary for the Aberystwyth National Eisteddfod of 1865. Yet as a young man he had been an eyewitness of *Rhyfel y Sais Bach* in the 1820s and would have been familiar with the Rebecca upheavals of the 1840s; this makes it less surprising that, as has already been mentioned in Chapter 13, in late 1868 or early 1869 he helped the poacher/murderer Wil Cefn Coch to escape to America (the source for this information is the series of columns of reminiscences of Victorian Cardiganshire published in the *Welsh Gazette* in the 1920s). He was, incidentally but perhaps not surprisingly, grandfather of David Ivon Jones, founder of the Communist Party of South Africa.

William Powell led a charmed and unopposed electoral life, unaffected by his desultory parliamentary attendance or by the faint stirrings of Radicalism in Aberystwyth just described, but Pryse Pryse eventually ran into opposition at the borough election of 1841 in the form of the Tory J.S. Harford of Falcondale. The mayor of Cardigan once more returned both men, since the Aberystwyth poll books had been lost somewhere on the road to Cardigan! The House of Commons found in favour of Pryse, and the Powell-Tory Pryse-Whig polarity continued by mutual agreement. Pryse died after the uncontested election of 1847, and was succeeded by his son Pryse Loveden, who had learnt Welsh, and who was sufficiently radical to support the ballot in place of public voting. Loveden was opposed in 1852 by the Tory, John Inglis Jones of Derry Ormond, but carried the day, only to hear that a number of farmers who had voted for him had been expelled by their Tory landlords, including Powell of Nanteos. At last the feudalism of Cardiganshire's tenantry was crumbling, though at serious cost to those brave enough to follow their consciences rather than their leaders. The policy of expelling tenants was to cost the Tories dear in rural Wales.

Although the Anglican squirearchy continued in mid-century to dominate Welsh politics, their power was beginning to ebb. In 1852 In Cardiff Walter Coffin, a Unitarian coal prospector, became the first Welsh Dissenter elected to the Commons; in 1859 in Merionethshire a Liberal (replacing the former title Whig) lawyer, David Williams, narrowly lost to W.W.E. Wynne, the local Tory squire. To Cardiganshire's shame no Liberal offered in that year, but in 1865 there was a collision of Liberal interests. Henry Richard of Tregaron (1812-88) represented a new generation; the son of the Revd Ebenezer Richard, he rose from being a draper's apprentice to a London pulpit; and in 1848 he had become secretary of the Peace Society. In 1865 he offered himself as Liberal candidate for the Cardiganshire county seat, but withdrew, gaining instead a famous victory in Merthyr Tudful in 1868. He had been unable to compete with the wealthy railway developer David Davies of Llandinam, who had contributed generously to many Calvinistic Methodist causes. It

SOME contemporary insight into the world of county politics can be gained from the career of Joseph Jenkins, 'the Welsh Swagman'. Farmer of Trecefel near Tregaron, he was recruited by the Nanteos Tory W.T.R. Powell to canvass for him in the 1859 election, which Jenkins did with vigour. He was equally zealous on behalf of the defeated Liberal David Davies in 1865, neglecting his farm to hobnob with the great, and drinking far too much. In 1868 he was pressed to support the Tory, Edmund Vaughan of Trawsgoed, a move which appalled his increasingly radical family and neighbours. After Vaughan's defeat Joseph Jenkins, his personal life and finances in tatters, deserted his family and all the causes in which he had believed, to migrate to Australia. His diaries have given him postumous fame.

Henry Richard's statue at Tregaron.

seems that the disappointed Richard never spoke to Davies again. Davies's generosity did not however carry the day in 1868; the squires, unable to find a Tory candidate, supported Sir Thomas Davies Lloyd of Bronwydd, who stood successfully under the Liberal label. But David Davies would return in good time.

The Reform Act of 1832 had been a damp squib as far as extending the franchise was concerned, but the 1867 Reform Act brought in serious change. The number of voters for the borough seat rose from 692 to 1,561, and for the county seat from 3,520 to 5,123. This did not destroy the influence of the smoke-filled rooms; in the bitter election of November 1868 Evan M. Richards, a wealthy Swansea Baptist, needed Gogerddan's support to achieve his narrow defeat of the Trawsgoed Tory. There were Tory complaints of the so-called 'Nonconformist screw', the pressure exerted from the pulpit by some Nonconformist ministers on behalf of the Liberals, while similar complaints were made against Tory parsons. The loudest accusations were made against Tory landlords (Trawsgoed, Nanteos, Alltyrodyn, Llanfair, Blaen-pant and Pigeonsford) who were accused of expelling some of their tenants for voting Liberal, and increasing the rents of others. The Cardiganshire election and its alleged malpractices figured prominently in the Commons select committee investigation of 1869, secured by the efforts of Henry Richard. Money was raised by popular subscription to compensate the ejected tenants, while the landlords protested that the expulsions were largely unconnected with politics. Henry Richard eventually admitted that there was not enough evidence to stand up in a court of law, and the House committee did not reach any decisive conclusions, but there was no need; the Liberal government brought in the secret ballot by an act of 1872.

In 1876 one last weapon against radicalism was used by John Lloyd Davies of Alltyrodyn, almost certainly at the instigation of his unscrupulous agent, Mason Allen. The Unitarian congregation at Llwynrhydowen occupied a chapel built on land leased from Alltyrodyn. Using a clause in the tenancy agreement, and blaming the minister William Thomas (Gwilym Marles, uncle of Dylan Thomas) for his preaching of the Liberal cause in 1868 and 1874, the landowner expelled the congregation from their chapel on 29 October 1876 and locked the gates. Gwilym Marles was denied

POLITICAL EVICTIONS IN WALES.

Dear Sir,

At a Meeting, held at Aberystwyth on the 4th of October last, it was considered desirable to convene a Conference for the consideration of the best means of assisting Electors who have suffered for the conscientious exercise of the Franchise, and of protecting such as may hereafter be subjected to such pressure.

In pursuance of the above resolution I am desired to convene the

CONFERENCE

AT THE TEMPERANCE HALL, ABERYSTWYTH,

On Tuesday, the 16th inst.

The Chair to be taken by E. M. RICHARDS, Esq., M.P., at 11 o'clock.

A PUBLIC MEETING

Will be held in the Evening, at the same place, at Seven o'Clock,

OSBORNE MORGAN, Esq., M.P., in the Chair.

I shall be glad to know at an early date whether we can count upon your presence.

Yours faithfully,

JOHN MATTHEWS,

Chairman of the Provisional Committee.

Aberystwyth, Nov. 5, 1869.

A public meeting notice following the 1868 general election. [National Library of Wales]

access even to the graveyard where his wife had been buried. The expulsion may have been technically if marginally justifiable on legal grounds, but it was a terrible political mistake; the cause of the expelled congregation was taken up by the Liberal press across Britain. Sympathy and money poured in, and the congregation built a new chapel. When in 1879 John Lloyd Davies died childless, his sister inherited the estate; almost her first act was to come by train to Llandysul with the announced purpose of handing back the keys of the original chapel to the congregation. The horses were unhitched from her carriage, which was then drawn by relays of young men to Llwynrhydowen for the ceremony. Gwilym Marles was too ill to witness this dramatic event; broken in health, his was the first burial in the new chapel's graveyard.

Llwynrhydowen chapel.

The nascent radicalism of the county was not strong enough to overwhelm traditional rural conservatism. Although Thomas Edward Lloyd of Coedmor was the last Tory to represent the county, having defeated E.M. Richards in 1874, but losing in 1880 to Lewis Pugh Pugh of Aber-mad, nevertheless the next generations of Liberal candidates can best be described as Whigs. In 1885 the borough seat was abolished, leaving one seat only with 12,308 voters. It was taken by David Davies of Llandinam, canvassing as 'the Working Man's Friend', who easily defeated the Tory Matthew Vaughan Davies, squire of Tan-y-bwlch.

David Davies was no radical. He used his wealth to buy land, and voted against Irish Home Rule. The radicalisation of the rest of Nonconformist Wales was now going ahead rapidly, with outstanding members such as T.E. Ellis of Merionethshire and Stuart Rendel of Montgomeryshire representing the new Welsh Liberal movement in the House. When Gladstone's government fell on the Irish home rule issue in 1886, David Davies announced himself as a Liberal Unionist, since he had no time for the Irish cause, and the county's 'real' Liberals cast about for an adequate candidate. They settled on the Haverfordwest lawyer W. Bowen Rowlands, and in an extremely noisy campaign Rowlands defeated Davies by nine votes. This Liberal success was soon followed by the county council elections of 1889, dealt with below; they proved a Liberal triumph in all Welsh counties except Breconshire. At Westminster governments came in and went out through a revolving door of Tories and Liberals: the landed interest, once divided between Whigs and Tories, was now largely Tory, and at the same time was losing its grip on power, while Irish Home Rule was the issue which determined how often the door revolved.

CARDIGANSHIRE ELECTION,
1880.

Mr. L. P. PUGH begs to thank the Electors for the hearty promises of support he has received, and to inform them that his name will be SECOND on the Ballot Paper. Each Voter has only *One Vote*, and in Voting for Mr. Pugh, a X should be placed opposite his name as below.

1	LLOYD. Thomas Edward Lloyd, Coedmore, in the County of Cardigan, Esquire.	
2	PUGH. Lewis Pugh Pugh, Abermaide, in the County of Cardigan, Esquire.	X

Under the Ballot it is absolutely impossible for any one to tell which way any Voter has Voted, unless informed by the Voter himself; and Mr. David Davies, M.P., has offered £1,000 to any one who can prove how any individual Voter has Voted.

Please Turn Over.

An election poster of 1880; Pugh was in fact victorious. [National Library of Wales]

Unfortunately Bowen Rowlands was not of the parliamentary calibre of Ellis and Rendel, but he sat until 1895 when he became a judge; the Liberal government of Rosebery disintegrated and Tory rule resumed for ten years. The Liberal nomination for Cardiganshire for the general election of 1895 was a surprise – the Tory candidate of 1885, Matthew Vaughan Davies, had turned his coat, realising that his former party was now permanently doomed to failure in Cardiganshire. It seems extraordinary today that this non-Welsh-speaking Anglican squire should have been chosen to represent the county which had found David Davies old-fashioned, and that the owner of Tan-y-bwlch was now supposedly part of a movement which included T.E. Ellis and Lloyd George. The genuine radicalism of south Cardiganshire Unitarians or the growing Aberystwyth intelligentsia never found expression in parliamentary terms, though in local politics, as will be seen below, Liberalism was more active. But Vaughan Davies was not burdened by debt as were so many of his class, nor had he any record of turning tenants out. So the 1895 election in Cardiganshire was a reversion to earlier times, with the Liberal (really a Whig) squire Vaughan Davies challenged unsuccessfully by a Tory squire, J.C. Harford of Falcondale.

The turncoat won, and Cardiganshire parliamentary politics fell into a coma. Vaughan Davies rarely spoke in the House; the county's Liberal party became moribund, such finance as was necessary being provided largely by Davies. He won in the general elections of 1900, 1906 and the first election of 1910, each time against another of the county's Tory squireens, and was unopposed at the second election of 1910 and in 1918. In the approach to the 1918 election the *Cardigan and Tivy-side Advertiser*, commenting on the inevitable nomination of Vaughan Davies, was ready to admit that he could not be regarded as an 'an ideal representative for such a Progressive county,' (whether the county was really 'progressive' is another matter). He was especially vague about whether he supported Lloyd George or Asquith, apparently persuading both sides of his integrity! However, if Cardiganshire was poorly represented in Parliament, there were signs of life elsewhere in the county, and we must turn aside for a while to examine them briefly.

THE farm labourers' miserable plight had been recognised long ago by the poet Evan Thomas Rhys (see Chapter 22). Writing before 1770, he described the World's Three Slaves as the Labourer, the Cobbler (he was one himself) and the Dog. The labourer has to walk to work before sunrise through mud and muck; he's lucky to have turnips to eat before returning in the dark to his pale wife, and their children crying for food.

* * *

The success of the Liberals in the county council elections was not the only sign of political change in Cardiganshire. By 1889 a few farm labourers in Cellan were ready to protest against their grim lives, though in vain. David Pretty cites the slavery of hiring fairs, the miserable pay, the menace of tuberculosis, the endless hours of toil, the filth of the stable loft, the misery of tied cottages, and the threat of an old age in the workhouse. Joseph Arch, the early pioneer of agricultural unionism in England in the 1870s, had no disciples in Wales for another twenty years (interestingly, later generations of his family are well represented in Ceredigion to this day). Any kind of unionism was slow in developing in the county, but by 1892 a Fabian Society had been founded in Dyffryn Orllwyn, organised by David Jones, cousin of the pioneer socialist Dr. E. Pan Jones. In 1894 David Jones gave evidence on behalf of the labourers to the Land Commission: the workers were no more than white slaves, their wages were lower than in any other Welsh county. But the farm labourers were scattered, their numbers declining and their morale low, unlike the Teifi valley wool-workers, who in 1901 formed their own union and successfully struck for better pay in 1903.

After that late but promising start by the wool-workers, unionism was slow to develop in Cardiganshire, but by 1912 members of the Amalgamated Society of

Railway Servants at Aberystwyth had formed the North Cardiganshire Trades Union and Labour Council. Other manifestations followed, including the Teifi District Labourers' and Fishermen's Union of 1916. World War I made life for the labourers still worse, since the Women's Land Army and prisoners of war could be employed for even lower wages, while farmers were profiting from ever higher prices. In 1917 T.E. Nicholas, the socialist, minister and poet, set out to lead a campaign in the county on behalf of the farm labourers, appealing to them to support the National Agricultural Labourers' and Rural Workers' Union (N.A.L.R.W.U.). The first branch was established in Llanilar, where Richard Llewelyn Jones served as secretary until 1974! Other branches quickly followed. In 1918 John Davies of Llangeitho, a friend of Keir Hardy, was appointed N.A.L.R.W.U. organiser in south-west Wales; he later ran the Workers' Educational Association across Wales. At first the work went ahead vigorously, but the agricultural depression which began in 1921 virtually destroyed the movement. The guaranteed prices and minimum wages brought in by the government during the war were done away with. Half the eighteen branches of N.A.L.R.W.U. disbanded by 1922; by 1927 only Llanilar remained. David Pretty calls the agricultural labourers' movement 'the revolt that failed'. The hapless labourers voted with their feet, leaving the land for good.

* * *

To return to parliamentary politics, in 1921 Vaughan Davies, was sent upstairs to the Other Place as Lord Ystwyth, his request for the title Lord Ceredigion having been rejected as too ambitious for a humble baron! He was the first Cardi ever to sit in the House of Lords, since the county's only peers, the Lisburnes, held an Irish, not an 'English' title. The county's Liberals plunged into fierce internal combat and a series of four elections in four years. For the by-election W. Llewelyn Williams, a long-time supporter of T.E. Ellis, and a competent writer on Welsh history, was adopted by the Asquithian county Liberal association, and opposed by Ernest Evans, a local man who had been Lloyd George's private secretary. The contest was acrimonious and, remarkably enough for the time and place, the two most prominent campaigners were both women: Violet Bonham-Carter, daughter of Herbert Asquith, spoke on Williams's behalf and Margaret Lloyd George on behalf of Evans, making some sixty speeches. In the event Ernest Evans carried the day thanks to Conservative support; Lloyd George was still a hero to the Welsh, although he was only in power thanks to the Conservative-dominated coalition. One consequence of the internal party strife was the creation of two separate Liberal clubs in Aberystwyth; the *Cambrian News* supported the Lloyd George Coalitionists and the *Welsh Gazette* the Asquithians, known to their opponents as the 'Wee Frees'.

When the coalition collapsed in 1922, Ernest Evans clung to the seat with a shrunken majority against the Glamorgan-born barrister and Asquithian Rhys Hopkin Morris in another battle of two Liberals, but in the 1923 general election the Tories intervened in the form of the seventh Earl of Lisburne, the family's last electoral fling in the county almost three centuries after they had first reached the House of Commons. Although the earl came last, he deprived Ernest Evans of his coalition-Conservative support, and so Hopkin Morris triumphed over Evans by 5,000 votes. By the time of the 1924 general election the Liberals were exhausted and the Tories downhearted, so that Morris was returned without opposition. This period of four elections, three of them fiercely contested, certainly restored political life in the county. When I came to live in Cardiganshire in the early 1960s there was still much talk in political circles of the strife of the early 1920s, and it was intriguing to find that the local political colours were still Blue for Liberals, Red for Tories.

At the election of 1929 Hopkin Morris easily beat off the Conservative challenge of the Teifi valley squire Colonel E.C.L. Fitzwilliam, and at the election of 1931 he gained a huge majority of 13,000 against the first-ever Labour candidate in the county, John Lloyd Jones, a Cardiganshire-born schoolteacher working in Ebbw Vale. As we have just seen, there had long been 'labour' activity in Cardiganshire, and a county Labour party branch had been established at Lampeter in 1919.

Rhys Hopkin Morris became a London stipendiary magistrate in 1932 and stood down from politics; he had won five elections (one unopposed) in ten years. At the by-election there were three candidates, but the new Liberal choice, D. Owen Evans of Llangrannog, took half the votes, the rest being divided between Colonel Fitzwilliam and another Labour candidate, a Senghennydd Baptist minister, D.M. Jones. D.O. Evans, who was a vice-president of the huge Mond Nickel company, had been sniffing around for the nomination as early as 1918, writing coded pieces for the *Cambrian News*; eventually his patience was rewarded. The Conservatives did not stand in 1935, and to many people's surprise a new Labour candidate, Ronw Moelwyn Hughes of Cardigan, polled over ten thousand votes; nevertheless D.O. Evans still had a majority of five thousand. The county's voters did not care that nationally the Liberal party was now a rump nor that their MP was not deeply involved in county life; Liberalism still prevailed over much of 'Welsh' Wales, though moribund elsewhere. P.J.Madgwick's study of the county's politics emphasises the complex ebb and flow of opinion, often inconsistent and self-contradictory, among the county's political groupings and public opinion in the pre-opinion-poll age.

* * *

Local government in Wales and England was for centuries the perquisite of the gentry, operating in the countryside largely through Quarter Sessions, which dealt with a wide range of responsibilities as well as acting as a magistrates' court. Cardigan and Aberystwyth both had municipal bodies under mayors; they were largely self-perpetuating oligarchies with more status than power, since they functioned under the eye of the major gentry families; Cardigan's Common Council did however have more power than Aberystwyth's Court Leet. Even the changes brought about by the Municipal Corporations Act of 1835 did not bring about

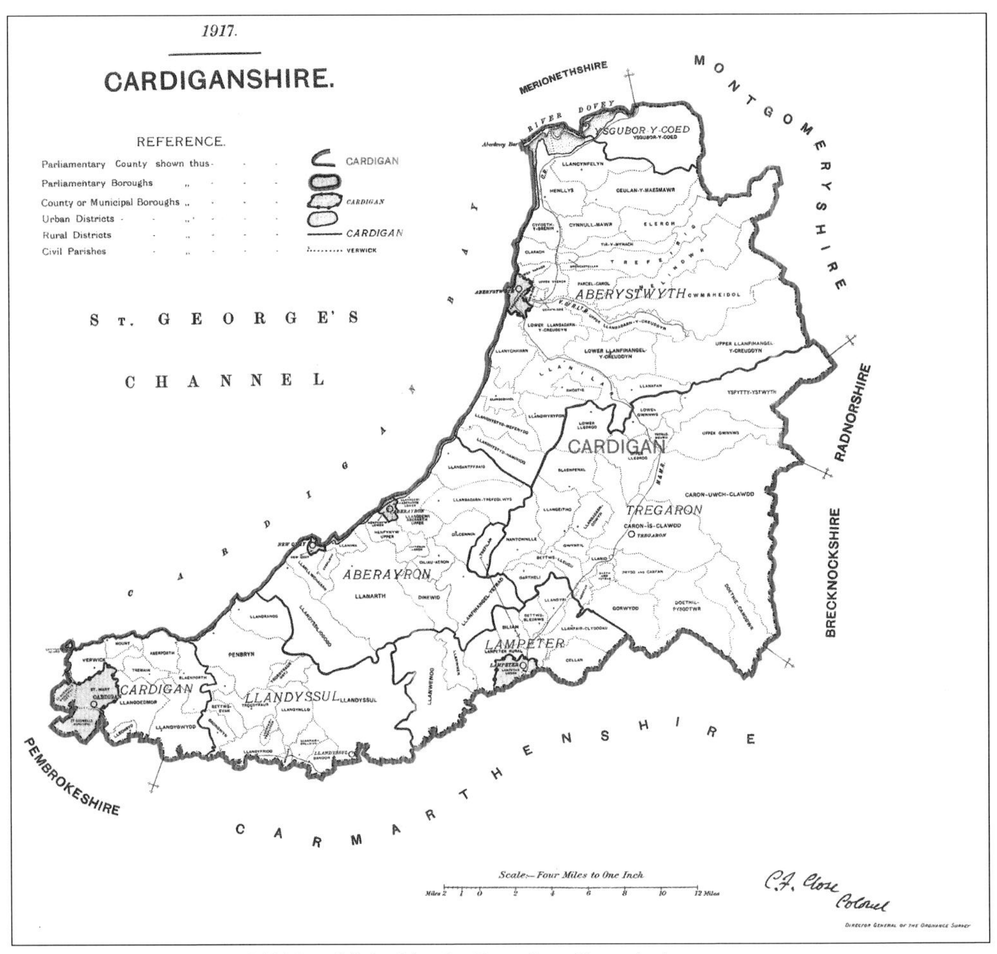

Local government map of 1917, published by the Boundary Commission.

dramatic reform; voters and councillors had to satisfy a property qualification, but since 1828 they no longer had to be Anglicans. Moreover Aberystwyth had secured through Parliament the right to an Improvement Commission with powers to clean, pave, light and water the town, to raise rates and borrow money.

More profound change came through two developments. One was the development of an urban middle class in both Aberystwyth and Cardigan, consisting of merchants and shopkeepers, lawyers, land agents, printers, and, in the case of Aberystwyth, mining entrepreneurs; hoteliers and craftsmen aspired to this level, where teachers and ministers also belonged. An increasing number of these men were Nonconformist in practice and Liberal by inclination, who took delight in cultural activities such as concerts and eisteddfodau. This group was activated at least in part by the Church rate scandal of the 1830s mentioned above.

A second source of change was the result of the policy of successive London governments in bringing in reforms which were to be administered by local elected Boards. Such important bodies as the Poor Law Unions, the police and above all the elementary schools were all controlled by boards. Control of these, as we have already seen in Chapter 17 in the case of school boards, became a tussle between Church and Chapel, Tory and Liberal (though some Liberals were Church-folk). This was epitomised in the long battle at Aberystwyth, described by Steven Thompson, to control the Downie Trust and the board of the Aberystwyth hospital. There does not seem to be any suggestion that either side sought control for the express purpose of securing favours for their party; rather was control simply a trophy, a proof that 'our' side was stronger than 'theirs'. The result was a damaging division which weakened the growing middle class in Nonconformist rural Wales.

The process of more general participation in the political process, the relinquishing of radical action such as the food-riot in favour of such constitutional activities as the petitioning of Parliament referred to above, continued slowly throughout much of the 19th century. In 1850 Aberystwyth people burnt the *Times* to express their sympathy with developments in Hungary and their disapproval of Tory attitudes, sending a petition to Lord Palmerston in favour of Hungarian independence and against Austrian imperialism.

THE almost incestuous relationship between religion and politics in the county is emphasised in David Jenkins's story of the county's police standing committee in 1888. The tithe conflict was still raging, and of the 24 members, 12 (all churchmen) supported the payment of tithes, while 12, including the chairman, did not. A new chief constable had to be appointed; three times the committee, thanks to the chairman, voted against the proposed local candidate, a churchman. Finally the committee appointed an outsider, who was a Calvinistic Methodist.

Despite their various difficulties, the ad hoc growth of elected bodies was a valuable preparation for the introduction of local councils through the act of 1888, followed by nationwide elections in 1889. The results were widely seen as a colossal snub to the Conservative and gentry interests; of the thirteen Welsh counties, only Breconshire elected a council which was recognisably of that interest. In Cardiganshire such eminent gentry figures as Sir Marteine Lloyd of Bronwydd, Thomas Waddingham of Hafod and Henry Bonsall of Cwmcynfelyn were all defeated by respectively a farmer, a postmaster and a coal merchant. Lord Lisburne, however, was elected unopposed for Strata Florida, and there were also other representatives of the landowning class. As David Jenkins emphasises, they were and remained personally popular, but were not acceptable as local leaders. Thirty-eight councillors acknowledged Liberal adherence and ten were Conservatives. This initial acknowledgement of loyalty to Liberalism or Conservativism soon gave way to a reluctance to identify with parties, and the Independent label became usual, with unopposed returns of sitting candidates frequent – a characteristic of a deferential community. By 1973, when the original Cardiganshire County Council was on the eve of dissolution, only one Plaid Cymru member had been elected as a party representative.

The first county councils did not at first replace the existing elected ad hoc governmental boards; councils' responsibilities were limited, and Cardiganshire's council budget for 1890 was only £12,440. However the second Local Government

Act, passed in 1894, gave the county councils additional powers and also created councils for urban districts (Cardigan, New Quay, Aberaeron, Aberystwyth, Lampeter), rural districts (Teifiside, Aberaeron, Tregaron, Aberystwyth) and parishes. Education was taken over by the county councils in two stages: intermediate schools in 1889 and elementary schools in 1902. Poor Law administration was handed over to counties by an Act of 1929. There were some obvious problems of division of responsibility between the different council tiers; thus 'health' became a county council responsibility, but sanitation, water, drainage, rubbish disposal, dairy registration and treatment of infections, all related to health, were matters for district authorities (for a brief treatment of health in the county, see Chapter 20). Improvement of the county's roads and bridges became a priority in the 1920s and '30s with increasing traffic, including the need for milk-lorries to gain access to hundreds of farm entrances where churns had to be collected every day. The two World Wars placed huge burdens on all local services, and by 1945 rural Wales as a whole stood in desperate need of better services.

* * *

Is Cardiganshire radical, or was it ever? For generations it has been traditional (an ironic word) to think so. The political scientist P.J. Madgwick devoted a chapter to the subject in his 1973 book, judging that the answer depends on how radicalism is defined. Interestingly, he concluded, in terms of the surveys he and his collaborators used, that 'Cardiganshire-born people are less radical proportionately than persons [living in the county] from elsewhere in Wales, or England.' He found that the term meant different things to different people, but that 'radicalism is one element in the political culture of Cardiganshire . . . part of the rhetoric of Cardiganshire politics, and the rhetoric imparts a certain style to a less certainly radical substance.' It is hard to disagree at all strongly with those conclusions a generation later, while reviewing the more distant past, we can see that Cardiganshire remained in the grip of the gentry rather longer than many Welsh counties, and was never wedded to the idea of government centralism.

Four politicians of a later vintage (see Chapter 25)

John Morris and Elystan Morgan in 1988; both are now life peers.

[Courtesy of the Cambrian News]

Geraint Howells, later Lord Geraint.

[Courtesy of the Cambrian News]

Cynog Dafis.

[National Library of Wales]

20. The Poor and the Sick

The quadruplets' gravestone at Ysbyty Cynfyn.

There is no more terrifying evidence of the double threat of poverty and disease than that to be found on two gravestones in the churchyard of Ysbyty Cynfyn. One records the burials on 23 February 1856 of Catherine Hughes, Elizabeth Hughes and Margaret Hughes of Nant Syddion, each of them three days old. On 1 March Isaac Hughes of Nantsyddion was buried – aged ten days. He was the fourth and last of the quadruplets born alive to Isaac Hughes and his wife. Now it was hardly to be expected that even one of four such tiny babies could possibly have survived in the conditions of the time. But the Reaper had not finished with the family of Nant Syddion. On 5 March Hugh Hughes of Nant Syddion was buried, aged five years. On 8 March the father himself was buried, aged 31 years; he and Hugh are commemorated on a separate stone. Finally on 12 March Hannah Hughes, aged three, was buried, and commemorated on the same stone as the quads. Local tradition has it that the shattered mother left the area and went to Australia with her last living child of the seven born to her; it seems clear that some such infection as typhus had killed the elder Isaac and the two elder children. The gravestones are unbearably moving, not least for the simple Welsh verse inscribed beneath the names of the quadruplets, which loses so much in translation:

Or un groth run dydd y daethom,	From the same womb the same day we came,
Or un bronau y sugnasom;	From the same breasts we sucked;
Yn run beddrod y gorweddwn,	In the same grave we lie together,
Yr un diwrnod y cyfodwn.	On the same day we'll rise again.

Nearly two hundred years earlier a traveller in Cardiganshire had noted how poor many people were. In 1684 Thomas Dineley visited much of Wales in the entourage of the Duke of Beaufort, Lord President of the Council, and kept a sketchbook-diary of the journey. In Cardiganshire he noted: 'The Vulgar here are most miserable and low as the rich are happy and high both to an extream; The Poorer sort for bread, eat Oaten Cakes, and drink beer small made of Oaten malt, some drink onely water for necessity . . .'

We have it on the best authority that the poor are always with us – but in Wales they are not easily traced in the medieval or early modern records. The miserable hovels in which they eked out life have sunk into the ground, their ragged clothes have not survived in museums, such wretched furniture as they had has long been used for firewood. For us to comprehend the mind-set of the poorest Welsh people in the early modern period is nearly as difficult as grasping that of Bronze Age folk. They are largely hidden from us. Yet the problem (always 'the problem') of the poor has always exercised ruling authorities everywhere. The Roman authorities provided bread and circuses for the multitude to keep them from rioting; Christian teaching sought to provoke the conscience of the fortunate, offering rewards in heaven for those who were charitable on earth. With the population growth in the 16th century, and the closure of the monasteries, the authorities in England and Wales worried about the impotent poor (who were deserving but cost money) and the idle poor (potential criminals), but there were also the labouring poor, whose lives were one long struggle for survival. It was to cope with these people that the Elizabethan Poor Laws were created, laying the responsibility on the parish vestry meeting to administer the poor-rate levied on property every year.

Our knowledge of poverty in medieval Cardiganshire is scant in the extreme. There was 'the Hospitall of Maudlyns' at Cardigan, founded 'to find certain impotent and deceased [*sic.* diseased] persons for ever'; this seems to suggest that this little institution, poorly endowed as it was, served the dual purpose of a medieval hospice and chantry. The monastic institutions at Llanllŷr and Strata Florida must also have offered charity to the poor. All were swept away at the Reformation; the state was slow to respond, preferring where possible to use the whip rather than coin of the realm.

In Cardiganshire we can recognise the labouring poor by the early 17th century, because some of them, both men and women, made wills. When Evan ap Henry of Llanfihangel Genau'r-glyn died in 1618, he left his all: his pot, his pan, his coffer and a few other implements, together generously valued at 18 shillings, to his daughter who had 'cared for her father olde & beddridden, being languishing after the death of her mother.' John Llewelyn of Llanfihangel-y-Creuddyn was a cobbler; before his death in 1665 he had a will drawn up in favour of James Parry, gentleman, who was his landlord, to receive all his worldly wealth – less than one pound. Presumably Llewelyn did this in lieu of unpaid rent.

For the 1670s we have the evidence of the annual Hearth Tax, which is a useful guide to the size of gentry properties, with mansions like Maesyfelin and Gogerddan having sixteen hearths. It was effectively a household tax – but roughly half the households in every parish were considered too poor to pay the tax at all. When we reach the 18th century, then the evidence begins to multiply, thanks to the survival of a number of parish vestry books which throw an extraordinary light on the misery of many.

The 1790 case of baby William Abel of Lampeter, detailed in the Lampeter parish vestry book, illustrates the kind of problems that abandonment, poverty and death bring in their wake. William was not illegitimate, but his father Stephen had gone to London, though whether to seek work to support his family or simply to abandon them we cannot know; the latter seems more likely. In April 1790 William's mother Sarah died. The baby was farmed out to David Davies of Cwmhenryd for eighteen pence a week by the parish overseers, while word was sent to his father. By December the overseers had despaired of a response and sought a warrant to be served on Stephen Abel. Enoch Nathaniel of Llanwenog was hired for a guinea to go to London to serve the warrant, with the reward of a further guinea if he succeeded. He failed; in the summer of 1791 a Mrs Evans agreed to take the baby to London to give him to his father. This plan also failed. Back in Lampeter baby William survived, and seems to have grown into a stroppy little boy, since he needed to be moved several times. In October 1798 he was apprenticed to Evan Evans of Abergranell for seven years, and the vestry paid for a suit and two shirts for him; he then disappears from view. The vestrymen, it should be added, would usually comfort themselves after their efforts; meetings were always adjourned from church to tavern, where the poor rates paid for large quantities of ale. Officials of today's Child Support Agency would immediately recognise the problems of baby William.

Life at the present day is hard for those who earn only the minimum wage, or who depend on social security allowances, but it is not realistic to compare the circumstances of today with those surrounding ordinary men, women and children in pre-20th-century Cardiganshire. Some were born to poverty, some had poverty thrust upon them, some declined into poverty. Injury or sickness could reduce the best of workmen to sudden indigence; a fire at home might destroy the tools on which he depended for his living. A valued horse's unexpected death was a severe crisis to a travelling craftsman. Bereavement, especially the loss of a husband, could bring destitution in its wake for widow and children if remarriage were not possible. All such circumstances drove people onto parish relief. Old age did not mean retirement; men and women worked till they could work no more, and then depended on their relations or the parish. A seduced unmarried girl might find herself pregnant and workless, tempted to kill her baby, as did Jane Evan of Cardigan in 1661, and many others from time to time. A small farmer in debt might have mortgaged his lands and have to give up all hope of passing them to his son, as John Thomas Llewelyn of Caron was forced to do in 1609, abandoning his land to the wealthy

THE awful nature of the poorest housing has been well summarised by Brian Howells: 'they were mostly mud-walled, with thatched roofs kept together with hay-rope bandages and wattle-and-daub chimneys. Often they consisted only of a simple room open to the roof . . . sometimes [having] a *crogloft* or cockloft.' Water came from a stream or well; sanitation and any form of privacy were non-existent. The worst conditions of all existed in the *tai unnos*, thrown up overnight, and only improved with the passage of time and the barest minimum of resources.

Stedmans from whom the mortgage moneys, spent by the time of his death, had come. Some poor folk might benefit from charitable gifts bequeathed by the wealthier, often to be divided among the virtuous poor of a parish as loaves of bread. Most of the wealthy, however, left little or nothing to charity; indeed, the miserliness of the great majority of the rich over the centuries is not sufficiently noticed by historians. Charity, of course, begins at home.

Mud-walled cottage at Penrhyn-coch, now demolished.

The Hearth Tax records of the 1670s suggest that at least a quarter of the population of Cardiganshire lived in what was then regarded as poverty; today we should be utterly appalled by their conditions of life. Admittedly the Poor Laws were intended to temper the wind to shorn and sick lambs; every parish had to appoint overseers of the poor, who raised a poor rate on landholders and eked it out to claimants with the consent of the ratepayers. Cardiganshire records of payment to the poor hardly exist before 1700; those which survive from the 18th century show that women formed the large majority of the poorest folk, as has always been the case. All sorts and conditions of people came before the vestry meetings where their fates were allotted; the lame, the blind, the aged, the sick, the pregnant unmarried and the subsequent illegitimate babies, the mentally handicapped like 'Evan the Idiot' of Lampeter, who in late 18th-century Lampeter was moved annually from farm to farm, with a warning that he should not be abused. A family man forced to serve in the militia would ask the vestry to pay for a substitute, which they would willingly do, so that his wife and children would not come on the parish, although it might cost £20. Handicapped or aged adults would receive a small allowance; babies and idiots might be farmed out, which must have been a grim prospect for most. Children who survived until the age of seven would be apprenticed, and then disappear from record. Pregnant unmarried women would be brought before a JP to swear to the paternity of their child, or despatched to their home parishes, while the fathers would be pursued, often ineffectually, to secure marriage or maintenance. In the mid-18th century at least one parish, Llanwenog, anticipated later developments by building a 'poor-house' which lasted until the Lampeter workhouse was erected.

All kinds of petty problems might come before a parish vestry. Discharged soldiers and sailors on their way home could claim maintenance for a night. Corpses of vagrants had to be buried. Medicines could be provided; in 1788 Lampeter vestry paid the cost of bringing sea water which it was felt might cure the cobbler's apprentice of an unspecified ailment, an early Cardiganshire acknowledgement of the newly popular medicinal use of sea water. In 1803 the vestry paid for a man to seek help in a London hospital. In 1800 Thomas Evan, a cobbler or saddler, was given money to buy leather so that he could pursue his craft. The vestry was responsible for paying for the slaughter of vermin – crows, foxes and moles: Lampeter paid out ten shillings for three foxes in 1793. George Eyre Evans, who spent much time reading the county's parish records, noted that when an orphan child at Mwnt was put out to a wet-nurse, it was the nurse's husband who was paid for the service.

One method of avoiding the disaster of poverty was to join a friendly society. Their history goes back in Wales to 1744, and the first in Cardiganshire were founded at Sgubor y Coed (1760) and Esgair-mwyn (1765). Alun Eurig Davies traced at least 34 such societies in the county. Llandysul boasted *Cymdeithas Gyfeillgar Tyssul Sant*, *Cymdeithas Fuddiannol Llandyssul*, *Cymdeithas Gyfeillgar Christmasia*, *Cymdeithas Fuddiannol y Cilgwyn* as well as the Good Templars and the Afon Teifi Lodge of the Order of Ancient Britons. Cardigan had its 'Friendly Society of Tradesmen and Inhabitants of the County-Town of Cardigan and the Neighbourhood thereof', founded in 1770, and many others. Emma Lile has investigated the Aberystwyth societies in some detail, among them the Society of Gentlemen, the Ancient Britons, the Padarn Fawr Society and the Husbandry Society. They usually met in public houses, and their economic purpose was to ensure payment of sickness benefit and funeral costs out of regular subscriptions. But they served another purpose, that of giving social status to working-class men, who might parade through their town behind a brass band carrying a huge banner, or wear the uniform of the Oddfellows, a national movement with four lodges in Aberystwyth. There were a few societies intended for women, such as the Princess Victoria Female Benefit Society; Aberystwyth also had a branch of the Girls' Friendly Society. All societies insisted on standards of moral behaviour; drunkenness or (in the women's societies) unmarried pregnancy led to suspension or expulsion with forfeiture of previous payments.

By the end of the 18th century the county's population was growing rapidly, and therefore the number of poor and incapable also grew. Inflation caused by the wars with France from 1793 onwards proved an ever-increasing burden on ratepayers, and corn prices rose, leading to riots at Aberystwyth in 1795, when lead miners broke into storehouses to carry away the corn they needed to survive. Poverty was like an endemic disease; so was inflation. Early in the 18th century ten pounds a year had sufficed to meet the expenses of Lampeter vestry; by 1780 it was fifty pounds a year, in 1795 it was a hundred pounds a year, and in 1812 it had reached the extraordinary figure of £395. By the 1820s poverty in Cardiganshire was a grim spectacle, not unlike the 'congested districts' of western Ireland. The increasing number of travellers in Wales, both from England and farther off, were struck by Welsh poverty, and particularly by poverty in Cardiganshire. The earthen cottages so common through the county were described as 'the worst mansions for human beings this side of the Tweed'. The poorer farmers were hardly better off than their labourers. In 1817 David Williams, squire of Bronmeuric, who worked energetically for the benefit of the poor, wrote that: 'The poor are attempting to prolong life by swallowing barley meal and water – boiling nettles etc . . . hundreds have been in the constant habit of begging from door to door . . . I fear half the labouring poor will perish as things are, before next harvest.'

Cottages at Pontsaeson between Cross Inn and Trefilan.

Responses to this grim state of affairs were varied. Young women (*merched y gerddi*) walked to London and Surrey, knitting as they went, to work in gardens there, returning at the end of the season. Domestic service, the most usual employment for girls, could, as Jill Barber has shown, lead to considerable suffering at the hands of abusing employers, including forced sexual intercourse (see Chapter 10). Men crossed the mountains to seek temporary farm employment, or moved south to the industrial valleys, sending money home to their families, a practice which continued into living memory; in the 1921 census 1,449 Cardiganshire men were recorded as working in the coal mines of south Wales. Some men and women worked at home producing yarn and cloth; others built the squatters' *tai unnos* described above while local officials turned a blind eye, since with a little land the squatters would not be a drain on the parish. Even a farm servant who had struck a bargain with a farmer at one of the annual fairs for a year's employment was not always safe; one farmer near Cardigan,

EMIGRATION figures by parish for migration to the U.S.A. were calculated by Bob Owen. Between 1831 and 1851, he counted 4,101 Cardiganshire people who had moved directly to the U.S. Among the contributory parishes were Llangeitho (321), Llanbadarn Fawr (311), Llan-non (225), Blaenpennal (215), Llanrhystud (159), Llangwyryfon (144), Cilcennin (129), Llannarth (125), cylch Tal-y-bont (113) and Lledrod (102).

who had so savagely beaten his farmhand that the man had run away, then prosecuted him for breach of contract, but was exposed in court for the brute that he was.

A more drastic remedy than squatting or temporary movement was temporary or permanent migration. Welsh people had of course been moving to England for centuries. The prospects for advancement might attract them, or maybe the prospect of escape from the restrictions of their supportive but tight-knit communities. In the 17th century some had been taken as bond-servants to the West Indian sugar plantations; Bob Owen identified at least thirty such from Cardiganshire among those of Welsh origin; one was a twelve-year-old boy who could hardly have given informed consent for what was virtually kidnapping into slavery. Others had crossed the Atlantic to escape from religious intolerance or to seek a better life. Thomas Johnes of Hafod commented in 1801 that 'vast emigrations are going to America from this County; we can but ill spare them.' The post-war depression of 1815 onwards drove a wave of Welsh people westwards, including some from Cardiganshire. Thomas Davies of Cardigan organised a voyage from the port to New Brunswick, Canada, in 1819, and the brig *Active* carried some 200 emigrants through a frightful storm on a six-week voyage which resulted in the successful foundation of the settlement of Cardigan. (Incidentally, the origins of Cardigan in Victoria, Australia, are not known to me as yet). The 1840s saw another strong movement to the United States, and by 1862 public meetings were being held in the county to discuss the Patagonia project, but most of the 1,865 emigrants were from north Wales.

Dr Anne Knowles has analysed 19th-century Welsh emigration in great detail, and has demonstrated how Cardiganshire men, with or followed by their families, tended to choose from three destinations: London (where, as mentioned in Chapter 11, many became involved in milk retailing), Merthyr Tudful (largely for the iron industry) and abroad. Overseas emigration sometimes followed an earlier move to south Wales or London. London maintained a flourishing Cardiganshire Society, whose annual handbook for 1933-34 contains the names of seven hundred subscribers. There was even a Ceredigion masonic lodge. Of the overseas destinations, the USA was the most popular, particularly Ohio, and especially from mid-Cardiganshire and Mynydd Bach; many of these folk sailed directly from Cardiganshire ports, others from Liverpool, while others had moved first to Merthyr Tudful, but were then attracted overseas. There they tended to occupy land in a not dissimilar pattern to that of their home society, and created, although only for a few generations, chapel-centred communities like those they had left behind. Among the descendants of emigrant Cardis were Harriet Beecher Stowe and Frank Lloyd Wright.

Although there were many emigrants to the USA from other parts of Wales, it is not surprising that the first handbook for Welsh migrants was the work of a Cardi, Edward Jones, who emigrated to Cincinatti in 1831; he published his *Teithiwr Americanaidd* at Aberystwyth in 1837. He was familiar with the state of Ohio, and promoted the counties of Jackson and Gallia, which became major centres for Welsh migrants, especially from Cardiganshire's Mynydd Bach, largely as a result of his efforts.

THE 1901 Census for Llanddewi Aberarth gives an example of a family who returned from America. David Williams and his wife Jane, both 45, both born in the parish, were then farming Pantyronen. Their 15-year-old son Albert had been born in Minnesota, U.S.A., while younger children aged 10, 6 and 5 had been born in Aber-arth. *Atgofion Ruth Mynachlog* (1939) describes a scene at Liverpool docks in 1879. Owen Evans of Mydroilyn and his wife set sail for America without one of their younger children, who resolutely refused to part from his uncle, and returned to relatives in Cardiganshire. My thanks to Mrs Auronwy James for these references.

A number of emigrants eventually returned to Cardiganshire, a reflux which has not yet been investigated; it may have been the result of a failure to thrive in the new environment, or simply *hiraeth*. The 1881 Census shows thirty people living in Cardiganshire who had been born in the USA, of whom some were apparently returnees or the children of returnees; others were American women who had married Welshmen, while several were clearly not of Welsh origin, like Eugenie Fleury, aged 19, who was employed as a live-in governess at the Bridge Street girls' boarding school at 26-27 Bridge Street, Aberystwyth, run by Elizabeth Jones, wife of the University College registrar, Evan Penllyn Jones.

The rapid growth of the British population in the 19th century meant that the old Poor Law system had become totally inadequate; the new Poor Law of 1834 laid down that counties should be divided into Unions, and in 1837 five were formed in Cardiganshire: Aberystwyth, Tregaron, Lampeter, Aberaeron and Cardigan (which included 17 Pembrokeshire parishes); there was vocal opposition to the new law, but no organised movement. Boards of Guardians were elected by ratepayers and property owners, and in Cardiganshire their membership was dominated by farmers or clergymen, though the first chairmen in four Unions of the five were landed gentlemen. Sir Edmund Head, an assistant commissioner for Cardiganshire answerable to the government, commented that 'the smallness of the farms in Cardiganshire and the poverty of the tenants creates a sort of common interest prospectively at least between them and the paupers.' Relations between the government's commissioners and the Cardiganshire Guardians were often difficult, especially in the case of Tregaron. The Welsh language, seen as a hindrance to communication, took some of the blame from the civil servants; the civil servant Nassau Senior referred to 'the misfortune of a distinct language'. The unpaid Guardians for their part resented the salaries paid to their officials, of whom there were 82 in the county by 1850.

The Poor Act of 1834 was an attempt to impose uniformity across Britain, which was sheer folly. The conditions in Manchester and Merthyr Tudful, with their pullulating industrial populations, were totally different from those in Rhaeadr and Tregaron, tiny centres of thinly scattered populations. The creation of such barracks and their administration in the countryside was far more expensive than the use of outdoor relief. The Act also had the unfortunate effect of virtually relieving fathers of illegitimate children from the likelihood of paying maintenance. It laid down squarely that 'a bastard should be what Providence appears to have ordained that it should be, a burden on its mother' – a barely veiled affirmation that women bear Eve's responsibility for the Fall of Man. It was not enough that a mother swore to a man's paternity; she needed witnesses, who were naturally reluctant, even if they could be found. It is of course true that prior to 1834 an unscrupulous woman might lie on oath, but the virtually complete reversal of legal responsibility drove women to abandonment and infanticide. Deserted wives could likewise be pressed into the loathed workhouse, rather than be given assistance to find employment, as Grace Hagen has shown was the case in south-west Wales. Misery and squalor, not to mention violent men, pursued poor women throughout the 19th century and into the 20th.

The Guardians were given the oversight of paid staff, the relieving officers, clerks, medical officers, and masters and matrons of the workhouses which the Boards were responsible for building. Workhouses were opened in Aberaeron (1839), Cardigan (1840) and Aberystwyth (1841); Tregaron and Lampeter were extremely laggard, only providing workhouses in 1876 after decades of nagging by the authorities. In fact, only the severest cases were accommodated in the workhouses, which were much too large; most paupers, of whom the great majority were aged over 70, continued for some time to receive outdoor relief as if no law had been passed – on occasion for reasons which the commissioners deplored, as when relief was paid in Llanilar to 'Thomas Roberts towards hay for his cow £1.12s.6d'. The Tregaron Union accounts for 1855 show that relief, usually between one and five shillings a week, was being paid to 389 named individuals, eleven married couples and three other family pairs. Relief was also given to 29 named individuals in other unions and 127 unnamed vagrants. The payments for the year totalled £1183.12s.11d. Of the named individuals, eighty per cent were women (mostly widows), further proof, if more were needed, of how women suffered severe economic injustice if they had no male partner, and since men died younger than women then as now, many women could expect to end their lives on the parish.

The decline in the county's population from mid-century brought a reduction of pressure on the system, and changes of government policy at the turn of the century began its break-up; social reforms such as labour exchanges and unemployment insurance, followed by the old-age pension, were in turn followed by the closures of the workhouses at Aberaeron (1914) and Tregaron (1915), both of which eventually became hospitals, with Aberaeron's 'cottage hospital' under county council management. The others survived until the National Assistance Act of 1948 under the official title of Public Assistance Institutions. Cardigan workhouse was eventually adapted as a block of flats.

The workhouses only dealt with a small minority of the poor, mostly those who were too helpless to survive outside an institution. With the growth in the 19th

The abandoned Aberystwyth workhouse, before demolition. [Ceredigion County Library]

century of government and council involvement in social care, with the increasing coverage of all aspects of life in local newspapers, the miserable lives of the wretched of the earth can be traced in Victorian and modern Cardiganshire. Here a farm hovel with only one bed shared by the farmer and his daughter pregnant by her father, there an urban hovel without fire or light and a man's corpse on the floor; the *Welsh Gazette*, the *Cambrian News* and the *Cardigan and Tivy-side Advertiser* carried many such stories, and the latter two titles continue to carry stories of violence and abuse when they occur.

Health and Sickness

The story of disease and death in Cardiganshire has barely been touched upon by historians, for the good reason that at least before 1800 there is little material. A few unconnected details may survive; for example, it is known that a piece of land at Ystrad Meurig was set aside for the use of medieval lepers; this is all the more likely in that Ystrad Meurig belonged to the Knights of St John of the Hospital at Jerusalem, well known for their nursing skills. Nantycleifion ('the sick people's stream') still flows by the site of the nunnery at Llanllŷr, and in the parish of

Llandygwydd is Ffynnon Gripil, whose name suggests one source of healing for the sick and maimed. The medieval hospital at Cardigan has already been mentioned.

Causes of fatalities are only known in the case of inquests on sudden deaths; numerous verdicts of coroners' juries survive before 1830 in the records of the Court of Great Sessions. David Howells has written of the fearful outbreaks of disease in 18th-century Wales; Lampeter was affected in 1738 and Aberystwyth in 1743, probably by smallpox. In 1796, wrote a correspondent from Llanbadarn Fawr, 'upwards of six score little ones were buried of the small pox at Llanbadarn since it came to the neighbourhood – besides the great numbers buried elsewhere.' These flashes of information are candles in the darkness of our ignorance. Even in the case of the wealthiest gentry it is rare for a cause of death to be noted; the *Gentleman's Magazine* recorded in 1780 that the Revd Dr William Powell of Nanteos had dropped dead in a London street, but whether it was a stroke or a heart attack that killed him is not known; incidentally he was not a doctor of medicine but of civil law. Deaths in childbirth might be inferred by relating burials of young women to christenings or subsequent infant funerals, but this is not an easy task.

Nor has the early history of medical practice in the county yet been traced. Though there were certainly doctors in Aberystwyth and Cardigan before 1800, the majority of the population would have used home remedies or turned to the local *dyn hysbys* ('cunning man'); before the establishment of the Medical Register in 1858 anyone could practise as a doctor. Folk remedies survived into the 20th century; it was widely believed that a child suffering from rickets could be cured by cutting its ear! In 1827 the Lampeter Board of Guardians negotiated with local medical practitioners to provide medicines and surgical appliances ('except trusses'). By 1840 they were inviting doctors to tender for contracts to provide midwifery services and surgical operations. However a visiting inspector in 1841

The Tregaron Board of Guardians, all male, though the majority of their charges were women and children. [Ceredigion County Library]

was appalled by the lack of services and by the payment of money to a single doctor even though he was incapacitated by gout. In 1840 the law required Guardians to provide vaccination, but Tregaron Union resisted this requirement stoutly, as they resisted much else; it was common practice for many meetings (not only at Tregaron) to be postponed in order to discover whether other Unions were taking action or not.

Inevitably it was Aberystwyth, as the largest town, that was best served. By 1834 there were two dispensaries in the town, both in Great Darkgate Street, and several doctors are known by name. The most interesting was Dr Richard Williams, who built a bath-house near the north end of the promenade on the site once known as Penbryndioddef, now occupied by a shelter; his building can be seen in early photographs. This provided sea-water bathing without the effort of entering the sea. The Aberystwyth Infirmary and Cardiganshire General Hospital was opened in 1838, and occupied several sites in succession before settling at North Road in new buildings which were begun in 1885 and extended in 1923 and 1939. The word 'infirmary' had by then been dropped from the title. A separate maternity building administered by the hospital was opened in Caradog Road in 1934. An isolation facility was established first in 1911 on Tan-y-bwlch beach near the bridge over the Ystwyth, and administered by Aberystwyth council. It was quite inadequate, but only in 1946 was Tan-y-bwlch mansion bought as a replacement, and quickly brought into use during the 1946 Aberystwyth outbreak of typhoid described below.

LIFE in Cardigan's Mwldan slum has been graphically described by Idris Mathias, born in Foundry Court in 1924 and growing up in appalling conditions in a three-roomed house. 'To the outsider, Mwldan may be a place of magic; a romantic, legendary place breathing sea breezes carried in on the Teifi flood: to me it was hell on earth.' However, he tells the story of his childhood with Rabelaisian relish, despite the frightful experiences, in his book, *Last of the Mwldan*. The slum was cleared in 1937.

Cholera, the terrifying intestinal disease which could by supper time kill a man who had been healthy at breakfast, firmly links together the problems of poverty and ill-health. Crowded housing and water sources polluted by cesspits were the sources of infection which killed thousands in the mid-19th century; Aberystwyth seems to have been fortunate in avoiding cholera, but cases were reported in Cardigan in 1866, and typhoid was a more frequent visitor to both towns. Scarlet fever killed 36 in Aberystwyth, mostly small children, in a single outbreak in 1872. This is hardly surprising given the insanitary conditions prevailing everywhere, but especially in places like Cardigan's Mwldan slum, horribly polluted by a slaughterhouse, and the courts between Aberystwyth's main streets, by the harbour and in Trefechan.

Although the process of improving municipal government began in 1835, progress was pathetically slow. Town commissioners like those at Aberystwyth kept themselves in power and spent or borrowed as little as was convenient. At Aberystwyth the first sewers were laid in the 1850s, but all kinds of abuses hampered the development of the system, which was only completed (more or less)

An Aberystwyth court in Eastgate Street before remodelling.

Windmill court, Eastgate Street, before remodelling.

in 1925, and meant polluting the sea instead of the land. This revolting practice, common to almost all British seaside towns, ports and resorts, was only ended in the 1990s. The first sewer was laid in Cardigan in the late 1880s, and the town's coverage was only completed in 1939. The development of water reservoirs and mains supplies was equally haphazard both in the towns and across the county. Nevertheless, serious supervision by health officials brought about considerable improvements by 1900.

Pulmonary tuberculosis was the acknowledged scourge of Cardiganshire in the late 19th and early 20th centuries. In the 1920s the death rate for the county was the highest in the land, nearly double that for Wales and England as a whole; the Welsh rural counties, with their poor, dark and damp housing and crowded conditions, were hotbeds of the disease. The Medical Officer, Dr Ernest Jones, commented in 1930 on 'that fear of fresh air so often found among cottagers' which was part of the pattern of infection. The King George V Welsh National Memorial Association was set up by the Welsh county councils to combat the disease, administering chest hospitals throughout Wales, including the Tregaron hospital and sanatoria at Llanybydder and Machynlleth. Improvement began before the advent of new drugs; in 1942 Dr Jones was able to tell the Minister of Health, who was visiting Aberystwyth, that the county death-rate from TB had fallen, though still above the rate for England and Wales; he attributed the improvement to the disappearance of lead-mining.

Tuberculosis was not the county's biggest killer; there were more deaths between 1920 and 1926 from arteriosclerosis (243) and cancer (156), both diseases mostly of the elderly, than TB (120). But it was a debilitating disease which particularly affected and slowly killed the young and middle-aged; it lowered morale, there were no drugs to cure it and sanatorium treatment was expensive, and a cure could take two years. The county's medical staff during the 1920s and '30s struggled to ensure improved milk supplies, cleaner water and better sanitation both in schools and in the county as a whole. It is hard for those without very long memories to realise that in the 1920s the populations not only of farms and villages but of New Quay, Aberaeron, Tregaron and Tal-y-bont drew their water from wells and had no flush toilets; the only sewers were the county's rivers and streams. In 1930 Dr Jones commented on the lack of means of disposing of rubbish, and on the misuse of rivers: 'the banks of the rivers are often made offensive to sight and smell by insanitary deposits.'

Given the general state of medicine and living conditions it is not surprising that the general death-rate among children was high. In 1927 there were 47 child deaths in the county, Dr Jones commenting that they were mostly from poor homes, and many were illegitimate; he remarked particularly on domestic overcrowding, poor sanitation and maternal ignorance of the dietary needs of both mothers and children. In later reports he insisted time after time on the unsuitability of the cottagers' diet of 'white bread and tea', on unwise shopping and rural unwillingness to cultivate vegetable gardens. He claimed that country people had lost touch with the healthy diet of their ancestors, but this seems to have been a romantic view of the past; the grim diet of the rural poor has been briefly described in an earlier chapter. In 1940 Dr Jones was still concerned for the county's children; he reported to the council that 20% were undernourished, and that the county's voluntary scheme for providing school meals was failing. The number of schools in the scheme had dropped from 71 to 42, and of the 35 schools in the Aberystwyth area, only three offered school lunches.

The county's medical services toiled diligently to improve the general state of health. In 1930 there was still a shortage of midwives and district nurses in some areas; the MOH commented, knowing his councillors as he did, that unsuccessful pregnancies were not just a cause of suffering, but represented an economic loss. Similarly he argued that provision of school meals would represent a great saving in later medical expenses. In 1931 the first Schools Dental Officer was appointed, although the need had been obvious decades earlier; in 1915 an earlier MOH had commented that 45% of the county's children had four or more carious teeth. In 1933 the new dentist saw 1,275 child patients and extracted 3,440 teeth, filling another 686; the figure is a comment both on the poor state of child dental health and on the robust methods then current of dealing with the problem, extraction being swifter and cheaper than filling.

The arrival of 1,647 evacuee schoolchildren and mothers with babies at Aberystwyth over the first four days of September 1939 posed a crisis admirably shouldered by both the local communities and the Health staff. The evacuees were from Liverpool, and the city had to lend Cardiganshire four nurses and a dentist to cope with the sudden influx. The MOH commented on the generally poor state of the children's health and their lack of clothing, praising local women for their generosity in ensuring clothes and shoes for those in need. He also remarked on the general improvement in the evacuees' health after six months in sea and country air.

The awful conditions in which so many of the British population lived before 1939 – poor housing, poor diet, poor water, no adequate medical services – became the targets of post-war governments. Diet was improved for many by wartime and post-war rationing, council housing was greatly extended, water supplies slowly improved (though much sewage was dumped untreated into the sea) and the National Health Service brought improvements to deal with a whole range of problems. Welfare payments were improved and child allowances brought in, which eased many burdens, as briefly surveyed in Chapter 25 below.

* * *

Fear of madness continues to haunt society today, and in the recent past it cast a darker shadow still. There is surely no more alarming Welsh historical writing than Russell Davies's chapter on mental illness and suicide in his study of Carmarthenshire from 1870 to 1920, *Secret Sins*. The very objectivity of his style is all the more effective in describing the fate of hundreds of mentally sick men and women, especially the poor wretches, many Cardis among them, who for all kinds of reasons were locked up in the 'Joint Counties Lunatic Asylum' at Carmarthen, opened in 1865, and who once incarcerated were rarely released. In 1899 23% of the inmates were from Cardiganshire. Davies's descriptions of the ways they were treated simply beggar belief. The controlling authorities, both medical and political, had various interests to protect, especially keeping down costs, while shame and ignorance kept the general public from involvement, except as groups of callous spectators. Davies cites a newspaper report of 1908 in which an inmate of the Carmarthen asylum, asked why he laughed, replied, 'I'm laughing at the likes of them being out and the likes of us being in.'

Prior to 1865 society had to deal with lunatics as best it could. Most were kept at home by their relatives, who tried to keep them completely concealed from view or only let out into the garden at night, practices which continued in Anglesey and Ceredigion in the 1960s and '70s (I speak as a witness). 'Village idiots' have long been a well-known feature of the rural scene in European countries, and can be found in the stories of Guy de Maupassant and Caradoc Evans as well as in official documents. For example, 'Evan the Idiot' figures in the Lampeter Vestry Book between 1778 and 1794. An illegitimate child, he was regularly put out to be cared for by the lowest bidder, and in a year when no one was willing to be paid a pound or two for his annual keep, then Evan had to go from house to house, a week at a time. The overseers had to warn that he should not be abused, a sure sign that abuse was happening. He must, one hopes, have been marginally better off than he would have been chained up in the Asylum.

The well-known traditional verdict on suicide, 'while the balance of the mind was disturbed', was a formula to enable the victim to be buried in consecrated ground, since the law used to follow the Christian teaching that suicide is a mortal sin. It certainly links suicide effectively with insanity, and offers a simplistic explanation for an act whose consequences for family and neighbours can be

Cottages at Blaen-plwyf, now demolished.

dreadful. There was a considerable increase in suicides in the late 19th century, conveniently blamed on the stress of industrialised urban life, but suicide in Carmarthenshire was more common in rural than urban districts, and it certainly figured, and alas continues to figure, in rural Ceredigion.

Plenty of reasons were given for individual suicides: disappointment in love and desertion in marriage, unemployment and money worries, religious terror and fears generated by World War I were common motives. But an unquantifiable factor was the dismal quality of so many people's lives which affected both physical and mental health. Davies quotes a government doctor's report to the Privy Council in 1864 that in Welsh farming 'nothing but the sternest frugality can hope to find any gain . . . men and women are going down to the lowest point of strength at which it is possible to live . . . [they are] a debilitated and scrofulous people.' This is not an expression of English detestation or scorn of the Welsh, simply a pointed comment on conditions from which more public commentators in Wales usually averted their eyes, preferring the vision of the whitewashed cottage and the crowded chapel.

Note: 'Miracle Oil'

In 1993 T. Llew Jones and Dafydd Wyn Jones published an intriguing account of the brothers Daniel and John Evans of Ferwig, who during the 1900s became widely known for their 'miracle oil' which was said to have cured hundreds of cancer patients. In 1906 the *Daily Mail* sent a reporter to investigate the phenomenon; he was impressed by their religious sincerity and lack of interest in fame. The *British Medical Journal* did not investigate the claims made for them but denounced them as quacks, while the Cancer Research Committee offered to investigate but on condition that the brothers revealed the recipe for their oil, which they refused to do. Interest had waned by 1910, but John Evans's son Rees knew the recipe, and with the support of the Marquis of Bute and attestations of his success from Marie Corelli and Hannen Swaffer, figures of the day well-known to the public, he was by 1928 practising with success in London. However, a lawsuit against him in 1930 damaged his reputation although he was not found guilty of any fraud. He continued practising in some obscurity until in 1946 the journalist Fyfe Robertson took an interest in him, and in 1950 the *Picture Post* published an account of Evans's remarkably successful work with the 'Cardigan cure' at a hospital in Newark, New Jersey, under the observation of qualified doctors. However, an investigation launched by Aneurin Bevan in 1950, whose results were presented to the House of Commons by the Tory minister Iain Macleod in 1952, was sceptical. It seems that the secret of the Cardigan cure died with Rees Evans in 1959.

21. Counting the People

Just as Ceredigion is a land clearly distinguished from its neighbours by natural boundaries, so there was, as late as the turn of the 20th century, a fairly distinct population. In 1901 nine inhabitants of every ten had been born in Cardiganshire, a situation which was to change drastically during the next ten decades. This does not mean that the whole population had ever been static. We have seen in an earlier chapter that there was considerable population movement and replacement during the Norman incursions, including attempts at replacing the native population with Flemish and other settlers. Merchants and miners had arrived from England and beyond in the 17th century. In the 18th and 19th centuries there were more influxes of men into the lead-mining districts, though little has yet been done to determine on what scale this happened; in 1881 there were 125 Cornish-born people in Cardiganshire, most but not all connected with the lead-mines. Thirty-seven of them were children who had come with their parents.

IN a study of eleven parishes in north Cardiganshire, G.J. Lewis showed that 'in 1851 only 21 per cent of the adult population was born within the parish of residence. A further 26 per cent had moved within the eleven parishes under study, and 42 per cent from a series of surrounding parishes… Only 9.5 per cent came from outside north Cardiganshire.' Farmers and traders were the most sedentary, professional men (teachers, policemen, ministers of religion) the most mobile. Lewis attributes the increasing mobility of the population after 1871 to improved literacy (people could read advertisements), higher wages (to be able to buy newspapers and eventually purchase bicycles) and more leisure time, enabling would-be lovers to travel further.

As well as migration, there was also movement within the county in search of employment and land tenure. With the growth of population and land hunger in the period 1780-1840 many people moved onto waste land and set up their *tai unnos*, many of which were later abandoned; their ruins or replacements can be seen above Ysbyty Ystwyth and in many places on the rougher hill-lands which nobody had previously been cultivating with any enthusiasm. A successful tenant farmer might seek a larger holding, and even if he were to obtain it on the same estate, the change could mean crossing parish boundaries. Marriage too was frequently across parish boundaries, but rarely at any considerable distance, since frequent travel for the purpose of courting was usually impossible. The result would be that, though the bride would be married in her own parish, she would then move to live with her husband.

Such was the shortage of employment that there was also temporary emigration; *merched y gerddi*, the travelling garden-women, some bringing their children, would walk from mid-Cardiganshire along the drovers' roads to the market-gardens round London for several months and then return; some might be fortunate enough to find more permanent employment in domestic service, while others may have formed lasting relationships or even returned pregnant. Men would spend months or years in the mining valleys of the south before returning. Some came back from London; even some of those who took the giant leap of emigration to America returned home. Boys and men from the coastal parishes went to sea, where many died. Some returned home to retirement, others must have stayed away permanently.

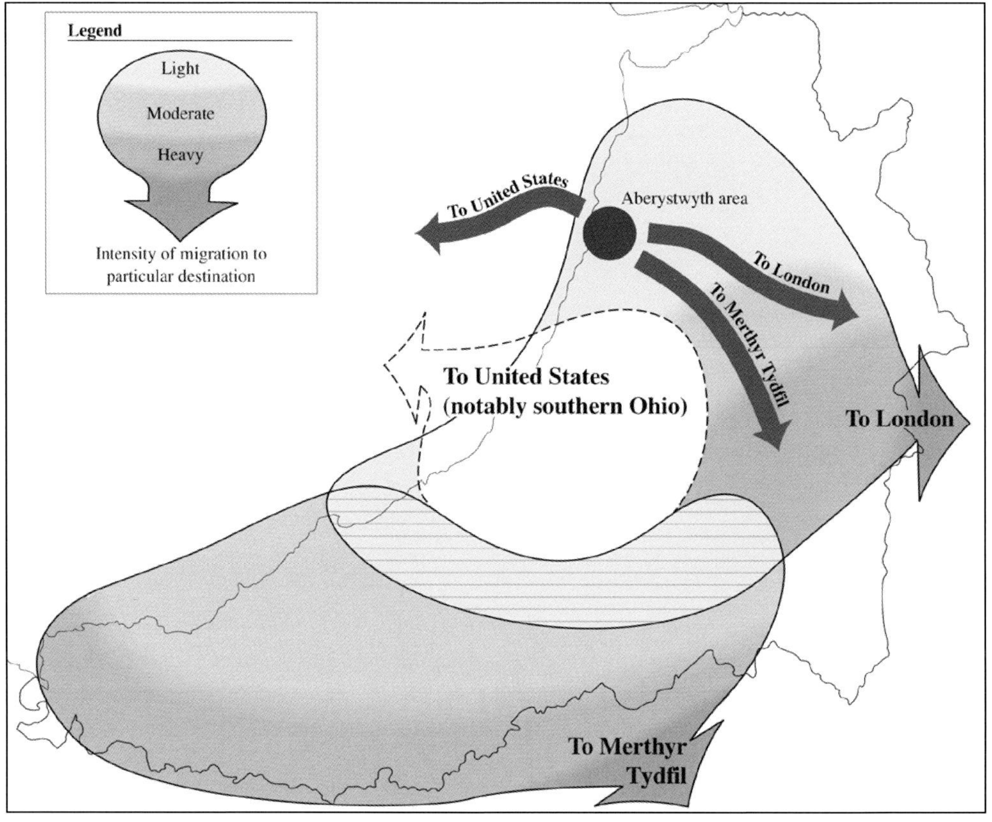

Schematic map demonstrating the destinations of Ceredigion emigrants *c*1835-50, by Anne Kelly Knowles.

[Courtesy of the Chicago University Press]

Before the first census of Britain was held in 1801 our knowledge of the kingdom's population is vague. Unfortunately it is even more vague for Wales, where the kind of documentation which could be used to estimate the population during the historical period is in short supply – and especially short for Cardiganshire. The first means of attempting a crude guess at the population of Cardiganshire comes from Bishop Richard Davies's returns for the diocese of St David's for 1563. He estimated the number of families in the county as 3,483. In 1720 Emanuel Bowen's *Britannia Depicta* of 1720 offers a figure of 'above 3163' houses, which seems to suggest little change from the 1,563 number of households. Even if we accept that as a reasonable estimate of the number of households, everything depends on the number we reckon as an average household or family. The Davies-Bowen figures suggest a rather low population figure, perhaps 20,000, but given that the Census figure of 1801 was 42,956, the figure at 1720 must surely have been nearer 30,000. Much of the rest of this section of the chapter is an elementary summary of the work of J.W. Aitchison and Harold Carter.

The census is inherently unreliable; it is usually reckoned that there may be a 10% margin of error in the early 19th-century figures, and margins of error and distortion certainly remain to the present day. A small population like that of Ceredigion is especially open to distortion, as will be seen below; this makes comparisons from decade to decade difficult. For example, in the 1891 census a larger area was included within the county than was normal either before or since. The 1921 census shows a temporary reversal of the decline which lasted from the high point of 1871 (74,000) to the low point of 1951 (53,000); this was apparently because in that year it was held in the summer rather than the spring, so that the numerous visitors to the county's resorts were included. The slight increase in population in 1961 may have been due to the capital works at Cwmrheidol, where the hydro-electric scheme was being created, bringing an influx of workers to the county. The startling increase from 1991 to 2001 is at least partly due to the inclusion of Aberystwyth's and Lampeter's student populations; this also distorts other statistics like percentages of the population born outside Wales and the percentage of Welsh-speakers in the county to such an extent that comparisons are almost unsustainable.

Below are simple lists of Census population totals, with figures rounded to the nearest thousand for the sake of clarity:

1801 43,000
1811 53,000 (dramatic increase)
1821 58,000 (the rate of increase has slowed)
1831 65,000 (the rate has increased again)
1841 66,000 (a drastic slow-down in growth)
1851 71,000 (a greater increase)
1861 73,000 (another slow-down)
1871 74,000 (continued slow increase; decline now beginning)

This was a period of rapid growth in the population of Wales and England, but the growth was much slower in rural Wales than in the industrial areas, and several rural counties actually went into decrease from 1851; that Ceredigion did not do so until after 1871 was probably due to the lead industry, which only declined from the 1870s. The slow rate of growth compared with the industrial areas was not for lack of babies; anyone studying the county's rural parish registers for the period 1800-40 when they are fairly inclusive will be impressed by the way births dramatically outweigh deaths; the slowness in growth was of course due to migration.

This had been made clear to me when studying the 19th-century church and census records for the parish of lower Llanfihangel-y-Creuddyn (rural, with little lead-mining); the population according to the census was barely increasing at all, even though births were well ahead of deaths. The simple answer is that people migrated, and that on a large scale; in the 1970s I could trace only two families in the parish which had been there in 1870. It is clear that migration covers a whole geographical spectrum, from movement to the next parish to crossing the Atlantic. An extreme case of outmigration is presented by Ystumtuen, a high mountain hamlet near Ponterwyd. It was the creation of the lead industry, and with the abandoning of the mines the population slowly moved away until in 1960 there was virtually no one in residence at all; the houses were mostly shells. Today however it is once more inhabited, by incomers; population replacement is complete.

Several factors helped inflate the county's natural population increase; the cultivation of potatoes may have been responsible in the earlier decades of the 19th century, and certainly the lead industry's boom decades in the third quarter of the century brought in additional population. But after 1871 the hidden loss of population can no longer be concealed (figures are rounded up or down to the nearest thousand except in the case of 2001):

1871 74,000
1881 71,000
1891 63,000 (a startling drop)
1901 62,000
1911 59,000
1921 61,000 (an anomaly caused by inclusion of summer tourists)
1931 56,000 (this figure should be compared with 1911, not 1921)
1951 53,000
1961 54,000 (small increase)
1971 55,000 (small increase continues)
1981 56,000
1991 61,000
2001 74,941 (grossly inflated by student numbers; see below)

The steady drop after 1871 is simply explained by the catastrophic decline in the lead-mining industry and the continuing decay of agricultural employment under the impact of cheap foreign food and of mechanisation; young people migrated, leaving an ageing population and a declining birth rate. By the last quarter of the 20th century male farm labourers had largely disappeared from the county, as had female farm and domestic servants. The decline between 1931 and 1951 would have been worse without the influx of Polish ex-servicemen and their families, most of whom settled in the Teifi valley (see Chapter 24). The increase in population from 1961 is largely due to the influx of retirees and people from outside Wales seeking escape from the urban rat-race. This increase conceals the continuing loss of the indigenous population, the Cardis, not only by continued out-migration, but because the indigenous birth-rate has for much of the 20th century been exceeded by the death-rate.

The statistics demonstrate a growth in the county's population of 14% between 1991 and 2001, a freak caused by the inclusion for the first time of the student

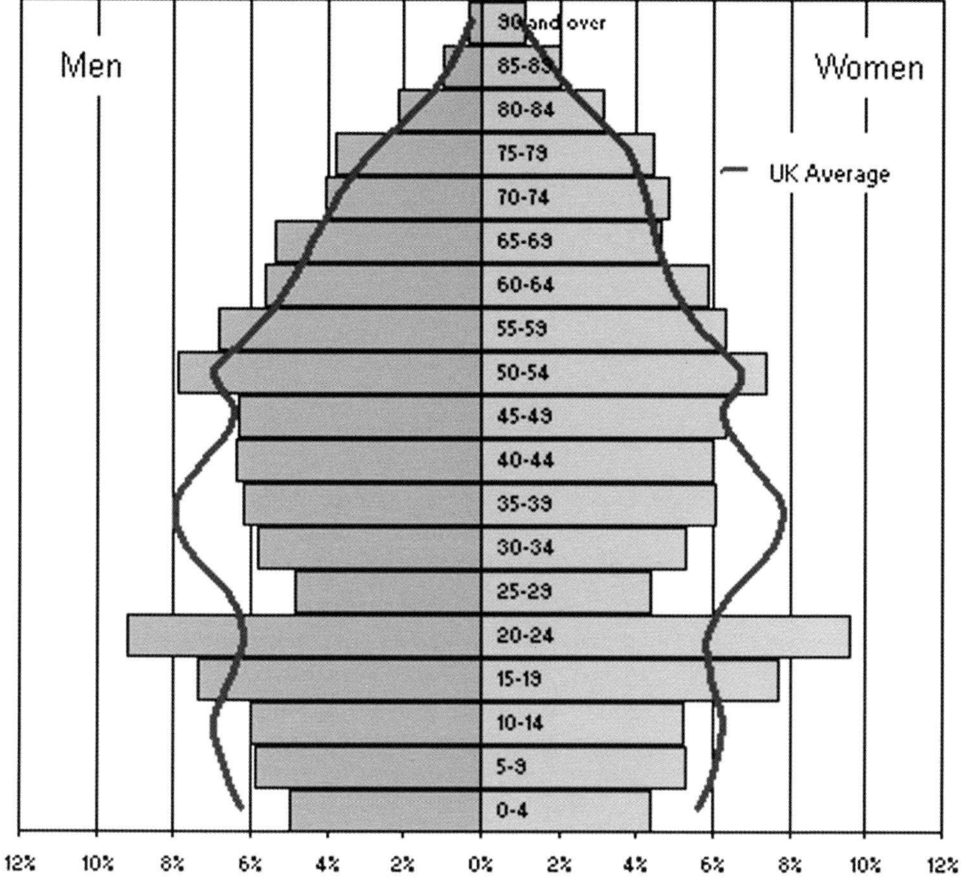

The 2001 Census pyramid for Ceredigion's population; note the effect of the student population in distorting the image.

populations of Aberystwyth and Lampeter. The next-largest increases among Welsh authorities were of 6% in Powys and Monmouthshire, and one may legitimately presume that the real increase in Ceredigion's population was about 6%. As it is, many of the county's 2001 statistics are unreliable. For example, by the 1991 census, 35.6% of the county's population had been born in England; population replacement was well under way. The figure for 2001 indicates that 41.4% were born *outside Wales*, which is not quite the same thing, but is in any case questionable because of the presence of some 6,000 or more students from beyond Offa's Dyke. The accompanying population pyramid shows clearly how difficult the figures are to interpret: there are far more in the 15-19 and 20-24 age groups than would have been counted out of term. This also affects the language figures, discussed below, and indeed the very age-structure purportedly demonstrated by the pyramid. The average age of the Cardi in 2001 was 40, that of the population of Wales and England was 38. But had students been excluded, the average age of the Cardi would have been a good deal higher.

The population pyramid reliably demonstrates an obvious decline in the birth rate, which will seriously affect the county's schools in the next decade. Less obviously, it shows a gender imbalance favouring women. Until recent times this was normal; although 105 boys are born for every 100 girls, it was usual for males to be outnumbered by the end of the second decade of life. It is of course well-known that women also live longer than men and always seem to have done so, even in the days of high maternal mortality while giving birth, so such an imbalance is natural from the age of fifty. However, the Cardiganshire shortfall in male numbers is marked; in six successive censuses it was the highest in England and Wales, and must have affected the birth rate. The explanation in the past seems to be that Cardiganshire men were more likely to be economic migrants than women; for example, there were 2,292 men from the county living in Merthyr Tudful in 1851. There was also temporary migration; men (including married men) would move to the coal-mining valleys and send money back home to their smallholdings, eventually returning themselves. In 1891 there were 14,737 Cardiganshire-born people living in Glamorgan, equivalent to almost a quarter of those still living at home (62,630).

There has of course been much movement within the county, not only in search of tenancies but from the countryside to the towns. The growth of Aberystwyth was not all due to the creation of the University College and the National Library; during the 19th century it became a town with its own critical mass, offering a wide range of employment, much of which was taken up by people moving from the immediate hinterland. After 1960 the popularity of the motor car has made commuting possible, so that the town's residential growth is supplemented by daily travel, some of it for surprising distances. Villages such as Bow Street and Penrhyn-coch have become almost entirely dormitories for Aberystwyth's working population. Less favoured parts of the hinterland – Cwmystwyth, Mynydd Bach, Ystumtuen – have at various times been drastically drained of their populations. Cwmystwyth in particular lost many families (from 1881 with the failure of lead mining) at a time before incomers had started to take over semi-derelict properties; in 1891 a quarter of Cwmystwyth's houses were unoccupied. The pupils of Cwmystwyth school in 1930 made a list of all the empty properties in the district; by 1990 only one had been rehabilitated and was in use. Many such properties were on land so marginal, so swept by rain and mist, that they had no attraction for anyone; such ruins are typical of the areas which had first been inhabited by the squatters who built the *tai unnos* between 1750 and 1850 at the time of land-hunger. Anne Knowles has drawn attention to the reluctance of these *pobl yr ymylon*, the marginal folk of rural north Cardiganshire, to surrender their grip on the little land that they owned, preferring seasonal to permanent migration whenever possible, turning their hands to whatever mite of additional income they might gain. One of the many difficulties of understanding the Census returns of the past is that people could only declare one source of income (miner, farmer, servant, etc.), though many were multi-skilled. As Knowles points out, these survival strategies which were intended to maintain a rural, land- and family-based way of life, actually bought into industrial and consumer capitalism.

The social historian David Jenkins, writing in 1949, showed how complex were relationships and identities in the communities of south Cardiganshire. Beginning with population statistics, he examined the people of Aber-porth, showing a complex of local loyalties. The first loyalty was of course to family, and he indicated how this had been weakened by ongoing emigration from the community, only to be replaced by incomers without any local family ties. Then there were relationships to the local community, in this case Aber-porth itself or to a single farm, and to chapel or public house. This complex of relationships had been severely readjusted with the creation of the Royal Aircraft Establishment, staffed largely by incomers (*pobol dwad*) rather than locals (*pobol y lle*). Jenkins further distinguished between two lifestyles, *buchedd A* and *buchedd B*; the first group lived through the Welsh language and chapel, observed Sunday and tended to avoid public houses, were thrifty and pursued education. The second group, of course, tended away from those identifying marks.

The late Emrys Jones made a similar study of Tregaron, emphasising – as did David Jenkins – the importance of religion and the Welsh language in the community. Using population statistics, he was able to show how different from the rest of the population were the ages of first marriage and the gender imbalance. Age of marriage was much later: 25% of men and 15% of women married after the age of 35, compared with figures for England and Wales of 7% and 4% respectively. These two studies of communities in the county, one a coastal village, the other a small market town, are no longer valid as descriptions of Aber-porth and Tregaron today, but they are wonderful reminders of how much has changed since 1950 in the population and social organisation of Ceredigion communities.

The Welsh Language in Ceredigion

Prior to the census of 1891 no direct and comprehensive attempt was made to ascertain the status of the Welsh language in Wales. Russell Davies has offered for south-west Wales a valuable survey of the travellers' accounts, of the religious statistics, and of the 'Blue Books' of 1847 insofar as they bear on the language. The evidence suggests that, on the whole, Cardiganshire was overwhelmingly Welsh-speaking. It is however hard to agree with Davies's claim, based on the 1851 Religious Census, that : 'Within Cardiganshire, no church held English-only services, nineteen conducted bilingual services and in sixty-nine the language of worship was Welsh.' In

STRANGE numerals in oral use in the county were published in 1924 by David Thomas, as used by elderly men in south Cardiganshire; one series began *în, tô, târ, câr* . . . Thomas believed them to be a survival from the days of post-Roman Irish settlement, and was supported in his belief by the great Norwegian Celticist Alf Sommerfelt. Later Thomas found another version in Goginan. However the Irish scholar David Greene has shown that they cannot be ancient, but probably derive from migrant Irish workers of the 18th or early 19th century employed to count sheep. Many of these workers would have been monoglot Irish-speakers.

fact the religious census says little about the language of services, but Ieuan Gwynedd Jones and David Williams, the editors, included language statements based on a parliamentary return of 1850 entitled 'Numbers of Services performed in each Church and Chapel in Wales'. The return shows that English-only services were held every Sunday in Cardigan and in St Michael's Aberystwyth (two English services and one Welsh in both) while Llanafan and Llanllwchaearn had two services in Welsh and one in English; Llangoedmor and Llandygwydd churches had one service in English and one in Welsh. Clearly Aberystwyth and Cardigan had considerable pockets of English speakers, and English services might be expected in a parish like Llanafan, home of Lord Lisburne. Davies's otherwise excellent general account of the evidence for anglicisation, and the forces working on its behalf, reminds us of the mobility even of pre-railway rural people, of their commercial contacts and of the importance of the maritime communities. There were always travellers, both tourist and commercial. Outsiders came to the county's fairs to sell their goods. With the increasing speed of movement and of contact, mass-produced goods with English labels, promoted almost always by English advertisements, were filling the shops. Some aspects of anglicisation are a little bizarre; why did Welsh farmers give their horses English names and their cows Welsh ones? Why were the fishing-boats of Aberystwyth in 1700 all named in English?

Despite the overwhelming prevalence of Welsh in Cardiganshire during the 18th and 19th century, there is an interesting difference between the status of Welsh as a *written* language in south-west Wales and in north-west Wales. From 1700 onwards some Welshmen were willing to write probate documents, especially wills and inventories, in Welsh. They only represent roughly half of one per cent of the probate documents in the National Library, but whereas in the diocese of Bangor there are 772 sets of documents with one or more in Welsh, in St David's there are only 85, and of those, only 22 are from Cardiganshire, fewer than the 35 from the parish of Llanfaelog, Anglesey. Moreover, but for the efforts of one man, Thomas Harry of Cardigan, the number would be even smaller; he wrote four wills for Cardigan men and two for Mwnt between 1789 and 1813. Unfortunately I have not been able to find out anything about him. Moreover, though Harry's use of Welsh is competent enough, there is nothing in the Cardiganshire Welsh wills (only one inventory survives) comparable to the vigour and confidence of the language in scores of the Bangor documents. Why this should be, in a county which otherwise has produced more than its share of Welsh-language poets, prose-writers and scholars, is not easily understood, except in the context of a long tradition of popular uncertainty in south Wales generally about the status of formal Welsh, compared with a greater northern readiness to acknowledge the language, a readiness which continues to the present day.

Patriots have often put much responsibility for anglicisation on the shoulders of the Welsh gentry, and it is true that their desire for social contact with their English equivalents, their desire for English education, their seeking after English heiresses, their hopes of obtaining high office, their desire to appoint non-Welsh gamekeepers for obvious reasons, and other factors, all meant that by 1800 the majority of the

Welsh gentry, even in Cardiganshire, had either abandoned the Welsh language or used it as a second language to communicate with lesser folk. That did not necessarily mean absolute contempt for the language, and some actually learnt it; the sixth earl of Lisburne learnt Welsh and insisted that his funeral (in 1889) should be entirely in Welsh. Sir Marteine Lloyd of Bronwydd (d.1937) was well-known for his efforts to speak Welsh. But the role of the Cardiganshire gentry in anglicising the county was as nothing compared with the slowly developing power of commerce, education and government, to which must be added the processes of in- and out-migration and intermarriage. In 1800 it is reasonable to suppose not only that the vast majority of Cardiganshire people were monoglot Welsh-speakers, but that English interfered little in their daily lives. However it must be remembered that the 1818 government report on the education of the poor claimed: 'The Cambro-British is an expiring language, and it were fortunate for Wales if they had but one language . . . the ancient Britons [!] are very partial to the English tongue.' Certainly by 1900 the 50% monoglot speakers would have been well aware of the pressure of English, particularly as they themselves were an ageing group; two decades of compulsory education had put English in the way of the younger generation, aided by all the forces of modernisation. As Russell Davies says, 'British society began to take precedence over local society'; inevitably the new British language began to displace the old British tongue.

Studies of Aberystwyth by Robert Smith and of Tregaron by Gwenfair Parry illuminate the life of the Welsh language in two very different Cardiganshire communities in 1891. Aberystwyth, despite its vigorous Welsh chapel and cultural life, was the Cardiganshire community with the highest percentage of monoglot English-speakers (always remembering that such terms are subjective) at 21%. Already, however, children aged 2-5 were 26% English monoglot. Given the forces of education and commerce, given the fact that governance and public life were conducted largely in English, given the English newspapers which reported town and county life, it is obvious that English in Aberystwyth was well-placed for growth. In 1891 13% of the town's population had been born beyond Offa's Dyke. Few of these had serious incentives to learn Welsh; if they picked it up, all well and good, but there were no classes for those who might have been persuaded to learn. Features still well-known in Welsh society are evident from the data: in 44% of homes where one parent was monoglot English, the children are recorded as monoglot English. Only in four homes where both parents spoke English only are the children recorded as being able to speak Welsh. There was no learning of Welsh in school and little on the street. There were several centres where English was absolutely dominant: the Cambrian Railway company deliberately employed English-speaking staff, the military barracks was overwhelmingly anglophone, as were the homes of some of the University College staff – where incidentally English was the only medium of instruction – while the children of a number of the Welsh-speaking clergy and ministers are recorded as monoglot English.

Tregaron with its environs was almost as different from Aberystwyth in 1891 as it is today. Although the little town functioned successfully as a commercial centre, the area was not economically flourishing; the woollen trade was past its best, the lead industry had collapsed and agriculture was not as strong as it had been. While Aberystwyth was growing; Tregaron was losing population to emigration. It was a thoroughly Welsh community; 99% of the population spoke Welsh, 83% were monoglot Welsh. A significant number of men in the district worked in the lead mines. Especially interesting are the 48 individuals who had moved to the area having been born beyond Offa's Dyke. Twenty-seven of them spoke Welsh; ten of them were probably children of Welsh migrants to England who had returned to the parental country.

Although Tregaron was overwhelmingly Welsh in speech – in 1891 it was the most Welsh-speaking area in the most Welsh-speaking county in Wales – agents of change already existed in the community. The most drastic was the negative factor of out-migration, but other factors were present. The professional men in the area, the careeer role models, were nearly all bilingual. The rector and his wife were Welsh-speakers, but their children are described as monoglot English; if true, that means that they could not communicate with the majority of the district's children. The figures in this matter are especially interesting. Aberystwyth was the first Welsh area to elect a school board, in 1870; Tregaron's board was forced on it by the government in 1874. By 1891 the children of Tregaron, at least in theory, had had fifteen years' exposure to education which must have been – again, at least in theory – overwhelmingly English. Yet according to the 1891 census, 75% of the children aged 6-14 were monoglot Welsh, and so were 76% of those aged 15-24. This is less surprising since four of the eleven teachers in the area counted themselves monoglot Welsh speakers!

* * *

In 1901, so the census for that year tells us, 93% of the county's population spoke Welsh; 50.4% spoke Welsh only. Census figures of course are suspect for all kind of reasons. People misunderstand questions, people do not always tell the truth. A proportion of the population, by accident or design, never make a census return. The language question is so cut and dried as to cause difficulties of various kinds. What constitutes an ability to speak Welsh or English? In the census all are their own judges of their ability. Attitudes to Welsh have always been complex; some are proud of it, some ashamed, many ambivalent. Then there are difficulties of comparison which face the researcher. Thus the 'Welsh question' was asked for the first time in the 1891 census, but as we have seen, the registration area treated as Cardiganshire was larger than the county as reckoned from 1901 onwards. Moreover in 1891 the language question was asked of all individuals over the age of two; from 1901 it was asked of all over the age of three. So a simple comparison between 1891 and 1901 is impossible; as a matter of interest, the figures for 1891 for the larger unit were 95% Welsh speakers, with 74.4% monoglot Welsh. The apparent *increase* in the percentage of Welsh-speakers between 1921 (82%) and 1931 (87%) is due to the anomaly of the 1921 census described earlier; many holiday-makers on the Cardiganshire coast were from the anthracite coalfield communities.

There is little evidence at the end of the 19th century of serious concern in the county about the future of the language, though the original Welsh Language Society, founded in 1885 by Dan Isaac Davies, whose concern was to ensure the use of the language in the school curriculum ostensibly to improve the teaching of English, had held meetings in the county during the 1880s. But despite the overwhelming percentage of Welsh-speakers at the turn of the 20th century, there were threatening signs of erosion. The school system was overwhelmingly English-medium, largely ignoring not only the language but its culture. This was not a matter of public concern; success in English was seen as essential for 'getting on in the world'. Schools, and the two university colleges, were very willing to employ staff without concern about their ability to speak Welsh; this was part of a more general process by which incomers moved into the county, mainly for employment at this time, later for retirement. Local government and the more remote operations of national government functioned almost entirely in English. Then there were the summer visitors, who spent much time in Aberystwyth, Borth, Aberaeron and some coastal villages, and who had to be catered for in English. The coming first of the railways and, by 1910, of the motor car, made it much easier for them to come, and the railways were more convenient than ships as a way for local young people to leave the county. All this meant that the towns in particular were centres of anglicisation, though the countryside remained overwhelmingly Welsh-speaking.

The decline in the percentage of Welsh-speakers between 1901 (93%) and 1931 (87%) seems quite slow (especially remembering the men who died in the Great War), though at the same time the percentage of monoglots declined from 50% to 20%. The next thirty years, however, saw the rate of decline accelerating; from 87% in 1931 it fell by 1971 to 67% – the decade 1961-71 being particularly damaging. There was a slight deceleration between 1971 and 1991, but it still meant that in 1991 only 59% of the county's population claimed to speak Welsh, of whom a percentage would have been second-language speakers.

The figures for Welsh in the 2001 Census are not easy to compare with those for previous decades. As far as the overall totals and percentages are concerned, they are affected by the inclusion of thousands of students from beyond Offa's Dyke. They are also complicated by a new and complex set of categories, laid out below with figures for Ceredigion's population aged 3+:

1. Understands spoken Welsh only:	5211
2. Speaks Welsh but does not read or write it:	3635
3. Speaks and reads but does not write Welsh:	1990
4. Speaks reads and writes Welsh:	32147
5. Other combinations of skills:	1652

The inclusion of category 1 for the first time meant that 44,635 or 61.2% of the population claimed (or admitted) some skill in Welsh. John Aitchison and Harold Carter's 2004 analysis of the language figures for Wales points out some apparent paradoxes. That figure of 61.2 is larger than the 59.1% who claimed in 1991 to be

Welsh-speakers, but we are not comparing like with like. Aitchison and Carter compare the totals of categories 2-5, very reasonably defining them as 'Welsh-speakers'. The totals for 1991 and 2001 are as follows:

1991: 36026 2001: 37772.

That looks reasonably good for the language, since it represents an increased number of Welsh-speakers. But expressed as percentages of the population the figures are not so good:

1991: 59.1% speak Welsh 2001: 51.8%

Again, we may suspect that the student-surplus of 2001 is at least partly to blame, but any suspicion of complacency must be dismissed. Welsh in Ceredigion is threatened, not only by emigration of Welsh-speakers and immigration of non-Welsh-speakers, not only by intermarriage, but by the declining birthrate so obvious in the population pyramid.

The 20th century had added its own factors to the other threats which had already begun to erode the Welsh language in its heartlands. The two World Wars killed hundreds of Cardiganshire men, of whom the vast majority would have been Welsh-speakers, while teaching English to monoglot Welsh-speakers who survived the ordeal. Migration, temporary or permanent, continued throughout the period. Organised religion slowly lost its appeal, especially to young adults. Tourism continued, with caravan parks partly displacing the use of bed-and-breakfasts, and there was a growth in the number of second homes. First radio and then television brought the linguistic boundary onto almost every hearth. The popular English-medium press had its own impact. Aled G. Jones cites research by Emrys Jones into popular readership in Tregaron, still overwhelmingly Welsh-speaking at the time of the research in the mid-1940s. Between 1920 and 1945 the population's reading matter had shifted significantly from Welsh-language books to English-language periodicals and papers. From the 1960s onwards came a steady stream of incomers, taking part in a process known as counterurbanisation – abandoning urban life for the countryside in areas like Ceredigion. They are not just retirees, but families with young children whose impact on the linguistic situation of the village schools they attended has been dramatic. Aitchison and Carter characterise the out- and in-migration processes as the 'exchange of a Welsh-speaking population for an English one'.

The reaction to this situation has been partly dealt with in discussing education in Chapters 17 and 25. To anticipate, Welsh gained considerable ground in the curriculum of many elementary schools, but remained simply a subject in the secondary schools until the late 1960s, and that is how it remains for the majority of pupils; the bilingual secondary schools at Aberystwyth and Llandysul, and Welsh-medium courses in certain other schools, are largely a holding operation, and they do not even reach every Welsh-speaking pupil, since some parents choose English-medium education for their children.

Aberystwyth was the major centre for anglicisation in the county, but it nevertheless gave birth to several movements which became national in their impact on Wales and the Welsh language. One, the Welsh Language Society, is briefly dealt with in Chapter 25. Two were the creations of Sir Ifan ab Owen Edwards (1895-1970), who was appointed a member of the University College staff in 1921. His remarkable vision of what became Urdd Gobaith Cymru (the Welsh League of Youth), established in 1922, with its headquarters in Aberystwyth, its camps, school and village groups, its annual games, its National Youth Eisteddfod and its continuation of the children's magazines established by his father Sir Owen M. Edwards, played an enormous role in language maintenance among young people; the first permanent Urdd youth camp still flourishes at Llangrannog, making a valuable contribution to employment and the economy. Sir Ifan's second and equally remarkable contribution came in 1939: he saw the impact that a wave of English evacuees would have on the Aberystwyth junior school attended by his son Owen, and created a tiny private school in which Welsh was the medium of teaching. The experiment survived, to be taken over in 1951 by the county's education committee, and from it sprang the whole 'bilingual school' movement which has done so much across Wales in both language maintenance and extension.

22. The Use of Languages: Dialect, Literature and the Press

Far too much Welsh breath has been wasted on the supposed superiority of one dialect of Welsh to another, a debate first noted by Gerald of Wales, who remarked that while some favoured the Welsh of north Wales as the 'best' Welsh, there were others who most appreciated the Welsh of Ceredigion. The discussion has always been futile, since speakers of 'good' Welsh can be found anywhere in Wales, and so can speakers of 'bad' Welsh. Such judgments are often made on the grounds that one region or another has supposedly borrowed fewer English terms; for example, southerners are often condemned for using words such as *danjerus* rather than *peryglus* or *masiwn* not *saer maen*, but such criticisms do not come well from northerners who use *stalwyn* for *march* or *fflïo* for *hedfan*. Every area-dialect borrows English terms; my Ceredigion favourite is found in the north of the county and in Meirionnydd, where 'hedge' is not the usual *perth* or *clawdd*, but *shetin*, from English 'setting', as in 'quickset' meaning a hawthorn hedge, not from 'shut-in' as local folk-etymology has it.

Of course definitions of 'north' Welsh, 'south' Welsh or even 'Ceredigion' Welsh are virtually useless, since there are no clear linguistic boundaries between one region and another. Alan R. Thomas's 1973 atlas of Welsh dialect shows clearly a series of boundaries running in many directions across Wales, separating not only 'north-south' terminology but also sound changes such as the well-known difference between *capal* and *capel*. For Ceredigion Thomas distinguishes two areas; one he calls 'Lower Midlands', covering north Ceredigion as bounded by the Dyfi, Rheidol/Ystwyth and Pumlumon; the other he calls 'Teifi Valley', though it reaches down to Carmarthen. In vocabulary, the Dyfi marks the well-known division between *tadcu* and *taid*, *nawr* and *rwan*, while the rather shaky line between *cadno* and *llwynog*, *da* and *gwartheg*, *gwahadden* and *twrch daear* runs roughly speaking along the Rheidol. The Aeron is the boundary between *pownd* and *pwys*, *hwpo* and *gwthio*. A few words are characteristic (more or less) of the county as a whole, e.g. *lôn fach* for a narrow lane, while others are confined to smaller areas. Thus the delightful *cisys* (< 'kisses') is the Rheidol-Ystwyth word for 'sweets', now alas disappearing; *tropas*

IWAN WMFFRE, in his study of the county's place-names, identifies not two but four separate dialect areas. The smallest is the northernmost tip of the county, where the influence of Powys is strong. Next is 'Penweddigeg', reaching south roughly as far as the Ystwyth fault. The rest of the county divides approximately between south-east (like the Welsh of Carmarthenshire) and south-west, related to the Welsh of north Pembrokeshire. These areas all melt into each other. Wmffre lays emphasis on the weakening of dialect variation, and in his study was only willing to use informants born in or before 1930.

represents 'soot' between New Quay and the Rheidol valley. *Clewyn*, 'a boil', *hether* for 'heifer' and *gwynio* 'to ache' are all characteristic of the north of the county. Cardiganshire dialect provides the excellent term *safati* (literally 'stand to it') for a buttress.

To speak of boundaries in dialect is actually misleading; by and large dialect usages shade into each other, rather than stop and start at a particular line. Moreover the social changes of the past two centuries have greatly affected dialect. Literacy in Welsh has made people aware of 'standard' (usually Biblical) terms, even when they continue to use dialect. Social and mechanical mobility have meant that young people seeking marriage partners have a wider geographical field of choice, and so inevitably the language of the hearth will be a compromise, and thus affect the everyday language of the children. Primary school teachers have a considerable influence on the language of their charges, though I know of no study of this in Ceredigion.

It is well known to scholars that dialect boundaries shift, marking stages of advance and retreat. It will bear repeating that the word *parc* is the standard word, south of New Quay, for a field, but the Aberystwyth suburb-name of Penparcau, and the occurrence of the field-name *Cae Parc* in the Ystwyth valley in the 19th century, show clearly that *parc* was once a standard word as far north as the Rheidol valley. (The English word 'park' incidentally, originally meant simply an enclosed piece of land, hence its Welsh meaning). *Cadno*, the well-known southern word for 'fox', is found in northern Cardiganshire place-names where orally the northern *llwynog* is now the standard term.

Some of the richness of Ceredigion spoken Welsh has been harvested by Huw Evans and Marian Davies, and by Erwyd Howells. It's true that a number of the expressions Howells notes can be found well beyond the county's borders. Two local sayings I can warrant from personal experience. In the Rheidol valley a person who is feeling the cold may say *Ma' 'nwylo i'n siarad Saesneg* ('my hands are talking English'); the explanation is that rubbing cold hands together produces a sibilant sound reminiscent of a language – English – where to Welsh ears the sound of 's' is much more evident than it is in Welsh. A serious village scandal caused so much gossip that a village senior was provoked to say to me *Bydd ci arall â'i gynffon ar dân wthnos nesa* – 'there'll be another dog with its tail on fire next week'. It is deeply to be regretted that the profound stresses the Welsh language is now enduring threaten not just its existence but the verbal variety and creativity which makes it so wonderfully rich.

This linguistic richness was for centuries the medium for a tradition of story-telling, folk-song and ballad-singing now virtually extinct. Llinos M. Davies's *Crochan Ceredigion* is a collection of folktales from Cardiganshire sources about the fairies, corpse-candles and phantom funerals, about witches and cunning men, about giants and mermaids. Intermingled with these in her collection are stories from literary sources, some of which have already been cited in earlier chapters of this volume.

The best-known of Cardiganshire's ballads was *Morgan Jones o'r Dolau Gwyrddion*, Dolau Gwyrddion being a farm west of Lampeter on the A475 to

TAITH Y CARDI

O Landyssul i Lundain.

Yn ystod pa un y daeth i gyffyrddiad a'r WIDW FACH LAN.

Arall-eiriad o'r " Charming Young Widow."

I LIVE in Llandyssul, yn Shir Aberteifi,
A letter inform me my uncle wass ded—
To ask me in a minet to go up to Llundain,
As canoedd o bunau was left me, twass said ;
So I wass determin to go on my shwrne,
And booko my ticket—first class I was fain !
But if I wass go third-class I wass never engounter
The Widw Fach Lân I wass see in the train !

Y Widw and me side by side sit together,
In the carredge wass no one but us and no more,
Distawrwydd wass broken by my purty companion,
Who ask me the time by the watch I wass wore ;
Wrth gwrs I wass tell her, and then conversashwn
Wass speaking between us, yndeed, till my brain
Wass go on the bendro, — 'ro'wn i bron myn'd yn wallgof
Gyda'r Widw Fach Lân I wass see in the train.

She wass so taliedd I venter to ask her
How old wass the child she wass have on her brest ;
" Ah ! sir, " she wass say, and she did llefain shockin
And the plentyn she carry to her bosom she prest,
" When you speak of my child I'm quite brokenhearted—
His father, my husband, Oh ! my heart breaks with pain ; "

— 1 —

A favourite Cardiganshire ballad, printed by J.D. Lewis, Llandysul, *c*1900.

Llanwnnen. It tells a typically tragic story of the ill-fated love between Morgan Jones and Mary Watkin, whose father forbids their marriage; she dies in Morgan's arms, and he expires soon after, so the two are buried in the same grave. The ballad's author, blind Dafydd Jones of Dolau Bach, Llanybydder (1803-68), only a few miles from Dolau Gwyrddion, was one of the most productive of 19th-century Welsh ballad-singers. Years after his death people remembered him as a tall man in a serge hat, guided by his daughter, with a strong but sweet voice. Evan Jones has listed a number of Cardiganshire ballad-writers: Stephen Jones of Aberystwyth, Dafydd Rice of Cefnmabws (who fought at Trafalgar in 1805), Joel Rowland of Blaen-plwyf, John Morgans of Brynyrychen and Benjamin Evans of Aberaeron. Cardiganshire ballads commemorate accidents in the lead mines, the great storm of 1846, and comically describe an outing to Aberystwyth in an excursion train. A few individuals continued the tradition of singing ballads after the age of composition had died; the late Bertie Stephens was perhaps the last in the county. The last printer of ballads in the county was J.D. Lewis of Llandysul.

JONATHAN CEREDIG DAVIES (1859-1932) produced a detailed and localised but unscholarly collection of local folklore in his *Folk-Lore of West and Mid-Wales* (Aberystwyth, 1911). This strange man printed the 438 pages of his autobiography on a tiny hand-press at his home in Llanddewibrefi. He wrote a booklet and a novel about Patagonia, which he had visited, and an account of his travels in Australia.

Story-telling, folk-songs and ballad-singing were simply some oral aspects of a rich folk-culture of beliefs, ceremonies and practices which were largely common to the folk-culture of Wales and to a great extent of Western Europe. This is sufficiently evident from Meyrick's introduction to *The History of the County of Cardigan* (1907 edition), which in dealing with 'ancient customs and superstitions now remaining in Cardiganshire' brings together everything he had read about Welsh customs, including bobbing for apples, the *plygain* (carol singing early on Christmas morning), corpse candles, vigils for the dead and marriage customs, none of which are or were peculiar to Cardiganshire. At least two wedding customs lasted into the 20th century. One was firing off guns, which led to a tragedy at Beulah in 1916 when a bride on her way to her wedding was shot dead by a 16-year-old lad mishandling his father's gun. Much less harmful was the custom, which may yet survive, of children hindering a bride's progress to church by holding a rope across the road until they are paid. The phantom funeral is known in Cardiganshire as the *toili*, which does not simply indicate the local pronunciation of *teulu* ('a family'), but refers to *Teulu Gwyn ap Nudd*, as I was assured by the late Bedwyr Lewis Jones. *Teulu* originally meant 'war-band' or bodyguard, and since Gwyn ap Nudd was king of the fairies a vision of the *toili* was a doubly alarming event for those who experienced it.

A much earlier source than Meyrick for Cardiganshire superstitions is *The Certainty of the World of the Spirits* by the Shropshire divine Richard Baxter, printed in 1691. In it he published letters from John Davis, vicar of Genau'r Glyn, who had seen corpse-candles at Llanrhystud, and from the Puritan John Lewis of

Glasgrug, who had been warned of the future death of his child. Easier of access are the general studies of Welsh folklore and custom by T.Gwynn Jones, Evan Isaac and Trefor Owen listed at the end of this chapter. T. Gwynn Jones includes a good deal of Cardiganshire material in his book, which is not surprising since he was working in Aberystwyth and had many contacts to provide him with material about the cunning men still operating in the county, and about recent cases of witchcraft and of folk-healing. Volumes of parish history may include chapters on folklore and custom, as in *Hanes Plwyf Llandysul* by W.J. Davies (Llandysul, 1896). One feature of folk-culture which seems completely absent from surviving information about Cardiganshire is dancing; Welsh dance seems to have been valued for longer in the east and south-east than in west Wales. And what would one not give to hear Francis Thomas, 'the blind crowder of Cardigan', playing his *crwth*.

* * *

Ceredigion has made a centuries' long contribution to Welsh literature. Earlier chapters of this book deal briefly with aspects of the earlier literature produced in Ceredigion: the involvement of Rhuddlan Teifi (Highmead) in the fourth branch of the *Four Branches of the Mabinogi*, the *Chronicle of the Princes*, the poetry of Rhygyfarch, of Dafydd ap Gwilym, the family of Parc Rhydderch and the visits of poets from elsewhere to praise the families of Tywyn and Gogerddan. Since Dafydd ap Gwilym was acknowledged during his own lifetime as a supremely gifted and influential poet, and given the visits to country houses already mentioned, it seems strange that Cardiganshire should only have produced two poets of note during the later medieval period. One, Ieuan ap Rhydderch, has already been referred to in Chapter 8 above; the other was Deio ab Ieuan Ddu, who flourished between 1440 and 1480. To judge from his twenty surviving poems, he travelled from *plas* to *plas* mostly within Cardiganshire praising their owners in the traditional manner, but there also survives his 'Satire on the Thief who Stole the Bard's Cattle', while his most interesting *cywydd* is that describing a journey through the county from commote to commote, beginning in the south and passing through Gwynionydd, Glyn Aeron, Anhuniog, Mefenydd, Creuddyn, Perfedd and Genau'r Glyn, naming many of the ancestor-figures of each district. Deio may have been from Perfedd commote himself, and according to tradition was buried at Llangynfelyn.

Although later poets from elsewhere continued to visit the county, after the death of Deio ab Ieuan Ddu there seems in Cardiganshire to be a virtual and inexplicable absence of the kind of local poets who during the late 16th and early 17th centuries continued elsewhere in Wales to maintain the traditional *cynghanedd* and the *cywydd* and *englyn* forms, lasting in some areas long after the disappearance of what we would call the full-time professional poets. Glamorgan, Flintshire, Caernarfonshire, Anglesey and Merionethshire continued to produce such work well into the 18th century, after which it was given new life in the revamped eisteddfodau of 1789 onward. Instead Cardiganshire, and in particular the Teifi valley, became a vigorous literary centre for prose rather than poetry.

It would be overbold to claim for this literary activity the title of Enlightenment, that great movement of intellect which spread through Western Europe during the 18th century. Nevertheless some spark of that cast of mind may be detected in the development of theology in Wales and particularly in Cardiganshire, which ran through Arminianism towards Arianism and eventually Unitarianism. It is also to be detected in the work of that obscure figure Simon Thomas of Cilgwyn, Llangybi, who published *Hanes y Byd a'i Amseroedd* ('A History of the World and its Times') in 1718, with a second edition in 1724 under the title *Llyfr Gwybodaeth y Cymro* ('The Welshman's Book of Knowledge'). This was the first miniscule attempt in Welsh to interest readers in the nature of the universe and the discoveries of the great English scientists, and was reprinted several times. The classicizing aspect of the Enlightenment is to be glimpsed not only in the educational work of Edward Richard of Ystrad Meurig, but in his poetry, particularly his exercises in pastoral.

James Davies, better known as Iaco ap Dewi (1648-1722) was another early figure of importance in the Teifi valley group of writers – they can hardly be called a 'school'. Born in Llandysul, he seems to have been trained as a copyist, and he applied himself to the copying of Welsh manuscripts, living alone in almost hermit-like conditions. He was familiar with *cynghanedd*, though his few efforts at poetry are insignificant, but he and his fellow scholar Samuel Williams copied, in National Library of Wales Llanstephan manuscript 133, one of the most important collections of poetry of the earlier centuries. He scraped at least part of his living by translating religious texts into Welsh, eight of which were published. Whereas Iaco ap Dewi was a dissenter, Samuel Williams of Llandyfrïog (*c*1660 – *c*1722) was a priest who became rector of Llangynllo. He copied numerous manuscripts of earlier Welsh literature and translated a number of religious works from English to Welsh, but none was published. He composed some of the Teifi valley carols known as *halsingod* and published the only collection to appear in print, in 1718. Figures like Iaco ap Dewi and Samuel Williams represent a bridging point in Welsh culture between the era of the manuscript and the age of printing. Copying manuscripts remained important in a country without public libraries, cheap publishing and mass literacy.

Samuel Williams is less well known than his son Moses Williams (1685-1742), already mentioned in Chapter 16 above, for his work in promoting the Welsh Bible. Born in Cellan parish, Moses Williams had been an assistant at Oxford to Edward Lhuyd, the great polymath who, in spite of his Cardiganshire mother, cannot rightly be considered part of the tradition of Cardiganshire culture. Williams became a priest after Lhuyd's death, and from 1715 to 1732 held livings at Llanwenog and Defynnog (Breconshire). Apart from his extensive religious publications, he produced a remarkable bibliography of Welsh printed books in 1717 and was responsible for the first printed edition of the Laws of Hywel Dda (1730). He had hoped to publish a major collection of early Welsh literature and other works of importance, including the Welsh Triads, but lack of patronage hindered his efforts, though he was an admired friend of some of the great English scholars of his day, and can be claimed as an Enlightenment figure.

Another major figure in the Teifi valley literary circle was Theophilus Evans (1693-1767), of Penywenallt, near Newcastle Emlyn. He spent time as curate to Moses Williams at Defynnog before his appointment as vicar of Llandyfrïog in 1722 and then a series of livings in Breconshire. Apart from his religious publications, his literary ambition was the promotion of the glories of the Welsh past, which he achieved in the extraordinary *Drych y Prif Oesoedd* ('A Mirror of the First Ages'), published in 1716 and greatly enlarged in 1740, with numerous later reprints, including an English translation first published in the USA in 1834. He borrowed as fact from Geoffrey of Monmouth the myth of the Trojan origin of the British people before moving to the Roman and Saxon invasions. The 'Treachery of the Long Knives' figures prominently, as does King Arthur; the author then leaps past the laws of Hywel Dda to Llywelyn the Last and the Morals of the Welsh with barely time to draw breath before beginning a second part setting out in a highly tendentious manner the history of Christianity in Britain. This extraordinary farrago, in lively Welsh, was not surprisingly much more popular and influential among the Welsh people than the solemn English of William Wynne's 1697 *History of Wales* or William Warrington's 1786 *History of Wales*, and it continued to be reprinted into the 19th century.

Much more scholarly was the work of William Gambold (1672-1728) of Cardigan, who after graduating at Oxford, where he knew Edward Lhuyd, returned to Wales to be vicar of Puncheston, north Pembrokeshire. He worked zealously on a Welsh dictionary, but could not find support to publish it; however, his *Grammar of the Welsh Language* (1727) was only the second book in the English language to be published in Wales, and the first grammar of Welsh to be published in English.

Isaac Carter's pioneer press commemorated at Adpar.

David Davis of Castell Hywel has already been mentioned in Chapter 17 for his work in education. Born near Llangybi and pupil of the fine Baptist historian Joshua Thomas, Davis was a minor but genuine Enlightenment figure, who sympathised with the French Revolution and who, at a meeting in Birmingham after the mob's destruction of Joseph Priestley's house and laboratory, proposed a motion condemning the vandalism. As a poet, Davis was long remembered for his Welsh translation of Thomas Gray's 'Elegy in a Country Churchyard', and his fine chain of *englynion* to the ruined mansion of Peterwell. His poetry, including a translation of one of Sappho's best-known love lyrics, was published in *Telyn Dewi* in 1824, with many reprints, the last in 1927.

With so much literary activity in the area, it is less surprising than it might otherwise seem that the first legitimate Welsh printing press was set up in 1718 by Isaac Carter at Adpar on the north bank of the Teifi, a symbolic event that is rightly commemorated by a memorial there, though after four years Carter sensibly moved to Carmarthen, the largest town in Wales at the time, which eventually replaced Shrewsbury as the most important centre for printing and publishing Welsh books. One way of publishing was for the author to secure subscribers who would pay at least part of the cost of the book beforehand, thus enabling the printer to engage in the work; sometimes lists of subscribers' names appear in the volume. The minor gentry of the Teifi valley were still sufficiently Welsh in language and interest to sponsor publication of worthy books; thus Walter Lloyd of Coedmor and Stephen Parry of Noyadd Trevawr ensured the appearance of Alban Thomas's translation *Dwysfawr Rym Buchedd Grefyddol* (1722).

Although many of the prose writers described above could turn out verses in *cynghanedd*, carols and hymns, the writing of verse was largely left to others. That verse was being composed in the area in the early 18th century is evident from what little is known of Evan Griffith of Tŵr-gwyn, Troed-yr-aur, who in 1701 ventured to an eisteddfod held in a tavern at Machynlleth, where his work was soundly drubbed by poets from Gwynedd. Another who preferred verse to prose was Siencyn Thomas (1690-1762) of Llechryd, a bootmaker-poet and dissenting preacher from Bryngwyn in south Cardiganshire. Siencyn's printed work, which includes a delightful poem in praise of Youth, is in the free metres, not *cynghanedd*, but his son John Jenkin (1716-96) studied the strict metres, attended an eisteddfod at Llanidloes and was at least partly responsible for an eisteddfod at Cardigan in 1773. He was a prolific versifier; some of his work is typical of Welsh 'occasional' poetry: 'A Song to wish Success to the new Ship *Hebog*', 'A Song asking for a Periwig for an Old Man', as well as a number of elegies.

Literary activity was of course not confined to the Teifi valley. Evan Thomas Rhys of Llwyndafydd (*c*1710 – *c*1770) was another poet and bootmaker; he had the posthumous good fortune to be included (under the name Evan Thomas) in the *Oxford Book of Welsh Verse* thanks to his savage epigram addressed to the gentlewoman who had impounded his goat, likening its beard to that of her mother and its horns to those of her father (implying that she was a bastard). His work was collected together seventy years after his death in *Diliau'r Awen* (1842); like the epigram already described, it is essentially verse for occasions. He lampoons the great preacher Daniel Rowland for displacing Jesus from his throne in favour of Prejudice, and when widowed, rejects in an *englyn* the advice of his friends to marry a young lass, preferring a woman who's already had her family, and who'll look after him well. The subscribers' list includes a wide social sweep: ships' captains from New Quay figure alongside carpenters, an auctioneer, an ironmonger, two publicans, a tanner, several shipwrights, numerous clerics and the squires of Pigeonsford and Llanina.

This tradition of versification was widespread throughout the southern half of the county. The Aeron valley produced poets throughout the 19th century, of whom the best known was Cerngoch (John Jenkins, 1820-94), brother of Joseph Jenkins the 'Welsh Swagman' mentioned in Chapter 19; they were great-nephews of David Davis of Castell Hywel. He farmed Penbryn-mawr on the Llanllŷr estate, and his verse was in the 'occasional' tradition of Evan Thomas Rhys; neither man saw his verses printed in his lifetime, but their wit and aptness made them well-known orally. Indeed, some of Cerngoch's bawdy work has never been printed, but remained known locally well into the 20th century.

Works by the earlier poets named above had already been collected together many years after their deaths in a substantial volume, *Blodau Dyfed* (1824), by one of a new generation, Daniel Evans (1792-1846), better known as Daniel Ddu o Geredigion. The volume contains work largely by Cardiganshire men, but its publication was due mainly to the support of Carmarthenshire subscribers. The book includes several poems by the greatest of Cardiganshire's 18th-century men-of-letters, Evan Evans, Ieuan Fardd (1731-88). From Cynhawdre, Swyddffynnon, Ieuan was born in what seems, at least in retrospect, to have been an area of the county entirely devoid of poets other than his schoolmaster Edward Richard and Richard's friend Lewis Morris (1701-65). Ieuan's training in *cynghanedd* and the traditional metres was entirely due to Morris, who brought his bardic learning from his native Anglesey, but did not share it widely in his adopted county; indeed, adopted is not the right word, for with very few exceptions Morris despised the *Teifisiaid* (Cardis) almost as much as he detested *plant Alis* (the English). His pupil Ieuan was a fluent classical scholar, but an early addiction to the bottle meant that his efforts to achieve promotion in the Church from humble curacies were always bound to fail. It did not however hinder him from copying many important Welsh literary manuscripts, and from corresponding with leading Welsh and English scholars of the day.

Ieuan's greatest single contribution to Welsh culture was his remarkable trilingual volume *Some Specimens of the Poetry of the Antient Welsh Bards* (1764), setting out in print for the first time examples of the poetry of Aneirin, Taliesin and the poets of the Welsh princes. Instead of the romanticising falsifications of Macpherson's *Ossian*, Ieuan adhered firmly to his originals. His poetry is less valuable, but his *cywydd* expressing his longing for his own land is remarkable not only for its invocation of the beauty of the river Teifi, but for its address to Wales as a whole, praising its mountains, valleys and rivers in a way no Welsh poet had ever done before; his *englynion* on the court of Ifor Hael, patron of Dafydd ap Gwilym, are among the best-known verses in the Welsh language. Ieuan was not the only Cardiganshire scholar-priest; Thomas

CEREDIGION'S first woman of letters since the Matchless Orinda was Cranogwen (Sarah Jane Rees, 1839-1916) of Llangrannog, teacher of navigation (in which she had practical experience as well as theoretical knowledge) and of sol-fa music. At the Aberystwyth Eisteddfod of 1865 she won a prize for a poem on the subject of the 'Wedding Ring'. She edited the first successful Welsh-language journal for women, *Y Frythones*, and founded *Undeb Dirwestol Merched y De*, the Women's Temperance Movement for South Wales, in 1901 (see also Chapters 10 and 17.

Thomas (1776-1847) rector of Aber-porth, published in 1822 his weightily-titled *Memoirs of Owen Glendower (Owain Glyndwr) with a sketch of the History of the Ancient Britons from the Conquest of Wales by Edward the First, to the Present Time*, in which he includes an account of the 1797 French invasion of Fishguard.

Ieuan Fardd died in wretched poverty at his parental home before the eisteddfod emerged from the back rooms of taverns from 1789 onwards, and while the refurbished festivals held at Corwen, Abergavenny, Carmarthen and elsewhere did a good deal for the prestige of the Welsh language, the standard of poetry was dismal, as exemplified in the dreary work of Daniel Ddu o Geredigion, winner of numerous eisteddfod competitions before he turned critic and eventually committed suicide. For the rest of the 19th century Welsh literature was printed in greater volume than ever before, but with little increase in talent. Literary life, as opposed to real creativity, continued. Among many largely forgotten figures may be mentioned John Jones, 'Ivon' (1820-98; see Chapter 19), grocer, secretary of the Aberystwyth National Eisteddfod of 1865 and friend of Daniel Silvan Evans; they co-edited a popular volume, *Ysten Sioned* (1882). Another leading figure in the town's cultural life was the musician Edward Edwards, Pencerdd Ceredigion (1816-97). There was a similar level of activity in 19th-century Cardigan, embodied in the Cardigan Literary, Scientific and Mechanics Institution, founded in 1847.

Earlier decades of the 19th century had seen the success of provincial eisteddfodau, especially at Abergavenny. With the spread of the railways and journalism, the 'national' eisteddfod movement was getting under way after 1858, and in January 1864 a public meeting in Aberystwyth was held to discuss the proclamation of the eisteddfod for 1865. It was an extremely acrimonious meeting, but Llew Llwyfo carried the day in favour of going ahead. The eisteddfod was organised by John Ivon Jones. Financially it was a success, and

THE story of the many eisteddfodau of Cardiganshire (other than that of 1865) remains to be written. The National returned to Aberystwyth in 1916, 1952 and 1992; to Cardigan in 1942 and 1976, and to Lampeter in 1984. A 'semi-national' at Cardigan in 1909 became Gŵyl Fawr Aberteifi, and flourishes still. Sir David James's Pantyfedwen foundation sponsors two eisteddfodau at Pontrhydfendigaid and Lampeter (founded in 1964 and 1967 respectively). A few of the once-numerous local eisteddfodau continue; the national Cerdd Dant festival is a frequent visitor to the county; the Urdd National Youth Eisteddfod comes less often, but the county's schools are always well-represented wherever it may be held; district and county qualifying meetings are keenly contested.

Forgotten poets of Cardigan.

from Tuesday till Friday the orators and lecturers boomed out their addresses, all in English, in a vast wooden pavilion holding 6,000. Hugh Owen the educationist, an enthusiast for everything the other side of Offa's Dyke, had for the first time foisted his Social Science Section onto the festival. Many were the complaints about the prizes withheld on the classic grounds *Neb yn deilwng* (no one worthy), and there were darker allegations.

The Anglesey poet-priest Nicander (Morris Williams) had entered an ode for the Chair competition; the abrasive adjudicator Caledfryn (William Williams), an uncompromising Congregationalist, withheld the prize. Another priest, Penbryn-born Gwynionydd (Benjamin Williams), who had entered the competition for a biographical dictionary of Cardiganshire worthies, saw the prize go to a fellow-Churchman, Griffith Jones of Caernarfon. Gwynionydd was furious, denouncing the injustice in the press, and both men published their volumes; there is no doubt that the judges were wrong! As for the unending stream of English from the platform, the temperature in the pavilion must have chilled when the fine scholar Ioan Pedr of Bala rose to ask why there was so little Welsh used. Many agreed with him, but no explanation was given, and little changed on the Eisteddfod platform for generations.

Despite the energetic bardic activity described above, the product was transient in value. Scholarship, however, and the drive towards raising the level of education in Wales, benefited hugely from Cardiganshire men. Lewis Edwards of Pwllcenawon, Penllwyn (1809-87) was one of the great educationists of the mid-century; Daniel Silvan Evans (1818-1903) of Llannarth was the finest Welsh lexicographer of the century, and Sir John Rhŷs (1840-1915), born John Rees at Aberceiro, Cwmrheidol, the greatest Celtic scholar of his time. Since the only one of these three to live and work in the county was Silvan Evans, and that only for brief periods, it is unnecessary to pursue their careers in this volume.

The same is true of two later figures: Griffith John Williams (1892-1963) from Cellan, professor of Welsh at the University College of Wales, Cardiff, and the writer-historian William Ambrose Bebb (1894-1955), who though his childhood home was at Gamer Fawr farm beside the B4343 from Pontrhydfendigaid to Tregaron, where he is commemorated, spent his career in Bangor. Halfway between 'natives' and the 'exiles', so to speak, is Thomas Richards (1878-1962) of Tal-y-bont, one of the great Welsh librarians, whose career was wholly spent in Maesteg

THE name of Sir Samuel Rush Meyrick (1783-1848), the first county historian, deserves the greatest respect. He was an English lawyer and antiquary who in 1803 married Mary Parry of Llwyn Hywel, Llanilar, and was cut off by his father. By 1809, aged only 25, he had completed his massive *History and Antiquities of Cardiganshire*. The first half is a useful study of Welsh history and culture, and of mining and agriculture in Cardiganshire, followed by a geographical description of the county. The second half of the book is a gazetteer of the county's parishes and gentry families. The reprint of 1907 includes a number of valuable appendices, listing the county's sheriffs and members of Parliament, and notes on the county families. His other works, on genealogy and medieval armour, are still used by scholars.

and then Bangor but whose volumes of reminiscences about his Cardiganshire childhood deserve mention here. A fully-fledged native was Evan Daniel Jones (1903-1987) of Llangeitho, National Librarian of Wales from 1958 till 1969. Always known as 'E.D.', he was greatly respected for his scholarship and much loved for his unassuming and genial character. His living successors in the world of scholarship are simply too numerous to mention.

To move from scholarship back to creative writing, the turn of the 20th century saw a remarkable fissure dividing Cardiganshire's authors. Poets emerged who continued to write in Welsh, and do so to the present day (see below), but creative prose got off to a better start in English than in Welsh. Anne Evans, better known as Allen Raine (1836-1908) was born in Newcastle Emlyn, and was a great-granddaughter of David Davis, Castell Hywel. It was only in the 1890s, when she had made her home in Penbryn, that she was able to publish a series of novels, mostly dealing with life in Wales, some of which were enormously popular – *A Welsh Singer*, *Torn Sails*, *A Welsh Witch* and many others, now largely but not entirely forgotten. Her Welsh-language equivalent, so to speak, was Elizabeth Mary Jones (1877-1953), known as Moelona, and born in Rhydlewis, one of thirteen children. Of her thirty books for adults and children, her *Teulu Bach Nantoer* (1913) became a classic. But whereas Allen Raine and Moelona were lauded for their work, another south Cardiganshire author was vilified when his first volume appeared in 1915.

Allen Raine (Anne Adalisa Puddicombe, neé Evans).
[National Library of Wales]

THE National Library of Wales, one of the last fruits of the national revival of the late 19th century, was sited in Aberystwyth at the insistence of its greatest benefactor, Sir John Williams. It opened modestly in the Assembly Rooms, Laura Place, in 1909 while waiting for seven years for the first of its major buildings to be completed. Apart from the prestige and cultural benefits deriving from the presence of a great library, both town and county profit from the library's employment of nearly three hundred staff and the visits of scholars and members of the public from near and far. A much smaller but valuable collection of books is in the Founder's Library at the University of Wales, Lampeter.

The book was *My People*, a collection of short stories by Caradoc Evans (1878-1945). Although born south of the Teifi, he spent his childhood in Rhydlewis and eventually took to journalism in London. *My People* was a savage excoriation of Cardiganshire village life, caricaturing in particular the relationship between community and chapel, savaging the status-seeking money-grubbing hypocrisy of ministers and elders. The book was followed by several more volumes of equally vigorous short stories and a number of less successful novels. The Welsh raised howls of protest at *My People*, not only for the matter but the language of his stories. Evans invented a peculiar Anglo-Welsh patois of his own, such as was never spoken anywhere in Wales; it seems at first glance or hearing (his stories read aloud particularly well) like a combination of literally translated Welsh and a Welsh form of Biblical English, but many of the most colourful expressions are of his own devising. Despite all the protest he returned to live in the county and eked out a penniless existence in New Cross; he lies buried in Horeb chapel cemetery.

The National Library before 1937 [postcard source].

Another great Anglo-Welsh writer had a lesser association with Cardiganshire, but since it influenced his work, Dylan Thomas (1914-1953) should be mentioned here. Although his most popular work, *Under Milk Wood*, is most often associated with Laugharne in Carmarthenshire, the descriptions of Llareggub village are at least partly reminiscent of New Quay, where Thomas lived in 1944-45; this is clear from the early sketch 'Quite Early One Morning'. Thomas had previously lived for a while in Tal-sarn. There is now a Ceredigion Dylan Thomas Trail for visitors to follow.

To revert to Welsh-language writing, J.J. Williams of Llandre (1869-1954) and his friend Dewi Morgan of Rhydypennau were both successful poets in the National Eisteddfod, and represent a bridge from Victorianism into the 20th century. Many of the best-known early 20th-century Cardiganshire poets were deeply rooted in their local landscapes; some of them are perceived as belonging to recognised groups, others as outright individualists like Dewi Emrys (David Emrys James, 1881-1952), born at New Quay, buried at Talgarreg. The most influential group was that known as *Beirdd y Mynydd Bach* because of their common origin, but in fact they were very different as men and poets. Edward Prosser Rhys (1900-45) caused something of a sensation in 1924 with his crown-winning Eisteddfod poem *Atgof* (Memory); he worked as an extremely effective journalist and publisher in Aberystwyth until his early death. J.M. Edwards (1903-78), actually born in Llanrhystud rather than on the slopes of Mynydd Bach, spent his career teaching in Barry; he was crowned three times at National Eisteddfodau, and is noted as an early exponent of *vers libre* in Welsh. B.T. Hopkins (1897-1981) passed his lifetime farming at Blaenpennal; he composed in the traditional metres and his fine cywydd, *Rhos Helyg*, celebrates the beauty of the land and the decline of the old rural ways. Another group of poets is known as *Beirdd Ffair Rhos*, whose most influential figure was Evan Jenkins (1895-1959).

There has been a tradition of families of poets in Wales for centuries – several of the poets of the Welsh princes were related, and the 'Phylipiaid' of Ardudwy were particularly productive. But there has never been a family group of poets like *Bois y Cilie*. The blacksmith-farmer-poet Jeremiah Jones (1855-1902) of Cilie farm, Llangrannog, fathered twelve children; six of the seven boys were poets, and several more have emerged in succeeding generations. Their careers, like their writings, were extraordinarily varied, but two must be named, the much-loved figures always known as Isfoel (Dafydd Jones, 1881-1968) and Alun Cilie (Alun Jeremiah Jones,

Poets Gerallt Jones, Isfoel, Dic Jones, Alun Cilie, S.B. Jones, T. Llew Jones and Tydfor.

[Courtesy of T. Llew Jones]

1897-1975). Alun Cilie fostered a group of poets in the Blaen-porth and Llangrannog area, the most distinguished of whom is undoubtedly the farmer-poet-broadcaster Dic Jones (b.1934). Also associated with the family both by marriage and poetry is the prolific T. Llew Jones (b.1915), twice chaired at the National Eisteddfod, and much appreciated by generations of children and young people for his novels and poems. Other poets not related directly to any of these groups and now themselves veterans also emerged in the county, including J.R. Jones of Tal-y-bont, Vernon Jones of Bow Street, John Roderick Rees of Pen-uwch, Donald Evans of Talgarreg and Idris Reynolds of Brynhoffnant. I ask forgiveness of anyone I may have omitted.

In contrast to the above are three figures who stand by themselves. Sarnicol was the pen-name of Thomas Jacob Thomas (1873-1945) of Capel Cynon, Llandysul, a poet whose pen was dipped in acid, the best of modern Welsh epigrammatists. Idwal Jones (1895-1937) of Lampeter was also a humorist, but very different to Sarnicol. His practical jokes and eccentric headship of Devil's Bridge school made him well-known in the small world of west Wales, while his dramatic sketches and popular songs delighted audiences throughout the country; he fell victim to tuberculosis, the curse of generations of Cardiganshire youth. James Kitchener Davies (1902-52), reared on the damp edges of Tregaron bog, then in Banbury and later in Blaengarw, Glamorgan, spent his adult life in the latter county but his childhood experiences in Cardiganshire are vividly, indeed luridly brought to life in his finest dramatic poem, *Meini Gwagedd*. The grim tubercular claustrophobia of the work does not make easy viewing or listening, but nothing better explains what drove thousands to leave the grim subsistence life of the Cardiganshire back-country, even though the author was mourning the passing of a way of life, not rejoicing in its death.

Centenary Memorial of Sarnicol.

In this attempt to outline the literary tradition in Ceredigion, it would be wrong not to refer to those figures from elsewhere who settled in the county either for life or a substantial period. But to claim (while avoiding the names of living persons) that T. Gwynn Jones, Sir Thomas Parry-Williams, Sir Thomas Parry, D. Gwenallt Jones are or were part of that tradition would be folly; nor does the protean figure of Saunders Lewis, who spent his wilderness years in the county, belong to this outline. Aberystwyth's university status has been a magnet to major scholars and writers from elsewhere, and they have enriched the circles in which they moved. But they are national figures not local figures, whereas – to choose a single example – Dic Jones is both a national and local figure as far as Ceredigion is concerned.

Printing and Journalism

Reference has already been made above to the first legitimate printing press in Wales, set up at Adpar by Isaac Carter in 1718. It was an isolated phenomenon, for Carter soon moved to Carmarthen; the county remained printless for the rest of the century. Unique in another way was the first press in north Cardiganshire, established by Thomas Johnes of Hafod in 1803 especially to print his own translations of the great medieval French chroniclers. The work was beautifully done and the books are now collectors' items. The Hafod press was however a forerunner of the Gregynog Press rather than part of the general spread of printing throughout Welsh towns and some villages from the 1780s onwards. Printing had reached Machynlleth in 1789 and Dolgellau in 1798, but Aberystwyth was slow to join the trend. Only in 1809 did John James, bookbinder and minister of Bethel Baptist chapel, set up a press in 47, Bridge Street in partnership with Samuel Williams, who did the actual printing. James sold out to Williams in 1812, who continued printing until his death in 1820, when his wife Esther continued the press, first under her own name, then in partnership with her son Philip from 1847. It was at her press that Aberystwyth's earliest periodicals appeared, the *Hanesydd, neu hyfforddwr misol* (1823) and the *Trysorfa Ieuenctyd* (1828). It may seem strange that it took so long for periodicals to become established in Wales, but apart from stamp duty (repealed in 1855) and the high cost of production and difficulties of distribution, government fears of Jacobinism and Chartism meant that informers were always ready to report publications to the Home Office, and conservative magistrates were equally ready to convict papers accused of publishing subversive or libellous material. Hoaxers were ready to submit items whose truth was difficult to verify. The distribution problem which plagued Welsh publication eased with the coming of the railways, but was never solved in a country lacking a capital city.

Esther Williams's first competition came from John Cox, who began printing in 1824 to a higher standard than the products of the Williams press, and who was favoured by churchmen to do their work. He printed the early Anglo-Welsh novel *The Adventures and Vagaries of Twm Shôn Catti* (1828) by T.J. Llewelyn Prichard. In 1840 he began the first Aberystwyth newspaper of which copies survive, *The Demetian Mirror or Aberystwith Reporter and Visitants' Informant*, chiefly directed

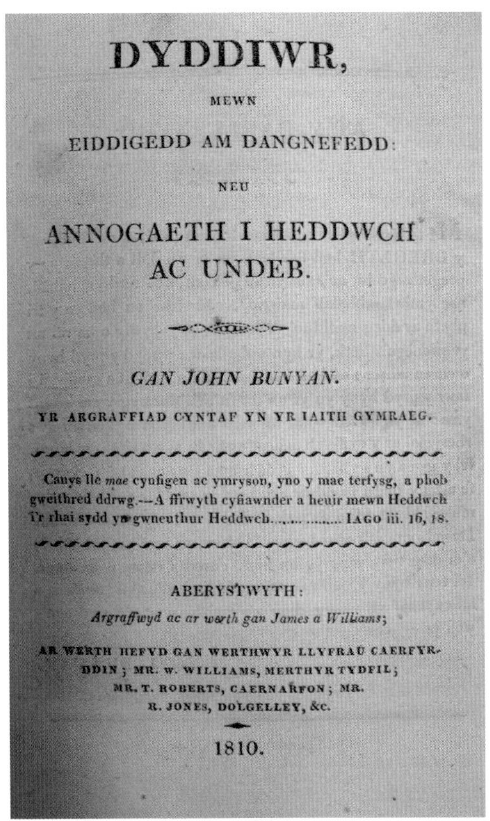

DYDDIWR,

MEWN

EIDDIGEDD AM DANGNEFEDD:

NEU

ANNOGAETH I HEDDWCH AC UNDEB.

GAN JOHN BUNYAN.

YR ARGRAFFIAD CYNTAF YN YR IAITH GYMRAEG.

Canys lle *mae* cynfigen ac ymryson, yno y mae terfysg, a phob gweithred ddrwg.—A ffrwyth cyfiawnder a heuir mewn Heddwch i'r rhai sydd yn gwneuthur Heddwch.............. IAGO iii. 16, 18.

ABERYSTWYTH:

Argraffwyd ac ar werth gan James a Williams;

AR WERTH HEFYD GAN WERTHWYR LLYFRAU CAERFYRDDIN; MR. W. WILLIAMS, MERTHYR TYDFIL; MR. T. ROBERTS, CAERNARFON; MR. R. JONES, DOLGELLEY, &c.

1810.

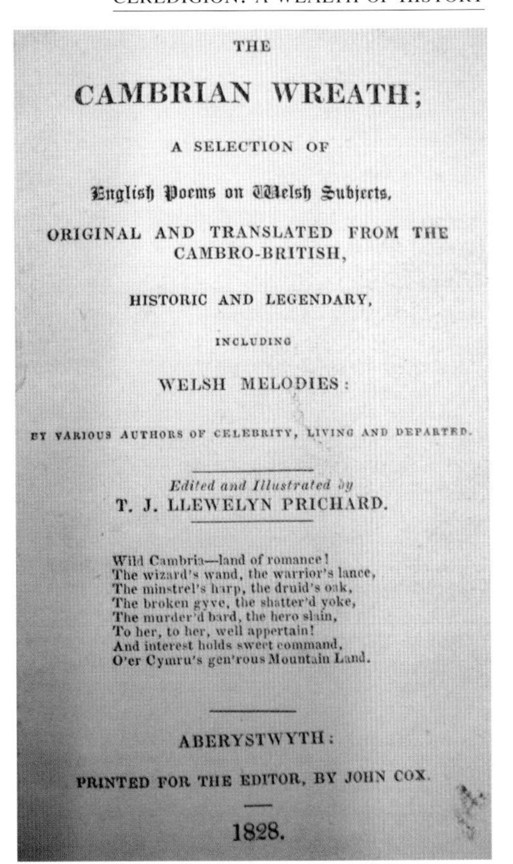

THE

CAMBRIAN WREATH;

A SELECTION OF

English Poems on Welsh Subjects,

ORIGINAL AND TRANSLATED FROM THE CAMBRO-BRITISH,

HISTORIC AND LEGENDARY,

INCLUDING

WELSH MELODIES:

BY VARIOUS AUTHORS OF CELEBRITY, LIVING AND DEPARTED.

Edited and Illustrated by
T. J. LLEWELYN PRICHARD.

Wild Cambria—land of romance!
The wizard's wand, the warrior's lance,
The minstrel's harp, the druid's oak,
The broken gyve, the shatter'd yoke,
The murder'd bard, the hero slain,
To her, to her, well appertain!
And interest holds sweet command,
O'er Cymru's gen'rous Mountain Land.

ABERYSTWYTH:

PRINTED FOR THE EDITOR, BY JOHN COX.

1828.

Examples of early Aberystwyth printing.

to the holiday trade; six numbers were published in August and September, 1840. Among his later publications were two volumes of the adolescent poems of George Powell of Nanteos. He died in 1870, and the press was carried on for three years by two sisters, and then by a former Cox employee until his death in 1881. Another competitor for Esther Williams came in the form of her own nephew Samuel Thomas, who brought the Swansea press of Joseph 'Gomer' Harris to the town in 1828, together with the established periodical *Lleuad yr Oes*. He persuaded the controversial David Owen, 'Brutus', to become its editor, and for a while Brutus kept a school in Llanbadarn Fawr, but both magazine and editor soon moved to Llandovery. In 1839 yet another Aberystwyth press began work, that of David Jenkins who had formerly worked with Esther Williams and then with John Cox. Among his publications was the first attempt at a Welsh musical periodical, *Blodau Cerdd*, the musical work of Ieuan Gwyllt, and the first successful newspaper, the *Aberystwyth Observer*; no early copies apparently survive, but it seems to have begun in January 1859 and continued publication until 1915.

It was the arrival of John Gibson in Aberystwyth in 1873 that transformed journalism in west Wales. The *Cambrian News*, was in origin a Liberal paper published in Bala by the owners of the *Oswestry Advertiser*. Gibson, a Lancaster man of humble origins who had gained printing experience, began work with the Oswestry paper. He soon proved he had journalistic talent, and was sent to Aberystwyth to take charge of the *Cambrian News*, then printed in Bala. His vigorously expressed views on a range of topics soon won him admirers and critics; he was strongly in favour of the Welsh national revival currently in progress, and became a powerful advocate of women's suffrage. He also had a biting sense of humour which often offended local pomposity; after an especially bitter row in 1879 involving prestigious members of the oddly-titled 'Smokey-Faced Club' and abuse of drinking hours which led to a question being asked in the House of Commons, it was agreed that the *Cambrian News* should be bought from the Oswestry owners by Gibson, whose supporters lent him the money to do so, and the paper began to be printed in Aberystwyth in 1880. Gibson continued to campaign energetically for municipal improvements in the town as well as offering pungent and knowledgeable comment on current affairs in general. It was said of him that 'every public man in the counties of Cardigan and Merioneth lived in fear of being dipped in his inkpot.' He was widely respected in the world of British journalism, and was knighted in 1915 shortly before his death. One has only to compare the editorial material of the *Cambrian News* during Gibson's lifetime with that of the contemporary *Cardigan and Tivy-side Advertiser* (a perfectly adequate purveyor of local news) to realise the superiority of the former.

THE DEMETIAN MIRROR;

OR,

Aberystwith Reporter, & Visitants' Informant,

FORMING A

RECORD OF LOCAL EVENTS, AND CHANNEL OF GENERAL INFORMATION.

PUBLISHED AT ABERYSTWITH, EARLY EVERY SATURDAY MORNING, BY J. COX, AT HIS LIBRARY, 30, PIER STREET

VOL. I. No. 1.] SATURDAY, AUGUST 15TH, 1840. [Price 3½d.

ADDRESS.

ANY person who has been accustomed to converse with the intelligent classes of society annually resorting to this rapidly-improving and highly favored Watering Place, must have often heard from them expressions of surprise at the non-existence of any thing like a Newspaper, or medium of communicating public information on matters of local and general interest: whilst others having information which they have felt a desire to convey have had adequate knowledge of our "Sayings and Doings" cannot be acquired and imparted by them; if, therefore, benefit will be derived by a more extended knowledge of our place and its attractions, it will be seen that we, at home, who are interested, must do the work.

By the establishment of this small Weekly Periodical, which is intended as a faithful chronicle of local events, and a vehicle of information to the Visitants, both by Advertisement and otherwise.—the Inhabitants and

POLITICAL OR PARTY DISCUSSIONS will form no part of the Demetian Mirror, though brief reports of what is actually taking place will occasionally be given, without the addition of any tint or shade of colouring whatever. Every effort will be made to render it as attractive as similar Periodicals, by the publication, independently of Advertisements, of any incident or occurrence of interest, in the Town or Neighbourhood; an accurate List of the Arrivals, Departures, and Fashionable Move-

An early Aberystwyth newspaper.

Gibson's independent turn of mind became less and less acceptable to the Liberals who had originally supported the *Cambrian News*; in 1899 George Rees of Lampeter, helped by a number of influential people, set up the *Welsh Gazette* as a competitor. Despite its partly political origins, the paper seems in retrospect to have been most successful in attracting writers on Welsh culture and especially local history. George Eyre Evans and David Samuel, both respected local historians, contributed regularly, and its Welsh-language columns of reminiscences are also useful to latter-day historians. However, the *Gazette* was never as well capitalised as the *Cambrian News*, and it ceased publication in 1964, whereas the *Cambrian News* became an important printing firm as well as the newspaper's publisher. In 1900 Aberystwyth, though not rivalling contemporary Caernarfon, must have been a comparatively exciting place for journalism, with three weekly newpapers (the *Cambrian News*, *Welsh Gazette* and *Aberystwyth Observer*) competing with each other, as well as with the *Cardigan County Times* (published in Welshpool; it was a western version of the *Montgomeryshire Times*) and the *Cardigan Bay Visitor*, published in a wide range of local editions.

To complete the story of Aberystwyth printing and publishing, mention must be made first of the National Library of Wales, which has printed and published a number of books over the years, many of them gems of printing technology, and of E. Prosser Rhys, whose poetry has already figured above. Rhys worked for the *Welsh Gazette* and then in Caernarfon for the *Herald Cymraeg*. He returned to Aberystwyth in 1923 to edit the long-established *Baner ac Amserau Cymru* and to found Gwasg Aberystwyth, setting an extraordinarily high literary standard in his choice of publications, and running the Welsh Books Club, which successfully published some fifty titles.

The development of printing in Cardigan is a little obscure. One Evan Jones printed there in 1815, but virtually nothing is known of him. By 1825 if not before Isaac Thomas was running a jobbing press and began keeping copies of everything printed. By a fine combination of neglect and good fortune news of the survival of this extraordinary archive of ephemera reached the ears of the then recently-appointed National Librarian John Ballinger, and consequently it formed an early and treasured acquisition. Thomas's *Almanac y Cymro* was published from about 1835 till 1940 without a break. His son Owen William Thomas founded *The Cardigan and Tivy-side Advertiser* in 1866; it still flourishes, though printed in Haverfordwest, having seen off several short-lived weekly titles such as the *Cardigan Herald*, the *Cardigan Observer* and the *Cardigan Record*. Owen Thomas's three sons inherited the press one after another, all dying young, and it passed to their sister Margaret in 1916; she died in 1939, ending the family connection.

It was about 1870 that Jenkin Davies began the first press in Lampeter, and he became known as a printer of ballads. Another press, founded about 1880 by T.D. Davies at Caxton Hall, was bought in 1897 by the portentously named 'Welsh Church Press and Printing Company Limited', with much august support. It published the Church magazines *Y Llan* and *Yr Haul*; by 1918 the company had folded, and other printers were found for the periodicals.

Among Cardiganshire printers John David Lewis of Llandysul (1859-1914) is one of the most interesting. He belonged to the breed of country scholars who have not yet entirely disappeared from the county; a passionate bibliophile, he accumulated a fine collection of ballads and local publications, and was very ready to publish good volumes of local history. In 1892 he installed a printing press behind the shop he had inherited from his father and hired a printer from Llannerch-y-medd. By 1901 he had abandoned the general store in favour of bookselling and publishing, usually under the name *Gwasg Gomer*, the Gomerian Press, a last indirect flourishing of the long-held belief that the Welsh language was traceable to the Biblical patriarch Gomer (Cymraeg < Gomer-aeg!). Despite this Baptist connection, the Lewis family have always been at the heart of the Unitarian movement. At J.D. Lewis's death his eldest son Dafydd, joined by his brothers after they had completed war service, continued and expanded the printing and publishing work, including the publication of the cultural periodical *Y Genhinen*. The second World War did not interrupt the presses, which were always kept abreast of the latest technology; at the time of writing Gwasg Gomer publishes more copies of more titles than any other Welsh publisher. It is the only one of many Welsh printing-publishing firms of the 19th century to have adapted successfully and prolifically to modern print technology. Under a third generation of Lewises, the cousins John and Hugh, and with a fourth generation already in harness, the press makes an invaluable contribution to Welsh and local culture as well as to the economy of Llandysul.

Occasional printing was carried out in Tregaron and Aberaeron at various times, but it was in Tal-y-bont that Robat Gruffudd began one of the most exciting ventures in 20th-century Welsh publishing, Gwasg y Lolfa. He had already published the first number of his annual *Lol* (= Nonsense) in 1965, which included the first-ever nude spread across the centre pages of any Welsh-language publication, causing ructions at the time, and bringing excellent publicity. The first book Gruffudd published, through a Cardiff printer, was *Hyfryd Iawn*, the lively disquisitions of the Cardi humorist Eirwyn Pont-siân. New printing technology made publication and printing a much easier process than in the days of type-setting and hot metal. Robat Gruffudd saw not only the potential for original novels for children but the fact that there was a new young-adult readership in Welsh Wales, many of them associated with *Cymdeithas yr Iaith Gymraeg*, whose periodical was printed at Y Lolfa. The company was eventually able to buy the redundant Tal-y-bont police station and court-room and expand the business, now run by the brothers Lefi and Garmon Gruffudd.

* * *

J.D. Lewis and Prosser Rhys were Cardiganshire men native to the county, who devoted their careers to working here and who made a giant contribution to the promotion of Welsh literature throughout Wales. A third giant deserves to be celebrated with them – Alun R. Edwards, whose inspirational work in running the county's library service and in the creation of the College of Librarianship will be described in Chapter 25. Alun Edwards succeeded in promoting a number of schemes for the encouragement of Welsh reading and publication. Within the county he inspired the creation of Welsh reading groups and of the Cardiganshire Books

Society, involved mainly in the publication of Welsh books of Cardiganshire interest, especially a remarkable series of autobiographies; it was capitalised with money from the county's share of Church endowments. He oversaw the Welsh book stamps scheme, and the distribution of boxes of books before Christmastime for sale in village shops. He inspired the move to gain a government subsidy for the publication of Welsh books in order to overcome the problems of cost, design, distribution and sales which so handicapped the traditional Welsh printer-publishers. He also ensured a cooperative scheme between the county libraries of Wales for the guaranteed purchase of Welsh books likely to prove popular with readers.

Alun R. Edwards [Courtesy of Ceredigion County Library]

Ideas bubbled from Alun Edwards's busy imagination, the greatest of which was the establishment of the Welsh Books Council. It was typical of the man that he was perfectly happy to start this scheme in the most modest way, with a part-time organiser, Enid Morgan, in a corner of his own office for want of any other space; the first full-time organiser, Alun Creunant Davies, began work in 1965. By the time he retired in 1987 the Council employed 35 staff, divided between the headquarters in the former Catholic college, Castell Brychan, and a distribution centre now located in the Llanbadarn industrial estate. The whole organisation continues to flourish on a subsidised financial basis which even Alun Edwards could scarcely have dreamed possible. He was always the first to praise the support given him by the Cardiganshire County Council. Not that the councillors always accepted his plans immediately; he told me once that the secret of getting his own way was always to acknowledge sincerely that the councillors were right, to take the rejected plan away, hone and polish it and then take it back to committee as often as necessary until he won acceptance. The progress made in Welsh politics since 1951 when the first, minimal recognition of Wales in governmental matters was made, through the creation of the Welsh Office and Secretary of State in 1964, to the Welsh Assembly (which unfortunately Alun did not live to see) is well and positively illuminated by the progress made in Welsh publication largely inspired by one man from Llanio.

23. Entertainment and the Arts

What we know of public entertainment in Cardiganshire only emerges into view in the 19th century, and it was a largely urban phenomenon. Cardigan town was visited during the age of Victoria by the Christy Minstrels, the Cambro-American Concert Company, Mr E.C. Pugh the famed thought-reader, the Royal Marines band, numerous circuses, Herr Pareezer's Dioramas and Prussian Choir, and by Sanger's Waxworks exhibition, not to mention a string of less notable attractions. Towns could provide a venue for the show, accommodation for performers, and access to an audience. True, the numerous annual country fairs had long provided entertainment, though much less spectacular and noisy than that associated today with Aberystwyth's November fair. Menageries travelled the highroads and byroads; a touring elephant died in Tregaron in 1848 and was buried behind the Talbot Inn. Country men played *cnapan* and their bloody-nosed games of football; the annual Hen Galan game between Llandysul and Llanwenog was notorious for its savagery. The goals were seven miles apart; those who had horses rode them while the rest were on foot. There were no agreed rules, and by 1842 Enoch James, vicar of Llandysul, had succeeded in replacing the semi-riot with a Sunday Schools festival, but primitive football with both sexes participating lasted elsewhere in the county for several more decades. In the summer, country people might take their rare days of leisure at the seaside; a comic Welsh ballad tells how a naïve young man from the country who took the excursion train to Aberystwyth lost his chance with his girlfriend to a sophisticated town slicker. When these mixed groups of young people reached the beach they were quite happy to plunge naked together into the sea – how could they have afforded the modesty of costumes or bathing machines?

Tre-saith beach.

The gentry had their own ideas of entertainment bound up largely with the shedding of blood, whether of fish, bird or mammal. Fishing and otter-hunting were for the summer, while winter was the time for fox-hunting, hare-coursing and shooting game. Virtually all the gentry took part in these activities, though E. Crompton Ll. Fitzwilliam of Cilgwyn ran counter to his Tivyside peers in expressing his loathing of fox-hunting. His son, in the way so common to sons, differed entirely and spent far too much time and cash on the sport his father detested. The Pryses of Gogerddan, like other great gentry families, kept game books, and these survive for the whole of the 19th century. Gogerddan owned four separate lakes or ponds and had stream and river fishing rights as well; trout, sewin and perch were the usual catches. The angling books make frequent notes of the state of the weather, and occasionally of other matters, as in 1873, 'Someone has watered my bottle of gin.'

Huntsmen and hounds at Trawsgoed, 1888. [Courtesy of the Earl of Lisburne]

The game books carefully list all the kills made; partridge, woodcock, hares, mallard, snipe and rabbits were consistently shot throughout the winters of the 19th century. Pheasants too, though very scarce before 1830, were killed in increasing numbers, suggesting a growing emphasis on breeding. The gentry aimed their guns at a wide variety of birds; the Gogerddan records include wild geese, teal, scaup, curlews, herons, red and black grouse, golden plover, lapwings, moorhens, land and water rails, moorhens and greenshank. The Trawsgoed game books mention a bittern on Tregaron bog, shot by the sixth earl of Lisburne in 1892. The Gogerddan game books often record gifts of game, because sometimes more creatures were shot than the household could possibly consume: local ladies, local vicars and the mayor of Aberystwyth's annual feast were all beneficiaries. There are intriguing entries: it was noted for May 4th, 1881, that 'Pryse Pryse returned from Australia'. Accidents happened:

> [15.11.1805] On this unfortunate day Mr T. Jones of Machynlleth in shooting at a Water Rail killed the Poor Dog 'Grieg' the Favorite of his Mistress, and the Gift of her Friend.'

Worse happened at Trawsgoed; the sixth earl of Lisburne noted for 27 September 1890, 'Poor old Derry shot. Recovering.' This was probably his cousin Jones of Derry Ormond. Or was it a favourite dog? In the meantime, the estates' gamekeepers were slaughtering crows and hawks, weasels and stoats, in the interests of sport.

Although the Pryses shot their game every winter, their greatest love was hunting. Printed booklets survive recording the pedigrees of the Gogerddan pack of hounds; others in the hand of Sir Pryse Pryse (d.1906) record in extraordinary detail every day's hunting. The family's north Cardiganshire estate offered endless opportunities for chasing foxes (no mention is made of otters, though there are reports of Pryse involvement with otter hunting in the *Aberystwyth Observer*). The strain on the Gogerddan estate's finances was so great that Sir Pryse recorded with some emotion how a crisis struck in the early 1890s:

> At the end of this season [1893-94] I was compelled to give up hunting the country owing to want of means. It had been a hard struggle to keep things going as long as I had done. But it was a great blow to me after all my hard work and trouble to have to part with my hounds when I had got them to such perfection . . . I sold the hounds to Mr Vaughan Davies of Tan-y-bwlch for £100. Much less than I could have obtained in the open market . . . I would now give a good deal not to have let this man have one single one of my hounds, but have let them go elsewhere. I do not think a man could go through a more bitter experience than I had to, the two seasons Mr Vaughan Davies kept the hounds. I saw the pack . . . being humbugged, bullied and spoilt every day they went out . . .

In fact Vaughan Davies sold the pack in spring 1896, and in 1897, after representations by his tenants, Sir Pryse once more invested in hounds. It may seem surprising that the tenants sought the continuation of hunting; Sir Pryse describes enthusiastically how pack and horsemen crashed across a turnip field in pursuit of their inedible quarry. But the hunt gave employment, since horses and hounds need to be fed and bedded, as well as providing a colourful and popular spectacle, and the foxes needed to be kept down. After World War II, however, the Gogerddan hunt gradually faded away, despite the valiant efforts of the last Lady Pryse, who died in 1993. At the southern end of the county too, hunting was a favourite occupation of the squires; Teifiside hunting can be traced back at least to 1736, and in 1765 a Georgian silver stirrup cup became the Hunt's property, to be filled with port and emptied by the Master. Colourful accounts of hunts appeared in the *Cardigan and Tivy-side Advertiser* from time to time, but the Boer War put an end to the annual hunt ball. The Tivyside Hunt still exists, but at the time of writing it seems doomed.

The most considerable field entertainment provided by the Gogerddan estate was horse-racing. The level ground between the mansion and Bow Street was the site of a race-track on which annual August meetings were held until part of the track was sold off to Thomas Savin for the Aberystwyth railway. The *Demetian Mirror* gives an account of the 1840 meeting, observing that a new grandstand had been built on stone foundations. The meeting was badly affected by rain, but five races were held on each day. The Pryse family entered horses in all but one race, winning four. The race ball at the Assembly Rooms is described as having been a brilliant affair; quadrilles were danced and champagne drunk until 4 a.m. The Nanteos Hunt ran steeplechase meetings on the ground east of Pendinas. Today trotting races are the county's main equine sport; the Tregaron races last for three days in August, and attract many entries from England and Ireland.

David Whitney's header for Aberystwyth knocks Hereford United out of the Welsh Cup in 1972.
[Courtesy of Alan Blair]

Outdoor sports derived from England – cricket, rugby and football – gradually replaced the savage village battles of cnapan, and in particular became an alternative to the bloodier field sports enjoyed legally by the gentry and illegally by poachers and their customers. The Cardigan Cricket Club was active in the 1840s, and the *Demetian Mirror* of 1840 records the August activities of the Aberystwyth Cricket Club; a game between 'University men' and members of the club suggests that bowling skills exceeded batting, since in four innings the total of runs was only 136; the University men were victorious. Like the race-goers, the cricketers celebrated with dancing. More recently, for a few golden years from 1955, Glamorgan played a local team annually on the University cricket field. From 1974 the best talent in the north of the county was gathered in the Llanilar cricket club and was, until its enforced demise in 1987, one of the best village teams in Wales, but cricket continues in Ceredigion's towns and a few villages.

The *Demetian Mirror* also notes the activities of the Society of Rheidol Archers, founded in 1832; archery and croquet were the only outdoor activities considered suitable for ladies before the later invention of lawn tennis, which was taken up in Teifiside and Aberystwyth. Dr Leslie Baker-Jones has published details of these and other sports in Cardigan and the Teifi valley, including women's hockey, polo, rowing, swimming, golf, bowls and cycling. Cardigan rugby and soccer are first recorded in 1878 and 1879 respectively. The Gwalia Skating Rink (for roller skating) was opened in Cardigan in 1910.

Women's sporting activities at Aberystwyth were given a fillip when the numbers of women attending the University College increased in the 1880s. Miss E.A. Carpenter, the first warden of the new women's hostel, encouraged her students to take part in games. She encouraged hockey and presided over the women's rowing club, founded in 1890. These activities were handicapped by poor equipment, the

THE history of Ceredigion cricket took a great leap forward after the drafting of this chapter, thanks to Robin Varley's valuable book on Aberystwyth cricket. Early matches from 1830 were played at Gogerddan and later in Aberystwyth, and gentry influence (Pryse, Lisburne, Gilbertson, Richardes) was strong for many decades. Games were played against Pembrokeshire, against a Cambridge team (probably a collection of visitors to the town), and Dolgellau. In 1861 the Ceredigion Cricket Club was formed, and the arrival of the railway made games against Ystrad Meurig college, Lampeter, Newtown and more distant clubs possible. Lovesgrove, Cardigan, Gogerddan, U.C.W. and Aberystwyth Schools all provided opposition, as did scratch teams of visitors. By 1908 the Ceredigion club had faded out, but other teams in Aberystwyth and the county kept the game alive, while the gentry influence and social activities diminished in importance.

Aberaeron schoolgirls playing hockey, pre-1914. [National Library of Wales]

obligation to wear long loose skirts and the ban on male spectators! The ban was eventually lifted in 1899, and spectators of both sexes went to sporting activities, many of them expressly to talk to each other, since elsewhere male and female students could only speak to each other after a formal introduction. Other games were slow to develop; tennis and gymnastics were not taken seriously, and women did not take part in the college sports day until 1919, when a relay race was arranged. Despite all these hindrances, women's sports and games eventually gained serious attention, and influenced gender attitudes in the north Cardiganshire community.

The growing love of sport saw Aberystwyth develop its golf course, tennis courts and bowling greens. Aberystwyth soccer has had its history written in painstaking detail by Peter Parry and Brian Lile; the town football club traces its story back to 1884, but teams were playing occasional games in the 1870s. Unfortunately entries for rugby, soccer and cricket in the county are not to be found in the indexes of *Ceredigion* nor of the *County History*. Sport does figure, though not in the index, in *The History of the University College of Wales Aberystwyth 1872-1972* by Dr E.L. Ellis, himself a noted amateur footballer for the Aberystwyth club. He describes the 1920s as a golden age of sport in the college, with the XV winning the British University Rugby championship in 1927.

Public meetings, much more popular as entertainment then than now, could demand great powers of endurance from those attending. At a St David's Day meeting in Cardigan in 1917 the audience listened to eight speakers who dealt with the Welsh Character, the Welsh language and its literature, Wales and the English, Cardigan in the Middle Ages, the Institutions of Wales, Famous Welshmen, Our Celtic Relations, and the Heroes of Wales. This marathon agenda, with its eight male lecturers, was interspersed with songs by five different soloists, all women.

Inevitably there was more public entertainment in Aberystwyth than anywhere else in the county, and it has been well described by R.F. Walker. There were two major driving forces for entertainment in the town – the tourist industry and the University College in recent times. However, theatre companies visited Aberystwyth from 1789 if not before; various buildings were pressed into temporary use. The Assembly Rooms in Laura Place were built by subscription in 1820 for the 'quality' to take refuge from the *hoi polloi*; they could dance and play cards there, read the newspapers and play billiards. A purpose-built theatre in Thespian Street did not last long (1831-45), leaving only the street's name as a memento. Prior to the arrival of the railway, visitors could make trips by coach, and even board the paddle-steamer *Plynlymon* for a day trip to Bardsey and back.

THE St David's Gentlemen's Club claims to have been founded in 1780. W.J. Lewis does not admit the claim; he believed that the Social Club founded in that year continued until 1888. A St David's Club was begun separately in 1838 but its fate is not known. The present St David's Club was formed in 1890 by members of the Social Club joining with members of the Masonic lodge whose premises can be recognised in Market St. This was the first Aberystwyth club to have its own premises; it moved to its present Eastgate St. location in 1903.

The arrival of the railway brought new crowds and the building of the pier, the bath houses and new hotels, the Queen's (now county offices) seeking with its Victorian grandeur to displace the Belle Vue and the Talbot as *the* place to stay. Trains enabled visiting entertainment to reach the town more easily; perhaps the climax was the arrival on six special trains of Buffalo Bill Cody's Wild West Show. Meanwhile the University College began from 1884 to make its contribution of musical and dramatic performances. There were several venues to choose from: the Pier pavilion, the Assembly Rooms, the Queen's and the Temperance Hall; this latter like the Assembly Rooms was also used for public lectures, meetings and concerts. Even Constitution Hill had its Victoria Hall as well as the original camera obscura. There was a roller-rink in Portland Street in the 1880s, and the Coliseum (1905) provided a stage for music hall, drama and opera before giving way to cinema. A purpose-built cinema had been provided in Market Street in 1910; it burnt down in 1934. The vast College Hall held 2,500; built in 1923, it too was burnt down, but not before many fine concerts had been given there. The King's Hall (1933), built by the council in a challenging form of art deco modernism, provided a versatile substitute for nearly fifty years, and its loss is mourned.

Professional theatre, opera and music hall were not wiped out by the arrival of the cinema in 1910; amateur groups of town and gown held on particularly well, and numerous village drama groups flourished, while Aberystwyth's summer pierrot company performed regularly, surviving the hiatus of World War I. But the long duration of World War II and new developments afterwards seriously affected later developments. In 1950 the arrival of television marked a change that affected both the cinema and live amateur entertainment; this was a period characterised by the post-war decline of many seaside towns, and Aberystwyth lost several of its hotels, most notably the Queen's, which closed in 1951. However, the town was not destined to suffer as much as many of its rivals; car- and coach-borne tourists replaced the weekly and fortnightly visitors, and the post-1960 expansion of the University was a major driving force in the district economy. With increasing prosperity and governmental willingness to support the arts, new levels of subsidy became available, and Aberystwyth benefited magnificently with the building of the Arts Centre, with its Great Hall (1970) and Theatr y Werin (1972), not to mention more recent developments on the site.

John Roberts, Telynor Cymru (1816-94), at Trawsgoed in 1888.

[Courtesy of the Earl of Lisburne]

The county's smaller towns were not barren of entertainment. Travelling players visited Cardigan at least as early as 1825. The old Shire Hall provided the first venue, which eventually moved to the Angel Inn. At various times Cardigan folk were entertained by a Turkish Gypsy troupe, the Christy Minstrels and Sir Frank Benson's Shakespeare Company, which also visited Aberystwyth. The Pavilion cinema was built in 1912 and operated profitably for many years, staging plays as well as showing films; eventually it became a snooker hall. However a new initiative emerged in Cardigan with the creation in 1988, in a disused slaughterhouse, of the Mwldan Arts Centre as a cinema-cum-theatre with art gallery and café. It has proved so popular that with European funding an ambitious £7 million pound project has seen it extended and developed to house more studio space and an additional auditorium. The smaller but lively theatre at Felin-fach in the Aeron valley, a site long associated with tertiary education, provides an excellent centre for Welsh-language drama and local presentations.

Music

To attempt a summary of Ceredigion musical life in a few pages would be a foolish enterprise, nearly as foolish as it would be to overlook the subject. Reference has already been made to the county's ballad and folk-song tradition. Rhidian Griffiths has given a valuable account of the development of hymnody and classical music. Choral singing developed in the early 19th century with the appearance of both

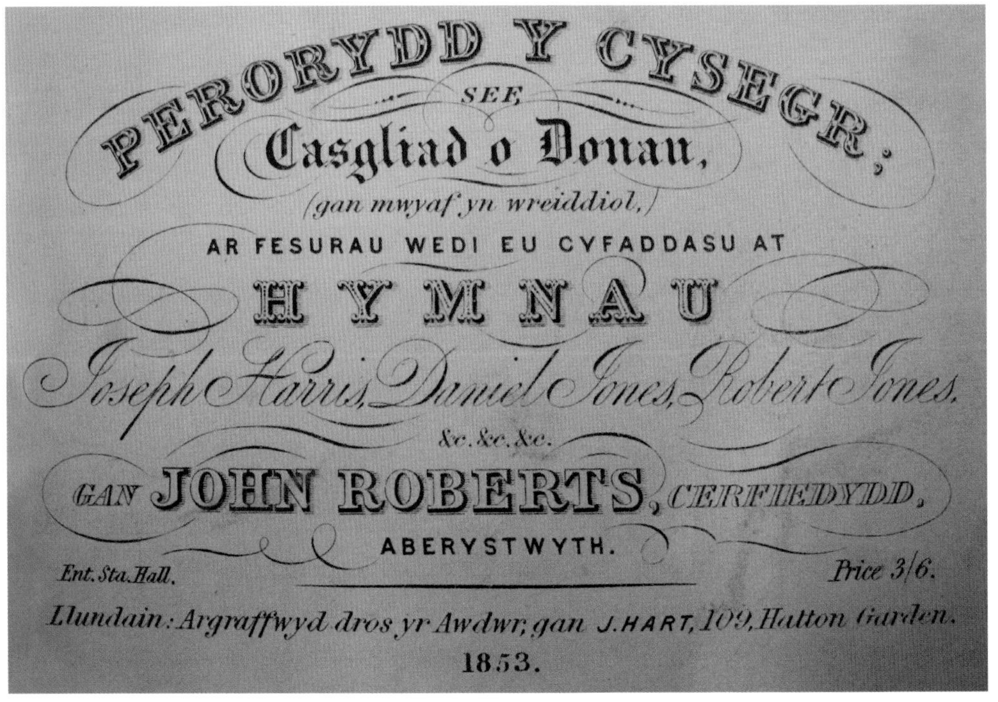
PERORYDD Y CYSEGR;
SEF
Casgliad o Donau,
(gan mwyaf yn wreiddiol,)
AR FESURAU WEDI EU CYFADDASU AT
HYMNAU
Joseph Harris, Daniel Jones, Robert Jones,
&c. &c. &c.
GAN JOHN ROBERTS, CERFIEDYDD,
ABERYSTWYTH.
Ent. Sta. Hall. Price 3/6.
Llundain: Argraffwyd dros yr Awdwr; gan J. HART, 109, Hatton Garden.
1853.

Perorydd y Cysegr by Ieuan Gwyllt.

peripatetic and resident singing teachers, who did much work with church and chapel congregations. A music society was founded at Aberystwyth in 1830; by 1852 the Tabernacle Choral Society was giving concerts at the Assembly Rooms. Choirs for adults and for children sprang up in Aberystwyth, Tregaron and Cardigan, and small groups competed in local eisteddfodau. At the Carmarthen National Eisteddfod of 1911 four Cardiganshire choirs won first prizes in their respective competitions. After World War I standards of musical literacy declined somewhat, but Aberystwyth's male voice choir and choral society have reached the 21st century, along with smaller rural choirs from Aberaeron and from the Ystwyth and Teifi valleys. Aberystwyth has several times hosted the national festival of *cerdd dant.*

The mid-19th-century primacy of Aberystwyth as a centre of congregational singing fed the choral tradition already described. Cardiganshire's leading musician of the age was John Roberts (Ieuan Gwyllt, 1822-77) of Tanrhiwfelen, Aberystwyth, who made a permanent contribution to the editing of Welsh hymnody. He was one of the early teachers to promote tonic sol-fa, that system of notation which was cheaper to print and easier to learn than staff notation. The singing festival (*y gymanfa ganu*) flourished from this time onwards and well into the 20th century, but like other chapel activities it is much diminished. Organs began to be installed in chapels from the 1870s. Cardiganshire continued to produce its own musicians; the most notable composer from the county was R.S. Hughes (1855-93), though he had to make the inevitable move to London to gain a musical education, eventually settling in Caernarfonshire and making his living as an organist, adjudicator, teacher and accompanist.

Inevitably the University College came to play a leading rôle in Aberystwyth's musical life. The music department opened under Joseph Parry in 1874, just two years after the college's inauguration, and helped give women a place in the institution. Parry only stayed for six not very happy years, but his famous hymn *Aberystwyth* gave Protestant Christianity one of its great tunes and sent the town's name to many corners of the world. After Parry the college did not appoint another music professor until 1919, when the generosity of the Davies sisters of Llandinam and Gregynog brought Walford Davies (later knighted) to Aberystwyth as professor of music. These were the great days of Aberystwyth music; Boult, Elgar, Bartók, Vaughan Williams, Edward German, Gustav Holst, Sir Henry Wood all came to the annual musical festival, as did the London Symphony Orchestra. Walford Davies had wonderful support from Charles Clements, the great pianist and organist, and from David de Lloyd, who eventually succeeded him in 1927.

One of the most fruitful developments at Aberystwyth in more recent times was the founding in 1972 of the Philomusica of Aberystwyth, an orchestra for amateur instrumentalists of high calibre. Many of these were the product of the county's secondary schools; the Education Committee had employed peripatetic instrumental teachers of high standard, producing an excellent youth orchestra conducted by the Music Organiser Alan Wynne Jones, who served the county for more than twenty-five years. The county annually took an extraordinarily high percentage of places in the National Youth Orchestra of Wales. Aberystwyth also has a long tradition of silver-band music. More recently Ysgol Gerdd Ceredigion (the Ceredigion Music School) actually based in the Teifi valley and drawing on a wide area, has enjoyed considerable success.

Gorsedd of bards at the 1916 Aberystwyth National Eisteddfod. [National Library of Wales]

The Visual Arts

Painting in Cardiganshire must have begun with the sacred decoration of medieval churches, now all vanished. Artistic patronage passed to the gentry, who desired to emblazon their genealogies in the form of family portraits; these formed a valuable part of every major family's heirlooms. A few of the most valuable have survived, as in the case of Sir Marmaduke Lloyd of Maesyfelin, and a splendid anonymous portrait of Sir John Vaughan of Trawsgoed. Among the later, known artists who painted family members are William Roos and Sir Gerald Kelly, who in the 1920s painted the beautiful Countess of Lisburne for a fee equal to more than half the annual rental of the estate; perhaps her wealthy father footed the bill. The kernel of the fine Trawsgoed portrait archive still survives in family ownership, though now housed in England. The Gogerddan collection, including work by Van Dyck, was mostly sold off by the Pryse family, who replaced the originals with copies, but a good group portrait of three Pryse brothers and a dramatic hunt picture, both by Hugh Hughes, are in the National Library. The Nanteos collection was sadly fragmented by deaths and sales; the Lawrence portrait of Thomas Powell (d.1797) survives, but not in Wales; some of the collection has returned, with attributions lost, to the mansion.

Thomas Johnes of Hafod brought his Grand Tour collection of pictures and memorabilia to his Gothic mountain palace in the 1780s, and in 1807 he had a brief catalogue printed on the Hafod press. It included works by, or attributed to Rembrandt, Caravaggio, Van Dyck, Claude, Salvator Rosa and Romney. An art historian might well be able to trace the subsequent history of this collection; it is not known what may have been burnt when the house was gutted by fire, but the remarkable icon of Elijah (which is named in the catalogue) is to be seen today in St David's cathedral. The picture was said to have been brought back from the east by the crusaders, and to have been in the possession of Talyllychau abbey, but this is a typically romantic attribution; the work is actually 17th-century Cretan, far too late for the crusaders but a splendid piece nevertheless. Johnes also loved sculpture, commissioning busts of himself, his wife Jane and daughter Marianne, as well as a ravishing carving of Jane Johnes as Thetis, and of course the enormous marble memorial to his daughter which was destroyed when Eglwysnewydd church took fire in 1932; well-meaning firemen hosed down the hot sculpture with cold water and the stone shattered.

There was of course more to Thomas Johnes than his own direct buying of art. His whole Hafod project was a work of landscape art, a development of the ideas of the sublime and picturesque promulgated by his cousin Richard Payne Knight and his Aberystwyth neighbour Sir Uvedale Price. The mansion and landscape were celebrated in painting and sketch by Thomas Jones of Pencerrig, by John 'Warwick' Smith and by J.M.W. Turner, and by the pen of George Cumberland, author of *An Attempt to Describe Hafod*. Even the porcelain was decorated with landscape paintings. The critic Geoffrey Grigson saw the influence of Hafod's landscape on Coleridge's great poem *Kubla Khan*: the pleasure dome, the gardens and sinuous rills, the green hill and cedarn cover were all there – even the caves of ice, if the Hafod ice-house

Greek icon, formerly at Hafod Uchdryd.
[Courtesy of the Dean and Chapter of St David's Cathedral]

could be so transmogrified. Nor was Hafod with its environs the only attraction to artists: Rowlandson, Ibbetson, David Cox senior and junior, John Varley and others painted Aberystwyth castle and the harbour, Devil's Bridge and Cardigan. Among more recent artists to work in the area was John Piper, who was strongly affected by the ruins of Hafod in the 1950s.

After Thomas Johnes the most interesting local patron of the arts was George Powell of Nanteos (1842-82). He was owner of the estate only for the last four years of his rather short life, but during his youth he had a sufficient allowance to indulge his catholic tastes in a phenomenal number of directions. He published two volumes of his mawkish adolescent poems while only eighteen; he befriended Algernon Swinburne, who shared his taste for homosexual masochism, and corresponded with Henry Longfellow. Equally interested in music, he attended the first performances of Wagner's *Ring* cycle in Bayreuth and dined with the composer; contrary to popular belief, Wagner did not visit Nanteos nor draw inspiration for his *Parsifal* from his acquaintance with Powell (nor for that matter did Handel visit Hafod as used to be popularly believed). George Powell knew Clara Schumann well, and encountered the teenaged Guy de Maupassant, whose recollections of Powell's Normandy summer ménage with Swinburne are colourful in the extreme; he apparently brought over rent-boys from London and dined on roast monkey. At the same time he helped finance Sir Frederick Ouseley's College of Church Music at Tenbury and later supported music at the fledgling University College in Aberystwyth. The most remarkable and fruitful aspect of his dilettantism derived from his passion for Iceland. Powell visited the island, then under Danish rule, generously supported the Icelandic movement for independence and subsidised the production of two large volumes of Icelandic legends which he almost certainly helped to edit.

Powell also had a taste for the visual arts; he was friendly with a number of minor artists in London's bohemian circles to whom he gave commissions, and himself sketched; he also collected a large number of paintings, drawings and objets d'art. George Powell was not merely a collector for his own private delight. He offered his collections to the Aberystwyth borough council, but government regulations prevented expenditure on such a pioneering project; most of the collection was eventually bequeathed to the new University College of Wales, where his benefaction is always acknowledged.

Although his plan for a gallery fell through, George Powell would be gratified by the number of art galleries now open in the town. The largest is the National Library of Wales, which regularly accommodates two temporary exhibitions, often by living artists, as well as displaying a choice of its own treasures; the Library's own art collection runs to thousands of works, mostly landscapes and portraits. The University's Art department, housed in the Edward Davies building, exhibits both students' work and items from the college's own valuable collection. The Arts Centre on Pen-glais hill now has two galleries as well as a permanent exhibit of works from the University's large collection of ceramics. On a smaller scale the Ceredigion Museum accommodates exhibitions by living artists as well as works by local artists of the past. Of these the most prominent was George Worthington, who settled in the town in the Victorian era and made a living as a photographer and painter. Until his death in 1934 he was a familiar figure on the seafront and at the harbour. He must have produced hundreds of oil paintings; his favourite subjects were Llanbadarn church and marine scenes, but he loved to paint fantasies of highland scenery from his imagination, and he also decorated fireplaces and items of furniture. Worthington is by no means an important artist; some of his late work is execrable, but at his best it can be lively. A more interesting artist is the unknown mid-Victorian person known as the 'Aberystwyth Naïve' painter, whose work brilliantly records local scenes and events.

Mary Lloyd Jones. [photo by Tina Carr]

Thanks in part to the George Powell bequest, the University at Aberystwyth has had a long though sometimes passive role in the fine arts, a passivity clear from the subject's absence from Dr Ellis's history of the College. Art was in fact taught in the Education Department, enjoyed a brief period of independence in the 1930s. The college's holdings had been increased in the 1920s and 1930s by the generosity of the Davies sisters of Gregynog and other important patrons. Until the early 1970s, the teaching of Art at the University College continued a weakly existence within the Education Department, sustained by the best efforts of Lambert Gapper and David Tinker, both distinguished artists. In 1973 David Tinker succeeded in persuading the University to restore independence to what was now called the Visual Art department, now housed with its extensive collections in the elegant Edward Davies building on the Buarth.

Cardiganshire bred or gave a home to a number of distinguished painters during the twentieth century. It would be impossible to name them all, but acknowledgement must be made of John Elwyn, principally for his Ceredigion landscapes, of George Chapman, who although he is known for his paintings of the Welsh industrial valleys preferred to live in Aberaeron, and of the influential art teachers Hywel Harries and Ogwyn Davies. To represent their generation I have chosen Mary Lloyd Jones, originally of Pontarfynach but now at home in Aberystwyth, who works in many media on a wide range of subjects, but often returns to her native county's landscape for inspiration.

ARCHITECTURE

This is a difficult topic to deal with at a time when the long-promised Ceredigion 'Pevsner' is expected to appear but has not yet been published. Moreover, I have already attempted comment on many aspects of the subject in a number of different chapters. The first stone buildings in the county were the castles at Cardigan, Ystrad Meurig and Aberystwyth, and the early churches. Domestic building seems to have depended largely on wood and cloam (borrowed into Welsh as *clom*), a mixture of earth (clay if possible), straw and/or horsehair. Simple crucks supported a thatched roof, with a chimney fashioned of hazel wattle-and-daub. The walls were made thick and then whitewashed; so long as the roof functioned, these walls could last a long time, and some inhabited cottages in the county still have such walls. During the 20th century the thatch disappeared entirely, either covered over with corrugated iron or entirely replaced with other modern materials. In recent years several buildings south of the Aeron have once more been thatched, and most attractive they look.

Gentry houses have already been the subject of comment; the most obvious feature of their architecture in the county is simply that hardly anything survives from before 1700, other than Wern Newydd and Strata Florida (the latter much altered). The reason for this virtual clean sweep is still a matter of debate; the simplest explanation is the comparative poverty of the county, but Merionethshire, surely not that much richer than Cardiganshire, has far more early buildings. It has also been suggested to me that local stone does not endure in the long term, but Aberystwyth castle surely contradicts that. It might even be argued that Cardiganshire men were able to rebuild because of an increase in wealth which did not affect Merionethshire, but the subject is still in the air.

What is clear is that there was a huge rebuilding of ordinary farmhouses during the 19th century, and a similar sweep through the county's churches, most of which are Victorian, many of them with no trace of the preceding building. The same process happened with many chapels; the second half of the 19th century saw not only additional foundations, but extensive rebuilding and restoration of existing chapels. These developments were to a considerable extent the result of growing prosperity. Farmhouses underwent another prosperity-driven revamp after World War II; some were entirely abandoned to use for storage while comfortable, characterless villas or bungalows housed the family in well-earned comfort; others were re-roofed, re-windowed, re-doored and re-floored.

Many of Ceredigion's villages are of recent growth. Examination of estate maps of the late 18th century and of the Tithe and early Ordnance Survey maps shows that many places, for example Llangrannog and Llwyncelyn, hardly existed before the 19th century. Some are simply ribbon developments along main roads (Pen-parc, Taliesin, Bow Street), while others accreted round chapels, even taking the name of the chapel for the community. Many of the best-known villages were maritime communities of the Victorian period: Aber-porth, Llangrannog and Borth are examples. Some villages were mainly mining communities: Tal-y-bont, Pont-rhyd-y-groes and Llanafan come to mind, though Tal-y-bont had three woollen mills, while Llanafan also served as an 'estate' village, accommodating workers on the Trawsgoed estate. Several villages have some claim to antiquity; Llanfihangel-y-Creuddyn has been described elsewhere, while Llanbadarn Fawr certainly, and Ysbyty Ystwyth and Llanilar possibly, deserve consideration. Mydroilyn gives no obvious hint of antiquity, but its location makes it one of the county's more attractive villages.

The county's towns underwent similar drastic changes. The oldest town houses are late 18th century in appearance, though some may have older fabric behind the Georgian façades. There are plenty of attractive buildings from the period 1780-1840 to be found in Aberystwyth, Aberaeron and Cardigan. The view of Aberystwyth from Pendinas or Craig-lais shows how the roofed heart of the town has retained its slates, while 20th-century developments are largely tiled; earlier houses in all towns are faced in stucco or local stone, while later houses may be brick or breeze blocks with stone fascias. Bricks were made in Abermagwr in the 18th century; I lived for sixteen years in the last surviving house of local bricks, Tan-yr-allt.

Aberaeron's 'postage-stamp' house.

There are some worthwhile buildings scattered through the county. Nanteos and Mynachdy mansions and Llanwenog church have already been singled out in earlier chapters. The house called Westminster in Aberystwyth's Bridge Street is quite the finest town house in the county, though Aberaeron has many excellent houses, one of which appeared on a United Kingdom postage stamp as an example of 'Welsh Stucco'. The original college building at Lampeter and the National Library of Wales would give dignity to any county or city in Britain. Cardigan, while lacking the institutions of Aberystwyth, has its splendid bridge and warehouse, with the 18th-century courthouse building on the crest of the hill, and an attractive web of narrow streets. Among modern buildings the University's Physics block at Aberystwyth also figured on a postage stamp. There are two modern houses at the north end of Borth which are still controversial; perhaps the finest modern building which I would like to claim for the county is the West Wales Wildlife Trust's headquarters on the south side of the Teifi; the reserve is almost entirely in Ceredigion, but the building is actually just on the south side of the border. While one must deplore the uglification of much modern building in the county as in the rest of Wales, there still remains much to appreciate.

Pioneer modern architecture at Borth.

24. Cardiganshire at War

This was not an easy chapter to write. By coincidence the Bush-Blair war on Iraq was raging during the time of its preparation in 2003; there was a hideous irony in the fact that in 1914-18, 1939-45 and again in 2003 the *Cardigan and Tivy-side Advertiser* carried items about local women preparing comforts for troops in battle, especially as in both 1914-18 and 2003 Welsh troops were involved in Iraq, known as Mesopotamia in the earlier war. Cardiganshire men had of course been fighting in wars throughout history; a major difference between previous campaigns and the two World Wars was that in the latter full-time military service became compulsory, while the civilian population was involved in a way that had never occurred before. True, the Norman incursions had been violent and the eventual changes brought about by conquest were far-reaching indeed, but they took centuries; the period 1914-45 would bring about more rapid change than had ever been seen before, and the two wars played a considerable part. A more practical difficulty is the shortage of historical discussion of the two wars as they affected Cardiganshire; ironically, the official histories of both wars were partly written in the National Library of Wales.

The contrast between the two World Wars is as startling in the microcosm of Ceredigion as it is in a British perspective. The two conflicts began quite differently. The First World War (WWI) must have come as a considerable surprise to the majority of the population who either depended on the local newspapers or read no secular periodicals at all. Even for those who in 1914 read newspapers, there was little to prepare them mentally, and there was virtually no practical preparation at all; WWI broke on Cardiganshire quite suddenly. The *Cardigan and Tivy-side Advertiser* for 24 July contained no mention of any possible trouble; the 31 July issue had a paragraph headed 'Will it be War?' and the 7 August number had a large spread. Suddenly the paper began to contain accounts of recruits for the Army and Navy leaving Cardigan, of the arrest of German spies who turned out to be a Leicester couple on holiday, of the provision of

ABERYSTWYTH'S WWI began in hysteria. Among the many who were taken by surprise in Europe and had to hurry home from holiday was Aberystwyth's distinguished professor of Modern and Oriental languages, Carl Hermann Ethé, with his wife. Such was the instant hatred of 'the Hun' that a vile mob, encouraged by several leading members of the town community, ensured that the couple, as well as an unfortunate Englishman called Schott who had a German wife, were driven from Aberystwyth. The College authorities behaved with dignity and honour in ensuring Ethé's pension in the teeth of town council protests, which included the withdrawal of a £30 grant to the college and the resignation of the town's mayor, enraged by the attitude of the college authorities, four months after Ethé's death in 1917. A plaque in Old College commemorates him .

comforts for the troops. The county Red Cross was active. The mayor of Cardigan, Boer War veteran Captain Picton Evans, left the town for active service, seen off by a crowd summoned by the town crier; he was to suffer frostbite and dysentery at Gallipoli and was wounded at Gaza before dying in September 1918 in a military hospital, aged 46. By October the first prisoner-of war from the county was reported and the first major recruiting meeting was held, addressed by the county gentry and a local minister, the Revd Towyn Jones, who announced that having been for years a son of peace, he was now a man of war. Horses began to be requisitioned for military use.

In 1939, in contrast with 1914, the prospect of war was rarely out of the *Cardigan and Tivy-side Advertiser* all year. In January there was encouragement to register for Voluntary National Service; in February the paper was commenting on Hitler, Chamberlain and Roosevelt, and on the huge national budget for armaments. The annexation of Czechoslovakia in March brought gloomy prognostications, and in April Brigadier-General Lewis Pugh Evans VC, who had been Ceredigion's WWI war hero, was recruiting for the Territorial Army. In June lectures were being given in Cardigan on first aid for Air Raid Precautions (ARP) volunteers, and the Women's Land Army was in training. Large numbers of soldiers camped at Aberporth in August, but the deteriorating international situation sent the last campful hurrying back to London. On 8 September the *Tivy-side* announced grimly WE ARE AT WAR! By then evacuees were already arriving in Aberystwyth.

The second contrast between the two wars lies in the different modes of engagement of the county. To put it crudely, in WWI Cardiganshire went away to war, while in 1939-45 war came to Cardiganshire – not in the same way of course as it did to Kent or Swansea, but it impinged more on daily life than had the war of '14-18. True, soldiers were billeted in Aberystwyth in 1914 – six trains brought thousands of Territorials to the town, to the relief of the lodging-house keepers, whose season had been threatened with disaster by the exodus of visitors. But there were no training bases in the county, no experimental arms facilities, no visible signs of defences, no air raids. It was only comparatively slowly that the war came to affect everyday life. There were no evacuees; instead scores of Belgian refugees were given a hospitable welcome and housed in Aberystwyth, Cardigan and elsewhere across the county, initially at the expense of the Davies sisters of Gregynog. A number of them were professional artists and musicians who did their best to contribute to local culture; among their surviving legacies are sculptures in Llanwenog and Llanfihangel-y-Creuddyn churches. An inanimate class of refugees was formed by a selection of the treasures of the British Museum's library (now the British Library), stored at the partly-built National Library of Wales as a refuge from Zeppelin raids. Prisoners of war were accommodated in the county in both wars, but their presence was much more limited in WWI; for instance, German officers were accommodated in the little mansion of Aberllolwyn, Llanfarian.

Deaths began early; the first reported in the *Tivy-side* (23 October 1914) was of a Cardigan private who, asleep in his tent in camp in England, was accidentally shot dead at 4am by a jumpy sentry four hundred yards away. On 30 October the paper

Belgian refugees at Cardigan, 1914. [National Library of Wales]

announced the death of the only son and heir of Sir Marteine Lloyd, Bronwydd; in fact he had only been wounded, but he returned to the front and was actually killed in September 1916. Eventually small numbers of German prisoners of war were sent to work on farms between Lampeter and Aberaeron, and were well treated locally, but county councillors in north Cardiganshire, full of ignorant rage against the Bosche, threatened reprisals, only to be rebuked by their chairman, J.M. Howell, who suggested that it was 'the privilege of Britishers to treat German prisoners with Christian consideration.'

Whereas in 1939 conscription was introduced immediately, along with tribunals for conscientious objectors, in WWI every effort was made to avoid compulsion. Instead regular recruiting meetings were held across the county. Women were addressed as well as men; Mrs Thora Drummond, who was, until the outbreak of war one of the leaders of the militant suffragette movement, addressed a patriotic meeting for women at the Coliseum, Aberystwyth on Saturday 31st July, 1915, encouraging women to send their men to fight. Despite these efforts, the problems of recruiting enough young men soon came to the fore. Sons of the gentry joined without question, as indeed did some of their fathers. Sir Edward Webley-Parry-Pryse of Gogerddan, a veteran of the Boer War, was the county's chief recruiting officer, but after a year he gave up the post and went at the age of 53 to serve in France, which destroyed his health; he was invalided out and died in 1918. Young men in the towns were readier to volunteer than farmers' sons, for whom there was less social pressure to join up and more economic pressure to stay at home; the authorities complained of an attitude crystallised in the remark, 'I'll go when they fetch me'.

Hundreds of men sought exemption on the grounds that they were indispensable to the war effort, especially in agriculture; the papers of the Cardiganshire Great

War Tribunals at the National Library await their researcher. There were local tribunals, a county appeal tribunal and a national appeal tribunal, and differences could arise between them, as when the Aberaeron Urban local tribunal members resigned en bloc because of a decision by the county appeal body. Not every conscientious objector was sent to Dartmoor; employment with the Friends' Ambulance Unit or the YMCA were acceptable in some cases. Many appeals were allowed for a month or two in order to get the harvest in, or in one case 'after the Stallion Season' after which the men were expected to enlist. In May 1918 the shortage of recruits drove the government to insist that 30,000 farm workers should be enlisted, of which Cardiganshire's share was 425, and the task of deciding who should go was transferred to the County War Agricultural Committee. The County Appeal Tribunal met for the last time on 14 September 1918.

Few expressed any doubts about the validity of the war, and even fewer were willing to support the pacifist stand of the poet T.E. Nicholas (1878-1971), Congregationalist minister in Llangybi and Llanddewibrefi, who from the start condemned the war outright in the *Tivy-side*'s columns, scorning the anonymity which sheltered his newspaper critics; eventually he left his congregations to become a dentist. One conscientious objector who caused a furore was Dr D.J. Davies, teacher of French at Ardwyn Grammar School, Aberystwyth. In 1917 he appeared before a tribunal, and as a result the school governors passed a resolution that he should be dismissed. On two successive days in November the boys of the school refused to attend classes, and instead marched round the town to express their support for their teacher. Only the efforts of the headmaster prevented the girls from joining in; he persuaded them that it would not be 'ladylike or comely'. Another governors' meeting early in 1918, full of unseemly vituperation, eventually rescinded the dismissal resolution, but only thanks to the chairman's casting vote.

A British anti-submarine reconnaissance airship over Lampeter, 1918. [National Library of Wales]

The public contributed with extraordinary generosity to money-raising campaigns; in the two months December 1916 – January 1917 the Cardiganshire elementary schools collected £35,652.5s.2d. in War Savings. In September 1918 there was a 'War Weapons Week' as part of a war bonds scheme; Cardiganshire's response was astonishing. Cardigan and district, set a target of £15,000, actually raised £150,000, while the people of the Aberystwyth area raised a total of £682,448. This was the highest amount raised in Britain, given by one of the poorest districts in the country, and the second highest in the whole British Empire.

Slowly the war in Cardiganshire became more than the problem of recruiting young men for the Front, though long reports of tribunals of men, supported by their employers, seeking exemption from service, filled many columns in the *Tivy-side* and the *Cambrian News*. Bread and meat became more expensive, butter was scarce and price control panels were formed, though rationing was not brought in until the critical summer of 1918. Huge quantities of blackberries were picked and sent to factories for jam-making under schemes sponsored by the government; much of the picking was done by schoolchildren. Both newspapers began to carry reports of the experiences of Cardiganshire men. The Cardigan Company of Territorials served with the 1st/4th Welsh Regiment in the Dardanelles; twenty were wounded and one killed. By March 1916 there were regular reports of deaths of local men at sea or at the front, sometimes two or three at a time. A single page of the *Cambrian News* (19 May 1916) carried pictures of 26 local servicemen of whom one had been killed, one had been missing for a year, one was wounded and five had been invalided home with various illnesses.

WWI parade in front of Old College. [National Library of Wales]

It was widely believed by soldiers fighting in France that people at home had little understanding of the horrors of trench warfare, and this is obviously true in the profoundest sense. But anyone who read their local newspapers gained at least some small knowledge of what was going on. This derived partly from the growing casualty lists and their local impact, but also from reports sent home by soldiers at the front or derived from interviews with soldiers who were convalescent or on leave. Although letters from the front published in the local newspapers included a good deal of forced cheerfulness, mud and rats figured quite strongly in their accounts. The constant nagging of recruiting meetings and the endless reports on registration tribunals meant that a good part of every newspaper issue dealt with the war. Public speakers did not always spout jingoisms; in March 1916 J. Hugh Edwards, MP, addressed an Aberystwyth public meeting in which he used phrases like 'nauseating horrors', 'the hellishness of war' and its 'barbaric loathsomeness'. Then there was the presence of many convalescent servicemen, housed at the Theological College, Aberystwyth, Trawsgoed mansion and other country houses, to remind people of the troops' suffering.

The government was mindful of the need to involve the population at the local level; in April 1916 a captured German gun was ceremonially presented to the town of Aberystwyth on loan. Later a tank called 'Julian' was brought to Aberystwyth to raise funds for the war. It arrived by train and lumbered by a roundabout route to a site in North Parade, giving an exhibition of its 'climbing and destructive powers' on the way; tanks notoriously chew up road surfaces. Another tank stayed in Aberystwyth and ended up on the barbican of Aberystwyth castle; it was scrapped before WWII. Post-war reminders of the wartime horrors emerged with the return of a number of men who had been prisoners of war in Germany; they had almost starved to death, and perhaps may not have grasped that by the end their captors were starving too.

Aberystwyth made an important contribution to Welsh culture by insisting on holding the National Eisteddfod, postponed in 1915, during the following August. The *Times* thundered against it; why were the Welsh singing when Welsh soldiers were shedding their blood? Lloyd George, despite all the pressures on him, made his usual eisteddfod visit and laid about him from the stage with all his customary fire and panache. The *Times* was scorned; why should not the Welsh sing? Was not this part of what they were fighting for? Although reduced to three days, the festival was a great success, particularly the first-ever Eisteddfod *cymanfa ganu* or hymn-singing festival, now a regular feature.

The steady trickle of deaths and woundings gradually increased during 1916 and later. Families lost one, two or three sons. By 1918 the *Cambrian News* and the *Cardigan and Tivy-side Advertiser* bear evident signs of utter war-weariness, though by September it was clear that the war had been won. Nevertheless the deaths continued; one of the last was that of Lieutenant 'Billy' Powell, the 19-year-old heir to Nanteos, who was killed only a few days before November 11, shot according to local tradition by his own men, reluctant to follow him 'over the top' when the war was obviously ending. Like Sir Edward Webley Parry-Pryse, Billy Powell's father Edward Athelstan Powell, although in his forties, had volunteered for army service and had his health ruined in Mesopotamia. The member of the county's gentry who emerged from the war with the most distinction was Lewis Pugh Evans, who won the Victoria Cross for gallantry at Zonnebeke in Belgium.

Though peace was greeted with flags, bunting, drums, processions and church bells, the 1918 rejoicing was comparatively subdued, and the matter of commemorating the dead occupied many minds. In 1915 the government had decided to forbid the repatriation for home burial of the war dead, creating instead the haunting war cemeteries of eastern France and Belgium. This, as Angela Gaffney has argued, though understandable in the interest of egalitarianism, prevented the bereaved from experiencing a proper closure through a funeral farewell process. Few could afford to make pilgrimages to the military cemeteries, but large numbers of the deceased had no known grave; they had vanished into the mud or been blown to smithereens. The process of forming local commemoration committees acted as some form of substitute, but disputes were inevitable. Local councils and committees across Wales were largely hostile to the idea of a Welsh national memorial; it was only thanks to the efforts of the *Western Mail* that one came into existence in Cardiff in 1928. An equally basic issue was whether memorials were to be symbolic (tablet, column, sculpture) or serviceable (memorial hall, hospital). Because general coordination of effort was perceived to be impossible, commemoration occurred at a number of levels, and so a man's name might occur on tablets in his school, his church or chapel and on his community memorial. By 1922 Cardigan's local efforts had turned the Priory mansion into the Cardigan and District War Memorial Hospital, opened by Dame Margaret Lloyd George, but despite the financial sacrifice involved, the mayor drove forward a campaign for a cenotaph, unveiled a year later, which he said was originally inspired by appeals made to him by bereaved families. The county has a number of Memorial Halls, notably those in Llandysul, Tregaron and Aberaeron. Quite the strangest memorial is to be found in Aberystwyth's Age Concern offices, formerly the Alexandra Road elementary school. The craft teacher there produced an extraordinary wooden contraption with revolving batons, and the names of former pupils written on them in Iolo Morganwg's fake druidic alphabet, *Coelbren y Beirdd*.

Aberystwyth's magnificent war memorial.

The University College at Aberystwyth purchased the town's Old Assembly Rooms as a students' union and war memorial; the tablet of names is still *in situ*, but the union is now elsewhere. Typically of university memorials, the number of names is startlingly long, since so many graduates became officers, who were prime targets for enemy snipers. David Davies, son of the railway builder, endowed the University's chair of International Politics as a commemoration of the many former students killed. Lampeter commissioned the Welsh sculptor Goscombe John to provide a statue with a rather special formula in its inscription: 'To the immortal memory of the men of Lampeter and of Nurse Richards . . .' Aberystwyth commissioned one of the finest memorials in Wales from the Italian sculptor Mario Rutelli, at the then vast expense of £10,000. At the unveiling the crowd was startled by the magnificent naked bosom of the figure of Peace. Apart from the structure's splendour, it is remarkably well-engineered and has withstood the buffets of 1930s storms which overthrew most of the pier and tore great rents in the north promenade. Rutelli also created the Aberystwyth Tabernacl's striking memorial, with its enigmatic motto: 'Gadawed i Dduw egluro ei Hun' (let God explain Himself). Llanbadarn Fawr ran into trouble by using only English and Latin on its memorial; a Welsh-language tablet was added after considerable protest. No-one in Penrhyn-coch or elsewhere objected when a white quartz prehistoric standing-stone was appropriated for memorial use in the village square. The only public war memorial to an individual known to me is the lonely cross dedicated to Lieutenant Powell of Nanteos at Southgate, Aberystwyth. So many were the memorials that when the time came in 1945 to commemorate the newly dead, there was room for the mercifully smaller numbers of names to be inscribed on additional plaques rather than a need for new monuments.

* * *

As already suggested, there was a far greater state of readiness for war by September 1939 than there had been in 1914, both at national and local level. Aberystwyth town council had its emergency committee ready, and was busy making arrangements to receive thousands of evacuees, who arrived in large numbers during the first days of September. They were a huge burden on health and education services, but were made very welcome. Less welcome were visiting parents, some of whom expected to be fed on the host families' ration-books. Air raid precaution arrangements were announced in the press in minute detail, gas masks were issued, blackout and petrol rationing enforced, and by 22 September the *Tivy-side* was already announcing that local merchant seamen had survived attacks on their ships by U-boats.

Details about the Home Guard, rationing and the occasional bombing figured in the local newspapers. When the Local Defence Volunteers (later the Home Guard) had been formed in 1940, the Lord Lieutenant, Lord Lisburne, took command of the county's volunteers, but was almost immediately recalled to his WWI regiment, the Welsh Guards. Two battalions were formed originally, one in Cardigan and one in Aberystwyth; eventually a third was based in Lampeter. Thousands of men who were too old or unfit for full-time service, or who were in reserved occupations, trained with varying levels of competence and enthusiasm; others trained as aircraft spotters. There was a radar station at Allt-lwyd mansion, between Llanrhystud and Llannon, and radar masts on Constitution Hill, Aberystwyth; strategic observation and defensive points were manned, including the tower of Aberystwyth castle, the castle at Cardigan and Trichrug hill in mid-county.

Other serious preparations for invasion affected the county. The government's fear of German invasion was not confined to south-east England; there was genuine concern that Hitler might invade Ireland and attack Britain through Wales, especially the south-west. There, after all, the French had landed to support Owain Glyn Dŵr, Henry Tudor had landed in 1485, and the 'last invasion' happened in

The 1940 anti-tank trench crosses the A487 N.E. of Brynhoffnant, bottom right. RAF photo of 1946.
[Crown copyright: Royal Commission on Ancient & Historical Monuments, Wales]

1797. Concrete pill-boxes sprouted in many places: four in Aberystwyth harbour (of which one survives), fourteen at the Aber-porth airstrip; another survivor still defends Lampeter bridge. Across England and Wales the government developed a 'deep defence' strategy, a series of obstacles to invading German armies. In Cardiganshire this involved, among other things, a thirty-mile 'stop-line' from New Quay to the Tywi valley, designed to prevent the advance of tanks. Where natural obstacles could not be exploited, a broad, two-metres-deep trench was dug, with the spoil forming an embankment. Although mostly filled in, either deliberately or by erosion, these earthworks can still be traced from the air.

As well as preparations made for defence, a good deal of military billeting and training took place in Cardiganshire. Although the University College at Aberystwyth continued to function (with more female than male students), some of its buildings were used for training RAF personnel, whose headquarters were in the Queen's Hotel (now the County Offices). The Forum cinema in Bath Street became a NAAFI welfare centre and the Bath Street Wesleyan church a servicemen's canteen. Most Aberystwyth hotels were requisitioned for war purposes, only the Talbot remaining open to the public. As well as accommodating large numbers of service personnel at various stages of the war, the county had two Italian prisoner-of-war camps, at Llan-non and Henllan; a remarkable Catholic chapel, built in 1940 as a dormitory but converted and decorated by the Henllan prisoners, still survives in private ownership.

Another aspect of Cardiganshire's war was the development of research facilities. The Projectile Development Establishment, as it was originally known, opened at Aber-porth in 1940 for testing and improving weapons; it worked in collaboration with the Caerwent rocket propellant factory, run by the Royal Navy. The PDE grew up alongside Aber-porth's RAF training base for operations against air attack; gunners were trained, as were radar and searchlight operators. It then developed as an aircrew training facility, with a grass airstrip, the only one in the county, used at one time by Spitfires. There was also a secret facility for testing guided weapons and rocket-fuel at Ynys-las, opened in 1944 to develop surface-to-air missiles as replacements for anti-aircraft guns, which by then were largely obsolete.

A well-kept secret in both wars was the storage in Wales of artistic treasures from London. The Blaenau Ffestiniog slate mines have had a good deal of publicity as the long-unrevealed WWII secret store for the contents of London's National Gallery, but they were not the only Welsh hiding-place for national treasures. Gwyn Davies has listed 72 institutions, some Welsh, some London-based, some of overseas origin, whose artistic and archival treasures were sheltered at the National Library. Pictures from the National Gallery in London, some of which must already have spent WWI at Aberystwyth, came first to the National Library, whence they were moved to Trawsgoed mansion, and from there in 1941 to Blaenau Ffestiniog. Ironically the Library was a useful landmark for Luftwaffe bombers on their way to bomb Belfast, Liverpool and Glasgow, and remained inviolate.

Cardiganshire was certainly privileged by comparison with London and other bombed cities such as Swansea and Cardiff, and life was less restricted than on the south-east coast of England, where beaches were closed and mined, where piers were blown up, where access was restricted to residents, and where towns were often attacked by surprise hit-and-run air raids; when those ceased in 1944, they were replaced by the still more alarming V1 flying bombs and V2 rockets. Nevertheless the county did not escape wholly unscathed. Gwyn Davies has listed a number of occasions on which bombs fell on the county, all between August 1940 and October 1941. Nobody was killed or injured, but the night of 25 September 1941 must have been spectacular at Mydroilyn, since forty-three bombs fell around the village, and near Llannarth and Pont-siân. One British warplane crashed in the sea and four on land within the county, with a number of deaths.

By 1942 the *Cambrian News* was carrying regular reports of court proceedings dealing with offenders against blackout regulations (including a farmer who burnt some gorse), failure to plough designated land, overcharging for food, the sale of clothing coupons, and on one occasion with thieving and violent soldiers. In 1943 the county's Chief Constable J.J. Lloyd Williams resigned following investigation of police accounts; he had been responsible for over-lavish expenditure on petrol for travel and improper use of police cars, coupled with irregularities in the accounts.

1942 saw another wartime National Eisteddfod held in the county, this time at Cardigan; again Lloyd George spoke from the platform, though more briefly than he had done in 1916 – his health and powers were failing. As in WWI, the county made large financial sacrifices; in 1942, given a target of £400,000 for 'Warship Week', Cardiganshire raised £568,000. In 1943, for 'Wings for Victory' week, the county raised £616,682, well above its target of £500,000. December 1942 saw the worst accident of its kind in the county; five soldiers on an exercise on Aberystwyth beach at the north end of the promenade were swept into the sea by a freak wave and drowned.

Little has been written specifically about Cardiganshire people's war service overseas. Royal Artillery batteries from Aberystwyth and Cardigan served in World War II, which also saw a considerable number of Aberystwyth men serving in the Burma campaign; their sacrificial efforts are commemorated in a window in Llanbadarn Fawr church. Among the Cardiganshire men taken prisoner was the late Frank Evans, whose dire experiences at the hands of the Japanese nevertheless led, thanks to his determination, to the establishment of a reconciliatory relationship between Aberystwyth and the town of Kyoto, Japan, with school twinning as a lasting result.

Although the two World Wars both ended with fireworks and rejoicing, as well as mourning for the dead, and though people were determined to carry on as before, the wars were not simply obstacles to the general flow of life, they were huge catalysts which accelerated the forces of change in modern life – as much so in Ceredigion as elsewhere. It

ONE result of WWII which could not have been anticipated in 1939 was the settling of Polish ex-servicemen in the county, most but not all of them in the Teifi valley. Many reared families here, and gave new life to the Roman Catholic churches at Cardigan and Lampeter, creating a Social Centre in the latter. The Polish Society of Cardiganshire held annual Harvest Home festivals into the 1970s, but the society ceased to exist in that decade; its papers are in the National Library. The full story of the Poles in Ceredigion has yet to be written.

was not simply a matter of the deaths of many hundreds of young men. All lives were changed to some degree; thousands had experiences, both hideous and exhilarating, that they would not otherwise have had. The Welsh language certainly suffered, and that not only by the premature deaths of hundreds of speakers. The very fabric of society was changed; disillusion and cynicism helped contribute to the steady decline in chapel attendance, while people who otherwise might have stayed moved away from the area. The alteration in the status of women, already in train since the 1860s, accelerated. The realisation during WWI, forced by the German U-boat campaign, that the country depended on imports for over 90% of its timber led to widespread afforestation which has so changed the upland appearance of Wales. Agriculture, the county's main industry, was certainly affected deeply. It is widely accepted that the drive from 1940 onwards to make the country less dependent on food imports, sustained as it was after the war, helped change the nature of farming. Agriculture was not allowed to relapse into depression after 1945 as had happened in the 1920s; instead, mechanisation and the general drive for productivity would change the landscape. The longest-lasting activity in the county deriving from WWII is the RAE/DERA/Qinetiq establishment at Aber-porth (see next chapter).

25. Cardiganshire Yesterday: Ceredigion Today

A Cardiganshire farmer's wife once said to me that of the great changes she had seen – running hot water, water closets in the house and the coming of electricity – the one she had appreciated the most was the arrival in the farmyard of the mobile library van for her to choose her books. Hers may have been a minority choice, but it shows a particular appreciation of change and its benefits. Mutability is the great theme of history and literature, the inevitable change which not only drives each of us from cradle to grave but raises and overthrows tyrants, kingdoms and even mountains. All is change, if not necessarily decay. What is now Ceredigion, and was Ceredigion a millennium ago, was once the muddy bed of a great ocean, part of a plate which drifted up from south of the Equator and was slowly transformed by the inexorable powers of nature. Its landscape is still being transformed, more rapidly than ever before, by human influence, and we are of course at liberty to try to imagine a Ceredigion that still exists, nameless, some time in the future when the human race no longer controls the planet.

Cwmystwyth in 1900 and 1990: neater, tidier and emptier.

The aim of this concluding chapter is to trace some of those changes which have developed since 1945, since I have tried to close previous chapters at roughly – very roughly – that time, though with several exceptions, such as population, where it seemed impossible to break the narrative run. It is clear that change is an even more fundamental theme than in previous chapters, since change seems, at least to living spectators and participants, to have accelerated during our own time. To take an initial example, although the increased number of caravans since 1945, when they were virtually unknown, doesn't match the astonishing efflorescence on the north Wales coast, nevertheless it is considerable. The Ceredigion District Planning Authority, in an undated report (?1980), counted 3,554 'permanent' caravans on or very close to the coast, with another thousand-plus within a mile of the coast.

Is this a problem, or the answer to a problem?

Clearly the actual appearance of Ceredigion has changed considerably since 1945. Although most of today's roads were then already under tarmac, little had been done to straighten out the most awkward bends and expand the bottlenecks. Hedgerows and ditches were kept in good order by the combined efforts of farmers and county council labourers ('lengthsmen'). There were few or no caravan parks; the Clarach valley, for example, was still empty of chalets and trailers. The 'villafication' of housing had already begun, and villages were already tending to stretch along their streets in ribbons. Council-housing projects were under way, but the crowding of brick-stone-and-tiled houses into fields had hardly begun, processes which would give an entirely new meaning to the word 'estate'. Some hundreds of cottages made largely of earth, their thatched roofs now covered with corrugated iron, were still occupied. Farmhouses remained unmodernised, their farmyards full of life and muck.

In the mid-20th century agriculture was still fundamental to Cardiganshire's economy, with a bright future. World War II had brought guaranteed prices, effectively in return for increased production; mixed farming enjoyed a last brief flourish. When the war finished, prices were not allowed to collapse as had happened after previous major conflicts, and Cardiganshire's mountain farmers gained the benefit of support under the Hill Farming Act of 1946, support which was continued under the European Community from 1973, now the European Union. This meant a subsidy per head of sheep (mountain cattle were less favoured), and a consequent five-fold rise in the numbers of sheep kept. This obliged farmers to improve pasture with nitrogen (*glas cwdyn* – 'green in a bag') and subsidised lime, but overgrazing was often apparent. More cattle could be kept, thanks to the change from hay to silage, which began in the mid 1940s but was at first restricted by the physical effort involved before the arrival of the forage harvester. The virtual disappearance of hay, together with the use of nitrogen and herbicides, reduced the county's wild-flower populations to small pockets here and there. Another development was the rapidly increasing use of artificial insemination of cattle, which led to a huge improvement in the calibre of the county's stock. For a generation this work was done by specialists who visited farms in turn; nowadays farmers have acquired the skills and equipment necessary. The work of improvement once carried out by the pioneer county agricultural societies has been continued in divers forms, including the work of *Cymdeithasau Tir Glas*, local groups of farmers who run competitions with outside judges to award prizes for land improvement.

Agri-industry in the Aeron valley.

THE Cardiganshire-London community's most typical manifestation was its connection with dairying in London; three of the best-known London Welshmen of their day were active in dairying. Two of them were father and son, David Alban Davies (1873-1951) and his son Jenkin Alban Davies (1901-68). Both were great benefactors of Welsh and Cardiganshire culture; the former gave Pen-glais mansion and 200 acres to the University College at Aberystwyth. The third was Sir David James (1887-1967) who like Jenkin Alban Davies was born in London, but after a time at the family home, Pantyfedwen, at Strata Florida, he returned to London and set up home in Sussex. He turned from dairying to cinema ownership, and astutely sold his chain of cinemas at the market peak. Though domiciled in Sussex, he too gave generously to Welsh causes, including both the Church in Wales and the nonconformist denominations. He endowed the eisteddfodau at Lampeter and Pontrhydfendigaid and set up the Pantyfedwen Trust.

For a generation after 1945 milk production, stimulated by 'school milk' from 1946, sustained many farms and supplied the two creameries at Pont Llanio and Felin-fach. In 1984 the European Community, bothered by apparent over-production of milk and butter, imposed the quota system on milk producers. A wave of protests was followed by a gradual exodus from production, which gained momentum in 1994 when the abolition of the Milk Marketing Board in 1994 saw an end to guaranteed prices. Both creameries ceased operation, though Felin-fach saw the development of private dairying companies, and at Dol-y-bont Rachel's creamery continues to operate under that name, though no longer under the same ownership. The once-familiar sight of roadside churns on concrete stands has entirely vanished, and only rarely are motorists delayed by a herd of cattle – always black-and-white – en route between field and farmyard. Instead the county's cattle are mostly reared in suckler herds for meat, and largely sold in the county's markets at Aberystwyth, Tregaron, Lampeter and Cardigan.

Increasing forestry post-1945 brought more employment to *cefn gwlad*, the countryside. This was some compensation for the ongoing drop in agricultural employment, though with the growth of technology the number of forestry employees eventually declined, and the houses specially built for them were sold off. During the years after 1945 the Forestry Commission modified its stark geometrical and monoculture plantations in favour of landscaping and mixed planting, beginning in the dramatic landscape of the Ystwyth gorge. In 1901 there were 10,663 people earning their living on the land in Cardiganshire; the number was 3,240 in 1991. Whereas there was a fairly consistent decline in the number of farm labourers employed, the number of farmers remained stable for some periods and then changed; there was for example an actual increase between 1980 and 1986, but this was followed by a decline. The statistics are not entirely reliable, since census figures do not allow for farmers who are actually following a second occupation because their farms make little or no profit. Other sources of agricultural employment at first or second hand are the Clynderwen and Cardiganshire Agricultural Cooperative at Aberystwyth, Cardigan and Tregaron, the Meat and Livestock Commissions and the Farmers' Union of Wales, both with headquarters at Aberystwyth, and agricultural machinery contractors.

The Cardigan Wildlife Centre. [Courtesy of Mike Snow and the West Wales Naturalists' Trust]

So many issues of political, economic and environmental interest and importance are involved in agriculture and agricultural policies that it would be over-ambitious to attempt to deal with them here, but two things can be said. The first is that recent changes in the European Common Agricultural Policy will certainly lead to further major changes, perhaps most obviously in a reduction in sheep numbers, with far-reaching consequences for the rural environment. Whether farmers will be able to cope by diversification remains to be seen. Secondly – despite the darker legacy which has already been dealt with in Chapter 19, and although Cardiganshire farmers and families are much reduced in number, with a lesser share in the overall wealth of the community – their importance at the core of the county's life remains vital. This is still the county's premier Welsh-speaking industry. These are men and women who in spite of every obstacle still maintain rural life as best they can in

HORSE-BREEDING has long been one of the most successful aspects of Ceredigion farming. In 1915 there were 48 horse-fairs in the county, and although most have faded away, 32 present-day studs are listed in the Welsh Pony and Cob Society's history; the Society's head office is in Aberystwyth. Cardiganshire and Montgomeryshire are the heartland of these breeds. The Trefaes stud at Beulah has sold Welsh cobs to Australia, South America and to the king of Nepal, and has marketed Welsh ponies worldwide; other studs in the county are similarly active. Legendary cob stallions such as Brenin Gwalia are still spoken of with awe decades after their deaths.

changing circumstances. They have faced the challenges of wind and weather, of acid rain and soil erosion, of poor natural drainage, of foot-and-mouth, of fickle markets and of government and European policies which are usually well-meant but sometimes blundering, even disastrous. In such circumstances, and remembering their contribution to the Co-operative movement and to the Royal Welsh Agricultural Show from the beginning, Cardiganshire's farmers have contributed hugely to Welsh agriculture. Nor should one forget men like Dic Jones and J.R. Jones, farmers and poets with a proud contribution to national and local culture.

* * *

Major contributions have been made to the county's post-war economy by two large government-driven projects. The hydro-electric scheme at Cwmrheidol gave so much temporary employment that it skewed the 1961 census figures. More extensive employment was given by the Royal Aircraft Establishment centre at Aber-porth, whose World War II origins have been described in Chapter 24. After the end of the war the Aber-porth base and its airstrip were retained, the airstrip relaid in tarmac, and the complex of buildings on the headland south of Aber-porth became a major launch site for testing weapons, particularly the first British sea-to-air missiles. Weapons were aimed at large floating targets or at flying drones sent down from RAF Llanbedr in Merionethshire. The presence of the RAE was an enormous economic boost for south Cardiganshire, though unemployment remained chronic; in 1997 there was 12% unemployment in the area, and the closure of textile factories at Cardigan has made matters more difficult still. The RAE employment pattern was classic; servicing was done by local labour but the higher staff echelons were, inevitably, filled by incomers. Particularly welcome were the apprenticeships annually awarded to boys from local secondary schools. Less welcome were the occasional echoing booms from the launches and the requirement on fishing and pleasure boats to avoid a large area of the bay. It is not easy to disentangle the impact of RAE/DERA on the Welsh language in the area from that of tourism, retirement and second-home ownership in general.

The RAE was eventually restructured as the Defence Test and Evaluation Organisation (DTEO), conducting all kinds of trials at Aber-porth, including the training of dogs, and the airstrip continued in use for liaison flights and trials activities. In 1995 the DTEO was amalgamated with other bodies as part of the Defence Evaluation and Research Agency (DERA), and in 2001 DERA became part of a public-private partnership QinetiQ, and the airstrip was leased to a private individual. Qinetiq is a major centre of innovation in Britain, with its main centres at Malvern and

NUCLEAR power in Cardiganshire? This potentially massive project never got off the ground. In June 1957 officials of the Central Electricity Authority and Cardiganshire County Council inspected the Llanrhystud flats for suitability for establishing a nuclear power station, but Trawsfynydd and Wylfa gained preference. The site, like others, would have had a forty-year working life and a two-to-ten-thousand-year after-life.

Farnborough. At the time of writing the defence research facilities offer less employment than previously, and a plan is afoot to develop a business park on part of the site, with the airstrip developed for public use.

The 2001 Census gives some idea of the spread of paid employment in Ceredigion at the beginning of the 21st century, though the figures contain surprises. They are best presented as a table, in percentage terms, using the Census categories:-

the motor trade (16.75% – a remarkable figure)
education (12.44%)
health and social work (11.72%)
agriculture, hunting and forestry (8.64%: this is the second highest figure for the 22 Welsh local authorities)
manufacturing (7.86%)
construction (7.76%)
hotels and catering (7.75%)
real estate, renting and business activities (7.53%)
public administration and defence (6.18%)
transport, storage, communication (4.32)

Other categories are insignificant; tourism does not figure as a separate group. Gender differences are significant: four times as many women as men are involved in health and social work; twice as many women as men in education and hotel/catering work. Men dominate construction, agriculture and manufacturing, but in the motor trade, public administration and real estate the gender percentages are roughly equal. The figure for the motor trade is hard to credit. The figure for the construction industry (which represents 13.42% of employed males) is interesting in view of the current perceived shortage of workers: at the time of writing the considerable workforce engaged in restoring Alexandra Hall on Aberystwyth's seafront derives partly from eastern Europe, and will probably all move on when the work is over.

* * *

The sea for centuries had provided a highway for commerce and employment both on ship and shore, and although much shrunken in its importance since the west Wales shipping heyday of the mid-19th century, it can never be ignored. Shipbuilding died in the 1880s but the building of boats continued. A boatbuilding yard at Aberystwyth, on the site now occupied by the fire-station, was busy until 1948 in the building of wooden ships' lifeboats, and 25-ton fishing boats for the Pacific islands. Shipbuilding returned in the 1980s to the estuary of the river Leri, where it flows into the Dyfi, with the creation of F.L. Steelcraft, building and repairing an eclectic range of steel vessels, some of them seagoing tugboats. This company, now Steelcraft Kit, can claim to have built as many boats in thirty years as were built in Aberystwyth in a century, though not of comparable tonnage.

Ships – as opposed to boats – are now only rarely seen close to the Ceredigion coast, and a sight like the visit of a large detachment of the Home Fleet to

Aberystwyth in 1911 is hardly likely ever to be seen again. A converted Norwegian whaler of 1912, the *Ocean Defender*, twice visited Aberystwyth harbour during the 1990s, and the cadet training brig *Royalist* was the first square-rigger to tie up in the harbour for a century. The Greenpeace vessel *Rainbow Warrior* has also sailed into the bay. The most significant single development of the 1990s on the Ceredigion coast was the creation of the Aberystwyth marina. The sleepy atmosphere of the tidal harbour vanished with the dredging of the mudflats which created a permanent basin, the installation of pontoons and the creation of a large complex of waterside buildings.

Elsewhere, little has changed recently. A small development at Aberaeron has created a permanent pool of water favoured by ducks as well as yachts, but the harbour itself remains tidal. The river is now spanned by a useful but visually incongruous wooden footbridge. Cardigan's oldest warehouse now houses an excellent maritime heritage exhibition, while downstream a small Fleetwood trawler, abandoned here some years ago by her crew, rots sadly on a muddy bank. Dredging the Teifi would be drastically expensive, but would give a tremendous fillip to maritime life in such a picturesque estuary. Virtually the whole present and future of maritime activity on the Ceredigion coast is to do with pleasure-boating and yachting. Yacht clubs have replaced shipping offices as centres of activity. The biggest dates in the calendar are those for the lifting of boats from the water in the autumn, and their re-launching in the spring. However, a few traditionally-minded folk may still prefer the oily, fishy smells of the town quay at Aberystwyth to the varnish and ever-clinking stays of the numerous yachts and dinghies on the marina, though all must be grateful for the deeper water that the marina provides. Nor has commercial fishing vanished, as has been seen in Chapter 17 above. The real importance of the Ceredigion coast today is not in shipping as such, but in the tourism which on sunny days fills beaches and coves from Mwnt to Ynys-las. On such days the wise resident of the county will prefer to walk the county's many miles of footpaths, bridleways and green lanes, or explore the Cambrian mountains.

As for the railways which so completely displaced the sea as the principal mode of economic travel and transport, the most recent phase of railway history in Cardiganshire has been almost entirely that of closures. The last line to arrive was the first to go; passenger services between Lampeter and Aberaeron ceased in 1951; goods services beyond Felin-fach stopped in 1965 and finally the line shut altogether in 1973 when the daily milk-train from the Green-grove creamery ceased – 45 miles of line to Carmarthen had been kept open for this single train since the cessation of service from the Pont Llanio creamery in 1970. The Cardi Bach ceased to run between Whitland and Cardigan in 1962 and goods trains stopped the following year. Passenger trains from Pencader to Newcastle Emlyn ran for the last time in 1952, but freight continued until 1975. Services on the Carmarthen-Aberystwyth line began to shrivel away in 1963 with the withdrawal of many freight facilities, and passenger trains finished in 1965, following the recommendations of the Beeching report of 1963 and a flood which breached the line in the Ystwyth valley. The last freight carried to Aberystwyth was petrol and diesel; the siding still exists but has been closed for years.

With the closure of the Aberystwyth-Carmarthen line, Aberystwyth ceased to be a connecting-point between north and south Wales; one cannot travel by rail from one half of the country to the other without passing through Craven Arms and Shrewsbury. Indeed, though I can offer no proof whatsoever, there is an interesting rumour that the line to Aberystwyth was kept open as part of an emergency evacuation plan in case of nuclear war; only readers who remember the Cuba crisis of 1962 will know the level of fear that people felt during the early 1960s. The only beneficiary of the line's closure was the Vale of Rheidol service, which was redirected to the old Manchester-Milford Carmarthen line platform. The Aberystwyth line to Machynlleth and Shrewsbury has so far survived, though much attenuated. The Cambrian Coast Express was withdrawn, special trains have virtually ceased, though the occasional visit of a steam locomotive still happens. Summer trains can be desperately overloaded. Freight services have ended, sidings have gone, the old buildings have either been destroyed or taken over by the Vale of Rheidol. Signals became radio-controlled. Only Borth station remains open between Aberystwyth and Machynlleth; the stations at Bow Street, Llandre, Ynys-las and Glandyfi were all closed. Railway employment in Aberystwyth is reduced to a few clerks and the Vale of Rheidol employees. The main station building is now a public house. Passengers, now relabelled customers, either contemplate the vandalised and trackless platform opposite or squeeze into a small but pleasant buffet room. However, the service to London is faster than twenty years ago, even when a daily locomotive-drawn train ran through to Euston, and the views over the Dyfi estuary are as fine as ever.

Meanwhile the Vale of Rheidol railway was threatened from time to time. It had become part of the GWR after the amalgamation of 1922, and of British Railways (later British Rail) in 1948. BR continued to run it, but threatened closure or sale every so often, thus gaining for the line the backing of a Supporters' Association, and help from the Welsh Tourist Board. Eventually BR sold the line, not to the consortium of employees which was the popular choice, but to the Brecon Mountain Railway, who have run it successfully. Unfortunately the company does not use volunteer aid and so the line lacks the atmospheric buzz to be found in the voluntarily-supported lines elsewhere in Wales. In addition to the Vale of Rheidol line, two narrow-gauge railways were mooted for the county using closed standard-gauge trackbeds. The first, at Henllan in the Teifi valley, using part of the old line to Newcastle Emlyn, has operated a two-mile track successfully every summer since 1986. The second, in the Ystwyth valley, failed.

* * *

Politics is certainly a field where change in the county has been considerable. True, the Cardis did not care when in 1945 the Labour party achieved its first landslide victory across Britain and brought on huge social change. The victorious Liberal candidate in the county, who had only a Labour opponent, was Roderic Bowen, a young barrister from Aber-porth, at the time one of only twelve Liberal MPs left in the House, seven of whom were from Wales. Despite criticism of his frequent absences from the House, criticism which dogged him for the rest of his parliamentary career, Bowen successfully defended the seat in 1950 against both Labour and Conservatives, and against Labour alone in 1951 and 1955. In 1959 there were two novelties; one was the first Plaid Cymru candidate, Gareth Evans, a university mathematics lecturer at Swansea. The second was the county's first woman parliamentary candidate, Loti Rees Hughes for Labour; the fact that she has had no successor is a clear reflection of Welsh anti-feminism in parliamentary politics. Despite all the attacks on Bowen's part-time parliamentary attendance, he defeated both aspirants. It is worth noting that although it took another 33 years for Plaid Cymru to achieve success in the county, the county council had frequently voted in favour of 'Home Rule' for Wales, which was of course a Liberal policy.

By the time of the 1964 general election the zest had gone out of the Cardiganshire hustings as elsewhere; village meetings were shrunken, and candidates found themselves preaching to the dutiful converted. More comfortable housing, and in particular the entertainment provided by television, seemed to have sapped whatever political vigour there might have been in the county. For the first time since 1950 a Conservative candidate came forward, together with Labour and Plaid Cymru, but once again Roderic Bowen held off all comers, though with a much diminished majority; by this time there were only two Liberal MPs left in Wales. The new Labour government had only a tiny minority, and Bowen's 1965 acceptance of the post of Deputy Speaker was widely seen as a further betrayal of the voters, on top of his patchy voting record. His promotion, if such it was, did not last long.

At the 1966 election the Labour party played a trump card. Elystan Morgan, a native of Bow Street and an ambitious and personable young barrister, had previously fought several elections as Plaid Cymru candidate for Wrexham and then in 1964 for Merioneth; he was vice-president of Plaid and regarded as Gwynfor Evans's natural heir as the party's president. His Merionethshire failure in 1964 against a weak Labour candidate was such a profound personal disappointment that he joined Labour, and despite the odium which that switch attracted from some quarters he was able to draw enough votes from Plaid Cymru and the Liberals to destroy Bowen's occupancy of the seat. Elystan Morgan was certainly the ablest representative the county had had for generations, and his ability was recognised by swift promotion to a junior ministry in the Home Office, which he handled effectively. As a result he

Roderick Bowen, seen with Norah Isaac, first head teacher of the Lluest Welsh School.

[National Library of Wales]

was able to hold the seat in 1970 when across the United Kingdom Labour succumbed to a surprising defeat at the hands of Edward Heath's Conservatives; the Liberals clung to second place while Plaid Cymru drove the Conservatives to the bottom of the poll.

However, all was not propitious for Elystan Morgan. For 1974 the Liberals had chosen an outstanding candidate in the person of Geraint Howells, an enormously likeable farmer deeply embedded in the life of the county, unlike previous Liberal candidates. His readiness at agricultural shows to strip off his jacket, don an apron, seize a sheep and shear it by hand was only one of his many assets; his memory for faces, his family involvement in Welsh culture (he was secretary of the Ponterwyd eisteddfod for years), his impish sense of humour, were all widely appreciated. He had local experience as a county councillor, and was crucially involved in the establishment of the bilingual secondary school at Aberystwyth, whereas Elystan Morgan, who had supported such schools elsewhere in Wales, opposed the Aberystwyth development. This move did him considerable damage among those Plaid Cymru voters who had supported him previously. When Edward Heath challenged Britain to re-elect him in February 1974 Labour squeezed into power with a bare majority, but Geraint Howells swept the Liberals back into occupancy of Ceredigion. He maintained his position in the second election of that year against Elystan Morgan, and again in 1979, 1983 and 1987 against other opponents when Conservatives claimed second place. The 1983 and 1987 elections were fought in an extended constituency, Ceredigion and Pembrokeshire North; on both occasions the Plaid Cymru candidate, Cynog Dafis, was fourth in the poll and Howells victorious. Little could either man have dreamed in either year of what might yet befall.

Gwynfor Evans's remarkable triumph at the Carmarthen by-election in the summer of 1966 had been ironic indeed in view of Elystan Morgan's apparent belief that no Plaid Cymru candidate would ever reach Westminster. It was followed by the 1974 Plaid Cymru victories of Dafydd Elis Tomos in Merionethshire and Dafydd Wigley in Caernarfon. Geraint Howells's deeply ingrained broad-minded Welshness sat very easily with this changing scene, and it seemed that Ceredigion was his as long as he chose to keep it. Through the 1980s, however, Wales had suffered so much at the hands of the Thatcher government that it seems in retrospect that, whatever might happen elsewhere, there were sufficient Ceredigion voters who felt that Geraint Howells, good Welshman as he was, had had a long innings and it might be time for a change. Plaid Cymru was able to bring off its own trump card, an alliance with the Green Party which was sincerely entered into by Plaid Cymru's faithful candidate, Cynog Dafis, whose dogged determination, intelligence and personal dignity had acquired wide respect. He defeated Howells by three thousand votes in 1992 and defeated a Labour candidate in 1997 by nearly seven thousand; Geraint Howells had meanwhile accepted nomination to the upper House as Lord Geraint; he had been preceded there by Lord Elystan (Morgan), and both were followed there by the most important Cardiganshire-born politician of his or any generation since Sir John Vaughan, namely John Morris, long-time Labour MP for Aberavon, Secretary of State for Wales, the first Cardi ever to become a Knight of the Garter.

The 1997 Labour landslide brought constitutional change to Wales for the first time since the age of Henry VIII. The Callaghan Labour government of 1976-79 had, without any real conviction, offered Wales the chance to vote for a Welsh assembly, but the proposal was soundly defeated even in Gwynedd. By 1997, however, eighteen years of Conservative government had helped bring enormous changes to Wales, especially the decimation of the steel industry, the virtual elimination of coal mining and the BSE catastrophe in cattle rearing. A series of Secretaries of State for Wales had favoured a variety of policies and presented a range of personae, from the comparative successes of Peter Thomas in the Heath government and Peter Walker in the 1980s to the hated governor-generalship of the widely-loathed John Redwood, who left his mark on Ceredigion's economy and morale by shutting down the Ministry of Agriculture's operations at Trawsgoed mansion. Despite the Conservatives' reluctant establishment of a Welsh-medium television service and extended legal and educational support for the Welsh language, Wales voted the Conservatives out of every constituency in Wales in 1997, and the 1998 referendum for the Assembly brought success by a hair's breadth – but by a large margin in Ceredigion, which went on to elect Plaid Cymru's Elin Jones as its Assembly Member in 1999 and again in 2003. Cynog Dafis, who gained membership of the Assembly through the 'list', found the dual burden of service in Cardiff Bay and Westminster too heavy, and chose to serve the Assembly. This brought about Plaid Cymru's first ever by-election defence of a parliamentary seat, and success for its candidate Simon Thomas, who held the seat again in the general election of 2001.

* * *

The difficulties faced by county councillors and officers running such a small authority as Cardiganshire were well exemplified in 1945, when the county rate had to be increased by 20% and became the highest in England and Wales. Despite many improvements, standards of living in rural Cardiganshire, as in much of rural Wales, inevitably lagged behind life in the towns. Electricity (not a local government responsibility) was not brought to many villages and farms until the 1960s; piped water, drainage and sewerage were then still far from satisfactory, though these difficulties have been largely resolved. John Gibson had campaigned in the *Cambrian News* early in the 20th century for Aberystwyth to deal with its own sewage rather than pump it into the sea; only in the 1990s was this finally brought about.

Planning has not been the easiest of tasks; like many rural authorities, Cardiganshire did not take readily to planning procedures as laid down in the Town and Country Planning Act of 1947, and from time to time Cardiganshire and Ceredigion planning committees have been criticised, even in the House of Commons. Their task has not been easy; complaints that too many houses are built, thus encouraging too many incomers and anglicisation, are countered by pointing out that a shortage of houses drives up prices beyond the reach of local people; the issue is complex. In any case, selective housing policies might well be liable to prosecution under anti-discrimination laws. In fact it tends to be local people who prefer new houses, while outsiders prefer older dwellings. Perhaps more to the point is the all-British problem of a loss of visual taste which has allowed slate and lime-wash to be replaced by garish bricks and tiles in the name of convenience and economy. Heavily subsidised wind farms have proved more controversial; hard-pressed farmers gain income, and electricity is produced without atmospheric pollution, but tourism is hardly likely to be encouraged in Wales's precious wilderness areas by the creation of giant wind turbines in the Cambrian mountains, however elegant they are as machines.

The county has been more consistently successful in the field of education and library service originally developed by Alun R. Edwards (see also Chapter 22), which became one of the best in Wales and England, thanks to the librarian's skill and the county council's support – and that despite the dreadfully inadequate accommodation still in use today. Such support was all the more remarkable if it be remembered that, as J. Graham Jones has pointed out, because the rateable value of properties was so low, the product of the penny rate in the county was the lowest in all the counties of England and Wales.

As in all local authorities, the calibre of county councillors has varied considerably, but Cardiganshire certainly produced a number of interesting figures, and of those, a surprising percentage came from among the county's Unitarians. Many were 'characters' and one figure must stand for many, J.M. Lloyd Thomas (1868-1955), whose career fell neatly into two halves. Born in Llannarth, he converted to Unitarianism, and had a highly individual career as an ordained minister in Glamorgan, Nottingham and Birmingham, supporting the more extreme wing of the suffragette movement and the cause of the Boers. Eventually he proclaimed himself to be a Free Catholic and set up his own church. However in 1932 he gave up his ministry and returned to live in Llannarth; he became a county councillor, serving on numerous bodies, and enthusiastically supporting a number of causes, including Alun R. Edwards's development of Llyfrgell Ceredigion, the county music service, pony-trekking and the encouragement of Welsh breeds of cattle and horses.

The 1974 abolition of the urban and rural district councils, the replacement of civil parish councils by 'community councils', and the reduction of what was now officially named 'Ceredigion' to the status of a district within the new county of Dyfed, were changes sorely felt and much criticised within the old county. Carmarthen was seen as being a long way away, and those who knew that the standards of many school buildings and the library services in the old Carmarthenshire were much inferior to those of Cardiganshire were not unnaturally concerned for the future, especially as the new county rates represented a considerable increase on the old, and since the sixteen Ceredigion representatives were outnumbered both by Pembrokeshire and Carmarthenshire councillors. It was unfortunate that the international oil crisis of that time brought in fierce government economies which were felt painfully in the new county halls and district offices. For the first time county councillors were paid for attendance at meetings, and since they were involved in much more travelling their expenses rose; this did not increase their popularity among the general public.

The Dyfed authority lasted barely twenty years; the Heath government had created it, it suffered under Wilson, Callaghan and Thatcher, the Major government abolished it. There is, however, a residual Dyfed authority: from 1974 the three combining counties had one Lord Lieutenant and one annually-appointed High Sheriff, and these two offices remain in existence. All else changed; the old county of Cardiganshire was from 1996 the new county of Ceredigion, this time an all-purpose authority with no district councils beneath it, only community councils with very limited responsibilities; without this change it is doubtful whether devolution would have squeaked through in 1998. The new counties had less authority; governmental centralisation in London and Cardiff left the counties with less to decide in the way of policy but a huge amount of administration, though in education much has been devolved to individual schools. The county's profounder economic, social and linguistic problems, discussed by generations of councillors, have hardly changed and are beyond the power of local government to solve; although the population is no longer shrinking, it is still an elderly population and the county still has an insecure economic base.

Perhaps the most difficult aspect of Ceredigion's practical problems was revealed in a 2002 government Land Registry report. The average house price for Ceredigion at that time was £99,225, compared with Monmouthshire (£142,381) at the top and Merthyr Tudful (£46,119) at the bottom of the list of the 22 Welsh local authorities. Ceredigion houses were the fourth most expensive in Wales. In the table of income per head, Ceredigion's figure was £17,684, while the Vale of Glamorgan was highest at £22,854 and Blaenau Gwent lowest at £16,209; this meant that Ceredigion incomes were fourth from bottom of the table. No other county in Wales showed such an unfavourable contrast between house prices and incomes. In house prices, even Pembrokeshire houses (£94,608) were cheaper than Ceredigion's, suggesting that problems other than those of second homes lay at the root of Ceredigion's difficulties. By the time of revising this chapter in 2004, these house-prices were already hugely increased.

The new Ceredigion all-purpose authority settled to its responsibilities with a mixed team of old and new faces among both the councillors and the officers. The council has forty-two members representing thirty-six wards. At the time of writing (late 2004) there are three party groups: sixteen Independents, sixteen Plaid Cymru, nine Liberal Democrats, and one Independent Labour. Those figures represent a considerable weakening of the Independents from their previous control of the council with twenty-three members. Much of the discussion and real decision-making happen in an inner cabinet of nine members. The range of responsibilities undertaken by an authority governing fewer than 80,000 people is astonishing, for although governments of both parties in recent decades have centralised decision-making and policy in London and Cardiff, actual administration at local level seems to increase from year to year. From the limited expenditure of £12,440 in 1889-90, Ceredigion will spend £114 million in 2003-04 – roughly £10,500 for every man, woman and child.

Of that £114 million, much is spent on education, which has changed enormously since 1945. It was then that the county produced a development plan which foresaw the end of all-age elementary schools and the concentration of all pupils of 11+ in secondary schools. The original purpose was to create 'bilateral' (all ability or 'grammar-modern') schools for Aberystwyth (two separate bilaterals), Tregaron, Aberaeron, Lampeter, Llandysul and Cardigan; the term 'comprehensive' had not yet come into local use, though comprehensive schools were already being established in Anglesey. The Ministry of Education accepted the bilateral structure for Tregaron, Lampeter and Aberaeron, but preferred separate grammar and modern schools elsewhere. Ironically, when comprehensive schools became the norm, Llandysul was to become eventually the last grammar school in Wales, although the local authority had not wanted it to be a grammar school in the first place! In 1973 Aberystwyth was reorganised into two comprehensives, Penweddig (bilingual) and Penglais (English-medium).

THE name of Jac L. Williams (1918-77) was for a generation synonymous with bilingual education. Born in Aberarth, he was a vigorous public commentator on matters linguistic, and he made the Department of Education at U.C.W. Aberystwyth from 1960 until his death (and indeed beyond) the major centre in Wales for the development of bilingual education, for which he campaigned throughout his career. His opposition to the establishment of a Welsh-language television channel brought him into conflict with many, but he thrived on debate, never abandoning courtesy.

The creation of Penweddig, the first bilingual secondary school in a Welsh-speaking area (the previous five had been established in Flintshire and Glamorgan) was due to the dedicated campaigning by groups of parents in the teeth of fierce opposition from a small group of critics, who had the grace to disband when defeated; both schools quickly proved themselves highly successful, setting a pattern which led to Llandysul also becoming a bilingual school, Ysgol Dyffryn Teifi. Welsh-medium education in south-west Wales owes a huge debt to W.J. Phillips, director of education briefly for Cardiganshire, then for Dyfed when that authority took the county over in 1974; it was largely through his guidance that councillors, aware of parental involvement, were willing to establish bilingual schools on the Penweddig model at Llanelli, Carmarthen, in the Gwendraeth valley and at Crymych. The county's further education establishments at Cardigan, Aberystwyth and Felin-fach eventually merged into Coleg Ceredigion, with the phasing out of provision at Felin-fach.

These reforms of secondary education had a drastic effect on younger children; junior schools no longer had pupils over the age of eleven, and increasingly did not have to worry about the 11+ examination. The primitive sanitary conditions which had prevailed in many schools were modernised. Kitchens had to be installed either in individual schools or in an area centre, since school meals had to be provided for all who wanted them, as well as school milk. Some primary schools had to survive with small numbers; in the 1960s there were still one-teacher schools in the county. School closure was always stoutly resisted, most successfully in the case of Trefeurig, where the opening of a new school at Penrhyn-coch in the early 1970s was meant to make the closure of the former possible. There was a parent-teacher rebellion, and the authority revoked the closure; Trefeurig survives to the present day, because new housing at Penrhyn-coch meant that the new school was inadequate virtually from the beginning. The issue is certain to haunt communities and their councillors in the immediate future, since the 2001 Census showed fewer children in the 0-5 age-group than in the 6-10 cohort.

* * *

As if it were not enough that Cardiganshire had two university institutions, for a while even that achievement was excelled; the Welsh College of Librarianship, inspired by Alun R. Edwards, was established at Llanbadarn in 1964, and the Welsh College of Agriculture was created in 1970, both teaching to higher-education standards. Until the two bodies were swallowed up by the University College (which itself was later re-branded as the University of Wales, Aberystwyth), Cardiganshire had four degree-giving bodies, not to mention the two theological colleges in Aberystwyth, one Congregationalist, one Presbyterian, and for a while a Roman Catholic college at Castell Brychan, now home of the Welsh Books Council.

Life has not always been smooth for either of the Aberystwyth or Lampeter university institutions. At Aberystwyth the controversial appointment of Goronwy Rees as principal in 1953 was followed by fierce debate, and he resigned in 1957; dignity was restored with the appointment of Thomas Parry to the post. There was fierce resistance in the 1960s by some of the staff against the development of a bilingual policy for teaching and administration. The 1980s were economically tough for the college; the departments of Chemistry, Music, Philosophy and Classics were all closed, and then and later other departments were amalgamated, though others came into existence. Lampeter, as already mentioned, faces a chronic recruiting problem.

With the founding of the National Library of Wales, the Welsh Plant Breeding Station at Gogerddan (now the Institute for Grassland and Environmental Research), with the growth of the University at Aberystwyth to some 8,000 students at the time of writing, with the establishment of the prestigious University of Wales Centre for Advanced Welsh and Celtic Studies, Aberystwyth and the county have been hugely endowed with cultural responsibilities and opportunities. Education is one of Ceredigion's biggest industries, employing thousands, from university vice-chancellors and school head teachers to porters, cooks, cleaners and school bus-drivers. The county has a centuries-long record of distinguished educational practice of which it can be justly proud, which is best exemplified by a statistic from the 2001 Census. This is not the fact that 21.7% of inhabitants aged 16 or over had degrees or higher professional qualifications, the third highest percentage in Wales; that may be partly accounted for by incomers to the two university staffs. More directly to the county's credit is that the 24.99% with *no* qualifications at all is the lowest figure among the twenty-two Welsh local authorities; unfortunately this figure is rendered worthless by the overplus of well-qualified students.

* * *

Health was and is a key issue in local government. Ironically it was the return of peace which brought the county's greatest health crisis of the century to Aberystwyth and ensured adverse coverage in London's newspapers. Typhoid had been an occasional visitor to Aberystwyth during the 1930s, but from 1941 till 1945 there had not been a single case. The summer of 1946 was a good one for the town; the holiday trade was picking up, the battleship *George V* was anchored in the bay and the Welsh Guards paraded in the town. Ice cream was back on sale after the lean wartime years; unfortunately one of the vendors, who sold regularly outside the Alexandra Road primary school, was, unknown to himself, a carrier of typhoid, and he occasionally neglected the hygiene precautions he was legally bound to take. In the summer of 1945 several local doctors found themselves treating patients with a variety of unpleasant symptoms.

The borough's Medical Officer, Dr D.I. Evans, reacted swiftly; samples were rapidly confirmed as typhoid, the ice cream source detected, and the 44 beds in the new isolation hospital was suddenly so full that an appeal went out to hospitals in south Wales to accept Aberystwyth patients, and all were dealt with. Other sufferers emerged across England, all of whom had visited Aberystwyth and eaten the same ice cream. Fortunately the strain of typhoid was not as virulent as the disease can be on occasion, and of the 210 known cases only four died.

Working for the Cardiganshire health service must have been both rewarding and frustrating. The shortage of resources in such a small authority, the stubborn persistence of tuberculosis, problems of water, sewage, housing and diet called for the greatest patience and persistence. But health service revolution eventually arrived. In 1948, with medical services and hospital provision no longer dependent on charity or the ability to pay, Aberystwyth's hospital became the provider of services for mid-Wales as far as Machynlleth, Newtown and Lampeter. With the building in 1966 of a new hospital on the Bronglais site of the old workhouse, the North Road buildings became a geriatric unit for nearly thirty years, until the unit was transferred to new accommodation in the Bronglais hospital.

Not that the National Health Service solved every problem in the county. Ambulances had to be provided by the county council, and according to Ernest Jones's successor Dr Iestyn Morgan Watkin, the service in the mid-1950s was dismal in the extreme. The vehicles were boneshakers, drivers were untrained in any kind of medicine and the vehicles contained no oxygen, radio-telephones or other equipment. Reform came in a typically Cardiganshire way. A pedestrian was knocked down in Ponterwyd and seriously injured. By sheer chance the MOH happened to be on the scene and phoned for an ambulance; he had immediately recognised the agitated car driver as a county councillor. The duty ambulance driver refused to set out from Aberystwyth until he had finished his tea, while the duty attendant had to be summoned from a football match; the vehicle reached Ponterwyd ninety minutes after being called. Following the unfortunate pedestrian's death an inquest was held at which the coroner was naturally appalled by the state of the ambulance service, and the *Cambrian News* made much of the story. The result was the provision of four well-equipped Mercedes-Benz ambulances for service in the county.

In a sense both everything and nothing has changed. Everything, in that well-trained general practitioners are available for all, dispensing modern drugs and sending patients where necessary to well-equipped hospitals. Efficient water supplies and sewage disposal are everywhere. True, there is a shortage of dental treatment in the National Health system in Ceredigion as elsewhere, but the situation is still a great deal better than it once was, when poorly qualified men worked foot-treadle drills – though extraction was the general rule. Yet nothing has changed in that the county is, as it was in the 1920s, a place where children and young people are in short supply, and where the imbalance of age means a heavy workload for the system in terms of the diseases and general health problems of the elderly.

* * *

One of Sir Ifan ab Owen Edwards's major contributions to Welsh language youth culture (already referred to in Chapter 22 above) was that he managed to keep both Urdd Gobaith Cymru and his pioneer Welsh-medium primary school out of political controversy. Post-World War II Cardiganshire was still very much a Welsh-speaking area – but as in the rest of Wales, the county's governmental and administrative life was almost entirely English-medium, particularly as far as documentation was concerned. It was only in the late 1950s and early 1960s, with the Beasley family's beginnings of a revolt against English-only local rate demands, followed by Saunders Lewis's sensational radio lecture *Tynged yr Iaith* ('The Fate of the Language'), that matters began to change. On a February Saturday afternoon in 1963 a group of young men and women responded to Saunders Lewis's lecture by sticking posters on the walls and windows of the Aberystwyth Post Office demanding official recognition for the language. Some frustrated members then moved to Trefechan bridge and sat down on the roadway, blocking traffic. The furore which ensued led to the foundation of *Cymdeithas yr Iaith Gymraeg*, the Welsh Language Society, whose activities have done so much to raise the profile and status of the language in government and commerce, and which has always had its national office in Aberystwyth.

The 1960s saw a burgeoning of Welsh-language movements which were part of the same wave as the growth of Welsh-medium schools and the Language Society. None was so intimately linked with Ceredigion as those, but the county saw the spread of *papurau bro*, community papers such as *Y Tincer*, *Gambo*, *Barcud* and *Yr Angor* which brought printed Welsh into hundreds of homes and kept groups of devoted supporters busy writing, editing and distributing their papers. This movement had been made possible by access to cheap offset-litho printing, which obviated the use of metal type. Branches of *Merched y Wawr*, the women's group movement begun at Parc, Bala, spread through Ceredigion, with its headquarters in Aberystwyth. Young Farmers' Clubs, although not operating a monoglot Welsh policy, were strongholds of Welsh-language activity among young people. *Menter Teifi* (technically just outside Ceredigion, since its base is in Newcastle Emlyn) was established in 1979 to encourage local economic initiative. With the development of

BBC's Radio Cymru and the founding of Radio Ceredigion there was for the first time a potential of choice between Welsh-language radio programmes, though the material on each tended to be similar. On the other hand the influx of migrants, the presence of the television on almost every hearth, the globalising power of English and the decline of organised religion have severely eroded the confidence of Ceredigion's Welsh-speaking communities. The apparent deterioration of the long-term prospects for agriculture as a viable industry are particularly menacing, since agriculture is a major domain of the Welsh language.

The various councils which have governed the county – Cardiganshire, Dyfed, Ceredigion – have on the whole responded well to the demands made on them for bilingual services and education. But the in-migration issue is one which Welsh local authorities as a whole have found intractable and they have shied away from the drastic remedies proposed in some quarters. Ceredigion's housing policies are fiercely criticised by pressure groups such as *Cymuned* ('Community'); the paradox is that building fewer houses would force up prices even further, thus pressing younger people to move away. Nor has the National Assembly in Cardiff taken up the challenge. The Welsh language, the language of the overwhelming majority of Cardis for more than a thousand years, is on the cusp of survival. The best that can be hoped, as Aitchison and Carter optimistically suggest, is that 'rather than the slow eradication of the language which seemed likely at mid-century, a widespread bilingualism seems now much more likely.'

* * *

To those old enough to remember a different period, the decline of organised religion in the county, as over Wales in general, is a major change. It is true that in 2001 the census question on religion showed 70.8% claiming to be Christian, only just below the figure for Wales and England, but 19.7% claimed no religion, as opposed to 14.8% for Wales and England, possibly reflecting the student overplus. But the claim to be Christian is hardly borne out by the evidence of one's own eyes every Sunday, nor by such details that are available elsewhere. The decline has been long-term. The high point in Cardiganshire's Calvinistic Methodist membership was 6,750 communicants in 1906; after that there was a steady decline, and in 1971 the figure was 4,199. The real catastrophe

sic transit... Dewi Prys Thomas's Siloh chapel frontage of the 1960s has now vanished as if it had never been.

was in Sunday School membership, which, with the arrival of compulsory schooling in the 1870s, went immediately into steady decline, from 10,071 in 1873 to 1,280 in 1971. Nearly as striking was the decline in 'attenders', those who were not full members; they fell from 14,103 in 1873 to 6,659 in 1953. An individual Congregationalist chapel whose reports survive, Seion in Baker Street, Aberystwyth, shows a slow decline in membership between 1907 (483 full members) and 1985 (304 members). What is not clear from such statistics is whether – as one strongly suspects – attendance has declined even more steeply than membership, and that the number of young members has declined more steeply still.

It is clear that there was a particularly serious decline in attendance by children and young people; there was also a less obvious decrease in the percentage of active adult males, though they absolutely dominated all public aspects of chapel and church life for much of the 20th century; women were only able to emerge in leadership roles in default of men. The slow decline in the denominations which set in across Wales after 1926 became steeper after 1950. In Wales as a whole the 500,000+ nonconformist members of 1926 had been reduced by 1972 to 220,600, and there has been a considerable reduction since then. True, the Church in Wales was able to cheer itself with its increasing numbers of Easter communicants between 1945 and 1960, but thereafter the Church too began to suffer serious losses. Easter communicants in Wales dropped from 181,000 in 1962 to 136,000 in 1982, and now number fewer than 100,000. Separate figures for the Church in Ceredigion are not easy to come by, but it is clear that the drastic secularisation of rural Welsh life, helped on by the declining percentage of Welsh-speakers and the loss of natural Welsh-speaking communities, is as evident in Ceredigion churches as elsewhere.

When Cardiganshire's population decline was finally reversed after 1961, it was due almost entirely to the influx of non-Welsh-speakers, many of whom were unchurched and virtually all of whom found Welsh nonconformity inaccessible and unsympathetic, though some of them have helped maintain Anglican churches that would otherwise have been closed by now. Equally if not more complex was the development of alternative cultures: football, radio, television, the motor car, shopping. One aspect of the change worth exploring is the professionalisation of so many areas of life. Professional teachers, supported by professional administrators, using expensive equipment in purpose-built schools, have made the efforts of many volunteers in Sunday School look amateurish in comparison. Amateur activities in drama and music can hardly compete with the offerings of television and the recording industry. Another aspect, not easy to analyse, is the fragmentation of society, the continuing development of the autonomy of individuals and their consequent and inevitable loss of social responsibility.

Much research remains to be done on the dechristianisation of Wales, but it seems unlikely to be carried out because the subject of religion is not seen as intellectually fashionable. Nevertheless, in Ceredigion as elsewhere, a whole way of life has changed. No neighbour would now dare criticise another for mowing his lawn on Sunday as still happened in the 1960s. Triple attendance on Sunday (*cwrdd bore, Ysgol Sul, cwrdd nos*) hardly exists any more outside the larger towns; many chapels have difficulty filling their pulpits and a few pews once on a Sunday, let alone twice. Prayer-meetings, singing practices to prepare for the *gymanfa ganu*, preaching festivals are steadily weakening where not extinct. John Davies has attributed much of the general change in modern culture to central heating in our homes, an idea well worth contemplating. Why struggle out of doors on a winter's night to sit on hard benches in a chilly church, chapel or vestry now that more than one room in the home is warm and comfortable?

THE Cardiganshire Unitarian tradition remained vigorous into the 20th century. A single chapel, Pantydefaid at Prengwyn, produced a dozen ministers for the cause. In the 20th century such well-known figures in the county and beyond as T. Oswald Williams, his brother Gwarnant, D. Jacob Davies and the Lewis family of publishers at Llandysul were or are all Unitarians. But there has been the same shrinkage of ministry and congregations as in other denominations; according to the South Wales Unitarian website there are still fourteen congregations in the county, but only five have services every Sunday.

Naturally enough, the last chapels to be opened have usually been the first to close, either to fall into ruin or to be sold and developed as homes. Some Ceredigion chapels have already disappeared entirely, such as that at Ysbyty Ystwyth, at the time of writing, a heap of rubble, and the fine Sunday School building at Trefechan, Aberystwyth. Others have been turned into warehouses or have been, so to speak, domesticated. This is now happening even in places, such as Pisgah and Moriah on the Aberystwyth-Devil's Bridge road, which gained their names from their chapels. Churches are following suit; the little church at Blaen-plwyf is now a tasteful home, while the former church at Sarnau has sprouted a domestic excrescence quite out of architectural keeping with the original building.

Of course there are still some vigorous churches and chapels which it would be invidious to name – mostly urban. A factor which has both contributed to the general breakdown of Welsh Christian life and been a result of that breakdown is the disappearance of the professional ministry from many areas. In 1930 it was claimed that there were more in full-time religious employment in Cardiganshire than there were teachers! The modern shortage is usually blamed on the lack of recruits, in other words the lack of young people with the faith to commit to a life of sacrifice. Such a decline has been self-propelled, so to speak, not simply because there are fewer believers, but because shrinking congregations cannot or do not make the sacrificial effort to pay full-time ministers properly, even if they can be found. These joint reasons explain why some large areas are now without any resident minister, while those in post have numerous small congregations. Thus in 1987 the Presbyterian chapels in Tal-y-bont, Llanbadarn Fawr, Borth, Coedgruffudd, Comins-coch and Bow Street were all brought under one minister. The Church in Wales, though it lost many of its endowments in 1920, made a huge effort to raise money to maintain a professional structure and thereby a more regular ministry, but it still suffers from the simple shortage of faithful recruits and poor rewards, and in particular the export of Welsh-speaking priests has been replaced by bringing in

Welsh learners from elsewhere in Wales and beyond – without them, the Church in Wales would hardly be able to staff even its linked parishes in the Welsh-speaking countryside.

There are however other aspects to contemporary Ceredigion's religious life than Christianity. The considerable numbers of overseas students attending the two universities include many Moslems, and there is a well-endowed centre for Islamic and Jewish Studies within the college at Lampeter. Many Hasidic Jews spend group holidays at Aberystwyth and are conspicuous by their dress. There must certainly be Hindus and Buddhists among the student population, and these faiths have had a certain following elsewhere; for some time in the 1970s there was a 'Divine Light' mission at Cnwch-coch, and there is a Buddhist presence in Cwmrheidol, while the Bahai are present in Borth. Whether any of these faiths will achieve more than transient populations in Ceredigion remains to be seen.

* * *

Given that Ceredigion has been a clearly defined unit for over a thousand years, it is hardly surprising that native inhabitants identify themselves strongly as 'Cardis' vis-à-vis other Welsh people, with their own pride and sense of humour, much of which is self-mocking. Inevitably this self-identification has been seriously weakened by the process of population replacement that is happening in the county. Even if we admit that there is a serious distortion in the 2001 Census evidence that 42% of the population had been born outside Wales, we must still accept that at least 30% of the population are from beyond the Welsh border. On the other hand, one might have supposed that the comparative ubiquity of the car would have helped bind the population together; the car is, however, a fragmenter of society rather than a bond. In any case, Ceredigion is too large and its communities too diffuse for most people to know the whole area really well, nor is there a single large centre for meeting and shopping. North of Synod Inn the influence of Aberystwyth is felt, and beyond Aberystwyth, Machynlleth and Shrewsbury. For the region south of a line from Lampeter to Synod Inn, Cardigan exerts a certain pull, and beyond Lampeter and Cardigan are the attractions of Swansea, Carmarthen and Haverfordwest. Within the county there is a vague yet obvious north-south divide: the villages of Aber-banc, Trebedw, Penrhiw-pâl and Coed-y-bryn are as strange to the northern Cardi as are

ABERYSTWYTH, although not a county town, is a virtual alternative capital of Wales. Its central position (equally difficult to reach from all parts!) nevertheless drew the Methodist Fathers there in 1823 to write their church constitution, and the opening of the University College (1872) and the establishment of the National Library (1909) gave the town serious weight as a national cultural centre. Numerous bodies have their Welsh headquarters in the town, among them the Welsh Language Society, the Forestry Commission, the Welsh Nursery School Movement, the Farmers' Union of Wales, the Welsh Pony and Cob Society, the Welsh Books Council, the Centre for Advanced Welsh and Celtic Studies, Merched y Wawr, the National Union of Teachers of Wales (UCAC).

Penrhyn-coch, Swyddffynnon, Trefeurig and Ysbyty Ystwyth to the Cardis of the south – and how many Cardis know where Fforest yr Esgob lies? Moreover there are clear differences in speech between north and south, as for example between native Welsh-speakers from Blaenannerch and from Tal-y-bont. Ceredigion is a complex land, indeed a microcosm of Wales itself.

There are of course levels of community within the county which do reach all the way from Dyfi to Teifi. County councillors and officials meet together regularly; head teachers and teachers foregather; farmers know each other either face-to-face at marts or at one or two removes. Since the *Cambrian News* prints different editions for the north and for the south of the county, overlapping southward in competition with the *Tivy-side Advertiser*, they tend to serve lesser communities than the whole county, as by their nature do the *papurau bro*. In the field of culture, the county is in effect divided into thirds: Cardigan serves its area through Theatr Mwldan, Lampeter and Aberaeron are served by Felin-fach, while Aberystwyth, with the superior resources of the University Arts Centre as well as the town cinema, offers concerts, musicals, drama, cinema and art to a wider area than simply the north of the county, not to mention a choice of bookshops better than are available in Welsh cities and towns ten times its size. It is my sincere hope that through those shops, and the county's other bookshops, readers of this book, both native and incomer, may enrich their knowledge of this lovely and ever-fascinating little kingdom of Ceredigion.

Brenin Gwalia with his owner Mr David Rees. Happily, horse-rearing of the highest calibre still flourishes in Ceredigion. [Courtesy of The Welsh Pony and Cob Society]

Devil's Bridge, by Alfred Worthington.

Afterword: Ceredigion in the Future

by Owen Watkin, Chief Executive, Ceredigion County Council

Ceredigion's most enduring element is, of course, its geographical location. For a millennium and more, this has shaped its social identity more distinctively than any number of Statutes and Acts could ever hope to do.

However, if in the past its location may have kept the outside world at bay, or at least put it in a position to mould the influences of that world to its own shape, the rapid and pervasive impact of modern communication systems has radically eroded that remoteness. Over the last few decades, the television, internet and mobile phone have each in turn put paid to any notions of splendid isolation. And this technological revolution seems set to continue, further establishing the people of Ceredigion as citizens of the world, and allowing them to access that fast-moving world without having to move elsewhere.

Indeed it seems that its location seems more likely to draw people in than drive them out; unless, of course, you are one of those many young people who continue to see the bright lights of the cities - as much Cardiff now as London - as an escape from the shortage of opportunities and lack of material wealth in the county.

But what effect will this population movement have on the nature of the inherent society? No legislature can lawfully restrict freedom of movement. The challenge therefore is to protect the values and cultures of the society so that the best of our heritage can survive. Welsh-language culture has proved remarkably hardy in this respect, overcoming the pressures placed on it, like the infamous 'Welsh Not', with a mixture of resoluteness and innovation which is envied by minority language groups throughout Europe. Remarkable strides have been made in educating children in the use of Welsh, and each child reaching the age to move to secondary school should have a fundamental understanding and ability to use and understand the language. Support from parents who do not themselves speak Welsh for their children to attend Welsh-medium secondary schools is a growing feature. While this is happening, the educational achievements of the county's schools are the best in Wales. However the outward movement of a significant proportion of young people and the exponential increase in incomers is certain to put a strain on the education system to cope, while many of those coming to Ceredigion do not have children of school age.

A significant feature of those who come is their general goodwill towards the language and cultures of the area and their willingness to attempt to learn Welsh, some achieving exceptional success. But is this enough? To retain strong communities that have a sense of belonging, there has to be a very strong commitment by both the incomer and the resident to adapt and absorb. Being part of a community, as understood in Ceredigion, means being settled in an area, showing a willingness to dedicate time and energy to sustain the well-being of the community, and most importantly, to acknowledge and accept the values of that community. It is difficult to say whether the society still has the capacity to absorb these continuous changes without a dramatic dilution of those values that have given the county its enviable cultural identity.

But the concept of what constitutes society has altered. In the 1920s, Ceredigion was more homogeneous than in the last fifty years or so, which have seen the evolution of alternative communities and societies existing in parallel but with varying points of interaction and commonality. These groups, however, seem to be growing ever more distinct, often because people are encouraged to join activities by friends or contacts, and so, being self-selective, they become self-perpetuating. And as the population increases and becomes more complex in its composition, it is likely that this pattern of separate and parallel communities will continue. The Welsh-speaking community, for example, will, no doubt, maintain its considerable influence on the culture of the county as a whole but will gradually diminish as the dominant influence.

In contrast to the cultural values of the community, prospects for the economy may be brighter. GDP is, admittedly, low, according the area special support from European Structural Funds. A large part of the economy is dependent on public-sector organizations: the two universities, the local authority, NAW presence and a number of other significant institutions. The county is also remarkable for the absence of large or medium-size businesses and for its significant cohort of self-employed workers, often one-man firms. Unemployment is low, but wages are also low, with many examples of pluri-employment. Tourism has exceeded agriculture as the biggest sector producer.

Increasing interest in organic and high-quality, locally-produced foods give grounds for optimism. Changed patterns of purchasing, with greater reliance on locally-resourced materials and produce, should encourage the creation of sustainable local business and job opportunities. The towns of the county are buoyant despite, in some cases, what appear to be body blows suffered by the re-location of work, sometimes to other parts of the world where production costs are far lower. Towns are beginning to be regarded as leaders in Mid-Wales, drawing customers in and their relatively unspoilt nature provides an attraction to tourists who seek individuality rather than conformity. Indeed, the environment will continue to add to the wealth of the area: those who wish to enjoy the delights of the coastline and mountains and inland areas are often those who are also able to pay for the opportunities afforded by such places.

Although it might be claimed that the future will be like the past but more so, reality shows it never actually turns out that way. We may be allowed some structural calm for a period, but the influence of the National Assembly on the way our public institutions operate is sure to have far-reaching consequences, as witnessed, for example, by the way in which changes in the National Health Service have led to increased interaction with the local authority, in terms of social care and preventative health measures.

The County Council itself has already felt the impact of such changes. By Act of

Parliament, and with the active encouragement of the Assembly, a small political executive has been created within the local authority charged with the responsibility of delivering services. Consequently, local democracy is changing: an increasing emphasis on consulting the community, instead of relying on the elected representatives as the authentic voice of that community, will change the position of those councillors in society. And with these re-evaluations of role, along with increased external scrutiny of how the local authority manages itself, changes are also afoot that may bring solutions imposed from outside that are at odds with the established political culture of Ceredigion.

Sources and further reading by chapters.

References to the *Cardiganshire County History* have been simplified, since they are so numerous. The full titles of the two volumes so far published, under the general editorship of Emeritus Professor Ieuan Gwynedd Jones, are:

J.L. Davies and D.P. Kirby (eds) *Cardiganshire County History Volume 1: from the Earliest Times to the Coming of the Normans* (Cardiff, 1994).
Geraint H. Jenkins and Ieuan Gwynedd Jones (eds) *Cardiganshire County History Volume 3: Cardiganshire in Modern Times* (Cardiff, 1998).

References to annual publications are made simply to the year, without the encumbrance of volumes and numbers.

Several works are cited in more than one chapter, and are therefore listed here, rather than under chapter headings. References to David Jenkins (unless otherwise noted) are to his fascinating book *The Agricultural Community in South-West Wales at the turn of the Twentieth Century* (Cardiff, 1971), suffused with both knowledge and wisdom. Captain Jenkin Jones's diary of 1819, to which reference is made in several chapters, is to be found in *Historical Society of West Wales Transactions* volume 1 (1911). The relevant section is pp. 116-27. I have derived information in a number of chapters from the following books by W.J. Lewis:

Born on a Perilous Rock: Aberystwyth Past and Present (Aberystwyth, 1980).
'The Gateway to Wales': a History of Cardigan (Carmarthen, 1990).
A History of Lampeter (Cyngor Sir Ceredigion, 1997).

I have also derived material in several chapters from two volumes titled *'Those were the days': a History of Cardigan, the Locality and its People*, published in 1991 and 1992 'by the Cardigan & Tivy-side Advertiser from source material supplied by Donald Davies.' Several other sources are quoted in more than one chapter, but I have not multiplied the references.

Web-surfers will know more sites than I do, but the Ceredigion County Council's site, the National Library of Wales, Genuki, Wikipedia and the BBC are good starting places, and there is a remarkable local site for Llancynfelyn, all of which can be accessed through Google or Mozilla Firefox, as can information on most places in the county.

CHAPTER 1. THE NATURE OF THE LAND.

From the *Cardiganshire County History*, volume I:

D.Q. Bowen, 'The Land of Cardiganshire', 3-20.
C.C. Rudeforth, 'Soils and Land Use', 21-25.
P.D. Moore, 'The History of Vegetation in Cardiganshire', 26-42.
A.O. Chater, 'The Higher Plants and Vegetation of Cardiganshire', 43-75.
William Condry, 'The Vertebrate Animals of Cardiganshire', 76-90.
Adrian Fowles, 'The Lepidoptera of Cardiganshire', 91-104.

See also:

Denis Bates, 'The Aberystwyth Grits', and 'The Plynlimon area', and Edward
Watson, 'Periglacial Slope Deposits at Morfa-Bychan, near Aberystwyth' in M.G. Bassett (ed.), *Geological Excursions in Dyfed, South-West Wales* (Cardiff, 1982).

R. Cave & B.A. Hains (eds), *Geology of the country between Aberystwyth and Machynlleth* (HMSO London 1986).
CADW, *Register of Landscapes, Parks and Gardens of Special Historic Interest in Wales, I: Parks and Gardens: Carmarthenshire, Ceredigion and Pembrokeshire* (Cardiff, 2002). *II:1 Landscapes of Historic Interest in Wales* (Cardiff, 2001).
R.J. [Moore-] Colyer, *The Teifi: Scenery and Antiquities of a Welsh River* (Llandysul, 1987).
M.R. Dobson (ed.) *The Aberystwyth District* (Geologists' Association, 1995).
David James,' *Ceredigion: a Natural History* (Aberystwyth, 2001).
R.G. Stapledon (ed.), *A Survey of the Agricultural and Waste Lands of Wales* (London, 1936).

Chapter 2: Naming Ceredigion.

Iwan Wmffre, *The Place-names of Cardiganshire*, (Oxford 2004).

See also:

Melville Richards, 'Local Government in Cardiganshire', *Ceredigion* (1962) 272-82.
Melville Richards, *Welsh Administrative and Territorial Units* (Cardiff, 1969).

Chapter 3. Cairns and Hill forts.

From the *Cardiganshire County History*, volume I:

C.S. Briggs, 'The Bronze Age', 124-218.
J.L. Davies & A.H.A. Hogg, 'The Iron Age', 219-74.
R.A. Dodgson, 'Early Society and Economy', 343-64.
C.H. Houlder, 'The Stone Age', 107-23.

See also:

Richard Bradley, 'Mental and material landscapes in prehistoric Britain', in Della Hooke (ed.), *Landscape: the richest historical record* (Society for Landscape Studies, 2000) 1-12.
David Browne & Toby Driver, *Bryngaer Pen Dinas Hill-Fort: a Prehistoric Fortress at Aberystwyth* (Aberystwyth, 2001).
Vicki Cummings & Alasdair Whittle, *Places of Special Virtue: Megaliths in the Neolithic Landscapes of Wales* (Oxford, 2004).
Steve Jones, *The Descent of Men* (London, 2002).
Frances Lynch, Stephen Aldhouse-Green & Jeffrey L. Davies, *Prehistoric Wales* (Alan Sutton, 2000).
Kenneth Murphy, 'Plas Gogerddan, Dyfed: A Multi-Period Burial and Ritual Site', *Archaeological Journal* 149 (1992) 1-38.

Chapter 4. Romans in Ceredigion.

Cardiganshire County History, vol. I : J.L.Davies, 'The Roman Period', 275-317.

See also:

C.J. Arnold & J.L. Davies, *Roman and Early Medieval Wales* (Sutton, 2000)
J. Cantrell & A.Rylance, *Sarn Helen: Walking a Roman Road through Wales* (Milnthorpe, 1992).
Jeffrey L. Davies & T.G. Driver, 'The Discovery of a Roman coin hoard at Salem, Trefeurig', *Ceredigion* (1999) 1-4.

Chapter 5. The Early Kingdom.

From the *Cardiganshire County History* volume I:

R.A.Dodgson, 'Early Society and Economy', 343-64.
D.P.Kirby, 'The Political Development of Ceredigion, *c*. 400-1081'. 318-42.
D.P.Kirby, 'The Coming of Christianity', 365-77.
Heather James, 'The Archaeology of Early Christianity in Cardiganshire', 397-407.
Padraig O Riain, 'The Saints of Cardiganshire', 378-96.
W.Gwyn Thomas, 'The Early Christian Monuments'. 407-20.

See also:

Jane Carter, 'Santesau Ceredigion', *Ceredigion* (1998) 1-10.
Gillian L. Conway, 'Towards a Cultural Context for the Eleventh-century Llanbadarn Manuscripts', *Ceredigion* (1997) 9-28.
Wendy Davies, *Wales in the Early Middle Ages* (Leicester, 1982).
Wendy Davies, *Patterns of Power in Early Wales* (Oxford, 1990).
N.Edwards and A.Lane (eds.) *Early Medieval Settlements in Wales AD 400-1100* (Cardiff, 1988).
M. Lapidge, 'The Welsh-Latin poetry of Sulien's family', *Studia Celtica* 8/9 (1973-4) 68-106.
Charles Thomas & David Howlett, *'Vita Sancti Paterni': The Life of Saint Padarn and the Original Miniu* (Lampeter, 2003; published as volume 33 of *Trivium*).

Chapter 6. Resisting the Invaders.

R.R.Davies, *The Age of Conquest* (Oxford, 1987).
J. Goronwy Edwards, 'The Normans and the Welsh March', *Proceedings of the British Academy* (1956) esp. 164-67.
Ralph Griffiths, *Conquerors and Conquered in Medieval Wales*, chapters 16-18 (Cardiff, 1994).
Nerys Ann Jones & Huw Pryce, *Yr Arglwydd Rhys* (Cardiff, 1996).
Thomas Jones, *Brut y Tywysogion or the Chronicle of the Princes: Red Book of Hergest Version* (Cardiff, 1955).
D.J.C. King, 'The Castles of Cardiganshire', *Ceredigion* (1956) 50-69.
J.E.Lloyd, *A History of Wales from the Earliest Times to the Edwardian Conquest* (London, 1939).
J.E.Lloyd, *The Story of Ceredigion* (Cardiff, 1937).
Kari Maund, *The Welsh Kings* (Stroud, 2000).
Roger Turvey, *The Lord Rhys, Prince of Deheubarth* (Llandysul, 1997).

Chapter 7. Peace and Rebellion: Cardiganshire 1276-1543.

(See also for the previous chapter)

R.R. Davies, *The Revolt of Owain Glyn Dŵr* (Oxford, 1995).
Ralph A. Griffiths, *The Principality of Wales in the later Middle Ages* I (Cardiff, 1972).
Ralph A. Griffiths, *Conquerors and Conquered in Medieval Wales* (Cardiff, 1994).
T. Jones Pierce, 'Medieval Cardiganshire – a Study in Social Origins', *Ceredigion* III (1959) 265-83, reprinted in idem, *Medieval Welsh Society* (Cardiff, 1972).
Myvanwy Rhys, *Ministers' Accounts for West Wales 1277-1306* (London, 1926).
D. Hywel Roberts, 'Noddi Beirdd yng Ngheredigion – rhai agweddau', *Ceredigion* VII (1972) 14-39.
D.Hywel Roberts, 'Noddwyr y Beirdd yn Sir Aberteifi', *Llên Cymru* X (1968) 76-109.
I.J. Sanders, 'Trade and Industry in some Cardiganshire Towns in the Middle Ages', *Ceredigion* (1959) 316-36.

I.J. Sanders, 'The Boroughs of Aberystwyth and Cardigan in the Early Fourteenth Century', *Bulletin of the Board of Celtic Studies* (1954) 282-93.
Llinos B. Smith, 'Cannwyl Disbwyll a Dosbarth', *Ceredigion* X (1986) 229-53.
A.J. Taylor, *The King's Works in Wales 1277-1330* (London, 1974).
J.W.Willis-Bund, *The Black Book of St. David's* (London, 1902).

I am indebted to Professor J. Beverley Smith for a copy of the unpublished 1268 survey of Cardigan, held at Longleat house.

Chapter 8. The Church: Llanbadarn Fawr to Llangeitho.

James Cunnane, 'Ceredigion and the Old Faith', *Ceredigion* (1994) 3-34.
J.T. Evans, *The Church Plate of Cardiganshire* (Stow-on-the-Wold, 1914).
Madeleine Gray, 'The Diocese of St David's in 1563', in *The Journal of Welsh Religious History* 5 (1997) 48-50.
Colin Gresham, 'Medieval Parish and Township Boundaries in Gwynedd', *Bulletin of the Board of Celtic Studies* (1987), 137-49.
Geraint H. Jenkins, *The Foundations of Modern Wales: Wales 1642-1780* (Oxford, 1987).
Geraint H. Jenkins, 'Bywiogrwydd Crefyddol a Llenyddol Dyffryn Teifi, 1689-1740' in idem, *Cadw Tŷ mewn Cwmwl Tystion* (Llandysul, 1990) 103-52.
E.D. Jones, 'Ymneilltuaeth Gynnar yng Ngheredigion', *Ceredigion* 1961, 96-112.
Francis Jones, 'The Wells of Ceredigion', *Llawlyfr Cymdeithas Ceredigion Llundain* VII (1951-2) 21-27.
Phyllis Kinney & Meredydd Evans, *Canu'r Cymry* (1984).
F.R. Lewis, *The History of Llanbadarn Fawr, Cardiganshire, in the Middle Ages* (Llandysul, 1938).
T. Mardy Rees, *The Quakers in Wales* (Carmarthen, 1925).
Erasmus Saunders, *A View of the State of Religion in the Diocese of St. David's about the beginning of the 18th Century* (London, 1721; reprint Cardiff, 1949).
David H. Williams, *Atlas of Cistercian Lands in Wales* (Cardiff, 1990).
Glanmor Williams, *The Welsh Church from Conquest to Reformation* (Cardiff, 1962).

Chapter 9. Civil Society, Civil War.

Material for gentry life is derived largely from the probate and estate records held in the National Library of Wales. Material for the Civil Wars is drawn from the *Calendars of State Papers: Domestic* for 1644-60, and the *Calendar of the Committee for the Advance of Money* covering the period, published in London by the Stationery Office.

See also:

Leslie Baker-Jones, *Princelings Privilege and Power: The Tivyside Gentry in their Community* (Llandysul, 1999).
Howell A. Lloyd, *The Gentry of South-West Wales 1540-1640* (Cardiff, 1968).
Gerald Morgan, *A Welsh House and its Family: the Vaughans of Trawsgoed* (Llandysul, 1997).
Gerald Morgan (ed.) *Nanteos: A Welsh House and its Families* (Llandysul, 2001).
Bethan Phillips, *Peterwell* (Llandysul, 1983).
Michael Roberts, '"More Prone to be Idle and Riotous than the English"? Attitudes to Male Behaviour in Early Modern Wales' in M.Roberts & Simone Clarke, *Women and Gender in Early Modern Wales* (Cardiff, 2000).
Ruth Spalding, *The Diary of Bulstrode Whitelocke 1605-1675* (Oxford, 1990).
W. Ogwen Williams, 'Some Notes on Tudor Cardiganshire', *Ceredigion* (1969) 137-49.

Chapter 10. Women's Lives in Cardiganshire

This chapter is an amplified version of an article published in the 2001 issue of *Ceredigion*. The material is mostly derived from original documents in the National Library of Wales: the Gaol Files and Plea Rolls of the Great Sessions records; the Cardiganshire Quarter Sessions minutes; parish vestry books and the records of the Presbyterian Church of Wales. I am most grateful to Mrs Auronwy James for making available to me her research on the story of Jane Lloyd's marriage, first published in my *Helyntion y Cardi* (Aberystwyth, 1997), and to Michael Freeman for the references to Aberystwyth suffrage meetings. See also:

Kay Cook & Neil Evans, *The Women's Suffrage Movement in Wales, 1890-1918*, in Angela John (ed.), *Our Mothers' Land: Chapters in Welsh Women's History 1830-1939* (Cardiff, 1991) 159-88.
Lesley Davison, 'Spinsters were Doing it for Themselves: Independence and the Single Woman in Early Eighteenth-Century Rural Wales', in Michael Roberts and Simone Clarke, *Women and Gender in Early Modern Wales* (Cardiff, 2000), 186-209.
Sir John Gibson, *The Emancipation of Women* (ed. W. Gareth Evans; Gwasg Gomer, (1992).
Ceridwen Lloyd-Morgan, 'From Temperance to Suffrage?', in Angela John (ed.), *Our Mothers' Land: Chapters in Welsh Women's History 1830-1939* (Cardiff, 1991) 135-58.
Gerald Morgan, 'Women's Wills in West Wales, 1600-1700', *Transactions of the Honourable Society of Cymmrodorion* 1993, 95-114.
Gerald Morgan, 'Dowries for Daughters in West Wales, 1500-1700', *Welsh History Review*, 17 (1995) 534-49.
Ruth Spalding, ed. *The Diary of Bulstrode Whitelocke 1605-1675* (Oxford, 1990).
Lawrence Stone, *Uncertain Unions and Broken Lives* (Oxford, 1995).
Patrick Thomas, *Orinda* (Cardiff, 1998).
Eryn M. White, 'Women, Religion and Education in Eighteenth-Century Wales', in Michael Roberts and Simone Clarke, *Women and Gender in Early Modern Wales* (Cardiff, 2000). 210-33.

Chapter 11. Growing, Getting and Spending

From the *Cardiganshire County History* volume III:

D.I. Bateman, 'Cardiganshire Agriculture in the Twentieth Century: an Economic Perspective', 113-34.
David Jenkins, 'Land and Community around the Close of the Nineteenth Century', 94-112.
J. Geraint Jenkins, 'Rural Industries in Cardiganshire', 135-59.
Anne Kelly Knowles, 'The Structure of Rural Society in North Cardiganshire, 1800-1850', 76-93.
R.J. Moore-Colyer, 'Agriculture and Land Occupation in Eighteenth- and Nineteenth-Century Ceredigion', 19-50.
R.J. Moore-Colyer, 'The Landed Gentry of Ceredigion', 51-75.

See also:

Jill Barber, 'A Fair and Just Demand'? Tithe Unrest in Cardiganshire, 1796-1823', *Welsh History Review* 16 (1992) 177-206.
Richard J. Moore-Colyer, *A Land of Pure Delight* (Llandysul, 1992) pp. 26-35.
Richard J. [Moore-] Colyer, *The Welsh Cattle Drovers* (Cardiff, 1976).
J. Llefelys Davies, 'A Milk Enterprise at Felinfach', *Llawlyfr Cymdeithas Ceredigion Llundain* (1952-52) 30-32.

Wynne Davies, *One Hundred Glorious Years: The Welsh Pony and Cob Society 1902-2001* (Aberystwyth, 2001).
Cledwyn Fychan, 'Lluestau Blaenrheidol', *Ceredigion* 1966, 246-63.
David W. Howell, 'The Agricultural Community of Cardiganshire in the Eighteenth Century' *Ceredigion* (1993) 64-86).
Brian Howells, 'Social and Agrarian Change in Early Modern Cardiganshire', *Ceredigion* (1974-5) 257-72.
D.G. Lloyd Hughes, *Y Diwydiant Gwlân yn Nyffryn Teifi: Pencader a'r Cylch* (Llanrwst, 2004).
Evan L. James, 'The Freeholders' in John Rowlands, *Welsh Family History: a Guide to Research* (Aberystwyth, 1993) 269-79.
Dafydd Jenkins, *Thomas Johnes o'r Hafod* (Cardiff, 1948).
David Jenkins, *The Agricultural Community in South-West Wales at the turn of the Twentieth Century* (Cardiff, 1971).
J.Geraint Jenkins, *Life and Tradition in Rural Wales* (London, 1976).
J.Geraint Jenkins, *The Welsh Woollen Industry* (Cardiff, 1969).
Evan Jones, *Cerdded Hen Ffeiriau* (Aberystwyth, 1972).
J. Eurfyl J. Jones, 'Fairs in Cardiganshire', *Transactions of the Cardiganshire Antiquarian Society* (1930) 94-110.
David Ceri Jones, 'The Board of Agriculture, Walter Davies ('Gwallter Mechain') and Cardiganshire, c.1794-1815', *Ceredigion* (2001) 79-100.
Rheinallt Llwyd (ed.) *Llanrhystud Llanddeiniol* (Llanrhystud, 2004).
David Thomas, *Cau'r Tiroedd Comin* (Liverpool, n.d.).
Gareth W. Williams, 'The disenchantment of the World Crisis and Change in Cardiganshire', *Ceredigion* 1983, 303-321.

Chapter 12. Lead, Silver, Zinc

Cardiganshire County History, volume III: W.J. Lewis, 'Lead Mining in Cardiganshire' 160-81.

See also:

David Bick, 'Remnants of Mining in Ceredigion before the 19th Century', *Ceredigion* (1978) 355-59.
David Bick, *Frongoch Lead & Silver Mine* (Sheffield, 1986).
David Bick & Philip Wyn Davies, *Lewis Morris and the Cardiganshire Mines* (Aberystwyth, 1994).
David Bick, *Waller's Description of the Mines in Cardiganshire* (Black Dwarf, 2004).
George C. Boon, *Cardiganshire Silver and the Aberystwyth Mint* (Cardiff, 1981).
Roger Burt, *John Taylor: mining entrepreneur and engineer 1779-1863* (Buxton, 1977).
Roger Burt, Peter Waite, Ray Burnley *The Mines of Cardiganshire* (Exeter, n.d.).
Tina Carr & Annemarie Schöne, *Pigs & Ingots: the Lead/Silver Mines of Cardiganshire* (Tal-y-bont, 1993)
Mary A.E. Green, *Calendar of State Papers, Domestic Series, of the Reign of James I, 1623-25* (London, 1859).
George Hall, 'A Note on the Decline of Mining in Cardiganshire', *Ceredigion* (1972) 85-88.
Simon S.J. Hughes, *The Cwmystwyth Mines* (1981).
W. Jones-Edwards, *Ar Lethrau Ffair Rhos* (Aberystwyth, 1963).
W.J.Lewis, *Lead Mining in Wales* (Cardiff, 1967).
W.J.Lewis, 'Lead Mining in Cardiganshire', *Cardiganshire County History*, vol.3, chapter 8.
Jennifer Macve, 'The Search for Zinc Blende in Mid-Cardiganshire during World War II', *Ceredigion* (1991) 271-88.

Marilyn Palmer, *"The Richest in All Wales!" The Welsh Potosi of Esgair Hir . . .* (Sheffield, 1983).
R.J. Prichard, *The Rheidol United Mines* (Sheffield, 1985).
Simon Timberlake, 'An archaeological examination of some early mining leats and hushing remains in upland Wales', *Archaeology in Wales* 43 (2003). This usefully lists some of his recent publications.

Chapter 13. The County Gentry: Zenith and Nadir

Cardiganshire County History, volume III: R. Moore-Colyer, 'The Landed Gentry of Cardiganshire', 51-75.

See also:

Leslie Baker-Jones, *Princelings Privilege and Power: The Tivyside Gentry in their Community* (Llandysul, 1999).
Jill Barber, 'The Problem of Debt: the Papers of Charles Parry, Solicitor 1844-1855' *National Library of Wales Journal* (1993) 197-217.
Francis Jones, *Historic Cardiganshire Homes and their Families* (Brawdy Books, 2000).
R. Moore-Colyer, *A Land of Pure Delight: Selections from the letters of Thomas Johnes of Hafod 1748-1816* (Llandysul, 1992).
Janet Joel, *Nanteos* (privately published, 1995).
Elizabeth Inglis-Jones, *Peacocks in Paradise* (London, 1950).
Thomas Lloyd, *The Lost Houses of Wales* (London, 1986).
Gerald Morgan, *A Welsh House and its Family: the Vaughans of Trawsgoed* (Llandysul, 1997).
Gerald Morgan, 'Twf a Diflaniad Ystadau Dyffryn Ystwyth', *Ceredigion* (1997) 29-43.
Gerald Morgan (ed.) *Nanteos: A Welsh House and its Families* (Llandysul, 2001).
Richard Gareth Owen, 'My Dear Reverend Cousin', *Ceredigion* (1977) 224-36.
CADW, *Carmarthenshire, Ceredigion and Pembrokeshire: Register of Landscapes, Parks and Gardens of Special Historic Interest in Wales: Part 1 Parks and Gardens* ((Cardiff, 2002).
Caroline Palmer, 'A History of Tanybwlch Estate, Aberystwyth', *Ceredigion* (2001) 37-78.
Caroline Palmer, with Penny David & Ros Laidlaw, *Historic Parks and Gardens in Ceredigion* (Llandeilo, 2004).
Bethan Phillips, *Peterwell* (Llandysul, 1983).
Richard Suggett, *John Nash: Architect – Pensaer* (Aberystwyth, 1995).
Herbert M. Vaughan, *The South Wales Squires* (London, 1926; Carmarthen, 1988).

I am grateful to Dr Jill Barber for details of the Parry vs Jones feud and the Llidiardau murder case referred to above. Dr John Davies kindly told me of the Pugh memorial in Calcutta. Ivon's involvement in the escape of Wil Cefn Coch is described in the *Welsh Gazette*, 24 May 1945.

Chapter 14. Order and Disorder

Much of the material is derived from Great Sessions Gaol Files, minutes of Quarter Sessions and from the *Cardigan and Tivy-side Advertiser*.

Deirdre Beddoe, 'Eleanor James: Cardiganshire's Only Female Transportee to Australia', *Ceredigion* (1978) 320-22.
George Eyre Evans, *Cardiganshire* (Aberystwyth, 1903).
Howell Evans, *County of Cardigan: A Retrospect of the Nineteenth Century relating especially to Crime and its Prevention, the Administration of Justice, and the creation of the Police Force* (Aberystwyth, 1901).

Sharon Howard, 'Riotous Community: Crowds, Politics and Society in Wales *c*.1700-1840', *Welsh History Review* 20.iv 656-86.

David [J.V.] Jones, *Before Rebecca: Popular Protests in Wales 1793-1835* (London, 1973)

David J.V. Jones, *Crime in Nineteenth-Century Wales* (Cardiff, 1992).

Emrys Jones, 'Tregaron: the Sociology of a Market Town in Central Cardiganshire' in Elwyn Davies & Alwyn D. Rees (eds) *Welsh Rural Communities* (Cardiff, 1960) 65-117.

Bryn Owen, *History of the Welsh Militia and Volunteer Corps 1757-1908: Carmarthenshire, Pembrokeshire and Cardiganshire (Part 1) Regiments of Militia* (Wrexham, 1995)

Richard Suggett, 'Slander in Early-Modern Wales', *Bulletin of the Board of Celtic Studies*, XXXIX (1992) 119-53.

Gareth W. Williams, 'The disenchantment of the World Crisis and Change in Cardiganshire', *Ceredigion* 1983, 303-321.

J.W. Willis-Bund, *Cardiganshire Constabulary. Rules, Orders and Guide to Constables, also a Short History of the Force*. (Aberystwyth, 1897).

CHAPTER 15. 'BOANERGES WAS HIS NAME': CHRISTIANITY IN CARDIGANSHIRE

From the *Cardiganshire County History*, volume III:

Geraint H. Jenkins, 'The Established Church and Dissent in Eighteenth-Century Cardiganshire', 453-477.

Ieuan Gwynedd Jones, 'Church and Chapel in Cardiganshire, 1811-1914', 478-507.

See also:

John Aaron, *Torf Ardderchog: Teithiau Cristnogol Trwy Gymru: Ceredigion a Phenfro* (Bridgend, 1992).

David Barnes, *People of Seion* (Llandysul, 1995).

Tom Beynon published excerpts from Howel Harris's journals relating to

Cardiganshire in the *Cylchgrawn Cymdeithas Hanes Eglwys Methodistiaid Calfinaidd Cymru* (The Journal of the Historical Society of the Welsh Calvinistic Methodist Church) from March 1945 to December 1947, i.e. volumes 30-32.

D. Elwyn Davies, *They Thought for Themselves* (Llandysul, 1982).

D.R. & Z.S. Cledlyn Davies, *Hanes Plwyf Llanwenog* (Aberystwyth, 1939).

Russell Davies, *Secret Sins: Sex, Violence & Society in Carmarthenshire 1870-1920* (Cardiff, 1996).

Eifion Evans, *The Welsh Revival of 1904* (Bridgend, 1969).

Lewis Evans, *Braslun o Hanes Henaduriaeth Gogledd Aberteifi* (Caernarfon, 1972).

Peter Freeman, 'The effect of the Oxford Movement on some election campaigns in Wales in the mid-nineteenth century', *National Library of Wales Journal* XXXI, 4 (Winter 2000) 369-80.

David Jenkins, *O Blas Gogerddan i Horeb* (Aberystwyth, 1993).

Kathryn Jenkins, 'Pantycelyn a'r Cardis', *Ceredigion* 1993, 41-63.

Ieuan Gwynedd Jones & David Williams, *The Religious Census of 1851: a Calendar of the Returns Relating to Wales*, Vol.1, South Wales. (Cardiff, 1976).

Nerys Ann Jones, *Capel y Garn c.1793-1993* (no date or place of publication).

O.W.Jones, *Isaac Williams and His Circle* (London, 1971).

R. Tudur Jones, *Ffydd ac Argyfwng Cenedl: Hanes Crefydd yng Nghymru 1890-1914* (Swansea, 1982).

D. Densil Morgan, *The Span of the Cross: Christian Religion and Society in Wales 1914-2000* (Cardiff, 1999).

Thomas Phillips, *The Welsh Revival: its origin and development* (1860; reprint Edinburgh, 1989)

Erasmus Saunders, *A View of the State of Religion in the Diocese of St. David's* (London, 1721; reprint Cardiff 1949).
Eryn M. White, *Praidd Bach y Bugail Mawr* (Llandysul, 1995).

The reports of the Cardigan branch of the Bible Society 1813-20 are to be found in National Library of Wales MS 4415A. The account of the Penbryn tithe troubles is drawn from the relevant issues of *The Cardigan and Tivy-side Advertiser*, with thanks to Helen Palmer of the Ceredigion Record Office.

CHAPTER 16. THE CARDI GOES TO SCHOOL.

From the *Cardiganshire County History*, volume III:

W. Gareth Evans, 'Education in Cardiganshire 1700-1974', 540-69.
Gwyn Jenkins, 'Cultural Institutions in Cardiganshire', 602-17.

See also:

Dan Davies & William T. Hughes, *Atgofion Dau Grefftwr* (Aberystwyth, 1963).
E.L. Ellis, *The University College of Wales, Aberystwyth 1872-1972* (Cardiff, 1972)
W.H. Harris, 'St David's College, Lampeter' *Ceredigion* I (1950) 43-52.
Idris Mathias, *Last of the Mwldan* (Llandysul, 1998).
D.G. Osborne-Jones, *Edward Richard of Ystrad Meurig* (Carmarthen, 1934).
S.C. Passmore, 'The Revd. John Pugh, Motygido, Llannarth (1690-1763) and his School', *Ceredigion* (1996) 33-48.
Lisa Pennant, *Tai Bach a Thai Mas* (Aberystwyth, 2000).
D.T.W. Price, *Yr Esgob Burgess a Choleg Llanbedr / Bishop Burgess and Lampeter College* (Cardiff, 1987).
Gwyneth Tyson Roberts, *The Language of the Blue Books: the Perfect Instrument of Empire* (Cardiff, 1998).
Malcolm Seaborne, *Schools in Wales 1500-1900; a Social and Architectural History* (Denbigh, 1992). (Contains a useful bibliography of local publications).
Robert Smith, *Schools, Politics and Society: Elementary Education in Wales 1870-1902* (Cardiff, 1999).
A.L. Trott, 'The Implementation of the 1870 Education Act in Cardiganshire during the period 1870-1880', *Ceredigion* Vol. 3, 207-30.
J. Roger Webster, *Old College Aberystwyth* (Cardiff, 1995).

CHAPTER 17. LIVING BY WATER.

From the *Cardiganshire County History*, volume III:

David Jenkins, 'Shipping and Shipbuilding', 182-97.
Moelwyn Williams, 'Commercial Relations', 198-211.

See also:

Mark Bullen, *Customs, Curios and Contraband Part 2: Artefacts and Smuggling* (no date or place of publication).
Reginald Davies, 'Cyfrifiad Morwyr Cymru', *Cardiganshire Family History Journal* (II, 2, June 1999) 37-8.
Terry Davies, *Borth: a Seaborn Village* (Llanrwst, 2004).

David Jenkins, *Jenkins Brothers of Cardiff: a Ceredigion Family's Shipping Ventures* (Cardiff, 1985).
J. Geraint Jenkins, *Maritime Heritage: the Ships and Seamen of Southern Ceredigion* (Llandysul, 1982).
J. Geraint Jenkins, *The Coracle* (Newton Abbot, 1982; Carmarthen, 1988).
J. Geraint Jenkins, *Traddodiad y Môr* (Llanrwst, 2004).
D. Lewis Jones, 'Aberaeron: the Community and Seafaring, 1800-1900', in *Ceredigion* (1969) 201-42.
E.A. Lewis, 'The Port Books of the Port of Cardigan in Elizbaethan and Stuart Times' *Cardiganshire Antiquarian Society Transactions* VII (1930) 21-49.
L.Haydn Lewis, *Penodau yn Hanes Aberaeron a'r Cylch* (Llandysul, 1970).
W.J.Lewis, *New Quay and Llanarth* (no date or place).
W.J.Lewis, *The Gateway to Wales: a History of Cardigan* (Carmarthen, 1990).
Gerald Morgan, *North Cardiganshire Shipbuilding 1700-1880* (Aberystwyth, 1992).
Gerald Morgan, 'The Wrecking of Aberystwyth Ships and other Disasters', *Maritime Wales* 16 (1994) 9-19.
Gerald Morgan, 'Thomas Jones of Aberystwyth, Shipowner', *Maritime Wales* 17 (1995) 28-53.
Susan Campbell-Passmore, *Farmers and Figureheads: the Port of New Quay and its Hinterland* (Carmarthen, 1992).

CHAPTER 18. GETTING ABOUT, GETTING OUT

Arthur Chater, 'Inscriptions on Bridges in Ceredigion', *Ceredigion* (1978) 329-54.
Richard [Moore-]Colyer, *Roads and Trackways of Wales* (Ashbourne, 1984).
Ron Cowell, 'An early history of the Aberystwyth post office', *Ceredigion* (2000) 44-58.
Dewi Davies, 'The Early Years of the Turnpike Trust in Cardiganshire' *Ceredigion* (2003) 7-20.
David Holding & Tony Moyes: *History of British Bus Services: South Wales* (London, 1986).
J.S.Holden, *The Manchester and Milford Railway* (Oakwood Press, 1979).
R.W. Kidner, *The Cambrian Railways* (Oakwood Press, 2nd edn 1992).
Roger Padfield and Barrie Burgess, *The Teifi Valley Railway* (Haverfordwest, 1974).
M.R.C. Price, *The Whitland and Cardigan Railway* (Oakwood Press, 1975).
M.R.C. Price, *The Lampeter, Aberayron and New Quay Light Railway* (Oakwood Press, 1995).
Duncan Roberts, *Crosville 3: the Successors* (N.B.C. Books, 2001).
Herbert Williams, *Stage Coaches in Wales* (Barry, 1977).

I am indebted to Richard Hartnup for discussing with me the ancient roadways of Ceredigion, and to Michael Freeman for much help.

CHAPTER 19. POLITICS AND LOCAL GOVERNMENT.

From the *Cardiganshire County History*, volume III:

P.D.G. Thomas, ' Parliamentary Representation: From the Glorious Revolution to the French Revolution, 1688-1789', 342-67.
Margaret M. Escott, 'Parliamentary Representation: From the French Revolution to the Passage of the Reform Bill, 1790-1832', 368-86.
Roland G. Thorne, Parliamentary Representation: From the First to the Third Reform Acts, 1832-1885', 387-406.
J. Graham Jones, 'Cardiganshire Politics, 1885-1974', 407-429.
J. Graham Jones, 'The Cardiganshire County Council, 1889-1974', 430-452.

See also:-

P.W. Hasler, *The House of Commons 1558-1603* (H.M.S.O. 1981).
John Hughes, *A History of the Parliamentary Representation of the County of Cardigan* (Aberystwyth, 1849).
Arnold James & John E. Thomas, *Union to Reform: a History of the Parliamentary Representation of Wales 1536-1832* (Llandysul, 1986).
David Jenkins, 'The Pryse Family of Gogerddan II', *National Library of Wales Journal* VIII, 176-193.
Ieuan Gwynedd Jones, 'The Rebuilding of St. Michael's Church, Aberystwyth', *Ceredigion* (1973) 117-30.
Ieuan Gwynedd Jones (ed.), *Aberystwyth 1277-1977* (Llandysul, 1977).
Marian Henry Jones, 'Hungarian Sufferings: an Aberystwyth Meeting', *Ceredigion* (1978) 310-19.
P.J.Madgwick with Non Griffiths & Valerie Walker, *The Politics of Rural Wales: A Study of Cardiganshire* (London, 1973).
Aubrey J. Martin, *Hanes Llwynrhydowen* (Llandysul, 1977).
Samuel Rush Meyrick, *The History and Antiquities of the County of Cardigan*.
The Brecon edition of 1907 contains valuable additional material, particularly on MPs, provided anonymously.
Sir Lewis Namier & John Brookes, *The House of Commons 1754-1790* vol. 3 (H.M.S.O. 1964).
Bethan Phillips, *Pity the Swagman: The Australian Odyssey of a Victorian Diarist* (Aberystwyth, 2002).
David Pretty, *The Rural Revolt that Failed: Farm Workers' Trade Unions in Wales 1889-1950* (Cardiff, 1989).
David Pretty, 'Gwrthryfel y Gweithwyr Gwledig yng Ngheredigion 1889-1950', *Ceredigion* (1989) 41-57.
Romney Sedgwick, *The House of Commons 1715-1754* vol. 1 (H.M.S.O. 1970).
Robert Smith, '"Enlightened, Radical Cardiganshire": David Ivon Jones and his Native County,' *Ceredigion* (1995) 102-12.
Lucy Lloyd Theakston & John Davies, *Some Family Records and Pedigrees of the Lloyds of Allt yr Odyn, Castell Hywel, Ffos y Bleiddiaid, Gilfach Wen, Llan Llyr and Waun Ifor* (Oxford, 1913).
Steven Thompson, '"Without any distinction of sect, or creed, or politics"?: Charity and Hospital Provision in Nineteenth-Century Aberystwyth'. *Ceredigion* (2003) 38-56.
David Williams, 'Chartism in Wales' in Asa Briggs (ed.) *Chartist Studies* (London, 1959) 220-48.

Chapter 20. The Poor and the Sick

Cardiganshire County History, volume III: Alun Eirug Davies, 'Poor Law Administration in Cardiganshire, 1750-1948' in *Cardiganshire County History* III, pp. 323-41.

See also:

Alun Eirug Davies, 'Some aspects of the operation of the old Poor Law in Cardiganshire, 1750-1834', *Ceredigion* 1968, 1-44.
Alun Eirug Davies, 'The New Poor Law in a Rural Area 1834-1850', *Ceredigion* (1978) 245-90.
D.R. & Z.S. Cledlyn Davies, *Hanes Plwyf Llanwenog* (Aberystwyth, 1939).
Donald Davies, *"Those were the Days": A History of Cardigan, the Locality and its People*, volume 1 (Cardigan, 1991).
Thomas Dineley, *The Account of the Official Progress of His Grace Henry Duke of Beaufort through Wales in 1684* (London, 1888).
George Eyre Evans, *Cardiganshire: a Personal Survey of Some of its Antiquities, Chapels, Churches, Fonts, Plate, and Registers*. (Aberystwyth, 1903).

Grace Hagen, 'Women and Poverty in south-west Wales, 1834-1914', *Llafur* VII, 3-4, 21-33.
David W. Howell, *The Rural Poor in Eighteenth-Century Wales* (Cardiff, 2000).
Glyn Penrhyn Jones, *Newyn a Haint yng Nghymru* (Caernarfon, 1962).
T. Llew Jones & Dafydd Wyn Jones, *Cancer Curers – or Quacks? The story of a secret herbal remedy* (Llandysul, 1993).
Anne Kelly Knowles, *Calvinists Incorporated: Welsh immigrants on Ohio's industrial frontier* (Chicago,1997).
Emma Lile, 'Friendly Societies in Aberystwyth and their Contribution towards Cultural and Social Life', *Ceredigion*, 1997, 67-78.
W.J.Lewis, 'The Condition of Labour in Mid-Cardiganshire in the early nineteenth century', *Ceredigion* (1963) 321-35.
Gerald Morgan, 'Bottom of the heap: identifying the poor in west Wales records 1600-1680), *Llafur* VII, 9 (1996) 13-28.
Bob Owen, 'Ymfudo o Sir Aberteifi i Unol Daleithiau America o 1654 hyd 1860', *Ceredigion* (1954) 160-69 & (1955) 225-40.
Bob Owen, 'O Sir Aberteifi i Jackson a Gallia, Ohio', *Llawlyfr Cymdeithas Ceredigion Llundain* XI (1955-56) 17-21.
Helen Palmer, 'Documentary evidence on the lives of the poor in the later nineteenth century in Cardiganshire', *Ceredigion* (1998) 11-30.

Some information is drawn from the Reports of the County Medical Officer of Health for the 1920s and 1930s, and from the special report on the Aberystwyth typhoid outbreak by Dr D.I. Evans kindly lent to me by Dr John Hughes.

CHAPTER 21. COUNTING THE PEOPLE

From the *Cardiganshire County History*, volume III:

J.W. Aitchison & Harold Carter, 'The Population of Cardiganshire', 1-19.
J.W. Aitchison & Harold Carter, 'The Welsh Language in Cardiganshire 1891-1991' 570-87.
Anne Kelly Knowles, 'The Structure of Rural Society in North Cardiganshire, 1800-1850', 76-93.

See also:

J.W. Aitchison & Harold Carter, *Spreading the Word: the Welsh Language 2001* (Tal-y-bont, 2004).
E. Alwyn Benjamin, *Footprints on the Sands of Time: Aberystwyth 1800-1880* (Carmarthen, 1986).
Russell Davies, 'Language and Community in South-West Wales *c*.1800-1914' in Geraint H. Jenkins, *Language and Community in the Nineteenth Century* (Cardiff, 1998) 101-23.
Elwyn Davies & Alwyn D. Rees, *Welsh Rural Communities* (Cardiff, 1960), for the chapters on Aber-porth by David Jenkins and on Tregaron by Emrys Jones.
Madeleine Gray, 'The Diocese of St David's in 1563', in *The Journal of Welsh Religious History* 5 (1997) 48-50.
David Greene, 'The Irish Numerals of Cardiganshire', *Studia Celtica* X/XI (1975-76) 305-11.
Garth Hughes, Peter Midmore and Anne-Marie Sherwood, 'The Welsh Language and Agricultural Communities in the Twentieth Century' in Geraint H. Jenkins & Mari A. Williams, *The Welsh Language in the Twentieth Century* (Cardiff, 2000) 551-76.
Aled Jones, *Press, Politics and Society: a History of Journalism in Wales* (Cardiff, 1993).
G.J. Lewis, 'Mobility, Locality and Demographic Change: the case of north Cardiganshire', *Welsh History Review* 9, no.3 (1979) 347-61.
Gwenfair Parry, 'Tregaron (Cardiganshire)' in Gwenfair Parry & Mari A. Williams *The Welsh Language and the 1891 Census* (Cardiff, 1999) 279-96.

Robert Smith, 'Aberystwyth (Cardiganshire)' in Gwenfair Parry & Mari A. Williams *The Welsh Language and the 1891 Census* (Cardiff, 1999) 255-277.
Iolo Wyn Williams (ed.), *Gorau Arf: Hanes Sefydlu Ysgolion Cymraeg 1939-2000*, (Tal-y-bont, 2002).
John Williams-Davies, 'Merched y Gerddi', *Ceredigion* (1978) 291-303.

Chapter 22. The use of Languages, Literature and the Press

Jonathan Ceredig Davies, *Folk-Lore of West and Mid-Wales* (Aberystwyth, 1911).
Llinos M. Davies, *Crochan Ceredigion* (Aberystwyth, 1992).
Lyn Ebenezer, *Cerddi Ceredigion* (Llandysul, 2003).
Emyr Edwards (ed.) *Beirdd y Mynydd Bach* (Barddas, 1999).
Huw Edwards, 'Ceredig', in *Y Casglwr* (December, 1979).
Huw Evans & Marian Davies, *Fyl'na Weden I: Blas ar dafodiaith canol Ceredigion* Llanrwst, 2000.
Erwyd Howells, *Dim ond Pen Gair* (Aberystwyth, 1990).
Erwyd Howells, *Cof Gorau, Cof Llyfr* (Aberystwyth, 2001).
Evan Isaac, *Coelion Cymru* (Aberystwyth, 1938).
Jenkin James, *Gemau Ceredigion* (Cardiff, n.d.).
Geraint H. Jenkins, *Literature, Religion and Society in Wales 1660-1730* (Cardiff, 1978).
Geraint H. Jenkins, *Cadw Tŷ mewn Cwmwl Tystion* (Llandysul, 1990).
Geraint H. Jenkins, *Theophilus Evans (1693-1767) Y Dyn, Ei Deulu, a'i Oes* (1993).
Aled Jones, 'Sir John Gibson and the *Cambrian News*', *Ceredigion* (1994) 57-83.
Evan Jones, *Cerdded Hen Ffeiriau* (Aberystwyth, 1972).
J. Tysul Jones, 'John David Lewis a Hanes Gwasg Gomer', *Ceredigion* (1976) 26-49.
Nerys Ann Jones (gol.) *Oedi yng Nghwmni Beirdd Pentrefi Gogledd Ceredigion* (Tal-y-bont, 1992).
T.Gwynn Jones, *Welsh Folklore and Custom* (London, 1930).
T. Llew Jones, *Awen Aberteifi* (Llandybïe, 1961).
Tegwyn Jones, *Eisteddfod Genedlaethol Aberystwyth 1865* (Aberystwyth, 1992).
W.J. Lewis, *'The Gateway to Wales': a History of Cardigan* (Dyfed County Council, 1990).
Rheinallt Llwyd, 'Rhai o Feirdd y Mynydd Bach', *Ceredigion* (2002) 61-78.
S.R. Meyrick, *The History of the County of Cardigan* (new edition Brecon, 1907).
E.G. Millward, 'Beirdd Ceredigion yn Oes Victoria', *Ceredigion* (1990), 171-90.
Gerald Morgan, 'Ewyllysiau Cymraeg 1539-1858', *Cof Cenedl* XII (1990) 33-67.
Trefor M. Owen, *Welsh Folk Customs* (numerous reprints and revisions).
D. Hywel E. Roberts, 'Almanac *Y Cymro*', *Ceredigion* (1995) 62-85.
Alan R. Thomas, *The Linguistic Geography of Wales* (Cardiff, 1973).
Huw Walters, 'Dau Ysbryd Cylchgronol o Dref Aberystwyth', *Ceredigion* (1993) 87-96.
G.J.Williams, 'Daniel Ddu o Geredigion a'i gyfnod' *Y Llenor*, V (1926) 48.

Chapter 23. Entertainment and the Arts

From the *Cardiganshire County History* volume III:

Rhidian Griffiths, 'Music and Popular Culture', 588-601.
R.F. Walker, 'Entertainment in Aberystwyth 1780-1977', 114-27.
R.F. Walker, 'Tourism in Cardiganshire, 1774-1974', 299-322.

See also:

Leslie Baker-Jones, *Princelings, Privilege and Power: the Tivyside Gentry in their Community* (Llandysul, 1999).
George Cumberland, *An Attempt to Describe Hafod* (1795; new edn. ed. Jennifer Macve & Andrew Sclater (Hafod, 1996)).
E.L. Ellis, *The University College of Wales, Aberystwyth 1872-1972* (Cardiff, 1972).
Tegwyn Jones, *Eisteddfod Genedlaethol Aberystwyth 1865* (Aberystwyth, 1992).
Emma Lile, 'Chwaraeon Tymhorol yng Nghymru cyn y Chwyldro Diwydiannol', *Cof Cenedl* XVIII (2003) 71-98.
W.J. Lewis, *'The Gateway to Wales': a History of Cardigan* (Dyfed County Council, 1990).
Emma Lile, 'Menywod a Chwaraeon: Athletwragedd yng Ngholeg Prifysgol Cymru, Aberystwyth, *ca.* 1880-1914.' *Ceredigion* (2000) 59-72.
S.R. Meyrick, *The History of the County of Cardigan* (new edition Brecon, 1907).
Gerald Morgan, *Nanteos: A Welsh House and its Families* (Llandysul, 2001).
Trefor M. Owen, *Welsh Folk Customs* (numerous reprints and revisions).
Peter Parry & Brian Lile, *The Old Black and Green: Aberystwyth Town F.C. 1884-1984* (Aberystwyth, 1987).
Robin A. Varley, *'All that could be desired': a History of Cricket in Aberystwyth 1830-1997* (Aberystwyth, 2004).

CHAPTER 24. CARDIGANSHIRE AT WAR

Apart from material on the Ethé scandal, not much has been written about World War I in Cardiganshire. It does not figure in the index of the *Cardiganshire County History* volume III, though referred to by R.F. Walker in his chapter on tourism. Particularly lacking anywhere (other than on war memorials) is information about the county's considerable contribution to the Merchant Navy. For World War II I am much indebted to Mr Medwyn Parry of the Royal Commission on Ancient and Historical Monuments Wales. Dr Michael Freeman of the Ceredigion Museum kindly gave me details of recent exhibits concerning the wars. The other main sources used for both wars are the *Cardiganshire and Tivy-side Advertiser* and the *Cambrian News*. See also:

Gwyn Davies, 'Ceredigion in the Second World War', *Ceredigion* (2000) 81-93.
E.L. Ellis, *The University College of Wales, Aberystwyth 1872-1972* (Cardiff, 1972).
Angela Gaffney, 'The Great War in Wales: Memory and Monuments in Ceredigion', *Ceredigion* (2001) 137-53.
Tegwyn Jones, 'Erlid yn Aberystwyth 1914-17: Achos Hermann Ethé', *Ceredigion* (2001) 119-35.
Moira Vincentelli, 'The Davies Family and Belgian Refugee Artists & Musicians in Wales', *National Library of Wales Journal* XXII (1981) 226-33.

CHAPTER 25. CARDIGANSHIRE YESTERDAY: CEREDIGION TODAY

A reading list for this chapter would be far too long! Researching the late 20th century is far more difficult than one might imagine. Some of the material has already been listed at the end of the relevant earlier chapters, including chapters of the *Cardiganshire County History* volume III and recent articles in *Ceredigion*, as well as a variety of volumes of local interest, especially the various books of photographs which have been published in recent years. The government's Census 2001 web-site is invaluable, though not especially user-friendly. A number of details are owed to conversations with individuals mentioned in the Foreword.

Index

There are so many personal and place-names in this book that to index every occurrence would be tedious to both compiler and reader. Every effort has been made to include all significant names and categories. The letter 'b' indicates the text boxes.

CARDIGANSHIRE

SIR ABERTEIFI.

Reference to the Unions

1 *Machynlleth Part*
2 *Aberystwith*
3 *Aberaeron*
4 *Tregaron*
5 *Cardigan Part*
6 *Newcastle Emlyn Part*
7 *Lampeter Part*

CARDIGAN BAY

ABERAERON

New Quay Head

Henvynyw

Llanllwchairn

Llanina

Llandysilio Gogo

Llanarth

Ynys Lochtyn I.

Dihewyd

Llangranog

Mydroilyn

Cardigan I.

Mount

Penbryn

Aberporth

Verwic

Blaenporth

Tremaen

Bettws Ieuvan or Bettws Evan

CARDIGAN

Llangoedmore

Troedyraur

Llandygwidd

Llangunllo

Brongwyn

Llandyvriog

Llanvair Orllwyn

NEWCASTLE EMLYN

Henllan

Bangor

Llandyssil

PEMBROKE SH.

C A R M A

WILLIAM MACKENZIE